CHARLES WILLIAMS

This is the first full biography of Charles Williams (1886–1945), an extraordinary and controversial figure who was a central member of the Inklings—the group of Oxford writers that included C.S. Lewis and J.R.R. Tolkien. Charles Williams—novelist, poet, theologian, magician, and guru—was the strangest, most multi-talented, and most controversial member of the group.

He was a pioneering fantasy writer, who still has a cult following. C.S. Lewis thought his poems on King Arthur and the Holy Grail were among the best poetry of the twentieth century for 'the soaring and gorgeous novelty of their technique, and their profound wisdom'. But Williams was full of contradictions. An influential theologian, Williams was also deeply involved in the occult, experimenting extensively with magic, practising erotically-tinged rituals, and acquiring a following of devoted disciples.

Membership of the Inklings, whom he joined at the outbreak of the Second World War, was only the final phase in a remarkable career. From a poor back-ground in working-class London, Charles Williams rose to become an influen-tial publisher, a successful dramatist, and an innovative literary critic. His friends and admirers included T.S. Eliot, W.H. Auden, Dylan Thomas, and the young Philip Larkin.

A charismatic personality, he held left-wing political views, and believed that the Christian churches had dangerously undervalued sexuality. To redress the balance, he developed a 'Romantic Theology', aiming at an approach to God through sexual love. He became the most admired lecturer in wartime Oxford, influencing a generation of young writers before dying suddenly at the height of his powers.

This biography draws on a wealth of documents, letters, and private papers, many never before opened to researchers, and on more than twenty interviews with people who knew Williams. It vividly recreates the bizarre and dramatic life of this strange, uneasy genius, of whom Eliot wrote, 'For him there was no frontier between the material and the spiritual world.'

Grevel Lindop was formerly Professor of Romantic and Early Victorian Studies at the University of Manchester. His previous books include *The Opium-Eater: A Life of Thomas De Quincey; A Literary Guide to the Lake District; Travels on the Dance Floor*, which was a BBC Radio 4 Book of the Week; and a twenty-one volume edition of *The Works of Thomas De Quincey*. He has published six collections of poems, and his *Selected Poems* appeared in 2000. He lives in Manchester, where he now works as a freelance writer.

CHARLES WILLIAMS

THE THIRD INKLING

GREVEL LINDOP

OXFORD
UNIVERSITY PRESS

OXFORD
UNIVERSITY PRESS

Great Clarendon Street, Oxford, OX2 6DP,
United Kingdom

Oxford University Press is a department of the University of Oxford.
It furthers the University's objective of excellence in research, scholarship,
and education by publishing worldwide. Oxford is a registered trade mark of
Oxford University Press in the UK and in certain other countries

© Grevel Lindop 2015

The moral rights of the author have been asserted

First published 2015
First published in paperback 2017

Impression: 1

Published in the United States of America by Oxford University Press
198 Madison Avenue, New York, NY 10016, United States of America

British Library Cataloguing in Publication Data
Data available

Library of Congress Cataloging in Publication Data
Data available

ISBN 978-0-19-928415-3 (Hbk.)
ISBN 978-0-19-880643-1 (Pbk.)

Printed in Great Britain by
Clays Ltd, St Ives plc

Cover images: (L-R): Charles Williams, OUP Archives, reprinted by
permission of the Secretary to the Delegates of Oxford University Press;
C. S. Lewis © National Portrait Gallery, London; J. R. R. Tolkien
© Haywood Magee/Stringer/Getty Images. Background:
© iStock.com/Ann_Mei, © iStock.com/Henk Badenhorst

In Memory of Lance Cousins
(1942–2015)
– who first suggested I read Charles Williams

Preface

In his last two books of poems (*Taliessin Through Logres* and *The Region of the Summer Stars*) Charles Williams was, I believe, a great poet. I state this at the outset for two reasons: first, because it has been my reason for writing this book; and second, because, of all the many things I have to say about him, it is the most likely to be overlooked.

In the 1930s and '40s, Williams was quite famous. He was a popular novelist, a prominent critic and reviewer, a notable dramatist, and in Christian circles—which in Britain were bigger and more inclusive then than now—an influential thinker, speaker, and writer. During the Second World War, backed by the enthusiasm of T. S. Eliot, W. H. Auden, and C. S. Lewis, he was recognized as an important poet. Yet today he is largely forgotten. This came about partly through an accident of timing. Williams died in the last days of the war, one week after VE Day. The world had other things to think about, and the flurry of tributes, celebrations, and debates which normally follows the untimely death of a significant author could not happen. And there were other difficulties. Raymond Hunt, his de facto literary executor, had no experience in marketing an author, and his temperament—cautious, punctilious, indecisive—led him to dither about how to reissue Williams's work, and what to do about uncollected writings. Moreover, the post-war paper shortage made it hard to get books into print. The upshot was that little of Williams's work was available. Meanwhile, his widow, Michal *alias* Florence, would not countenance either a biography or, in the short term, a volume of his letters—both of which would have done a great deal to keep his name and work current. She knew that her husband had been in love with someone else, and was not prepared to have this made public. She thought of biography simply as muck-raking. She adhered to a naïve view that literary merit would tell in the long run, and that posterity would one day recognize her husband's work. Perhaps she was right.

In so far as Charles Williams is remembered today, it is chiefly as a member of the Inklings, the group of Oxford writers whose other central members were C. S. Lewis and J. R. R. Tolkien. His photograph hangs on the wall of the Eagle and Child pub in Oxford, and Humphrey Carpenter's 1978 group biography, *The Inklings: C. S. Lewis, J. R. R. Tolkien, Charles Williams and their Friends*, did something to keep him from oblivion. But Carpenter's portrait, vivid and broadly accurate though it is, is no more than a sketch. Williams's personal life was both strange and troubled. The sensibilities of those still living had to be considered; many papers were not in public collections, and some that were remained under embargo until well into the twenty-first century.

It is now time for the whole story to be told, and for Charles Williams to be reassessed. This book is by no means an unmixed advocacy. Williams's work ranges from the great to the embarrassingly bad; his personal conduct from the generous and heroic to the selfish and manipulative. As a writer he has always retained small followings amongst groups of readers who communicate too little with each other. Lovers of fantastic fiction (especially in the United States) have enjoyed his novels; Christians have debated his theology; those interested in the occult have been aware of him as a member of esoteric groups, drawing on magical symbolism and experience in his novels. A few scholars of English Literature have retained an interest in his poetry, which belongs beside that of Eliot and Yeats as a late, densely symbolist flowering of modernism in English. I have tried to put the whole picture together, and to show that once it is assembled, a figure formerly regarded as somewhat mystifying becomes comprehensible, and much more interesting. At the beginning of his career, Williams was a minor Edwardian poet, associating with Robert Bridges, Lascelles Abercrombie, and Alice Meynell. In his last years he was not only an Inkling; he was also the companion of Kingsley Amis and Philip Larkin. Though his writing was very different from theirs, he shared many of their social attitudes and had been, in his way, an 'angry young man'. He was the only left-wing Inkling. It is time for him to be read again, and understood better, and I hope that this biography can begin a process of reassessment.

Acknowledgements

As Charles Williams remarked, quoting Milton, ' "The grateful mind / By owing owes not" – But it never did a grateful mind any harm to acknowledge its indebtedness.'[1] A vast number of other people have helped with this book. I began to collect material for a biography in 1998, the idea having crystallized during a series of conversations with Anne Ridler. She subsequently supported the project by the loan of a large body of papers now in the Bodleian, and by giving two lengthy interviews despite being desperately ill ('I never get tired when I talk about Charles', she told me). I owe a great debt to Bruce Hunter (the executor of the estate of Michael Williams), who not only granted permission to quote from Williams's published and unpublished writings, but lent me the body of family papers which formed the foundation of this book. He has been a constant benign presence without whose support it could never have been written.

I am also extremely grateful to Roddy McDougall, who was generously encouraging and has kindly allowed me to quote from the letters of Phyllis McDougall.

For allowing me to record their memories of Williams, I must thank Brenda Boughton, Anne Dreydel, Christopher Fry, Jane Greenham, Mary Guillemard, John Heath-Stubbs, Helen King, Lois Lang-Sims, Anne Ridler, Margaret Routley, Johanne Schuller, Anne Spalding, Ruth Spalding, Joy Stephenson, Joan Wallis, and Kate Welbourne. I only regret that not all of them lived long enough to see the book finished. Gavin Ashenden kindly lent the records of his interviews with Joan Wallis and Phyllis McDougall. The alumni officers of St Anne's and St Hilda's Colleges, Oxford, undertook the labour of forwarding my standard letter to every graduate who had read English during the war years, thereby enabling me to hear from a considerable number who remembered Williams: too many to list here, alas, though each one contributed something to the picture.

1. CW to Margaret Douglas, 23 September 1941, Wade CWP.

The staff of many libraries and archives have made an invaluable contribution. I have often been in daily dialogue with Judith Priestman, Curator of Literary Manuscripts at the Department of Special Collections, Bodleian Libraries, Oxford, and with Laura Schmidt, Archivist at the Marion E. Wade Center, Wheaton College, Illinois. Both have helped in countless ways, and I would have been lost without them. I am also indebted to Marjorie Lamp Mead, Associate Director of the Wade Center; and to the late Christopher W. Mitchell, sometime Director of the Wade Center, who (alas) died whilst the book was in preparation. At the Bodleian I also thank Colin Harris of the Special Collections Reading Room; and Stephen Hebron, who gave invaluable help with illustrations. I thank the staff of the St Albans Library (especially Elanor Cowland), the British Library, the Manchester Record Office, the University of Manchester Library (especially Victoria Flood and Victoria Garlick of the Document Supply Unit), the John Rylands Library, the National Archives at Kew, the archives of University College London, and the Warburg Institute. Michael Highstead, Archivist at St Albans School, showed me the school and its documents; Fr Graeme Rowlands opened to me St Silas the Martyr, Kentish Town, and its records and publications. Martin Maw, Archivist of the Oxford University Press, not only guided me through the vaults at Walton Street but tirelessly helped and advised throughout the writing of the book.

Several owners generously allowed me to read and quote from their private papers: Glen Cavaliero shared letters from Michal Williams; Joy Cooper supplied writings by Ralph Binfield; Oliver Hawkins and Mrs Barbara Hawkins opened to me the Meynell archives at Greatham; Gillian Lunn lent letters from Thelma Shuttleworth; Diana Sparkes gave me access to papers of Hubert Foss. With great generosity, Michael J. Paulus Jr made available his research into Williams's part in the publication of Kierkegaard in English. I also thank the owners of Charles Williams's tarot cards, and of A. E. Waite's diaries and his *Record of the Holy House*, both of whom wish to remain anonymous. Anonymity must likewise veil my gratitude to the physician who, as a student, happened to be present at Williams's final operation and supplied an account of it.

For advice, information, and help of many kinds I thank Joan Abrams, Jeannie Brook Barnett, Jeff Cooper, Terry Drummond, Paul Ellis, Anne Grimwade, Michael Hampel, Genevieve Hawkins, Kerryl Lynne Henderson, Sørina Higgins, Geoffrey Hill, John Kelly, Hermione Lee, Dorothy Lewis,

Joan Light, Thelma Roberts, Helena Scott, Richard Sturch, Isabel Syed, Mrs R. Tarling, Christina Walkley, Martin Wilkinson, Helen Wheeler, John Wing, and Duncan Wu. Eileen Mable gave valuable help with research in St Albans. Colin Smythe discovered important, previously unknown photographs. David Llewellyn Dodds answered many queries and shared the benefits of a lifetime of scholarship.

The book could not have been written without the support of the Charles Williams Society, whose Council and members over more than forty years loyally pursued their mission of fostering the understanding and appreciation of Charles Williams and his work. Their journal, archive, and accumulated knowledge have proved indispensable. I thank Sandy Feneley and Paul Monod at the Centre for Medieval and Renaissance Studies, Oxford, where the archive is deposited, for their patient and generous help.

Gavin Ashenden, Stephen Barber, Edward Gauntlett, R. A. Gilbert, Philip Heselton, Brian Horne, Nigel Jackson, and Martin Maw read the entire book, chapter by chapter, as it was written. Their knowledge and advice were invaluable—though I have not always done what they advised, and I remain responsible for all errors of fact or judgement. Lois Lang-Sims also generously gave her time and energy to reading my draft; her letters were an inspiration, and it was reassuring to have the comments of someone who had known Williams so well. She died, aged 97, just after the book was finished.

Extracts from unpublished letters by T.S. Eliot and from his Introduction to *All Hallows' Eve* are reprinted by permission of Faber and Faber Ltd and the T. S. Eliot Estate. Extracts from the writings of C.S. Lewis are copyright © C. S. Lewis Pte. Ltd and are reprinted by permission. Letters of Phyllis McDougall (*née* Jones) are quoted by kind permission of Roddy McDougall. Charles Williams's letter to Jean Smith is quoted by permission of Martin Ferguson Smith. Extracts from the writings of Charles Williams are quoted by permission of Bruce Hunter. In a few cases, it has proved impossible to trace copyright holders. I should be very glad to hear from anyone I have missed.

My research was generously supported by a Clyde S. Kilby Research Grant from Wheaton College, Illinois; by grants from the Charles Williams Society, and from the Society of the Inner Light; and by a period as an Invited Visiting Scholar at St John's College, Oxford, for which I thank the President and Fellows of the College.

I am grateful for the help and expertise of Jane Turnbull, my agent, and Andrew McNeillie, Rachel Platt, and Jacqueline Baker, my editors at the Oxford University Press. And I cannot praise too much the patience of my wife Amanda, over ten years during which Charles Williams was almost as prominent a lodger in our home as he once was at 9 South Parks Road, Oxford.

Grevel Lindop

September 2014

Contents

List of Illustrations

Figures

Plates

Illustrations Credits

Plates 2, 4, 5, 7, 22 are reproduced by permission of the Bodleian Libraries, Oxford (Bodleian MS. Photogr. c. 554, folios 2, 5, 6, 8, and 10); plates 27, 29, 34, and 35 are reproduced by permission of the Charles Williams Society; plates 28, 30, 31, and 32 are reproduced by permission of Jeannie Moyo, for the estate of Anne Spalding; plates 11, 12, 13, and Figure 1 are reproduced by permission of R.A. Gilbert; plates 1, 3, 6, 8, 9, 10, 20, 21, 23, 25, and 26 are reproduced by permission of Bruce Hunter; plate 36 is used by permission of The Marion E. Wade Center, Wheaton College, Wheaton, IL.; plate 16 is reproduced by permission of Roddy McDougall; plates 14, 15, 17, 19, 24, and Figure 3 are reproduced by permission of Oxford University Press; plate 18 is reproduced by permission of Neil Scott.

List of Abbreviations

Anne Ridler Interview 1	Anne Ridler, interviewed by the author on 16 April 1998
Anne Ridler Interview 2	Anne Ridler, interviewed by the author on 17 July 2001
Anne Spalding Interview	Anne Spalding, interviewed by the author on 14 April 1998
Beinecke	The Beineke Rare Book and Manuscript Library, Yale University, New Haven, CT
Bodleian	Department of Special Collections, Bodleian Library, University of Oxford
Bodleian, ARP	Uncatalogued papers bequeathed by Anne Ridler to the Bodleian Library
Brenda Boughton Interview	Brenda Boughton, interviewed by the author on 5 February 2002
Carpenter	Humphrey Carpenter, *The Inklings: C.S. Lewis, J.R.R. Tolkien, Charles Williams and Their Friends* (London: Allen and Unwin, 1978)
C.S. Lewis, *Collected Letters* II	Walter Hooper, ed., *The Collected Letters of C.S. Lewis*, Volume II: *Books, Broadcasts and the War, 1931–1949* (New York: Harper San Francisco, 2004)
CWSN	*The Charles Williams Society Newsletter*
CWSA	Charles Williams Society Archive, Centre for Medieval and Renaissance Studies, St Michael's Hall, Shoe Lane, Oxford
Essays Presented to Charles Williams	*Essays presented to Charles Williams, with a Memoir by C.S. Lewis* (London: Oxford University Press, 1947)
Greatham	Meynell archive, Humphrey's Homestead, Greatham, Pulborough, Sussex

Hadfield (1959)	Hadfield, Alice Mary, *An Introduction to Charles Williams* (London: Robert Hale, 1959)
Hadfield (1983)	Hadfield, Alice Mary, *Charles Williams: An Exploration of his Life and Work* (New York and Oxford: Oxford University Press, 1983)
Helen King Interview	Helen King, interviewed by the author on 2 May 2001
Joan Wallis interview 1	Joan Wallis, interviewed by Gavin Ashenden and Stephen Medcalfe on 16 May 1992
Joan Wallis interview 2	Joan Wallis, interviewed by the author on 7 February 2001
Johanne Schuller Interview	Johanne Schuller, interviewed by the author on 22 June 1996
John Heath-Stubbs Interview	John Heath-Stubbs, interviewed by the author on 14 November 2000
Joy Stephenson Interview	Joy Stephenson, interviewed by the author on 6 February 2002
King	King, Roma, ed., *From Serge to Michal: Letters from Charles Williams to his Wife, Florence, 1939–1945* (Ohio: Kent State University Press, 2002)
Letters to Lalage	Lang-Sims, Lois, *Letters to Lalage: The Letters of Charles Williams to Lois Lang-Sims* (Ohio: Kent State University Press, 1989)
Lois Lang-Sims Interview	Lois Lang-Sims, interviewed by the author on 11 April 2001
Mary Guillemard Interview	Mary Guillemard, interviewed by the author on 20 June 2005
Phyllis McDougall Interview	Phyllis McDougall, interviewed by Gavin Ashenden and Stephen Medcalfe on 21 February 1992
Ridler (1958)	Williams, Charles, *The Image of the City and Other Essays*, ed. Ridler, Anne (London: Oxford University Press, 1958)
Ruth Spalding Interview	Ruth Spalding, interviewed by the author on 26 May 2005
TLS	*Times Literary Supplement*
Wade	The Marion E. Wade Center of Wheaton College, Illinois

Wade, CWMS	Charles Williams Manuscripts at the Marion E. Wade Center
Wade, CWP	Charles Williams Papers at the Marion E. Wade Center
Wade, CWP (Lindop)	Uncatalogued items in the Charles Williams Papers at the Marion E. Wade Center, identifiable from the preliminary list prepared by Grevel Lindop
Wade, WFPA	The Williams Family Papers Archive at the Marion E. Wade Center

Note to the Reader

Until the 1950s, it was customary to refer to 'the Oxford University Press', or 'the O.U.P.', with the definite article. Many of those whom I interviewed for this biography still did so. For this reason, for consistency, and to convey a sense of the period, I have followed this usage throughout.

In his letters, Williams had a trick of sometimes breaking off mid-sentence, leaving two, three, or four dots for rhetorical effect. To avoid confusion, I have indicated all my own cuts in quoted material, from whatever source, by three dots enclosed in square brackets thus: [...]; other dots are in the original text.

In the absence of any standard edition of Charles Williams's novels, references to his fiction are given by title and chapter only.

G.L.

'Ex umbris et imaginibus ad Veritatem'
'From shadows and images to the Truth'

– Cardinal Newman (as quoted in Charles Williams's *Commonplace Book*)

Prologue

Oxford, 5 February 1940. A cold Monday morning with snow on the pavements. Inside the Divinity School, Oxford University's fifteenth-century Gothic lecture hall, you can see your own breath on the chilly air. The stone-carved room, with its magnificent fan-vaulted ceiling, is crammed with the mixed student body of wartime Oxford. Most are women; the rest are largely young men straight from school: many awaiting call up and some in uniform, ready for training later in the day. Britain has been at war with Nazi Germany for five months: Hitler has invaded Poland, and is expected soon to attack France. But it is not news from the war that causes the buzz of suppressed excitement pervading the room. Often the audience for the second lecture of a series is smaller than for the first. This time it is larger: many who were here last week have brought friends, to see and hear something out of the ordinary.

As the nearby clock of St Mary's Church strikes eleven, three men sweep into the hall and up the central aisle between the chairs. At left and right, black gowns billowing behind them, are two well-known characters, leading members of the English Faculty: on one side, the domed forehead and burly physique of C.S. Lewis, Fellow in English at Magdalen College; on the other—slighter, smaller, with downturned mouth and piercing eyes—J.R.R. Tolkien, Professor of Anglo-Saxon. Between them strides an unlikely figure. Tall and angular, with a deeply lined face, gownless, in a blueish-grey business suit and round spectacles, darting quick glances about the room, he seems as full of anticipation as the students. When he mounts the platform, leaving his companions to find their seats in the front row, there is a glint of something like mischief in his eyes as he surveys his audience.

This is Charles Williams, the new Lecturer in English Literature. He clutches a rolled-up sheaf of papers in one hand but having set them on the lectern he never looks at them again. He launches into his lecture, which is on Milton's poetic masque *Comus*—the second of a term's course on Milton's works—and those already startled by his unacademic appearance are further shocked by his voice, which is not the usual refined 'Oxford' accent, but a sharp, plebeian enunciation. Almost Cockney, certainly with some sort of 'London' twang, it comes close to grating on the ear. But within a minute or two any resistance aroused by these unorthodox tones melts away.

Williams speaks as if *Comus* were of immediate and vital importance to himself and every member of the audience, and needs urgently to be discussed and understood. He seems to know *Comus*—and indeed all of Milton's poetry—by heart, plucking apt quotations out of the air as he goes. He charms the audience with his wit, his irony, his passionate urgency. He strides about the stage, gesturing with tense but expressive hands, clutching for the exact word and then firing it off with a piercing look at this or that student. He seems to speak out of the side of his mouth, and this—together with his accent—gives his words a curious personal intensity. Reciting poetry, he makes it a hypnotic incantation, but also a sensuous delight, enjoying it as if the sounds and rhythms of the words can be savoured like nectar, and sure that the audience will relish them too.

But he also understands the students' resistance, their scepticism, their doubts. *Comus*, he explains, is about chastity, a virtue undervalued in the present age but of the utmost importance, which we may choose to reject— that is our right—but which we must first understand. In the ancient world, he tells them, chastity was not merely abstinence. It was spiritual power. His hearers are spellbound. They sense that they are listening to someone who knows, and means, what he says; someone who has lived poetry, who has it in his blood and bones, and can speak to them about vital issues in their lives. The beauty of Milton's verse and the sacredness of virginity become, for an hour, the most important things in the world.

Then, far too quickly, time is up. Williams is already off the platform, with a quick conspiratorial smile to his friends in the front row, and striding from the room, leaving his audience dazed, exhilarated, inspired. Most leave the lecture determined to read *Comus* as soon as possible. Some already plan to persuade their colleges—by hook or by crook—to let them have Charles Williams as their tutor, next term if not this.

Lewis and Tolkien follow Williams at a more leisurely pace. In a few minutes they will reconvene at a nearby pub to drink and discuss the lecture.

Lewis has already made up his mind. 'Simply as criticism', he will later recall, 'it was superb because here was a man who really started from the same point of view as Milton and really cared with every fibre of his being about "the sage and serious doctrine of virginity".' Indeed, 'That beautiful carved room had probably not witnessed anything so important since some of the great mediaeval or Reformation lectures. I have at last, if only for once, seen a university doing what it was founded to do: teaching wisdom.'

That wisdom was hard-won and fraught with bitter paradox. The charismatic lecturer who celebrated chastity bore the emotional scars of a painful fourteen-year love affair which had brought his marriage close to breaking point. With an encyclopaedic knowledge of English poetry and unrivalled critical insight, he did not possess a university degree and could lecture at Oxford only because the Second World War had called away so many faculty members. At Oxford he was an anomaly: a restless Londoner who found 'Oxford, however nice, still a kind of *parody* of London'; a worldly wise publisher with a head for business, more at home with a cigarette and a sandwich in a Ludgate Hill wine bar than with the pipesmoke and claret of an Oxford common-room. He was beginning to be recognized as an important poet with a brilliantly original cycle of Arthurian poems admired by T. S. Eliot and W. H. Auden, amongst others. An important Anglican theologian and interpreter of Christian doctrine, he was also a trained occultist who continued to practise magical rituals with erotic and even sadistic elements to them. And what he meant by 'chastity' was something profoundly different from what Lewis, Tolkien, and the rest of his audience imagined.

To understand this extraordinary man who changed so many people's lives—this important English poet who has been almost forgotten—we must turn first to the drab streets of north London in the late years of the nineteenth century.

I

From Holloway to Silvania

As an adult, Charles Williams was not much interested in childhood, his own or anyone else's. From his early years he preserved no precocious sayings, no revealing anecdotes. He never claimed that his poetry was the outcome of an intense early vision. Indeed, the only story we have about his earliest years concerns a loss of vision. It was perhaps the most important thing that ever happened to him.

His mother took him to play every morning in the open fields at Highbury, one of the green spaces which dotted the suburban sprawl of Victorian north London. They knew when it was time to go home by looking at a public clock across the field. At five years old, Charles had measles. When he was better, 'Charles went for his usual walk to the field, and looking round said, "Oh, the clock's gone." '[1] The measles had damaged his eyes. From that time on, he had no distant vision. His world would consist increasingly of words: books, stories, conversation, ideas, poems—and the images they evoked. The physical world would always be, for him, a little unreal. Much later, he would write of what he thought to be:

> [a] fairly common experience – the moment when it seems that anything might turn into anything else [...] A room, a street, a field, becomes unsure. The edge of a possibility of utter alteration intrudes. A door, untouched, might close; a picture might walk; a tree might speak; an animal might not be an animal; a man might not be a man. One may be with a friend, and a terror will take one even while his admirable voice is speaking; one will be with a lover and the hand will become a different and terrifying thing, moving in one's own like a malicious intruder, too real for anything but fear.[2]

Charles was intensely imaginative; but his lifelong sense that the world could at any moment dissolve into a magical realm of sinister unreality or heavenly illumination was perhaps founded on a lifetime's visual uncertainty.

He did not wear glasses; his parents failed to notice that he was hampered by poor sight. They had other worries: his father, Walter Williams, was going blind, and the firm which employed him as a clerk was in decline. Charles would always remember the poverty of his childhood. 'The terrible insecurity of all life smiled through the windows of our schoolrooms',[3] he wrote; and, in a poem, 'My childhood knew too well the fate / that hangs o'er servants, and the strait / wherethrough the large unneeded go'. The lines suggest a childhood darkened by the fear of absolute poverty, the abyss of the 'unneeded' for whom there was no recourse but the workhouse.

The Williams family lived at the lowest edge of shabby-genteel respectability. When Charles was born, on 20 September 1886, his parents—Walter the clerk and his wife Mary, a former milliner—rented three upstairs rooms in a small terrace house at 3 Spencer Road (now Caedmon Road), Holloway.[4] They moved, perhaps when Charles's sister Edith was born in November 1889, to rent a whole house at 76 Canonbury Road, Islington.[5] Here, on one of north London's busiest highways, their neighbours were clerks and governesses, railway workers, carpenters, a stonecarver, a policeman, and a piano-maker.

Charles's father, Walter Williams, was a melancholy man, and he came from a dysfunctional family. The Williamses had lived in London since the early nineteenth century and had an adventurous streak. Charles's great-uncle Richard, a devout Christian with poetic talents, went to sea and in 1846, aged twenty-five, was 'wash'd overboard in A Gale of wind' near Naples. Richard's brother Henry disappeared in the wilderness of North Queensland, Australia, in 1878, prospecting for gold. The third brother, Charles's paternal grandfather, Charles George Robert Williams (1819–86), had an unadventurous but still troubled life. An Islington watchmaker, he was a fiercely republican atheist. His wife died in 1848, two days after giving birth to twin boys. Williams named his sons Charles Cromwell and Richard Walter Stansby but, true to his atheism, refused to have them baptized. Little Charles Cromwell died after only eight months. Walter, the surviving twin, was sent to live with his maternal grandmother. Five years later, in 1853, Charles George remarried. His new wife, Susan, was ten years younger than he and the marriage was unhappy.[6] If Charles George had hoped to provide an affectionate stepmother for Walter, he was disappointed. Five-year-old Walter remained with his grandmother, and instead Charles George's newly acquired mother-in-law moved in.[7] Twelve years later, in 1865, Susan gave birth to a daughter, Lilian, who thus became seventeen-year-old Walter's half-sister. Susan Williams abandoned her husband,[8] and the 1881 census shows Charles George living alone with sixteen-year-old Lilian. After this nothing is known of her. Like her mother, Lilian simply vanishes from the record.

From this unhappy background, a motherless surviving twin displaced from his father's household, Walter Williams emerged a cautious, serious, and intellectual youth. He learned French and German and found work as a foreign correspondence clerk. He also sent poems and stories to magazines and gradually became a successful part-time author. He became engaged to Mary Wall, a milliner, the daughter of a West Country cabinetmaker.[9] Their engagement was a long one because part of Walter's earnings went to support his father. Why Charles George, a watchmaker in his sixties, needed his son to support him, is not known. Perhaps he was losing his sight; there was apparently some hereditary eye problem in the family, quite apart from measles.

In April 1884, the 36-year-old Walter Williams belatedly had himself christened,[10] so that he and Mary could have a church wedding. They were married at St Matthew's, Islington, in May.[11] Walter perhaps became 'Christian' to please his bride. He practised his religion conscientiously, but showed no interest in religious ideas. Like many thoughtful late Victorians, he may have seen Christianity chiefly as a moral code with Jesus as its heroic, but human, founder. Still, from now on the Williamses would be a sober, churchgoing family, and Charles Walter Stansby Williams was baptized at St Anne's, Finsbury Park, on 7 November 1886, when he was seven weeks old.

Edith was born three years later. From their earliest days the children were used to evening prayers at home with their parents, and they were soon taken to church at least once, and often twice, on Sundays. Charles first went to morning service when he was about three and a half. He enjoyed it, and demanded to be taken every Sunday: Edith later recalled that he had 'screaming fits [...] when weather or illness prevented him from going'.[12] Church must have provided something—perhaps not least sheer entertainment—that the rather dull Williams home life lacked. Mostly the family went to St Anne's, Finsbury Park. The children enjoyed the walk: Edith remembered herself and Charles 'running and skipping along the quiet streets and the rough open grass space by the railway goods depot'. Charles 'used to march into church as if he owned the place'. He joined in the hymns energetically and somewhat tunelessly.[13]

For he was, and would remain, tone deaf. Music, which might have enhanced his visually stinted world, was not available to him. Its place was taken by poetry. The world of the Williams children was verbally a rich one—though never a quiet one, with the constant vibration of nearby freight trains and the rumble of horse-drawn wagons on Canonbury Road in the background. Walter Williams, a literate and conscientious father, read to the children and recited poems. Charles could read well by the time he was five, and his parents scraped together money to send him to a private infants' school, St Mary Magdalene.[14] The sight of their father writing was as normal to the children as the sound of his voice reading. Until Walter's eyes began to fail seriously, he spent his spare time writing prolifically for magazines. A scrapbook of his work survives, holding more than eighty short stories, two hundred poems, and twenty-odd articles. They appeared in cheap popular magazines aimed at the just-literate poor—*The National Temperance Mirror*, *The Family Herald*, *Crystal Stories*—and a few superior journals such as *All the Year Round* and *Household Words*. His poems were sentimental and nostalgic, and his articles mainly on poets—simple introductions to Longfellow and Goldsmith, Burns and Clare—or liberal political figures (Abraham Lincoln, or republicans such as Mazzini and Cavour). Walter Williams carried forward something of his father's radicalism.

Walter's fiction embodies the anxious ethical code of the 'respectable' late-Victorian poor, warning its readers against debt, dishonesty, and—above all—drink. With titles such as 'A Hidden Sacrifice', 'A Terrible Warning', and 'Harry's Temptation', their simple, melodramatic plots deliver the message that a single lapse of moral judgement, which often means specifically a single sip of alcohol, can lead to the abyss: disgrace, prison, madness, death.

Walter was not the only author in the family. Five miles away, at Leyton on London's eastern outskirts, lived Charles's uncle and aunt, Charles and Alice Wall. Aunt Alice worked in the humblest branch of literature: she wrote the verses to go inside greetings cards.[15] But her brother Charles Wall (1860–1943) provided a link with the world of learning. Having studied in Paris,[16] Wall worked as 'artist and engraver on wood', producing illustrations for books and magazines.[17] He wrote books on church architecture and local history, illustrated with his own drawings, and was an authority on prehistoric monuments, contributing chapters on early earthworks to the authoritative *Victoria County Histories*.

Wall's religious inclinations were High Church. A committed Anglo-Catholic, he cherished an idealistic view of the Middle Ages as 'days of mystic loveliness and poetical beauty', and of Britain as 'a shrine, [whose] soil is permeated with the dust of her saints'.[18] If anyone in Charles Williams's childhood fired the boy with romantic spiritual enthusiasm, it was surely his uncle Charles Wall. He spent a good deal of time with his aunt and uncle; years later, he recalled his 'childhood wanderings' along the Essex Road and how he 'used to walk over to Leyton' to see them.[19] Visits to the Walls offered an escape from constricting home life.

Other relatives provided occasional holidays. There were cousins at Brighton and Lowestoft, so Charles and Edith would spend a fortnight at the seaside. Edith recalled how important they felt when they were sent to Brighton by train, looked after by the guard, and 'how Charles had loved the Brighton Aquarium, and the slot machines on the West Pier', and riding on Volk's Electric Railway, 'in a little coach with no sides but a striped awning and looped curtains' until all their pocket money was gone.[20]

Besides the measles that damaged Charles's sight, one other childhood illness would have momentous consequences, though it passed almost unnoticed at the time. Charles contracted intestinal tuberculosis from drinking unpasteurized milk—the normal cheap milk of the day. There would have been a few days of fever, followed by apparently complete recovery. Undiagnosed, it left Charles with intestinal scarring and would cause problems in his later life.

Meanwhile, Walter Williams's blindness progressed. After 1891 he wrote no more for the magazines, and by 1894 he was nearly blind. In the same year, his company went out of business. Charles was eight years old and Edith six. The family faced destitution. A doctor—paid for with who knows what scrimping and saving—told Walter that to keep what was left of his sight he must move out of London's polluted air.[21] It was a desperate situation.

★   ★   ★

It was Charles Wall who provided the answer. He suggested that the family move to St Albans and open a shop selling stationery and artists' materials. He found premises for them at 15 Victoria Street, near the town centre, and 'helped with the arrangements, the borrowing of money and the buying of stock', financing part of the business himself.[22]

St Albans, a small town in Hertfordshire 20 miles north of London, was a sound choice. The town's 'clean air' was much publicized by developers who built new housing there to take advantage of the Midland Railway's commuter trains to London. St Albans was still a picturesque town with half-timbered buildings, a medieval market cross, and a magnificent abbey founded in 1077 near the spot where St Alban, a Roman soldier and the first British Christian martyr, had been killed in AD 300. It was a magnet for tourists and watercolourists. If you could sell artists' materials anywhere, you could sell them in St Albans.

For Charles and Edith, the change must have been astonishing. Their home was now a small shop called the Art Depot, squeezed between a tobacconist and a tailor. Behind the shop and house was a cottage garden filled with vegetables and fruit trees, and in summer masses of strawberries and rhubarb, overtopped by ranks of pea plants. The garden path, clustered in spring with drifts of snowdrops, led through a hedge into a field. It was idyllic. But the Art Depot was never prosperous. Wall had bought too much stock, and soon withdrew from partnership, leaving the business 'considerably in debt'.[23] Mary Williams, who had a better business head than her husband, managed the shop, but soon creditors were 'clamouring for payment'. To make ends meet Mary let out rooms to lodgers,[24] and made the children's clothes herself, even tailoring an Eton jacket for Charles.[25] Life was a struggle. The children, however, thoroughly enjoyed it. Edith in particular loved the garden, where she and Charles would play for hours.[26] For three years after the move Edith was home-schooled by her father in the room behind the shop: lessons were 'strict', but often interrupted when the shop-bell rang and Walter had to serve a customer, so that she could run outside. 'I can never remember being punished for this', she recalled.[27] The children were given little 'gardens' of their own where they could grow things, though Charles—already the quintessential townee—was not interested. And on winter nights Mary Williams would sometimes turn the garden path into a slide for the children by throwing down a bucketful of water to freeze ready for the morning.[28]

Seven-year-old Charles, in home-made shirts, attended the Abbey National School in Spicer Street—an indication of how hard up the family was: national schools were charity-funded parish schools for poor children. Classrooms were sometimes half-empty, as children stayed home to help their families with straw-plaiting (for hats) or other cottage industries.[29] What the curriculum was, we don't know; but there would have been much learning by heart—multiplication tables, spellings, and dates, but also poetry, which the children had to memorize. The foundations of Charles's knowledge of English poetry would have been laid at Spicer Street, though he learned as much again from his highly literate father, who introduced him to his own favourite authors, including Charles Dickens, Thomas Macaulay, and Samuel Taylor Coleridge. On Sundays, when only 'serious' reading was allowed, Charles was allowed to enjoy the science fiction of Jules Verne as well as *The Pilgrim's Progress* and stories from Roman history.[30] Walter, as Edith recalled, would:

> pursue any fresh point until he knew the answer [...] this meant that there were books on all kinds of subjects to which Charles had free access, but whereas Father's interest extended to any subject, Charles was concerned mainly with history and literature.[31]

Walter made sure that the children were given alternatives to religious dogmatism and learned to treat history's radical sceptics with respect. Charles would remember his father explaining how 'pious' people spoke 'slander [...] Of Voltaire and Tom Paine'.[32] Walter also told them how his own atheist father enjoyed proclaiming that 'religion certainly couldn't last' and that 'no Englishman had a use for the priest'. Charles George liked to discredit the Bible with conundrums like 'Who was Cain's wife?' Adam and Eve had just the two sons, Cain and Abel, but the Bible says that 'Cain knew his wife': so who was she? Again, 'What clothes did Christ wear when he rose?' If he left the grave-clothes behind in the tomb, did he go about naked?[33] Walter did such a good job that Edith, at around the age of eleven, secretly became an atheist, attending church only to please her parents.[34] Charles himself had no doubts. But, from childhood on, he was well aware of the case against Christianity.

Charles and Walter liked exploring St Albans and its outskirts, an area full of history. Nearby were the excavations at Verulamium, one of Britain's largest Roman cities. St Albans Abbey was built partly of bricks salvaged from Roman ruins. A group of cottages called 'Battle Mount' commemorated the two Battles of St Albans during the Wars of the Roses, in 1455 and 1461. In 1555, under the Catholic Queen Mary, a Protestant baker, George Tankerfield, had been burned to death near the Abbey, in the open space called Romeland—a space that the Williams family crossed every Sunday on their way to services at the Abbey. Two miles away, at Gorhambury, were the ruins of the house of Sir Francis Bacon (1561–1626), author, pioneer scientist, and Chancellor of England under James I. Walter must have talked endlessly to his children about these vivid local events and characters.

Not that all of St Albans was picturesque. The sordid St Albans brickfields had been described with horrific power half a century earlier by Dickens in

Bleak House, and, well into the 1920s, St Albans had grim slums with little sanitation. Meanwhile, new housing estates were being erected, and a battalion of estate agents flourished by persuading Londoners to move to smart new houses on the town's perpetually receding outskirts. Still, St Albans had a vivid social life. There was a cattle market every Wednesday, where longhorned highland cattle were sold,[35] and a lively street market on Saturdays.[36] Theatre was provided by amateur companies, and by the touring Shakespeare company of Philip 'Ben' Greet, last of the great nineteenth-century actor-managers, which visited regularly.[37] Charles's first experience of Shakespeare in performance probably came through full-blooded, larger-than-life productions mounted by Greet and his company, in which Sybil Thorndike and other notables made their debuts. St Albans was a rich environment for a child, and it left indelible traces. When in Charles Williams's novels we meet a bustling small town with its chapels, markets, muddy building sites, country-house grounds open for amateur dramatics, a history of martyrdom, and a strong sense of local democracy, we are encountering the St Albans of his childhood.

★   ★   ★

The little school in Spicer Street proved its worth: when he was thirteen Charles won a scholarship to St Albans Grammar School, entering in January 1899.[38] (Edith would spend the rest of her schooldays at a little school in College Street, run by a Miss Crouch.) The family must have been jubilant at Charles's success. St Albans Grammar School was the best educational establishment in town, with a history going back to Anglo-Saxon times. It occupied the old Abbey Gateway, a medieval building housing the massive arch leading to the Abbey precincts. Classrooms were on three floors, connected by two wide stone spiral staircases, one on each side of the gateway arch. High-ceilinged and vaulted, some without fireplaces, the rooms were freezing in winter. Where fireplaces did exist, their stone canopies carried medieval graffiti. Several rooms had stone corbels featuring the heads of men, animals, and grotesque demons. One room had an enormous semicircular 'cope table' once used for laying out the embroidered copes or cloaks worn by abbots and bishops. Too big to be removed from the building, it had remained there for centuries.

The school's most famous Old Boy had been a pope. This was Nicholas Breakspear (1100–59), better known as Adrian (or 'Hadrian') IV: the only

English pope. Walking to school in the mornings along Romeland, climbing the spiral staircase to a medieval room with a view over the Abbey, and reflecting on his papal predecessor, Charles must have felt a powerful depth of time and history. The school had only seventy pupils (all boys) but it was flourishing and up to date. When Charles arrived, a new chemical laboratory had just opened,[39] though Charles was more interested in two other innovations, a lending library and a school magazine, *The Albanian*—'a lively affair with competitions, drawings, cartoons, bits of occasional verse, etc'.[40] He certainly contributed to the magazine,[41] but no copies from his time have survived.

Socially, the school was mixed. In Charles's year the boys' parents included civil servants, clergymen, and a 'Professor of Music', besides an auctioneer, a draper, a carpenter, a tailor, a maltster, a builder, a farmer, and the 'Organising Secretary to the County Council'. Charles was one of the poorest pupils, but he made a friend at once. George Robinson, four months older than Charles, entered school on the same day. A farmer's son from Harpenden, he too was a scholarship boy. The two became very close both inside and outside school: George Robinson gives us the first glimpse of Charles as others saw him. 'In appearance', he recalled, 'Charles as a boy was of average build and stature standing rather stockily on his feet but with something of a peering, groping effect. One knew instinctively that his eyesight was not good.'[42]

The Grammar School emphasized games, with full lists of cricket and football fixtures, but Charles and George did their best to avoid them. 'By temperament', George recalled, 'we both fell into the category of "swots", anathema to the conventional boy, and this fact I suppose caused us to find in each other some mutual support and solace.'[43] They liked the same books, loving historical romance and fantasy. Favourites were Alexandre Dumas and Anthony Hope's *The Prisoner of Zenda*, Jules Verne, and Nathaniel Hawthorne (*The Scarlet Letter* in particular). They also liked Max Pemberton (a former pupil), author of *The Iron Pirate* and other adventure tales. Charles was keen on Dickens. George liked Walter Scott, but Charles thought the novels were too packed with lumps of historical information.[44] There were chances to take part in theatrical performances, as the school put on an annual play or pageant, on some episode in the town's history. 'Most of the boys', George Robinson recalled, 'tolerated the whole affair, some loathed it but Charles and I loved it. For years in the Williams home there was an old photograph showing Charles as a disappointed lover glowering at a thirteenth-century wedding group in which I was the bridegroom.'

There was theatre at home too. Edith recalled, 'We had charades, amateur theatricals, parlour-games at Christmas-time, and at any time quite a lot of reciting in unison, Father, Charles and I. Our amateur theatricals at home were mostly small plays written by Father. Occasionally we launched into something more ambitious e.g. *As You Like It*.'[45] Charles acted enthusiastically, with a preference for 'character' parts, and enjoyed 'making up stories and plays with a comic dramatic vein'.[46] He wrote poetry, and showed it to his father for critical comment.[47] He also tried his hand at fiction, taking his father's stories as the model. In December 1899, almost a year after he started at the Grammar School, the *Temperance Record* published his first story, credited to 'A Young Writer' (Charles was thirteen). 'My Cousin Dick' tells of a widower with a small daughter who one evening, instead of taking care of his child, goes to the 'Blue Eagle', where he gets drunk, gambles, and quarrels with a man who 'in the heat of the moment, flung a pot at his head'. Dick is brought home unconscious on a hurdle. On recovering, Dick 'declared that from that day he would touch no more spirits, and he never has', admitting that 'had it not been for that blow he should have become a confirmed drunkard'.[48] The 700-word story is a perfect miniature of the type of tale Walter Williams had written by the bushel for similar magazines.

★   ★   ★

Much of Charles's spare time, however, was spent with George Robinson in Silvania. A central European Catholic country, bordered by Laesingen, Stralenheim, Ornstein, and Lillienburg, Silvania was a constitutional monarchy ruled by His Imperial Highness Prince Rudolph and boasting an impressive array of knightly orders, including the Order of the Golden Cross, the Order of St Brendan, the Order of the Lion, and the Order of Maximilian V. Most important was the Order of the Black Gauntlet: 'Very rarely bestowed. Badge: A Gauntlet in iron, from a black ribbon. Motto: Terribilis.'

The political and military fortunes of this imaginary nation (partly modelled on Ruritania from *The Prisoner of Zenda*), its laws, genealogies, court ceremonies, anarchist plots, and literary history, kept Charles and George constantly busy. Like the Brontë sisters with Gondal, or C.S. Lewis and his brother Warren with Boxen, they inhabited an ever-proliferating fantasy kingdom. The ongoing serial was partly written and partly acted out, with Edith also taking part. George Robinson remembered it as:

> a sort of running drama, concerning one Prince Rudolph [...] Princess Rosalind and a Baron de Bracey (!), a comic character in the Falstaff vein. I was usually Rudolph, C's sister Edith the Princess and Charles was Baron de Bracey, in which character he showed a very ripe sense of humour and power of dramatic portrayal.[49]

Charles loved inventing Silvania's laws, constitution, and history, and concocting rituals for its orders of knighthood—for example, the 'Ceremony of Installation of Knight Imperial of the Golden Cross: "Dost thou here absolutely renounce all religions save and except only the Christian, which is the only true one?" [...] Then the Prince shall place the white scarf around the man, and give into his hands a sheathed sword, saying "I give thee this sword; use it well and nobly".'[50] At least one Silvanian play was written, and Charles wrote similar material for the school magazine.

He underwent his first real initiation on 27 March 1901, aged fourteen, when he was confirmed as a member of the Church of England. The priest who prepared him for confirmation found him formidable and muttered that Charles had 'too many brains for him'.[51] Used to debating with his liberal father and his Anglo-Catholic uncle, Charles already raised questions that went well beyond the basics of confirmation class. George Robinson noted the striking confidence of the adolescent Charles's behaviour in church. Tone deaf, he chanted the psalms 'not at all *sotto voce*... in a beautiful rhythm but no tune whatsoever'. Nor was he especially serious: Robinson recalled 'his giggles (in church) when he caught sight of two old ladies with bonnets and big cloaks shining with myriads of beads, singing out loud and strong, "Drunkards in the gate have made songs about me"'.[52] But there was an underlying seriousness. Once confirmed, Charles began attending Holy Communion at 7 a.m. on the first Sunday of every month; soon he took to attending 'more and more often'.[53] He enjoyed, and needed, the ritual—which allowed a sense of immediate contact with the spiritual.

By the summer of 1901 Charles and George had become star pupils. At school they 'carried off most of the form prizes',[54] and in December passed the Cambridge Local Examinations, Charles in Second Class and George in

First.[55] They also won County Council scholarships to University College London.[56] Both boys seemed destined for higher education. At UCL, where they would start in January 1902,[57] they would work for their matriculation exam, which would qualify them for a degree course at the same college. The Silvania fantasy went on as vigorously as ever, but reality was about to change immensely.

2

'The Most Talkative
Young Man'

On 13 January 1902 Charles Williams and George Robinson caught the early train to London. A short walk along the crowded Euston Road (easier for Charles to negotiate now that he was equipped with glasses) brought them to Gower Street and the entrance to University College London. Climbing the stone steps to UCL's pillared portico and entering the labyrinth of corridors and lecture rooms within must have been daunting for two fifteen-year-olds. Alarming in a different way was the mummified corpse of the philosopher Jeremy Bentham, keeping watch in the entrance hall from his glass-fronted wooden sentry-box. Bentham, believing that society should, rather than erect statues to its great men, publicly display their mummified bodies, had set an example by stipulating that his own should be on show. His gaping cadaver, complete with wide-brimmed hat, was a familiar presence to students and the butt of many scurrilous jokes.

George reflected later, 'The County Scholarship scheme was then in its early stages and the education authority did not know what it was doing in pitching boys of 15 into Univ. Coll. Certainly the two boys concerned experienced some bewilderment.'[58] They found themselves amongst 775 students in the Faculty of Arts, and—owing to a mismatch between school and university calendars—beginning in the second term of the academic year.[59] The pre-degree course was a broad one, taken over two years. Both boys registered for Latin, Maths, English, History, French, and General Science, paying fourteen guineas (£14.70) for the two remaining terms.[60] Though their scholarships covered this, it was a large sum: Charles's parents had rented their first home for ten shillings (fifty pence) a week.[61] Two terms at UCL cost the equivalent of six months' rent. And while Charles studied he could not earn.

The boys soon became used to the morning trip to London followed by a day of lectures: a familiar routine but a stimulating one. UCL, a progressive institution founded in 1826 to offer university education to all, without distinction of religion, sex, or politics, was an intellectual powerhouse, and its lecturers and professors taught the teenage 'matriculation' students as well as the undergraduates. English was taught by R. W. Chambers, the renowned scholar-critic, and W. P. Ker, author of *Epic and Romance*, the classic study of medieval narrative poetry. Latin classes were taken by the irascible genius A.E. Housman, whose *Shropshire Lad*, published quietly six years earlier, was just starting to gain popularity. In the crowded corridors between classes the boys might have glimpsed T.W. Rhys Davids, pioneer translator of Buddhist scriptures into English; James Sully and William McDougall, founding fathers of modern psychology; and the world's leading Egyptologist, Flinders Petrie. There was a fine library, and a Students' Union catering for an ebullient and outspoken student body; Charles joined exuberant college celebrations when the Second Boer War ended in June 1902.[62]

Charles was a conscientious student, even though the syllabus was unexciting. In first-year Latin he studied Cicero's *De Senectute*. Maths covered arithmetic, algebra, and geometry; French was grammar, composition, and *Half-Hours with Modern French Authors*. English didn't involve much literature: it was 'History and Structure of the Language' and 'Syntax, composition &c'. History was studied up to the end of the seventeenth century.[63]

Charles and George still elaborated their Silvania fantasy on the St Albans train—they were, after all, only fifteen—but they were growing apart.[64] George used to read in a somewhat random fashion, but Charles was 'much the more studious', and spent most of his time in the college library, studying or writing poems. Poetry had now become his chief preoccupation, and here the boys diverged. George enjoyed ballads in the style of Longfellow but his taste in poetry was unadventurous. He was baffled by the things that Charles was now writing: imitating the manner of the 'Celtic Twilight', for example, in poems like those of the early Yeats, saturated with an imagined, romantic Irishness:

> Who passes? Ho, the fight-worn, song-praised lords,
>   The heroes of our ancient legendry,
>   The royal riders of our land and sea; –
> Ho, way for Fingal and the Fenian kings![65]

Or exploring other mythologies, as in a poem which enlists Yggdrasill, the world-tree of Norse myth, as a symbol of the eternal and numinous persisting within the material and mundane:

> Roaring upwards in the wind,
> All the might of all things ill
> Loosened upon Igdrasil.
>
> Yet this trunk for ever blows
> In the raspberry and the rose,
> And the bark our fingers clutch
> Is iron railing to the touch,
> All the grass beneath out feet
> Is the pavement of the street,
> And the storm that racks and rends
> The quiet voices of our friends.[66]

Or following the 'Decadent' *fin de siècle* poets—Dowson, Wilde, and others who had sought beauty in the forbidden and the perverse—to revel, with adolescent daring, in the darkest and most guilty regions of his own imagination:

> To the Unknown Goddess
> Ah, sweet, be kind—possess me; tis this flight
>   I grudge; dear queen, be passionate and near!
> Are not all close corruptions thine, the sight
>   of uncleaned gutters in the heart, the sheer
> dizziness of decay, whose rising smell
>   makes the entranced soul sick with its own glee
> to be a part of what it hates most? quell
>   the fugitive moments of lucidity,
> and make me loathe and make me lust. Dear Power,
>   sole truth whereof our aching nerves are fond,
> thou who alone canst never shrink or cower,
>   having thyself, and having naught beyond:
> be wholly I now—head to slinking feet;
> and to thyself with my voice murmur *Sweet!*[67]

The pleasures of blasphemy extended to a gleeful, though not very coherent, address to Satan himself:

> Our father who wert once in heaven (the old
> ineffable incantation serves to-day),
> hallowed be thy name within thy cold

malicious devildom, thy sceptre sway
unhindered all our kingdoms, that thy will
be throughout earth accomplished, through this earth
of our most sterile bodies, till it kill
hopes and beliefs with charity, human mirth
hence satisfaction, hence completion, rise ...[68]

These early poems are undated, but clearly Charles Williams was in a ferment of experiment. 'I could not follow him in his adventures into poetry', George Robinson recalled.[69] 'Charles's more reflective outpourings were beyond me. I forget the poem and its subject but something he had written and shown to me was completely obscure and I must have told him so too bluntly. I can feel even now that sensation of a gate shutting between us.'[70]

★   ★   ★

In January 1903, despite having missed one term's tuition, the boys passed their matriculation exam,[71] and they registered for the Bachelor of Arts degree.[72] They continued with French, History, English, Maths, and Latin (studying Ovid's *Tristia* and Livy's *History*).[73] But, for Charles, money was a perpetual worry. Poverty was expensive: students received a guinea discount if they paid a year's fees at the beginning of the autumn term. George paid his twenty guineas at once, but Charles had to pay in two instalments, eight guineas and fourteen.[74] With the Art Depot struggling, scholarship money was being depleted for family expenses. Charles resumed his studies in September 1903 but the college accounts show him paying various guinea and half-guinea fees to the tutors 'in arrear'. In January 1904 he paid fees only for English, French, and Latin. And there the record ends. In the spring of 1904 he and his family gave up the struggle and he withdrew. It was the end of his formal education.

It was a bitter time, for Charles and the whole family. Later Charles would recall 'the doubts which he had felt about his own powers, and the dark look of a future empty of prospects'.[75] He had not even been able to use all of his county scholarship, which should have supported him until the end of 1904. George Robinson recalled rumours that Charles had been offered a scholarship at Oxford.[76] But no such scholarship would solve the problem, for the reality was that Charles had to earn money to support the family. He had taken Civil Service examinations in October 1903 but had not done well enough to be offered work.[77] Edith recalled a wretched time at 36 Victoria Street 'with their father frustrated by blindness and their mother overworked trying to feed and clothe the family, do the housework and shopping, and increasingly help with the hardly profitable shop'.[78] 'This', Edith wrote, 'may have been partly responsible for the nervous explosions which Charles developed during his adolescence, which in turn, may have accounted for the shakiness of hand which lasted for the rest of his life.'[79]

As before, the resourceful Charles Wall found a solution. Through his contacts in the religious book trade, he heard of an opening and told the Williams family.[80] The job was humble enough: it was at the Methodist New Connection Book Room in Holborn, London, and mainly involved packing books for transit,[81] but it meant a weekly wage. Charles applied and was accepted.

It was probably also Wall who introduced his nephew to what would become a favourite novel: *Hadrian the Seventh*, by Frederick Rolfe. Published in 1904, it tells of an impoverished English writer, an unsuccessful aspirant to the priesthood, suddenly elevated through a wildly improbable concatenation of circumstances to the papacy. Taking the name Hadrian in memory of the previous English pope, the hero proceeds to reform the Vatican, defuse international crises, and generally solve the world's problems before dying heroically, the victim of an assassin. The novel, a blatant piece of wish-fulfilment on the part of its disgruntled Catholic-convert author, must have had immediate resonance for Charles, recalling Adrian IV, his predecessor at St Albans Grammar School, and communicating a romanticized but highly critical view of the Vatican. And perhaps its vision of a forlorn and penniless intellectual suddenly elevated to the world's most exalted seat provided Charles with a consoling fantasy. Another important discovery was the Roman Catholic writer G.K. Chesterton. Charles read his novel *The Napoleon of Notting Hill* in 1904 or 1905, and was captivated. Thereafter 'the most important thing in the universe' was Chesterton's witty, argumentative weekly column in the *Daily News*, which Charles hurried out to buy every Saturday.[82]

Meanwhile, autumn 1904 found eighteen-year-old Charles again catching the early train to London, on his way to the Methodist Book Room at 30 Furnivall Street, Holborn. If he met former UCL friends on the train, there must have been some sad and embarrassing moments. The Book Room was the publishing office of the 'New Connexion', a breakaway sector of the Methodist Church. It distributed hymn books, religious pamphlets, and magazines, mostly sent in bulk to schools and missions. Charles probably served at the counter as well as organizing consignments for shipment. It was drudgery, but it was a first, precarious rung on the ladder of the book trade. And he made strenuous efforts to resume his fractured education by enrolling for evening classes at the Working Men's College in Crowndale Road, just north of Euston.[83] Founded in the 1850s by Christian Socialist philanthropists, the Working Men's College provided an acceptable replacement for UCL, with a good library and comfortable common rooms where staff and students mingled. Meals were available; there were debates and student societies. Here he made two new friends, Ernest Nottingham and E.K. Bennett. Others came to him through the Book Room itself. A colleague, Harold Eyers, introduced him to a debating society in Holborn, and so to one of his own friends, Frederick Page. As Page recalled, the debating society members soon recognized Charles as 'a man with a very wonderful mind'.[84] They welcomed him with open arms and he, Bennett, Nottingham, Eyers, and Page were soon firm friends. And back at St Albans, Charles joined an informal church discussion group known as the Theological Smokers, where he would meet George Robinson from time to time, 'always on approachable if not closely intimate terms'. The Smokers (all male) met, George recalled:

> over pipes and cigarettes coffee and cakes [and] explored the universe, regretted nonconformity, had a sneaking regard for but kept a wary eye on His Holiness – all very jolly but somewhat enlivened by the fondness which Charles and I both had for changing our position half way through the discussions so that we could see what was on the other side.[85]

Meetings were monthly, at members' houses, and the topics were serious: for example, 'What were the principles of the Reformation?', 'Sunday Observance', 'The Church of England in relation to other religious bodies', and 'The Report of the Royal Commission on Ecclesiastical Discipline'. The last topic looks especially significant: the 'Smokers' were High Church in their views, and the Royal Commission in 1906 had recommended greater leeway for ceremonial in church services, implying toleration for Anglo-Catholic practices. 'Charles was in his element at these gatherings', George remembered, 'talking a mixture of sound common sense and mysticism enlivened with jibes and japes'. Charles and others often continued the discussions 'half the night afterwards'.[86]

Charles was thinking for himself, and losing his former closeness to his father. He was wryly self-aware about the process. As he told a friend many years later:

> I could show you, I think, the very point in St Albans where, just as I was posting a letter, it occurred to me that when my father said X I despised it, and when any one of my friends said X I thought it was extremely intelligent. It is in our blood; we are furious with our parents before we know it.[87]

Several of Charles's lifelong habits crystallized during this period: the use of paradox, turning an argument back to front to confuse an opponent or just to find out what would happen; the long hours after work devoted to evening classes or intense debate; reading and writing while on the move, amidst all kinds of distractions, with poetry often written on the train to and from work. Even his smoking probably began at this time. Henceforth rarely without a cigarette, he would be, to the end of his days, a theological smoker.

★   ★   ★

Some childhood things lingered on. An affectionate letter of August 1905 from 'Charlie' to sixteen-year-old Edith (*'Mademoiselle et chère soeur'*), who was staying with relatives at the seaside, shows Silvania still flourishing, even without George. Edith was learning shorthand and practising it in her letters. Charles learned a little himself, and suggested mysteriously, '(By-the-way, if you will do a little more of Silvania, will you refer to me in your next letter in shorthand characters? *Don't* say anything about it, & *don't* if you *would rather not*.)'[88] Was he embarrassed at clinging to their private fantasy, or did he simply enjoy secrecy?

In 1907, however, imagination began to illuminate reality in far more profound ways. First the town of St Albans was transformed. Historical pageants were in fashion, and in the summer of 1907 life in Charles's home town was dominated by the St Albans Pageant. The Pageant ran daily from 15 to 20 July, at an arena amid the ruins of Roman Verulamium, five minutes' walk from the Abbey. A huge exercise in community theatre, the Pageant involved some 2,000 performers, mostly townspeople in period costume, including 'Troups of Horsemen and Horsewomen, Knights in Armour, &c.', together with 'A Narrative Chorus of 100 voices' and 'a complete Orchestra of talented Musicians',[89] dramatizing great events from the town's history. These included the capture of Verulamium by Julius Caesar from the British chieftain Cassivelaunus and his Druids in 54 BC; the sack of the town by Boadicea in AD 61; the martyrdom of St Alban; the Peasants' Revolt of 1381; the Second Battle of St Albans in 1461; and Queen Elizabeth's visit in 1572. For the spectators, there was a specially constructed 4,000-seat grandstand. Railway companies ran excursion trains and tickets were marketed by Thomas Cook.

During the days of this extravaganza the streets of St Albans were filled with a motley assortment of Druids, Tudor ladies, and armoured knights. A local historian recalls:

> the performers dressed at home and walked or drove to the pageant ground, and one laughed to see a Roman soldier strolling along smoking a pipe, and a Briton in skins riding a bicycle. One saw an Elizabethan lady in brocade (probably the drawing-room curtains cut up), walking arm-in-arm with a cross-gartered Saxon in a yellow wig and long drooping moustache.[90]

It was as if time had become transparent, its distances dissolved. People from all epochs formed a single community on the town's streets. Whether Charles took any active part is unknown. His sister Edith was certainly involved, appearing as an early Tudor lady.[91] The Pageant made a deep impression. It showed Charles new possibilities in theatre, and a different way to consider time. One day he would write a civic pageant of his own.

★ ★ ★

20 September 1907 was Charles's twenty-first birthday. How, if at all, he celebrated, we don't know, but he was now legally of age. As a poet he had not yet found an individual voice and was still unpublished, but he had achieved a fully competent verse technique, exemplified by the poem he presented to Edith in November, for her birthday:

> At the World's End
> Long hast thou waited, O Soul of mine,
>   Long hast thou stayed by the far world's end,
> Where the many lamps of the City shine,
>   Where the voices of many greetings blend? [. . .]
>
> Yet thou art patient to watch and wait,
>   And ever I see thee as I dream,
> By the entering-in of the Gladsome Gate,
>   Where the blazoned shields of the knighthood gleam.

> They break the bread and they pour the wine,
> Master for servant, and friend for friend!
> Ah, shall I come to thee, Soul of Mine,
> To the City set by the far world's end?[92]

The poem blends the chivalric vision of Silvania ('blazoned shields of the knighthood') with glimpses of mysticism—the Soul, the bread and the wine, the spiritual City. There is also a paradoxical dynamic between egalitarianism and hierarchy: the wine is poured by 'Master for servant, and friend for friend'. There are masters and servants; but the master serves, and all are friends. Religion, romance, and politics are blended.

Like other young members of the Abbey congregation he had been conscripted into lending a hand with Sunday School activities, and one evening at Christmas 1907 found himself helping to run a children's party at the Abbey. There was a nativity play, and he was surrounded by an unruly mob of excited children in makeshift costumes when he found his attention suddenly riveted by a young woman nearby. Her looks were striking: she had piercing eyes, a cloud of dark hair, and a commanding manner. She was beautiful; and watching her deal calmly and firmly with the children he found her beauty, momentarily, to be more than earthly. Something shone within her, or through her, which he perceived as spiritual—a revelation of absolute beauty which gave him a kind of shock. And then the pandemonium of the children's party closed in again.

He managed to exchange a few words with the girl, and introduce himself. She told him her name was Florence Conway. At first he was tongue-tied with shyness, but she helped him and soon he began to talk—unstoppably, as it seemed. 'For the first five minutes of our meeting', she recalled, 'I thought him the most silent, withdrawn young man I had ever met. For the next five minutes I thought him the nicest young man I had ever met. For the rest of the evening I thought him the most talkative young man I had ever met, and still the nicest.' They slipped away from the party and strolled out into the cool air, under the stars and the walls of the Abbey. It was a magical sight: 'The pleasant Abbey meadows tilting gently down to the river seemed to reverse their slope to gaze at us as we passed by', Florence remembered. 'As we walked under the great cedar tree its branches were as gigantic arms upheld to bless. And as we walked Charles talked. He talked of Browning.'[93] Perhaps it was something of a monologue, but neither of them cared. They were happy together. And when they had said goodnight and Charles turned back towards 36 Victoria Street, he realized he was in

love. Something extraordinary had happened, in the most mundane circumstances. But then again, had it not been a kind of Nativity, an incarnation, or birth of Love itself in human form? Was it accident that he had been
surrounded by kings and shepherds, the archetypal figures of the Christmas
story? When, much later, he came to write a poem about that evening, this
was how he remembered it: a miraculous blend of the mundane and the
mythical:

> Where did you meet your love, young man?
>   Where did you meet your love?
> 'I met my love in a crowded room,
>   With a carven roof above.'
>
> What did you say to your love, young man,
>   With all your mother wit?
> ' "How hot it is!" or "How do you do?"
>   And there was an end of it!'
>
> Who was beside you then, young man?
>   Who was beside you then?
> 'Gaspar, Melchior, Balthazar,
>   And a crowd of shepherd-men!'
>
> What did you say to them, young man,
>   Silently, through the din?
> ' "Princes, when ye come in to her,
>   I pray you, lead me in." '[94]

3

The Silver Stair

Florence Sarah Conway—known in the family as 'Flo'—was born on 23 May 1886, the youngest of five girls. Like the Williamses, the Conways had left London in financial disarray. Edward Conway had been a builders' merchant, trading in the Canonbury Road near Charles's childhood home.[95] But in 1885 the business failed and the family moved to St Albans, where Conway now worked in a hardware shop. Florence had been born just after the move.

In a crowded household, Florence had to fight for her share of attention. She was bright, impulsive, and noisy. Stories were told of her, aged three, at play in the nearby churchyard, joining a funeral party during a hymn and cheerfully exhorting the widow to 'Sing up!'; of her finding an old Welsh high-crowned hat in the house one Sunday, putting it on and trotting into church calling out 'Look at my new bonnet!' Pretty and sparky, with quick wit and a sharp tongue, she was also a romantic. Said to take after her French great-grandmother, she felt herself a little exotic, and disliked her first name (taken from long-suffering Florence Dombey, heroine of Dickens's *Dombey and Son*, which her mother had enjoyed during pregnancy).[96] Florence had joined the St Albans Pageant as a 'Lady of the time of King Edward VI'; her photograph—with her dressed in a sweeping skirt and a high 'horned' head-dress with veil, taken on her twenty-first birthday—adorned the Pageant's official programme. It was an image she treasured.

Her father, James Conway, knew the countryside and loved field sports, not least as an amateur poacher. He took Florence with him, teaching her about birds and animals, and showing her how to tickle trout: finding a fish in its lurking place under the bank and gently stroking its belly with a finger, lulling it into a trance before pulling it out onto the grass.[97] But Florence also read a good deal and had enjoyed school; she had decided to become a teacher. When she met Charles Williams she was working as a classroom assistant, before starting a teacher-training course.

Both Charles and Florence were busy with work and family duties: Florence recalled that often they were 'abundantly thankful to see one another occasionally from opposite sides of the road'.[98] But they walked together in the countryside around St Albans, continuing the kind of literary conversation they had begun that Christmas night at the Abbey. Charles was shy, and discussion perhaps provided a pretext for meeting. Years later, Florence remembered 'those walks and literary conversations' as 'lovely'; but she added, 'we never talked of love'.[99]

★ ★ ★

For the first six months of the relationship, Charles toiled in his humble job at the Methodist Book Room. Then the Book Room closed down.[100] Luckily Fred Page, his friend from the debating club, worked at the London branch of the Oxford University Press, where he was proofreading a seventeen-volume edition of Thackeray. 'This', he recalled, 'was more than a full-time job, and I was asked if there was anyone I could recommend to come as my assistant.' He mentioned Charles, who was appointed and began work in the Paper, Printing, and Proof-Reading Department of the Press on 9 June 1908.[101] 'For eight years', Page recalled, 'we sat side by side in different parts of Amen Corner, one of us reading aloud to the other, who checked the proofs.'[102]

Charles Williams had joined one of the world's great publishing houses. The Oxford University Press traced its origins to the fifteenth century, when the first book had been printed at Oxford. For the next few centuries its business centred on printing Bibles, for which it held a special license. In the 1860s it entered the lucrative school textbook market, developing into a fast-growing business. Originally based solely in Oxford, 'the OUP' (as employees called it) opened a London office to promote its wares, and the London branch began to commission and publish its own books. Thus a division of labour had developed: the Oxford end of the business published scholarly books, mostly under the prestigious 'Clarendon Press' imprint, while the London branch produced textbooks, and books for the general market. The 'London' and 'Oxford' businesses were twin publishing houses— but conjoined twins, for their finances were interconnected and they used the same printing presses. The head of the London office was known, confusingly, as the 'Publisher'; his opposite number at Oxford, equally strangely, was called the 'Secretary', because technically he was Secretary to the

Delegates, a panel of Oxford academics who oversaw the Press. There was lively rivalry between employees in the two camps. The 'Oxford' staff prided itself on producing works of scholarship and fine printing, and looked down on the plebeian productions of the money-grubbing London business. The 'London' staff, on the other hand, boasted of getting the real work done, facing the challenges of a competitive business, making money without which the self-important Oxford business would collapse.

'Amen Corner' (the first word pronounced to rhyme with 'stamen', *never* with 'Carmen') was the OUP's busy London headquarters, occupying a block of buildings on Ave Maria Lane, between the monumental domes of the Central Criminal Court (the Old Bailey) and St Paul's Cathedral. Traces of London's ancient City Wall, built by the Romans, ran 100 yards away. Behind the building was Stationers' Hall, where the first printers of Shakespeare and Jonson had registered their work. Nearby on Paternoster Row, the block's northern limit, Charles's artist uncle, Charles Wall, now a publisher too, had the offices of his Talbot Press. London's General Post Office and Central Telegraph office, nerve centres of the British Empire's communications, were two blocks to the north. Charles must have felt he had arrived at the centre of the world.

It was, though, a somewhat chaotic centre. Amen Corner had grown with the business, starting from a single office and taking over neighbouring premises, removing walls and knocking doors through as it went. By 1908 it had become a bewildering labyrinth of rooms, staircases, and passages with offices improvised in all kinds of uncomfortable corners. It was easy to get lost, and easy to lose oneself on purpose. So long as Charles and Fred Page got their proofreading done, they were free to perch, more or less unnoticed, in any spot they could find around the untidy building. By the end of 1908 Thackeray was complete, so the two friends spent the next seven years proofreading other books. That might seem a long time to be kept as mere proofreaders, but at Amen Corner there was no planned career progression and no training. New employees were simply given some humble job and expected to get on with it, absorbing the business of publishing by osmosis from the incessant bustle around them. Charles was lucky to be given such a meaningful task as proofreading. Geoffrey Faber, joining the Press a few years later, recalled being 'given some catalogues, a few extremely terse instructions', and being set to cutting slips of paper from printed sheets and gluing them onto pages of foolscap to make a list of Oxford books.[103] But the Press rewarded loyalty. Williams knew that if he were diligent, he could expect a job for life. And after all, the OUP may not have seemed very different in atmosphere from the Methodist Book Room. Much of the business consisted of Bibles, prayer books, and hymnals, and there was a strongly selling list of popular religious anthologies: *The Vision of Righteousness*, *Voices of Comfort*, *A Book of Sorrow*, and other saccharine titles.

Perched on shabby chairs in some cubby hole or quiet half-landing at Amen Corner, Fred Page and Charles Williams found plenty of time to chat about things other than proofs. In particular, they discussed poetry: Williams's own, and other people's. Page had a particular interest in Coventry Patmore, a controversial poet and Roman Catholic convert who had died just over a decade earlier, in 1896. To say that Page was enthusiastic about Patmore would be inadequate. 'Obsessed' might be more accurate. He read Patmore's works intensively, and was determined to discover everything he could about Patmore's life and writings.

Patmore (1823–96) is nowadays remembered as the author of *The Angel in the House*, a novel-in-verse about courtship and marriage. The poem suggested, daringly, that sexual love between man and woman could be a spiritual path, a way to God. In a later sequence of poems, *The Unknown Eros*, Patmore had gone on to alarm critics by elaborating in fiercely sensual imagery his view that God's love for the human soul is of the same kind as (though infinitely stronger than) the lover's erotic desire for his partner. God, in Patmore's view, is the Lover and Bridegroom of the soul, and their union should take place, ecstatically, in the human body, whose purpose is to be a 'Little, sequester'd pleasure-house / For God and for His Spouse'—the Spouse being the individual soul.[104] Victorian readers found these ideas daunting. Some critics described such passages merely as 'mystical' and 'obscure'; others were more outspoken. An example was Sir Shane Leslie, who wrote that the poems 'left Swinburne' (then regarded as a daringly erotic poet) 'panting in his gilded brothel'.[105]

Patmore had left mysteries in his wake. Certain poems in *The Unknown Eros* seemed to hint, startlingly, that mystical experience might be found by combining chastity with intense sexual desire. In his poem 'The Contract', Patmore depicted the first meeting of Adam with Eve. Adam invites his love to a bridal bed of roses; but Eve suggests that, just as in the heavens Venus and the sun stay always separate, so she and Adam too should place 'a voluntary bar' to their desires and refrain from physical union. They will touch, and they will kiss, but he is to promise that they shall remain virgins. Adam promises, and at once experiences 'Joy [that] comes down from Heaven in floods and shocks, / As from Mount Abora comes the avalanche.'[106] Another poem, 'Deliciae Sapientiae de Amore', sings the praises of unconsummated love ('O, spousals high; / O, doctrine blest, / unutterable in even the happiest sigh'), and again praises the example of the planet which never touches the sun, but is content

> once in his long year
> With praeternuptial ecstasy and fear [...]
> With hastening pace to come
> Nearer, though never near,
> His Love
> And always inaccessible sweet Home;
> There on his path doubly to burn,
> Kiss'd by her doubled light.[107]

And in 'The Child's Purchase', Patmore praises the marriage of the Virgin Mary with St Joseph, a relationship filled with 'Such rapture of refusal that no kiss / Ever seal'd wedlock so conjoint with bliss.'[108] Unlike most advocates of chastity, who recommended suppression of sexual desire, Patmore seemed to believe that desire should be experienced to the full—but not satisfied.

Exactly what Patmore *had* believed, however, was tantalizingly hard to discover. In the last decade of his life he had written a prose work, *Sponsa Dei* ('The Bride of God'), which, according to his friend, the critic Edmund Gosse, had summed up his views on 'the significance of physical love in religion'. Gosse, reading the book in manuscript, found it 'certainly audacious' but also a 'masterpiece'.[109] Nonetheless, *Sponsa Dei* was bound to be deeply controversial. Fearing that 'some parts of the book were too daring to be safely placed in all hands', Patmore showed the manuscript to the poet and Jesuit priest, Gerard Manley Hopkins, who had returned it to him with the enigmatic remark, 'That's telling secrets'.[110] Hopkins had followed this with an agitated letter warning Patmore of 'the abuses high contemplation is subject to', and mentioning the sexual aberrations of various unorthodox mystics.[111] Patmore, alarmed, burnt the manuscript.[112] Fred Page was fascinated by Patmore's poems, his ideas, and the enigma of the vanished masterpiece, *Sponsa Dei*. He discussed Patmore's poetry with Charles Williams, and if Williams had not read Patmore before, he did now. The two young men found Patmore's literary brew of religion, poetry, and sex irresistibly fascinating.

Meanwhile, Charles was working on his own poems, and writing about his love for Florence. One January night, probably in 1910, Florence was on her way home through the snow after a lecture, when, as she recalled:

> almost within sight of home, Charles overtook me. He put a parcel into my hands saying he had written a Sonnet Sequence called *The Silver Stair*. Its theme was Renunciation. Would I read it and tell him my opinion? And he fled. I thought 'Oh dear! Is he going to enter a monastery?' [...]
>
> I read *The Silver Stair* by flickering candle-light in my cold attic room. There were eighty-two sonnets and I read them all. So lovely they seemed; I read them again and yet again. Comprehension dawned and I cried aloud 'Why, I believe they are about me!' I read them again to make quite sure.
>
> Next day I wrote my first letter to Charles. It seemed to please him and though *The Silver Stair* had Renunciation for its theme our walks continued.[113]

★   ★   ★

The parcel that Florence had unwrapped in her chilly bedroom contained Williams's first substantial poetic work: a sequence of eighty-two sonnets. They were not easy to understand. No wonder Florence 'read them again and yet again'. Highly wrought in elaborate, old-world diction, the sonnets bristled with difficult ideas expressed in prickly and convoluted phrases. Williams had become, like his father, a skilful writer of sonnets, but he lacked the poetic resources to express the complex ideas he wanted to convey.

The Silver Stair depicts a disillusioned man, who has heard of love but never experienced it. One night all this changes, when he sees a woman from whose face the Divine seems to shine forth. The sonnets go on to examine love from a great many angles. Some make grandiose startling spiritual claims: this lady was 'Foreshadowed on the mind of God' from before time;[114] the praises usually given to the Blessed Virgin should be brought 'as a tribute' to her.[115] Yet he wishes his love to be secret, and 'will not call her, lest there be / God or some angel listening in the void'.[116] Such ideas seem, in Christian terms, to verge on blasphemy.

Elsewhere he develops a total identification between Love and Christ. Two sonnets depict Love bound and manacled, dragged by soldiers amongst 'fierce hands and hate and faces grim', and carrying 'The Cross whereon is our redemption nailed'. When Love 'fail[s] / Beneath it', its weight is taken by Mary Magdalene, a prostitute, who carries it despite stones and insults hurled by the crowd. And Williams implies that the Love he identifies with

Christ is not merely a selfless spiritual love, but also *eros*, the love of the body and of physical desire. Sonnet LXVII tells us that 'all soft passion [and] all sweet content' are manifestations of 'God the Holy Ghost', and ends with a triumphant paean to the many kinds of love: 'All lives of lovers are His song of love, [...] The silver and the golden stairs are His, / The altar His – yea, His the lupanar.'

'Lupanar'—a word as rare in 1910 as it is today—means 'brothel'. Florence probably had no idea what it meant.

But *The Silver Stair* was not a plea for sexual freedom. The clue is in the title. Throughout the sonnets, silver symbolizes virginity, whilst gold represents consummated love. Thus 'The silver and the golden stairs' are contrasted paths: love lived in celibacy, and love physically fulfilled. Towards the end of the sequence the message is stated with particular force. Sonnet LXXX portrays a 'bridal night' when other lovers will be 'stretched on the golden couch of their delight'; but the poet envisages greeting the day with '[trumpet] notes of silver', while:

> Toward white gates, down many a shouting street,
> Masters of hope and passion and sorrow, we,
> With clash of sword on shield, move and acclaim
> The Solemn Feast of Love's Virginity.

★   ★   ★

The Silver Stair shows Williams sharing Patmore's enthusiasm for celibacy in sexual love. Telling Florence that the poems were about 'Renunciation', he meant renunciation not of their relationship but of sexual consummation. Since respectable couples in 1910 were not expected to have sex before marriage, this might not seem very startling. But Williams envisaged celibacy between lovers as leading to a special spiritual state, perhaps even replacing marriage. Florence, reading the manuscript alone in her chilly bedroom, understood little of this. Williams's convoluted language stood in the way. She thought the poems 'lovely', and was flattered. But it would have been unlike her to offer unmixed praise. Though her letter thanking him for the sonnets has not survived, she later recalled what she called its 'forthright' concluding sentence: 'One day you will be a true poet and right at the end of your life you will be writing poetry that other poets will praise.'[117] Probably she told him the sonnets were *on the way* to being true poetry; that they showed promise. She adds, in her late recollection of the episode,

'Whatever the demerits of those sonnets as poetry, I loved them.'[118] That is not fulsome, but it probably expresses her honest feelings.

It was certainly like Florence to be 'forthright'. In the course of their walks she was embarrassed by Charles's habit of quoting, at full volume and with suitable gestures, his favourite passages of poetry. Sometimes heads turned and people stared. Florence rebuked him. Shy in other ways, Charles cared nothing for this. He teased her by citing the biblical example of King David and his wife Michal: 'David danced before the Lord with all his might; and [...] Michal Saul's daughter looked through a window, and saw King David leaping and dancing before the Lord; and she despised him in her heart.'[119] He took to calling her 'Michal', and she so much preferred this grand and masculine-sounding name to the hated 'Flo' that she adopted it. For the rest of her life she would be known as Michal.

It came naturally to Charles to confer nicknames, perhaps because he, Edith, and George had identified so readily with their characters in the Silvania saga. But the name he had found for Florence was dangerous, embodying an unresolved tension in the relationship. In the Bible story, Michal is a killjoy, her criticism of David punished with barrenness: 'Therefore Michal the daughter of Saul had no child unto the day of her death.'[120] It was an ominous choice.

* * *

Like Charles, Michal was developing a career. After teacher training, in 1910 she began a year's teaching experience to become fully qualified. Meanwhile Charles caught the train each morning to Holborn Viaduct, then walked to Amen Corner, stopping at a barber's shop for a shave, since the hand tremor which had persisted since the 'nervous explosions' of his adolescence left him unable to shave without risk of cutting himself. After work he might go to an evening class or discussion group, getting back to St Albans on a late train, reading or writing as he travelled.

And Fred Page found a new opportunity to help him. Pursuing his mission to learn everything possible about Coventry Patmore, Page had taken to writing to anyone who had known the poet. In 1907 he had introduced himself to the poet and journalist Alice Meynell, an intimate friend of Patmore in his last years. Alice and her husband Wilfrid were a hospitable pair, and Page had become a regular visitor at their London flat in Granville Place, just behind Oxford Street. After reading *The Silver Stair*, Page decided it was time to introduce Williams. On 3 May 1911 he wrote to Alice Meynell, asking if he might bring 'a most remarkable sequence of eighty-three [*sic*] sonnets on the life of virginity' and their author:

> Mr. Charles Williams. It is, I believe you will agree with me, such a sequence as should have had Rossetti, Patmore and Francis Thompson for audience. I ought to say that I am writing without Mr. Williams's knowledge, but he is so modest and diffident that he will make no efforts towards getting these and many other poems published, but I know that a favourable opinion from you would be an incentive.[121]

He enclosed three sonnets—admitting 'it is a fault that each of his sonnets should read like a riddle'. But his advocacy succeeded; on 27 May he took his friend to meet the Meynells.

At age sixty-three Alice Meynell was at the height of her reputation as poet and essayist. She and Wilfrid had been youthful converts to Roman Catholicism; both were from privileged backgrounds but had started without money: Wilfrid because he had alienated his colliery-owning Quaker father, and Alice because her aristocratic-bohemian parents had been of precarious means. They had made their way by hard work as journalists, and by their hospitality, holding frequent parties and (in modern parlance) 'networking' extensively. The centre of a consciously 'Catholic' literary coterie, they lived above the offices of Burns and Oates, leading Catholic publishers, whom Wilfrid served as literary adviser. He also edited the *Dublin Review*, a prominent Catholic literary magazine. Alice's friendship with the elderly Coventry Patmore had been a sentimental entanglement so intense that Wilfrid had had to warn Patmore away from his wife in decisive terms. More famously, in 1888 Wilfrid Meynell had discovered the devout Catholic poet Francis Thompson, author of *The Hound of Heaven*, living on the streets of London as an alcoholic opium-addict. The Meynells had published his poems and supported Thompson until his death in 1907—which had left something of a gap in their lives, for they enjoyed fostering needy Catholic talent. Page had picked a good moment to introduce a new protégé.

Williams's account of his first visit, in a letter to his aunt, is tinged with social comedy. Alice Meynell, with her *grande dame* manner and literary name-dropping, presented an alarming spectacle:

> Well, to describe Saturday. The first meeting with Our lady of Criticism [...] is a positive shock. She is moderately tall – about my height, perhaps hardly; has no looks at all; a manner which is not gush & not affectation, but smacks at first

of both. [...] I think the peculiarity is in the sound of her words, – if I knew music I would note them for you. 'O-o-h Wilfrid!' – something like that. [...]

One tastes there the 'tone' of the real literary culture [...] The names that crop up casually & are dismissed! [...] 'Aubrey de Vere once said to me...' 'Meredith used to argue...': besides of course the spiritual powers of Patmore and Thompson. Another thing is the curiously matter-of-fact acceptance of religious facts. Prayer is spoken of perfectly easily, & as a matter of course, with none of the 'when we...um...m'm...er...in short, pray!!' of ordinary English conversation. [...]

After we had been there some minutes [...] she opened the ball by 'leading me out'. 'I wonder if you would mind me pointing out to you a few things I thought might be altered in your poems. I have marked a few places – while I was reading them the second time, I hope you don't mind.'

Myself—(not quite grasping that *Alice Meynell* was speaking thus apologetically to *me* –) But – my sonnets?! But I am only too grateful for any trouble that Mrs Meynell has taken – [...] I have only been afraid that Mr Page rather thrust them on your attention. She admitted that whenever one hears of sonnets there is a faint momentary qualm, 'but it was nothing in this case. They are so beautiful, so wonderfully beautiful!' (!) And 'the idea is *quite* clear: it is only here and there...'[122]

After lunch, they went over the sonnets together. Alice Meynell was enthusiastic: ' "This is a really great one: but then—so many of them are great." '

We stayed till about six. When I took up the book in order to go, Wilfrid Meynell asked me when he was to have them in print? I answered that I had never considered that matter seriously.

Did I not think I ought to?

Again I said that with the vast amount written at the present day, verse should be either very beautiful indeed, or else the thought should be important, should in fact be *urgent* for publication.

Off they went again. Wilfrid Meynell considered that the beauty justified it: 'in fairness to you, Mr. Williams, they should be published.' As for the lady, 'O-o-h, but don't you think it is urgent?'

I said again that if Mrs Meynell thought so –

She answered that there was a whole system of thought in them. (!)

Wilfrid explained that the poems could be published fairly cheaply—250 copies could be printed for two shillings and sixpence each—and promised to subscribe £5 in advance, for forty copies. So, Williams reported:

the upshot of the whole matter was: that I promised to make the few alterations Mrs Meynell had suggested, & to think out a title for each one (which

Fred Page is now doing, while I criticize), & to seriously consider, in the light of the offered five pounds, the possibility of publication. Mrs Meynell asked me to go again, and I escaped.[123]

By the end of the month the titles had been drafted, and Page took the manuscript to Granville Street to see if the Meynells approved of them. He was also working on an explanatory preface to the poems. Williams prepared to visit Alice Meynell again, confessing, 'I have been reading and considering the sequence with [...] altogether new ideas of its worth. Your name has, if one may say so, carried so much weight for so long that it seems hardly credible, even now, that you are interested in it.'[124]

But reality had to be faced. In July, Williams admitted that he could not afford to pay anything towards the cost of publication. 'There is', he explained, 'an urgent need for my own earnings at home'; and his friends were no more prosperous.[125] Thus it looked as if *The Silver Stair* would remain unpublished. Still, he continued writing new poems, and visiting the Meynells. He also promised to send 'the scheme of a dramatic poem dealing with the clash of the ecclesiastical and the mystical [...] somewhere about 900 A.D.'[126] And Alice Meynell placed one of his new poems, 'Proserpina', in the *Saturday Review*, a prominent magazine.[127]

By February 1912, rather than leave the sonnets unpublished, the Meynells had offered to meet the entire cost of publication.[128] The final text went to Herbert and Daniel, publishers, on 25 March.[129] By mid-May Williams was correcting galley proofs and arranging permission for the quotation from W.B.Yeats's *The Shadowy Waters*, which was to go on the title page—including the strikingly apposite lines:

> It is love that I am seeking for,
> But of a beautiful, unheard-of kind
> That is not in the world.

The sonnets retained Fred Page's titles to help the reader, but the 'prose argument' was dropped—fortunately, since Fred's preamble, written from somewhere on the wilder shores of literary Catholic devotion, would have deterred most readers.

The Silver Stair crawled towards publication with frustrating slowness. On 24 July Wilfrid Meynell was 'wondering why no news of the volume came'.[130] Three days later Williams had checked the first thirty-two pages of revised proofs, and with Wilfrid promising 500 copies, reflected, 'The number of copies "staggers" me; to hurl so many copies on the world seems presumption—but of course I agree and accept very gratefully.'[131] At last, on 14 October, Meynell announced:

> My dear Mr Williams,
> I hold the first copy of your book in my hands, with joy. Does it not look a beautiful offering for her in whose lasting honour it was written? [...] I want to make a meeting and carry a toast to the health of your book.[132]

Williams received copies on 12 November. He wrote at once thanking Wilfrid Meynell 'for the thought, trouble, time, and labour which you have spent on the least of minor poets. [...] On my word, I almost begin to admire the poetry! [...] I sign myself, Protector of the Poor, Ever yours most gratefully, Charles Williams.'[133] He inscribed a copy for the Meynells, 'To the Givers'.[134]

Predictably, a religious sonnet sequence by an unknown poet made little impact. Copies went to Hilaire Belloc, G.K. Chesterton, May Sinclair, and Lascelles Abercrombie. The first two were prominent Catholic authors, May Sinclair a writer and suffragette, and Abercrombie a well-known poet. Only Belloc acknowledged the book, and even he did not review it, though Alice Meynell had no qualms about reviewing it favourably, writing, 'Poetry is a region of the mind, and the author of the *Silver Stair* lives there.'[135]

The most encouraging response came from Sir Walter Raleigh, Professor of English Literature at Oxford, to whom Humphrey Milford, the OUP's newly appointed Assistant Secretary, had sent a copy. Raleigh wrote back:

> It is a wonderful little book; [...] no doubt about it; real poetry. More like Rossetti than anyone else...It really is as if the author had not suspected that there was such a thing as Love, & had discovered it and written about it before, or almost before, any touch of familiarity had fallen on it. [...] It completely knocks out some other new verse that came with it.[136]

★   ★   ★

But perhaps, by introducing Williams to the Meynells, the well-intentioned Page had done him a disservice. Even as *The Silver Stair* worked its way through the press, Harold Munro at the Poetry Bookshop in London was publishing *Georgian Poetry, 1911–12*, an anthology intended to revitalize English poetry with realism and colloquial language. And that same summer, an ambitious 27-year-old American poet, Ezra Pound, was meeting in London with two other poets, Hilda Doolittle and Richard Aldington, to elaborate the principles of what they would call 'Imagism', which included 'Direct treatment of the "thing" whether subjective or objective', and the use of free verse instead of rhyme and metre. Together, Georgians and Imagists would sweep away everything Alice Meynell stood for. Refined sentiments, archaic diction, and intricately patterned stanzas already looked outdated; the coming war would put an end to their prevalence in poetry. In due course Williams would find his own way to modernism, but by encouraging him to link himself so firmly to the Meynells, the well-meaning Fred Page may have set back his friend's poetic development by ten or even twenty years. In the summer of 1912, however, Williams's thoughts were far from such reflections. He held in his hands a solid, well-printed volume of his own poems, and his ambitions were growing. He was writing a play, and making plans to compose an Arthurian epic.

4

'Marriages are Made
in Heaven'

Charles's play owed a good deal to his uncle, Charles Wall. In 1910 Wall had published *Relics of the Passion*, a book surveying relics of the crucifixion venerated in European churches: fragments of the True Cross, pieces of Christ's garment, vessels containing his supposed blood, and such things as the famous Turin Shroud. Wall also summarized legends of the Holy Grail. But the largest category concerned the Crown of Thorns worn by Christ at the crucifixion. Wall listed fifty-six churches displaying individual thorns, or the entire crown.

The book stirred Williams's imagination. By late 1911 he was planning a play to be called *The Chapel of the Thorn*,[137] about a struggle for possession of a thorn from Christ's crown and the chapel where it was housed. He finished it in August 1912, soon after seeing *The Silver Stair* through the press. The play is set in the early Middle Ages, outside the chapel, which, with its relic, is guarded by a solitary priest, Joachim, and his young acolyte, Michael. The play depicts a three-cornered struggle between mysticism, represented by Joachim; the Church, represented by the local abbot, Innocent; and paganism, in the form of Amael, a bard and high priest of the old gods. Abbot Innocent wants to wall in the chapel and take the thorn so that it will draw pilgrims to his abbey. Joachim, the mystic, believing only in the value of direct communion with God and lacking respect for the church hierarchy, wants to keep the thorn at his humble chapel, and has the local villagers' promise that they will fight to keep the chapel independent. What Joachim does not know is that the villagers are concerned only because the chapel has been built over the tomb of Druhild, a pagan hero who, they believe, will one day rise from the dead. For their Christianity is only superficial: whilst the women venerate the Virgin Mary, the men are pagan to the core, clinging tenaciously to the old gods and to their custom of buying young women to keep, alongside their wives, as concubines or 'chamber-maids'.

The play consists largely of debates between the three viewpoints of mystic, ecclesiastic, and pagan bard. Joachim sees the Church as a mere agent of exploitation, and believes that its rules are pointless since only direct spiritual experience has any value. Abbot Innocent, however, argues that such a view, with its trust in love and freedom, is too demanding for ordinary people. For their own good, they need authority and rules. In the name of the Church he is ready to use force to seize the chapel and take away the thorn.

Amael, the pagan bard, representing a heroic and brutal world, speaks much of the play's best poetry. He admits that he has performed human sacrifice:

> Twice hath my hand lain over mortal eyes,
> While, with the incantation of the Fire,
> I struck forth human blood upon the stone!

But he can also be modest:

> I am a little dust
> Blown from the ruined temples of the gods
> And troubled by the feet of the white Christ
> When he goes through the land.[138]

Amael's most important relationship is with Michael, Joachim's young acolyte. Joachim hopes that if the thorn can be retained, Michael will one day take his place as priest of the chapel. But Michael longs for a life of adventure: his heart is stirred by Amael's tales. Amael urges him to leave the tame life of the chapel and sail with him to learn magic, poetry, and the harp:

> Is it time in youth
> To wait upon white altars? Hark, the gods
> Sing at their feasting, not as hermits sing!
> We servants of the gods have heard their song,
> And some of us are mad with their delight,
> And some are lords of ships and raids and fire,
> And some have crept into the black bear's den
> With a torch and a spear and slain him: but we all
> Are heroes, princes, champions![139]

In the play's second and final act, Abbot Innocent placates the villagers by agreeing not to wall in the chapel—a promise he clearly intends to break.

Joachim is forced to hand over the thorn and wanders off alone into the hills, while young Michael slips away to sail with the pagan ships for a life of poetry and adventure. The tension between Church, inner spiritual life, and paganism remains unresolved—probably because Williams sympathizes with all three viewpoints. Intellectually he acknowledges the case for the Church's authority; but his heart is with the mysticism of Joachim; and he responds viscerally to the pagan glitter of Amael's world. The energies and tensions that will form his major poetry are already seething in *The Chapel of the Thorn*. The play's debate is his inner drama. Alice Meynell, however, never acknowledged the play's value. Until May 1915 she kept promising to discuss it with Williams;[140] but she never did. It seems odd that she showed so little interest. Did she find the play disturbing—suggesting, perhaps, that Williams, like the acolyte Michael, might break away from the path set out for him by his elders and betters?

★ ★ ★

Williams was not unduly troubled by Alice Meynell's lack of interest in his play, probably because he was thinking seriously about writing an Arthurian epic. The Victorian age had been rich in Arthurian poems—most famously, Tennyson's *Idylls of the King* and Swinburne's *Tristram of Lyonesse*, both completed in the 1880s. Williams wrote, many years later, that his desire to tackle the theme began 'in a vague disappointment with the way in which Tennyson treated the Hallows of the Grail in [his poem] "Balin and Balan" [...] It was clear that the great and awful myth of the Grail had not been treated adequately in English verse.'[141] To him, the Arthurian material was never merely 'legends'; it was a *myth*—a timeless, universal story with many meanings. And the quest for the Holy Grail was not just one Arthurian episode among many. The Grail—the cup used by Jesus at the Last Supper, held by Joseph of Arimathea to collect Jesus' blood at the crucifixion, and finally brought to Britain—was the original vessel of Communion, the archetypal chalice of the Mass. The Grail represented the coming together of God and man, heaven and earth. For Williams it was the Arthurian myth's central symbol and culmination.

Recalling the early days at Amen Corner, Fred Page wrote, 'Very much more than Thackeray it was C.W.'s plan of a poem on the Arthurian myths that we discussed',[142] implying that they discussed it as early as 1908. Certainly around 1911 Williams began to keep a commonplace book, where

he noted ideas for the poem, and his research for its materials. It is a fascinating document of an ambitious young poet's mind at work.[143] The first
entry, a line from Tennyson, stands alone at the top of the page. It looks like
a declaration of intent, and it reads:

'His epic, his King Arthur, some twelve books.'

We can guess when the volume was started because Williams used a 'dummy'
from the Press: a blank volume made for trying out a binding for the 1911
Concise Oxford Dictionary. Williams must have helped himself to the mock-up
when it was no longer needed. Newspaper clippings pasted in later suggest
that he added material, probably until 1916. At first he did not intend the
book exclusively for Arthurian notes. Three pages contain extracts from
Rossetti's translation of the *Vita Nuova*—Dante's account of his love for
Beatrice and the poems he made of it. But after that the book is filled with
plans for the epic, as Williams thinks, reads, and makes connections. The
essential focus of the poem, he thought, would be the Grail:

> *The Grail?*, really, the one fixed point – the Reality. It is, in truth, other things
> which move & it which is still... The Wine, = the Blood, = the quintessence
> of the world.... The knights who achieve see Galahad as a crimson-pulsing
> pillar of fire... & feel all things as the movement of the Grail-wine.[144]

Arthur, he notes, should not be a Christ figure, but imperfect, loving his
Queen Guinevere through 'pride, rather than real love' because he is 'in
love with his love (= himself)'. His kingdom, to be called Logres (a Welsh-
derived name used in the early sources), might represent 'the achievements
of men (medicine, aeroplanes, logical thought, intensive agriculture, &c) in
the midst of the darkness and evil chances which surround them'. Love
would be vitally important: 'Love, as God, and as the Way, [are] to dominate
the poem.' The knights might embody different types of love—Tristram as
'fated love', Lancelot 'sinful love', Perceval 'human love', and Galahad
'Divine love'. Or Perceval might represent 'virginal love: he rarely sees his
mistress, but their souls dwell holily together' (a little like Charles and
Michal)? Key characters—potentially more interesting than the knights—
are sketched out: 'The three great men of Arthur's household: Dubric, the
ecclesiastic & priest[;] Merlin, the wizard & "scientist"[;] Taliessin, the artist, poet, singer.'

There are political ideas: the Round Table might represent both 'the
visible Church [and] the visible Republic'; the Holy Grail could 'appear to

a native-born churl, the slave of a Roman lord'. The knights might be 'champions, orators, and almost embodiments' of guilds of craftsmen in Camelot—to 'include the idea of the common people'. Would there, he wonders, be 'any real objection to time & distance being ignored, & Mohammedan knights introduced'? One might 'Bring Arthur & his sur-roundings [...] forward & parallel to Charlemagne & his surroundings in France, A.D. 800: so as to obtain the full effect of Islam, in Africa, in Spain.' An Indian knight could be brought in—requiring information about Buddhism.

Williams ransacks books of every kind for material that will help him turn the Arthurian story into global myth. He notes many versions of the Arthurian legends, including Malory's *Morte D'Arthur* and the *Mabinogion*. Jessie Weston's scholarly Arthurian studies figure, alongside books on Celtic literature and on the Roman occupation of Britain—including Charles Wall's book on *Ancient Earthworks*. He studies Frazer's *Golden Bough* for cults of sacrificed gods who might relate to the wounded Fisher King of the Grail stories. He reads Wallis Budge on ancient Egypt, and Prescott's *Conquest of Mexico*, to find out if Osiris and Quetzalcoatl have anything to add. He reads about Greek oracles and the Gnostics. And to develop his ideas about imaginative spiritual power, good and bad, he explores magic, mysticism, and the borders between. Arthur Machen's *The Great God Pan* is noted alongside the idea that Pan might be Merlin's father; E. Nesbitt's *Story of the Amulet* is quoted: 'Knowledge that Time & Space are only modes of thought – "is not this the beginning of all magic?"' He studies books on the Salem witches, as well as A.E. Waite's *Hidden Church of the Holy Graal* and *Mysteries of Magic*. And—though this is not listed in the *Commonplace Book*—he reads Evelyn Underhill's classic study, *Mysticism*.[145]

The notes show a powerful poetic imagination at work as—in Coleridge's words—it 'dissolves, diffuses, dissipates' its materials 'in order to recreate'. The intensity with which Williams's notes interconnect myth, history, geography, and mysticism, piling one on another to generate possibilities of rich symbolism, are deeply impressive. There was just one problem: apart from a few stray lines, he found himself unable to write the poem. He gave up, probably some time in 1916. The material would gestate in his mind for another twenty years; meanwhile his energies would be directed elsewhere.

There was only one immediate small result. *The Pageant of Gwent*, per-formed at Abergavenny in August 1913, included a minstrel's song about

Arthur and Guinevere with words by Charles Williams.[146] How the poem found its way to Abergavenny remains a mystery.

★ ★ ★

No letters between Charles and Michal have survived from these years, so we can only guess how their relationship developed. In 1913, when they had been courting for five years, Michal began a year's teacher training in Bishops Stortford, 30 miles from St Albans, so they saw even less of one another. But at some point they became engaged, though they would not marry until 1917: a nine-year wait, probably caused by their families' poverty.

Williams felt painfully aware of his own narrow circumstances when he and Fred Page visited the Meynells in the summer of 1913 at Humphrey's Homestead, the Sussex farmhouse they had recently bought and enlarged with a beautiful library whose shelves were just starting to fill up with finely bound books, between portraits of Alice's famous literary friends. Elegant French windows opened onto a garden with a view of meadows beyond. Page told Alice that Williams had 'a dramatic poem in two acts, and a "Book of Hours", to show you; as well as a drama and an epic(!) not yet written'.[147] The dramatic poem was *The Chapel of the Thorn*; what the 'Book of Hours' may have been, we don't know. Alice, hospitable and encouraging though she was, was not always the soul of tact. 'The public has been so surprisingly kind as to buy my edition of 2500 of [my] essays', she wrote afterwards to the author of the unsold and almost unreviewed *Silver Stair*, 'leaving me without any copies for presents. When the second edition comes in, I shall seize two for you and Mr Page.'[148] Williams left the manuscript of *The Chapel of the Thorn* for her comments, and she promised to discuss it 'in the early autumn';[149] but autumn came and went with no word. At last, in late May 1915, a note in her swirling, swooping calligraphy arrived, asking rhetorically 'Why have I kept your drama so long?' She had read it, she wrote, with 'profound admiration', but felt the early pages were undramatic and needed revision. She never mentioned it again and it simply faded from view.

Meanwhile, in early summer 1914, with the epic simmering in the background, Williams continued to send new short poems to the Meynells, and he and Page, who had together proofread Cary's translation of the *Divine Comedy* at the Press,[150] discussed Dante's *Vita Nuova*. It connected in many ways with their interest in Patmore. Dante's treatise on love and creativity has been called 'a Christian tantric text' recounting 'Dante's effort to channel and concentrate erotic desire for the sake of a Christ-centred spiritual intensity and focus'.[151] Page, preoccupied as ever with Patmore, spent his summer holiday at the seaside, tracking down people who had known the poet. On 29 June 1914 he wrote to Williams:

> Dear Poet,
>   I was minded to send you a truthful account of my yesterday's adventures at Hastings, and then comes the shock of the Austrian assassination, but it shan't detain me long: I am no publicist. [...] But at least it helps to show on what a volcano our civilization is built: how quickly we might be in the midst of a European-Asiatic war.[152]

The moment of prophecy induced by the assassination of Archduke Franz Ferdinand at Sarajevo soon passed; in the next paragraph Fred turned back to an account of his visit to Coventry Patmore's former house at Hastings.

★ ★ ★

But within a month, the 'volcano' was erupting. Following the Archduke's murder by a Bosnian Serb, armies of the Austro-Hungarian Empire invaded Serbia. One by one other nations were drawn in and Europe, criss-crossed by tense alliances and antagonisms, began to tear itself apart. Britain entered the war on 4 August, and by October the conflict on the Western Front was settling into the stagnation of trench warfare. Williams's friends Harold Eyers and Ernest Nottingham joined the army promptly, whilst E.K. Bennett, his friend from the Working Men's College, corresponded with pacifist writers such as Romain Rolland and Goldsworthy Lowes Dickinson, trying to organize international resistance to the war.[153] Williams, imaginatively deep in Arthur's Dark Age Britain and the end of the Roman Empire, was able to maintain a certain detachment as, in November, he drafted a sonnet for the coming New Year:

> When Goths and Visigoths, Burgundians, Huns,
>   Burned march and province, suburb and high Rome,
>   Till, far aloof in Bethlehem, Jerome
> Saw that tremendous City's final suns,
> Was there no privacy of little ones,
>   Nor kings nor senators, in some small home,
>   Who still changed greeting, as we may while come,
> O'er sea, Byzantium's and Chalons' guns?[154]

Civilisations rise and fall, in other words, but what really matters is the inward, spiritual life of families in 'small homes'. His Aunt Alice, more pugnacious, composed a robust verse for that year's commercial Christmas card:

> We've had many goods from Germany
> As every Briton knows
> Before our sometime friends became
> Our false and cruel foes:
>
> But there's one true British product
> That will put those foes to flight,
> And thats the good old British pluck
> That stands for truth and right.[155]

The war took a severe toll on Amen House. By 1917 about 100 men, roughly one-third of the staff, had enlisted.[156] Charles Williams's circle of friends began to suffer early on, when Harold Eyers was killed on 20 May 1915. Williams commemorated him in a poem:

> O the songs we shall not sing!
>   O the deeds we shall not do!
> O the robbed hours that shall bring
>   In your thought's place thoughts of you![157]

In June 1917 Ernest Nottingham was killed too.[158] Fred Page was called up in July 1916; by late October he was in the trenches 'somewhere underneath Ypres' (which suggests that he was involved in the Battle of Passchendaele).[159] He ended the year alive but suffering from 'depression and rheumatism'.[160]

Williams, with his hand tremor and poor sight, was unfit for military service, but went for a medical examination. The doctor, he reported, 'refused me, [...] saying that I should be in the hospital half the time, and that he couldn't think of anything I could safely be used for'.[161] Perhaps he was recalled for further examination as casualties mounted and the War Office became less particular, because in May 1917 he still thought that he 'might be in the Army' by late summer.[162] But it did not happen. He was given spare-time 'war work' to do at St Albans, and dug trenches in London's Hyde Park for infantry training.[163]

★   ★   ★

Keen to assemble another publishable volume of poems, Williams continued sending poems to Alice Meynell, and in December 1914 she wrote with detailed criticisms. She complained of 'rather crowded lines sometimes, [and] very long syllables together. [...] But I think all these sonnets have a great classic beauty and tragedy. [...] The new ones are deeply interesting. But I find them sometimes rather difficult. I think the *meanings* are rather crowded.'[164] In September 1915, she wrote more enthusiastically:

> What can be greater in poetry? I am not extravagant either in thought or word; [...] I know that what I feel is inadequate, and what I can say much more inadequate, in praise of poetry so great. It puts me to much discipline! both of understanding, and, when I achieve full understanding, of love. [165]

Despite hints that he was packing too much complexity into his poems, Williams must have been immensely encouraged. Yet by 14 July 1916 he was finding it hard to write. Perhaps a phase was coming to an end. 'It may be the war or it may be growth', he told Alice, 'but I don't seem able to write lately—unlike some of the poets and men of letters. During the last eighteen months I've only done "Waking Ode for Easter", a "Dedication", a poem called "The Wars" (but not about this one!) and one or two other short sets of verses.'[166]

But the idea of an Arthurian epic was still active in his mind, alongside the hope of publishing a new collection of short lyrics. In November 1916 he wrote to ask for help on both fronts. First, he wanted to know how Tennyson pronounced the name 'Galahad'. Did he give the first syllable a long 'a'?

> You see from this that I am still moved by the thought of an Arthurian – or rather a 'Grail' poem. If *you* say that Tennyson is final, I will promise to drop the idea at once. But perhaps.. Why were Tennyson and Patmore both so monarchical and Tory,—not so much in direct politics as in idea? It seems so strange that they were neither moved by the great dream of the Republic. And Tennyson makes the Grail an incident, instead of the very purpose of the Table. [...]

Second, he was thinking of submitting the new poems to the publisher Elkin Matthews. Could he mention Alice's name?[167]

She was ready to help (though significantly she avoided any comment on the plan for an epic) and urged him, 'pray let Mr. Elkin Matthews know of my very deep admiration for your poems. If you don't think it would seem too much prepared, I would willingly write a note. [...] Do let me know the fortunes of your poems.'[168] Williams asked her to write. But 'Alas, one sees too many versifiers and anthologists disappointed here at Amen Corner to have much hope!'[169] He sent off a typescript on 20 November, but Matthews rejected it. When the package returned to Amen Corner in the afternoon post, Williams 'in a temper threw it aside and marched out of the office at five-thirty'.[170]

Help came from an unexpected quarter. Henry Frowde had now retired from his post as 'Publisher', and been replaced by 36-year-old Humphrey Milford. Milford was an enigmatic figure. Educated at Winchester and New College, Oxford, he was a fine tennis player who had competed at Wimbledon. He also knew the ways of the Press, having served as Assistant Secretary in Oxford. Like many educated men of his time, he preserved in all circumstances an urbane and mildly genial manner which deflected any attempt to find out what he was really thinking or feeling. He could appear entirely unhelpful. When Geoffrey Faber, for example, completed his task of gluing catalogue slips on pieces of paper and went to ask Milford what to do next, Milford told him that a man with a first class degree should not need to ask for instructions, and sent him away again.[171] (Faber left the OUP and founded a world-famous publishing house of his own.) Yet Milford also had a genius for identifying talented people and giving them their head. With no obvious management system, he developed a fluid, organic way of working where tasks were handled by a flexible group of highly intelligent colleagues who shared the editorial processes almost intuitively, like family members. Often aloof and untalkative, Milford somehow encouraged the office to grow into a community, and presided over a period of huge expansion which would see the London OUP become a leading and innovative commercial publisher.

The morning after Williams stormed out of the office in despair, Milford arrived to find the typescript of the rejected poems on his own desk, where it had been placed by Fred Page, with a note suggesting that the poems deserved 'a better fate' than rejection by Elkin Matthews.[172] Milford had already noticed Williams as a talented man: it was he who had sent *The Silver Stair* to the Oxford Professor of English, Sir Walter Raleigh. He did the same with this new collection, asking Raleigh whether he would recommend publication. Raleigh reported favourably, and by the end of February 1917 Williams was discussing the final shape of his book with the Meynells.[173] The title chosen was *Poems of Conformity*, and in late June 500 copies were printed.[174] Williams inscribed one of them reverently:

> To Alice Meynell
> from her child and devotee
> Charles Williams.

★ ★ ★

By now, Charles and Michal were arranging their wedding. Michal, now qualified,[175] was teaching at the Soho Parish School in London. A date for the marriage crystallized during 1916, but it is hard to detect much enthusiasm in Williams's letters (those between Charles and Michal are lost). In July 1916 Charles wrote to Alice Meynell, 'As for marriage—it is good of you to ask. We did wonder about next year, but the whole financial position of my own people is so very unpleasant, and trade is so thin, that I sometimes think—' and he breaks off, to quote from a comic novel by Anthony Hope: ' "Marriages are made in heaven," said I. [...] "I thought of waiting till I got there." '[176]

There is a curious detachment about this: it doesn't sound like the remark of a man eager to marry.[177] In February 1917 the couple, hoping for an Easter wedding, were busy looking at houses and flats in north London.[178] But when Williams heard that the Serendipity Bookshop in Mayfair, owned by the Meynells' son Everard, was to close, he remarked, 'If I were to be in London by myself and if I didn't know my London rents, I should be tempted to try and take those rooms. For I have decided that poets—some poets— were not meant to be house & flat hunters.'[179] Is he edging his way as close as he dares to saying 'Some poets were not meant to marry'? When Wilfrid Meynell wrote 'Please say what you would like me to send you as a wedding-offering. If this is too embarrassing a question, I will take my luck',[180] Williams, who clearly *was* embarrassed, instead of referring the question to Michal (who would have had a practical answer ready) responded, 'I have thought of an offering—Will you and Mrs Meynell review the book?'[181] It is hard to believe that he meant this seriously, but the unavoidable impression is that he found it difficult to engage emotionally or imaginatively with the notion of his approaching marriage. Fortunately the Meynells sent a proper wedding present (though we don't know what it was).

Charles and Michal found a suitable flat at 18 Park Hill Road, Hampstead, and married on 12 April 1917, four days after Easter, on a Thursday afternoon when the shop was shut. The wedding, an almost painfully low-key affair, was celebrated at St Albans Abbey, probably in a side chapel, by the Rev. E.R. Evans, 'an old acquaintance from Sunday-school teaching days'. Although Michal had unmarried sisters, none were present as bridesmaids; instead she was attended by Charles's sister, Edith. Charles's friends were away in the trenches, so one Pickles, an acquaintance from the Press, did duty as best man.[182] The witnesses were Edith Williams and Michal's father, James Conway. Whether other members of the Conway family attended the wedding is unknown. After the ceremony the little party went back to the Williams's household in Victoria Street. The Conways probably felt that Florence was marrying beneath her. They may have expected the girls to repair the family fortunes through marriage; instead, Florence was tying herself to the myopic son of a struggling shopkeeper—and, they may have thought, one who had helped her adopt a new and rebellious identity as 'Michal'. Charles's entry in the register for his occupation, 'Editorial work', indicated a step up in the hierarchy of the Press; but the Conways perhaps saw him as a sort of clerk. There was no honeymoon, but they left that evening for their new flat in London, and the following day Williams wrote to thank the Meynells for their present, concluding, 'my wife (of how short a formality but how long a love) begs me to add her thanks to mine'.[183]

★   ★   ★

As *Poems of Conformity* approached publication, Humphrey Milford sent a copy of *The Silver Stair* to a friend, Olive Willis. She was headmistress of Downe House, a leading girls' boarding school in Kent. Having read the book, Olive Willis wrote to Williams in May, praising his work and inviting him to visit her at the London flat where she spent weekends. He replied, a little nervously, 'I should very much like to accept your invitation later on in the summer—if your reading of the second book leaves you still disposed to extend it. One never knows what effect an author's second book— especially a poet's—may have on those who liked his first.' She had asked about some puzzling passages in the sonnets, so he did his best to explain, concluding ruefully, 'I think [*Poems of Conformity* is] much plainer, only Mr. Milford doesn't agree with me, I'm afraid.'[184] The new book, when it appeared, did not deter her, and on 13 October, Charles and Michal went to meet Olive Willis at her flat. It was the beginning of a friendship which would have many good and unexpected consequences.

Poems of Conformity appeared at the end of June. A substantial collection of almost 130 pages, full of interesting ideas, it is very mixed in quality and has little internal coherence. Dedicated 'To Michal', the book opens with an epigraph from the Biblical Song of Songs, clearly referring to her: 'Who is she that looketh forth as the morning, fair as the moon, clear as the sun, terrible as an army with banners?' In general, Michal appears through the haze of the volume's elaborate rhetoric as an intimidating figure. A series of poems to daunting mythological females (Persephone, Andromache,

Hecuba, Cassandra) is followed by an excessively obscure poem, 'Conformity', which opens with five stanzas of anxiously elaborate justification to Michal for Charles's spending time writing poetry and seeing his friends—or rather, as the poem puts it:

> What cunning hours are pledged, O Song,
> Of privy meditations long
>   To thy director sway!
> Nor her imperial head withdrew
> Your right prerogatives from you,
>   Companions of my way!

Michal's 'imperial head' having been gracious enough to let him meet his male companions, Williams goes on to celebrate the 'rooms and roads of gay contest, / Journey and argument and jest, / From Kew to Harpenden' and to remember friends who have died in the war. The poem seems to use 'conformity' between people to signify something like 'love'—widening the book's unappealing title, which otherwise seems designed merely to proclaim religious orthodoxy.

But the book's central poems proclaim ideas which are far from orthodox. In *The Silver Stair*, Williams had hinted that God, and romantic love between man and woman, were the same thing. Now he takes the idea much further and starts to develop it systematically. The 'Sonnets' announce the idea explicitly:

> Too long the world – proud infidel! – hath kept
> Love's place of kisses unto man's much loss;
> Too long religion dreamed while lovers slept; –
> Now peers-at-arms all they assume the Cross.

To put it bluntly, sexual love and Christianity are linked—are perhaps even, in some sense, identical. Certain poems use the life of Christ to explore the idea in detail. 'Gratia Plena' presents the lovers' first meeting as an Annunciation; but the next poem, 'Presentation', predicts that their love will also undergo a crucifixion: 'What tragic moment [...] Shall cloud our Sun and shake our Earth?' 'Or shall – O dread of dreads! – by me, / Love come unto his end in thee?' It seems a curiously pessimistic poem. Still, despite the discouraging circumstances of their wedding day, and their combined sexual inexperience when (as Williams puts it) 'Our young virginities together went [...] toward Love's self', the poems suggest that they had developed a happy sexual relationship: *The Silver Stair*'s aspirations for

an ecstatic virginity-in-love are forgotten. The poem 'Churches' asks rhetorically why lovers should leave the delights of sex to get up and go to
church, and answers that religion shows love between man and woman as
having 'a quintessential unity' with all the other kinds of love, including the
spiritual. It even hints that orgasm is, or can be, a kind of Holy Communion.

Politics also features. 'The Wars' prophecies the coming of 'the Republic'
and celebrates the Russian Revolution of 1917—not the October Bolshevik
coup, but the March revolution, when a democratic Provisional Government
replaced the absolute rule of the czar. 'Now', writes Williams, 'all the world
is glad / For falling thrones of Petrograd.' In its ideas, *Poems of Conformity* is
anything but conformist. Yet its most ambitious poems are almost unread-
able. Archaic in language, and packed with complex thought which the
words struggle to express, they communicate only with great difficulty.
Alice Meynell and Fred Page approved the ideas (Meynell, surprisingly,
claiming to be a socialist as well as a feminist and a Catholic) but seem not
to have looked any further. Williams badly needed constructive criticism.
Modernist insights might have helped him disentangle his style; after all,
Yeats's *Responsibilities* had appeared in 1914 and Eliot's *Prufrock and Other
Observations* was published simultaneously with *Conformity*, in June 1917.
But there was no one to point to such influences. Alice Meynell still encouraged Williams to write ingenious lyrics like her own, a form that made his
work contrived and constricted. Sending her the new book on 3 July, he
wrote, 'If I hadn't read and admired you long before [my poems] never
would have been just what they are.'[185] It was only too true.

Alice reviewed the book favourably for *The Dublin Review*, praising
Williams for *not* being 'Georgian' or modernist; he was, she concluded,
'alone among the writers of his generation by the quality of his imagination
and even by the turn of his verse'. If there were other reviews, they have not
come to light. Despite his two published books, Williams was failing to
make any impression on the literary world. By the late summer of 1917,
however, he was embarking on a new adventure, and one stranger than any
he had yet undertaken. To understand how it came about, we must retrace
our steps a little.

5

The Initiate

In 1915, two men approached the Oxford University Press with a proposal for an anthology of 'mystical poetry'. They were D. H. S. Nicholson and the Rev. A. H. E. Lee. They wanted to make a selection of English poems from all periods dealing with mystical experience—not just religious poems, but poems presenting direct experience of spiritual reality.

It was a natural project for the OUP, whose London branch often published anthologies. The proposal went to Raleigh in Oxford, who approved it, and by August 1916 Nicholson and Lee had delivered their material. The book joined the growing list of important anthologies honoured with the title of 'Oxford Books' as *The Oxford Book of English Mystical Verse*. Yet reading the final typescript, Raleigh felt vaguely uneasy. 'I hope very strongly that there is not going to be a *movement*', he remarked: 'The good mystics are lone souls, and I can't imagine anything more nauseous than a fashionable mysticism.'[186] In detecting some hidden agenda Raleigh was remarkably acute, for a significant number of the anthology's modern contributors, including Aleister Crowley, Evelyn Underhill, A. E. Waite, W. B. Yeats, Edwin Ellis, and Arthur Machen, as well as the editors, Nicholson and Lee themselves, were current or former members of the Order of the Golden Dawn.

The Hermetic Order of the Golden Dawn had been established in London in 1888 by a group of Freemasons with esoteric interests. Among them was Samuel Liddell 'MacGregor' Mathers (1854–1918), a dedicated scholar of the occult and a strong personality. The Golden Dawn's object was 'to pursue the study of the Occult Sciences',[187] and by 1896 it boasted more than 300 members, in branches scattered across the United Kingdom. Membership was open to Masons and non-Masons, women as well as men. The Order's programme was to enlighten its members by teaching a variety of psychological and magical disciplines—meditation, visualization, the study of systems such as the Kabbala and the tarot, and the practice of ritual. Members advanced through 'grades', with entry into each grade marked by a dramatic ceremony designed to affect the candidate at a deep emotional level. The Golden Dawn was eclectic in its sources. Its symbolism drew on Christian, Egyptian, Jewish, and classical religions, besides various Renaissance systems, including the 'Enochian magic' of the Elizabethan sage John Dee. For it was a basic tenet of the Order that correspondences could be found between different spiritual systems, allowing a synthesis to be created.

Although some had a genuine interest in mysticism, much of the Golden Dawn's membership regarded the Order simply as a school of occultism. Unauthorized groups met to experiment with clairvoyance, telepathy, astral travel, the invocation of spirits, and other magical practices. Tensions developed and in 1900 the Order split into factions, from which two main organizations emerged. One, which was strictly Christian and mystical in its orientation, was led by A. E. Waite, and was to be called The Independent and Rectified Rite of the Golden Dawn. The other, to be known as Stella Matutina ('The Morning Star'), was more magical in its interests. Existing members were given the choice of which one to join. Both groups were open to new members. Among those who joined Waite's Independent and Rectified Rite were the future anthologists, A. H. E. Lee and D. H. S. Nicholson.[188] But in 1914, after further arguments developed, Waite dissolved his organization. The following year, Nicholson and Lee brought the plan for their anthology to the Press.

Although *The Oxford Book of English Mystical Verse* would come out under the prestigious Clarendon Press imprint, the labour of getting permission from authors to reprint the poems was given to Charles Williams, at the OUP's London office, who found himself writing to Aleister Crowley, A. E. Waite, and W. B. Yeats,[189] amongst many others. Whether he knew it or not, he was now in touch with the leading occultists of the day.

★   ★   ★

Soon after Nicholson and Lee first brought their proposal to the Press, Williams sent a copy of *The Silver Stair* to A. E. Waite. During his Arthurian research he had read at least two of Waite's books: *The Mysteries of Magic* (1886), and *The Hidden Church of the Holy Graal* (1910), an analysis of the medieval Grail legends. Waite argued that the 'Graal' (as he spelled it, following Old French sources: the word is from Latin *gradalis*, a cup or platter) symbolized a direct, mystical communion with God more profound even than the sacramental communion of bread and wine administered by the churches. And Waite went further, dropping hints about 'Secret Orders' and 'high intimations which are communicated to those who seek',[190] suggesting that a path to mystical experience was open, even in the modern world, to those determined to find it. Williams must have been tantalized by these hints. Now Nicholson and Lee's anthology alerted him to the fact that Waite was also a poet. So, in the summer of 1915, he sent Waite a copy of *The Silver Stair*.[191] The timing was apt, for Waite had just established a new secret organization: the Fellowship of the Rosy Cross.[192]

Waite responded promptly, inviting Williams to visit. On Saturday 4 September he travelled to Waite's home at Ealing in west London. Arriving at the modest suburban residence he was greeted by the portly, moustached figure of Waite, and introduced to his twenty-six-year-old daughter, Sybil, who presented Williams with her album, which the visiting poet duly signed and dated.[193] The two men retired to Waite's study, where they could talk and smoke amidst Waite's extensive library of occult, alchemical, spiritualist, and mystical books and journals. With Waite's Fellowship of the Rosy Cross less than two months old, the *Mystical Poetry* anthology in preparation, and Williams primed with a knowledge of at least two of Waite's books, the conversation must have turned on poetry, mysticism, and the esoteric—including the Holy Grail. Probably Waite, not yet knowing Williams well enough, refrained from mentioning his Fellowship in any specific way. But he may have dropped hints about 'secret fraternities',[194] which it was possible to enter.

Fifty-seven-year-old Waite (the author of more than forty books, and describing himself in *Who's Who* as 'the exponent in poetical and prose writings of sacramental religion and the higher mysticism')[195] could be pompous and pedantic, but he was a mine of information about literature, history, and the occult, and could be critical and funny. He had been a successful writer of advertising copy for Horlick's, the malted milk drink; he knew many authors and a panoply of eccentrics from the occult world. Williams must have had a thoroughly entertaining time.

They kept in touch, and Williams visited again on 25 April, when Waite returned his book, and they had 'a long talk'.[196] Then, or soon after, Waite told him about the Fellowship of the Rosy Cross. In June 1917, Williams wrote to Waite telling him that he was now married, enclosing a copy of *Poems of*

Conformity, and, momentously, asking whether he might join Waite's secret Fellowship—and how much it would cost. Waite replied on 14 July, congratulating Williams on his marriage and calling *Poems of Conformity* 'very beautiful in thought and manner, very subtle in suggestion.' He continued:

> I give you God speed therefore in the path of love and in the path of song [...]
> And that leads me to that Order, about which I once spoke to you and which
> you now ask to join. It is concerned with the mystery of Divine Love unfolded
> in ritual and symbolism.[197]

Waite enclosed a 'Form of Profession' to be filled in and signed. Williams had also to choose a 'Sacramental Name'—a Latin motto which, Waite said, 'should express your hopes and desires on entering'. He added, cryptically, 'Your nervous trouble is no difficulty; it leads one to mention that in the [first] Grade the candidate is hoodwinked [i.e. blindfolded], but that he is in safe and loving keeping, so that there is no cause for anxiety.' We don't know what this 'nervous trouble' was: had Williams mentioned his occasional horrifying sense of unreality? 'As regards the "demands of a financial nature" ', Waite continued:

> I know very well of your material position in life. On the one hand there are
> expenses which cannot be avoided and on the other there are certain fees
> which can be reduced or set aside at need. It would be wrong of us to exclude
> or bar the progress of any one who ought to be with us on a mere question of
> money.

The expenses were real enough. Williams would need to go to a Mason's outfitter for 'a black cassock' and 'an enameled cross'. Also:

> As regards the Order itself, the Entrance Fee is one guinea and the subscription one Guinea. When another Grade is taken there is a Grade fee of 10/6
> (not a subscription, a payment once and for all). After the meetings we have a
> little supper together at a cost of 2/6 each, unless wine is taken. There is no
> obligation to have this meal, but of course it brings members together. Finally,
> the Rituals are printed and sold as cheaply as possible to members, the price
> being according to size. Most of them are 3/6 each. They can be borrowed and
> copied, but this involves labour. You must tell me frankly whether your circumstances permit such expenditure. In conclusion, please do not keep this
> Form of Profession too long, as it is against the rules.

The likely cost of his entrance to the Fellowship would be £4 10s 6d: a considerable sum in 1917, certainly more than half of Williams's weekly salary.

The 'Form of Profession' was a printed sheet headed with the motto *Benedictus Qui Venit in Nomine Domini* ('Blessed is he who cometh in the name of the Lord') and under it the mysterious title 'The Fellowship of the R∴ C∴'. By signing it, Williams would 'solemnly and sincerely affirm' that 'there is one Eternal Source and Principle, called God' from which 'the soul of man derives everlasting life'; that he wished to gain 'knowledge of my Source and Union with God in consciousness'; and that 'being on the Quest of God I ask of my own free will to be admitted into the Fellowship of the R∴ C∴, which communicates the knowledge of the Quest and its term in symbolism'.[198] ('Term' here meant 'purposed end' or 'goal'—a favourite usage of Waite's.) So the Fellowship was to help him on his mystical quest for union with God. Wisely, the document did not promise that he would achieve this goal; merely that he would gain 'knowledge of the Quest' and its end.

What had Waite told him about the Fellowship of the Rosy Cross? Certainly, he would have explained that it was a Rosicrucian organization—a group claiming to embody the principles set out in the mysterious Rosicrucian manifestos first published in Germany in 1614 and 1615. These two pamphlets had described a secret order of benevolent learned men, bearers of esoteric knowledge brought from the East by a certain Christian Rosenkreutz. The members of this organization, known as the Brotherhood of the Rosy Cross, were said to travel the world, teaching, healing the sick, and working for the good of humanity. In fact no such order existed, and historians now believe that the pamphlets were allegorical, not meant to be taken literally. Nonetheless, over the centuries numerous esoteric groups had been founded, calling themselves by similar titles, and 'Rosicrucianism' had become a recognized tradition. Since the Rosicrucian manifestos had been fictions, the title allowed the founders of groups a free hand in setting up whatever kind of esoteric organization they liked, though the name itself imposed some use of Christian imagery—often the symbol of a gold cross with a many-petalled rose at its centre.

What Waite told Williams, and how much Williams knew already, remains unclear. Waite had written a scholarly book on *The Real History of the Rosicrucians*, published in 1887, and knew quite well that no existing group could claim a genuine Rosicrucian pedigree. Indeed, he had written that 'all persons [...] who proclaim themselves to be Rosicrucians are simply members of pseudo-fraternities' and that their claims were essentially 'a lie'[199]—a statement that looked distinctly odd, now that Waite had his own 'Rosicrucian' group. Perhaps he simply kept quiet about this; or he may have explained to Williams that his Order's title represented aspiration, not historical fact.

The founders of the Golden Dawn had all been members of a Masonic organization known as Societas Rosicruciana in Anglia ('The Rosicrucian Society in England'). But the Golden Dawn had accepted practical magic— the use of paranormal methods to change the world in accordance with the magician's will. Waite would have none of this in his Fellowship of the Rosy Cross, which was to be strictly Christian and mystical, with no striving for magical powers. So what could he offer Williams? First, he could promise the companionship of dedicated fellow-seekers. Second, he could claim that in his Order, 'the mind is trained [...] firstly, in the sense of possibility, and, secondly, in the direction of consciousness, so that it may be overflowed by the experience of the experiment'[200]—that is, mental training would be given which might open the aspirant's consciousness to mystical experiences. Perhaps Waite spoke also of what could be achieved by 'the imagination raised in ecstasy'[201]—the use of visualization and other imaginative powers to bring the mind closer to God. In short, Williams could expect guidance, teaching, and encouragement; but nothing was guaranteed, and he would have to do the work himself. Nor did Waite pressure him to join. Motivation must come from Williams himself.

Naturally, the motivation was found. Fascinated by the writings of Patmore and Waite, inspired by his own intense experiences of love and poetry, and convinced that the dogmas of religion implied profound spiritual states that could transform one's being, Williams was ready to join such an enterprise as Waite's. Perhaps he recalled the elaborate knightly orders of his fantasy kingdom, Silvania—the Golden Cross, the Lion, the Black Gauntlet—and felt that they had foreshadowed a higher truth. He signed the Form of Profession on 18 July 1917. For his motto he chose 'Qui Sitit Veniat' ('Let him that is athirst come') from Revelation 22:17—the Bible's very last verse apart from St John's personal colophon. Waite replied on 6 September, telling him it would be 'convenient for the Fellowship to arrange for your Reception at the Autumnal Equinox, which will be celebrated on Friday, Sept 21st, beginning at 5 or 6 p.m. The Temple will be opened then in the Neophyte Grade.'[202] He reminded Williams to make sure that he had his robes ready.

And so the day came when Williams finished work at Amen Corner and set off along High Holborn and up Southampton Row against the scurrying Friday evening crowds, a tall thin young man carrying the small case that held his carefully folded robes, to enter, shyly, the Imperial Hotel in Russell Square. There is no full record of what followed, but we can attempt a reconstruction.[203]

★   ★   ★

Williams reaches the hotel a few minutes before six o'clock in the evening. Crossing the lobby to the reception desk, he feels anxious. Should he ask for Mr Waite, or, embarrassingly, for the Fellowship of the Rosy Cross? But before reaching the desk he is accosted by a man who checks his name, shakes his hand, and shows him upstairs to a small room where he is asked to hand over the robe, take off his shoes and socks, and remove jacket, waist-coat, collar, and tie. His personal property, he is told, will be safe. He may keep his spectacles. Then he is left to wait in his shirtsleeves.

After what seems a long time, the door opens and Williams sees a startling vision: it is the stranger, now barely recognizable, in a radiant blue robe with an orange collar. On his chest is a disc decorated with a Hebrew letter, and he carries a long staff with a staring eye at its top. Silently, he beckons Williams to follow. Along the corridor they enter a larger room, where a wooden prayer desk stands in front of a closed partition door. He is told to kneel at the desk. A scroll of stiff paper is put into his hand. The stranger slips out, leaving him alone. He calms himself and tries to pray, to open himself to the divine love and mercy. He asks to remain firm and pure in his intent. He abandons thought. Through the partition he hears muffled voices and sometimes the sharp bang of something striking the floor. He tries not to think but to remain clear and timeless, to sense light and mercy descending from above.

At length the door opens and the stranger returns. Fetching a jug, basin, and towel from one side of the room, he takes glasses and scroll, and washes and dries Williams's hands and face. As he does so, he announces, 'From a temple of the spirit, in the name of God and of His Light, I have come into the ways without, that I may bring you into a deeper knowledge of the world within. By the brotherhood at the heart of our fellowship, I bid you remember that what is begun here and now will find its fruition only when it ends in God.' He blindfolds Williams and fastens a coarse cloth garment around him. 'There is darkness on the eyes of the mind', Williams hears, 'but the mind shall enter into day. The yoke of the world is upon you, but the soul shall enter into freedom.'

There is a knocking, and some exchange of words which the dazed and disoriented Williams cannot take in. He feels hands encouraging him to stand, supporting him as his painfully stiff knees straighten. He is led forward. There are questions and answers in different voices, and then a question aimed peremptorily at himself: 'Inheritor of night and time, what seek you in the places of the soul?' Before Williams can think of an answer, his guide's voice answers for him: 'Through the darkness of time and night, I have come to the gate of the temple, looking for light within.' He is led forward several more steps, and a sonorous voice addresses him.

'We hold your signed application for admission to this Fellowship, which exists for the increase of spiritual knowledge. [...] Before your reception can proceed, it is necessary for you to take a solemn obligation [...] to observe the rule of the temples and never to disclose without, that which you learn within. [...] Are you willing to take this meet and salutary obser-vation?' Williams repeats after his guide: 'I desire the light of the house, and I take its laws upon me.'

He is led forward again. Noise now tells him that many more people are present. The authoritative voice resumes: 'Postulant in this home of the spirit, [...] in the name of the Lord of grace, who is the fountain of all our light, I bid you kneel down as a sign of worship and obedience. Give me your right hand, which I place upon this holy rose in the centre of the cos-mic cross.' Kneeling, Williams feels his hand pressed against a carved wooden surface which, he guesses, is the many-petalled rose of the Rosicrucian symbol. 'Lay your left hand in mine, as a pledge of the sacred and sincere intention that your heart brings into this Order.' Complying, he is told to bow his head and recite after his instructor:

'I, Charles Walter Stansby Williams, in the presence of the Eternal Father of Light, [...] and in the presence of the brethren who are gathered here together in the grace of his Divine name, do of my own will [...] most solemnly pledge the honour of my soul to hold inviolate the glory of the Rosy Cross and the mysteries contained therein. I will not speak of them in the world without when I go forth herefrom. I will not disclose the name of this Holy Temple but will keep all secrets of the sanctuary as I would keep those of my king and God. [...] I promise solemnly from this moment that I will persevere with courage and devotion in the path of divine sci-ence. [...] I certify hereby and hereon that I desire above all things the knowledge of the Rosy Cross, and I covenant that at no time and under no temptation will I apply it to the works of evil. [...] Deal with me, O Lord, in Thy mercy. [...]'

He is helped to rise. He is led about, turned in different directions; crosses are marked in water on his forehead; he smells incense burned close to him. Voices tell him that he is consecrated with water and with fire. Then he is made to kneel again. A voice announces 'Light in the place of Light, Light shining in the darkness, Light in the soul of man.' The blindfold is removed. Someone hands him his glasses. As his dazzled eyes adjust he sees before him a tall man in red and green robes, who announces, 'I am the witness of the Light, shining in the darkness of material things.' Around him are other figures in colourful robes. In front of him is a small altar, and on it a golden cross with a crimson rose at its centre. A dozen or more people, men and women, stand along the sides of the room. A short prayer is said and then Williams—legs shaky with exhaustion—is helped to his feet. The guide, the green-robed man, and another (in yellow and violet), join their wands over his head in a threefold arch, each welcoming him with a brief phrase to 'the Salvator Mundi Temple in the Fellowship of the Rosy Cross'. The coarse robe is removed and he is helped into his new black robe. Someone adds a white silk collar from which hangs a crimson cross. He is taken aside and—*at last*—allowed to sit down. Overwhelmed, elated, and exhausted, he listens to an explanation of the ritual he has just undergone—a wordy lecture of which, in his present state, he absorbs almost nothing. His attention focuses once more when a man in a reddish-brown cloak rises to announce: 'In the name of God who is our light [. . .] I testify that Charles Walter Stansby Williams, who will be known henceforth amongst us by the sacramental name of Frater Qui Sitit Veniat, has entered the portal of the Rosy Cross and has been admitted into our bond of the Fellowship in the Neophyte grade.'

Presiding on a throne some distance away is a figure whom Williams dimly recognizes as Waite—no longer his shabby-genteel suburban host but an impressive, white-robed figure with a white headdress and a wand surmounted by a triple cross. Waite makes a short speech of welcome; after which Williams finds that, mercifully, he is no longer the centre of attention. The ritual moves on to a celebration of the autumn equinox but he takes in little of the detail, as the coloured figures come and go gracefully, intoning their speeches, changing places in a slow, elaborate dance.

At the end, he must stand once more: as the most junior Neophyte, he has the job of doorkeeper and must check, symbolically, that the temple is secure. Finally he queues with his newly found Rosicrucian brothers and sisters at the altar for a brief act of Communion: eating a fragment of salted bread (symbolizing the element of earth, and its spirit); sipping wine (symbolizing the liquid element and the spiritual water of life); inhaling the scent of a rose (air, and the breath of the spirit of God); and holding his hand to the warmth of a lamp (fire, and inner purpose conforming to the divine will).

At last the Temple is closed. Williams is escorted, amid congratulations, introductions, and a few jokes, to the men's robing room. Restored to his suit and belongings, he follows the group thankfully to the supper room for a much-needed meal and a celebratory drink. When he emerges—elated, inspired, and exhausted—into Russell Square, he is surprised to find that it is barely eleven o'clock. He feels as if years have passed; and as if something has happened that will take him years to understand.

★   ★   ★

Around the time that Williams underwent his initiation, *Mystical Verse* was published. By then he knew its editors well. They were remarkable men. Forty-year-old Arthur Hugh Evelyn Lee (nicknamed 'Henry') was the Cambridge-educated curate of St Stephen's Church, St John's Wood, in north London. Deeply interested in mysticism, he had joined Waite's Independent and Rectified Rite of the Golden Dawn in 1908,[204] staying until Waite wound it up in 1914. It was perhaps in Waite's organization that Lee met Daniel Howard Sinclair Nicholson (born 1883), who had joined in 1910. Nicholson shared Lee's strong interest in mysticism, and in 1912 had published a translation of *Some Characteristics of the Interior Church* by the early nineteenth-century Russian mystic Lopukhin, with a foreword by Waite; and in 1913 he translated a *Handbook of Mystical Theology* by the eighteenth-century Jesuit Giovanni Scaramelli. Despite an eight-year age gap and other contrasts (Lee was single and celibate, Nicholson married but separated and living with another woman), the men were firm friends and the *Oxford Book* was a natural expression of their shared interests.

But their friendship took other forms. Every two weeks, they met with a few like-minded people at Lee's vicarage to explore spiritual matters. And they invited Williams to join them. It became a regular habit. As Williams recalled, Lee:

> was profoundly interested in the mystical schools of all kinds, although he tested their final value by their fruits in the Christian sense. [...] He had and practised a very high capacity for friendship. The knowledge of him over many

years which his friends had – I myself for more than twenty, and others for many more – were, I suppose, completely unclouded by any dispute beyond the intellectual discussions in which he, as well as we, delighted. For the greater part of those twenty years he and I and two others met for an evening once a fortnight or so, when there was nothing to do but talk; and those evenings were always happy[.][205]

If we take this literally, there were four regulars at these gatherings: Lee, Nicholson, Williams, and another. The fourth may have been R.R. Graves, a lay-reader at Lee's church, who later described Lee as:

> the happy combination of the mystic, the scholar and the Christian philosopher, tempered by a kindly sense of humour. [...] It was during those memorable hours spent in his study that one realised the depth and beauty of his mind, as he would open up fascinating avenues of thought.
>
> It was his love of contemplation and meditation which carried him into a realm so little understood by his casual acquaintances.[206]

A still more likely member was the Rev. Basil Arthur Lester—another former member of Waite's 'Independent and Rectified' version of the Golden Dawn,[207] and a lifelong friend of Lee.[208] Williams also knew Lester[209]: they probably met at Lee's evening discussions.

It was around 1919 that 'Henry' Lee first invited Charles Williams to these gatherings. And we can guess at the topics discussed, because providentially a notebook belonging to Lee has survived.[210] It is written from both ends; the front is dated 1912; the other end contains material from books first published in 1918. So it spans the period when Lee and Williams became friends. It contains notes on alchemy, kabbala, and astrology; on yogic and other breathing exercises, some treated as Christian practice ('Inspire through the Spiritual Centre saying *Christ* during three steps'); and on the transformation of sexual energy for spiritual purposes.

One section of the book is headed 'Notes on Alchemy by N.O.M.' The initials stand for '*Non Omnis Moriar*' ('I shall not altogether die'), a magical motto of William Wynn Westcott, a founder of the Golden Dawn. And the notes end with 'S.A.'—representing another of Westcott's secret names, '*Sapere Aude*' ('Dare to be Wise'). The notes are in fact Lee's notes on 'Golden Dawn Flying Roll No. VII', a lecture by Westcott. The bizarrely named Flying Rolls were instructional lectures, supplied by Westcott and Mathers for the Golden Dawn's advanced students of magic. Their name was derived from the biblical Book of Zechariah (5:1–4): 'And [the angel] said unto me,

What seest thou? And I answered, I see a flying roll; the length thereof is twenty cubits, and the breadth thereof ten cubits.' The angel explains that the 'roll'—a *scroll* in modern parlance—will 'cut off' thieves and perjurers: 'it shall enter into the house of the thief, and into the house of him that sweareth falsely [...] and it shall remain in the midst of his house, and shall consume it with the timbers thereof and the stones thereof.' The allusion was meant as a warning to anyone obtaining Golden Dawn documents by theft or deception. And if Lee had access to one Flying Roll, he probably had access to more. There were, in fact, thirty-four of them and besides alchemy they dealt with clairvoyance, talismans, astral travel, magical implements, the Enochian tablets, and many other magical devices and procedures.[211]

How had Lee obtained such material? Were he and his house about to be consumed by angels avenging theft or perjury? Not at all. Magicians copying the Flying Rolls were required to label them with an address for return in case of the holder's sudden death. Lee took this precaution, and the front cover of the book bears his signed instruction that in case of his death it must be returned to 'Dr Carnegie Dixon'. Dr William Eliot Carnegie Dickson [*sic*] was a long-standing member of the Golden Dawn. When the organization split in 1903, Dickson did not join Waite's Christian 'Independent and Rectified' Golden Dawn but the magically inclined Stella Matutina. Around 1916 he gravitated to a London temple of this organization called The Secret College—a local branch of the Stella Matutina intended for Freemasons. The notes on the manuscript suggest that at the time when Williams became Lee's friend, Lee was learning Golden Dawn magic under Dickson's tutelage.

And was this magic discussed on Sunday evenings at the St John's Wood vicarage? Probably. Anne Ridler, who knew Nicholson, Lee, and Williams in the 1930s, spoke of them all as former Golden Dawn members, and noted that all three were reluctant to discuss their activities:

> Nicholson and Lee, Henry Lee, who was a parish priest in Hampstead [*sic*] somewhere, and Charles [...] Yes, they had all been members of the Golden Dawn, and they'd all sloughed it off, and they wondered whether the vows of secrecy they had taken, which of course they believed in when sworn, still operated now they'd left it. And they decided that on the whole they did operate, so they didn't [talk]. Well, [Charles] used to talk in a general way about the ceremonies and how he liked to perform them properly.[212]

Anne Ridler may, of course, simply have been confused about which organization Williams had belonged to. But she recalled that Williams 'always spoke of himself as having belonged to the Golden Dawn'.[213] And it is quite possible that he had. For two decades he met regularly with a group consisting largely, if not entirely, of former Golden Dawn members. His host, Lee, was an active and current member; the others may have been too. To facilitate discussion and save embarrassing silences, they may well have arranged for Williams to be initiated—either (minimally, and perhaps in the privacy of Lee's study) into the moribund Independent and Rectified Rite or, more ceremonially, into the Stella Matutina. We may never know. But if Williams always said that he had belonged to the Golden Dawn, it is likely that he was speaking the exact truth.

As an odd footnote to all this, in a private collection there exists a copy, in Charles Williams's handwriting, of an advanced grade (known as the '5 = 6 Ritual') of the Independent and Rectified Rite of the Golden Dawn. Nothing is known of how it came to be made. One would not expect such a ritual to be shown to anyone who had not already passed that grade. Did Nicholson and Lee (or someone else) initiate Williams to that level? Again, we may never know. But the likelihood is that from 1919, if not earlier, Charles Williams was an initiate not only of Waite's Fellowship of the Rosy Cross, but also of one of the Golden Dawn's original branches—either the 'Independent and Rectified Rite' or the magically oriented Stella Matutina. He probably never told Waite about his parallel membership.

6

'The Satanist'

In October 1917, six weeks after Williams's Rosicrucian initiation, the Bolshevik revolution began in St Petersburg. Acutely aware of his family's poverty, Williams felt elated. 'I do not know in what particular way the Russian people experienced insecurity', he wrote later. 'But I know very well in what way the English did. There expanded over them a sky of iron from which the faces of their rulers looked down, uttering such phrases as "There must always be a margin of unemployment".' Now, in Russia, the 'iron sky' showed itself vulnerable: 'It seemed that the Earth shouted against it, and it broke. [...] I am not saying that we became Marxists or Communists. [...] But there [was] a half-hope that the Revolution would not fail.'[214]

Russia withdrew from the European war. America had entered in April 1917 as Britain's ally, virtually guaranteeing victory, but food rationing was introduced and when the war ended in November an influenza pandemic was raging (Michal had 'flu twice).[215] A general air of fatigue and discontent prevailed. For Charles and Michal, relief was afforded by Olive Willis, the generous headmistress of Downe House, who gave the couple a belated honeymoon in late July and early August at her cottage in the remote village of Aisholt in Somerset. Hunched into a small side-valley of the Quantock Hills, the cottage was an enchanting place. The poet Anne Ridler, who later knew it well, recalled:

> The cottage, Holcombe, lies in a plashy valley, nearly at the end of a lane that wanders off into a track to climb the combe: pink-washed and with its windows set so that they seem to be giving a rakish wink, it draws the guest into its dark, cool depths as though it never meant to let him go again. Garlic and wood-smoke made the special spell of Holcombe, and the stream running near its garden gate is still its music. The garlic grew somewhere near the door; in the sitting-room [was] the open hearth for logs.[216]

There was a fragrant rosemary bush by the front door. Cooking was by bot-
tled gas, lighting by candles.[217] It was a place of timeless tranquillity. Charles
and Michal spent ten days there, walking, relaxing, enjoying the scenery
and one another. On Sundays they went to the little medieval church at
Bagborough to attend Mass. In the evenings Charles read Saintsbury's *History
of English Prosody* and, he recalled, 'enjoyed it so much as to make me want to
try all sorts of new metres and things'.[218]

One evening, as they walked back to the cottage from Kilve, he talked
about his own poetry. 'Night was falling', Michal recalled:

> as we came to Alfoxten and soft shadows were descending on the combe.
> Though we were in country where Wordsworth had lived, and though 'a
> beauteous evening', it was to Tennyson's poem 'Now sleeps the crimson
> petal...' Charles turned for words to express the beauty of the night, and it
> was Tennyson's poetry, especially the *Idylls* that he discussed as we went on our
> way. Then he told me of his future intention to write an Arthurian Sequence
> with endeavour to give the work full dimension, and in a new medium as to
> form and style against the verse he was then writing, for which he expressed
> intense dissatisfaction. He spoke of the preparation such a work would entail
> and of the thought and meditation which must be given to its form and set-
> ting. He concluded: 'I shall make it my final poetry'.[219]

'We've had the nicest time of our lives', Charles wrote to Olive afterwards,
'and we're very glad we didn't have our honeymoon last year, or we couldn't
have had it this.'[220] Michal, who under her imperious manner was quite shy,
added a timid note, in tiny script: 'Thank you so much for this delightful
holiday. I have never really had my husband all to myself before and it has
been such a nice experience.'[221]

★   ★   ★

The plaintive admission—'I have never really had my husband all to
myself'—is striking. Ten days at Aisholt allowed an intimacy already rare in
their marriage. Michal was sure that Charles then first told her about 'his
future intention to write the Arthurian Sequence',[222] (though 'Sequence' is
a result of hindsight, for he still thought of it as one long poem). If so, he had
taken a remarkably long time to reveal his most cherished plans to his wife.
After all, he had been discussing the Arthurian poem with Fred Page and
Alice Meynell for the past five years. But he and Michal were not, generally,
spending much time together. Charles spent five and a half days each week

at the Press; working Saturday mornings was normal. Perhaps he still went to evening classes; some evenings were taken up by the Fellowship of the Rosy Cross, and one evening a fortnight by the esoteric group meeting at Lee's vicarage. At home, he spent much time writing poetry and reading intensively; he and Michal were together from lunchtime on Saturday, and on Sundays, often attending morning service at St Silas the Martyr, Kentish Town.

Sometimes they took the train to St Albans at weekends to see their families, but this was not an unmixed pleasure. Michal's family still disapproved of the marriage. 'My eldest sister', she recalled, 'told me that when my father saw me a few weeks after marriage he said "She has lost her looks & her gaiety & her confidence in life." '[223] Michal 'loved' Charles's family home with its walled garden, and thought the house 'attractive too—Victorian furniture polished & plain in design & no Victorian hotch-potch'. But she found Charles's parents unappealing. Walter Williams she thought:

> certainly not an intellectual. He was well read in a lick & pick sort of way – that is he had a deep enthusiasm for lyrical poetry but didn't bother with the profundities of the poets – I doubt whether he had ever been shaken as most of us are & Charles exaggeratedly so when reading Shakespeare & Milton & Wordsworth.[224]

And 'whereas Charles was superinteresting his papa was not, quite the contrary somewhat boring in fact'. Moreover, 'He hated the shop & could very much offend customers. Always accusing them of passing off 1d. for a half-crown.' And although she thought Charles's mother 'outstanding for ability & goodness' and 'excellent company', Michal sensed that she and Edith thoroughly disliked her, though they tried hard to hide it. On her side, Mary Williams found Michal alarmingly volatile: her summing-up was, 'Look what I got for a daughter-in-law! Worse than quicksilver to handle. Never knew what she would do, never knew what outrageous thing she would say.'[225] Clearly, relations with the in-laws did little to enhance the marriage. When Miss Pike, an old friend from St Albans, visited them in London, Michal remarked, ' "Married life isn't in the least what we thought it would be like." ' Charles said quickly, ' "What a lot of time we wasted, we should have married years and years ago." '[226] Charles's interjection sounds like a manoeuvre to steer the conversation away from dangerous ground.

Although she could write well on occasion, Michal was not highly literate. She never used joined-up handwriting, her grammar was erratic, and to the end of her life she never mastered the possessive form of her husband's name, often writing it as *Charle's*. Only indomitable optimism could have convinced anyone that she was capable of writing a book. Yet Williams must have thought it possible, for around 1918 Michal contracted with his uncle's Talbot Press to write a book on Christian symbolism. The idea can hardly have been hers. Probably it was an attempt by Charles to involve Michal in his own interests and line of work. Predictably, it was a disaster. The book, a straightforward guide to the meanings of the imagery found in the carvings, stained glass, and decorations of churches, was published in 1919 as by 'Michal Williams', but the writing—with its quotations from Blake's 'Proverbs of Hell' and Wordsworth's 'Tintern Abbey', and its original theological insights (such as that 'all meals—from the Blessed Sacrament to the hastiest lunch—symbolize the nourishment of men by the Divine Grace')[227]—is clearly Charles's, and both later confirmed this.[228] Michal's gloomy summary was, 'I wrote [it] (with Charles 99% assistance).'[229] One can imagine the frustration, the tears, the arguments. Michal was not cut out to be a writer, and it took some naïvety on Charles's part to try and make her into one.

★   ★   ★

At the Press, by contrast, he went from strength to strength. He was now an editor, his intelligence and efficiency all the more obvious amid the difficulties of working with 'a scratch war staff'.[230] Internal memos were signed with initials, and he was universally known as 'C.W.' His wit and talent for light verse were greatly appreciated. Fred Page, who rejoined the Press in 1918, none the worse for his war experiences, recalled:

> We were [...] a very merry crew: we wrote sonnets, each in turn supplying a line, C.W. supplying the rhymes; [...] [Williams] wrote poetry as fast as he wrote doggerel. I have seen him write a sonnet with his watch in his hand, and I have heard him improvise nonsense in rhymed couplets for about an hour on Christmas Eve.[231]

The inscrutable Humphrey Milford, nicknamed 'Caesar'—a title perhaps conferred by Williams—'would often keep Charles after office hours to talk about books and poetry'.[232]

The London OUP was responsible for the World's Classics, a popular reprint series. Its hardback volumes, small enough to fit into a pocket, sold in millions, rivalling the more famous Everyman's Library, published by Dent. Apart from an intention to publish 'classics'—whatever they might be—there was no clear policy of selection, and oddities were mixed in with the predictable major works of world literature. The series expanded rapidly; there was endless scope for enterprise, as well as the challenge of trying to outdo Everyman. Williams spent much of his time proposing, debating, commissioning, editing, and seeing through the Press new World's Classics volumes. The titles chosen were either out of copyright, or famous works by living authors who could be cajoled into accepting a minuscule royalty. Each volume was given a newly commissioned introduction, so there was constant correspondence with writers and translators. Williams and Page were also responsible for the Oxford Standard Authors, a series of larger one-volume editions of poets and a few prose writers, aimed at students and serious readers. This series too sold in large numbers. His energetic involvement with these two series meant that Williams was directly shaping what educated people perceived as the literary canon. Inclusion in the World's Classics or the Oxford Standard Authors conferred classic status. The effects on education and public culture were inconspicuous but profound.

The Press also took privately commissioned work. One such book was the first, limited, 1918 edition of the *Poems* of Gerard Manley Hopkins. Most of Hopkins's poetry had remained unpublished at his death in 1889 and this first cautious selection was arranged by his friend, the Poet Laureate Robert Bridges. Williams was probably involved in its publication, though the Press's records are incomplete and nothing about the book survives. Discontented with his own poetry and searching for new forms, Williams must have been intrigued by Hopkins's daring experiments with sound and metre. A copy was sent to Alice Meynell, as a leading Catholic poet and friend of Bridges; but when Williams asked for her opinion he received a swift rap over the knuckles: 'No, I cannot away with Gerard Hopkins's pranks. Nor do I see very much of his merit.'[233] And when he raised the question of free verse, the reaction was equally dismissive: 'As to *vers libre*, I think nothing [...] can be too strong in condemnation. It is because English prosody is so wonderfully liberal and various that I resent that license. Liberty should preclude license in verse, surely.'[234] If he were to find 'a new medium' for his poetry, he could expect no help from Alice Meynell.

In 1920 Gerard Hopkins, the poet's nephew, joined the OUP's London office. After war service he became Publicity Manager and, later, Editorial Advisor. He was fluent in French (becoming an admired translator) and had ambitions as a novelist: his first book, *A City in the Foreground*, was published the year after he joined the Press. A big, genial man, full of confidence and (according to Press gossip) a womanizer, he made a striking contrast to the small, fastidious, delicate-featured Fred Page and the lanky, mercurial Charles Williams; yet they soon became a triumvirate working seamlessly together. Projects in progress were passed around from one to another depending on who had time, expertise, or inclination, and letters signed by Humphrey Milford were often actually dictated by Page or Williams. Fred, Gerry, and 'C.W.' were remarkably free from territorial defensiveness. Far from causing confusion, this informal intimacy produced great efficiency.

Williams was now perfectly at ease taking a book all the way through from proposal to production. When James Rhoades's translation of *The Poems of Virgil* came up as a possible World's Classic, he read it and wrote a confident report on it:

> The chief praise of this translation is that it is straightforward prose, written as blank verse, but not much the worse for that [...] Of course Rhoades's remark on p. viii about B[lank] V[erse] being the metre of the English Epic is bunkum; he may be right, but it must be B.V. developed through a fresh and great mind – Browning or Wordsworth or Abercrombie – [...] the first two or three pages of Rhoades' translation are enough to put anyone off.

Still, subject to being 'made more English here and there' and 'keyed up' a little, Williams thought it likely to be 'a steadily, if slow selling' commercial proposition. The report shows both Williams's careful thinking about verse, and his defiantly conservative taste: placing minor contemporary Abercrombie alongside Browning and Wordsworth was eccentric even in 1920. He answers an in-house query about pages briskly: 'All our blank verse in the *World's Classics* seems to be 40 lines to the page. Rhoades has about 12540 lines, = 314 pp + 16 prelim. = 330 pp. Estimate of cost herewith.'[235]

He was also responsible for Aylmer Maude's translations of Tolstoy, many of which first appeared as World's Classics. This could be very laborious. In July 1920 he checked the whole of *What I Believe* against another translation to ensure that Maude, who worked largely without revision, had not skipped a paragraph. He checked quotations, dealt with Maude's proofs (sometimes inviting him home after work to sort out details), and arranged payments. And he was always ready to discuss the substance of books as well as their technicalities. When Maude, a member of the socialist Fabian Society, raised the matter of pacifism, Williams was ready with a considered view: the difficulty, he said, was that Jesus seemed:

> to justify both theses – resistance and non-resistance. In one place he forbids the use of swords; in another, 'he that hath a sword let him take it'. [...] My own inclination is to believe that certain people have a vocation to what one might call the 'direct' approach to God; i.e., they follow the contemplative life, they are celibate, without property, and do not use the sword. But the majority of men follow the indirect approach; they marry, have property, are engaged in the affairs of the world, and rightly at a crisis they use physical force. [...] Contemplatives of course don't marry; but for many men marriage is the beginning of the Way.[236]

In such work, enlivened by such discussion, Williams spent his days; though a note to Maude ('I will take care to be in up to twelve and after about two each day') indicates that generous lunch hours were the rule.[237]

★   ★   ★

And he was beginning to find his way as a critic. The process began with a bizarre shock early in February 1918. Turning to the letters page of the weekly *New Witness*, he was appalled to find a long letter, headed 'THE SATANIST', announcing that '*Poems of Conformity* has come hot from Hell.'

The author, Catholic critic Theodore Maynard, was answering J.S. Phillimore's review of the book a month before, which had greeted Williams's poems enthusiastically, praising their 'verbal and rhythmical beauty'. But Phillimore had hinted that the 'religious love poems' might be misunderstood—perhaps even 'misconceived as blasphemous', though he had acquitted Williams of religious unorthodoxy.[238] Maynard believed that Phillimore had been hoodwinked. 'I was half way through the volume before I discovered the clue to its meaning', he wrote. The book was 'a malicious attack upon the faith' and Williams a cunning pagan in disguise:

> To the Christian, marriage is a type of the mystical union of God with the soul. Mr. Williams, however, has lent his genius and scholarship to invert the process. Objects of Catholic devotion have been made by him symbolical of physical intercourse between sexes. Our Blessed Lady and the Son become the centre of the Eleusinian mysteries. He invokes the Queen of Heaven, Astarte, under the name of the Queen of Heaven, Mary.[239]

Maynard thought that Williams:

> must be one of the subtlest intellects of the day [and] the hideous secret impli-
> cations did not strike [other] innocent reviewers. Well, thank God I am not so
> innocent that I cannot recognise the devil when I see him! I read the poems
> and am reminded of the Satanists, those apostate clerks who say a Black Mass
> devised of lewd ritual [...] Like them, Mr. Williams decks out phallic worship
> in a chasuble[.]

To prove it, he quoted from 'Orthodoxy':

> Thy body's secret doctrines now
> Are seen and felt and known:
> More wisdom on thy breast I learn
> Than else upon my knees[.]

For Maynard at least, Williams's exploration of his sense that romantic love
could be a path to God had gone badly wrong.

Williams wrote to the magazine with 'vehement protest'. The two men
arranged to meet and talk at the offices of the *New Witness*. 'I found him a
man who looked less than twenty-five years old', Maynard recalled (Williams
was in fact thirty-one), 'trembling with nervousness and most embarrassingly deferential. He talked with staccato eagerness.'[240] Maynard quickly
realized that his vision of a depraved intellectual undermining Christianity
was wide of the mark. Williams was innocent and sincere, as well as acutely
intelligent and theologically informed. Charmed and impressed, Maynard
lunched with him the following week, when Williams—typically combining humility with exuberant love of paradox—agreed, having reread his
own poems, that they *could* be seen as Satanic, and was ready to side with
Maynard. The tables were turned: the critic found himself arguing that the
poems were blameless. He had detected the influence of Frazer's *Golden
Bough*; Williams confirmed this, and went further: 'That Paganism was in
many respects like Catholicism inclines him to believe in Catholicism.
A myth demonstrates a mystery.' The discussion continued as they walked
across Regent's Park together. Williams, by now on great form, claimed that,
'He ha[d] been so much occupied in discovering the extent, correlations,
and surprises of Christianity [...] that he never had time to stop and enquire
whether Christianity was true.' As for the erotic element in his verse,
Williams explained that when he had written about the 'secret doctrines' of
a woman's body, or told Michal that 'Thy person puts to utter trial / Creeds
and theologies', 'He did not mean that physical passion was a more certain

good than prayer, but only that there are many roads to faith, and that the road of human love has been the one followed by him.' So charmed was Maynard that he invited Williams to review his own next book. He came away convinced that Williams was 'Unquestionably a major poet'—though not perhaps 'quite free from serious heresy'—which Maynard thought could be corrected if only Williams would become a Roman Catholic. They remained friends, and Maynard's summing up was unequivocal: 'Williams came into my own life like a thunderbolt.'[241] It was a verdict that many would echo in the future.

Maynard found Williams so impressive that he recommended him to Hawkesyard Priory in Staffordshire, to lecture on 'religion in English Verse'.[242] Williams found the prospect a little intimidating, though it was also a stimulus to further reading. He told Olive Willis:

> The dark, guileful and picturesque Prior came to tea the other Sunday, robes and all. He seems to have an appalling knowledge of philosophy and I shrink from my commitments in the way of the lecture. In preparation for which I've been reading the *Prelude* and admire Wordsworth more than ever.[243]

The Prior was 'vastly astonished to find that [he] should not only know that Eternity doesn't mean going on for ever, but should possess 2 vols of Aquinas!'[244] Olive Willis suggested that Williams come and repeat his lecture for her pupils at Downe House. And, probably again through Olive Willis, he was asked in 1923 to lecture at one of the London County Council's Evening Institutes. So almost by chance Williams fell into lecturing on English Literature—something he had been doing in conversation for years. Himself a product of the evening-class system, he took to the work naturally. It became an important part of his life, with profound consequences.

He reviewed Maynard's poems for the *New Witness* in August 1918; other reviews followed. And in December 1920 the *Contemporary Review* published his first free-standing critical article, 'The Hero in English Verse'. It shows the brilliant leaps of insight and unexpected connections that would make Williams an outstanding critic. He reads Milton's Satan as a continuation of the Shakespearian tragic hero, and points out that some of Satan's speeches could equally well have been uttered by Christ in *Paradise Regained*. Both characters, he suggests, represent human heroism. Their experiences of suffering, torment, and resistance are our own.

★   ★   ★

Williams's initiation into the Fellowship of the Rosy Cross was not immediately followed by a flurry of activity. As a humble Neophyte he could
attend only the seasonal celebrations of solstice and equinox, and act as
doorkeeper when a new member was initiated. In everyday life, Waite's
Fellowship asked no specific work other than prayer, taking the sacraments,
and a constant attempt to keep in mind that 'the sole purpose of man's
sojourn in the material world is that he may attain union with the Divine'
and that 'the first work of the seeker after Divine Things is the purification
of his own nature'[245]—an intensification of things that any Christian might
(in theory) be aiming at.

But his progress in the Fellowship was rapid. Between September 1917
and July 1919 he passed through six grades in all: those of Neophyte, Zelator,
Theoreticus, Practicus, Philosophus, and Adeptus Minor. Each grade was
signified by a pair of numbers, indicating its correspondence to one of the
spheres on the Kabbalistic 'Tree of Life' diagram, which represents both the
unfolding of divine energy into the creation of the world, and the path of
mystical return to the divine source. Thus the Neophyte grade, regarded as
merely a threshold to the path, was indicated as 0=0. The next grade, Zelator,
was 1=10 (the first sphere on the path, which is also the tenth and last stage
in the emanation of divine energy). Then came Theoreticus, or 2=9 (second
stage of the path, ninth level of creation) and so on. Each grade had its
dramatic initiation ritual, and its list of 'Points of Contemplation', which
postulants had to study before taking the grade. The subject-matter and
imagery of each ritual corresponded to the symbolism of the appropriate
Kabbalistic sphere, so that the whole structure could be mapped onto the
'Tree of Life'. The aim of the process was deepening self-knowledge, and an
increasing conformity to the will of God.

Besides the Kabbala, the rituals drew on symbolism from alchemy and the
tarot. The Zelator ritual, for example, involved a bowl of earth to symbolize
the postulant's physical body and 'body of life', which he or she was to purify.
At the Theoreticus ritual, earth was again produced, this time said to be 'transmuted' into 'living and philosophical stones' for the building of the Temple.
The Zelator ritual and those beyond it each involved the display of a large
tarot card, specially painted, which symbolized the path to the next stage of
attainment, and which was explained to the postulant in a lengthy speech.

The more grades that an initiate took, the more rituals he or she was able
to attend. What began for Williams in 1917 as a matter of attending a ritual
probably every two or three months soon became a commitment to monthly,

three-weekly, and then fortnightly attendance. On 26 August 1919 Williams, or rather 'The Beloved Frater Qui Sitit, Veniat' was 'raised on the cross of Tiphereth' in the dramatic Adeptus Minor or 5=6 initiation, where the postulant was symbolically crucified: tied, standing, to a full-sized cross, vowing to 'offer up my life in sanctity on the mystical Cross of Christhood', dedicating his will, desire, mind, and body 'as one who has been betrothed in God and is seeking the word of union'. The ritual implied not just a commitment to union with God but an acceptance of whatever suffering the path to that union might entail. 'I will accept the cross in Christ', pledged Williams, 'that I may descend afterwards with Him into the valley of silence and may arise in the glory of His union.' After being unbound from the cross, he listened to the story of Christian Rosenkreutz as told in the original Rosicrucian manifestos, and watched the 'resurrection' of the apparently dead Chief Adept (the richly costumed Waite) from his tomb in an elaborately painted seven-sided sanctuary, probably constructed from screens. At the climax of the ritual, the Chief Adept told the postulant, 'This also is thine own story [...] I raise you into the company of adepts in the house of the Holy Spirit.'[246]

Williams was now an Adeptus Minor, his level of attainment on Waite's plan identified with the sphere of Tiphereth, the central point of the Kabbalistic Tree. Adeptship imposed obligations within the Fellowship. Williams began to take on important ceremonial roles: on 26 January and 11 March 1921, he was 'Proclamator et Lucifer' (announcer and bearer of the lamp)[247] and for six months from 23 September 1921 he was Master of the Temple,[248] presiding over the ceremonies: a major speaking role which entailed much learning by heart. Williams later recalled that 'most of the members [...] were content to read words from a script when it came to their turn, but that he himself took pleasure in memorizing what had to be said, so that he could celebrate with dignity'.[249] He believed that 'ceremony, rightly used, [...] gives a place to self-consciousness, and a means whereby self-consciousness may be lost in the consciousness of the office filled or the ritual carried out'.[250]

The Fellowship of the Rosy Cross included both men and women, and it would have been quite possible for Michal to join. But she showed no interest. Her only known comment is:

Waite [...] suggested Charles becoming an initiate of his order which I think he ran as a profitable side line. Charles did so & told me the whole thing was exclusively for the Order & he might not reveal the ritual & never did I ask one thing about it & I didnt know its name [...] I think there is too much made out of his connection with this very phony Order. & I dont think it influenced him in any way.[251]

Far from being 'profitable', the Order survived on a shoestring and the idealistic Waite was always poor. But Michal was temperamentally averse to such things, and Charles's membership gradually placed another barrier between them.

Alongside his ritual practice with Waite's Fellowship, from 1919 Williams was a regular presence at 'Henry' Lee's evening gatherings, which took place on Sundays after Evensong.[252] We cannot eavesdrop on their gatherings, for no record survives of what they discussed or did. But we can hazard some guesses, based on the known interests of Lee and Nicholson, the chief members of the group.

Lee's main preoccupations, to judge by his publications and his surviving notebook, were alchemy, and 'animal magnetism'—that is, the magical uses of hypnotism. He probably saw these topics as essentially one, for he was deeply interested in the work of Mary Anne Atwood (1817–1910),[253] who had taught that the chemical operations spoken of in alchemical texts were really allegories for a process of spiritual transformation, aimed at transmuting the 'base metal' of the ordinary sinful human being into the pure 'gold' of a purified person in contact with God. The 'vessel' in which this took place was the human body and mind; the operation of 'refinement' or 'distillation' was the experience of repeated hypnotic trance. Lee's notebook contains notes on Atwood and several other 'spiritual alchemists', and in 1927 he would translate a French classic of 'animal magnetism', *Magnetism and Magic* by Baron du Potet de Sennevoy. That Williams took part in discussions of such matters at Lee's vicarage is virtually certain, for a late page in his Commonplace Book contains notes on an article about Mary Anne Atwood—surely recommended by Lee.

Lee was also impressed by the works of Henry Proctor, who advocated celibacy so that the retained male 'seed' could be 'transmuted into a vitalising fluid, the elixir of life, which restores life to the body, in every part, first to the physical and then to the mental, and finally to the spiritual'.[254] To achieve this, Proctor recommended a system of breathing exercises. One should:

> lie passively or sit erect and fix the mind upon the idea of drawing up the vital fluid to the Solar Plexus. Then breathing steadily and filling the whole body

with air at each inhalation, you will be conscious of the upward passage of
the elixir of life and will feel its stimulating effect upon the whole system. [...]
By this means our life can be continually renewed[.][255]

Citing the enormous lifespans of the Old Testament patriarchs—Noah, for
example, who lived for 950 years—Proctor claimed that even 'the last enemy,
DEATH' might be defeated. He even hinted, though his declamatory prose is
not very clear, that it might be possible to die and return to life:

Pioneers are wanted to lead the way, to offer their bodies, living sacrifices; to
lay down their lives for the good of mankind, as Jesus laid down His, but having laid it down, to take it again, and so bearing about in their bodies the
energizing power of His death, that His life may be manifested.[256]

'Henry' Lee sought out Proctor's strange books in the British Museum
Library, and took detailed notes. It seems likely that they were discussed at
his evening meetings.

The group's other leading figure, D. H. S. Nicholson, was more conventional, though he also held some unorthodox views. In his book on St Francis
of Assisi, he mentioned the possibility that 'the spirit could be nourished
by the transmuted desires and activities of the body'.[257] Nicholson believed
in reincarnation, and theorized that after a life of asceticism a soul, having
'gained due ascendance over its body', might be reborn into the world 'as
one of those to whom [...] the need for repression is entirely foreign', and
might 'turn to the sanctified fulfilment of the body's functions with the
utmost naturalness'.[258]

Such ideas, with their questions as to how the desires and energies of the
body might be 'transmuted' into spiritual work, were surely debated at the
St John's Wood vicarage. Perhaps Lee's group even tried out Proctor's exercises, seeking to arouse the 'elixir of life' within themselves. If Williams
explored these matters, he may have connected them with Patmore's celebration of the mystical potential of unconsummated desire, and pondered
their relationship with his own sense of the connection between erotic love
and Christianity, and with the sacredness of the body as demonstrated by
Christ's incarnation.

★ ★ ★

How far Charles Williams's activities with Waite, Lee, and Nicholson could
be called 'magical' is an open question. It is also unclear whether their

emotional effect upon him was therapeutic or destabilizing. Writing to
Olive Willis in October 1918, he claimed that he was much happier, or at
any rate more stable, than in the past:

> It may be that one grows out of strong feelings, but for quite a time now there
> hasn't come on me personally such blackness of misery (for no particular rea-
> son) as used to descend. And this isn't thro' marriage, at least I think now, it was
> earlier. I don't mean 'despair'; simply wishing, as the King said in *The Napoleon
> of Notting Hill*, that God, having made the world in six days, had knocked it to
> bits in the next six.[259]

Certainly some of the new poems he was writing show depression being
kept at bay. There were a couple of robust political satires—'Abdications'
celebrates the end of the war with delight at the fall of czarism and the
Hapsburg Empire, and a poem from February 1919 greets the 'improved'
unemployment figures with heavy irony:

> Sing songs about the table
> And psalms within the kirk,
> For the exact percentage
> Of people out of work
>
> Is only six point five, my boys,
> Is only six point five,
> Not more than six point five per cent
> Are sorry they're alive.[260]

But these remained unpublished. The poems he showed to Alice Meynell
and which went into his next book, *Divorce*, take a very different tone. Several
show him haunted, psychologically at least, by friends who died in the war:

> To walls and window-curtains cling
> Your voices at each breakfasting,
> As the cups pass from hand to hand,
> Crying for drink in No Man's Land.

'In a London Office' depicts even Amen Corner as a nightmare:

> Seven bodies round me spin
> Live tentacles, to snare
> And drag my mind therein
> Out of the open air.
> Before me a blank wall
> Is built; I cannot flee,

> I feel the thin threads crawl
> Tightening over me.

Three 'Experiments' in free verse—a first timid experiment in modernism—begin with 'Traffic', pervaded by a curious sense of unreality:

> These shapes of brown and black painted horses,
> These bright dabs on the street
> Like motor-buses, –
> If I stood in front of them, would they crush me?
> Surely not: I should find
> They were cut out of paper, cardboard, or tinned metal,
> They and their riders and all the hats and parasols on them,
> Thin, almost two-dimensioned [...]

Many of the poems to Michal are also disturbing. The last of 'Four Sonnets' suggests that, in making love, we consent to all the past suffering that led to this moment—our ancestors underwent 'severity', and nature, through evolution, hides 'a past of massacre' in the body of the beloved: 'Thus I in you deliberately embrace / Nature, and all her warfare on our race.' Other poems hint at guilt or disharmony.

'To Michal: On Forgiveness' makes it clear that there have been rows:

> fault of madness or of sloth
> Has wrecked our often plighted troth,
> And all your angers, justly moved,
> Lighten upon this earth you loved

– 'this earth', of course, being Charles.

After this, one might expect the book's title, *Divorce*, to have a marital relevance, but the title poem, addressed to Charles's father, treats 'divorce' as a synonym for 'renunciation' and praises Walter Williams, a little uncomfortably, for the way he is letting go, in old age, of worldly concerns and attachments. Yet the book's most striking poems are precisely about the impossibility of disconnecting. Every good has some connection to evil; every pleasure hides a history of suffering. Even the German Kaiser—an object of British loathing—is seen as a reflection of ourselves 'since he bears our sins and we bear his'. It is comforting to think that God (or 'Love') can forgive him, because it means God may be able to forgive us too. This sense of implication—that no one and nothing is separate, that everything impinges upon (and pays for) everything else—would grow and deepen to become an insight central to Williams's life and work.

He had sent the poems, as he finished them, to Alice Meynell. Her responses continued fulsome but bland. 'My admiration of your work is, as I hope you know, very deep', she wrote: 'At first I thought these last two poems too difficult, but that was only because of my feebleness of mind.'[261] Williams badly needed stringent criticism from an informed reader. What he mostly got was, to put it bluntly, gush. *Divorce* is the work of a poet who has lost his way. The OUP published it in the spring of 1920 and Williams reverently inscribed a copy 'For his teacher, Alice Meynell'.[262] Meanwhile, he and Fred were helping her assemble a volume of essays, *The Second Person Singular*. She was tired, and already suffering from the cancer that would kill her within two years.

7

'Why the Devil Does Anyone Ever Get Married?'

I n the summer of 1920, a certain John Pellow reviewed *Divorce* favourably in a magazine called *New Highway*. He and Williams began to correspond, and Pellow turned out to be a kindred spirit. A civil servant, four years younger than Williams, he was an aspiring poet: some of his work had appeared in the 1918–19 volume of the popular *Georgian Poetry* anthology. He had a wide interest in religion, which included sympathy with High Church views. Charles and Michal invited Pellow for dinner in February 1921, and he recalled how Charles startled him by opening the front door with a sweeping bow, then racing ahead of him up the long five-flight stair-case to the flat.[263] There Pellow was introduced to 'the duchess-like presence' of Michal. He found Williams:

> a talkative jolly fellow. His 'R's are 'W's, and his voice rises at times rather unpleasantly towards cracking point. His wife who really is called Michal, a tall dark handsome girl. A certain little nervous simpering way which she has at first, wears off in time. She would have, I think, a sweet nature. She is a school teacher. They have the topmost floor of a high large house, and grumble at it [...] C.W. was much bucked by my notice in the *New Highway*. He had been a little depressed by his bad reviews, & began to discount the good opinions of Alice Meynell & Bridges (both old, he said).[264]

Pellow recalled, 'There was a torrent of talk—I never heard anything quite so brilliant. He encouraged you to talk, and you found you did talk better and more fluently. He regarded you as at least as intelligent as he.' The two poets praised each other's work, and commiserated over the literary world's neglect.[265]

In April, Williams returned the visit: 'Come early and be prepared to stay late', Pellow urged,[266] and in October Pellow came again to Hampstead.

The two poets shared a quirky sense of humour. Inviting Pellow to dinner, Williams wrote:

> You know the way so I need not draw little beautiful medieval charts with the four living creatures in the four corners, and the devil looking round the corner by Sodom, and St Joseph sticking his staff in the ground by Glastonbury, and Keats walking in his garden, and Coventry Patmore in his, and the least of your servants looking out of his window expecting you.[267]

He also told Pellow to 'bring some of the poems that the editors won't have'.[268] He was prepared to give practical help: he showed Pellow's poems to Milford with a recommendation to publish,[269] and the resulting book, *Parentalia*, appeared in 1923.

Naturally the two poets discussed and exchanged books. Williams recommended Rolfe's novels, and Pellow duly read *Hadrian VII*.[270] They pored over the illustrated three-volume edition of William Blake's *Works*, edited with esoteric commentary by W.B. Yeats and Edwin Ellis; Pellow was 'Glad to know that [Williams] finds Ellis & Yeats "elucidations" more obscure than the prophet himself.'[271] Pellow suggested promising books for the World's Classics,[272] and Williams told him 'One of these days I will *read* Chaucer, not just read him'[273]—a significant distinction. *Reading*, with emphasis, meant careful, thoughtful reading, with critical works within reach—the kind of reading he did when preparing his lectures. But he never came to enjoy Chaucer.

Pellow was a safe confidant for the frustrations that Williams felt with his job, his writing, and his family. This was, Pellow recalled, 'a time when Charles was in a state of acute depression about the world generally'.[274] In January 1922 he was apologizing for not having seen Pellow lately because an aunt had fallen ill in November, and:

> till Christmas we spent our weekends at her rooms: not, you understand, being useful, but visiting the sick in Evangelical fashion. I drew the line at reading the Bible (which anyhow she didn't want—not being what one would call *really* religious, although feeling that CHURCH, not *the* Church, nor a church, but just CHURCH, plays an important though vague and not essential part, in life), but I bought medicine & talked gossip & patted a dog & scratched a parrot [...] I hope the Church gave itself indigestion on Christmas Day, & the World all along[.]

At work, he said, his latest task had been to compile a dull, patriotic school poetry anthology as factotum to V. H. Collins, who was, he said, 'an atheist?

well, in that entourage—and one of many loves, and the lord of the educational side', and the book was:

> not a book to be vain about: scissors and paste and much toil. He had the idea, I did the toil. *Poems of Home and Overseas*—the title almost makes me weep; with Mrs Hemans and Conan Doyle and O. W. Holmes in and Shakespeare to round all up and Blake to give it an air and Kipling to give it a flag. [...] The book would have been much worse if it hadn't been for me. Mrs Hemans and Shakespeare without the Blake.[275]

The anthology is better than Williams admits. He even managed to include a new poem of his own—'Sub Specie Aeternitatis'; and the modern poet most represented is Edward Thomas, whose poem 'Words' stands at the end of the book—surely Williams's doing. Collins, described by a colleague as an 'incurable schoolmaster',[276] was no doubt infuriating to work with; but the letter shows Williams transparently envious of Collins's status at the Press and his success with women (his 'many loves'). This reflected both Williams's sense that he himself was professionally unsuccessful, and a perception that the pressures of domesticity were tightening around him. For Michal was now some four months pregnant.

★ ★ ★

The baby, a boy, was born on 18 June 1922. He was large and his birth was difficult. Williams seems to have had difficulty in adjusting emotionally to the situation, and deciding quite what he felt about having a son. Writing to Pellow with the news on 6 July, he worked his way round to it by way of a torrent of elaborate fantasy before coming to the point:

> However, all this is a parenthesis [...] a genuflection, an offering, a petition, a meditation, but not a facing facts, a letter, an information, a statement, a profit-&-loss account, a nothing more or less than, a worldly business, a real thing. We have the real thing here;—to be more accurate we have the worldly appearance of the real thing here. In the Divine & only true world of Eternity there exists (we find) a spirit who now thrusts himself into Time. I hope he likes it; his lamentations suggest a doubt. He arrived on the first Sunday after Trinity [...] He weighed [...] just over 9 lb on birth. He has a flat nose, a complexion 'wasted' Michal declares 'on a boy' and a temper—of the worst! His mother had a bad—and towards the end—rather touch and go time—but seems to be pulling round.
>
> I have (laus Deo) no conscious change of emotion: a child is a guest of a somewhat insistent temperament, rather difficult to get rid of, almost pushing;

a poor relation of a fairly pleasant kind. His little voice pulls at my ears; my
heartstrings are unplucked [...] No extraneous circumstances like children can
affect the Me: and I am sure I don't want to affect the Him.[277]

It is a very odd letter. The style—somewhere between Burton's *Anatomy of
Melancholy* and Charles Lamb's essay on 'Poor Relations'—betrays embarrassment; and Williams's insistence that his 'heartstrings are unplucked',
combined with his alarming admission that Michal has had a 'rather touch
and go' experience giving birth and now, eighteen days later, 'seems to be
pulling round', suggest that he is wholly out of his depth, trying to avoid
panic by cultivating detachment after what must have been a shocking and
frightening period. The remarkable claim that 'no extraneous circumstances'
can affect him is perhaps the key: he is terrified of the changes that must
come.

The little boy was baptized on 18 July at St Silas's, Kentish Town, and
named Michael Stansby. His godfather was 'Henry' Lee. It seems odd that
Michael should have been given a name so similar to the one his mother
had acquired. They are distinct—*Michal* in Hebrew means 'brook' or 'stream',
whilst *Michael* is the rhetorical question, 'Who is like God?'—but in English
their pronunciation is virtually identical and must have caused endless confusion, not least for Michael himself.

Williams seems to have maintained an unusual degree of emotional
detachment from his son. In his letters to Pellow—where, admittedly, he
made a practice of letting off steam—Michael figures chiefly as an obstacle
to the continuance of normal life:

> O my dear Pellow [he writes], how intelligent our Lord was! 'I come not to
> bring peace but a sword': I am sure a baby brings a sword, to slay all the happy
> little innocent busynesses of one's life [...] But he is a nuisance: does one write
> verse? Never. A hundred unfinished poems lie about the flat.[278]

Most new parents are startled by their child's demanding dependency. The
strain of sleeplessness and wrecked plans take a severe toll. And Williams was
in modern terms a 'workaholic', who liked to be working for most of his
waking hours: if not at the office, then writing and purposefully reading
at home. Some of his comments are normal enough, as when (perhaps late
in 1922) he told Olive Willis that he, Michal, and Michael were going to
St Albans because 'One has to be as nice as one can to one's people, that our
days may be long in the land', adding, 'More than our nights are: Michael
being sometimes distressed with his rash, and at other times overwhelmingly

anxious to play.'[279] Pellow recalled that Michael 'could not be left at night. He had to be fetched and marched up and down on Charles' shoulder. He recited pages and pages of Milton to the poor child [who] did not like it. [...] You could not carry on much intelligent conversation in an atmosphere like that, so we alternated meeting at his home to meeting for luncheon in Newgate Street, round the corner from Amen House.'[280] But when visits to the Pellows were cancelled at short notice, there are hints that Charles thought Michal was fussing needlessly. Apologizing for one visit likely to be missed, he wrote: 'It appears that the young star usually sleeps till getting on for one, and then wakes for his food. And Michal is reluctant to wake him in case it should tend to make him a little peevish, for the afternoon. I don't think it would but you never know.'[281] When, a couple of months later, Williams visited the Pellows—presumably alone—his host recorded that:

> He also held forth on his favourite paradox—that there is no natural affection between parents & children [...] & from that he got on to love—this he was discussing with Cecily [John Pellow's wife] who strongly disagreed with all he said. He said he had loved his wife to his knowledge not more than half a dozen times during the whole of their acquaintance—he too used love—not as applying to day to day domestic affection—but love in its highest sense—all absorbing, all surrendering, self-obliterating, Love the Jealous, the Terrible God, the destroyer of illusions &c.[282]

Whatever his exacting criteria for real love, it seems that the difficulties of parenthood were leading Williams subtly to resent Michal and her preoccupation with their son. In July 1925, when Williams cancelled a visit because of Michael's whooping cough, Pellow noted, 'A letter came from C.W.—a wail of protest and deliberate gloom.'[283]

What some of these 'wails' were like we can judge from a couple of surviving letters:

> Why the devil [wrote Williams on 4 July 1925] does anyone ever get married? What does marriage, and its consequences do for any human but cause disappointment, misery, disillusion, unhappiness, strife, tumult, weariness, boredom, sickness, malevolence, hatred, cruelty, stubbornness, anger, torment? And other things. If I were not married I should come over this afternoon [...] As it is I shall go home and find Michael with what is undoubtedly whooping cough; and my wife reduced by several sleepless nights to a bilious attack [...] I hate feeling that I alone am sheltering, protecting, amusing, and generally dealing with, the everlasting energy of the young. I wasn't meant for it.[284]

Then, as humour returned, he added a 'Theological Footnote': 'P.S. (also N.B.): Everything in the above letter is to be understood according to the Mind of Christendom as defined by the principles of Romantic Theology'; and then a 'Personal Footnote': 'N.B. (also P.S.): My wife is a dear.'

Pellow, who had children himself, viewed his friend's self-pitying histrionics with detachment. His comments on Michael show, by contrast, how chilly are Williams's remarks about his son. In September 1923 he notes that Charles and Michal visited, 'bringing Michael with them, a fine sturdy little fellow, now learning to walk. C.W. confesses himself devoid of parental enthusiasm; the child is not an unmixed blessing; when he wakes them at 2 a.m., Charles does not love him.'[285] In May 1924, Pellow notes, 'Michael— now two-and-twenty months—a charming little fellow, who can talk and walk.'[286] In Williams's comments, one looks in vain for any such warmth.

Yet the poems he wrote for Michael, full of love and tenderness, tell a different story. Forced to stride up and down, up and down at night with the child on his shoulder, he composed a delightful 'Walking Song' to soothe him:

> Here we go a-walking, so softly, so softly,
> Down the world, round the world, back to London town,
> To see the waters and the whales, the emus and the mandarins,
> To see the Chinese mandarins, each in a silken gown.

The poem, full of fairy-tale imagery, ranges playfully over the wide world before returning to home and bed. A 'Night Song' draws on Williams's occult knowledge, elaborating traditions of bedtime prayer by invoking the 'vast quaternion' of the four archangels of the elements—Raphael Prince of Air, Gabriel of Water, Michael of Fire, and Auriel of Earth— to guard the little boy's bed. And a free verse poem, 'Contemplation', charmingly captures a moment when father and son stare in wonder at each other:

> Actually, child, I am a god
> Communing with you, a god:
> We from our eternal stations
> Behold in their infinite complexity the designs of the Almighty,
> And among them, far away, tiny, unimportant,
> Our age,
> And in it, tinier, less important,
> A town, a street, a cradle,
> And two mortalities, each solemnly regarding the other.

But things were not easy. Williams hinted to Pellow that money worries were in the background, and a subject of argument.[287] When Pellow told the Williamses about a suitable house for sale, Charles thanked him but admitted that they couldn't yet afford it. Michal thought they should buy 'next year' in the interests of their son, but she too was afraid of the commitment: according to Charles, her refrain was, 'O I don't want to buy, Serge, I don't want to buy'.[288] ('Serge' was, strangely, her private name for Charles.) 'I don't believe anyone but the mystic', Williams wrote, 'can actually appreciate the beauty or value of money!'[289]

★   ★   ★

When Michael was around eighteen months old Williams began to give evening lectures. The London County Council had set up a series of Evening Institutes, and invited him to give twenty-five lectures on Modern Literature at Poplar, east London, beginning in the autumn of 1923.[290] The sessions—a one-hour lecture followed by tea and discussion—would be on Thursdays, from 7.30 to 9.30 p.m. Williams took the job mainly for the fees, but he was shy of the audience, and afraid his views would be unpopular. In July, Pellow reported, 'The prospect appals him.'[291] As the date crept nearer he adopted a tone of bravado, writing to Olive Willis in August: 'Audaciously I plunge into the County Council lecturing this winter, very doubtful of success in hitting the hearts and minds of an audience in *Poplar*. [. . .] You might occasionally pray for me on Thursday evenings—Chrysostom perhaps would be a good saint to invoke.'[292]

Chrysostom, whose name means 'Golden Mouthed', is the patron saint of lecturers. His blessing must have been granted, for the lectures were a success. They required much preparation, which meant burning more midnight oil whilst the tired Michal coped with the fractious Michael; and Williams, a natural perfectionist, was dissatisfied. But he gained confidence. The lectures, he told Olive Willis:

> haven't gone too badly, though they [. . .] make me feel like a burglar creeping through the house while the Nine young Muses in the Nine small beds are all asleep upstairs [. . .] I am unhappy about them in some remote way—possibly because each of them ought really to take a year to write, and I haven't the time.[293]

He was soon a confident and increasingly charismatic lecturer. Thelma Mills, an elementary schoolteacher, encountered him in 1926, at the New

Park Road Women's Institute (an evening college for women) in Streatham, south of the Thames. Here, on a September evening, she recalled that a 'group of some 15 assorted ladies', ranging in age from nineteen to fifty-six, sit waiting for a course on Shakespeare. The bossy Principal of the college arrives, 'an autocratic, Queen-Victoria-like little lady':

> ushered in ceremoniously by the new lecturer who fetches up beside her, slim, tallish, dark, with old-fashioned pince nez. He bows his head in acknowledgment of her introduction, and proceeds to bow her out. She seems a little taken aback at being played off her own stage... still! Shutting the door, the Presence returns to the table, fishes a fistful of notes from one pocket and a watch from another, places them squarely on the table before him, and is off!—literally. To and fro he pranced before us, hands in pockets jingling keys and coins, as a spate of words fell from those mobile lips—oration, quotation, incantation [...] and all in that strange voice and odd accent. It was terrific and we didn't understand a word of it. After an hour he stopped as suddenly as he had begun, checking with the watch and flinging himself onto the wooden chair as if it were a divan and he the great Tamburlaine, having disposed of the 'pampered jades of Asia', now ready 'to entertain divine Zenocrate'. [...] We crept out stunned, and returned wondering how we'd get through an hour's discussion with this strange phenomenon. We needn't have bothered. By the end we were hooked. We had never known till then how clever we all were. We looked at each other with new eyes, and at our lecturer with a wild surmise. The accent wouldn't suit Miss Massey [the Principal], but we heard it as they heard the Apostles at Pentecost, each in his own tongue.[294]

Williams never lowered his level to suit the audience, but it didn't matter. His sincerity and enthusiasm carried people along. His prodigious memory for poetry made his recitation fluent and hypnotic, and he spoke every word as if straight from the heart—rendered curiously memorable by his harsh voice and north London accent. A listener to one of Williams's lectures recalled his reciting the opening lines of *Paradise Lost* as:

> Of man's first disobedience an' the fruit
> Of that ferbidden tree, 'oose mortal tiste
> Brort death into the world and all our wow...
> Sing, 'eavenly muse, that on the sicred top...[295]

He could command a room, hold attention, and transform the atmosphere. In discussion he listened with the utmost care and courtesy; rephrasing the halting insights of his students, he showed them that they had been on the edge of profound perceptions all along. And he believed that poetry was not just an ornament to life but a testimony to its deepest, most personal meanings, relevant to each individual:

> Charles related everything he said about everything and everybody to us and ours. [The poets'] lives and works—which we had been hearing about with appropriate dates and relations to their times and tides of fortune—their lives and loves and ours, he insisted, were an integral part of Life itself.[296]

The schoolteacher Thelma Mills wrote: 'Charles Williams exploded into my life without warning', adding, 'I wish I could give you some idea of the sheer fun of it!'[297] From now on, lecturing—once, twice, sometimes three times a week during term time—was central to his life. It was through lecturing that he developed his ideas, built up material for his books, and made friends. But it came at a cost. Michal, as so often, felt excluded. Years later she summed it up with her usual precision: 'I know nothing of the City Literary circle except that twice a week I sat up till nearly midnight to minister to an exhausted man after his lectures.'[298]

★ ★ ★

And still he worked conscientiously within Waite's Fellowship of the Rosy Cross. Between November 1922 and January 1925 he participated in twenty rituals, at irregular intervals. Sometimes months would pass between gatherings; at other times, such as October 1923, he would attend three in one month. Several times he was 'Proclamator et Lucifer', carrying the symbolic lamp, giving commands, and declaiming spiritual teachings. At other times he was 'Third Celebrant', wearing an orange robe with a blue girdle, guiding candidates, male and female, through the $5 = 6$ initiation and binding them to the Cross of Tiphereth on which they would offer their lives to God. It required responsibility, confidence, and a great deal of memorizing.

All this was expected as part of his personal development and progress in the Order. After nearly four years of such work, in June 1923, he went on to take the $6 = 5$ grade, which was that of Adeptus Major. The records show that 'Frater Qui Sitit Veniat [...] received the Rite of Sepulture, was Raised by the Kiss of Peace, and Received Speech in the Rose.' The ritual was a stirring one, in which the postulant was again bound upon a cross, where he had to repeat a solemn pledge—a renewed and stronger version of his original oath of secrecy—before undergoing a symbolic 'Death of the Self'. He was placed on a bier, his eyes closed and his body covered by a red pall.

There he remained until a priestess, veiled from head to foot, revived him by pressing a red rose against his lips. The ritual represented the death of the worldly aspects of the personality ('whatever in his natural personality has no place or state in eternity') and the pressure of the rose symbolized the 'Kiss of the Shekhinah'—an encounter with the 'Dwelling of God' or divine presence in the created universe, envisaged in Kabbalistic mysticism as feminine. The grade of Adeptus Major in Waite's system corresponded to the Kabbalistic sphere of Geburah, or 'Severity', and represented a daunting point of self-dedication.

Over the following months Williams again acted as Third Celebrant, or Master of the Temple, until 10 July 1924, when he took the grade of Adeptus Exemptus $7 = 4$, corresponding to the Kabbalistic sphere of Chesed, or 'Mercy'. This was his most demanding initiation yet. It required a commitment not only to one's own spiritual path, but to all those one might meet who were capable of spiritual development. As Waite's 'Prolegomena' to the grade explained, 'he who attains the grade of Exempt Adept is an ordained priest and teacher', who leaves the sphere of Chesed 'for a life of ministration in the holy assembly from the side of mercy'. The Adeptus Exemptus initiation was the Fellowship's equivalent of ordination as a priest, and one was expected to take it with due seriousness. Preparation for the ritual required spending a day in silent prayer, reflecting:

> on spiritual love as the key to the grand mysteries; and on the power and the grace which are essential to one who having been drawn to things that are eternal, should receive a commission to lead others in the path. The silence of the postulant must be preserved until his mouth is opened in the course of the ceremony itself.[299]

The day that this initiation took place, 10 July, was a Thursday, so presumably Williams had taken a day or two off work. Where did he spend his day of silence? Perhaps he stayed with 'Henry' Lee, away from the pressures of the Hampstead flat. The ritual was long and demanding. It also heightened the element of sexual tension which had been subtly introduced at the previous grade with the appearance of the Priestess and her rose. In the Adeptus Exemptus initiation, the Priestess played an equal part with the male Celebrant (on this occasion Waite himself). Symbolizing union with God, the object of the ceremony was declared by the Priestess to be 'the living Union of the lover and beloved in mind and heart and will'. This was repeated at many points: 'The spirit is the heavenly spouse, and the spouse is Christ.' It was the erotic symbolism—familiar from Coventry Patmore and from earlier mystical sources—of the human soul as bride of the divine lover. Williams, who had long identified romantic love as a manifestation of God, must have found it inspiring and deeply congenial.

Until late in the ritual, the postulant had to remain silent. Even the oath—undertaking to 'impart the Word', and to 'draw unto me the chosen hearts, from the deeps beyond Malkuth, through all the holy houses of the Rosy Cross'—was taken silently, 'in the inmost heart and secret soul'. Much of the practical business of the initiation was done by the Priestess: it was she who drew him between the pillars of the temple, led him to the altar, offered him wine (representing 'the ecstasy of Divine Love'), placed a symbolic dagger in his hands (which he had to kiss), and so on. Finally, the Celebrant in Chief and the Priestess joined hands over the altar, 'In the union of the Lover and the Beloved, world without end',[300] as they closed the temple.

Williams would take one further initiation, but not one that conferred a new grade. 'Adeptus Exemptus, 7=4' was as far as he went in the Fellowship. The grade's commitment to teach and to help, and its affinity with the Kabbalistic sphere of Chesed, the Divine Mercy, stayed with him. To the end of his life, he would use 'Under the Mercy' as a favourite phrase of blessing or farewell.

★   ★   ★

Although the Fellowship of the Rosy Cross had no formal course of studies, its members were not left without instruction. They were given copies of each ritual in which they participated, so as to prepare their 'lines'. Each grade had 'Points of Contemplation' on which the postulant had to meditate, and up to the grade of Philosophus there were standard lists of questions and answers to learn. The texts drew on the whole range of Christian mysticism, with liberal infusions of Kabbala and alchemy. Moreover, members of the Order surely read the works of their Chief Magus, A.E. Waite himself—especially his 1913 book on the Kabbala, *The Secret Doctrine in Israel*. Williams was certainly enthusiastic about it. Michal remembered that Charles 'deeply admired' it,[301] and Anne Ridler recalled:

It was *The Secret Doctrine in Israel* [...] which interested him most—and he continued to admire it, for he recommended me to read it, when I knew him in the thirties. It is a study of a Jewish mystical work, the *Zohar*, and includes

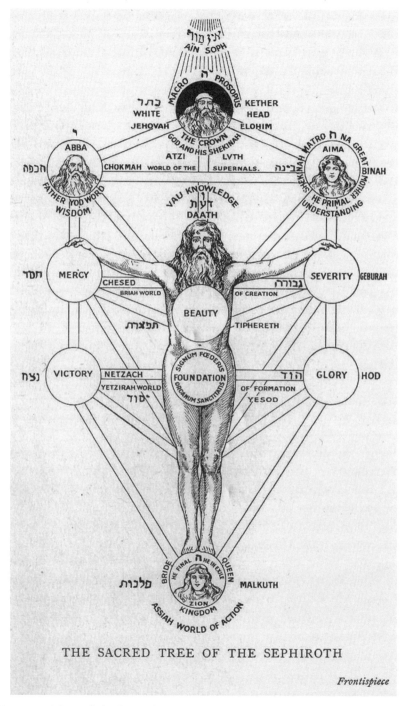

THE SACRED TREE OF THE SEPHIROTH

Frontispiece

Figure 1. The male body on the Sephirotic Tree: from *The Secret Doctrine in Israel*

much of the lore which is found in Golden Dawn teachings. [...] The frontispiece shows a diagram [Figure 1] of the Sephirotic Tree laid out upon the figure of a man, with the different properties related to the parts of the body—e.g. *Chesed*, Mercy, is at the right hand, *Geburah*, Severity, at the left. In this book, I believe, are the foundations of Williams's thought about the symbolism of the body, and of his lifelong attempt to develop an adequate theology of marriage[.][302]

His doings with Lee and his group in the early 1920s remain mysterious. But we know that Lee arranged for someone to draw up his friend's horoscope. We know this because in 1934 Williams told Anne Ridler, 'My horoscope—I must show you my horoscope one day—said I should be a destructive force, or lesser words to that effect, but I never believed it: neither the destruction nor the force. But I occasionally wonder...'[303] In 1942, he added:

> I have been reading my horoscope which I found. Lee had it done by someone he knew when I was about 35 or so. It has some odd things. It prophesies great commercial success—no, sorry, financial: that is its chief error. But it also says that at 41 I 'enter the period of Mars which will remain operative until 56 years of age'. Mars! Venus is weak: I might be 'happier & more successful unmarried' (only I should have done nothing), but I 'may remain celibate throughout my life unless at 57 I come under the influence of Jupiter's greater periods'.[304]

Williams was thirty-five in 1921. The horoscope has disappeared but presumably his study of occult and mystical ideas with Lee's group continued. One December, perhaps in 1924, Williams told Pellow that:

> The OUP [...] is madly plunging into a four-volume *Hermetica*—Hermes Trismegistus, Gnosticism, and so forth. I have collected as many as I could of the clean sheets of Volume I which shall be at your disposal if you want to read them some time. I don't know that there is anything *very* exciting bar a pleasant phrase about 'There was in the beginning Light and out of the Light arose a sound.' And even so, one should use the present tense of eternity: 'there is in the beginning...'[305]

No doubt the spare sheets of the *Hermetica*—a collection of Greek magical and mystical texts from the early Christian period—were taken to Lee's vicarage, passed around and discussed. They were not his only esoteric reading. Around 1922 he was reading two books by the Golden Dawn founder, William Wynn Westcott—*Numbers: Their Occult Power and Mystic Virtues* and *Sepher Yetzirah, Or, The Book of Creation*, a classic work of Jewish mysticism.[306] He also maintained an interest in the works of the theosophist G.R.S. Mead:

in 1918 he had read Mead's *Quests Old and New*;[307] in 1924 he was reading Mead's *Fragments of a Faith Forgotten*—picked up second hand, he told Pellow, for ninepence![308]

Since 'Henry' Lee had access to the Golden Dawn Flying Rolls, these may also have been discussed at the vicarage. If so, Williams would have acquired knowledge of many standard Golden Dawn techniques. These could have included meditation on tarot cards, in which the subject entered into the card's landscape and imaginatively 'explored' it; divination, using the elemental tools (pentacle, cup, wand, and dagger—assigned to earth, water, fire, and air); clairvoyance by means of 'tattwas'—cards bearing coloured symbols associated with the elements, and used to fix concentration; and magical self-defence, which could include drawing (or visualizing) a 'banishing pentagram' to keep evil influences at bay, or quietly picturing a protective layer of 'odic fluid' around one's body.

Certainly Williams's intellectual and spiritual life was now both intense and colourful. New and stimulating groups of friends had replaced the old Theological Smokers. Once a fortnight Lee's group met; in between, there were lively lecture audiences. And, at intervals, Williams could immerse himself in vivid ritual practice with Waite's Fellowship. But Michal was left out. Williams did not intend this, however: though it did not occur to him to try to enter her world, he would have welcomed her to his. He had already tried to make her into a writer. Had she been a different person with other talents, she might have become his co-author in literature and his High Priestess in ritual. But these were not her strengths. And so the lively, impulsive girl who had ranged the countryside with her sporting father found herself trapped in a dull London flat coping with a difficult toddler whilst her husband was, mostly, elsewhere.

8

Romantic Theology

Despite pressure of work and discontent with his personal life, Williams continued through the early 1920s to write new poems. Unable to find a new poetic style, he strove, like the protagonist of Ezra Pound's 1920 poem *Hugh Selwyn Mauberley*:

> to resuscitate the dead art
> Of poetry; to maintain 'the sublime'
> In the old sense.

Many poets of the time faced the same problem: a stylized diction of 'thees' and 'thous', together with tidy rhyme and metre, made their poems seem dated. Yet the free verse practised by a handful of Imagists and the like mostly looked flat, and failed to flow. How could poetry in the post-war world appear fresh, vivid, and spontaneous, yet musical and powerful?

With apt symbolism, autumn 1922—the season in which Alice Meynell died—saw the publication of T. S. Eliot's *The Waste Land*. Eliot's poem was certainly 'modern', but to its first readers it also seemed chaotic—a welter of voices and fragments. Until its underlying unity began to emerge through repeated reading it was simply baffling. We don't know when Williams first read it, or whether, on doing so, he was struck by its affinities to his own central preoccupations, with its imagery drawn from Arthurian legend and its thirst for spiritual nourishment. He would later think deeply about Eliot's work, and Eliot would become a central figure in his life. But not yet.

Meanwhile, on Sundays, with Michal and Michael, he attended morning service at St Silas the Martyr, Kentish Town. The church was impressive—a tall brick basilica, its spacious interior lavishly decorated with statues of the saints, fine carvings, and stained glass. It was a bastion of the Anglo-Catholic tradition: a tradition that rejected the authority of the pope, but enjoyed all

Catholic practices, including private confession, prayers for the intercession of the saints, and devotion to the Blessed Virgin. The glimpses we have of Williams's own religious practice show him engaging fully with the ritual expressions of this tradition—as when he begins a poem to Michal with the line 'The ceremonial gestures end', and concludes it with 'I rise, I genuflect, I turn / To breakfast, and to you!' Gesture was important and natural to him; it would have been unthinkable to him that the body should not play its part in worship. Even the name he had given to his wife alluded, however problematically, to dancing before the Lord.

Charles and Michal had attended St Silas's ever since they moved to London in 1917. By May 1918 Williams was a sidesman, seeing to the seating and comfort of the churchgoers and taking the collections, a role he kept for the next five years. The congregation included many local artists and craftspeople, and was notable for the performance of religious plays within the church itself—the first English church since the Reformation to allow them. The first of these, *The Mystery of the Passion* by local author Benjamin Boulter, was performed at Easter 1918. The following years saw a series of other plays. Williams undoubtedly attended these and they inspired him to think afresh about the spiritual possibilities of drama. And between 1920 and 1928 he contributed fifteen poems to the parish magazine, most of them later collected into his published books.

Occasional editors were interested in his work. His poem 'Absence' appeared in the *London Mercury* in March 1922, and a sonnet, 'Sleep', was taken by *The Living Age*. Technically accomplished but archaic, 'Sleep' might have been written in the sixteenth century. It ends:

> How dost thou lure us from our late consent
> And our night prayers to light and ecstasy,
> Tempting us now, with our last waking breath,
> To ask no more, but only this, of death.

It contributed nothing new to poetic consciousness, and Williams must have known it. Pellow noted how ruefully Williams picked over remembered compliments:

Alice Meynell told him he was the greatest poet since Patmore & Fr[ancis] Thompson. Lascelles Abercrombie said of one of his sonnets that it was one wh[ich] the world would not willingly let die. Sir Walter Raleigh was also among his admirers. But said C.W. 'most of my admirers are dead (AM & Ralegh) or dying (the P[oet] L[aureate])!'[309]

Williams and Pellow compared wretched sales figures: *Poems of Conformity*, 158 copies; *Divorce*, 126. Pellow's *Parentalia* had sold 105.[310] Pellow thought Williams's lack of success was partly due to sectarianism: if he were a Roman Catholic 'he wd be boosted by all the Roman journals [. . .] and his books would *sell*'.[311] But he also thought Williams was too impatient. Reading a batch of his friend's new poems, Pellow liked some, but reflected that 'thought & expression haven't fused. [. . .] If they were my own work I should lay them aside for 3 months & then work over them thoroughly.'[312]

In originality, however, Pellow thought Williams second to none. Perhaps the most striking demonstration of this absolute independence of mind came in May 1923, when Charles showed him a new poem, 'On Pulling a Chain'. Full of alchemical imagery, it begins with an apology for possible disturbance caused by flushing the lavatory at night, and goes on to reflect on the generality of excretion:

> White classic poets, kings in hall
>   of judgement, bishops singing mass,
> maids lovelier than Helen, all
>   are brought to one uneasy pass,
>   with beasts that feed on flesh or grass[.]

The poem speculates that even heaven must have 'sewers fit' so that imperfection may be drained into lower realms and 'be brought to use again'. Even when 'the world' went to look upon the Crucifixion, catching a glimpse of the apparent triumph of hell:

> Therein hot furnaces they saw,
>   and scarrèd hands alchemical,
> pour and repour as bade the law,
>   vitriol, blood and bitter gall;
>   and heard one to another call
> the work was finished without flaw.

Finally the poem asks:

> Did our Lord in His fair body
>   bring a new miracle to pass
> and bid all food for strengthening be?
>   or was He as His mother was
>   as Pilate and as Caiaphas
> and all his chosen chivalry?

The answer seems to be that, in His body, 'that most strong crucible of pain' which He took on 'to try the great experiment', Christ too experienced these bodily functions. The poem takes spiritual acceptance of the body as far as possible. No physical process, it implies, is unholy. (Williams surely knew that the topic had been debated between Catholics and Gnostics— who denied the full physicality of Jesus—in the second century.) Pellow thought the poem 'an astonishing production—astonishing not bec[ause] of its delicate subject [. . .] but because of the daring way in which he achieves beauty'.[313]

But Williams's audacity was not to everyone's taste. When, in April 1923, the Dominican friars asked for a contribution to their magazine *Blackfriars*, he sent a poem called 'To Michal, on Bringing her Breakfast in Bed'. Naturally they rejected it.[314] To offer such a poem to a magazine edited by celibate friars was probably deliberate provocation. Williams felt strongly about Christianity's discomfort with the body, sexuality, and even marriage. In this he took a lead from Waite, who described celibacy as a 'virus' which had 'disordered the views of Christendom'.[315]

Williams was thinking again about Arthurian matters. In September 1923 he discussed with Pellow his ideas for a 'highly symbolic and sacramental' poetic treatment of the Grail legends,[316] and the following year revealed a decisive change in his thinking. He now planned not a single piece but a sequence of ballads. He asked Pellow about the pronunciation of 'Palomides', the name of the Saracen knight of the romances. He wanted to stress it on the second syllable, but had been told that most people stressed the third. 'Curse them!' he wrote in comic *chagrin*. 'And they thus ruin a stanza from the (unwritten) Graal ballads:

> In the high town of Ispahan
> (Where palmers walk on peas)
> Where redly smites the sacred morn
> On jewelled turbans that adorn
> The Persian divan, was he born,
> The prince Palomides.

Curse them again!!'[317] It is hard to tell how serious he was: the line about palmers and peas certainly sounds comic. But clearly he was thinking about the ballads, if not actually writing them.[318]

There was also a puzzling success, of a kind. The 1924 Paris Olympics included a poetry competition. Williams entered with 'Ceremonial Ode for the Opening of the Olympic Games', written in his worst high-flown style, and received an award by post. In August of that year, Pellow recorded: 'Lunched with Williams. He has been awarded a Diploma & Bronze Medal by the Olympic Games but is uneasy as to what it means, how many others have received awards, so is not boasting at present.'[319] His misgivings were justified, as reference sources cite Oliver St John Gogarty, Irish poet and friend of Joyce, as having won the same bronze medal. Perhaps other people did too. The episode remains mysterious.

★ ★ ★

The major project of the years 1922 to 1924, however, was the body of poems that would become his next book—as yet untitled. Freed from the pressure of Alice Meynell's opinions, Williams tried a range of stanza forms, and experimented again with free verse. The outstanding example of this is 'On Meeting Shakespeare':

> I saw Shakespeare
> In a tube station on the Central London:
> He was smoking a pipe,
> He had Sax Rohmer's best novel under his arm
> (In a cheap edition),
> And the *Evening News*.
> He was reading in the half-detached way one does.
> He had just come from an office
> And the notes for *The Merchant*
> Were in his pocket,
> Beginning (it was the first line he thought of)
> 'Still quiring to the young-eyed cherubins,'
> But his chief wish was to be earning more money.

The poem remakes Shakespeare in his own image as a plebeian modern author, balancing sublime poetry with cheap thrillers and the newspaper, and preoccupied with the difficulty of earning a living. In this curious self-portrait, the two poets meet, overlap, and merge.

However, the striking feature of most of these poems is the tone of horror and even nihilism they manifest, their sense of metaphysical dread in everyday surroundings. In 'Domesticity' the simplest domestic acts—'Bathing or lighting a fire or going downstairs'—are fraught with revulsion. To wash is to remember mass executions by drowning during the French Revolution.

When the poet lights a fire, 'the small flames scorch / Something other than wood' and he feels himself one with those who burned martyrs, or:

> my silent lips shout with the mob
> Where to-day in the West a screaming negro endures
> The last pains of death, and my food is cooked at his fire.

Replacing a book on the shelf, he feels himself sliding the last brick into place as some helpless prisoner is walled up, 'And I thrust the stone hastily in and turn and go.' Everything accuses: 'The very wallpaper stares straight ahead, / Seeming neither to whisper nor wink but to speak all the time / How beneath it the mortar is bloodily streaked.' He cannot separate himself from the pain and guilt of others. And there are dreadful uncertainties. In 'Theobald's Road' he waits to meet Michal but it occurs to him that:

> There must be many Theobald's Roads in the universe;
> Images of images; almost, not quite, identical;
> A little above, a little below, slanting across, here but not quite here[.]

Perhaps she has slipped into another dimension, and they will not meet again for many decades, or ever. 'As for the doctors, / They may call it loss of memory, they may call it madness.' 'Witchcraft' is a hymn to Satan—'Our Father who wert in heaven', as Williams writes, borrowing a line from a poem of his adolescence—spoken by a witch who adores the fallen arch-angel because only he can grant the ultimate delight of cruelty, which is 'To see our lovers weep / Under our word or kiss.'

There are other, happier poems: rhymes for children, and poems of love and marriage. But the originality and power are mostly in these poems of fear and disquiet. It is Williams's most powerful poetry since *The Silver Stair*, and seems to come from a period of mental suffering, in which his frightful sense of the unreality of his surroundings is compounded by a perception of evil in the world and in himself.

★　★　★

But a fundamental change was beginning in Williams's life, and in the life of the Oxford University Press. In spring 1924 the lease on Amen Corner expired; its offices had become cramped and inconvenient. So the Press took over Amen House in nearby Warwick Square. The move, an enormous upheaval, took most of February and the new building opened on 3 March.

Even more than the former offices, Amen House embodied the history and grandeur of London—and the Press. Its nucleus was a pair of elegant eighteenth-century town houses. New upper storeys of white stone had been added, with further offices behind, and a seven-storey warehouse with space for 750,000 books. In the basement, a glass panel revealed part of London's Roman wall. The ambience of Amen House (which remained the OUP's London headquarters until 1966) impressed itself strongly on employees, some of whom can still, in memory, walk over every floor of the place. A visitor would go up three steps and enter by double doors. On the left was the showroom, where 'customers [could] inspect Bibles [. . .] in every kind of plain or fancy leather binding, prayer books ditto, or leather bound editions of the World's Classics or Oxford Standard Authors',[320] and a selection of children's books. Opposite was 'a beautiful waiting room with fine furniture, a decorated plaster ceiling and Adam fireplace, and, leading off it, the social [. . .] centre of the Press, the Library'.[321] At the time of the move, there was no librarian. The first occupant of that post, a young woman called Phyllis Jones, would arrive nearly a month later.[322]

To reach the upper floors, you went to the back of the hall, encountering Sergeant Larner:

> elderly, scarred of face from the First World War, and dignified of demeanour, who receives visitors and, if necessary, transports them upwards in the small, hydraulically-powered lift which he works by pulling on a vertical cable running through roof and floor; and Miss Winnie Cox in the telephone cubby-hole next to the showroom, knitting interminable garments between calls. Miss Cox [. . .] made an internal telephone system almost unnecessary. If one wanted to know anything, one talked to Miss Cox.[323]

One floor up the 'broad, shallow staircase' above the showroom, in 'a magnificent room with an Adam ceiling' Humphrey Milford presided over his empire, helped by an assistant, who had his own small office; across the landing was Mr Cannon, the staff manager. (Milford also had a butler, 'frequently seen with his silver salver at mid-morning', an employee recalled.)[324] Also on the first floor were Gerry Hopkins, responsible for publicity, and the formidable Helen Peacock, Head of Production. Miss Peacock—'tall, plain, honest-looking, blunt of speech, with piled untidy greying hair pulled back in a bun, always dressed in blouse and skirt, the battleaxe of the Press', and its German expert—received manuscripts once the editors had finished with them, and 'got them estimated, designed and prepared for the printing office'.[325] Above was the binding office and then, through a swing

door and along a linoleum-floored corridor, the printing office, and finally
the room where Williams and Page worked as editors: officially, 'Readers
to the Press'.

Here, away from the public front of the Press, conditions closer to the old
huddle of Amen Corner soon re-established themselves. It took little time,
once the files and boxes were moved in from the old offices, for Charles and
Fred to dig themselves into a sort of nest, as recalled later by a colleague,
Charles Hadfield:

> CW, in his swivelling and tippable chair, sat on the right, Page on the left [in an
> armchair]. Beside CW was a hatstand upon which he would hang his coat and
> hat—he always wore a homburg—and slap his gloves, as soon as he entered. [...]
> Between the two desks was a chair for visitors, and above that file copies of all
> the Oxford Poets, containing every reported correction, ready for the next
> reprint. A similar set of nearly 500 World's Classics were on the shelves behind
> Fred Page, together with his favourite books—Alice Meynell, Chesterton,
> Swedenborg. Behind CW was a miscellaneous collection, including Middleton
> Murry, Malory, and, later, T.S. Eliot. Along the south wall were all the Oxford
> Standard Authors, Oxford Books of Verse, and a portrait of Henry James; and
> down behind CW's chair was a litter of his own manuscripts in wooden boxes.
> There wasn't a spare inch anywhere—the overflow of books from the room
> was guarded by Ralph Binfield [who arrived in 1927] next door. Although
> Ralph was CW's assistant, his and Page's room had no space for a third, so Ralph
> was accommodated in two square yards of the printing office[326]

Each editor had a wastepaper basket, but Williams, apparently:

> invariably missed [his], consequently there were always bits and pieces all over
> the floor! [...] CW smoked a lot and there was always a haze about his office.
> As I knocked and entered the room he would spin round in his swivel chair,
> which to me never looked safe, at the same time tipping the chair back at an
> alarming angle, often propping his feet up on the desk, and in that slanting
> position would raise his eyebrows (much exaggerating his rather shaggy
> appearance) and regard me with a questioning look.[327]

A cultural theorist could read a whole 'spatial poetics' in the structure of
Amen House. Ralph Binfield recalls, for example, that 'Humphrey Milford
had definite views about staircases'.[328] There were five in all, and lower echelons of staff were not supposed to use the 'elegantly-carpeted' main staircase,
so Williams and others avoided it after Milford arrived at 10 o'clock each
morning. They used another staircase at the rear—Williams, who scorned
the lift, bounding up it 'two at a time, hands in trouser pockets'.[329] Washrooms

were also a status symbol. Milford had his own, with curtains over the door. He preferred that employees did not see him emerging: 'Such carelessness earned an angry scowl.'[330] Other washrooms were reserved, in a hierarchy, one (on the first landing) for senior male staff; one (slightly below ground) for clerks, assistants, counting-house staff, and so on; and an even lower one, in the basement, for lorry drivers, cleaners, and the like. There were parallel arrangements, lacking the upper echelons, for female employees.

Whilst bathroom facilities descended, as it were, with one's status, office space ranked in the opposite direction, with the lowest-ranking employees at the top. Above Williams and Page, on the third floor, was the sales department. Humbler yet, on the fourth floor were the 'counting-house' staff—still, in 1924, working as their kind had done for hundreds of years, perched on high stools at counters, writing carefully by hand in leather-and-brass-bound ledgers. 'Cleaners [...] worked during the day; when the counting-house floor was scrubbed the clerks wound their legs around their high stools and got on with their job.'[331] There was a dining room for female employees, in order to save them from the perils of going into the city for lunch. Milford had his lunch cooked on the premises and served privately in his room. Other male staff foraged outside.

Williams's office overlooked the backyard of the Old Bailey, London's Central Criminal Court. Neighbouring buildings were obliged to have frosted glass in any windows overlooking the yard, but the Press—apparently privileged as a kind of national institution—had been allowed to have clear glass. From Williams's office one had 'an excellent view of prisoners being escorted into the Old Bailey',[332] and could even see into the disrobing room,[333] where judges retired on leaving the court. Any staring, however, would be met by a police sergeant's yell, 'Get away from those windows!'[334]

All this makes Amen House sound slightly grotesque, a kind of book-trade Gormenghast. Probably much of what went on was normal for the period. But the new building had a profound effect. It articulated the shape of a community: hierarchical and, in many ways, authoritarian—no trade unions allowed—but also close-knit, friendly, and united by a pride in producing and distributing good books. It was an article of faith that the OUP was the world's finest publisher, and employees were patronizing about neighbouring firms such as Hutchinson, or Hodder and Stoughton. The old offices had impeded work and communication. Amen House brought people together, put them in touch and made them visible to each other. Alice Mary Hadfield, who came to work there later, recalled it as 'a good place in which to work, human, interesting, exciting, full of personalities of all grades'.[335] As such it provided, literally, the stage on which the drama of Charles Williams's middle years would be played out.

★ ★ ★

No sooner had Williams settled into his new office than a crisis landed on his desk. Translator Aylmer Maude's enthusiasm for Tolstoy, whom he had known personally, verged on fanaticism, and acting as Maude's 'minder' within the Press was no joke—though Williams's colleagues sometimes treated it as one. 'Maude, a belligerent slave of the Russian novelist, [...] carried on a ceaseless correspondence in literary journals about every aspect of Tolstoy, even the spelling of his name.'[336] Perpetually argumentative, Maude was such a nuisance that sometimes when colleagues saw him coming across Warwick Square they would alert Williams, who would disappear down a back staircase, leaving him to others.

Early in 1924, an American publisher started issuing versions of Tolstoy by another translator, Nathan Dole, marketing them as 'for the first time a complete, authentic, and unexpurgated version'. Maude was furious, and encouraged the Press's New York branch to protest, pointing out that besides personally endorsing Maude's versions, Tolstoy had 'so disliked Mr. Dole's rendering that he would not even reply to his letters or give him any vestige of recognition'.[337] These comments brought rumblings from Dole and his lawyer, and on 19 May 1924 Williams received a telegram from Maude at Chelmsford: 'DOLE HAS SUED AMERICA FOR LIBEL PLEASE CALL HERE IMMEDIATELY'.[338] There seemed every prospect of an action—'Dole v. Oxford University Press'—in the American courts, and Williams had the uneasy task of supplying ammunition for Cravath, Henderson, and Degersdorff, the Press's New York attorneys, to prepare their defence. There followed hours of confabulation with the enraged Maude, in the office and at the Williams's home in Hampstead, as they disentangled exactly what Tolstoy had said and written to Maude, what Maude himself had said in print, what the Press had said to whom, and how much of all this could be proved.

Fortunately, Dole failed to pursue his action beyond its first hearing and, after causing Williams great anxiety, it lapsed. Reporting this narrow escape, the New York attorneys offered a few words of advice:

We take this opportunity [...] of urging upon you the desirability of avoiding the inclusion of statements of fact in literary criticism. [...] The statement

[...] that Tolstoy so disliked Mr. Dole's rendering that he would not even reply to his letters [...] caused us much concern, lest the court should hold that these words, if untrue, were libellous. [...] On this issue we would have had the burden of proof and, in view of Count Tolstoy's death, it would have been impossible for us to procure the evidence necessary to sustain our defense.

We are pointing this out [...] so that you may appreciate the distinction between statements of your own opinion concerning a man's work, which are in the nature of literary criticism, and statements of fact, which might, in many cases, be held libellous, if untrue.[339]

With that little sermon on the difference between opinion (safe) and fact (dangerous), the matter ended.

With Dole despatched, Williams was able to turn his attention to the usual editorial matters, writing a note for the World's Classics on possible endings to Dickens's unfinished novel *Edwin Drood*, and pressing on with his poetry. As far back as late 1922, he had told Olive Willis:

Mr. Milford, pursuing the Art of generosity, asked me the other day when the world was to be surprised and delighted by another volume of ME. But I have replied that one can't keep on thrusting oneself down the public, who are good judges, and that I think I ought to be silent [...] I do rather squirm at the awful picture of a very minor poet taking himself with dreadful solemnity.[340]

In the autumn of 1923, after the Press had rejected Williams's proposal for 'a small book on *English Dramatic Literature*',[341] he had again discussed his poetry with Milford, lamenting its lack of success; whereupon, he told Pellow that Milford 'offered me a reputation in the 21st century'.[342] But soon Milford suggested that the Press should publish another collection. Williams writhed, yet knew he would give in:

I simply *can't* bring myself to reject HSM's offer to do another book: I despise myself, but I like to see myself in print. I like to read them in a few years' time and think how good they are. 'My God, what genius I had'... and so on.[343]

So, once the Tolstoy crisis was over, he thought again about a book. He felt uncomfortable, with Milford, his employer, now cast as his patron too. He handled this by confronting it head-on, fulsomely celebrating Milford's patronage in two poems that almost bracket the new collection, which was to be called *Windows of Night*: an opening 'Prelude (To H.S.M.)', balanced by the penultimate 'To a Publisher'.

Both poems have, centrally, a political import. 'Prelude' presents Williams's poverty-stricken childhood as a time of fear, when he 'saw the blinding

tyrants smite / Their serving-folk with death or night / For avarice or
whim' and when even God's will ('The fitful poised Almighty threat'),
'though but few it seemed to strike / with madness, cancer, and their like, /
Yet taught all to despair.' In his early years he dared not expect happiness.
But now, he lives 'Beneath a courteous lord'—Milford himself—and offers
his verse to Milford, since 'your care / Sustains unharmed my household
stair'. Modelled on Renaissance poems addressed to an aristocratic patron,
the gratitude expressed in 'Prelude' is so humble, so tinged with self-pity,
that one cannot help suspecting that it hides a degree of unconscious resentment. It is hard to believe that the tight-lipped Milford was not slightly
embarrassed by it.

'To a Publisher' reads more positively. It takes its starting point from
St John's vision, in the Book of Revelation, of the New Jerusalem with its
twelve gates. Williams imagines this 'Free City' as having twelve guilds, each
with its different type of work, marching in 'exalted pageantry' through the
streets. Their place—his own and Milford's—will be amongst the people of
letters: poets, writers, editors, publishers, patrons, and printers. This ideal society will be ranked, yet egalitarian: 'For there in turn republican all are / Our
masters, and we theirs; so interchange / The hierarchical degrees afar.'

Both 'Prelude' and 'To a Publisher' show, unmistakably, the impact of
Amen House. Like the building, they celebrate the business as an ordered
hierarchy, with Milford as its ruler, taking its place in the City—London as
well as the visionary Jerusalem which it reflects—and proud of its work,
ideals, and traditions. The second poem reconciles Williams's egalitarian politics with his love of chivalric hierarchy, in the concept of a fluid system
where people change place, moving constantly up and down. The poems
mark a new stage in Williams's thinking. His workplace has crystallized as
part of his spiritual vision.

★   ★   ★

Completing the new book of poems, Williams embarked on another project close to his heart: an exposition of what he had come to think of as
'Romantic Theology'. Since his first meeting with Michal, which he recalled
as a revelation of essential love, he had believed that romantic love was a
religious experience; perhaps, as Patmore had claimed, the only spiritual
experience most people would ever have. Yet the Church undervalued it.
Marriage was a sacrament, and Christ's first miracle had been performed at

a wedding; but the Church entertained a lingering prejudice in favour of celibacy, and had never explored the theological meaning of the intense experience of being in love.

Romantic Theology was formulated first in his poetry. *The Silver Stair* had at some points identified Love—love between man and woman—with Christ. In later poems Williams had taken to using the word 'Love' where one would normally expect 'Christ' or 'God'—which had led Theodore Maynard to suspect that he was a pagan masquerading as a Christian. The experiment had been tried a little differently in *Scene from a Mystery*, a short piece which Williams had published in Chesterton's *New Witness* in December 1919. Essentially a nativity play, *Scene from a Mystery* is a highly stylized drama, featuring Mary and Joseph, shepherds and kings, Herod and Caiaphas, Satan and Gabriel, and 'Our Lord Love'—who seems to represent sometimes God the Father, sometimes Jesus, and sometimes the human quality of love. In the opening lines, Williams emphasizes that the drama can be viewed as either outward or inward—taking place in Judaea and Galilee, 'Or the profound depth of man's inmost soul'. Most readers surely took *Scene from a Mystery* as simply a daring dramatization of the commonplace that 'God is Love'.

This small script of 1919 held no suggestion that 'Love' meant erotic love. But among the poems which would appear in his still-untitled new book was 'Counsels of Perfection', a ballad in which a pair of 'wedded lovers' resting beneath a tree are coarsely rebuked by a 'preaching friar'. The bride replies:

> 'Thy versicles upon the road
> Cry: *Naught save God can be:*
> O foolishness! without our clear
> Response: *These too are He!*'

She claims that their love is poverty, chastity, and obedience all in one. The poem combatively asserts the equal value of the ways of love and of asceticism—what Williams would come to call the Ways of Affirmation and of Rejection. It also contains, in the words '*Naught save God can be [. . .] These too are He*', a first hint of the paradoxical aphorism which Williams would later use as a frequent basis for reflection: 'This also is Thou; neither is this Thou.'

In the summer of 1924, Williams began to set out in full his conviction that human sexual love was a path to the divine, and a direct manifestation of divinity. In late August, Pellow noted that his friend was 'writing Outlines of Romantic Theology, a prose version of Divorce and Conformity'.[344] Williams must have told Pellow that he was putting into prose ideas that had been central to his poetry since 1917. By early September a typed draft of *Outlines of Romantic Theology* was being read by Humphrey Milford, who sent it to the Bishop of Ripon for an opinion as to whether it was publishable. But Williams told Pellow on 5 September, 'I scribble away at *Romantic Theology*, a book which will probably affect profoundly the whole thought of the Universal Church.'[345] How seriously he meant this is not clear; nor is it clear how he could be 'scribbling away' at a book which was already typed and sent out for comments. Anyhow, the next day Williams told Pellow that the Bishop had reported:

> but secretly—at least, Caesar hides the document: which infuriates me. I have hinted at openness, but without effect. Caesar, in a private note to me, says (most charmingly): 'I fear this is not for us. It may be for all time and I may be like the poor Indian, but I am afraid of it and of you.'[346]

But Williams continued to work on the book, and ten days later told Pellow that 'with several *lacunae*, [it] is now finished'.[347] He added that he also had a title for his new collection of poems. It would be called *Windows of Night*. But work on *Romantic Theology* continued, and on 3 October he told Pellow—yet again—that '*Romantic Theology* is temporarily finished, but it is only in pencil and I don't know when I shall have it typed. However, it shall be yours when I do.'[348] The theme was so important to him, and so challenging, that he kept having new insights: 'temporarily finished' versions turned out to be merely *un*finished.

Outlines of Romantic Theology was certainly a daring work. It aimed at nothing less than establishing a new branch of theology, whose focus would be the experience of 'romantic love; that is, sexual love between a man and a woman'.[349] Williams argued that since love was a human experience of fundamental importance, the spiritual significance of erotic love was long overdue for attention. Most theologians had been celibate clerics, and, whilst they admitted marriage as a sacrament, 'it would be demanding too much [...] to expect them to be sensitive to the meaning and graces of a sacrament from which they have been debarred'.[350] Williams proposed to remedy the defect, and to do so by, essentially, 'a single formula: which is, the identification of love with Jesus Christ, and of marriage with His life'.[351]

He proceeded to find analogies or 'correspondences' between the experiences of love and marriage, and the life of Christ. Thus the moment of falling in love—the birth of love, as it were—corresponds to Christ's birth. Christ's baptism corresponds to the marriage ceremony. Love (like Christ in the wilderness) is tempted: as He was confronted with stones and invited to turn them to bread, so the lovers will have to live with 'the stones of depression, boredom, monotony, dislike' and realize that love will not magically transform these into something wonderful. Eventually love will have to undergo some form of crucifixion. One aspect of this is simply the fact of the lovers being bound to one another: 'The lover knows himself to be the cross upon which the Beloved is stretched, and she also of her lover', because 'the sense of being for ever intimately bound to another [...] when it is not repose is agony.' More intimately, 'intercourse between man and woman is, or at least is capable of being [...] a symbol of the Crucifixion'. Love can also undergo a resurrection, and an ascension—when 'there descends upon the lovers the indwelling grace of the Spirit, nourishing and sustaining them'. Williams cautions, however, that 'perhaps a happy marriage in this sense is as rare among marriages as a great saint among orthodox Christians'.[352]

Milford had probably been disingenuous in seeking advice from the Bishop of Ripon, who was unlikely to be pleased by such daring speculations. The episcopal eyebrows must have been raised at several points in Williams's argument—as when Williams rephrases the usual 'Jesus Christ our Lord' as 'Jesus Christ our Love',[353] or argues that in sexual intercourse between lovers:

> the presence of Love, that is of Christ, is sacramentally imparted by each to the other. If this act is not capable of being a sacrament, then it is difficult to see in what way marriage itself is more sacramental than any other occupation; [...] the Christ of the Eucharist and the Love of the marriage-night are indeed not two but one[354]

– so that making love may be, in effect, a form of the Mass.

Outlines of Romantic Theology was a challenge to the Church's traditional reticence on the subject of sexuality. But Williams was not writing in isolation. The dedication—'*To A.H.E.L., D.H.S.N., and F.P., whose book this is as much or more than mine*'—makes clear that its ideas had been discussed with 'Henry' Lee, Daniel Nicholson, and Fred Page. More strikingly still, there survives an unpublished sonnet by Williams entitled 'For Henry Preaching on Romantic Theology', showing that Lee not only knew of the doctrine but preached a sermon on it at St Stephen's.

A notable absence from Williams's dedication is A.E. Waite. Although Williams continued to attend gatherings of the Fellowship throughout

1924, neither his letters nor Waite's diary mention any social encounter. It seems they had no personal relationship outside their Rosicrucian activities. Rather, Waite is present in *Romantic Theology* by way of his book *The Secret Tradition in Israel*, a study of a Jewish mystical text, the *Zohar*. Waite condemns the Christian Churches' attitude to marriage as a 'failure', and their consecration of marriage as 'skin-deep [...] reluctant and half-hearted'— whereas, according to the *Zohar*, marriage is obligatory for those who would enter paradise, and at the moment of sexual intercourse 'the *absconditus sponsus* [secret bridegroom] enters into the body of the woman and is joined with the *abscondita sponsa* [secret bride]', thus reunifying the sacred Name of God which has been fragmented on earth.[355] This corresponds closely to Williams's view that sex, rightly experienced, is equivalent to the Mass. Williams confirms his debt to Waite in a footnote recommending the *Zohar* as 'extraordinarily valuable'.[356]

Williams's book was also, perhaps, an attempt to remind himself of the nature of marriage, as his relationship with Michal became increasingly difficult. And it is striking that children are barely mentioned. This is most conspicuous when he says of sexual intercourse that, 'There is no other human experience, except Death, which so enters into the life of the body; there is no other human experience which so binds the body to another being.'[357] He seems to have forgotten about childbirth.

★   ★   ★

The sudden decision to write about Romantic Theology in the summer of 1924 may have been prompted by something other than personal factors. For in July 1924 D.H.S. Nicholson published *The Marriage-Craft*—also a book about sex and marriage, and also dedicated to 'Henry' Lee. *The Marriage-Craft* purports to be a novel, but is really a philosophical dialogue. Its characters include Nicholson himself (as the narrator, Peter), Lee (as 'Henry'), and Charles Williams, thinly disguised as 'Ronald'.

The story opens with the narrator and Ronald on a crowded train, heading into Hertfordshire for a country walk. Ronald (Williams) is expounding his theories on sex:

> quite ingenious and quite audible—and quite undismayed by the cavernous silence of the carriage. After a more than usually improbable remark—something to the effect that there should be a law forbidding married couples to live

together for more than six months in the year—he had looked round innocently when a loud snort had broken the silence of his unwilling audience.[358]

During their walk they hatch a plan to hire a canal boat, assemble a diverse group of friends, and take a holiday on which they will, as Ronald expresses it, 'put our cards on the table and see if we can't find out what all this sex business, all this marriage tangle, really comes to'.[359] The plan goes ahead, and besides Peter (Nicholson) and Ronald (Williams), the party consists of Henry, a celibate clergyman with an interest in alchemy; an artist, Hillyard, and his theosophically inclined wife; Pearce, a boring barrister, and his wife Mary; Mona (Ronald's wife, childless and said to be 'seven or eight years' older than Ronald—details no doubt added to make it clear that she is *not* Michal!), and Eileen, who, it is delicately implied, is the narrator's mistress— an autobiographical touch, since Nicholson, though married, lived with another woman.[360]

On successive days, the party debates the purpose of sex (physical reproduction, mental creation, spiritual development, or all three?); celibacy, monogamy, and polygamy; the sacramental view of marriage; and 'The hope of transmutation'.[361] Henry reads aloud from Plato's *Symposium* and opines that 'the Grail, of course, stood for the whole sex mystery'. Ronald argues that secular marriage contracts should be renewable after a number of years, and that children should not be brought up by their parents. But it is the topic of transmutation, debated on the last day, which brings the most striking contributions. Henry asserts that if sexual energy could be transformed and applied to other purposes, 'It would be something greater than electricity [...] it would be greater, probably, even than the release of atomic energy.'[362] Alchemy was concerned with it; the Grail romances hint at it. 'Jewish secret tradition' and the *Zohar* are 'concerned with very little else'.[363] Hillyard admits that it is sexual energy that powers his art; his wife talks of the Eastern doctrine of Kundalini, the 'great serpent [...] coiled at the base of the spine', which can be aroused and raised to the brain, which can 'redirect it to any purpose it desires'.[364] Eileen argues that for a married person, 'if there is any possibility of transmutation, the only hope is to fall in love with somebody not your husband or your wife', so that 'there'd be a good deal left to transmute'.[365] The transmutation of sexual energy, in short, requires sexual frustration.

The dialogue of *The Marriage-Craft* probably allows us to get as close as we ever shall to eavesdropping on the discussions at Lee's vicarage. It can hardly be coincidence that Nicholson's novel and Williams's *Outlines of Romantic Theology* came into being so closely together in time. They are twin offspring of debates that took place in Lee's group.

Nicholson had been canny enough to sugar his esoteric pill with a coating of light fiction. Williams was less fortunate and, as autumn arrived, *Romantic Theology* remained without a publisher. But at any rate the new book of poems, *Windows of Night*, was ready. It went to press in November,[366] for publication in the first week of January 1925.

9

Phyllis

As soon as *Windows of Night* was published, Williams sent copies to Wilfrid Meynell and A.E. Housman.[367] Housman replied—considering his stringent critical standards and often devastating turn of phrase—with surprising warmth:

> I particularly admired the *Prelude*, *Prisoners*, and the sonnets *To Michal*; and that counts for more because I look askance at sonnets, a form of verse responsible for more sham poetry than any other. [...] Probably the most remarkable poem in the book is *Witchcraft*, though it is not, and indeed could hardly be, a perfect success.[368]

From him, this was high praise.

The new book made enough of an impression to be reviewed fairly widely. The results were mixed, as Williams told Pellow:

> You saw the *TLS*, I expect? 'Dull, but bright', as a man here used to say. The *Nation* snubbed me, the *Camb. Review* annihilated me. The *Glasgow Herald* discovered me; so did Drinkwater in the *Sunday Times*. The *Manchester Guardian* courteously disliked me; the *New Age* said I was an important poet who never wrote poetry (in effect); the *Morning Post* babbled; the *Oxford Magazine* liked me; *The Month* in a paragraph said I wasn't an R.C.; *Blackfriars* in three pages wished I was.[369]

None of this translated into sales: by June only about 150 copies had been sold. More excitingly, he reported, '*Who's Who* have asked me for a biography!!' and in June his confidence received a boost when *The Bookman* published a two-page article on his work, written by Eugene Mason, a minor Catholic poet and essayist, who had known and admired Williams for some time.[370] He remained a lifelong friend, though sadly almost nothing is known about the relationship. *Windows of Night* was certainly Williams's most powerful book so far, though Pellow attributed its pessimism to a touch of hypochondria: 'What Williams wants I told him is dumb-bells, & a cold bath every morning.'[371]

Pellow also had misgivings about *Outlines of Romantic Theology*. He thought it 'a rare & wonderful book',[372] but could not suppress doubts: 'The question is, whether his fundamental thesis is correct: the whole stands or falls with this. He applies it with extraordinary aptness & with what seems at the time much more than mere ingenuity—but that is not necessarily a proof of the thesis.'[373] And Williams in person took no pains to make his views palatable. In July, he came to dinner with the Pellows (Michal and Michael being at the seaside), and:

> We discussed Romantic Theology.
>   CW maintained his apparent paradox that he does not love his wife more than 2–3 times a year. He would limit the word Love to the supreme activity of the soul when the Beloved appears 'the perfection of living things' 'the A and Ω of creation' &c &c.—and would deny it to the mild affection which is the normal food of a happy marriage.
>   C[icely] & I contested this.[374]

In November, Fred Page recommended *Outlines of Romantic Theology* to Oswald Burdett, a fellow Patmore enthusiast who was a reader for a new publisher, Faber and Gwyer. Burdett seemed interested, though Williams, hardened by repeated disappointment, took a guarded view: 'I don't for a moment suppose they'll want it, and as their ghastly advertisement paragraphs make me ill, I don't know that I want them to. But if one leaves publication to chance, destiny, or God, one must give chance, destiny, or God a free hand.'[375] But the year ended without any response.

★ ★ ★

Meanwhile, Williams had turned his hand to a new kind of writing: one that merged popular fiction with politics and esoteric matters. After his last lecture of the summer term at the Poplar Evening Institute, he had taken the Tube home as usual. Like Shakespeare in his own recent poem, he was reading a thriller by Sax Rohmer, the creator of Dr Fu Manchu.[376] Finishing this piece of pulp fiction, it occurred to him that he too could write a thriller. 'So', he told Olive Willis:

> I did. It took me seven weeks: it was first thought of on 8 July and finished by the end of August. It runs to about 90,000 words, is called *Adepts of Africa* (its

original title was the *Black Bastard*, but he wasn't black, nor a bastard), and thinks in continents. There are S. African revolts, riots in Houndsditch, a Mass at Lambeth, a Prime Minister, a suicide, a man two centuries old... O it's a wonderful book. One of these days it shall be typed – and you shall read it. It keeps going off into conversations and discussions, and being dragged back to incident. [...] It is the joke of my life, and I love it as such.[377]

Whilst writing it he gave progress reports to Pellow: on 17 July, 'I have written a chapter and a half of a novel. (Negro World War and things.)';[378] and later, home with his family from the seaside, 'We are back. *The Black Bastard* has reached slip No. 213, and has returned with me. [...] The Prime Minister has wildly appeared and disappeared; there is a solemn ceremonial,—and a hypnotized Zulu king in Hampstead; two Jews of the fiercest; and I approach a Mass at Lambeth.'[379]

In the midst of writing the novel—on 27 July 1925, to be precise—Williams was raised to a new level in the Fellowship of the Rosy Cross, being 'integrated by Dispensation on the part of the Headship into the Blessed Company'.[380] 'By Dispensation' seems to mean that there was no actual ceremony: Waite simply decreed that Williams be deemed to have reached the 'Portal' of the fourth and highest level of the organization, the so-called 'Hidden Life of the Rosy Cross'. In Waite's system this Fourth Order corresponded, in Kabbalistic terms, to the realm of the Supernals—Kether, Hokhmah, and Binah—the highest spheres on the Sephirotic Tree. These represent a spiritual realm so profound that esoteric practitioners often regard it as unattainable, and indeed dangerous, to human consciousness. And for the time being, Williams went no further. There is no record of his attending the Fellowship again that year.

Quite what *Adepts of Africa* was like at this time we don't know, since only a much-revised version has survived. As we have it, however, it is broadly as described in Williams's letters of 1925. A kind of metaphysical thriller, it starts from the idea that Africa has revolted against its colonial masters, and African troops are now invading England. This is, of course, a satirical stroke: most of Williams's readers would have thought it only right and proper that England should have invaded Africa, so he neatly turns the tables. But it is also a matter of symbolism, for the invading powers—the 'High Executive'—issue proclamations addressed 'to all who owe their devotion to music, to poetry, to painting and sculpture, [and to] more than rational energy',[381] and to those who 'believe that in love and art and death rather than logic and science the kingdom of man lies'. In short, Williams (like his close contemporary

D.H. Lawrence) is attacking the philistinism, puritanism, and emotional repression of the England of his day. Thus the novel's protagonist, Roger Ingram, asks himself, 'Was Africa then within? Was all the war [...] but the shadow of the repression by which men held down their more natural energies?'[382]

Ingram is clearly a self-portrait of Williams. A professor of 'Applied Literature' at London University, and a passionate devotee of English poetry, he falls under the influence of a mysterious and charismatic stranger, Nigel Considine. Considine claims to be 200 years old, and to have achieved his immense vitality by the 'ritual transmutation of energy'—chiefly, it seems, sexual energy; though he argues that art, religion, and, indeed, all passions can be similarly transmuted. 'I have transmuted masculine sex into human life', he explains. 'I've done this with all things—whatever I have loved or hated, I have poured the strength of every love and hate into my own life and what is behind my life, and now I need love and hate no more.'[383] Considine's techniques, though never explained in detail, represent an extreme version of those methods of transmutation of energies, sexual and otherwise, discussed in A.H.E. Lee's circle and, to a lesser extent, in Waite's Fellowship. They recall the alchemical imagery of Waite's rituals, as well as Lee's notes on claims that transmutation of the sexual 'vital fluid' could give a lifespan of centuries. Considine masterminds the African invasion, but his prime goal is the conquest of death itself. He believes that a person sufficiently steeped in energies transmuted by his methods should be able to return from death. Joining Considine at his headquarters, Ingram witnesses the body of a dead disciple make small movements and seem on the point of reviving, but the experiment fails. Considine is eventually murdered by one of his own followers—a Judas figure egged on (ironically enough) by an Anglican vicar. Considine's body is hurried away by submarine, the African invasion collapses, and most of the characters rejoice in the destruction of Considine as a dangerous megalomaniac. But Ingram remains unsure as to how to judge him, and the novel ends with Ingram speculating about whether Considine may have been right, and whether he might after all return from the dead.

It is a deeply ambiguous ending. Considine is an unattractive figure, but he represents many things which were truly important to Williams: poetry, passion, devastating honesty, and the exploration of human energies—by esoteric means amongst others. The novel is untidy and too crammed with ideas and subplots. Despite the startling title—*The Black Bastard*—which

Williams used privately for the novel, it makes a powerful attack on racism in both its anti-African and anti-Semitic forms. And it confronts the reader with a question that must have preoccupied Williams at this time—the question of whether some form of inner work (meditation, alchemy, or ritual) could render life more profound and intense as well as more long-lasting, and if so whether such work was ethically right. Williams—the Adeptus Exemptus—was asking how far he could, and should, go on the path of adeptship. And he was leaving the question unanswered.

★   ★   ★

In the office, work went on as usual, with Williams's superiors regarding him as a serviceable factotum. He was often to be seen racing around the building on errands. A secretary who happened to be in Milford's 'huge' room, with its 'highly polished and slippery floor' one day recalled 'gazing in horror as poor CW almost measured his length on that floor when rushing in, as usual, to a "summons" from the Publisher for a consultation'.[384] When a school anthology of *Victorian Narrative Verse* was wanted for the OUP's Indian branch, V.H. Collins, head of the Education Department, remarked that they needn't pay an outside editor: 'Williams will do just as well.'[385] So Williams buckled down to the laborious task: selecting poems, tracing copyrights, correcting proofs, and writing an introduction aimed at students in Indian schools.

Ralph Binfield, who joined the Press as assistant to Williams and Page shortly afterwards, found it an enthralling experience to learn from these two 'patient tutors':

> A contrasted pair, the quiet, scholarly Page, who seldom moved from his chair, except to go to the British Museum, and the eloquent restless Charles Williams, looking almost in those days like a stage poet, with his pince-nez, his untidy hair and his trousers, always far too tightly braced in an age when businessmen's trousers were expected to caress the tops of his shoes. [...]
>
> From these two [...] I learned a great deal in a short time. Fred Page taught me the technicalities—how to compile an index to a book, how to annotate a school edition, how to read the various stages of proof. C.W. taught me gradually how ignorant I was. His precise evaluation of the various poets we published made me shy of putting any writers into categories, and especially of using loosely the word 'mystic' which for him was applied to only two or three of the many English poets. He taught me to avoid the trite and obvious.

Young Binfield would show Williams his own writing:

> 'What do you think of this poem/play/short story sir? I wrote it last night. It just came to me.' 'Well, it shouldn't have, poetry is hard work.' He always found the weaknesses at once. 'Oh, you've been reading Hardy. He did it better.' And while I talked, he wrote all the time, and as soon as I had gone someone else would come in to chat, while he still wrote on. Only when his telephone rang would he signal me to stop. 'I can do two things at once, but not three.'[386]

He had no time for Binfield's 'enthusiasms for pacifism and ecumenism': '"But why have Christians tortured each other Sir?"—"Because, my dear Binfield, they thought the opinions they held were important, and that the other people were wrong".'

At the end of 1925 Williams summed up his situation in a letter to Olive Willis:

> Marriage, age, fame—shall I report in order? Well, marriage proceeds—only not 'according to plan' because I never made any. It tends to be absorbed by paternity. [...] It is, I suppose, a mark of the period that paternity (as an idea) should appear eccentric and a trifle unpleasant. I *cannot* think of myself as a father; just occasionally, when I am playing with the Infant, I see far off, as in an illustration of 1850 in the *Sunday at Home*, a dreadful distortion of myself. It's the revolt, I think, of the contemporary imagination against its predecessor. The fatherhood of the fathers is visited upon their children and our teeth are set on edge. We can't, we daren't, be as consciously paternal. [...] Anyhow, the child is bound to be unhappy.
>
> Not that Michael is particularly—yet. [...] There are moments of mutual pleasure; we admire—very far this side of idolatry—one another. He appears moderately intelligent. [...] The end of the page suitably concludes him as a subject.
>
> Age...Nothing to be said about *that*. It just happens. I am conscious of a remote self-preservation instinct; that is, I realise that it is possible to cling to life as life and not for its satisfactions. [...] Man is capable of such unreason? Magnificent! But not for a suburban bourgeois of forty!
>
> Fame...Ah well, now! It is fame to be in the new *Whos' Who*, I suppose?.. The reviews, with a few exceptions, have been very kind. *The Oxford Magazine* loathed me; the *Nation* was nasty; the *London Mercury* ignored me. The *T.L.S.* and the *Manchester Guardian* were polite but unsympathetic. The *New Age* called me one of the most important poets of the day. And John Drinkwater admired me in the *Sunday Times*.[387]

He told her about the novel and enclosed, as a Christmas present, a book of T.S. Eliot's poems—probably *Poems: 1909–1925*, which had appeared in

November and included *The Waste Land*, 'Prufrock', and 'The Hollow Men'. Coincidentally, the book was published by Faber and Gwyer, the firm that Eliot had recently joined and which even then was mulling over *Outlines of Romantic Theology*.

And so 1926 began propitiously, with Burdett reporting on 2 January that he would strongly recommend *Romantic Theology* to Faber.[388] Sadly, things were not as simple as that. Two days later Pellow noted:

> Went along to Burdett in the evening [...] He admires the Outlines immensely—thinks it 'beautifully written' but it is an awkward length & suggests that C.W. should expand it, if he can do so without spoiling it. He dislikes the title also—or rather thinks it a bad one from the publisher's point of view; and he suggests a preface—written by Dean Inge (quite the last person who would do it, I suggested) [...] I doubt if Wms. would agree to this.[389]

In fact, the mercurial Williams came round. They discussed it over lunch and Pellow reported that:

> He was much amused with my tale [...] & violently indignant with Burdett's suggestion about the length, the preface & the title. But it didn't mean much & he adopted my suggestion for a title with enthusiasm: viz. *Intelletto d'Amore: An Introduction to Romantic Theology*.
>
> He is writing another novel—about the Holy Graal & Black Magic & an Archdeacon & has a third in view. I suggested he offer all three to F&G to bring out together as a trilogy. A magnificent idea he thought.[390]

The new title, incorporating a phrase from Dante, was surely worse than the original but no one seemed bothered by this; and while Faber continued to ruminate about *Romantic Theology* and *Adepts of Africa*, Williams went on with his new novel about the 'Holy Graal', provisionally entitled *The Corpse*.

Away from Hampstead and the OUP, industrial tensions were mounting. The war, foreign competition, and a strong pound sterling had damaged the British coal industry; mine owners were trying to cut wages and increase working hours. Negotiations with the Miners' Federation failed, and in support of the miners the Trade Union Congress declared a General Strike to begin on 3 May. The strike lasted nine days and brought much of the country to a standstill. Even at the OUP, a non-union workplace, a few hardy souls went on strike. They were dismissed and never worked there again.[391] Williams did not strike, but he sympathized with the miners. 'The miners, it seems, are beaten—by the Prince of the Powers of the Air; and there is none that doeth good, no, not one', he wrote, as the defeated drifted back to work.[392]

And there were further, final, difficulties with Faber and Gwyer. After weeks of complicated discussions about *Romantic Theology* and the novel, Williams summed up:

> Faber won't have it. Nor the novel. Why did I ever let myself show them to him? He has taken four months to think about it, and now he drags in the strike. God bless him!
>
> After you left [Burdett's report] with me I read it and wrote to O.B., disagreeing with all his suggestions, and saying should we pretend no-one wanted it. And he wrote and said no for God's sake send it to F and G at once I withdraw everything; so I did and F got another opinion which said it was too good to turn down and I went and saw him and at O.B.'s suggestion I sent F. the novel and he refused after a time and times to do *that* and Was I in a hurry for him to decide about *R. T.* and I said no but he might be as quick as he could and that was half-way through April and now he says the strike has adversely affected it and shall he return it or would I like to leave it with him for him to consider for 1927?
>
> What a man! Four months (and a preliminary one with O.B.) and still he doesn't like to let it quite out of his blasted claws! I dislike Mr. Faber very much.
>
> So it and the *B.B.* and the *Corpse* can all go away with the *Chapel of the Thorn*. Although there did seem a remote chance of another man—a printer who wants to be a publisher—doing the *B.B.*: so perhaps I won't bury that too deep. But it *is* a little annoying, isn't it? [...]
>
> I shall leave off writing books.[393]

Still *Romantic Theology* was not entirely given up. In July it was lent to a Methodist minister, S.G. Dimond, who responded ecstatically, and to the New Testament scholar Vincent Taylor. But neither could suggest a publisher.

The 'printer who wants to be a publisher' may have been Hubert Foss, head of the Press's newly established Music Department. Foss's kingdom was entered by Amen House's *other* front door, to the right of the main one, and boasted a grand piano in its reception room. Foss was one of Milford's intuitive, quick-fire appointments. Originally a sales representative, he had proposed an educational music book to Milford in 1922. Milford decided to open a music department, and immediately set Foss to run it. Foss was twenty-four years old and a flamboyant genius—a kindred spirit to Williams. He had won a scholarship to Oxford but failed to take it up through family poverty. He had edited a literary magazine with G.K. Chesterton. He wrote and composed, and dashed about the building puffing on a large cigar, counterpart to Williams's perpetual cigarette. Like Williams he was 'a workaholic, who, in addition to his extensive duties at OUP, would frequently work into the night on other projects'.[394] Manically energetic, charming, and persuasive, he had a knack for spotting new composers. During his career he signed up, amongst others, Vaughan Williams, 'Peter Warlock', Constant Lambert, William Walton, and Benjamin Britten. To these talents he added an interest in typography, and had designed a typeface for Henderson and Spalding, the firm who printed music for the OUP. He and Williams quickly became firm friends, often seen about Amen House talking, laughing, and plotting. Foss was a rationalist and religious sceptic, but this merely provided endless fodder for debates and jokes. They had begun collaborating even before the office move. Williams, despite knowing nothing about music, wrote three texts for music that Foss wanted to publish: 'The Moon' for music by Purcell; 'Beauty Lately' for Handel; and a translation of the medieval hymn 'Stabat Mater Dolorosa'. More important collaborations would follow, and in time Foss would indeed become one of Williams's publishers—but not yet.

In the summer of 1926, as his fortieth birthday approached, Williams found himself the author of an unpublished play, two unpublished novels, and an unpublished book of theology. No wonder the boxes of manuscript behind his chair in the office were overflowing. With determined friends like Foss, Pellow, and Page to help, perhaps *Romantic Theology* might still have found a publisher. But by the end of the summer Williams's attention was elsewhere. It had been captured by Phyllis Jones.

★   ★   ★

For this, as for so much else, Amen House was responsible; and, more specifically, its library. An employee described it as 'Long, low, beautifully-furnished, [and] book-lined throughout except where its front windows look out over Warwick Square'.[395] For editorial staff, the library had quickly became the building's social centre—a kind of senior common room where people gathered to relax, discuss, and debate. This process was not unconnected with the presence of the librarian, Phyllis Jones, who had taken up her post on 10 March 1924. Phyllis was blonde, pretty, lively, and twenty-two years old. Men found her fascinating—not least because, without being overtly flirtatious, she let it be seen that she adored men.

Born on 9 September 1901 in Tooting, south London, the daughter of a hosiery salesman,[396] Phyllis had been educated at a small private school and then, from 1918, at King's College for Women, Kensington (later part of the University of London), where she had studied 'Household and Social Science'. She became a science teacher at Hamilton House, a girls' boarding school in Tunbridge Wells, but left in 1923, in her own words, 'rather in disgrace owing to too flippant behaviour—in spite of getting girls through their School Certificate'.[397] 'Flippant behaviour' may have been a euphemism. Certainly before she joined the OUP there had been what she called 'affairs'—an army captain, and 'the young man who went to Keswick and got religion'.[398] Next she spent two months as nursery governess to a 'very grand' family 'in the depths of the country'.[399] When this job also ended, Phyllis found herself aimless at home and, as she recalled, 'my father said "I'm tired of you being at my tail, for goodness' sake go and find a job somewhere."'[400] (Robert Jones was housebound, suffering from tuberculosis.) Someone noticed an advertisement for a librarian at the Press, with no particular qualifications stipulated, so Phyllis applied, as did several others. Milford interviewed her and is said to have 'put three questions to her: "Do you read French?" "Yes." "Do you read Proust?" "No." "Do you suffer fools gladly?" "No." He turned to his secretary, Tommy Curtis, and said "She'll do. Send the rest away."'[401] Given Milford's methods and Phyllis's personal charm, this is quite credible.

Starting at the Press in March 1924, Phyllis soon got to know Williams by sight and sound. As she recalled:

> I remember Hubert Foss and Charles Williams coming down the stairs talking to each other and that's [...] really my first recollection of him; [...] then he took to coming into the library and walking round [...] I had to learn every book and where it was in the catalogue. So I went round every single book, priced it, found its place in the catalogue, and knew where it was [...] and while I was doing that I think Charles used to come in and out.[402]

By May 1926 she knew him much better than that. Williams, seeing in her a potential for editorial work and charmed by her beauty and energy, apparently involved her in some way when work began on the first two volumes of the Tolstoy Centenary Edition, which were to be published in 1928. His visits to the library during working hours became more frequent than ever. He later noted his attachment to her as having started sometime after Whitsuntide (23 May) 1926.[403]

When the holidays came in late July they found themselves, of the white-collar staff, almost alone in the vast building. Williams beguiled the time—a slack period in the publishing schedule—by writing, not a pastoral but its opposite, *An Urbanity*: a witty poem in seventeenth-century style, 'Wherein *Tityrus* laments to *Phyllida* the departure from town of various other personages of the Court, and takes occasion to consider the curious nature of the Creation':

> Ah *Phillida*, how far to-day
> the keepers of our treasure stray, [...]
> now only you and I are left
> twinkling across a hollow cleft.
>
> The entrance-hall is blank and bare;
> unfriendly lies the central stair.
> The first floor—O the first floor: dead!
> there were but three, and all are fled!

He goes on to sketch each colleague—given a suitable pastoral name, of course—on their travels. The formidable Miss Peacock, '*Dorinda*', is in Germany; '*Alexis*' (Gerry Hopkins) is in Italy, and they will hear all about it, because 'he is the type-writer by which / all things click into novels'; '*Colin*' (Fred Page) is away birdwatching; and Humphrey Milford— '*Caesar*'—is in Italy too. As an afterthought, Williams (or '*Tityrus*') recalls Hubert Foss:

> No, I forget—within his cells
> the master of the music dwells,—
> but how should folk like you and me
> break through his guarded privacy?

Having surveyed these five characters, he turns to various other, less attractive figures at the Press, and wonders why they were created:

> these five and us two, what remains
> worthy creation's growing pains?
> look round the House, say, what beside,
> if you were God, could you abide?

But he has to conclude that God had His own reasons for making them:

> they are not dreams (or so are we).
> He made them then? ah mystery!
> He made them? yes, that sigh subdue,
> He made them—AND HE LOVES THEM TOO.

There is even a glimpse of the Kabbala. Why do Helen Peacock and Phyllis Jones quarrel so often? Because they represent the opposite pillars—Justice and Mercy—of the Sephirotic Tree:

> His justice in *Dorinda*, true;
> His mercy, *Phillida*, in you
> (you, each a pillar of our morals—
> this is the reason of your quarrels[.]

He sent the poem first to Phyllis. It was also shown to Hubert Foss, who took it to Henderson and Spalding, the printers with whom he sometimes worked, and arranged to have it printed as an elegant pamphlet, which he designed. Charles Williams sent a copy to his sister Edith, with a letter:

> I wanted to send you a copy of the *Urbanity*. Only 25 copies have been printed, and those distributed with and in extreme secrecy. One day it may be worth guineas and guineas! Caesar is a little nervous, I think, but very well pleased; and calls Dorinda, whenever he has an opportunity, by that name.
>   Incidentally, I have suggested to him that I should like to publish another book of verse soon, and he assents. So I must do the finishing work on that.[404]

Milford was not the only person at the Press to adopt the new names. People started calling Hopkins 'Alexis' and Fred Page 'Colin'. Milford was already known informally as 'Caesar'. *An Urbanity* was a further step in the development of a community at Amen House. As the poem circulated, it mythologized the workplace. And at the heart of the myth, hidden as it were in plain sight, was the unadmitted truth that the relationship between Charles Williams and Phyllis Jones was more than just an ordinary friendship.

At first nothing was said openly, but when Phyllis went on holiday to Devon at the beginning of August, she and Charles missed each other enough to exchange letters. He told her that he had fallen and twisted his ankle; Michal had gone to visit her family, leaving him supplied with 'many cigarettes, & Mr. Freeman Wills Croft, & Mr. P.G. Wodehouse, & Mr. Edgar Wallace & *Punch* & so on.'[405] Phyllis replied sympathetically, addressing him as 'My dear Mr. Williams', and complained—missing the conversation at Amen House—that she had 'not talked with any really interesting people' and had been bored by:

> a perfectly dreadful woman who says she's a deaconess. [...] I do think there ought to be some third alternative for women besides marriage or becoming like this deaconess or the older objectionable spinsters that one knows. [...]

When you consider it, it is only very exceptional strong people like Miss
Peacock who don't marry & still remain jolly & decent.[406]

Her landlady's brother-in-law was 'a real die-hard Conservative' and she
wished she could see him argue with Miss Peacock: 'I expect Comrade
[Peacock] would get so fierce she wouldn't be able to speak.' And she hesi-
tated as to how to sign herself:

> How do I end?
> Yours very sincerely
> Yours affectionately
> either is true tho' a little inadequate
> Phyllis M. Jones.

Williams's letter enclosed a comic poem about Miss Peacock losing her
temper, 'Ad Pavonem Iracundum' ('To an Angry Peacock'), and (perhaps
with the deaconess in mind) asked, 'Why has the Church gathered to itself
so many detestable creatures all professing to adore Love—our burning and
terrific lord!' It also told her, apparently, 'that he has a mild feeling for a
dozen people, has pledged devotion to one; [and] has affection for two', [407]
of whom she is one. These declarations of 'affection' on both sides were not
hard to interpret.

Strangely it was Aylmer Maude, the troublesome translator of Tolstoy,
who now became a catalyst. Tatyana Tolstoy, the novelist's daughter, was to
give a lecture in London in early December,[408] with Maude translating.
Phyllis Jones and Charles Williams were sent on behalf of the Press—Phyllis
to sell books, and Charles to keep an eye on Maude. After the lecture,
Charles and Phyllis walked alone together to Victoria Station, where she
would catch her train home. As often happened with Williams, the conversation quickly became personal. He sensed that Phyllis was unhappy.
She was finding her family irksome, her father had lately died, and she
was frustrated by the limitations of her education. Soon, as they walked,
they were talking about prayer, and about the value of life. 'He probably
[asked] what did I feel about this and that and I said I thought it was all
pretty horrible, you know, and he probably said "Yes, it is but it isn't!"'
She was impressed that he seemed to understand her depression. 'He
never said "Oh, it's absolutely jolly, you've got everything, you ought to
be very happy!"—you see, he never made those fatuous remarks that
young people tend to expect.' Rather, 'he accepted that it was pretty grim
and life was...'[409]

Frustrated with his own career, his views tinged with the deep pessimism that colours *Windows of Night*, Williams was a melancholy but congenial companion on the dark street. When Phyllis spoke of her unhappiness, he amazed her by endorsing her feelings with ideas he would later use in a dramatic scene based on that night's conversation:

>   If
> we for a fraction of time could overhear
> the echo of one-millionth of the groan
> that issues from the world, we should be lost,
> maddened, self-slayers. Do not persuade yourself
> that you are anything but most miserable.
> Which being known, make profit out of it.
> Be happy.[410]

Happy, he argued, because suffering is an alchemical process which, if we accept it, can purify and perfect us. By the time the couple reached Victoria Station they felt that, despite the age gap, they understood one another and shared a predicament. At the station, Williams found himself very much tempted to kiss Phyllis.[411] Yet he held back, and they said a decorous good-night. But as her train pulled out of the station, he could no longer avoid admitting to himself that he was in love with her.

★   ★   ★

Williams later called it 'the second great shock of my existence'.[412] The first had been the dawn of his love for Michal. She had been Beatrice to his Dante—the inspiring and idealized woman who was the pole star of his life and work. But, over the years, ideal and reality had drifted apart. Michal was now a harassed housewife, often suffering back pain and much taken up with her frequently ill four-year-old son. As for Williams, he was now a hard-pressed editor, lecturer, and unsuccessful author, who knew that his wife could not really share his interests in theology or literature. The centre of his attention had long shifted away from home and settled in his ideas and his work, now embodied in the world of Amen House. And at the centre of Amen House was Phyllis—an accident, one might say, waiting to happen.

We don't know quite how soon Phyllis confessed that she felt something similar. A letter from early in their relationship shows her struggling to define her feelings:

I don't quite know how to start—but I feel I must make some sort of attempt to tell you what I feel about you—a thing I am powerless to do when I am with you. Am I in love with you?—No. Do I love you—yes. [...] You must see that you are bound to mean more to me that [*sic*] I do to you—You have your wife Mr Nicholson & others. The people who mean anything in my life are—my mother (about whom my feelings are mixed)—my friend at Bath. [...] I tried to consider how far I was justified in saying that I do love you but I could come to no sort of conclusion except that I do feel for you something that affects the part of being which I most desire to keep hidden from everyone. [...] have I rather overstated the point in giving you the truthfulness you asked for—if I had left this bunk until the morning I should probably have been less frank. [...] This letter is very untidy but my pillow didn't make a good desk. [...] I could go on for several pages [...] so I will stop & put this in your room.

Soon she told him she was in love with him. In a tender (undated) letter she imagined her future grandchildren asking:

'And did you never fall in love?' 'Not till I was 25 & then—[...] He called himself Charles Williams and he was at the Oxford Press but I called him Urban and I had a dark suspicion that he was not born of ordinary parents but that Merlin or some other magician brought him.'

—'What was he like granny?'

– 'Like no man you will ever know my children, tho' you should live to be a hundred & travel from one sea to another. [...] he came in to my world so slowly and surely & yet so swiftly, & he taught me all that I know that is worth knowing.'[413]

Phyllis was twenty-five on 9 September 1926—eleven days before Williams's fortieth birthday. 'Urban' was a shrewdly chosen nickname. Suggested by *An Urbanity*, it pinpointed Williams as the quintessential city-dweller, whilst alluding to his ceremonious and 'urbane' manners, and teasing him on his theological pretensions by identifying him with the most famous Urban of all—Pope Urban II, who instigated the First Crusade. Perhaps, for Williams, the name had some flattering redolence of Nicholas Breakspear and Hadrian VII—those English popes, real and imagined.

Williams noted that he first kissed Phyllis in early April, 1927—four months after that evening walk to Victoria Station. By then they were immersed in the intoxication of an office romance, an open secret to most of their colleagues. On Williams's side, there seems to have been no question either of telling Michal or of making physical love to Phyllis. He simply rejoiced in the emotional bliss of this new intimacy, and the creativity it stimulated. For he found himself inspired—not just with *An Urbanity*, but with other poems which soon grew into a long sequence, begun in 1926 and finished in 1927, which he would call *A Century of Poems for Celia*.[414] Discussing the creative transmutation of sexual energy, a character in Nicholson's novel had speculated that 'the only hope is to fall in love with somebody not [...] your wife [so that] there'd be a good deal left to transmute'.[415] Now Williams was making the experiment in earnest.

★ ★ ★

The new inspiration was critical as well as creative. Following his first careful reading of Eliot, Williams decided to offer the OUP a critical survey of contemporary poetry. In late September 1926 he sent to Milford a proposal for *Modern English Poets*.[416] About the same time, his evening lectures began again. He had been asked to lecture not only at Streatham but also for the City Literary Institute in Holborn, and he reckoned that it was now—with the delight of his new relationship with Phyllis to fire him—that 'the Lectures had really started'.[417] Thelma Mills, attending his Shakespeare lectures at Streatham, was, as we have seen, entranced by Williams. And it was not only by his extensive learning, his dramatic delivery, and the way he related the poetry to his students' own experiences. This naturally carried over into the coffee break, when Williams listened sympathetically to his students' problems and enthusiasms. Thelma recalled, 'He soon knew all about my innermost feelings and behaviour—and misbehaviour: I had never in all my 23 years had anyone like this to talk to!' He seemed equally open about his own personal life. Before long, 'we knew all about Michal, his wife, and her bad back, and why she was called Michal; and were always ready to hear about the latest cleverness of the young Michael—5, when we first heard how he had brought his parents tea in bed, with fearful care'.[418] After the classes, Thelma would often walk with Williams to his bus stop to continue the discussion. Her reaction was not unusual. In an all-female class, Williams's blend of charisma and approachableness rapidly made him an object of near adoration. Some students took to attending both series of lectures, so as not to miss anything. And when, early in 1927, Phyllis started attending his lectures, small predictable jealousies arose. 'Occasionally, the O.U.P. librarian came to our lectures', Thelma recalled, 'and held his entire attention through the coffee break. This had come to be, usually, mine, naturally!' As students became personal friends, they began to visit Williams at the Press. He had always been open to friends visiting him at work— D.H.S. Nicholson often came—and he would take them out to lunch nearby or offer them spare copies of books as they debated poetry, drama, and life.

Phyllis Jones was free to attend lectures because, after her father's death in late 1925, she recalled, 'My brother and I went to live in a boarding house in Bloomsbury [. . .] and I started going to all the literary institutes and listening to [. . .] what he believed, poetry and everything.'[419] The 'boarding house' was Lancaster House, in Upper Bedford Place. Probably Phyllis was supposed to be chaperoned by her brother Gerald. But as she remembered, 'It was a marvellous time for me because [. . .] I could do what I liked, nobody said "Well, what time will you be in?"'[420] With Phyllis in the audience, Williams's lectures were even more inspired; and she made daring proposals—for example, since they shared a taste for thrillers, that they should go to see *The Ghost Train*, Arnold Ridley's sensational play which was the hit of the 1926–27 season. From Williams's point of view the only shadow was that, at Lancaster House, Phyllis became friendly with a fellow boarder called Billy Somervaille, a bright young man studying to qualify as a company secretary and hoping to go into the oil business. No doubt she was mischievous enough to tease Williams about Billy from time to time. But Williams had his intellect and experience, his poetry, and his charismatic lecturing performances on his side. He did not feel seriously threatened.

10

'I Can't Do Without
You—I *Can't*'

Having given the leading characters at Amen House their new identities in *An Urbanity*, Williams and Foss wanted to take things further. Amen House had a Dramatic Society, so a play or pantomime for Christmas 1926 was the obvious answer. They hit on the idea of a masque. The masque was a Renaissance court entertainment, with aristocratic actors playing versions of themselves in a moral or allegorical setting, with music and spectacular costumes. The masque celebrated community—often the intimate community of a royal court or aristocratic household. The classic example, and one Williams loved, was Milton's *Comus*, which had music by the poet's friend Henry Lawes.

The masque was a perfect fit for Amen House as Williams and Foss envisaged it. Fred Page, Helen Peacock, Phyllis, and the others could play themselves, gently caricatured as Colin, Dorinda, Phyllida, and so on; there could be in-jokes aplenty about office life; and since masques were normally presented to entertain an aristocratic patron, Humphrey Milford—Caesar—could preside from a throne. Foss, a talented composer, would write the music.

Foss and Williams must have been beside themselves with glee as they planned this wonderful coup. It was a brilliant idea and they had exactly the gifts to bring it off. One might think that with editorial work, twice-weekly lectures, and writing poems for Phyllis, besides maintaining some sort of life with his wife and son, Williams would have been too busy to write and direct a masque. That would be to underestimate him. Late in 1926 he was not only writing the masque but working on a tragedy (*The Witch*) for his students at Balham, and on *A Myth of Shakespeare*—an episodic play for his students at the City Literary Institute to perform in April.[421]

Williams, like his fellow-workaholic Foss, generally slept little; with the suppressed excitement of Phyllis in mind, he now slept even less. He also wrote, thought, talked, and walked fast. Nor was his work for the Press neglected. Binfield recalled that though 'he never ceased writing':

> he did his O.U.P. work at such a pace that no one could complain because he wrote [...] in the firm's time. He would bounce into the office, hang up his hat, gloves and stick, and plunge straight into pages of verse which he had obviously been composing mentally on the tube or walking down Newgate Street and bounding up the stairs.[422]

Irene Smith, a 'junior' in the Correspondence Department, remembered the pace of his progress:

> When wishing to consult a colleague he would tear around the maze of corridors, dash up the stairs several at a time, often humming to himself and almost sending flying anyone in his path. On one occasion I collided with him round a corner during my early days at the Press, dropping a thick file of papers. He was full of remorse for his haste, helped me retrieve my jumbled collection of post and insisted on escorting me back to his office to help get the papers into some semblance of order, spreading them over the sheaves of papers already littered on his desk. Finally, as we made little progress between us, he phoned the head of my department, apologising profusely in his own inimitable way.[423]

The Masque of the Manuscript, as it came to be called, was planned for Christmas 1926, but was eventually performed in April. Williams directed it himself. Rehearsals went on for weeks—often (to exclude spectators) in his office. Foss's piano was moved from the Music Department to the library; tables and display cabinets were shifted. On 28 April, the day of performance, one end of the library, with its book-lined wall, was curtained off to become the stage. Facing it in solitary splendour was a 'throne' for Milford; behind him the room was filled with chairs for staff and visitors.

With the lightest possible touch, *The Masque of the Manuscript* performed a rite of initiation, death, and rebirth within Amen House. It showed how the manuscript, with all its imperfections, must die in order to be reborn as a perfect, fully finished book; and it hinted that people must undergo a similar process on their spiritual path. After a short prologue spoken by Williams, an unseen singer—Foss's wife Dora—sang 'The Carol of Amen House':

> Over this house a star
> Shines in the heavens high,

> Beauty remote and afar,
> Beauty that shall not die.

The Carol affirms that all makers of books, no less than Shakespeare himself, are seeking perfection and beauty. Through 'the toil that is given to do, [...] the search and the grinding pain' they follow a vision of 'peace and the perfect end!'

The curtains part to show Phyllida working in the library, surrounded by all the world's learning. The Manuscript, an untidy figure dressed in rags with streamers of paper hanging off her (played by a junior OUP employee) dances around the library, begging to be published. The Manuscript is an absurdly academic book—*A Short Treatise on Syrian Nouns as used in the Northern and Sub-Northern Towns in Five Hundred BC, with two maps and three charts*—a parody of the kind of unsaleable scholarly book which the London staff liked to think preoccupied their Oxford colleagues. Phyllida subjects the Manuscript to a ritual questioning, 'making the sign of the magical pentagram' in front of her and asking, 'Art thou purged as by fire and by water made clean?' To which the Manuscript replies, 'I mean what I say and I say what I mean.'

Williams had sent Phyllis a diagram to show exactly how the pentagram should be traced with the finger, explaining:

> This is the Banishing Pentagram of Magic, for the expulsion of demons, ghosts, and such like intruders. The pentagram should be carefully closed at the left bottom corner. The whole of this, and indeed of the opening dialogue, should be acted and spoken in the seriousness of high fantasy. It is a shadow of the Mysteries, and the mode by which manuscripts enter into achievement is similar to our own.[424]

Alexis and Dorinda—Gerry Hopkins and Helen Peacock—now edit the Manuscript, cutting off her tatters of paper, and Caesar, from his throne, signals his consent to publish her. But she must die as a manuscript before she can be reborn as a printed book. Alexis and Colin bring in a bier and lighted candles. She is laid on the bier and the stage is left in darkness except for the candles, whilst Alexis recites a poem about descent into the underworld. He concludes:

> And where is the Lodge and the Master, O there is the place of the East;
>   And where is the altar and offering, O there are the hands of the priest;
>   And the table is every way perfect, and the crown of the kingship goes well,
>   Since the feet of Dom Galahad entered, and he sat in the Perilous Sell.

These words echo Waite's rituals ('the Lodge and the Master') and the Arthurian myth, with the reference to Galahad, achiever of the Grail, taking his place in the Perilous 'Sell' or Seat. Then the erstwhile Manuscript is revived as the 'gloriously dressed' Book. The masque ends with a sung Ode to Mnemosyne—Greek goddess of memory and mother of the Muses—and an epilogue, spoken by Williams, darkening the mood by reminding the audience—and Caesar himself—of death.

The masque was a small triumph. Its simple ritual form, derived from Williams's Rosicrucian experience, gave it strong dramatic movement, and the gentle caricature of its actors—careful, pedantic Fred, argumentative Gerry, and straight-laced Helen Peacock all playing versions of themselves—delighted their friends. Williams had reflected back a harmonious view of his colleagues and the work they did, viewed as a spiritual process. He had also conducted a beneficent magical ritual at the centre of Amen House, with his colleagues as celebrants. No wonder everyone was delighted, and that the atmosphere of the workplace became, as many colleagues attested, even happier than before, despite the admitted 'toil and the grinding pain' of daily work.

★   ★   ★

The development of a love affair is always something of a mystery. Important events are invisible to outsiders, and the protagonists see things through a haze of emotion. In the case of Charles Williams and Phyllis Jones, although hundreds of letters survive, they are mostly undated, written to be left on a desk or sent by messenger and answered within hours. Years later, Williams told Raymond Hunt that, 'One great period [of the relationship] was from September 1926 to the First Masque in April 1927. After that everything went wrong—except, of course, the Holy Ghost.'[425] In reality, their happiness probably lasted a little longer than this cryptic remark suggests, into the summer of 1927.

Williams was selective about whom he told. Daniel Nicholson, whose own personal life was unorthodox, probably knew very soon after it began.[426] Less intimate friends were kept in the dark. At Christmas 1926, writing his characteristic end-of-year letters, Williams had described a dully uneventful year. 'Nothing ever happens to us', he told Pellow—perhaps salving his conscience by writing 'us' rather than 'me'—'at least nothing beyond domesticities.'[427] And to Olive Willis, he wrote that apart from starting a second novel:

> which had the Graal in and a modern Duke and a publisher's office and a corpse
> and black magic and an Archdeacon and the police and Prester John, [...]
> Nothing else has happened. The usual tiresomeness, a few poems, a wonder
> (once or twice) whether God was going to replenish the world with another
> infant—but it came to nothing, and I'm not sorry.[428]

One would never guess that for the past six months or so he had been preoccupied by a new love, and fired with a creative inspiration he had not felt
since writing *The Silver Stair*.

Phyllis was immensely excited at finding herself taken seriously by such
brilliant people as Williams and his friends. She writes:

> Shall I confess to you that I think at the moment I am a little conceited. You
> see I've never had anything like the past eighteen months before. If you could
> know what my college life was like [...] & then the gradual effect of here,
> which has come to a head in the last eighteen months. You liking me &
> DHSN thinking it worth while to talk to me & Alexis [...] Do you see? [...]
> to feel that people one admired, people one would choose to admire one—
> did do so.[429]

Frustrated by the narrowness of her education, she was thrilled by Williams's
deep knowledge of myth, literature, and theology:

> I love antiquity. It makes me sick with excitement & rage that I don't know
> more; & that I may know more. It gives me exactly the same feeling as when
> I have walked down Guildford St. [towards the British Museum] in a tearing
> hurry to catch up with all the terrible & beautiful things which seem to be
> waiting round the corner. But it isn't just the knowledge. I don't want only to
> *know* whom [*sic*] Arthur & Tristram were, I want to feel in my mind about them
> exactly as you write. Please write more about the Graal; I can't bear not to know
> who they all were & what they meant. I think your mind is a perfect, heavenly
> sort of British Museum (excuse the comparison) where all the things are alive,
> & that beautiful Aphrodite & the Demeter sits still & looks out. [...] Make
> them walk into my mind so that I know these things as you know them. [...]
> No one but you can do it.[430]

For Williams, admiration from a beautiful young woman was intoxicating.
And her questions set him thinking again about his long-delayed project for
a poem about Arthur and the 'Graal'. Later he would remind Phyllis of 'the
most happy chance by which you asked me to write to you about the

[Round] Table'. It began to dawn on him that their relationship, and his ambitions for poetry about the Grail, might come together. He could write love poems to her set in an Arthurian context. 'There', he reflected, 'the method lay.'[431]

And since Phyllis confided her troubles to him, he found himself becoming her spiritual adviser. Soon he was teaching her about 'attention' and 'the practice of the presence of God'.[432] He also suggested gently, 'You must read the Gospels one day for fun, and tell me what you make of Christ.' To mix spiritual teaching and erotic desire was to take on a dangerously ambiguous role. Soon he was in a painfully confused state. 'Polygamy', he told Phyllis:

> seems to have a great deal to be said for it [...] I am fastidious enough—let my twenty years of monogamy witness—but I thought I was stronger on the idea. [...] To which the Adversary: 'Quite, quite. In short, you commit spiritual adultery till you think you are in danger of being found out, and then kick an innocent companion into psychical mud.' And—there is Christmas.
>
> Yes, Celia my dear, there is Christmas. You know I don't think it is *only* because of the thousand domestic excuses that one can make that I have jumped at every chance to avoid the Sunday mass these last two or three weeks. [...] Plainly, I funk it. I funk the Communion unless...I am afraid I shall go to the Christmas Mass. I am afraid I accept the Divine Child and adore it.[433]

At home for the holiday, Charles and Phyllis exchanged letters, both admitting that they were bored. She complained of four dull days with her family. He (at St Albans with Michael, Michal, his parents, and Edith) admitted to feeling 'a slight interior boredom' once Michael had finished opening his presents on Christmas Day.[434] Both were being somewhat guarded—after all, these were letters sent to private addresses, a different matter from notes left on a desk at Amen House. But the impression is that life apart, even for a few days, was insipid. They craved the intensity of each other's company.

Williams was already writing poems for her. First came a sequence of twenty poems in which he calls her 'Dianeme' (a name taken from a poem by Herrick). It includes apologetic poems to Michal in which Williams tries to rationalize his emotional tensions:

> Think not, Fairest, that thy power
> ever dwindled for an hour,
> though my restless mind should seek

> once to know itself oblique,
> once to see what it would find
> if another should be kind

—and perceptive admissions of self-centredness:

> How darkly, Dianeme, I doubt
> I loved nor her nor thee;
> 'tis but myself myself admires,
> myself that's dear to me.

This initial outpouring was followed by more than 100 poems addressed to Phyllis as 'Celia'. The writing was obsessive: Phyllis was flattered but embarrassed. As she later recalled, 'poems pouring down on you, why, [if] you really get two or three poems in a week—it's difficult to say anything—"I like it", "I don't like it" or what! [...]—it's not easy to know how to react.'[435] And in truth the poems were, for the most part, doggerel: an unhappy flood of archaic language, overheated and demanding.

★   ★   ★

Fortunately Charles and Phyllis shared simpler tastes, including an appetite for crime novels, which they lent one another. Their lives became increasingly intertwined. A jokey note from Phyllis implies their constant companionship: 'Dr Yerks: "Do you know how to form a habit?" Me: "Yes. By going to see Urban every day at 1.45."' And Williams indulged her in luxuries he could ill afford. Phyllis writes:

> But look here is this pound offer genuine or not? Because if it is I'll do something about it. Why I could go & order my new hat *at once*. Think of that. Damn it all I've cost you enough money already this year, so either I ought to stop or it's gone past mattering: which do you think it is? [...] The truth is, darling, I do look nice when I'm well dressed & I don't see why all the talents one is supposed to develop should be the nice dull stodgy kind like thriftiness & punctuality.[436]

Soon the dynamic of their relationship—that of adoring pupil and authoritative teacher—was expressing itself in intricate games of fantasy. On 10 January 1927, Phyllis addressed an elaborate document, complete with ribbon and seals, 'To Charles Williams, Ambassador to the Imperial And Urbane Government, from Phyllis Jones on behalf of the Celian Sovereign State', apologizing for 'cheek', insolence, and other failings.

Williams had taken the name 'Celia' from Marvell's poem 'The Match', where Celia is a distillation of all the world's most precious substances. In Latin, 'Celia' means 'heavenly'. It was Williams's name for an ideal version of Phyllis; Phyllis as a manifestation of divine glory in female human form. And sometimes he certainly saw her that way. An undated but much later letter recalls some occasion when it happened on the steps of St Pancras Church:

> Celia [...] you shall be, before angels and men, what you were to me on the steps of St Pancras. [...] So you shall radiate the light out of which God made you; and purify your earthly tabernacle till the Shekinah shines through.[...] I saw you in the glory you had with God before the world began[.][437]

Or again:

> Your hair is the shrouded sun: I told you that. I wish you wouldn't have it cut: it is behind the white—no, the tinged marble of your neck like deep, deep, deep hangings of gold—like myths and legends and epics lying behind vision. [...] Show me your hands once more before you vanish in your cloud of fire, my royalty of Netzach.[438]

But Phyllis's document from the 'Celian Sovereign State', apologizing for cheek and insolence, tells another story. The games of master and pupil, stern teacher and naughty girl, were being acted out. Playfully, Williams began to give her spoof examination papers to answer, often on details of her own behaviour. He set essays on 'The difference between a promise, a statement and a pious hope', or on 'Why the female mind is incapable of punctuation' (Phyllis's was not always up to OUP standards). If the answers were unsatisfactory, small physical punishments would be exacted: a smack on the hand, or—with Phyllis perhaps bent over a desk or chair—on the bottom. No doubt this began with bits of office horseplay more tolerantly regarded in the 1920s than they would be today. But they developed further. One small note reads, in its entirety, 'The rod please Urban dear. Question 4 has exhausted me. I have thought for at least an hour but I can put down nothing more.'[439] Another reads:

> Lord of the faithful receive the thanks of thy slave and servant for thy generous and careful treatment. August Lord, thy slaves bowes [*sic*] herself before thee in thanks for the trouble taken over her. Behold tho' thy stripes did sting thy servant, & tho' thy rod was heavy upon her hand yet does she bow herself in submission before thee[.]

Phyllis joined in these games with enthusiasm, often adopting other personae:

Thank you, dear Professor for the leniency of your treatment—tho' was it a paper knife? It was an effective blow, that one, and it did sting, so did the others but only for the moment. [...]

> Your affec. Pupil
> Netta.[440]

Or, more dramatically:

Th-th-thank you, d-- d-- dear Professor for your lenient treatment (sobs)—it didn't h-- h-- hurt ve-very much, there were great weals on me but I didn't mind. Thank you for bothering, I know I deserved it. I know you can't help your beard & I'm sorry

> Phoebe.[441]

Williams, of course, had no beard. That was just part of the fantasy. And Phyllis was ready to take the initiative. Here is her plan (probably pure fantasy) for an ideal day out with Williams:

Come down to the office & meet you, proceed by taxi (say 10/-) to Harrods, spend £1 on silk stockings, £2 on a new hat & £2 on anything you wanted—books etc.

From there we should go to the toy dept & purchase 1 small cane, 1 delicate whip & anything else that took our fancy. = £6.

Have lunch somewhere very nice £1.

Go to a theatre in the afternoon £1.

From 6.0 to 12.0, I imagine, could be passed very pleasantly with dinner, a warm room, the Harrods purchases. Say £5.

Leaving £2 for extras, taxis, cigarettes, chocolate.[442]

For the Phyllis who revealed herself in such games, Williams coined yet another name: Circassia. This derived from the long literary tradition which identified Circassian women—white women from the northern Caucasus—as the most beautiful in the seraglio of the Turkish sultans. The name had connotations of both eroticism and slavery. Williams could thus think of his beloved as a kind of trinity. In heaven, so to speak, she was Celia; in Amen House, where she looked after the library, she was Phyllida; and in the secret sexual world where she flirted with him and courted punishment, she was Circassia.

The psychology behind these playfully sadomasochistic elements in the relationship can only be guessed at. Phyllis seems to have awakened something in Williams which had remained dormant in his marriage to Michal.

Perhaps such games of pain and power compensated for a sense of power-lessness in other areas of life. He might stage masques at the Press, but he remained a frustrated author and humble employee, at the mercy of Milford's whims. His sexual life with Michal had probably faded. Erotic play with Phyllis offered a kind of substitute without technically constitut-ing adultery; though emotional unfaithfulness could hardly have been taken much further. And, he believed, it generated inspiration. It provided, as Nicholson's book had put it, 'a lot to transmute'. For Phyllis, the game of submissive but naughty pupil offered endless possibilities for manipulation. By yielding, flirting, and playing on Williams's fantasies she could gain (at a time when she had lately lost her father) attention, affection, and control over the most interesting man she had ever encountered, a man 'Like no man you will ever know [...] tho' you should live to be a hundred & travel from one sea to another.'

And Williams taught her things she wanted to know—suggesting books for her to read, taking her to lectures, writing her letters about theology. And he introduced her to people. A casual reference in one of his letters to 'my uncle's room' suggests that he took her to meet Charles Wall.[443] And after 'Henry' Lee became Vicar of St Martin's, Kensal Rise in March 1926, they went there one Sunday to hear evensong and meet him. Phyllis wrote a comic poem about what happened, mocking her admirer's enthusiasm for this much-mentioned hero:

> I have, my child, proud Urban said,
>   A friend named Henry Lee.
> But for your sex he does not care –
>   – He lives in celibacy.

> But if you show yourself polite,
>   And remember he's of the élite
> I may *occasionally* mention his name
>   Now won't that be a treat.[444]

As a great privilege, Celia is taken to hear Henry preach. But, alas, someone else is taking the service:

> The bell has stopped, the organ sounds
> The choir boys enter, my heart bounds
> Within my breast to think that now,
> Within a second, Henry's brow
> Shall enter there & I shall spy –

> But what is this & may I die.
> If that thin voice that mere precision
> And Oh my God! Prayer book revision
> Oh Henry! Henry! Henry Lee
> When shall my eyes thy glory see?

Phyllis wants to peep in at the vicarage window and see the room where 'He sits e'en now with Nicholson!' But Urban sends her home, though himself staying—probably (though the poem does not say so) for his usual meeting with Lee's esoteric group. Phyllis ends by suggesting that Lee doesn't exist: 'No, you have no core or pith / Oh Henry Lee, you are a myth'.

Clearly, Phyllis was not without resources of her own; and she could use other admirers to maintain a balance. No doubt she kept Williams informed about her young admirer Billy Somervaille. Gerry Hopkins also provided ammunition:

> I was quite incapable of telling you last night [...] but I should have told you that I have allowed Alexis to kiss me [...] somehow that sign of his affection for me seemed to bring home with a rush to me how deplorably I was attached to you.[445]

Williams responded with a light-hearted poem 'On her flirting with Alexis': 'I do not blame Alexis, no one could: [...] but Celia, need you so *encourage* him?'[446] But jealousy—not least as an unpublished novelist—also prompted a vicious rhyme, 'On Alexis's Latest Novel':

> I wish that I could write as well,
>   as wittily, with such an air
> of knowledge born in cynic hell
>   and drunk with bitter-brewed despair [...]
>   all is as bare
> and filthy as a broken hovel
>   which long since was some leper's lair,
> in Mr. Hopkins' latest novel.[447]

Did Phyllis show the poem to Gerry? In time, Williams would learn that in Hopkins's hands a novel could be a dangerous weapon.

Inspired though she was by what Williams taught her about religion, Phyllis was delightfully open about the contradictions of her own hedonistic nature:

> What do I want? I don't know. I want my sweets from all shops. I want the jolly parts of the Christian creed. I want to have some connection with the

bits of St John & the apocalypse that I love & at the same time the freedom to indulge my senses. And I just don't see how I can do it. [...]

I should hate you not to like me to sit on your knee. Who is there who is so truly fond of me? Who else likes quite so much to have me put my arms round him? No one I believe. So in my supreme unselfishness I want to keep that. [...] I don't want to commit fornication; I don't want to be chaste. And there you are.[448]

But she was capable of delivering salutary shocks. Williams had expounded Romantic Theology to her and lent her his book, claiming to be indifferent about publication. Phyllis doubted this, and with clear-sighted naïvety pointed out a deeper problem:

Yes Urban I think you do make efforts towards publication; [...] But I think if it is to be published then the circumstances should be altered [...] It must I think be something to do with the fact that R[omantic]T[heology] has to do with God.[...] A public declaration of something which is more than a morality— & yet the circumstances have not been more than an immorality have they? I am drawn between seeming to make too much of these circumstances and the feeling that they should be altered if the book were to be published. I think the Captain Wright business finally decided my opinion, because any public position does bring with it a certain responsibility, doesn't it? It is better that the practice of public men should coincide with their theories.[449]

Captain Wright had written a book claiming that the Victorian Prime Minister Gladstone had had an immoral connection with prostitutes. Gladstone's family had lured Wright into a libel action which he lost, paying heavy costs. The case, a *cause célèbre* of early 1927, prompted debate about the relation between public service and private conduct. It had perhaps not struck Williams that people might find an incongruity between his current personal life and the theology of marriage that his book proposed. The question, once raised, became disturbing. For the time being, Williams made no further attempt to publish *Romantic Theology*.

Sometimes, indeed, he expressed disgust with his own behaviour:

All this unhappy afternoon
I have been dazed by an evil moon
that floats within me, and turns my dreams
into visions nearer the truth, it seems;
I am not I, and if we talked
of God and poetry as we walked,
it was that they should be panders both
to an old man, full of lust and sloth

> crawling and peeping and slinking about
> behind those masks, and only to find
> for his greasy, slimy, and feverish mind
> the thought that pleases him[...]
> It is five-fifteen; I have heard it strike,
> but all the hours seem much alike. [...]
> and the hours are gone where the bad hours go—
> into the mouth of a large crocodile,
> in the mud of a pit, with a terrible smile[.][450]

Perhaps such feelings affected his membership of the Fellowship of the Rosy Cross. Since 1917 he had been a diligent member, moving steadily up the grades. But after July 1925, when he reached the Portal of the Fourth Order, the Fellowship's records show no sign of Williams's attendance for some two years. On 29 July 1927 he took part in his last ritual: 'The Ceremony of Consecration on the Threshold of Sacred Mystery for the Watchers of the Holy House'. The ceremony seems to have been intended to admit the postulant—who was not Williams himself—into a state at the borderline of the realm of the Kabbalistic 'Supernals', the three highest spheres of the Sephirotic Tree. The postulant would ask for his body to be sanctified, so that 'soul transformed in God through flesh made pure, and justified by Holy Temple Rites, may bear faithful witness in the world'. The ceremony was written with a careful eye to the balancing of male and female elements, and aimed at what has been called a 'creative transmutation of sexual energy',[451] integrating the maleness and femaleness *within* each participant, and thereby lending power to the quest for mystical union with the divine.

It is an elaborate ceremony, involving imagery of lilies and roses and much antiphonal recitation between Priestess and High Priest. Containing no overt sexual imagery, it is said by those who have participated in it to create a very strong sense of sexual polarity. The reasons for Williams's decision to take no further part in the Order remain unknown. Perhaps he felt that he was already experiencing quite enough sexual polarity in his daily life. Perhaps he felt that the tangles of his relationship with Phyllis now compromised his commitment to the quest for mystical union with God. Whatever the reason, he took no further part in the Fellowship of the Rosy Cross. Waite visited him at the OUP in September 1928, probably to discuss his future relationship with the Order. There was no antagonism, and Waite wrote to him occasionally until 1931. The letters have not survived. Williams kept his robes and other regalia, but he also kept his vow of secrecy and never mentioned the Order to anyone. Nor did he tell Michal that he had left. They had never discussed his attendance at the Order, and it may already have served as cover for evenings with Phyllis.[452]

★ ★ ★

By the time of this last ritual, the relationship had reached crisis point. The daily bombardment of poems and letters, the elaborate games, the spiritual and literary instruction, the possessiveness—from a man who would neither make love to her nor propose marriage—was becoming an unbearable pressure. In the summer of 1927 Phyllis seems to have asked for an end to it. Williams agreed, and put on a brave face, writing:

> What a year! I don't really go back much—or only rather vaguely—before the end of last June. And the first Tolstoy. And then the [...] lecture. And the second Tolstoy. Do you remember offering to take me to 'The Ghost Train'? Yes, you liked me a little then. But instead I took your arm—which to me was much like a weekend at Brighton—and we talked about Almighty God. [...] We begin something new—and that also is a prelude. Will next year be sharper, sadder, but as precious as this past?[453]

He copied 100 of his poems into one of the Press's blank dummy volumes as *A Century of Poems for Celia*, and gave it to her, with a new poem for prelude:

> I shall choose out a hundred poems for you
> of all I have written since our love was new,
> of all that, in this sudden burst of days,
> I have written for your pleasure and your praise. [...]
> Never again, till time itself be ended,
> shall we by such a year of grace be friended.

Astonishingly, he seems also to have given a copy to Milford:[454] a sign of how deeply he trusted 'Caesar'; or, to put it another way, of how far Milford was complicit in the affair.

Williams meant to stay away from Phyllis, but was unable to sustain his resolution. He took to haunting Upper Bedford Place in the evenings. She later recalled, 'He would follow me through the streets, and really it was quite terrible sometimes. [...] I would be walking down one side of the street, and I would be conscious of him walking down the other side of the street. [...] And just sort of talking to himself.'[455] Though she did not say so, on some of these occasions she was probably going out with Billy Somervaille. Williams later used his memories of this horrible time in his novel *Descent into Hell*:

> He would not go to spy; he would go for a walk. He went out of the room, down the soft swift stairs of his mind, into the streets of his mind, to find the phantoms of his mind. He desired hell. [...] At a junction of the roads, as at a junction of his mind, he stopped and waited—to enjoy the night air. His enjoyment strained intently and viciously to hear the sounds of the night [...] He was not in ambush; he was out for a walk. [...] The moon was bright; he stood at the edge of his own skull's platform; desire to hate and desire not to hate struggled in him. In the moonlight, visible, audible, arm in arm, talking and laughing, they came. He saw them pass; his eyes grew blind. Presently he turned and went home.[456]

But Phyllis could not bear the separation either. The chronology is not clear, but at some point she wrote to him:

> I do not believe you would credit the feeling of utter desolation that has come over me. It began last night when I got into bed & realised that I should not be seeing you—it seemed more horrible than I can describe. [...] were it not that Binfield or anyone may come down my tears would blot the page. You can't, you mustn't try to shut me out from your heart. I can bear anything— the last year again anything, but not, O I can not bear this nightmare. [...] I can bear anything but don't I beseech you leave me alone.[457]

Williams replied in kind:

> I will never part from you if I can help it. I will never leave you if I can stay with you. I will never, whatever I may say, willingly of my own accord let you be without me if you want me still. I thought you might miss me, but I never thought that you would feel such a desolation[.][458]

The relationship entered a state of chronic instability. Periodically Williams would try to break it off, only to be dragged back by Phyllis's entreaties. Her plaints, when he tried to free himself, were heart-rending:

> I myself knew I should miss you but I had not [*sic*] idea that the whole place and neighbourhood would pain me with your absence. [...] The last weekend has shown me the kind of thing that I can't bear, the kind of thing that seems as if it would break my heart and eventually kill me.[459]

Sometimes she reacted with anger. In August 1928 Williams made a stilted leave-taking, the defensive superiority of his style betraying acute embarrassment:

> I thought you would like to be wished goodbye, dear Celia. I thought I would say it to you. I hope that any feeling of desolation has passed by now. [. . .] I do not think I have anything more to say. [. . .] When I have said goodbye, I have said everything.[460]

This, or some similarly patronizing letter, provoked Phyllis to a furious outburst fraught with painful home truths:

> I wish to God you'd stop telling me what *I* feel about your actions. [. . .] You're so bunged up with words & the images they create in your own mind that you're incapable of realising anyone else's conception of things. And as if it weren't enough that you should be born a distinguished poet but that you must try to tack on to yourself all the [*illegible*] traditions of a public school code of something or other. [. . .] But whats the good of talking to you. [. . .] Something, the devil or what not in you or through you is trying to tempt me; & to do what I don't know. But I damn well won't do it. I'll see you in hell first. [. . .]
>
> Of course I've done wrong things but I've never, never ceased to love you. [. . .] If you'd only for a few minutes cast away all the candles & the incense & junk you've set up round my image & see me not as a blasted saint but as an ordinary disgusting human being who nevertheless wants & will fight to get a relationship with you that has some semblance of love about it we might get on with the business. But no, you won't.
>
> But my God if you *ever* tell me again what your absence & withdrawal means to *me*; if you ever dare to assume again that you know what I'm thinking or feeling about you I'll wreck your blasted office so that even you'll be a little ashamed.[461]

There is no signature. The ink is smudged with tears.

In this overheated atmosphere, even religion became matter for emotional blackmail. At one point, to judge by Phyllis's response, Williams threatened to give up Christianity:

> I do dislike the idea of your renouncing Christianity, its silly & unreasonable, but there you are, & I dislike even more that you should disown 'agape'; for a time perhaps, 'until this tyranny be overpast'. But when the worst is over? No, that won't do will it? So you mustn't. Who will give me Christian books? Do you think you can prod people about things which you have ceased to care about yourself—so well, I mean? Wasn't that what made everything so real?[462]

But if he threatened to leave her, she would play the same card herself:

Dearest Urban you mustn't go away from me truly you mustn't. Something dreadful will happen to me if you do. [...] I shall forget God—you know I will: [...] The seeds of sin that you see in me will sprout & blossom. Besides I can't do without you - I *can't*. [...] I don't say - Please look after me but just – Don't decide to leave me alone.[463]

And so it went on, through 1928, 1929, and into the summer of 1930. Poems and letters, arguments and reconciliations, madness and attempts at sanity. Two notes, side-by-side in this archive of confused, undated correspondence, sum up poignantly the divided life that Williams was living through these years. The first:

My dearest Urban,
     Your letter has upset me dreadfully [...] I have read your letter once but I *daren't* read it again or I shall be really ill. You *must* come & see me [...] I know I've treated you badly & done everything beastly that one human being can do to another but I've never ceased to love & need you. [...] The night I came to the theatre with you & you left me sorrowfully I *did* go through torments when I got home. And because of those torments I *won't* read your letter again because it breaks down the whole of my defence against the misery which waits round the corner.[464]

And next to it:

Dear
     I hope you will find everything comfortable. There is 7/- on the dresser. Tell the milkman no milk Sunday or Monday.
     Best love till Saturday
     Michal.
     My coat may come back from the cleaners on Sat. morning. Could you give a cheque for 12s/6d if it does?[465]

There is, really, nothing more to say.

I I

Substitution

'From 1927 to 1930 was a dreadful period: even allowing for its goodness',[466] Williams wrote, with his usual touch of paradox. But the fact that he was going through hell during these years did not hinder his writing. On the contrary: empowered, perhaps, by the 'transmutation' of unfulfilled passion, he was beginning a period of ceaseless creativity.

His tragedy *The Witch* was written for his students at Balham to act in 1927. Undistinguished in plotting and verse, *The Witch* is striking as a portrayal of pure evil. Bess, the 'witch' of the title, lives in hunger and poverty, refusing charity lest it make her comfortable and thereby reduce her hatred for her neighbours. Her plotting results in the death of the local Squire's son, and the Squire's madness and despair. Its most striking moment is the ending, when Bess turns on the audience:

> And all you else,
> comfortable pleasant people through the world,
> [. . .] a thing goes wandering o'er the earth
> you cannot see, a thing that dark or day
> are all alike to, burrowing through all walls,
> that is madness, and is sickness, and is hate,
> and is a marvellous thing beyond all these—
> being that which first God saw when he beheld
> pure evil. Into your houses and your breasts,
> till you shall wither and look all awry
> with twisted faces, it shall slide along; [. . .]
> farewell, you comfortable folk, farewell,
> but this shall be among you till you die.

Maybe the actors relished this, but it must have made an uncomfortable evening for the audience. It was one of several works in which Williams would examine, without explanation or excuse, the nature of sheer, motiveless malevolence—something he would always associate with witchcraft.

In his dealings with authors he remained tactful, speaking as a vulnerable fellow-writer rather than as an omniscient publisher. To the poet Jean Smith, he suggested 'with a humility approaching abjectness' that she reconsider her use of the word 'strange', which she perhaps 'repeated rather a lot', confessing that:

> years and years ago a man objected to my using the word; he thought it had been used so much that it had lost its force. [...] O and 'the blackbird's flageo-let' comes in twice; I daresay you don't mind, I don't, but I mention it in case you should observe it yourself and think I hadn't.[467]

Such gentle hints improved the Press's publications and cemented close relationships with authors. A letter to Housman, proposing (unsuccessfully) a volume of his *Selected Prose*, blends judicious flattery with an appeal to stringent intellectual standards:

> It is not for me to praise Mr. Housman, but perhaps I may suggest that the qualities of your mind and style are the precise qualities of which at present men are very much in need; and that this re-publication would be a definite act against chaos and looseness and mess and in favour of strength and intellect and lucidity.[468]

The editing of anthologies continued as usual. Writing the Introduction for *Victorian Narrative Verse*, he praised Swinburne's Arthurian poems and attacked Tennyson for the pomposity of his King Arthur and his inadequate treatment of the Grail.[469] With Fred Page, he deputized for Milford in editing *The Oxford Book of Regency Verse*; Milford's name is on the title page, but the Preface, obviously by Williams, is full of his characteristic wit and quirky intelligence, as when he grumbles that in the Romantic period, 'Not only are "the majors so very major" but the minors "are so very minor"', or announces that 'Keats's *Ode to Autumn* is, without doubt, greater than Hood's. But it is conceivable that Keats himself might have had momentary doubts.' The task was made more fun by the involvement of Phyllis Jones, who is thanked 'for her ungrudging secretarial labours'.[470]

Having tried to make Michal an author, Williams did his best to lure Phyllis into producing books, and failed again. He arranged for her to edit *Selected Letters of Lord Chesterfield* for the World's Classics. Of course she could not do it, and made it another instance of her emotional dependency:

> I want you to keep me intelligent; I want you to rescue me from the slough of despondency. I can't bear you not to worry about my work. [...] I can't go on

[*sic*] my own: I can't learn poetry unless you tell me what to learn, nor do Chesterfield unless you help me, nor be good unless you tell me to be good. [. . .] It wasn't just a sex episode, I did try to *love* you & I do try still, tho' rather more selfishly.[471]

And, even more desperately:

the answer to it all is that I have sold my birthright for a mess of potage. I don't quite see why that is the answer, but it is. And as for what I will do for you, how can I do anything when you withdraw yourself? [. . .] And no one but you cares about the poets and antiquity: and even you will leave me in my mess of potage. So I can do nothing for you because you want none of the things I can do. [. . .] And you *can* do things for me so I ask you—to write Chesterfield, to buy me chocolate, not to leave me. [. . .]
How I will need Chesterfield.[472]

When Chesterfield appeared in 1929 the Introduction was credited to Phyllis but had been written by Williams.

He also, surprisingly, wrote for *The Dominant*, a music journal that Foss had launched in November 1927. Ignorant of music and having no ear for it, he made his first article, 'The One-Eared Man', a rueful confession that he had been 'born one-eared, an absurd caprice of nature [who] would not willingly abandon conversation in favour of music'.[473] His other article, 'The History of Critical Music', published in April 1928, is an ingenious intellectual fantasy, surveying modern music from the viewpoint of 1965. Music certainly occupied him at this period, even if he could not appreciate it. One of the *Poems for Celia* depicts him actually copying out music (perhaps for his own masque): 'Damn it, how long this bloody music takes [. . .] the time's changed; / I nearly missed it [. . .] The last bar, / yes, the last crochet. I put down my pen.'[474] Robin Milford, Humphrey's composer son, recalled: '[Williams] told me he regretted knowing nothing of music (tho. I remember him at a gramophone recital of Sibelius' works at O.U.P., & have wondered if he did not probably acquire by intelligence what he had been denied by nature)[.]'[475]

More congenial was the opportunity to review crime fiction for the *Daily News* (later the *News Chronicle*), a left-Liberal daily paper. It came through Norman Collins, who had joined the Publicity Department at Amen House. From a poor background, energetic and creative, Collins seemed made from the same stuff as Foss and Williams, with whom he soon became friendly. Collins left in 1929 to join the *News* and, knowing Williams's appetite for detective stories, signed him up. From January 1930 until February 1935 Williams contributed a fortnightly column, reviewing four or five thrillers in 350 words. It was the 'golden age' of the detective story, and his pieces were incisive and perceptive: in January 1934, for example, in one week he reviewed Dorothy L. Sayers's *The Nine Tailors*, S.S. Van Dine's *The Dragon Murder Case*, and Agatha Christie's *Murder on the Orient Express*, spotting them all as classics of their kind. He also found space for startling speculations—such as his demand for 'the admirable story yet to be written [in which] a new Jekyll-and-Hyde is himself at once the corpse, the murderer, the detector [...] the sub-conscious to murder the conscious and the sublimated to detect the crime. After all, most people hate themselves enough to do it.'[476] In the late twentieth century, similar ideas would be explored by innovative writers such as Philip K. Dick and Chuck Palahniuk. But Williams had them first.

★   ★   ★

During 1928 Williams and Foss had written a second Masque, *The Masque of Perusal*, for performance early in 1929. But in December Williams was called to St Albans, where his eighty-year-old father was dying. For the following month he visited often, though he spent much of his time by Walter's bed writing 'pages and pages' to Phyllis.[477] Walter died of heart failure on 10 January 1929; his funeral was held at St Albans Abbey.

At Amen House, preparations for the second masque went ahead. Curtains were put up,[478] furniture and piano were moved in, and the masque was performed on 8 February, Milford's fifty-second birthday. *The Masque of Perusal* takes up where the first masque left off. The book on Syrian nouns is sold to a writer (Foss) who seeks inspiration from the ancient language it describes. Once read, the book becomes a thought in the writer's mind. But it cannot express itself in a new book until it has found an answer to the question of why books should exist at all. The question is at first met only with crass commercial considerations (voiced by Gerry Hopkins) and well-meaning clichés (voiced by Fred Page—it says something for Williams's charm that he persuaded his colleagues to act these obvious caricatures of themselves), but finally receives the idealistic answer of 'labour and purity and peace'—voiced, of course, by Phillida. To represent the constraints on integrity in the publishing business, Phillida appears 'on a height, blindfolded and chained hand and foot'—a predicament that probably also satisfied some personal fantasy of

Williams's. Thought sets her free, and the characters perform a 'Procession of the Graal', with an inkpot to represent the Graal and the element of water; a pen for spear and fire; a piece of printer's type for the rod and 'spirit' or air; and paper to represent the earth element. The piece ends with an epilogue addressed to Milford as Caesar.

This second masque, though visually exciting, is more obscure than the first and seems to lack focus. Some of its audience were probably baffled, though the high jinks and music will have kept them entertained. Its fundamental question—why are we writing, why are we publishing, what is the point of anything at all?—may genuinely have been troubling Williams at this time. Perhaps some lack of clarity invaded the masque itself. Williams, however, was quite clear about the masques' purpose. To him, they were a presentation of the Mystical Way. In January 1929, shortly before *The Masque of Perusal* was performed, he offered Phyllis a long exposition in a letter. Like many of his letters, it was an essay directed *at* the person addressed, rather than a letter in the usual sense:

My dear Phillida,
There is (it is said) only one work which is pursued everywhere and at all times, from which nothing is alien and to which all things are directed (otherwise they are null and void). And that is the re-union of man and God. Of which also the Masques are a parable.[...]

The First Masque then was a presentation of the New Birth. It will be obvious to you that what happens to the soul of man happens to the works of man, and it seems to me that all good things done in goodwill are part of the revelation of infinite Perfection—publishing books, building bridges, adding up figures (or what other games the Counting House indulges in), playing tennis (which you do, I gather, so admirably) or anything else. So in the first presentation, the Manuscript is shown discussing some other state of being, namely, that of permanence and delighted usefulness: to be a printed Book—though she very vaguely understands what is meant by that. And after a certain distress and pain she enters into that state. This is the beginning of the Mystical Way. [...]

And then the Book or the soul naturally thinks that it has reached its End, and all's going to be cherries and apple-pie. Well, it isn't. The unhappy thing finds that it's just left there—nothing particular happens. [...]

But there comes a time when it has to go on.[...] The New Life begins to lay its tasks upon her. This has been told for centuries under the symbolism of the Quest of the Grail [...] And the Hymn of the Grail is true, if anything is. If in the saints then in us; if in us then in our work.

Printing, publication, sale,
Bear the Hallows of the Grail.

Yes: when I scribble a question about Leo the Isaurian on the margin of proofs or Alexis designs advertisements or Dorinda argues about percentages or you keep your books in their proper order. [. . .]

With the baffling of temptation, the redemption of capacities, the freeing of other thoughts and purposes, the completion of the task, the *Masque of Perusal* ends. The old division of the Mystical Way was into the Way of Purgation, the Way of Illumination, and the Way of Union. The first is in the First Masque, the second in the present, and the third awaits the will of God. . . .

I salute the Keeper—at the entrance to which Christian Rosycross came, after taking part in the Mysteries, with the breaking of the day, to be a doorkeeper.[479]

So whether they knew it or not, the staff of Amen House had now witnessed an initiation into the second stage of the Mystical Way. Blending workplace patterns with Rosicrucian ritual, Williams was aiming to instruct his colleagues, enhance the atmosphere of Amen House, and—equally important—keep Phyllis engaged with his ideas and his spiritual guidance.

★   ★   ★

As soon as the masque had been performed Williams turned his attention to St Martin's, Kensal Rise, where his *Rite of the Passion* was to form part of the three hours' Good Friday service on 29 March 1929. Performed 'with intervals of prayer, meditation and music', the *Rite* is a pageant-like verse play presenting the passion, crucifixion, and resurrection of Christ as 'Love'. When it was written is uncertain. Its style varies wildly: it incorporates several entire poems from *The Silver Stair*, and its general treatment is the same as that of the nativity story that Williams had published in *The New Witness* a decade earlier.

Lecturing continued as usual. He visited Downe House twice in 1930, to speak on Sir Francis Bacon and on Blake, and there were the evening lectures, with Williams always ready to dispense sympathy and advice to his students during break time. Some students guessed that he was unhappy, which nevertheless did not diminish their trust in him. He was open about his own confusion and vulnerability, and advised the practice of bearing pain and uncertainty, trusting that things would be for the best, rather than fretting for solutions.

Thelma Mills at Brixton, became especially close to him, and (though she was not a Christian) he began to take on for her too the role of spiritual advisor. They had lunch together once a month at a restaurant near Amen

House. He discussed sexual love and mysticism with her and told her, 'if Miss Massey [the college principal] ever wants to get rid of me I shall have a riotous last evening. I think I shall lecture on Havelock Ellis [the famous sexologist]. But hush! These fantasies are too wild for a sedate world.'[480]

More seriously, he told her:

'The kingdom of heaven is within'—and what is the kingdom of heaven? Love and lucidity—the advent of God—in all relationships and all occupations: not in sex only, nor in religion only, nor in art only nor in beauty only, but everywhere and at all times. But if the Kingdom is within, what I mean is that you must submit yourself to it. As for example—to empty the mind of thought, to still the emotions, to concentrate on God (and I do recommend God instead of Love—for, though they are the same word, Love has so many associations......though you may say, so has God. [...] The practice of the prayer of entire silence is one way of learning the mysteries of Love. But when you pray, *pray*; and when you play, *play* (and don't be too solemnly sacred[...]).[481]

He persuaded her to read the Song of Solomon. When she ridiculed the biblical glosses interpreting its subject as 'The love of Christ and his Church', he wrote:

My mind was a little fretted by your scorn of the chapter-headings [...] not that I want you to believe them unless you like; heavens, no! But I do want you to see that they are not there in order to water down the ecstasy of the *Song*—[...] They are there because the Church believes the fullest possible adoration known between mortal lovers to be 'as moonlight unto sunlight, as water unto wine' compared to the final rapture of the soul surrendering to God.[482]

To Thelma he first hinted at a discovery—or perhaps a rediscovery of something ancient. He invited her to lunch, to discuss, he said, something 'which has made me wonder whether the New Testament may not be merely true in some of its advice. All about "bearing one another's burdens". I have an awful (full of awe) feeling that one can.'[483] Following their discussion, he approached Thelma with a startling proposal. An inspector, he said, was to visit his class, and he was worried about it: 'The projected visit interferes; intrudes awkwardly; will not be dismissed; in fact, makes of the lecture a burden, which it is not, or certainly should not be.'[484] Would Thelma, he asked, be willing to take on the worry for him? If she would set herself to worry a little about the inspection, then he could get on with preparing the lecture, and giving it, without anxiety, knowing that she was taking care of it on his behalf.

He was proposing what he came to call 'substitution', whereby one person could voluntarily take over the suffering—mental or physical—of another, and so relieve it. He had long felt that everything—everyone—was connected. And he had wondered about the implications of such biblical passages as St Paul's 'Bear ye one another's burdens, and so fulfil the law of Christ' and 'we, being many, are [. . .] every one members one of another'. The ultimate example of the process was the Atonement, in which Christ had redeemed mankind from the burden of sin by taking it upon Himself. Reflecting that it might be possible to make conscious use of this principle, he began to experiment, perhaps in conjunction with members of 'Henry' Lee's group, with whom he certainly discussed the idea.[485] As he explained to Thelma, it should be possible for one person voluntarily to suffer anxiety, fear, or pain on behalf of another. The first person would then be relieved of the misery; and the second person would be better able to bear it, for it would have been chosen, without personal involvement. Thelma recalled:

> The image, Charles [said], is simply that of carrying someone's heavy shopping-bag or suitcase, & giving them a breather. *Not* of removing the contents & returning the container empty. Of course not. In fact [they] are given time to free [their] mind & flex [their] muscles, to feel free, for that while, of the whole thing. [. . .] C. had the lecture on & in his mind: [. . .] so: the lecture is imaged by the suitcase, which is an easy weight. [. . .] He could manage it himself certainly but it would be a chore *SO* What happier solution than that C. should ask his friend T. to carry the image of the Inspector's disturbance of his mental processes, & so relieve him, that he may lecture unperturbed.[486]

It seems uncharacteristic that Williams should have been worried about the inspection. Perhaps he simply chose it as a suitable test for the technique. Anyhow, Thelma agreed, and did her best; though it was an anticlimax, for the inspector failed to turn up. But other experiments followed, and Thelma began to use the method herself when it seemed called for. She documented one example:

> my young friend Enid who had a series of dental visits to make, & was in such terror of the approaching first, that she was quite distraught, told me. I got her to *name* the parts of her fear . . . The dreaded Chair itself, imagining the sharp prick of the needle, etc. etc. She was able to laugh—if ruefully—& admit that it sounded silly, put like that . . . Nevertheless, . . . I said that though the teeth, and the experience would be hers, the pain should be mine. Let her be *interested*, but not afraid. The chair is *comfortable*; relax in it: make it a *relaxation exercise*, especially relaxing at the moment of jab to *notice* . . . this & that & the

other, including *the fact* that the relaxation excludes the apprehension of pain to such an extent that one does not feel it....All right. [At the appointed time] I [...] had toothache (having *forgotten* my promise). She radiantly asserted that she had felt nothing, & could never be afraid of the dentist again.[487]

'Substitution' would become an important element in Williams's spiritual practice and ideas. He speculated that when we suffer, it is perhaps so that some other may benefit. When we are happy, someone else, perhaps quite unknown to us, has earned our happiness for us by their pain or effort. We live, quite literally, from and in one another; and all of us from and in God.

★ ★ ★

Phyllis's eager curiosity about Arthur and the Grail had reignited Williams's passion for the myth that had so long haunted him. Perhaps as early as December 1926 he had started again to write poems about the 'Matter of Britain'. And now they were poems that involved Phyllis. First came one which he called 'The Assumption of Caelia', in which he imagined the Celtic 'poet and warrior' Taliessin (King Arthur's court bard) singing to the King about a maiden he knew long ago in 'Byzantion', and of how she died and went to heaven. Her soul has all virtues, but is only named when the voice of God identifies her as 'Love-in-Caelia'. And rather than simply entering heaven, 'heaven opened from her; from her inmost soul / the Centre issued in the unchanging Whole'. As a perfect soul, that is, she already has heaven within her. Her 'assumption' into heaven is an instance of the mystical union with God which Williams had sought so long through prayer and ritual.

He was exploring the possibility of viewing Celia—the true, deepest nature of Phyllis—as an embodiment of spiritual perfection, a human manifestation of the mystical goal. Writing the poem, he found he was merging his love poetry, his mysticism, and his vision of the Arthurian myth. He was at last reaching the kind of poetry he had always wanted to write. And he saw that rather than attempt a long narrative, he could choose brief episodes from the Arthurian myth, or invent them and insert them *into* the myth, making them reflect his own immediate concerns. As he summed it up later, 'there the method lay'.[488]

More poems followed. In these, Williams meditated upon Phyllis's body, making it in turn a written text, a source of power through erotic constraint, and a microcosm of the Arthurian world. A poem called at first 'The Clothing of Celia' but later 'Tristram's Song to Iseult', shows the lovers—who cannot consummate their love, since Iseult is to be King Mark's bride—on their last night alone together, 'in a woodland refuge'. Tristram composes a poem for Iseult and, telling her 'now shalt thou my precious vellum be', writes it all over her naked body. The narrative describes how the poem, beginning at her brow, gradually spreads 'between the breasts [...] around the columned thighs' and onwards, until her entire body is covered with text. He allows her to wash the poem away again, but assures her, 'Champions shall honour thee but never so.' The poem, and the fantasy it embodies, are an astonishing example of poetry serving as substitute for sex. It clearly proclaims Williams's desire to make Phyllis indelibly his own by the intensity of his writing about her; his wish is that, once so written about, she will never quite be anyone else's. She may wash the writing off, but the poetry will stick.

'Lamoracke's Song to Morgause' tells of how Sir Lamoracke, in a 'turret chamber', wrestles with his lover, Queen Morgause, the adulterous wife of King Lot of Orkney. Lamoracke throws her, naked, on 'a bed of beaten gold' and ties her up with silken ropes. To her thus immobilized, he sings a love song, predicting the fall of the kingdom and promising to rescue her in the last battle. The third poem, 'Percivale's Song to Blanchefleur', is the most obviously magical, in that it makes the woman's body a microcosm. The notion that the human body may be viewed as a kind of map, model, or set of correspondences for the greater world has always been a central part of traditional worldviews. It is especially prominent in Kabbalistic thought, where a human figure is often pictured superimposed upon the Sephirotic Tree. Williams's new poem aimed at establishing Phyllis as a microcosm of Britain and the Arthurian world:

> This to record, beyond all myths, the myth
> of Britain and thy body one therewith;
> for coming on this night, sister, I saw
> astonished and adoring and in awe,
> how the tale means but thee and thou the tale,
> and after what dark manner the dark Grail
> is manifested and mistaken not
> through a shape fairer than is Camelot.[489]

The poem sets up a detailed system of correspondences between Phyllis's body and the Arthurian kingdom. Her ten fingers are the ten chief knights of the Round Table; the palms of her hands—'Centres of consecrating energy'—are the Bishops of Winchester and Canterbury. Her mind is

Lancelot, her eyes Merlin, her mouth the poet Taliessin. The 'shining top-most of the hair' is the King, her throat is Camelot, and her spine is the Law. Her left thigh is Sir Bors, and her right Sir Percivale—the two guardians of the Grail—and between them is 'the Mystery of Helayne', daughter of King Pelles, keeper of the Grail, and mother of Galahad, who achieved it:

> This is the destined and thrice holy place
> where is the Action and the last embrace[.]

In short, her vagina is the Grail. He ends by urging her to see in others too this sacred, cosmically ordered being: 'Wilt thou be perfect? teach thine eyes to see, / in all, in each, what thus I marked in thee.'

The ideas and images of these poems are fascinating. And Williams's style has begun to change. The language, though still archaic, is plainer and more direct. Williams is writing about things that are desperately important to him. And he told Phyllis that the poems were about her: 'though the poems are not what I could have wished, still Tristram does derive from your Circassian and inscribed hands, and Lamoracke from a not unworthy fantasy of you'.[490] That the poem about Lamoracke's binding of Morgause should be based on a 'fantasy' about Phyllis is hardly surprising. But how does 'Tristram's Song of Iseult' derive from her 'Circassian and inscribed hands'? Circassian, presumably, because they had been chastized, slave-like, in erotic games. But 'inscribed'? The answer is supplied by a note that Williams wrote in 1930 to Thelma Mills. After mentioning this poem, he asks: 'have you ever at least arranged for a pencilled message or name on your hands? It is a pleasant enough fantasy, I have found: slight, but happy. Do let me know if you find it amusing.'[491] Evidently he had written 'at least' in pencil on Phyllis's hands; the poem extends this into a vision of writing over her entire body. The practice—which seems to have had both fetishistic and magical aspects—would occur again, and with other women. Thelma, a strong-minded young woman, did not take up the suggestion.

These new Arthurian poems lay unpublished, until early in 1929, Hubert Foss made a proposal. He planned, with the printers Henderson and Spalding, to publish limited editions of fine books, which he would design. The imprint would be called the Sylvan Press, and he wanted its first book to be a volume of poems by Charles Williams. Williams offered nineteen poems from his recent work, including the group of erotic 'Arthurian' poems about Phyllis. The title was to be *Heroes and Kings*. Foss intended a sumptuous production: the book would be in folio format, on handmade paper, bound in scarlet silk with a gold-stamped design, and illustrated with wood engravings by Norman Janes, a well-known printmaker. Only 300 would be printed.

Although the book contained two poems about Michal, Williams saw it chiefly as a way of honouring Phyllis. He told her:

> It will be a beautiful book, but who is going to buy it I don't know. However, that doesn't matter. The purpose of it was other. It pleased Almighty God to set for the present—and perhaps for a little longer time—the praises of Celia in print before her; so that she may never entirely forget the beginnings of the great song that we proposed—from *The Clothing of Celia* upwards.[492]

In another letter he confirmed:

> that the four poems in *Heroes and Kings* of my Arthurian—the songs of Tristram, Palomides, Blanchefleur, and Taliessin—are due to you; [...] they are fresh; they haven't been done before; they are an expansion of English verse.
>
> This letter is yours and mine; but if by any chance you lose it or—anything, the copyright (I warn a hypothetical stranger) is mine. And it can't be published—in any way—unless I or my executors agree.
>
> Did I ever tell you that I suspect that I am a mild masochist as well as a mild sadist? But not happily with anyone but you. Because I hate all stirrings of sex apart from you.[493]

The idea that his letters might be published occurs more than once around this time, perhaps because he sensed that his poetry was improving. A few months later he wrote to Phyllis, 'Won't you have a time one of these days editing my letters to you for publication? When I say "editing" I *don't* mean "watering-down" but adding little notes here and there[.]'[494] It is good to know that he could contemplate publication of these letters without dilution.

Heroes and Kings appeared in February 1930. But Williams continued to write Arthurian poems, wondering whether Milford might publish them. On 28 February 1930, sending Milford a copy of *Heroes and Kings*, he wrote:

> *King Arthur*
> Nobody wants any poems about him any more—*nobody*. I sympathize with this feeling very much; I don't know that I do. But for twenty years I have always meant one day to annotate certain significances which neither Tennyson nor Morris nor Swinburne nor the rest took any notice of [...] But I have never known how to start. Another long, long poem on the Grail looked so depressing, and odes and things were not narrative enough. However, having been asked one week-end to write a few notes on the Arthurian legend, I wrote instead the poem which appears here as *Percivale's Song to Blanchefleur*,

and then in a moment's irritation *Tristram's Song to Iseult*. [...] And so, between
then and now, raised the number to nearly forty. I should think another twenty
or thirty would see it through. [...]

   If you turned them over, and found them dull (as they may be) or too *passée*,
and would say so, I should be more grateful than depressed. For I know—O
I know—how dull the story can be, and how easy a fluent romanticism.[495]

Perhaps the manuscript was then called *King Arthur*. (When it was retyped
ten years later, Williams would name it *The Advent of Galahad*.) But Milford
was not interested—fortunately, for Williams had not yet thrown off his
'fluent romanticism', though he could now pinpoint the problem. More
surprisingly, Milford agreed to consider publishing a volume of Williams's
plays the following year.

★ ★ ★

Alongside the poems, he had been working hard to complete the book on
modern English poets that he had proposed in 1926. The Clarendon Press,
the scholarly Oxford end of the business, had taken it on; but Williams
had not delivered. He later confessed, 'it took me three years to do [...] &
I never liked it—it was horrible'.[496] He completed the book in September
1929 but it was not published until February the following year, and instead
of *Modern English Poets* the title was changed to *Poetry at Present*. It is an odd
book, consisting of sixteen chapters, each surveying the work of a poet.
Among those included are Hardy, Housman, Kipling, Yeats, W.H. Davies,
Walter de la Mare, Chesterton, Masefield, Eliot, Robert Graves, and Edmund
Blunden. Each chapter is followed by a verse 'Endpiece', a short poem
by Williams in which he mimics the style and themes of the poet he has
just discussed. The best of these 'Endpieces' are mere pastiche; several are
excruciating—it is surprising that the Clarendon Press was willing to
countenance them.

   Despite the title, *Poetry at Present* was hardly an up-to-the-minute survey.
Hardy had died whilst it was being written. Most of the other poets were
over fifty; several were in their eighties. The selection was notably conservative. The original plan had been to deal only with 'English' poets (Yeats
and Eliot squeezed in because both had been technically 'British' for part of
their lives). But Englishness largely excluded modernism. When Robert
Graves and Laura Riding had published their *Survey of Modernist Poetry* a
couple of years earlier, they had discussed not only Eliot but Ezra Pound,

E.E. Cummings, Marianne Moore, Wallace Stevens, and Williams Carlos Williams—all of them American. If Charles Williams had heard of any of these writers, his book gives no sign of it.

Yet *Poetry at Present* does clearly show Williams's conservative taste starting to crack under the strain of his emotional experience. The Preface apologizes to Eliot, 'for whose work I profess a sincere and profound respect, though I fail to understand it'.[497] What he does understand is the horror portrayed in much of Eliot's early poetry. Commenting on Eliot's 'I have seen the eternal Footman hold my coat, and snicker / And in short, I was afraid', he identifies it as 'the experience, so common and so detestable, when the whole universe seems to be sniggering at one behind its hand'.[498] He adds, 'Mr Eliot's poetic experience of life would seem to be Hell varied by intense poetry. It is also, largely, our experience.' He sees why Eliot is writing a new kind of poetry. 'If only we could neglect it', he writes, 'and go back to our sound traditional versifiers.' But he knew that was impossible. He could no longer endure being merely a 'sound traditional versifier'. And as he signed the Preface to *Poetry at Present* in September 1929, the agent of change already lay amongst the papers on his desk.

★   ★   ★

Change came from what might have seemed the least likely source: the gravely ill, 85-year-old Robert Bridges. The poet had been a friend of Gerard Manley Hopkins, and held his manuscripts. Now the Oxford University Press had decided to publish the first mass-market edition of Hopkins's poems. An expensive limited edition had appeared in 1918, but this new edition would make Hopkins famous. In May 1929, Bridges wrote:

> Milford is now getting a 2nd Edition of Gerard Hopkins's poems ready. They have a man at the Press in London who writes elaborately and meta-physicopoetically in the manner of Donne and he is to be entrusted with the 'editing'—which is mainly the difficulty of knowing what to add to the old edition. He is coming to see me on Tuesday, and I am aware that he is amenable.[499]

The 'man at the Press' was Williams. His task was to add sixteen new poems, check the texts, and write a critical introduction—though Bridges would be credited as the editor. Williams finished his Introduction in July 1930.[500]

It was twelve years since Alice Meynell had warned him against 'Gerard Hopkins's pranks'. Looking freshly at the poet's work, in the wake of the excitement and disturbance stirred in him by a careful reading of Eliot, Williams was inspired, and his Introduction is full of enthusiasm. He sees Hopkins as drawing on basic sound qualities of the English language—those 'habits, especially alliterative, to which English verse is [...] accustomed'.[501] In Hopkins, he says, 'alliteration, repetition, interior rhyme, all do the same work: [...] they persuade us of the existence of a vital and surprising poetic energy'.[502] He concedes that the poems are difficult. Often, he says:

> intense apprehension of the subject provides two or more necessary words at the same time. [...] It is true that we cannot make haste when reading him, but that is what helps to make him difficult. The very race of the words and lines hurries to our emotion; our minds are left behind [...] because they cannot work at a quick enough rate.[503]

Like Milton, Hopkins has 'the simultaneous consciousness of a controlled universe, and yet of division, conflict, and crisis within that universe'.[504] Williams intensely shared that consciousness; and he could see how valuable such a style might be for exploring it. 'It is arguable', he wrote, 'that this is not the greatest kind of poetry; but it is also arguable that the greatest kind of poetry might easily arise out of this.'[505] Poets, he predicted, would draw new life from Hopkins: they 'will return to him as to a source not a channel of poetry; he is one who revivifies, not merely delights, equivalent genius'.[506]

If Williams needed to 'revivify' his poetry, then here was an answer. He began experimenting with Hopkins's style, as in this unpublished sonnet:

> Thy will be done on earth, as it is in heaven
>
> Sweet spirit, fleet spirit, why in such anguish pant
>   saying: *as it is, ah! in heaven, as in heaven thy will is done*
>   *so be it here!* then straining thyself to run
> towards the unaccomplished will thou seest in want
> of thy will to aid? So I once, who now recant,
>   saying, *as it is now in heaven*; look, that heaven is one
>   allwhere; that lovely truth, which here may none
> despoil or forbid, the perfected habitant
> of heaven is even now reckoned. This very will,
>   this act—delight, loss, ardour, whate'er it be—
> is already summed complete by the will's own skill.
> Thou hast but to know it:—this is the mere task given,

> fair spirit, rare spirit!—on earth the will perfectly
> done, *as it is, as it is oh! already in heaven.*[507]

He would never have published a poem as slavishly imitative of Hopkins as this, with its internal rhymes, strings of stressed monosyllables, exclamations ('*ah!*') in the midst of sentences, and disregard of usual word order. But now he was exercising: trying out the new tone, disrupting the smooth rhythms and end-stopped lines of his previous poetry, to pack it with struggle and thought.

★   ★   ★

Reactions to *Poetry at Present*, from some of the poets themselves, were surprisingly positive. Edmund Blunden called it 'capital and original'; Lascelles Abercrombie wrote, 'You've given me a splendid show, and [...] in a book which [...] is by far the best thing of its kind I know.' But perhaps they were just flattered to be included. Housman, Milford reported, grumbled that 'it praises all the poets too much'.[508] The book sold well and was reprinted.

Soon after its publication, something more important happened. An almost unnoticed presence at Amen House was Jo Harris, a junior typist. She hated her job, under a Head of Department who 'was not conducive to happiness'. She had thought Williams 'much too preoccupied to be so observant. But such was C.W.'s nature, always thoughtful and kind to the young', that he noticed, and arranged for her to be transferred: 'I was in the department for some time before I had working contact with him, and found myself typing (badly I'm sure) some correspondence for him. I think he must have needed extreme patience, but then he was one of the most patient men when dealing with the young.' Williams's kindness in rescuing Jo from her former boss was unexpectedly rewarded:

> He would admit that he was not a tidy man in the office and had occasional clean-ups. On one such occasion, after one paper basket was full he turned out a large typescript which he said could go as it had been refused by all the publishing houses. I said what a pity.[509]

Jo mentioned that she had nothing to read over the weekend. Williams shrugged, tossed her the typescript, and said, 'Do what you like with it.' It was *The Corpse*, the thriller rejected by Faber in 1926. Jo read it over the weekend, thoroughly enjoyed it, and on Monday sent it to a newly established publisher, Victor Gollancz.[510]

The result was a letter from Gollancz, dated 19 March 1930. The book, he said, had arrived just before he left the office on Tuesday and he had taken it home:

> Let me say at once that it is a very long time since I have enjoyed a book so much. I found in it great beauty, both literary and spiritual, as well as excitement. I rarely devote more than an hour and a half to the manuscript of a novel; but I had to read every word of this one and did not finish it until two o'clock this morning.
>
> I wanted to write to you at once, so that you might know how much I was personally delighted by the book. But I do not want at this stage to make you an offer. My own interest in this kind of book is so great that I have found it well not to trust my own judgement: and accordingly I have sent the manuscript on to a reader for a confirming opinion. I shall write to you again in the course of the next few days.
>
> Meanwhile, I should like you to be considering very carefully the question of the title. I feel absolutely certain that *The Corpse* won't do. [...] We must have an arresting title which suggests neither detection nor, I think, black magic or the Graal. I am inclined to think that any suggestion of the latter would 'put off' many readers, who will nevertheless enjoy the book when they are once persuaded to begin it.[511]

The reader's report was positive; Williams thought about titles and chose a phrase from Milton: *War in Heaven*.

The novel told a good tale, gripping at once with an unforgettable opening sentence: 'The telephone bell was ringing wildly, but without result, since there was no-one in the room but the corpse.' The action, tinged with horror and comedy, follows unremittingly from there. The book introduces Williams's finest fictional creation, Sir Giles Tumulty, 'explorer and antiquarian'. Utterly cynical, magnificently foul-mouthed and totally devoid of human decency, Tumulty is a splendid villain. Not himself a black magician, he likes to associate with such people because he enjoys watching them go mad and destroy themselves. Tumulty deduces, through antiquarian research, that the Holy Grail exists, and pinpoints its location. It is in fact the battered silver chalice which stands unused in the vestry of an English country church. He joins forces with a would-be magician, Gregory Persimmons, and they attempt to get their hands on the Grail, by force or deception, so that Gregory can use it for unholy purposes. They are opposed by the saintly Archdeacon of Fardles, by Lionel Rackstraw (a self-portrait of Williams in his most depressive mode) and by the Duke of the North Ridings, an idealistic Catholic nobleman (Williams, perhaps, as he saw himself in heroic fantasy).

There are car chases, blasphemous rituals, demonic enchantment—and debates about the status of the Grail. As a material object, is it really so important in itself? If so, could it be used for evil? Or is, as the Archdeacon proposes, 'any chalice of consecrated wine' of more value?[512] The villains are of course defeated. Having celebrated Mass with the Grail, the Archdeacon dies in an ecstatic moment of mystical union, 'the final stage of the Way'; and the Grail vanishes, 'dissolved and dilated into spreading colour'. The novel was a great advance on the still-unpublished *Adepts of Africa*. The pace was quicker, the characters sharper. The thriller form dominated, with metaphysical questions coming up incidentally as the story developed. No wonder Gollancz had been unable to put it down.

Published in June 1930, *War in Heaven* was moderately successful and brought what Gollancz called 'a small but satisfactory profit'.[513] He asked for another novel, so Williams sent *Adepts of Africa*, telling Gollancz:

it is only fair to warn you that it has been refused by several publishers [...] my own feeling is that I would make the alterations noted on the attached sheet, and then I think it might be quite bearable. [...] I had rather not spend much time on it, nor do I think it would be much better if I did.[514]

Gollancz found fault with the book, and in July Williams assured him, 'I agree with you entirely. I think I know what is wrong with it, but I am not sure whether the book is worth putting right.'[515] So it was again put aside. By then Williams was, in any case, already working on another novel.

★   ★   ★

In July 1930 Michal abruptly gave up her work as a teacher, perhaps exhausted with combining work and childcare. Writing to Olive Willis, Williams implied that she had had some sort of minor breakdown. 'Michal', he told her, 'has abandoned her school and is to be at home. And has been for two or three days.' He asked if she and Michael might go to Olive's cottage at Aisholt on 21 July; he would join them a few days later. 'I think the change will be for everyone's good', he added, 'and anyhow it was quite impossible for her to go on.'[516] The family spent a happy fortnight together at the remote cottage in the Quantock hills. But they were not altogether alone. Olive Willis owned several cottages in the village, and she planned to visit soon, with her friend Miss Nichol. On their first evening the family strolled over to a cottage further down the valley to see if she was there.

Michal knocked at the door, which was opened by a teenage girl who told them that Miss Willis had not arrived.

The following day, Williams passed the same girl with others in the lane. Then the Williams family went to see a display of water-divining or 'dowsing'. The dowser let them try his instruments (eight-year-old Michael claimed to have felt a twitch, the others nothing).[517] As they walked back, they were startled by the four girls jumping down into the road from one of the high banks flanking the lane. They introduced themselves as sixth-form pupils from Downe House: Mary Wright, Diana Hambro, Jean Wilson, and Anne Bradby. Williams did not recognize them but they knew him from his lectures at the school. The girls' footpath through the woods had led them to a steep slope above the road. There were amused apologies on both sides for the previous failures of recognition—Williams quite distressed and asking 'What *must* you think of me?'—and the girls invited the family to supper at 'their' cottage the next day.[518] Anne recalled that:

> Mary [Wright] was the only one of us who knew how to cook: she made an omelette or something! We none of us could cook and we were rather worried about giving them food, but they were so nice, and Michal his wife was always delightful in that way, very easy and welcoming; and then we went to supper with them and he read aloud both up there at their cottage in the evening, and also at a hut that Miss Willis had, high up on the opposite side of the valley to them, looking down over the village, the hillside—and it had a kind of veranda, we sat out on the veranda looking at the view, and he read aloud the poems [from] *Heroes and Kings* [...] We were deprecating about our appreciation and so on, his kindness in reading it; and he said 'Oh, well, any young poet enjoys reading,' he said, 'at least if you call 40 young!' which to us was rather comic![519]

By now Olive Willis was also in the party. But as so often, the events had a private meaning for Williams. He wrote to Phyllis, telling her that he had read poems about her—'under the proper veils of verse'—to the girls,[520] and these seem to have included those startling poems about the binding of Morgause and the 'inscribing' of Iseult.[521] He also read them parts of a new play he was working on, to be called *The Chaste Wanton*. As the title suggests, it was about his relationship with Phyllis. The girls were enchanted by Charles and Michal's kindness and hospitality, and by finding themselves treated as equals by a real poet. They also felt that Williams had some form of psychic sense. On a walk together, he claimed to identify the scene of a Dark Age battle between Saxons and Danes. Anne knew the spot, and confirmed that he had found the exact place. It was an uncanny moment: 'We felt this sort of strange—well—otherworldly feeling', recalled Mary. 'And we weren't at all the kind of girls who expected to feel this sort of thing! But he had such a powerful sort of personality that I dare say he could have persuaded us!'[522]

Secretly, Williams was suffering as much as ever, and sending letters to Phyllis:

> I will not say I miss you, because that doesn't describe it, but I may say that the leaves on the hedges remind me of you (I can't think why). [. . .] You needn't—indeed, you shall not answer this, because—O a hundred becauses. [. . .] And if you wrote it might upset my heart overmuch. Besides I should never believe it was for anything but an awful effort of pity.
>
> But if it should please God that you wrote me a little letter for me to have when I came back, if you *could*—I would rather have that than anything on earth (except you). However, I don't ask nor [sic] anything. [. . .] O Celia how impossibly unseparateable we sometimes seem to be! I love you, baby! I love you, defiant witch![523]

He was taking the typical workaholic's holiday. Little time was devoted to his family: during the two weeks, he reviewed one batch of crime novels and requested a second; wrote to the office about 'the autumn list'; went over *Many Dimensions*, his new novel-in-progress, wondering if he ought to cut out Lord Arglay, one of the central characters—'but I shrink from rewriting 270 slips'; and worked on his play *The Chaste Wanton*. He also found time to write 'A Song of the Myths', a 72-line poem inspired by the names of the four girls, Diana, Anne, Mary, and Jean:

> Above the rippling river, amid the swelling combes,
> in gardens fair and flowered, in low and lovely rooms,
> among the farms of Somerset, the sheep herds and the smiths,
> we walked by sun and starlight, and looked upon the myths.

The poem goes on to link the girls to their legendary namesakes: the Roman goddess Diana, St Anne the grandmother of Jesus, the Virgin Mary herself, and Jeanne d'Arc. On the last evening of the girls' visit, Williams invited them all to his cottage and read them more poems, including 'A Song of the Myths'. 'Certainly', Anne wrote, 'the time and the place took on all the splendour of a myth for me':[524]

> And I do remember our saying goodbye on the last evening at Aisholt—he walked down to our cottage with us—and saying goodbye to him, and going

into the cottage, which was completely dark as we had no electric light, and it was a kind of blackness which swallowed me up. Because somehow I thought I probably would never see him again, or anyway we wouldn't have any contact.[525]

As she went into the dark house to prepare for bed, she felt despair, knowing—as she had known for some days, really—that she was in love with him.

★   ★   ★

Having left school in July, Anne Bradby did not expect to see Charles Williams again. But she had taken some photographs of him and his family, so she sent them to the Press, and waited. Sure enough, one morning her brother called out, 'Anne, you've had a letter in a literary-looking hand-writing with a postmark from Hampstead!' Williams thanked her for the photos—'a gracious reminder of the happy days'—adding:

> The other remembrance ['A Song of the Myths'] shall follow in a few days: it has to be copied. I was thinking rather vaguely—if our Caesar publishes my book of dramatic pieces—of putting it in as an Epilogue—for memory's sake and love's.[526]

Anne replied, this time revealing her doubts about herself and her future. Williams replied, sending the poem and adding, comfortingly:

> you won't be a mediocre person.. not if your heart and mind accustom themselves to the high things... no, not even when you think you are. As of course you will think. [...] Do write to me occasionally if you feel inclined. Why should I have to wait till heaven to know how life treats you?[527]

Meanwhile, despite already having a novel and a play in progress, he was working on a third masque, to complete the mystical trilogy he had outlined to Phyllis the previous year. *The Masque of the Termination of Copyright* would show the freeing of the Book from all earthly ties when its copyright expired, fifty years after the author's death. It would then become 'one with thought': a part of all human culture, rather than the intellectual property of an individual. Williams imagined this as a parallel to the completion of the mystical quest, expiry of the Book's copyright symbolizing the moment when a soul lets go of worldly ties and merges with the Divine. He planned an elaborate series of scenes—the Council of the Gods, the Place of Dereliction, the Vestibule of Immortality—and proposed that Billy Somervaille should be given the role of Hermes, messenger of the Gods (even though, said Williams, he would be bound to flirt with Phyllis). 'You know the cupboards under the Library shelves?' he asked Phyllis:

> Do the shelves in them take out? And is there any way by which you could squeeze in to one? I'm afraid there wouldn't be room, but [...] I should have liked your arm to appear waving a duster or something and then you to scramble out. [...] Go and look and tell me if your slimness can squeeze in.[528]

Perhaps she thought she could, for after a prelude in which the Gods decide to reprint the Book, Williams wrote a scene in which the messenger of the Gods (called Perigot) seeks the one remaining copy in a horrible run-down second-hand bookshop. Here Phillida, now an oppressed maid-of-all-work, appears first as a hand waving a duster from a cupboard, and then scrambles out. The bookshop is a hellish parody of Amen House, a dusty junkpile of books run by Dorinda, a nagging harridan, and Alexis, a loutish layabout who throws away his money betting on horses. But Perigot unearths the precious Book amidst the rubbish, and the characters wake, as if out of a nightmare, to become again their true selves in Williams's idealized version of Amen House.

Many details are unclear, and the masque was never truly completed. Sombre in tone, and longer than the two earlier masques, it would have been a challenge to produce. Though Williams was loath to admit it, his radiant vision of his workplace was already becoming shadowed by pain and disappointment. He noted on the typescript that 'owing to various hindrances' the masque 'was never presented'.[529] But 'hindrances' was a mild word for traumatic events which were about to put the vision of the masques forever beyond recovery.

★   ★   ★

Thelma Mills was now engaged to be married. She no longer came to lectures, but still often saw Williams over lunch or at the Press. And he was still experimenting with her, using various forms of substitution and what might be called 'magical psychology'. Early in 1930, when she told him she often worried that she was a burden to him, he suggested a procedure:

> What you can do, my absurd child, is to write down on a piece of paper just as soon as you can—
>
>> I am making a fuss about nothing
>> But I am quite right to make a fuss about it.

I am a foolish little brat
But I am a child of lucidity.

There you are—and so you are. And put it into an envelope and send it to me;
that will cost you three ha'pence, and serve you right! And every time you
begin to worry—I say, *worry*—about being a burden you had better do it over
again.[530]

Now, in August 1930, he enlisted her help, admitting that he was anxious.
Phyllis was about to take a week's holiday riding in the Sussex countryside.
She was an experienced horsewoman; but Williams felt seriously worried,
and he asked Thelma if, in accordance with the principles of 'substitution',
she would 'hold' the worry for him.[531] She agreed, and he relaxed somewhat.
But, on 5 September,[532] a letter arrived confirming his worst forebodings:

Petworth Cottage Hospital.
My dearest Poet,
Where do you think your Celia is? In bed with a broken leg! And likely to be
in bed for a month unless I'm lucky. Isn't it putrid. I did it jumping & it hurt
like blazes, Urban. [...] The journey here in the springless station bus still
remains vivid in my mind but I'm not now in very real pain tho' rather irrita-
ble & sick about my holiday & worried about my Mater. Everyone has been
so kind but if only it hadn't happened.[533]

In a fever of anxiety Williams dropped his work and caught a train to
Petworth, some 35 miles away. But he was not the only person from the
Press to be hurrying down there. At some point—perhaps on his journey,
perhaps actually in the hospital—he encountered a flustered Gerry Hopkins.
And Hopkins, seeing that the game was up, confessed that for some time
past he and Phyllis had, in a fully physical sense, been lovers.[534]

12

Novels and the Poetic Mind

In *The Silver Stair*, written twenty years earlier, Williams had foreseen that love would be crucified. His *Romantic Theology* had elaborated: 'There are few lovers [in whom] there is not something akin to Judas and the abyss.'[535] It was true of him; it was true of Phyllis. He had betrayed Michal by loving Phyllis. Now Phyllis had betrayed him by her affair with Gerry—thick-skinned, well-off, cynical, *married* Gerry Hopkins. It was a shattering blow. It shook to the foundations his determination to idealize Phyllis, to see her as bearer of the Grail. He returned to London in turmoil.

Naturally he had assumed that Phyllis would eventually marry—some commonplace young man like Billy Somervaille, with whom she would lead an ordinary life, leaving their own enchanted territory of poetry and mysticism untouched. But Gerry Hopkins! His understanding of Phyllis was changed. A scrap of Shakespearian dialogue ran obsessively in his head: 'What hath she done, Prince, that can shame our mothers?'—'Nothing at all, unless that this were she.'

Most men would have cursed, and tried to get over their feelings. But it was not in Williams's nature to think that his most intense experiences could be mistaken. Rather, those experiences remained true, alongside whatever came later. Life's paradoxes must be lived. It *was* she, and it was *not* she. Those glimpses of Phyllis as an image of divine perfection—'radiating the light out of which God made [her]'—remained true. That—her heavenly aspect—was Celia. And Celia remained unchanged, whatever Phyllida (the practical, worldly aspect of Phyllis) might get up to in the mundane world—at Amen House, in her flat at Upper Bedford Place, wherever.

As for Phyllis, she found it a relief to have the air cleared; but she was determined to go on being Celia. After a few weeks in hospital—it was a complicated fracture—she wrote, with cheerful incoherence of metaphor:

> Darling Urban, [...] I'm quite sure my broken leg has washed away any misunderstandings we may have had—not that any of this really mattered, but if it can make you feel a little of how much I need you I shan't altogether regret the tiresome weeks. I did feel yesterday that you believed a little that I do love you.[536]

Williams must have been in a dreadful state when he arrived home that first day. Michal had perhaps already guessed the essentials of the situation. It became increasingly difficult to keep the secret. 'I don't know what Michal makes of it all', he told Phyllis:

> there are moments when I feel I must speak of it. But more when I feel as if it had all been handed to me, so to speak, in a parcel—'do what you will, only be happy. And let it rest there; Why drag it into talk?' [...] It is months and months since any kind of married intercourse took place—O ages. And I am not at all certain that this is not done for me. On the other hand, she may think my nature is *so*, and that's that. Only certainly my loss of appetite and the rest was put down to your being away.[537]

Evidently a painful charade was in progress. Sometime in the first few weeks Williams told Phyllis that Michal had turned down an invitation to join him in some excursion, 'because she thought it would be much better for me "to have a good tramp in Sussex"'. Apparently visits to Petworth were being rationalized as country walks. But also, 'on Saturday morning I was charged [by Michal], if you had written again, to go at once, not to come home but to go straight on. [...] It seemed to me—all things considered—a noble effort of agape's.'[538] At last, on 16 November, the truth was—more or less—acknowledged, when:

> there was a mild *éclaircissment* at home, in which, for the first time, in so many words, (or almost so many) I...what word can I use? I let it be clear that I loved and did love you. [...] The conversation was a little distressed but very amicable. Things seem to have returned to their normal life now, curiously enough. But wisely, too, for—in spite of Michal's impulses of goodwill—affairs at home can't be altered; and it would do no human being any good if they could be.[539]

Michal must long have sensed that something was wrong. If she had been in any doubt, she knew now. Over the following weeks *agape*—generous, unselfish love—was perhaps not her only response. Michal had a powerful temper. Some of her (perfectly natural, but less positive) reactions are suggested by comments made long afterwards: 'However much Charles seven year itch with the virgin tart masqueraded as love in excelsis, it was as sordid and unhealthy as are all such affairs. It lost him my love for ever, & my respect & I very much loathed being used as the inhabitant of a brothel which was my humiliating lot for years[.]'[540] As for Phyllis, 'The woman is a nasty bit of work.' No doubt all this and more was said. It also inconveniently slipped out that Charles had left Waite's Order quite some time before: 'He had not told me & I didnt know', Michal recalled, 'till Henry [Lee] made some reference to it. Charles didn't seem pleased about Henry's enquiry[,] probably it was cloak for his frequent absences at [sic] home & the matter was never mentioned again.'[541] Life in the Hampstead flat must have been wretched. Michael, now eight years old, must have been aware of the tension; he may have seen tears and arguments. Thelma Mills recalled that around 1931, Michael had a 'breakdown' and that after this, at times of stress, he would retreat into a deep depression.[542] Perhaps this was connected with the trouble over Phyllis.

Phyllis and Charles wrote to one another almost daily. 'O my dear', Williams wrote, 'I do so want the sight of you again. I feel that if I were half a man I should throw everything to the winds, and come and live in Petworth, so as to see you for two minutes every day.'[543] He took precautions at Amen House. 'I have', he told her, 'swept all the letters and private papers out of your drawer into a large envelope—which shall go in the safe or somewhere. [...] I don't like the idea of God knows who poking about there.'[544] He tried to be understanding about her involvement with Hopkins: 'I hadn't—and I blame myself a little—realized your need of and relation with him, anyhow not entirely', he wrote awkwardly. Nonetheless things were difficult, at Amen House as well as at the hospital:

GH [wrote Williams] preferred not to speak of anything more than the normal friendship, since he will—in that sense—keep me at arm's length and forget the past, and pretend we are equally concerned with a distressed invalid. [...] He told me on Tuesday morning that he thought of coming, and I assented with goodwill. But it was impossible, just impossible, for me to go down on Wednesday and ask him how long and when he was coming. [...] Alexis is a dear, and we are great friends, but we cannot occupy the same space at the same time—in any sense.[545]

But there were jealousies and recriminations. 'My dearest Urban', wrote Phyllis, in answer to some diatribe:

> Your letter has upset me dreadfully. [...] I *daren't* read it again or I shall be really ill. Oh God you can talk about & *lap* up everything you can about my 'peculiar needs' for other people but nothing under heaven or earth will make you believe my need for you. You *must* come & see me[.][546]

And again, 'Oh no, Mr Williams, you're wrong on one point, & I feel it an obligation to put you right. Wherever Mr Hopkins was last Saturday, he was not with me—so chase that little bee out of your bonnet & send it buzzing somewhere else.'[547]

★ ★ ★

Yet—astonishingly and typically—Williams continued to write fiction. In early summer he had started another metaphysical thriller, *Many Dimensions*, about a miraculous Stone, once the centrepiece of King Solomon's crown, which turns up in modern London. The Stone, which has the four Hebrew characters of the Tetragrammaton or holy name of God within it, has come into the possession of arch-villain Sir Giles Tumulty. It is infinitely divisible—it can be split without ever becoming smaller—and it can heal all diseases and allow instantaneous travel through time and space. It is also 'the end of desire'—a physical embodiment of the mystical goal of union with God. And Sir Giles intends to exploit and abuse it. Williams had described such a stone in 'Lilith', a poem in *Heroes and Kings*, where Solomon wears a ring with a stone wherein 'moved, flamelike, interwoven, uttering song, / the four intelligible letters'. The idea came from Waite's *Secret Doctrine in Israel*, where a similar stone 'was inscribed with the Divine Name before it was cast into the abyss'.[548]

Many Dimensions follows the same pattern as the previous novel, *War in Heaven*: a sacred object appears in the world; good and bad people fight over it and debate its meaning; at last evil is defeated, and the object—stone or grail—vanishes, whilst a good character who has identified with it dies in a kind of mystical union. The new novel, however, showed better construction and more credible characters than *War in Heaven*. Its treatment of time-travel may have been inspired by discussions in Lee's group of J. W. Dunne's *An Experiment with Time*, which had caused a sensation in 1927 (Lee later wrote a long article on Dunne in a co-Masonic journal).[549] Dunne's book argued for a multi-dimensional view of time and claimed that all of time—past, present, and future—is accessible to the mind, especially in sleep, and that dreams consist of a mixture of all three.

The Stone's extraordinary properties give ample scope for experiments by the monstrous Tumulty. To see if it can cheat death, he arranges for a condemned man at Wandsworth prison to grasp it during his execution by hanging (the man survives, horribly alive with a broken neck); and he induces a laboratory assistant, Pondon, to wish himself back into the previous day (Pondon vanishes, becoming trapped in a recurring time-loop where he keeps reaching the moment of his wish and going back again). *Many Dimensions* is the first fantasy novel to take speculations about time-travel significantly further than Wells's *The Time Machine*. No previous fiction had considered the possibility of becoming trapped in a 'loop' like Pondon's, and other passages raise still more complex problems, as when a character says, 'Supposing I project myself an hour forward and find I'm sitting in this room—and then suppose I return to the present and go to my bedroom and have myself locked in for two hours, say, how can I be doing what I saw myself doing?'[550] Tumulty tries to send himself forwards in time by ten minutes and is frustrated to find that he cannot tell whether or not anything unusual has happened, since he seems to have 'memories' of the intervening minutes, real or otherwise. Such problems would be explored a decade later by science-fiction writers such as Richard Matheson and Robert A. Heinlein, but Williams got there first. Nor does the originality end there. The quest of the novel's protagonists is not to use the Stone for power, but to rid the world of this troublesome transcendent object; at one point Arglay considers 'wishing himself into the heart of Vesuvius' with the Stone in order to destroy it. Both ideas would reappear in Tolkien's *The Lord of the Rings*.

For Williams, however, the novel's most important feature was its heroine, Chloe Burnett, whom he intended as a portrait of Phyllis. Chloe works as secretary to Lord Arglay, the Chief Justice of England—a paternalistic philosopher who resembles an idealized blend of Milford and Williams himself. She is efficient, intelligent, 'rather good-looking [and] avid of facts and ideas'.[551] She is naturally sensitive and just. Without being consciously religious, she has an immediate and spontaneous affinity with the Stone. 'You have a hint of the holy letters on your forehead', the Hajji (a Persian mystic) tells her.[552] She is a natural mystic, and as the novel progresses she becomes increasingly identified with the Stone. Eventually she becomes the pathway for its passage out of the world altogether.

Williams completed *Many Dimensions* during Phyllis's first two weeks in hospital. It might seem odd that he was able to write at a time of such stress, but that was precisely the point: it was in writing that he felt closest to Phyllis, that he could most firmly engage her attention, and to some extent control how she should see herself. He had discussed the novel with her for months, and now bowed to her wishes by killing off Sir Giles. A note dated 10 September 1930 reads: 'Pursuing laboriously the contract your Divinity established in the Tube train, [...] I have the honour to report that last night between twelve and one, [...] with some consciousness of inadequacy owing to your Serene Loveliness's unavoidable and multitudinous absence, I killed Sir Giles Tumulty.'[553] Tumulty, rashly wishing to 'get at' the stone whilst holding one of its types, is utterly destroyed: he is found 'twisted in every limb, and pierced and burnt all over as if by innumerable needle-points of fire'.[554] Williams sent Phyllis passages from the novel, with apologies: 'Chloe—I *am* sorry about the name—but it wasn't done on purpose, and only you and I will know.'[555] Completing it, he involved her in a small ritual to mark the occasion, asking her to copy out at once: 'On the 14th of September, in accordance with a vow and a compact, the brother of my [lovely *deleted*] imagination completed *Many Dimensions* without altering Chloe Burnett and my Lord Arglay.'[556]

He offered the novel to Gollancz, who replied, 'I am most eager to see *Many Dimensions* [...] In fact, I itch for it, so don't delay a moment!'[557] It appeared in January 1931.

★   ★   ★

The doctors had pronounced Phyllis's leg 'a beautiful set'.[558] But there were complications. It did not set properly and the pain continued. She was transferred urgently to the Westminster Hospital, the leg was reset, and she stayed until the end of October.[559] The hospital was near Amen House, so new difficulties arose. Visiting Phyllis, Williams might bump into Hopkins. But if he stayed away and Hopkins failed to visit, Phyllis, bored and lonely, would reproach him:

> Oh dear, oh dear, *Why* didn't you come. Really, if I didn't love you very much I should be furious. 40 undisturbed minutes you might have had. [...] Why in the names of all the gods of Greece didn't you say to G.H. 'if & at what time do you visit Phyllida?' [...] Instead of which you box yourself up in your room & do no good to any living person [...] I could shake you.[560]

He tried to aid Phyllis's recovery by magical means. Early in her stay at the Westminster he told her, 'I abandoned an instinct to masturbate last night so that I might offer the strength to you in God. And that, dear Celia, was that.'[561] There could be no clearer indication that he viewed sexual energy as a force that could be transmuted for chosen purposes. Phyllis also recalled that Williams 'tried something [. . .] when I was in hospital. I remember him telling me that he'd walked round and round the hospital.'[562] Sure enough, Williams's letter continues:

> I should add, knowing what Colin calls 'my interest in—' all sorts of things I oughtn't to be interested in, magic and all that, that I was very careful to go round *with* and not against the sun. Not *widdershins*, you know. It is good to obey the rituals in small things as in great—when you happen to know the rituals.

His circling of the building had the intention of directing energy towards Phyllis's healing. The letter continues placidly, 'What we really want is intelligent suggestions for the *World's Classics* next year.'[563] Phyllis told Williams she was plagued by bad dreams, and for a short time he was able to stop them by simply saying, 'You won't dream.'[564] And he continued her magical education, telling her:

> We are publishing a badly printed [. . .] but rather amusing book by Wallis Budge on *Amulets and Superstitions* which has some curious bits of information in. As it is 30/- nobody much will buy it, but there again you might like to look through it sometime. It has a chart of the sephirotic Tree of which I have talked to you (Only too much!).[565]

There is also one episode which is mysterious in every way. Involving the Stone, it must be connected with *Many Dimensions*—or with the poem 'Lilith', which had appeared the previous year. All we have is an undated letter from Williams:

> My dearest Life,
> Perhaps I mightn't have written *quite* as soon if I hadn't wanted to ask you to do something for me; and will you keep the change, which ought to be 5/-, for doing it?
>   Will you, if you have an opportunity, find a space between two seconds, and slip into the Stone of Suleiman Ben Daood, King in Jerusalem? If you take the first turning on the right there—but whether that is past, present or future I'm not clear, or all or none—you will, I think, find three tabernacles such as Peter wanted to build on the Mount of Transfiguration [. . .] And in them you may,

or may not, find three women living—O but living!—whose names you may know instinctively. Will you go to each of them in turn and say: 'He you know sends you a crown if you will take it,' and lay five silver shillings at her feet, and see if she has anything to say, or any sign to send. And then go to the next and do it again. If they all keep theirs, why, that will use up this pound note, which is why it is sent. But if any or all refuse—and if one does, they all will, then I will lend it to you yourself for ever and ever, but I will not give it to you. For I gave it to them this morning before I woke, and it is *corban*, devoted to the Lord. And if you ask me why I choose to do it in this way *now*, I shall say it is for a firmness and a resistance to temptation and a refusal of unbelief.

And the signs they will send, if they send, of their will, are that Celia sends me a kiss of the Evangel, and Phillida a line of verse murmured in my ear, and Circassia – I am afraid that Circassia would have to sit on my knee and be beaten. But contrariwise I shan't speak of the signs, and the crowns are theirs or yours for ever.[566]

This may be merely an elaborate joke. But it appears also to be a visualization exercise: Phyllis is to envisage herself entering the Stone and following a path inside it, to encounter three aspects of herself (as named by Williams) and make offerings; a 'crown' was five shillings—a quarter of a pound. The 'signs' expected are the usual ones, partly erotic, associated by Williams with the different facets of his beloved. But the notion that the women might have 'something to say' suggests an exercise in divination or mediumship. That Williams 'gave it to them this morning before [he] woke' perhaps indicates that the exercise began as a dream. 'Corban' is Hebrew, from Mark 7:11, meaning 'given to God'—particularly in fulfilment of a vow. There was a tradition, in magical groups descended from the Golden Dawn, of male magicians using female partners as mediums, or for travel on the 'astral plane'. Was Williams doing something similar?

In late October Phyllis left hospital and went to a farm near Petworth, to convalesce, her spirits undamped as ever. She was also determined to maintain her hold on Williams, displaying an attractive jealousy to keep him in line:

I will tell you what you may do. [...] You may walk with who you like anywhere you like but not thro' Clapham Park & not up Balham Hill & *not* to Euston & above all not in taxis, you may give them what you want of your mind you like but not just how & just where you talked with me. [...] When I am thoroughly used to the idea (not the reality of course!) of your walking about London with other persons of my sex (curse them all), then I will begin to consider the idea of your walks with them in the particular parts that I consider mine.[567]

Williams tried to be playful in return, but soon faltered:

> it isn't fair that the roads of South London should be sealed to my companions,
> if—or rather when—I have them. But it would be very hard work to open
> them. O Celia, [...] I think on the whole I am glad I was one of your lovers,
> if only I wasn't still so dreadfully yours.[568]

★ ★ ★

A consolation was his growing friendship with Anne Bradby. Anne was beautiful, blue-eyed, and brilliant. She had a gift for languages, a deep Christian faith, and a strong interest in poetry. Anne had first seen Williams a few months before, when he came, during her last term at Downe House, to lecture on Blake. She had been 'unprepared for the electrifying effect of his lecture: his eloquence, the passion with which he declaimed verse in his Cockney accent, and the characteristic gesture that accompanied moments of special intensity, hands raised in front of him in the shape of a cup.'[569] Even then she had felt some special link with him. 'I remember', she wrote, 'the fury with which I noticed a girl from one of the forms imitating his hands–uplifted gesture'.[570] Their meeting at Aisholt, and the poem Williams had written there for Anne and her friends, had strengthened the bond.

Anne keenly wanted to see more of him, but at the end of the summer she left with her parents for six months in Italy, visiting Rome, Florence, and Assisi. So she exchanged letters with him throughout the journey. When Anne, following her father's Low Church views, mocked 'the clouds of incense' at St Peter's, Williams quoted Chesterton, reminding her that the Roman Church had been good enough for such men as 'Raphael and Racine, [...] Dante and Descartes'.[571] And he was disarmingly open about his own responses. 'I went to see [*Antony and Cleopatra*] last week', he told her, 'and very nearly made a public exhibition of myself by quite abandonedly crying all through the later part.'[572] He recommended Clough's poem *Amours de Voyage* and, when Anne complained about the slow trams and long climb up the hill of St John Lateran in Rome, responded by reflecting on viewpoints, and how—if you were, as he put it, the Lateran Hill—people might:

> see you as houses and trams and a slow climb, and not see in you also the
> image of the Caelian Mount and the Church of Christendom and St Augustine

going out from the monastery upon it to the conversion of the Saxon thanes in yourself. But they, dear mother of the mother of God, will be wrong. It will be there all right.

It was clear that he was not speaking only of the Lateran Hill. And Anne helped him by sending information about Mantua, the setting of his new play *The Chaste Wanton*.

Phyllis had returned to London in early December. Milford, perhaps to allow the emotional temper at Amen House to cool, assigned her to oversee a Christmas display of Oxford books at Bumpus, the London bookshop. But the shop was chilly in the wrong sense, and Phyllis was not one to let her love-life languish. 'There is nothing to do here', she wrote to Williams on Bumpus letterhead:

> & we do it in an atmosphere compared with which the North Pole must be warm. [...] I do hope you can get tickets for Wednesday. Perhaps you could find me up here & we could have food together. Oh God, what a life this is, isn't it? Why on earth did I have to come here.
> My love
> Celia.[573]

She continued to balance neatly between humble disciple and charming flirt:

> Dearest Urban,
> Now that I'm beginning to dance and move about again it feels almost as though my body were rising from the grave & I'm so afraid of it running away with my mind & soul. But I do enjoy reading the History of Educational Thought, and I do think about God. But I don't think so very faithfully now of Billie in Java. Am I fickle dearest Urban?[574]

Billy Somervaille had passed his exams and gone to work for an oil company in Java.

When Phyllis received a copy of *Many Dimensions* she held back from identification with its innocently mystical heroine:

> it's a beautiful and imposing book [but] I can't help wondering whether an outsider will understand the significance of it. I mean why should Chloe do all that? Why should a quite ordinary secretary decide suddenly to believe in God. Isn't that what the reader will ask? [...] The beautiful parts are really lovely & extremely moving & I do think the end of Sir Giles almost too terrifying to read.[575]

This jarred uncomfortably with Williams's view of how she *ought* to be; he apparently suggested methods which might help in her conversion, including, perhaps, repetition of the 'Jesus prayer'. She replied:

> No, I do not think any of the methods you suggest would be likely to have any effect. It is possible the Psycho-Analyst suggestion might bring about a conversion of my sub-conscious self, but I do not think a mere mechanical repetition of a phrase would be likely to affect it. And the chanting idea would not fail to produce aught else but a mere irritation besides which in the present state of affairs I couldn't go on for longer than two or three days.[576]

On publication day, 12 January, Williams sent *Many Dimensions* to Olive Willis, telling her, 'It is one of the books "recommended" by the Book Society this month: and this seems a greater fantasy than anything in the book.'[577]

★   ★   ★

Phyllis returned to work at Amen House early in 1931. Whether or not the affair with Gerry Hopkins continued, we don't know. Her relationship with Williams, however, gradually settled into something like its old pattern—role-playing, private jokes, and punishments included. 'I do want to do all the things you suggest', Phyllis certified in a miniature document, '& to this I put my name & seal on this 27th day of April 1931. If I fail may I take the punishment you will justly mete out Oh my lord. Celia.'[578]

But the tensions of working alongside his rival (not to mention overwork and sleeplessness) led to occasional explosions on Williams's part. And Phyllis knew how to hit back:

> Its all very well isn't it, to be polite and charming in front of Mr. Viner & say *Would* you mind getting me this etc & no doubt Mr Viner will go back to the bindery filled with the thought of your delightful manner to your inferiors BUT would he have been so impressed if you had repeated your efforts of ten minutes ago? [...] I don't think its right that one minute people should rage up & down the Library flinging insulting remarks & the *very next* minute come back & pretend that they are incapable of being impolite, *just because they have an audience*. I may be wrong of course Mr. Williams *I'm* not infallible *I* never did think I couldn't go wrong but [...] I don't like people pretending to be polite when really they have fierce & terrible tempers & get upset at the slightest thing[.][579]

Yet Phyllis was as addicted to the relationship as he was. 'I wish you could believe that I needed you', she told him in another note:

> I have tried these last weeks to make you feel I did—but not very successfully perhaps. [...] Do you think, perhaps, no one wants me without sex, really & truly? I can't believe it. But I believe in you & I'm damned if I'll give the thing up just because *your* [*sic*] occasionally—well, I leave it to you to apply the word & I'm often lazy & disgusting.[580]

It was perhaps now that Williams privately expressed his bitter feelings in a series of harsh epigrams:

> *Do you write poems still? Still. Tell me why.*
> Well, much as beetles quiver as they die.

Or, deeply telling in its revelation of class-insecurity ('van' having the archaic sense of 'forehead'):

> One thought alone, I think, must strike
>   her unscarred, sleepy, golden van;
> one slight regret, one mild dislike –
>   that I am *not* a gentleman.

These are a few of many. The love that had once illuminated his life was now turning it to a waste land. He summed up the position in a bleak sonnet:

> Middle Age
> Why am I peevish? The half-rotten core
>   of a half-eaten apple, here I lie,
> maggots consuming me, and hear no more
>   Love and Intelligence even pass me by.
> To fourth-rate minds a fourth-rate mind I come,
>   and on the whole do no long-lasting harm;
> in my mid-age I find my mental home
>   among the geese that cackle through the farm.
> Kept for old sake's sake, my remembered past
>   stands, a Victorian heirloom, on the shelves
> of a few lives—cracked, not much like to last,
>   and out of fashion with their proper selves.
> This play of images, my thought, means—what?
> That meaning is not worth powder and shot.[581]

* * *

He was still lecturing on two evenings per week. In the spring and summer of
1931 he taught at the City Literary Institute (City Lit) in Holborn and the
Evening Institute in Tooting. The lectures were so inspiring that a body of
students now came to both series. Unhappiness, rather than making him intro-
verted and closed-off, led him to become ever more patient, sympathetic, and
open to his students. Literary discussion naturally led to talk about daily life and
problems. Students became friends and several—especially the women, who
were particularly susceptible to his wit and charm—would visit him at Amen
House and be taken for lunch or tea, to discuss difficulties with parents, boy-
friends, money, their career aspirations, or their religious highs and lows.
'C.W.'s young women' became a byword among the staff and some referred to
them as his 'chelas'—a Tibetan word for 'disciples'. And indeed, Williams sometimes addressed Thelma Mills playfully as 'My admired initiate'.[582] He told her:

> The gurus (I read the other day) in India sometimes make their disciples
> sweep out caves with their hair. Aren't you glad I'm not a guru? And yet that
> tradition—not of the hair but of discipleship—has lasted centuries. Its danger
> is that the.. what shall I say? Master, director, may be supposed to be 'better'
> than the postulant or pupil. That's where the Church is wise; it never suggests
> that the priest in confession is 'better' than the penitent.[583]

Thelma worked actively on her spiritual life under Williams's direction. At
one time—date unknown—she practised 'austerities' of some kind, and he
urged restraint:

> I never think a little austerity did anyone any harm; though I incline to suggest
> you should set a time-limit to whatever you decide to try out. Say a month,
> and see how you feel at the end of it—what you feel, rather. And tell me
> precisely what austerity you think of practising.[584]

He gave her small tasks to perform, to encourage awareness: 'I would have
you write a word on a slip of paper each day: what shall we say? *Vigilemus*
(which is to say, let us watch…) So you just put down *Vigilemus*, with the
date against it, each day until you come.' He encouraged her to discover
aspects of the divine within herself. He quoted his 'favourite line' from
Paradise Lost ('And thus the filial Godhead answering spake')—and told her,
'There's no reason why you shouldn't be a small Filial Godhead yourself.'[585]
He set her to memorize this and some neighbouring lines, a dialogue
between God the Father and the Son:

> This I my glory account,
> My exaltation, and my whole delight,

> That thou in me, well pleas'd, declare thy will
> Fulfilled, which to fulfil is all my bliss.

The intention was to help her discover the glory, and fulfilment of the divine will, in herself.

When Thelma was about to get married, he set her both self-examination and penance:

> If you were a member of the Holy Roman Church you would make a special confession before marriage—*not* being, I wonder if you would spend a few minutes deciding what is your worst fault (or—are your worst faults), as clearly and simply as you can, and tell me on Monday. I shall punish you for each—not for myself, this time—but so that you will believe afterwards that these are put wholly away. And then I should like you also to tell me, as clearly and simply as you can, what you want to be and do—in effect, your most firm resolutions. And these I will offer, 'as far as in me lies', to our sacred Lord that night.[586]

The punishment may have been physical: a much later letter (from 1940) threatens, jokingly, to give Thelma 'five on each hand with a cane' for some supposed offence. Thelma seems entirely untroubled: she mentions finding such incidents 'an uproarious joke'.[587] Unlike Phyllis she never responded flirtatiously and there is no sexual element in any of their letters.

Far from finding Williams's instructions oppressive, Thelma felt they gave shape and satisfaction to her inner life. 'He was always aware of the [...] sheer mystery, of the necessity of being, as you might say. If you got joy it was a bonus, but it was your business to find joy, [...] to accept everything with joy.' Also, 'He never stressed Christianity. He never gave impression of making a point or having a message.'[588] He made the spiritual life appear common sense. And he was quite open about his own sufferings. 'I sometimes feel that I am being something of a hypocrite', he wrote, perhaps in 1932:

> If *you* call yourself lazy, what about me? Here are five years of pain, and still the victory is unachieved—partly because the will is not yet converted. You will easily pass me on the Way.[589]

Anne Bradby too became a regular attender at the lectures. Returning from Italy in 1931, she had 'still had no clear idea of what [she] wanted to do'. She confided in Williams, who sympathized, telling her, she recalled, that 'as a young man he had felt the same, and classing himself as a "second-rate sensitive mind not at unity with itself" (Tennyson's description) he wrote:

"There do seem to be an awful lot of us about the world!" '[590] In the autumn Anne enrolled for a course in journalism at King's College, London and moved to a student hostel. And Williams began to hint to her about 'substitution':

> I don't think we have even begun to find out how much we can help one another. I believe that 'Bear one another's burdens' is a truth to which we have only dimly seen the way. I think we are alone, and that those solitudes are yet in communication—in short, I think two opposites are true. But there is laziness and pre-occupation and conceit and selfhood, and these dam the pure stream of Love. But the pure stream is there all right, and infinite. I do think that we can literally plunk all our bothers on some-one else, and take others' in turn. And sometime I will tell you how.[591]

★   ★   ★

Milford had agreed to consider a volume of plays for publication, so early in 1931 Williams submitted *Three Plays*. It was a dubious proposition. None of the plays had been professionally staged. *The Witch* had been a student play at Balham; *Rite of the Passion* had been performed once, at Lee's church; and *The Chaste Wanton*, an Elizabethan-style verse play, had never been performed at all. Milford rejected the book. But Williams persuaded Olive Willis to lobby on his behalf. Surprisingly, Milford gave way—perhaps through a kindly desire to buoy up Williams during a bad period—and in June 1931 *Three Plays* appeared.

The 'plays' were a motley collection, rendered still odder by being interspersed with apparently random poems. Three of these were Arthurian, most likely salvaged from the *King Arthur* collection that Williams had hoped to offer Milford, and the book concluded with 'Epilogue in Somerset: A Song of the Myths'—the poem he had written for Anne Bradby and friends at Aisholt.

He told Olive Willis that the book was 'Something of a mixture, but all in the Higher Unity'.[592] It may have seemed a bizarre ragbag, but in Williams's mind, which was nothing if not systematic, it was all perfectly coherent. 'Taliessin's Song of the Myths' depicts the disordered state of Logres (the mythic Britain) before King Arthur establishes order; it introduces *The Witch*, a play about pure evil. In 'Taliessin's Song of Byzantion' the bard comes to the court of the Emperor to ask for help (thus symbolizing the turning of the soul to God in prayer); this introduces *The Chaste Wanton*, a play about the beginnings of the Mystical Way. 'Taliessin's Song of the Setting of Galahad in the King's Bed' shows the moment when Galahad, achiever of the Grail, takes Arthur's place—symbolizing transcendence of the secular by the divine: a fitting prelude to *The Rite of the Passion*, portraying the redemption of humanity in the death and resurrection of Christ as Love. The book's 'Epilogue', 'A Song of the Myths', depicts a moment of bliss and beatitude in ordinary life, when loved friends are together in peace—'a place of Mystery, Love's Hierusalem, [...] Within an English garden'. It was a structure which made sense in Williams's personal mythology, where everything was timeless, and the patterns of Arthurian legend could embrace essential moments from history, the Bible, or personal life. But no reader could have made these connections. A pattern was there, but it was not being communicated.

Moreover, *Three Plays* caused tension at Amen House. *The Chaste Wanton* was, transparently, about Charles and Phyllis. It concerns the love between an unhappy duchess and a wandering alchemist who teaches her about the mystical way of transformation through 'toil, / attention, adoration, practice of love', before dying a tragic death. For those who knew about Williams and Phyllis, it must have seemed intolerably self-indulgent (everyone at Amen House, Williams told Phyllis, 'takes it for granted' that the play is about their relationship).[593] And Williams included a note which, in the light of recent events, certainly bore more than one interpretation: 'The title of *The Chaste Wanton* is due, I believe, to Mr. Gerard Hopkins, who dropped it casually in conversation as possible for a mock-Elizabethan play. But, before the amusement was begun, it or I had turned serious, and the title enlarged its meaning beyond its original scope.' Indeed. As for Michal, 'I thought both "Witch" and "Wanton" poor when I read them long ago', she wrote later, '& was sorry they were ever published.'[594] Perhaps it was *The Chaste Wanton* that suggested her own succinct title for Phyllis: 'the virgin tart'.[595]

Fred Page was deeply critical, though exactly what he said is unknown. The fraught state of Williams's nerves can be judged from the anxious, over-vehement tone of his reply:

> Either you have been reading something else and got them mixed, or I haven't written the play I thought I had.
>
> I say then—and I will, for once and with apologies, say it rudely, so that you may rudely contradict—that no-one who had read the C[haste]W[anton] could begin to say your Q.E.D. I say that the Q.E.D. has nothing *whatever* to

do with the play. [...] I say that nowhere, NOWHERE, through it all, do Vincenzo & the Duchess set anything at all above benevolence.[596]

He was comforted by Nicholson and Lee, who, he reported, 'just cried out' with joy and wonder at certain passages.[597] The play was dear to Williams for reasons that had nothing to do with literature, and he would not hear it criticized. By now, however, he was already writing a new novel.

★   ★   ★

Looking from the windows of a country house, saw the head and shoulders of a lion moving through a cornfield. It was known in the neighbourhood that this lion had escaped from a menagerie, and that it had killed a goat. Wondered if I could hit it from the window with my revolver, but decided that the range was too great. Decided to lie up alongside the track in the cornfield, and to wait till the beast repassed. Felt, however, that I should prefer to be armed with something better than a revolver. Went out to try to get a rifle.

The words are not by Williams, though they supplied his new novel with its dominating image, and suggested its title: *The Place of the Lion*. They were written by J. W. Dunne, in *An Experiment With Time*,[598] and are the record of a dream used by Dunne as evidence of precognition. Perhaps they had lodged in Williams's mind from a discussion at Lee's group in or around 1927. Their inner meaning for Williams, however, came from another and more surprising source: music. In June 1930 he attended a concert at the house of Hubert Foss, and—'one-eared' or not—had been moved to write a poem afterwards:

> How lovely music is!
> All the fair animals of the forest came
> running before a flame.
> There was a fire in the forest; this
> nor saw I nor felt –
> but herd by herd, company by company,
> beautiful things broke audibly:
> the fair birds flew,
> the fair beasts poured forth leaping in me,
> towards the temporal hut wherein my heart had dwelt.
> Hastily it withdrew,
> fearing the overthrow of walls and roof,
> hastily aloof.
> All in a wonder, a grace of sound,
> wild and ordered, fierce and controlled,

broke the quick rushing movement around.
I was rapt to behold
the lives, the forest lives, the lives of my life,
forgetting their strife,
surge towards the hut that was once a heart; but O
as it shook to its overthrow,
all stayed, all vanished, all ceased.
Bird and beast,
diverse multitudinous lives that came
hurrying, hurrying, hurrying from the flame
in the forest beyond my heart,
all that my thought spied
in the great incantation, the magical art,
vanished; the music died.[599]

The music suggested to Williams the liberation of primal energies—animal, glorious, and archetypal. It coalesced with the image of the escaped lion in the cornfield to provide the theme of his next novel, which would deal with the breaking through of archetypal energies into the world, revealing themselves first as animals: as *the* ultimate and original lion, pattern for all existing lions; as the archetypal and perfect butterfly; and so on—culminating in an unquenchable fire which will go out only when the magic that created it, and released uncontrolled archetypal energies, can be reversed. The crisis has been caused by a Mr Berringer, who runs a mystical 'Study Group' in the village. He has developed a practice of meditating on the archetypes (or Platonic forms, or underlying energies, or ideas, or angelical powers, or Celestials—they are never given a definitive name) through which the world comes into existence. His meditations have somehow made a kind of breach or tear in the fabric of reality, so that these fundamental spiritual powers are now entering the world, unmediated, and drawing their ordinary counterparts back into themselves. There is a prospect that the world will thus be gradually 'uncreated'—sucked back into the original spiritual energies from which it was made. The world is saved, of course, by the novel's protagonist, Anthony Durrant; but not before his intellectual girlfriend, the medievalist Damaris Tighe, has learnt by experience that the Platonic archetypes on which she has been complacently writing a thesis are real and terrifying forces, not quaint, outdated fancies.

The novel, Williams's most ambitious so far, a remarkable experiment in purposeful fantasy, is only partially successful. The characters are thin and there are passages where the narrative is hard to follow. *The Place of the Lion* is among his most ambitious works, but its execution lets it down. Or so it appears now. But for some readers of Williams's own generation, the book was life-changing. Many of those who read it in the 1930s and 1940s regarded it as his best, a novel which brought them illumination and altered the way they saw the world. Certainly Williams was doing something unique in the fiction of his time, dramatizing ideas drawn from Neoplatonism and the Kabbala. But the novel was timely. In 1931 the notion of apocalyptic energies threatening the destruction of the world was not mere fantasy: something very like it was really happening. Economic depression had struck two years previously; in Italy Mussolini had established a dictatorship; in Germany democracy had broken down and the government ruled by decree, with Hitler's National Socialist Party the second-largest in Parliament. In Stalin's Russia, collectivization was beginning, with mass deportations and executions. Everywhere there was a sense that events were out of control and terrifying forces rising to the surface. Anthony Durrant shares the feeling of many at the time, sensing that:

> he existed unhappily between two states of knowledge, between the world around him, the pleasant ordinary world in which one laughed at or discussed ideas, and a looming unseen world where ideas—or something, something living and terrible, passed on its own business, overthrowing minds, wrecking lives, and scattering destruction as it went.[600]

The novel went to Gollancz and was published in September 1931.

The notion that *everything* Williams wrote was about him and Phyllis had now taken firm root at Amen House. 'It will disgust you', he told Phyllis, 'to know that [Milford] thinks Damaris is you, and when I denied it he said there were a number of small traits which he was certain were you. I hope—and think—he is wrong. You weren't meant to be there at all.'[601]

★   ★   ★

In June the students at Downe House performed his play *A Myth of Shakespeare*: he took Michal to see it, and he told Olive, 'How lovely and moving it all was – the place, and the music and the girls and the dancing and the *Myth* and Himself. [. . .] It was a most exquisite business.'[602] In July a letter came from Professor Lewis Chase at Duke University, North Carolina. Chase wanted to include Williams's poems in a course he was planning, and asked about his early life and influences. Williams replied with a fascinating autobiographical letter:

I grew up in an English lower middle class household, and that meant (for me) two things (i) that literature and such things were a normally accepted part of life—that 'culture' (to use a dubious word) and history and so on were assumed to be a natural background [...] But it meant (ii) that there was never enough money, and that our family existed always on the edge of... as it never quite happened I don't know what, but some kind of imagined destruction.

As for my early reading, it was large and formless. My father encouraged me to read everything, and any lack was due to circumstances—not to prejudice [...] My father had a very strong feeling for the Jewish tradition—and to some extent he passed this on to me, though I was brought up just a straightforward Anglican.

There have been, I think, three imaginative shocks in my life. (1)—I don't know about chronologically—some sort of distinction of 'eternity' from 'ever-lastingness', and the notion of eternity as being the same thing as the existence of God: not a quality of, but the being of, perfection. (2) A profound intellectual sense—when I was about 21—that the relationship of romantic love *is* (not like, but *is*) the same thing as Christianity. (I don't mean that it is a good substitute, there are too many dangers.) You will find that a good deal of *Conformity* and *Divorce* is occupied with this idea. (3) A later intense realization of this, with an even greater sense of the profound and all but eternal union possible between human beings now; and of the awful capacities and graces that exist in Love. Also of the perfectly hellish capacities of our own 'unredeemed' nature.

In short, I should say (roughly, and possibly wrongly) that all my work was concerned (a) with the discovery of the nature of eternity, (b) with its action upon human beings, (c) with the dereliction of human beings in their perversion of this eternity. [...]

Ought I to say anything else? Physically I have always been most maddeningly hampered (a) by short sight (b) by a nervous trouble which a childish illness left with me; and both these things have interfered with a proper apprehension of the external world.[603]

Again, the unspecified 'nervous trouble' remains a mystery.

He was working on a new book of criticism, *The English Poetic Mind*,[604] as a follow-up to *Poetry at Present*. But it was not a firm commission. Sending part of the text in late September, he wrote anxiously to Kenneth Sisam, Assistant Secretary to the OUP:

Do take it if you can, because I don't want to be driven back *entirely* upon novels, which are much more paying. And if you would make them pay me as

much as ever they can now in advance and if you would tell me sometime
how much that would be—you would save a distracted head and a slightly-
disturbed household.[605]

He received £50, and used the book's draft text for his autumn lectures
both at the City Lit and at Tooting. Anne Bradby went regularly to both
series: so much was spontaneous that the 'same' lecture was not really the
same; and anyway, she simply wanted to see him. Often they met at the Tube
station and went together.[606]

The lectures must have had a particular intensity, for Williams's new critical study was also an attempt at making sense of the disaster which had
overtaken his personal life. Published by the Clarendon Press in 1932, *The
English Poetic Mind* was brilliant and deeply personal. Williams announced at
the outset that his object was to explore the turning point of Shakespeare's
Troilus and Cressida: the moment when Troilus realizes that Cressida has
betrayed him ('...Nothing at all, unless that this were she'). This was, of
course, the central trauma of his own recent life: the betrayal of his faith in
Phyllis. But Williams argued that some such moment—a point when the
seemingly impossible happens, a 'time when poetry imagines to itself a crisis
of utter overthrow and desolation',[607] was an experience *necessary* to poetry.
Those poets who could confront such a trauma in all its disorienting horror
went on to achieve greatness, and with it a new depth and serenity. Others
approached it and shied away, failing in the ultimate task.

It was an attempt to turn his own emotional trauma into a meaningful
ordeal, a poetic dark night of the soul from which he might emerge a better
poet. But Williams conducted the argument brilliantly. He found such emotional ordeals in Wordsworth's *Prelude*, at the point where the poet's beloved
England declares war on his equally beloved revolutionary France, producing a dreadful clash of loyalties. Another was the moment of inner crisis
described by Milton in *Paradise Lost*, when Satan lands on 'Niphates' top'
and, experiencing the hell within himself, pauses in his destructive mission,
wondering whether he should repent.

Williams gives Tennyson as an example of a poet who loses his nerve.
Lancelot, in the *Idylls of the King*, felt (Williams paraphrases) that 'he ought
not to love Guinevere, but he felt that all that was good in him rose from
that love, so that when he tries to separate the two moralities he goes mad,
but in his madness he beholds the Grail'.[608] But Tennyson shies away from
the horrific vision of sin and virtue *as one*, and makes Arthur simply deny it:

'Thou errest, Lancelot'. Tennyson fails the test. The depths of psychological and spiritual reality are too shocking for him to face.

As an investigation into poetic psychology, albeit based in Williams's own obsessions, all this is fascinating. But Williams makes it clear (paradoxically, in a book that emerged from a personal crisis) that he is not really concerned with the personal lives or beliefs of poets. The crisis, as it interests him, takes place *in poetry*. Criticism, he says, should 'explain poetry by poetry [...] because poetry is a thing *sui generis*'.[609] A poet's value lies, he says, 'in, and only in, the poems he writes—and not in what he means by them'.[610] Williams sweeps away all considerations of the poet's biography and intentions. In poems, it is poetry that speaks; and what does it speak about? It speaks about poetry.

In his insistence on the self-referential nature of poetry, Williams anticipates both Roland Barthes and Jacques Derrida. Yet he does so without the negative and destructive implications for meaning which those authors often convey. This is because he assumes that it is poetry itself which speaks; and he hints that poetry in the full sense may be the Holy Spirit. He does not argue these ideas out, step by step. He simply assumes them and applies them. *The English Poetic Mind* is a deeply difficult book; and it anticipates, sporadically and impressionistically, much of the literary theory which would emerge later in the twentieth century. Naturally it went unappreciated at the time. There were few reviews. The *Times Literary Supplement* had little idea of what Williams was talking about, and seemed frightened by the book's intensity, warning that: 'There is danger [...] in such insistence upon the essence and core of all, lest a kind of mental paralysis, an aesthetic "complex", may establish its dominion over us.'[611] It was left for Geoffrey Hill, in his 2005 Empson Lectures at Cambridge, to rediscover *The English Poetic Mind*, calling Williams 'a great critic' and the book itself a 'critical masterpiece'.[612]

★   ★   ★

Before Williams finished *The English Poetic Mind* he was already writing a new novel, *The Greater Trumps*, which would be about the tarot. Today, tarot cards are a familiar feature of life. In the 1930s they were much less known, though Eliot's *The Waste Land* had satirically drawn attention to them with Madame Sosostris and her 'wicked pack of cards'.

Exactly what Williams thought about the tarot, and how much he knew of its history, is unknown, since apart from *The Greater Trumps* he wrote nothing about it. But tarot cards featured in many of Waite's Rosicrucian rituals, where large hand-painted tarot trumps were displayed at key moments. Waite himself had written *The Pictorial Key to the Tarot* in 1911, and the artist Pamela Colman Smith had designed a pack to his precise specifications: published in 1910, it is available today as the 'Rider Waite' tarot deck.

One tarot pack owned by Charles Williams still exists, in private hands. It is the 'Marseille' tarot, the most traditional tarot generally available. With it is a small copy, bound in grey card, of Waite's *Key to the Tarot*, which was normally supplied with the 'Rider Waite' pack. This suggests that he once possessed that also—as one would expect of someone who belonged to the Fellowship of the Rosy Cross. Williams would also have been familiar with Waite's lecture to members of his Order—'The Tarot and the Rosy Cross'.[613] As a standard component of Golden Dawn lore, the tarot may well have been discussed also at Lee's Sunday evenings. Indeed, as if in a curious private joke, a central character of *The Greater Trumps* is called Henry Lee.

The Greater Trumps returns to the formula that had underpinned *War in Heaven* and *Many Dimensions*, in which an object of spiritual power is discovered, fought over, and finally, through the agency of a spiritually advanced person, vanishes from the world. In the new novel this object is the archetypal tarot—or rather two tarots. One is a mystical table on which seventy-eight miniature golden figures, representing the trumps and suit cards, perpetually dance, their movements corresponding to the perpetually changing balance of forces governing the cosmos. The other is the original tarot 'pack'—actually a set of hand-painted papyrus leaves, made in ancient Egypt and lost for aeons, from which all other packs are descended. The papyrus leaves have been separated from the table and its dancing figures for thousands of years, and it is believed that anyone who can bring them together once more will gain immense power.

Naturally, the components come within striking distance of each other soon after the novel opens. The papyrus leaves are inherited as part of a collection of playing cards by Lothair Coningsby, a petulant and self-centred elderly man, whose daughter Nancy is engaged to Henry Lee, a young barrister of gypsy descent. Henry's grandfather, Aaron Lee, happens, secretly, to be the hereditary custodian of the sacred table with its perpetually dancing tarot figures. Recognizing the cards in his future father-in-law's collection,

Henry Lee invites the Coningsbys for Christmas to the country house where Aaron Lee keeps the table and its dancers in a secret room. His intention is to persuade Lothair Coningsby to hand over the cards; and if he refuses, to murder him by magical means and take them.

The ingredients for a straightforward thriller are thus in place. But the novel's focus is not on the (rather silly) adventure story, but on the symbolism and meanings of the tarot, and how these relate to the inner states of the characters. We see all four suits of cards used magically to create the material elements to which they relate—most vividly when Henry attempts magical murder by using the court-cards of staves and cups (corresponding to air and water) to summon a blizzard in which he intends Lothair, who is out walking, to die of exposure.

The characters, too, are identified with cards—in this case the trumps. Lothair Coningsby, for example, who thinks himself the embodiment of solid good sense, is by profession a Warden in Lunacy (Williams has the title slightly wrong: it should be Master of Lunacy), a legal functionary who administered the affairs of mentally incapacitated people. The joke is that Lothair, a narrow-minded and spiritually obtuse curmudgeon, is clearly the Fool. His sister, the quiet but profoundly loving mystic Sybil, is the Empress; and so on. But as the novel progresses, each character experiences the nature of many cards. Henry Lee, seeing his overweening ambitions come to nothing, temporarily *becomes* the falling Tower of the tarot. Several characters, at times of painful suspense, become the Hanged Man. Likewise with the novel's external settings. A car driving out of London becomes the Chariot; a policeman directing traffic is seen momentarily as the Emperor.

Superficially little more than a lightweight thriller, *The Greater Trumps* is really a work of immense complexity, as its characters and episodes display the ever-changing patterns—the dance—of the tarot symbolism. And beyond its use of individual cards there are visionary passages: meditations on the elements; or a panorama, from the tarot chamber, of the world with its landscapes, human populations and armies, rivers, oceans, and spiritual movements all performing the endless dance which the tarot reflects. Williams could hardly have written all this without deep meditation on the tarot and its symbolism. Yet we know nothing of the work he must have done: not even whether it was done with Waite's organization, with Lee's group, or on his own initiative. The only trace is the novel itself.

His letters say little about the composition of *The Greater Trumps*, perhaps because Phyllis does not feature (the heroine Nancy in no way resembles her). But she is not completely absent from the novel. Sending her a copy of the newly published book in April 1932, Williams told her:

> This is really a secret note, which is why it is written so small, and between to-day and to-morrow, and the sweetness of your back and the roundness of your ears, and the way they offered themselves for kissing, and the golden top of your head when it turned itself to the wall. [...] Shall we put away all thought of any but you in my Trumps, and shall we say—as between us—that it, especially page 243 (but don't look at it till you come to it), is yours, because there is time enough to do what we choose to do. [...] the gladness I have to think that you are in my trumps. For the soul of it is more like you than Chloe's even (though she was nice, our Chloe).[614]

The page he mentions describes Nancy, reconciled in love with Henry, at the moment when the couple undertake their magical work of calming the snowstorm:

> She stood above the world, and her outstretched and downturned palms felt the shocks, and she laughed aloud to see the confusion of clubs striking upward [...] She laughed to feel the blows as once she had laughed and mocked at Henry when his fingers struck her palm; danger itself was turned into some delight of love.[615]

No doubt the passage was meant as 'especially' Phyllis's because it recalled their games of erotic punishment, in which Williams had frequently 'struck her palm' not only with his fingers but with pencils, rulers, and other things. *The Greater Trumps* is preoccupied with hands: almost everyone in the book is characterized by their hands, and at climactic points both the Tower and the Wheel of Fortune are seen as made entirely out of interlocked hands. Women's hands were a subject of fascination for Williams. 'You know I have always found my imagination preoccupied with the question of the wrist & the hand', he told Phyllis in an undated letter.[616] When Nancy approaches the tarot room to begin her benevolent magic, 'her palms were gently throbbing and tingling. [...] It might so easily have been disagreeable, but it was not disagreeable; it was exquisite.'[617] Such passages have their function in the story; but there is also a private meaning, where Williams optimistically reimagines those punishments from a female point of view—and finds them 'exquisite'.

Williams sent *The Greater Trumps* to Gollancz on 2 March 1932. Gollancz replied, 'My dear Charles: I absolutely adore it. The snow storm is the very finest thing you have done. Five hours you kept me up, reading every word of it. But, alas, we shan't sell it—it is the most difficult of the lot. [...] P.S. Agreement on Monday.'[618]

Gollancz published the novel, with his usual speed, in April; it was followed in May by *The English Poetic Mind* from Oxford's Clarendon Press. Rarely can one author have produced, almost simultaneously, two books so original and so different.

★ ★ ★

Williams still lectured from time to time at Downe House. He certainly made an impression on the pupils, though not always the impression intended. During the holidays, a Downe House pupil called Margery, for example, regaled her cousin Lois Lang-Sims (whom we shall meet later) with tales of an extraordinary lecturer, known to the pupils as 'Chas. Bill', who was wont to visit the school. As Lois recalled:

> No professional clown, it would seem, could have beaten his performances. In graphic imitation of his antics, my cousin would stride up and down an imaginary stage, grimacing like a maniacal monkey, clasping her arms about her as she mimicked his habit of seizing one of the stage curtains in a wild embrace while the school held its breath. 'We always think it's going to come down on his head when he does that, but it hasn't—yet.' Then, when I laughed, she would add firmly, in case I should underestimate the significance of having their own celebrity to be laughed at:
> 'Of course he's a famous poet. And I told you, didn't I, about him and Miss Willis?'
> 'I don't remember exactly. [...] Tell me again.'
> 'Well, someone was looking out of the window, and Chas. Bill and Miss Willis were in the garden. And he gave her a rose and she gave him a kiss.'[619]

The Downe students having performed *A Myth of Shakespeare* the previous summer, Williams supplied them in 1932 with a companion piece, *A Myth of Bacon*; he visited Downe for rehearsals, and directed the play on 25 June. Written in blank verse, it dramatizes scenes from the life of the philosopher and statesman Francis Bacon (1561–1626). Williams's view of Bacon is the one current in Rosicrucian circles, of a thinker dedicated to the betterment of humanity through the enlargement of knowledge—a mission given him by 'Salomon's House', a mysterious college of benevolent philosophers. Short and undistinguished, the play pleased Olive Willis, who requested another for next year. Williams offered 'a lighter thing [...] all about a

Christian fugitive and a naiad and a high priestess and two lovers. [...] Meanwhile I'm working against time to finish a novel before the holidays— when I want to do D.H. Lawrence, & meditate over the sequel to the *Poetic Mind*.'[620] And he gladly accepted Olive's invitation to the Williams family to stay at Downe for two weeks in the summer.

The novel he was trying to 'finish' was *Adepts of Africa*—now retitled *Shadows of Ecstasy*. It was a forlorn hope: Gollancz had rejected it two years before, and was unlikely to want a book he had so firmly turned down, however much rewritten. Sure enough, in late July he refused it again. Williams tried to keep his spirits up but he was tired and life seemed an arid business. When Anne Bradby, once again staying at Aisholt, wrote to him in late August, it brought an upsurge of poignant memories:

> It *was* a lovely time, and all of you were sweet, and do you remember [...] how you jumped over the hedge on top of us, and how we exchanged suppers, and how you brought me back something I'd left behind, and how we talked by the door, and how we went to church, and how (so the saints say and we try and believe) he doth not suffer his holy one to see corruption? So if I send you memories and blessings from London you will know that Aisholt is part of reality still. [...] I [...] wish you all happiness in Aisholt now and at all times and in the heavenly Aisholt that is known in and by the apparent. Lay a hand on the earth for me somewhere where we were together and bless it for me; and remember us all to it, sprinkle a little earth for each of us and say
>
>> 'And O ye Fountains, Meadows, Hills and Groves,
>> Forbode not any severing of our loves;
>> We only have relinquished one delight
>> To live beneath your more habitual sway.'[621]

13

'They Saved My Life by Three Hours'

As the autumn of 1932 drew on, Williams—forty-six in September—was busier than ever: manically, dangerously busy. For the Press, he was writing a prose version of Browning's *The Ring and the Book*, and abridging E. K. Chambers's life of Shakespeare (900 pages, two volumes); he was writing a life of Francis Bacon for the publisher Arthur Barker; he was revising *Shadows of Ecstasy* yet again; he was generating ideas for a new novel; he was reviewing four or five thrillers fortnightly for the *News Chronicle*. Even here he found space for original thinking. On 16 September, for example, he offered startling thoughts on capital punishment:

> Ought we 'to pity or punish?' to kill or to cure? The answer perhaps is that we must take a life for a life, but that the compensating life must be freely offered. There may yet be a lay order of men and women willing to offer themselves to be executed in the convicted criminal's place: thus we could unite mercy and judgment.[622]

In October he attended a conference at Chichester on religious drama, organized by Bishop George Bell.[623] Meanwhile, the Press wanted a sequel to *The English Poetic Mind*; lecturing at Tooting on 'Poetry and Philosophy', he planned (as before) to turn the lectures into a book. He told Anne Bradby:

> I've twelve evenings to fill instead of five, and as I'm not quite so demented on the subject, you're not so likely to have me pouring out a continual flood. [...] What they will be is *not* Poetry & Philosophy so much as an effort to work out, as it were, the kind of reason and the kind of power which exists in certain places along the development of the poetic mind—Pope, Spenser, the heroic play, Keats, Milton—& so on.[624]

He urged Anne and her friend Mary Wright, 'Invite yourselves to Hampstead or to the Press for lunch or something whenever you like. Or look in.'

The body of devoted lecture-goers grew steadily. Raymond Hunt, an engineer from Welwyn Garden City, became a lifelong devotee, attending every London lecture and following Williams when he spoke elsewhere, taking notes. Williams continued to be generous with his time, knowledge, enthusiasm—and books. One attendee, M. Joyce Taylor, recalled:

> After he'd spoken of Gerard Manley Hopkins I said I still didn't understand the poems & Charles immediately made an appointment to meet me one lunch hour. He spent that time going over the poems and explaining the language to me, and ended by giving me a copy of the Gerard Manley Hopkins collected edition with [his] introduction in it.[625]

Fitting private writing around unremitting work at Amen House, he told Anne Bradby that 'he reckoned to write nearly 7,000 words of prose in a weekend, or maybe 10,000 with the luck of no interruption'.[626] He could produce a book, or equivalent, in less than three months—at the expense, of course, of family life, which must have been minimal.

Surprisingly, in late autumn Gollancz accepted the much-revised *Shadows of Ecstasy*, Williams's weakest novel and the last one that Gollancz published. It came out just before Christmas. But the strain of it all was palpable. 'O Olive my dear', he groaned to Miss Willis:

> Bacon at Downe is one thing, and Bacon for a publisher (seventy-five thousand words!) is another. But I hurl myself at it—it was I who first remarked to the agent that I'd been looking F.B. up—and I've done the first draft of 60,000. Only I don't *really* understand the *Novum Organum* or Common Law or Chancery suits. No. Only he's paid me *some* money and I've spent it, so I must go on.[627]

★   ★   ★

In January 1933 a new project, and a new person, entered Amen House. The project was *The Oxford Dictionary of Quotations*, a brainchild of Milford, and the person was Alice Mary Smyth, who was to edit it: another Milford innovation, for she was the Press's first female editor. Tall, strikingly handsome, and red-haired, twenty-seven-year-old Alice Mary—she insisted on *both* names—was an Oxford history graduate who had done postgraduate study in the United States, at Mount Holyoke,

Massachusetts. She vividly recalled her introduction to Williams, and the Press, one Monday:

> I had joined the O.U.P. at Amen House that morning [...] at a salary of £4 a week. I was standing alone in a tiny little office with a glazed window, one chair, and three dictionaries of quotations issued by other publishers on a desk [...] when there were loud footsteps outside, and the door was thrown open by Gerard Hopkins and C.W., who had come down from their upstairs office to be nice to the new girl. They were both large men—C.W. was not so thin then—and they completely filled the office. They both had a lot to say about the horrors of life in the Press. The very mention of my job on quotations set C.W. off, reciting [Tennyson's] *Ulysses* I think, while Gerard Hopkins continued to talk, assuring me that 'C.W.' was always like that and I must just get used to it, as they all had. They asked me about myself and when I told them my academic qualifications C.W. said 'Lor!', and they both told me not to worry, none of the qualifications need bother me any more, I need have no fears of promotion or wealth once I was safely installed in the Oxford University Press. 'They won't throw you out either,' said Gerry generously. 'Not exactly. You will just be found mouldering away one day, forgotten for twenty years,' said C.W.
>
> I was astonished at the vitality of this pair, [and] at C.W., as he had knocked off *Ulysses* as one might recite the address from an envelope. [...] Then Gerard Hopkins went back to work and C.W. stayed. He began to talk seriously about my job.[628]

Alice Mary's desk was covered with stacks of cards. Ralph Binfield had been dismembering other dictionaries of quotations, cutting out the entries and pasting each one onto a card. Williams told Alice Mary that more—many more—were on their way down. Her job would be to go through the 100,000 or so cards, throw out the duplicates, then copy out the citations from all the remaining ones.

This was not how Alice Mary had pictured her future in publishing. 'I was appalled, and angry, at the vast, monotonous and brainless task which would take six months.' Williams's response was to light a cigarette and sit down. 'He said that it would be boring and monotonous, and that large stretches of everyone's life were that, and in itself that was nothing to complain of; that, brainless as it might seem, the work did require someone who knew the difference between Crabbe and Crashaw.' He asked her about herself, and seemed to think she was lucky to have come to London alone from the country: 'Clearly he thought all young people chafed at home and were burdened by their parents and families.' This surprised her. 'He recommended me to Phyllis Jones, the librarian next door to my office, told me to ask her for any help I needed, and not to despair, and went out', leaving Alice Mary thoughtful, and subtly disturbed. 'I remember feeling very different after he had gone, both more composed to the work and more uneasy about myself.'[629]

Once Alice Mary had weeded the duplicates and copied the first few hundred cards, 'starting at author A', the Quotation Committee convened. Known as 'Q', it met weekly for several years. The main members were Alice Mary, Hopkins, and Williams. Foss, Binfield, Milford, Helen Peacock, Phyllis Jones, and Raymond Goffin (head of the Indian branch) sometimes attended. Alice Mary would read out each quotation in turn and the others debated whether or not it was 'familiar': the criterion laid down by Milford, characteristically irritating but useful, was 'whether one would expect to find it in *The Times* fourth leader'. Alice Mary recalled:

> C.W. generally put his feet on the table and tilted his chair back horribly dangerously, and smoked, took off his glasses and rubbed his eyes, smuggled a pen and little pad out of his pocket and scratched out a word in a poem and wrote in another in his shaky hand, still balanced on two chair legs, and was always perfectly clear and accurate about every quotation. Sometimes he would exclaim, 'But the best bit has been left out'; or ' "*flared*", not "stared"—Good God in Heaven, "flared forth into the dark" '.
>
> We were a bunch of experts. C.W. knew everything, particularly everything on Shakespeare (*all* of him), Milton and Wordsworth, Malory, Marlowe and the Elizabethans, Donne and the metaphysicals, Pope, Keats, Tennyson, Bridges, Kipling, Chesterton. Gerard Hopkins was expert on eighteenth-century novelists, Fred Page on Patmore and the nineteenth century, Sir Humphrey on Browning, Meredith and Trollope. [. . .] Besides literature, C.W. knew a great deal about religion, history, magic, and witchcraft[.][630]

Alice Mary dealt with the Bible, hymns and the *Book of Common Prayer*. She had always been religious, and to her surprise found this a bond with Williams, who 'was pleased that I put forward all his favourite texts and hymn-verses'. Arguing over quotations from hymns led to 'some of the wilder quotation meetings', when people 'threw away all scruple about "familiarity" in their fury to include or exclude lines which were shreds of their own religious pasts'. There was also the temptation to sing:

> Can a woman's tender care
> Cease towards the child she bare?

was mooted. We yelled the answer,

> Yes, she may forgetful be,
> Yet will I remember thee,

and C.W. added 'Yes, by God, and you'd better look out when I do!' The after-noon we reached 'Light's abode, celestial Salem' [...] C.W. simply said, 'Well of course we must have the whole of the last verse.' Someone said 'No, too long,' and he began to chant

> Laud and honour to the Father,
> Laud and honour to the Son,
> Laud and honour to the Spirit,
> Ever three and ever one.

With one accord and no direction we all drew a deep breath, and roared,

> Con–sub–stan–tial, co–e–ter–nal,
> While unending ages run.

I can only suppose that people in the passage said 'C.W. must be in there.' We were a little shaken ourselves, and kept very much to business after that.[631]

It all sounds very jolly, but these hilarious moments were interludes in a punishing schedule. Williams was always in the office by 9 a.m., and would speak to no one until he had sat for half an hour writing hastily on one of the little spiral-bound reporters' pads he used for his personal work. He was putting on paper the material he had composed mentally between the Tube station and the office. During the day:

> he worked hard, in or out of the office. His lunches were scanty—a sandwich, a glass of sherry or his favourite hock[632] and soda-water, coffee and a ciga-rette—for eating and drinking were of little interest. The Press's work and his own were interchangeable. Often he worked through the lunch hour and also took work home. [...] His day did not stop when he slammed papers into drawers, put on his coat, gloves and hat and went downstairs, listened and glanced in case Phyllis might be coming out of the Library, had a word with anyone passing on the stairs, said good-night to Sergeant and Miss Cox the telephonist, crossed the square with his easy quick stride, turned into the home-going crowds in Warwick Lane and made for the tube station. Once or twice a week he would be lecturing, and not get home till ten.[633]

And then, after Michal had gone to bed, Alice Mary later learned, 'Charles would get out his books and notes' and work into the small hours.

★ ★ ★

And the relationship with Phyllis continued. They went to see *King Kong* together,[634] and Williams still trusted her with his most intimate thoughts. In late 1932 or early 1933 the English translation of Mario Praz's *The Romantic Agony* was going through the Press when someone raised the alarm: might this study of morbid, horrific, and sexual themes in European Romantic literature be obscene, and in danger of prosecution? With bizarre appropriateness, the proofs were sent to Charles Williams for a considered opinion. (Chance, or a sly decision on the part of the inscrutable Milford?) Williams gave the book a clean bill of health, but it set him thinking. He told Phyllis:

> It's a fantastic book, but it set me wishing again that we (we in general, the world, but inevitably you and I in particular) could find some way of bringing that province—I mean all that the words sadism, &c signify—*into* the general whole. Pathological, morbid, perverse—the words bleat out; but they call the saints the same. Some of these longings *are* almost insane, & certainly without the will of both they are tyranny. But tyranny is the misuse of power (our modern sense of the word anyhow), and what I want is to see bewilderment relieved by presentation of achieving power. 'Play' is all very well, and covers a lot, but there does seem to be some search for more than 'play'. It isn't mere symbolism either. The mistake they make, I mean the Romantic Agonists, is to push to extremer and extremer efforts without proportioning that by all other activities. They don't want the whole. But it's the whole that matters.[635]

And again:

> Don't, unless you have, look up sadist in the Dictionary; it will give you a wrong idea of me. I suspect the Marquis de Sade was really unpleasant, but in our moral England it's so difficult to find out. Eccelin da Romano was probably one, & perhaps Tiberius, & perhaps that Urban who read his breviary outside the torture-chambers. Whereas I wouldn't hurt a fly unless it made it perfectly clear that it liked it. And then only a little, and then only for the conversation. [...] Let be; I will tell you all about it one day or write a letter about it. When you leave the Press, I think; I should dislike it sooner.[636]

In the spring of 1933, however, several things happened which may or may not have been connected. Probably the first was the publication, in February, of Gerry Hopkins's seventh novel, *Nor Fish Nor Flesh*. It was based, unmistakably, on the triangular affair between himself, Phyllis, and Charles Williams—the latter crudely caricatured as the eccentric visionary artist Peter Meriden. The novel's plot, in essentials, is simple. Ralph Giffard, a prosperous middle-aged novelist, rents a room in his large house to the young artist Meriden. Meriden brings in his wake a pretty student artist, his pupil Joan Croft. Giffard assumes that they are having an affair; but he himself falls in love with Joan, and when he discovers that Meriden and Joan are not actually lovers, he proceeds to seduce her. Or nearly—for having persuaded Joan to come with him for a weekend at a country hotel, he delays and somehow the relationship fades away. Giffard realizes, belatedly, that Meriden is heartbroken, having been idealistically in love with Joan all along. Joan wanders away, sadder and wiser; Giffard himself settles down to write a novel about it.

Nor Fish Nor Flesh—the title's meaning is never very clear—is a poor novel: verbose, pretentious, and badly plotted. But Williams must have been sorely hurt by the clearly recognizable parody of himself. 'Meriden' has a working-class accent and a chip on his shoulder. His clothes are suavely sneered at: he wore 'City trousers that were a shade too short, and City sleeves that were a thought too long [...] garments that, however new, had, certainly, never been good.'[637] He has 'a curious exaggeration of manner, a faintly burlesqued air of deference that might have been mockery or might have been gaucherie'.[638] He gives people nicknames (dubbing the moneyed Giffard 'Maecenas', and Joan 'Perdita'). He is 'vociferous and gesticulating',[639] and philosophizes at the top of his voice in a theatre queue, drawing embarrassing attention. Giffard recognizes that Meriden is probably a genius, but manages to imply that genius is not really in good taste. Moreover, reversing their relative ages and emphasizing Giffard's wealth, Hopkins presents his own persona as the other man's patron. As for Joan, she is little more than a cipher: a nice, colourless young woman with no talent or intellect.

Nor Fish Nor Flesh was a breathtaking insult, to both Williams and Phyllis. It is almost incredible that Hopkins could have written and published it, knowing that he would continue to work alongside them. Had Phyllis mischievously shown Hopkins, years before, Williams's bitter verses 'On Alexis's latest novel'? If so, Alexis had his revenge now. Alice Mary recalled that 'Charles spent several ten minutes in [the] Library in emphatic disclaiming, correction and wrath.'[640] This lofty way of putting it surely understates his reaction. He must have been bitterly hurt and furiously angry. The only consolation might have been that one part of Hopkins's motivation was all too clear; for whilst Phyllis had ended her affair with Gerry, she remained as attached as ever to Charles. Gerry might or might not be sexually attractive; but 'Urban' had opened new worlds for her, shown her new sides of herself. That was what she truly valued.

At about the same time, Williams took a firm decision to stay away from Phyllis during working hours. Perhaps embarrassment over the novel was involved. Perhaps he simply decided it was time to pull himself together and avoid the tantalizing pain of seeing his beloved during the working day. For almost seven years the daily trip to Amen House had been enlivened by the expectation of seeing Phyllis. Now they would meet only at 'Q' and on other work-determined occasions. Whatever the details, Williams ceased to 'come downstairs' to drop into the room where she worked[641]—no longer the library, for Phyllis had been transferred to the Production Department, whilst Alice Mary Smyth took over as librarian—which, Alice Mary remarked, 'lowered the temperature, as [Milford] perhaps intended'.[642]

Meanwhile, the pace of Williams's work continued to increase as summer drew on. He wrote the introduction for a volume of Walter Savage Landor; he wrote a life of Macaulay for a book of *Short Biographies*; he reviewed for *Time and Tide*; he offered the Clarendon Press a book on *Prose at Present*, which was turned down, but he contracted to write a life of King James I for Arthur Barker.[643] Williams was not a good biographer. He had neither time nor skill for research into original sources (though he did sometimes consult published state papers), and his biographies are badly overwritten. This had much to do with length: the 1936 *Queen Elizabeth*, at 186 pages, is quite a good read, whereas the other biographies, twice the length, are at times so mannered as to be almost incomprehensible. Adept at spinning pages of psychological-metaphysical speculation which padded out a meagre factual content, he regarded the biographies as potboilers; though—as Eliot kindly said later—'he always boiled an honest pot',[644] and they received surprisingly tolerant reviews.

★   ★   ★

Even as Williams undertook this journeyman work he was trying to plan a new novel. Since the previous summer, he had been intensively reading D. H. Lawrence and reflecting on Lawrence's ideas about sex—ideas related to, but different from, his own. It was probably in late summer 1932 that he wrote to Phyllis:

> I have read *Kangaroo*—and am a little anti-D.H.L. at the moment. He does seem to be straining to tell us something which it's quite easy for us to

understand without this fuss. And it's no good his telling us about the dark phallic God unless he hints at why phallic. [...] I meditate on *Reason and Beauty in the P[oetic] M[ind]*, [...] on my lectures on the Drama, on the odd papers on *Poetry on Poetry*, &c.; on the novel on death and—at odd moments—on the White Column novel.—I feel as if the last ought to pull D.H.L. & other things all together & delimit a place & mode of exploration. Have you noticed that in the *Prelude* Wordsworth speaks of amorous delight, spiritual delight in love (adoration) and says this spiritual delight only exists with Imagination which equals

'absolute power
And Reason in her most exalted mood.'[645]

Two proposed novels are mentioned here. One, 'the novel on death', may be the first stirring of the idea for a story set in the afterlife, which would eventually become the 1944 novel *All Hallows' Eve*. But what was 'the White Column novel'? An answer is supplied by an unpublished, undated poem:

From a field of fragrant thyme
snakes of Aesculapius climb
up the shaft, compact of snows
their double shadow turns to rose.

Up the slender column tall
those twain snakes medicinal,
hugely coiling, clamber slow,
living in its living flow.

From their dark and ancient home
in the sacred base they come,
wisdom of the body twined
with the wisdom of the mind. [...]

He who for himself would know
Aesculapian science so,
let him, in Apollo's hour,
when the dayspring hath its power [...]

let him to that column's place
tiptoe come, and on its base,
white and curved and virginal,
lightly strike and lightly call,

till those sacred serpents come,
issuing from their ancient home,
up that shaft compact of snows
twining, touching it to rose,

till, with eyes of euphrasy
in his inner body he,
made as Aesculapius wise,
sees that column light the skies.[646]

Aesculapius was the Roman god of healing, his snake-wreathed staff a symbol of medicine. The poem makes it clear that the phallic-seeming 'white
column' is the current of energy which, according to many esoteric systems,
flows from the base of the body up the spinal column to the brain or crown
of the head. The energy is often pictured in serpent form: what yogic systems call 'Kundalini'. Perhaps Williams's work on revising *Shadows of Ecstasy*
had turned his thoughts once more towards 'transmutation of energy' and,
prompted by the example of Lawrence, he was casting about for more effective ways of treating the theme in fiction. Clearly the games with Phyllis
were also connected; indeed, the theme had been subtly present in his life
ever since his early studies of Patmore. But the 'white column' remains a
mystery, and the novel stayed unwritten.

★   ★   ★

For intellectual discussion and female company, Williams turned increasingly to Anne Bradby. Still studying for her diploma at King's College, she
attended his lectures with her friend Mary Wright; when he finished 'Poetry
and Philosophy' they signed up for his course on early Christian thought:

> The long trek by Tube meant that we missed supper, but what did that matter,
> when we were learning about the *Consolations* of Boethius and his definition
> of Eternity ('the full and perfect simultaneous enjoyment of interminable
> life')? However, Mary's mother insisted on making us sandwiches to eat in the
> Tube.[647]

They 'had lunch with Charles Williams in the wine vaults on Ludgate Hill
and returned to his little room at Amen House', and were even invited to
tea at the Williams's flat in Parkhill Road—a rare honour, granted probably
because Michal had already met them at Aisholt. In return, they took
Charles and Michal to a Chinese restaurant.

But Anne had a special rapport with Williams. She was writing poetry
herself; she confided her youthful troubles and anxieties to him, and he
responded honestly and wittily: 'You will recollect also that any pain of
yours (it doesn't matter about the cause) is one with the Cross. That cuts a
lot of ice, he added gloomily. Well. perhaps...' And, 'Nothing is what we

expect, and everything is much better. I have a horrid feeling that I'm having a perfectly happy life (though I may feel as if I were going off my head
sometimes) *if only I could see it so.* Curious!'[648] They trusted each other: with
Anne he could think aloud, or let his pen run on spontaneously, without
fear of being misunderstood. By the summer, he was treating her as a literary equal. In a letter thanking her for help over a detail in the *Bacon* biography, which he had finished at Easter, he enclosed proofs of the first
chapter, urging 'O but tell me where Mr. Eliot crashed over Milton; I
should love to know exactly where he was unintelligent' (no doubt referring to some controversial remark made at the Faber offices), and moves on
to theology: 'There are, I said once, only drugs & God. I'm inclined to alter
that now & say: Everything is both drugs & God; and man's choice is
whether he will know whatever is before him as drugs or as God.' He ends,
'I'm thinking of putting—did I tell you?—the doctrine of substituted love
into the next novel'—probably the first recorded reference to what became
Descent into Hell.[649]

On 17 August 1933 he told her:

> I've been rather attracted [...] by the idea of a series of poems using math-
> ematical diction; & by chance I tried this one out. If I had leisure I would do
> some more—one on planes; & one on the Angle (a very subtle & important
> one); and one on asymptotes;[650] & so on. [...] Read them as love-poems in the
> courteous metaphysical sense, & they become, perhaps, clearer.

He enclosed the poems—two love poems, entitled 'Euclid' I and II, using
imagery from geometry, in seventeenth-century 'metaphysical' style:

> did some hid Master draw
> the logic of Euclidean law,
> firing the proposition through
> by making diagrams of you?

—and so on. He told Anne that no one else had seen them: a sign of how
far he trusted her judgement. No one, he told her, yet fully understood
'substituted love': 'After all, we only discovered it as an experiential fact, by
chance, as it were; and I'm terrified out of my senses at the idea of going
further.' He added that he had 'tried out the chapter in the novel in which
Shakespeare (so to speak) explains the idea—not very clearly', and ended:

> Are there moments, Anne, when you wish you weren't refined & cultured &
> all that? [...] Everyone ought to be a little vulgar. Shakespeare was. That
> God!—Excuse this sudden parenthesis: the sight of my own futility disgusted

me. My new novel is all about the Cities of the Plain. The last two sentences
are darkly connected, though you won't see it.[651]

The 'new novel' would become the 1937 *Descent into Hell*. A note to
Raymond Hunt, arranging to meet him, confirms this, adding 'I've written
a beautiful chapter about suicide!'[652] *Descent into Hell* does indeed contain
a suicide.

★   ★   ★

That cheerful note to Hunt was written on Monday, 21 August 1933. But
before the time of his appointed meeting with Hunt the following Saturday,
Williams was feeling ill. Nausea was accompanied by bouts of severe stomach pain. No doubt he treated the symptoms with his usual casualness,
insisting they would pass, but late on Saturday it became obvious that he was
seriously ill. Michal called the doctor. An ambulance was summoned and
Williams, ashen-faced and in agony, was driven to University College
Hospital. X-rays were taken and at 2 o'clock on Sunday morning an emer-
gency operation for intussusception was performed.

Intussusception is a rare condition where part of the intestine folds back
inside itself: it is often compared to one section of a telescope sliding back
inside another. The intestine becomes blocked. Food cannot pass, the blood
supply is cut off, and an untreated patient usually dies within a few days.
Williams, it turned out, had pushed his luck to the limit. He was fortunate
to survive. The causes of intussusception are various, but in his case the
likely cause was adhesions—essentially, scar tissue—from an unnoticed
childhood infection with abdominal tuberculosis caught from milk, which
often carried bovine TB.[653] This had been aggravated by overwork and poor
diet. The midday sandwich, sherry, and cigarette would hardly sustain
healthy life.

A week later Williams was well enough to write to Phyllis:

Dearest,
I'm getting on, as they say, but never was so weak a creature. Since they saved
my life, they say, by three hours last Sunday morning, my mind has been wandering and I've been behaving in the most fantastic way. They give me two
ounces of milk every two hours, and that's all. [...] My wife was talking of
asking you to come with her & the others & I know not what because I didn't
understand quite. But she thought I couldn't bear it yet.[654]

The same day, Phyllis sent a note saying, he later recalled, 'that when she heard of [the illness] she knew quite clearly & coldly that she couldn't bear to contemplate life without me'.[655]

His recovery was not helped by a *faux pas* on the part of Fred Page. Aware that Michal knew about Charles's attachment to Phyllis, but not realizing that Michal imagined it to be a secret between herself and her husband, the guileless Fred said something to reveal that the affair was common knowledge at Amen House. Michal was horrified: what she had thought to be a private sorrow now appeared a public humiliation.[656] She felt that the entire editorial staff of the Press had connived over the affair. When Williams came to understand this latest phase in the endless slow-motion disaster, he commented resignedly, 'So far as I can understand—but my brain isn't really working—F.P.'s let off more devastation one way & another in the course of the first 24 hours than one would think possible!'[657] Nonetheless, Michal came to see him in the evenings, staying until around 8 p.m.[658]

By 17 September he was out of hospital, having insisted on leaving at the first possible moment. He told Anne Bradby:

> Actually there's been very little pain. [...] There's been extreme physical discomfort, but not more. There's also been extreme mental discomfort—nightmarish things. But in a feeble kind of way, as soon as the possibility arose, we asserted the Faith. (Though I do rather feel I ran away from the hospital—rather unShakespeareanly.)[659]

Soon he was able to take a cheerful tone about the whole business, telling Raymond Hunt, 'An absurd twist happened in my interior which all but twisted me—it seems—out of normal existence (at least—normal? but you know what I mean).'[660] Privately, he brooded on other possibilities. Long accustomed to symbolic thinking and to meditating on microcosm, macrocosm, and levels between, he sensed a homology between Amen House and his own body; between staircase and intestine. Could the crisis, he wondered, have been caused by his rigid decision not to visit Phyllis at work? 'Dearest', he wrote to her:

> (i) It's occurred to me that it's just possible that all this was the transference & disposal of the 'obstruction' that I allowed to exist in the matter of coming downstairs. As if our Lord, not proposing to stand more than six months of that kind of thing, hardened it into flesh and then had it removed. ?Fancy? I don't know.

(ii) I want to get up to the Press for a few moments this week; I'm writing to HSM suggesting Friday. I think I shall sleep better if I see you for even a second or two.[661]

He returned to Amen House around the middle of October,[662] but he was at work on his own writing—including preparing a series of lectures on 'The Metaphysical Tradition in English Poetry'—much sooner. He told Anne Bradby:

I go on very nicely, thank you: rather depressed & tearful at times, rather gloomy & selfish at others, but improving out of knowledge: so that everyone says I am looking much better than they expected, & I feel as if actually I had no more than had a tooth out & deceived them all. [...] I still get tired rather too quickly, & my mind revolts from James [I] & won't get on with the novel & dislikes Metaphysical Tradition & is bored with everything it reads. But that will pass.

And he continued to discuss theology with her:

I do think that the double challenge of 'This also is Thou' and 'Neither is this Thou', carried into everything, probably as much as any formula, assist the soul. They are an example of my momentarily pet obsession of asymptotes, and the point at which they do meet would be the Spiritual Marriage, after which (they say) is the Beatific Vision.[663]

From 20 October, eight weeks after the operation, he was lecturing again twice a week. And he gave a one-off lecture on 'The Supernatural' at Kingsway Hall on the 21st.

Ceaseless activity was driven partly by the need for money. When John Pellow wrote, after many years' silence, to ask about literary agents, Williams's reply was warm but harassed:

How nice to hear from you again! though I know it's all my fault. But keeping and educating (God help us!) a child—which is the explanation of all my books—does leave one negligent and evil in manners towards all one's friends. As for poetry—that was in my salad days, before I got busy providing toast for myself and others. But I occasionally long for the salad![664]

★   ★   ★

Despite his cheerful tone and renewed torrent of activity, Williams was noticeably changed after his brush with death. Always slim and angular, he now looked positively thin. His face was more deeply lined; his handwriting smaller and shakier. Yet his literary contacts continued to extend. He met Montgomery Belgion, a talkative literary journalist who delighted in making introductions. Belgion invited him to lunch in late October to meet the novelist L.H. Myers, who admired Williams's novels. More importantly, Belgion asked if Williams would like to meet T.S. Eliot. If so, he said, he could arrange for the Bloomsbury salon hostess Lady Ottoline Morrell to invite them both: 'If we propose teatime on the 1st [of November] and she agrees, it will be a private affair; if we propose the 2nd, it will be her weekly literary tea. So, choose [...] and let me know.'[665]

Even before writing his hesitant chapter on Eliot for *Poetry at Present*, Williams had been making a sidelong approach to the other poet. In 1928 he had commissioned Eliot to write an introduction to Wilkie Collins's *The Moonstone*. Then in 1930 he had written, cautiously, about the recently published *Ash Wednesday*:

> It will not perhaps displease you to know that Mr. Milford and Mr. Hopkins and I all, separately and together, agreed that it seemed to suggest to us that our great-grandchildren would find it great poetry; but that by the way. Without asking for meaning or interpretation or anything, it did just occur to us to wonder whether there were any—well, say, allusion—in the 'three leopards' or the 'unicorns dragging a gilded hearse' that one would perhaps be happier for recognizing. Dante or 'the Forest Philosophers of India' (my God!) or anything?[666]

Eliot's answer has not survived. Two years younger than Williams, Eliot was now a leading poet and critic, and an editor at Faber and Faber. In 1927 he had joined the Church of England, afterwards describing himself as 'classicist in literature, royalist in politics, and anglo-catholic in religion',[667] a position deeply congenial to Williams. As Eliot recalled, it was Lady Ottoline who had first encouraged him to read *War in Heaven*. A devotee of both theology and detective thrillers, Eliot had been delighted. Now, in 1933, they met at a 'literary tea' at her house in Gower Street:

> I remember [wrote Eliot] a man in spectacles, who appeared to combine a frail physique with exceptional vitality; whose features could be described as 'homely'—meaning by that word a face which is immediately attractive and subsequently remembered, without one's being able to explain either the attraction or the persistence of the impression. He appeared completely at ease in surroundings [...] which had intimidated many; and at the same time was modest and unassuming to the point of humility. [...] He talked easily and volubly, yet never imposed his talk; for he appeared always to be at the same

time preoccupied with the subject of conversation, and interested in, and aware of, the personalities of those to whom he was talking. One retained the impression that he was pleased and grateful for the opportunity of meeting the company, and yet that it was he who had conferred a favour—more than a favour, a kind of benediction.[668]

Soon they met again. Williams told Phyllis:

Ottoline Morrell wrote that [Eliot] was full of the first meeting, and most unusually. When I threw out [...] the suggestion that we might repeat the evening T.S.E. accepted with almost flattering haste. We conversed on theology and art. He is a nice creature. Belgion says he is normally much on his guard, but that he seems to drop it with us. I will try & tell you another time 'what was said'.[669]

Possibly the two men detected shared resonances beyond their common Anglo-Catholicism and publishing work. Both had less than satisfactory marriages (Eliot spectacularly so, since Vivienne was mentally ill and he lived apart from her). Each drew poetic inspiration from an unconsummated love affair. Eliot, indeed, had returned only the previous month from a chaste visit to Emily Hale, the Boston sweetheart of his youth, whom for many years he loved, and who loved him, though they would never marry. Like Williams, he believed in an exalted state of spiritual love, akin to Dante's for Beatrice, asking of Emily Hale, in their unconsummated relationship, 'an extraordinary feat: that her feeling should match his own need to transmute love into "Love", a distilled concentrate that would never evaporate'.[670] This was, of course, precisely what Williams had asked of Phyllis, and what she had, excusably, been unable to achieve.

Williams sent Eliot a copy of *The Place of the Lion*. Devouring it over a weekend, Eliot wrote thanking him, and praising *War in Heaven*:

I have never before met anyone who was interested in the [Grail] subject matter in quite the same way as myself. [...] I suppose what the ordinary reader gets out of your stories is just what he gets from a thousand other well built 'thrillers', but for me they mean something quite different and special, and I hope you will be inspired to write more. [...] I have found these two books so exciting that I am incapacitated from making any purely literary judgement of them; though the visualisation of the immaterial, and such scenes as the rippling of the ground in *The Place of the Lion*, seem to me marvellously successful.

It is surprising how few people seem to have any awareness of other than material realities, or of Good and Evil as having anything to do with the nature of things—as anything more than codes of conduct. I suppose it is because there is something so terrifying, like a blast of air from the North Pole, in spiritual realities that just natural cowardice and laziness make us all try to evade it as much of the time as we can.[671]

Eliot later told Helen Gardner that his famous phrase in 'Burnt Norton'—'At the still point of the turning world'—had been suggested by the description of the Fool at the centre of the dancing tarots in *The Greater Trumps*, which 'alone in the middle of all that curious dance did not move'.[672] He became a close friend of Williams, but also at times an object of rivalry. 'O but tell me where Mr. Eliot crashed over Milton', Williams had implored Anne Bradby—and something of that attitude remained.

Around the same time, Williams came to know Dylan Thomas. Binfield complained one day about the tediousness of some indexing he had to do. Williams responded, 'I have a young man in my class who would give his right arm to have your job', adding that the young man's name was Dylan Thomas.[673] Thomas had turned up at one of Williams's evening lectures, and been deeply impressed. Anne Bradby heard him tell Williams, '"Why, you come into the room and talk about Keats and Blake as if they were *alive*." '[674] He visited Williams's office, bringing poems; in January 1934 he wrote, 'Charles Williams [...] has read many of my poems but confesses that he does not understand them; they cannot be "pooh-poohed" but he could not say that he liked them.'[675] Later, Williams became more enthusiastic: in March 1936 he sent Raymond Hunt a proof sheet from the magazine *Life and Letters Today* containing the first seven sections of 'Altarwise by Owl-light', commenting 'I have not read them properly but they gave me considerable pleasure. Everyone tells me—and I think they may be right—that Mr Dylan Thomas is going to be very important.'[676] He supported Thomas's application to the Royal Literary Fund,[677] and around 1937 tried, unsuccessfully, to persuade the Press to publish a collection of his poems.[678]

★ ★ ★

Reason and Beauty in the Poetic Mind, Williams's third volume of criticism, appeared from the Clarendon Press in November 1933. Despite passages of brilliant criticism, it is less well-focused than the previous book, and harder to follow. It combines close readings of passages in Keats, Wordsworth, Milton, Shakespeare, and others with analysis of certain key words—among them 'reason', beauty', 'imagination'—which recur in their work. But the style is often impossibly contorted, and there are many misquotations. Its most important part is its opening chapter, 'The Ostentation of Verse', a profoundly original essay on form and metre in poetry. Williams argues that choice of verse form (Spenser's elaborate stanza, or Milton's blank verse) changes, and determines, what a poem can say and show. The poet 'determines to know the subject of his poem so, and not otherwise'.[679] Displaying its own arbitrariness, verse is thus more honest, though more artificial, than prose. The discussion anticipates insights which would later be expounded by French structuralists and Russian formalists. Yet reviewers ignored it, whilst the book's obvious weaknesses were denounced. 'I'm getting like George Eliot & Lord Tennyson', he confessed:

> I'm refusing to read bad reviews! *The Criterion* begins by saying what criticism ought to do, & added that I did none of these things—so I didn't read any more. [...] I'm sure it's very intelligent, but I shall never be humble enough to be taught by the *Criterion*.[680]

Edith Sitwell consoled him after a slashing review from the Cambridge critic F.R. Leavis:[681] 'Why, *of course* Mr Leavis called you a fool. Is there anybody of importance, with the exception of Mr. Eliot, who has *not* been called a fool by him?'[682] A more congenial critique was the one written by himself, in the *Week-End Review*, for a series where authors reviewed their own books. 'All of us have authors whom we cannot read properly', Williams declared, 'and I am sorry to say that Mr. Charles Williams is one of mine.' The article (illustrated by a calligraphic cartoon: Figure 2) is mostly, albeit wryly, an exposition of his actual views, but ends by pointing to a real danger, emphasized with disturbing hints of himself as *döppelganger*:

> Patterns are baleful things. [...] When, being very young, I sometimes thought I knew Mr. Williams, I should have warned him to beware of his pattern; if ever, 'some evening when the moon is blood', I meet him again in Holborn or in Ludgate Hill, I shall offer him the same warning.[683]

★ ★ ★

Much of his emotional support now came from Anne Bradby, who (while seeking permanent work in publishing) had been engaged by Williams:

> to select poems for the proposed *Oxford Book of Modern Verse* from a list of poets drawn up by Lascelles Abercrombie. [Abercrombie] had been commissioned by Oxford to edit the book, but was now too ill with diabetes to finish

Figure 2. Pen portrait: cartoon by 'Cola' from the *New English Weekly*, 1933

what he had begun. So for the whole of one winter [1933–4] I scanned the pages of poets good, bad, and indifferent, and selected what I thought best—I had of course no right of veto.[684]

Anne went on to edit a volume of *Shakespeare Criticism* for the World's Classics, which involved a year of intensive reading, guided by Williams. Visiting him in his office, she noticed how often he would be with 'his *great* friend' D.H.S. Nicholson, chatting or planning to slip out for coffee.[685] Anne also attended meetings of 'Q', where she observed the complicated web of Amen House relationships—Gerry Hopkins now among the admirers of the glamorous Alice Mary.[686] There was also a short-lived plan, conceived by Williams, for her to write a book on cant in English Literature (or, more positively, on '"Poetic Integrity" or Sincerity or what not'). It came to nothing.[687]

Anne continued to attend Williams's lectures, becoming class secretary, and occasionally exaggerated the number of students in order to keep the classes alive. She would walk with him afterwards:

> to the Tube station, or to the offices of G.K. Chesterton's paper *G.K.'s Weekly* to pick up books he was to review. I studied his poetry with a view to getting a selection published, and what was more important, I became his audience with a licence to criticize [...] About once a week after he left Amen House at 5.30 we would go to a café, and he would read the latest poem, or expound a theory about, say, the connexions between Logres and Britain, or the symbolism of Merlin. [...] And sometimes we lunched together in the City.[688]

This was at Shirreff's Wine Bar on Ludgate Hill: 'a sort of cellarish place; you sat in little cubicles, which was very good for talking'.[689] Williams confided in Anne about everything, telling her, 'I must say, Anne, I do simply & straightforwardly *like* your way of pointing out what my secret mind already knows, & doesn't say quite loudly enough.'[690] He showed her his *Century of Poems to Celia* and when he thought of a good line about God –'Thou only art, what none but Thou canst be'—he sent it to her in case it might be of use to 'either of us'. He asked her to write to him about *Reason and Beauty*, 'because I wanted to know how it struck you',[691] and when in January 1934 Gollancz rejected his new novel, *Descent into Hell* ('Very surprising! very annoying!! somewhat embarrassing!!!'),[692] he at once lent it Anne to read, no doubt hoping for consolation: 'It looks rather depressing in its present state; an air of rejection materializes in the very feel of the typescript. But 'twill serve I hope.'[693] In July it was rejected again, by Arthur Barker—though Barker, having just published *Bacon* to decent reviews, commissioned another biography, this time of John Wilmot, Earl of Rochester.[694] Williams considered offering Barker a life of Dante as well, but decided against it:[695] he had taken on the job of reading unsolicited manuscripts for Norman Collins, now an editor at Gollancz, and was 'swamped with MS. novels'.[696]

He tinkered with *Descent into Hell* throughout 1934, lending it to trusted readers. L.H. Myers, Williams reported, thought that '*Descent* has more genius than any of the novels. [...] But, he says, "the style, as well as the matter, is so odd." I must read it again from that point of view.'[697] And other ideas for novels bubbled up. He met a nurse, who:

> remarked that lunatics *are* worse at the changes of the moon, & I thought of the tides, & wondered about writing a novel on the moon—not like Mr. Wells, but about the lunar influence: Artemis, perhaps. The lunar light transfusing the earth—a cold terrible inhuman influence thrilling us.[698]

But the idea went no further.

In March 1934 Anne went to Italy. Williams kept her informed about the lectures. There were now four a week: at Downe House in Berkshire on Mondays and Thursdays, and in London on Wednesdays and Fridays. 'Somehow time seems a little full', he ruminated, 'and yet, you know, I'm essentially lazy.' The London series that he gave on metaphysical poetry went 'awfully deep':

> The means of union between the Shakespearean & Miltonic universes. Time in the Sonnets—the conception of some outside-Time event in the Metaphysicals. And in the Nativity Ode. As not in Shakespeare. It sounds almost better like that than it really did sound. I can never live up to my titles. (Nor could anyone else.)[699]

When Anne returned, he gave her a bundle of typescript containing all the poems he had written since 1926, as well as a more recent group which were, he said:

> different: I've played for—O a long while, with the possibility of doing a set of (more or less) love poems, but a little more...something or other.. than most. But how far these—which are the Ianthe poems—are related to the others I simply do not know. Whether, in the imagination, Celia is Ianthe, I honestly can't tell. I'm sure she isn't, outside it![700]

It is not clear what 'the Ianthe poems' were. But it *is* clear that, as a poet, he had lurched to a halt. He could neither abandon the poems he had written, nor move on. He wanted Anne to solve the problem for him. The situation was typified by the day in May 1934 when he tore up a batch of poems, then changed his mind, stuck the fragments together and handed them to her. He wrote:

> To do *nothing*, to leave them, seems so weak & futile (I refer only to the best). Yet to destroy them all . . . Or . . . But anyhow do as you suggest. [. . .] There are large lacunae [. . .] so it's a little difficult to get the effect; but you may as well see them.

Yet in the same letter he toys with the idea of Anne smuggling some of them into the *Oxford Book of Modern Verse*, under a pseudonym: 'it even struck me that Simon Pollard was a nice nondescript name. I should have liked Simon Arglay, but perhaps not! But is it the thing?' [701] He was in a state of utter confusion.

He now confided completely in Anne, working with her, in or out of the office, on a daily basis. Did any hints of sadism emerge? Only very slightly:

> Once [Anne recalled], when he used to come to my flat to have supper—and we did embrace—he once gave me a *tremendous* hard pinch on my arm which left a blue mark for several days which my mother asked me about. And he said 'Well, that's given you something to think about!' Well it did! [702]

Naturally, her response was not in any way flirtatious, and it never happened again. Occasional fantasies surfaced in letters: in May 1934 he threatened to ask about her progress on some editing job, predicting:

> you'll probably be PERT. And then before one can say or do anything all the Dryads in Broceliande will carry you off in their shining shimmering midst. But I won't stand for it; I shall transfix them with a charm, & there will you be all stuck in a bramble, and tied on to it with Merlin's own girdle till you've learnt a hundred lines of the most argumentative part of *Paradise Regained* by heart. [703]

Broceliande was the great western forest of Arthurian tradition. When Anne went on holiday in July 1934, he wrote:

> I made a small discovery: the 'inward eye' of Wordsworth's *Daffodils* must be the same as the eye in the *Intimations* that 'kept watch o'er man's mortality'.— Of no immediate importance, but a Link!
> With which gift, I release you, except for an unbreakable thread about your ankle: if you feel anything pulling you it will be that. Thank you for your

interest, thank you for your work, thank you for you.. the words I really mean
are 'keeping me up to it'. Put your conscience in a bag, & anything that you
think might worry it put in another & keep for me. It is an imposition upon
you—& you mustn't let it be: you can always do me fifty lines instead—a
much pleasanter kind, curiously, in some relationships!⁷⁰⁴

The fantasies of control are gentle, strangely mixed with advice and literary
discussion. Anne was both wise and tolerant. Unlike Phyllis she never used
these urges as means for manipulation. Instead she allowed Williams to discuss, and acknowledge, his own strangeness. Many years later, she recalled,
'He used to make a joke of it and say we didn't know the half of it, and that
if he grew to old age, he'd be discovered as one of the dirty old men in the
park or something like that.'⁷⁰⁵

To speak in this way must have been a solace for him.

★   ★   ★

And solace was needed. Billy Somervaille had returned from Java, where he
was making a successful career in the oil business. He proposed marriage,
and Phyllis—tired of the pressures of Amen House, where she might meet
two married and dissatisfied admirers round any corner—was considering
whether to accept him. She insisted on discussing it with the weary and
battered Williams. 'The problem of Benediction here for some time has
been: does Phillida go to Java or not?' he told Anne Bradby. 'Having died
once, I shan't again either way, so I'm comparatively detached. But it's all
very curious and a little difficult. And no-one knows his or her own mind
for two minutes together.'⁷⁰⁶

At last Phyllis decided. She would marry Billy. And it would happen fast:
she would leave the Press on Friday, August 29 and be married on Monday
morning. She wrote to tell Gerry Hopkins, who was in Ireland, and Williams
also wrote—with some completely unrealistic notion that Gerry might stop
the wedding. 'It seemed to me necessary to my own justice', he told Anne,
'to write, saying: "if you want to act, & can act, act." There is, I suppose, a
faint possibility that he may rush back & do something. But I do not much
think it. And it will anger my heart if he does. Improperly.' Gerry replied—
begging Williams to 'make her wait':

> But I do not see what I can do, [he told Anne] even if I would. I can't ring up
> Celia & beg her to postpone everything. [...] And if there were any power in
> me over her, still I'm not clear that I ought to use it for Gerry as against Billy.

I'm sorry about him; and I am everlastingly grateful that my experience of death came first. He 'ought to have talked to me'. And I—I—I—high heavens, I!—am to help *him!*[707]

He tried to be stoical, but he was in turmoil. 'There is now no more to do', he told Anne in a long and anguished letter:

but I shall sit here and do it. 'This also is Thou, neither is this Thou.' We are all alternately bright & polite—no, that's not fair. It seems the maddest ending to so much beauty & pain & hunger & work & the rest of it; & I am obsessed by a sense of all the time I have wasted [...]

   It occasionally occurs to me that Christian morality & Christian marriage & Downe & other places & things would disapprove. But I'm not very much moved. And yet, if we admit the Celian relationship as permissable, what lowest vulgarity of mere sensual grab can we forbid? However, I will discuss principles for the next five years—& probably for ever. I am simply marvellous at discussing principles.

The letter mixes blame of himself with blame of Phyllis—and with an irrational sense that he should somehow have exercised control over her:

It is absurd how easily the evenings at home pass. I mean, of course, there is a large pain in my toe or heart or liver or somewhere; but there isn't the irritation & darkness I should have expected myself to feel, considering that an erroneous emotion protests that all possibilities of beauty are—But as it has done that at intervals for seven years, I do know it *is* erroneous; it is the self-hood, the illusion. [It is] partly because of the evil in me, since I do not love Celia & Billy & G.H. with complete & utter goodwill; partly because of weakness—I ought never to have let Billy get a foot in, and I ought to have exercised some kind of authority. But it's easy to say so now—[708]

The paragraph breaks off with a scrawl. He resumes, to tell Anne that Phyllis—as if she had not hurt him enough—has 'indicated that she would like [him] to have a few words with Billy' but then changed her mind.

   The letter keeps returning to the idea that Phyllis—or rather Celia—is his *creation*:

The worst of it is that I made her—yes, by God! spiritually, mentally, and in Amen House. Others have admired my handiwork, but little they did towards marking it. 'Incestuous passion of a creator'! It sounds like a headline in the *Demiurgic Times*. What was I saying? O yes. I made her, & she—if she did not make she shaped Billy, & Billy has profited by the shaping[...] I realize that, eight years ago, I envisaged a mutual sanctity, communicated, interchanged, infinitely beautiful and—can it be? talked of? Alas, it isn't in the nature of sanctity to be *so*.

He even hints that he might have considered divorce:

> There was a time—a rather dreadful time—when Michal, half in love and half in pride, would have divorced me; if I had willed. But (and would I? God knows; Gerry was already on the scene, and apart from him—I don't know. At present especially I don't know) one cannot send a child to school, & so on, & so on on five hundred a year and what one makes beside—say, seven hundred. But it annoys me sometimes. Unfair, of course; I sulkily insist on being unfair.

And he rises to a Faustian climax—undercut by a moment of realism:

> Morals & marriage & Downe notwithstanding, I can't repent—I can't, I don't, I won't. On the Judgement Day, I won't.. unless my whole vision is altered. [...] And yet it's all *wrong*, all wrong. [...] 'This also—damn & blast!—is He.' O I am in a temper—I wish I had several bottles of wine & a mad masochist of the most ingenious kind. And in six months' time shall I have forgotten?[709]

The following day he was able to take a lighter tone: 'As Dante told us— there is but one heaven. It is (I feel) a mistake; it would be nice if there were a peculiar Javanese one, & Billy & G.H. were pushed into it, & told to stop there.'[710] But the torment continued. On Saturday morning, the day after Phyllis left, he went to the office—empty now of her magic—and felt better than expected, which he attributed to Anne's taking on the pain, in substitution for him. He went home at lunchtime, and then:

> God help us in a thousand ways, who do you think has just rung up? Billy. 'Phyllis wondered if I would come round & see her.' My people [Michal and Michael] were out—praise God! Does Celia...no, I'm defeated. If they hadn't been coming back, in the rush of the moment I should probably have gone. [...] I should have taken a taxi—shaken to the nerves.[711]

On Sunday evening he went to visit his old friend Eugene Mason. As he walked back over Hornsey Rise, a white-haired gentleman handed him a tract. With a smile and a bow, Williams took it. Glancing down, he read the opening words:

AND THERE WAS **DARKNESS** OVER THE WHOLE EARTH.[712]

Then Monday came. He turned down an invitation to the wedding,[713] and while Phyllis—Celia, Phyllida, Circassia—married William George Somervaille, chartered accountant, at the Marylebone Register Office, Charles Williams sat in a restaurant with the publisher Arthur Barker, smiling and drinking 'more than usual of Caesar's wine', to celebrate the publication of *James I*.[714]

14

'I'm Becoming a Myth to Myself'

'Well,' Williams told Anne Bradby the next day,

> —it happened. In the *Times* this morning. All nice and neat. 'Quietly,' said the notice. [...] It gives me a curious effect of an age-long clock stopping. [...] There is, now, no occasion either to be at Amen House or not to be. For the first time for eight years, it doesn't matter a bit. Curious.

Everything was a blank. Standing in his office, he stared at *James I*: '(a surprisingly tedious book, my dear Miss Bradby! unbelievably unrelated to anything in heaven or earth [...]).' Somewhere, he reflected—'in the strong room here I suppose'—were all those letters Phyllis had sent during his illness, saying 'she couldn't bear to contemplate life without me, [...] And then the outer world caught us again, & we were both strange & obstinate, & there was Gerry, & up to the very end...and now the clock stops.'[715] A few things were left. There was work, and threats of an open-plan office, which Williams resisted because he wanted privacy with visitors: 'There are, occasionally, Souls, & I must have scattered a lot of seed in nine years in my own little place, which I couldn't so well throw in public',[716] he told Anne. (Often, though, discussions with colleagues or friends on spiritual matters took place on the stairs, a fact so well known that in April 1935 *The Lantern*, the staff magazine, carried a neat caricature of Williams striding upstairs, hands in pockets, over verses captioned 'The Rite of the Stairs' [Figure 3]. They were by Ralph Binfield, who was clearly well aware of Williams's ritualistic tendencies.)

But there was still poetry; and there was Anne. The two were now closely connected. Twenty-six years younger than he, Anne had exactly the fresh viewpoint he needed at this crisis in his life. For, approaching his forty-eighth birthday in September 1934, Williams had lost his way as a poet. Since the

THE RITE OF THE STAIRS

When the Poet agilely
up the stairs springs,
think not he wantonly
maketh him wings,
recking no order
of escalate things.

In the pattern of thought
each stair has its place,
each landing has brought
contemplative grace;

the new carpet's woof
in his prose one may trace.

The learned commentator
who, years hence, prepares
to guide the viator
through his thoroughfares,
will reprint a plan
of the O.U.P. stairs.

SCAPIN

Figure 3. The Rite of the Stairs: verse by Ralph Binfield, cartoon by an unknown hand, 1935

unsatisfactory *King Arthur* in early 1930, he had written almost no verse. He was stuck, and he knew it. Yet he had not rejected poetry. Rather, he had devoted his most intense efforts to understanding it. He had surveyed the work of other poets in *Poetry at Present*, and had gone on to deep analysis of what poetry could say about itself in *The English Poetic Mind*, followed by fundamental thoughts on poetic form in *Reason and Beauty*. He had seen the possibilities in Hopkins's experiments in verse, and had privately tried them out. Moreover, in the space of a year he had nearly died, and had lost the second great love of his life. It was a situation full of challenge and potential.

In talk with Anne, his Arthurian interests naturally came up. He gave her the commonplace book in which he had once collected material for an Arthurian epic, and by July 1934 they were discussing the idea that he might resume the Arthurian poems, in a different manner. He was nervous about changing his style, but Anne coaxed him along and reassured him. 'This new playing with verse makes me feel almost shy', he told her, sending a draft of what would become a new 'Prelude' to the Arthurian sequence. 'But you have an admirable way of soothing one's uncertainty whilst maintaining an integrity of judgement.'[717] And in August, after discussing metre, he wrote, 'Re-reading, by accident, our Arthur, I was struck by the idea that the coming of the High Prince to Camelot & the vision of the Grail might correspond to a kind of sense of life—just ordinary life—as one thing.'[718] Whatever this means, it shows they were debating his Grail vision, and the project was now '*our* Arthur'. Williams was sharing his poetry as he had never shared it before.

Anne was the ideal confidante (she would later become, as Anne Ridler, a notable poet in her own right), and in a gentler way she did for Williams what Ezra Pound had done for Yeats twenty years before, providing a modernist sensibility to help the older poet revitalize his work. Her knowledge of poetry had been deepened by her research for the *Oxford Book of Modern Verse*, and she was writing herself, using free verse. She recalled that Williams:

> always seemed to be writing very late at night, and he used to bring new Taliessin poems which he'd just written to me, to discuss them. [. . .] I was very much aware that sometimes he tended to use, to fall into, poetic diction. [. . .] He lived so much in books and the lines were always so much in his head that I'm not sure he always knew when he was using it.[719]

Anne supplied that self-awareness, keeping him from lapsing into old habits.

Instead of an epic, Williams pursued the idea of writing lyrics and short narratives focused on particular incidents from the Arthurian mythos, trusting readers to know enough of the traditional stories to make sense of what he wrote. In this way he could concentrate on episodes that inspired him; and as in *Heroes and Kings* the pivotal figure was the bard Taliessin. Like Tennyson, Williams spelt the name with a double 's'—the usual spelling is 'Taliesin'—perhaps to clarify the pronunciation: four syllables, with the stress on the third: 'Tally-ESS-in'.

Anne was vital to the creative process. He shared with her his developing thoughts on metre, sending her (probably in late 1934) part of a lecture or essay on the subject: 'English verse derives a certain quality of its own from its very uncertainty. There is no common agreement on the proper management of the stresses [...] But that very dispute will reveal unexpected powers in the whole line.'[720] Most of their work together is beyond recovery: Williams generally threw away his drafts. Only a couple of fragments survive to give us a glimpse of their collaboration. Towards the end of 1934 he sent her the following list (the queries are his):

The Poems of Taliessin
Prelude[?]
Logres
The Return of Taliessin
The King's Crowning
The School of the Poets
Palomides
Gareth
Dinadan & Iseult
The King's Justice
The Monks' Carol
The Passing of Merlin
Palomides at the Christening
Taliessin's Meditation
Galahad in the King's Bed
The Riding of Galahad
Mordred
The Pope's Letter [?]
The Last Voyage
Lancelot's Mass

Some idea of Anne's work on the poems can be got from her undated response to a batch of 'poems to date old & new':

> As they are at present I should be doubtful about including:—
>   Song of La Belle Iseult & Sir Dinadan.
>   Carol sung by the Monks
>   Song of the Riding of Galahad
>   Taliessin's Song of the Passing of Merlin
> & I'm not sure about Mordred's Song of the Kingdom.
>   What about the Birth of Galahad & his Farewell?
> And Percivale's song which was printed in *New English Poetry*?
> And then there were one or two lines I wanted to ask you about from the new poems.
> *Taliessin in the School of the Poets.*
> 'Taliessin's shadow, the depth of the width...' seems a little awkward.
> And what does 'no hope' mean in the last verse but two, please?
> *Taliessin's Meditation...*
> I am not sure whether I understand the connection with Merlin & the pall. Is it that the four-pointed pall was half-rent & the altar was behind?
>   Also, it begins with 'Four *points* the world gave'; then how are they 'dimensions at last undimensioned'?
>   Towards the end,—'And a new point that has none.' Does it matter there being no verb for that?
>   Lastly: 'The junction of the two diagonals was pointed,'—mightn't it be better altered to 'was a point'? because if you say 'pointed' you give the sense of another dimension.[721]

And Williams revised readily. Helped by Anne's critical probing, he transformed old poems and wrote new ones: poems forged with much hard work, amidst intense discussion, from the autumn of 1934 onwards. The first, as Anne recalled, was 'Taliessin's Return', completed in September 1934. Its first stanza, full of freshness and vigour—seemingly a young man's poem despite Williams's forty-eight years—surely celebrates this liberation into a new style, a rebirth into true poetry:

> The seas were left behind;
> in a harbour of Logres
> lightly I came to land
> under a roaring wind.
> Strained were the golden sails,
> the masts of the galley creaked
> as it rode for the Golden Horn
> and I for the hills of Wales.

Drafts of other poems followed rapidly: 'The Vision of Empire' in October; 'Taliessin in the School of the Poets' in November; 'Percivale at Carbonek' in February; 'The Crowning of Arthur' in April; 'The Star of Percivale' in July.[722]

Identifying with Taliessin, the sixth-century Celtic bard whom he imagined as court poet to King Arthur (an Arthur imagined as a local king under the Byzantine empire), Williams was returning not only to his long-standing Arthurian vision but to the rich tensions of his early play, *The Chapel of the Thorn*. For Taliessin, 'born of the Druids by the sea, / drank also in the schools of Gaul'. Pagan and Christian, he brings together the figures of pagan bard and Christian mystic from that early drama. Both were sides of Williams himself, who thus found, at last, a voice that spoke from the deepest parts of his being, and its deepest contradictions.

He let go of his old stylistic habits, and of any anxieties about making himself understood by the average reader. Perhaps he sensed that this was his last chance to make something of the grand plan he had cherished all his life. His vision was rich and complex: an amalgam of myth, history, theology, esoteric systems (alchemy, Kabbala, ritual magic), his personal views—and obsessions—about love and sex. Over the years all these had fermented in his mind, forming elaborate patterns embodying deep insight and powerful feelings. And he was lucky: the 1930s were the great age of 'difficult' poetry. With the available examples of Hopkins, Eliot, and the later Yeats, no poet need feel inhibited about expressing complex ideas in dense language. And there was Dylan Thomas. Sending Anne a further draft of the 'Prelude', Williams wrote, flippantly, 'Herewith. Pretty soon I shall abolish the Prelude altogether. Or else leave any odd stanzas I like with no care for intellectual co-ordination. Dylan Thomas & so on.'[723] The remark is frivolous, and unfair to Thomas; but it shows—all the more clearly for its casualness—how even the example of Thomas allowed Williams to relax, to please himself. And the 'Prelude' was not abandoned. Four years later, after many revisions, it would appear at the head of the sequence—sharp, chiselled, cryptic, resonant even at first reading, and, for readers who persisted and pondered, based on a fully coherent logic:

> Recalcitrant tribes heard;
> orthodox wisdom sprang in Caucasia and Thule;
> the glory of the Emperor stretched to the ends of the world.
>
> In the season of midmost Sophia
> the word of the Emperor established a kingdom in Britain;
> they sang in Sophia the immaculate conception of wisdom.

Carbonek, Camelot, Caucasia,
were gates and containers, intermediations of light;
geography breathing geometry, the double-fledged Logos.

Miraculously, absurdly, the most unlikely thing had happened. Charles
Williams had begun to write major poetry, poetry fit to stand beside the
work of his great contemporaries: poetry that deserved to last.

★ ★ ★

Anne continued to hunt for a job in publishing. Williams found her more
work for the Press, and suggested she write *A Word Book of English Poetry*—'a
collection of the important words in great passages of English verse' with
quotations juxtaposing the lines where they occurred, with 'notes upon the
illumination caused by that propinquity'. He listed as examples a few words
he felt should be included: *Hand, Glory, Lordship, Faculties, Metaphysical,
Bewildering.*[724] It was an idea he had applied in his own criticism, tracing
continuities and contrasts in the use of key words by different poets. Anne
did not follow up the idea. Again, Williams was ahead of his time: such
explorations would be made in future by William Empson (*The Structure of
Complex Words*, 1951), C.S. Lewis (*Studies in Words*, 1960), and Raymond
Williams (*Keywords*, 1976).

News of Phyllis drifted back to the office. Alice Mary had seen her and
Billy on honeymoon, and reported that Phyllis was having 'a difficult time'
and had 'fainted under sheer emotional stress'. She was reported to have
said 'Of course, I couldn't leave C.W.' Williams commented, 'Whether she
has arranged to divorce Billy in five years' time I don't know',[725] a malicious speculation but percipient: the marriage would last less than four
years. In Java, Phyllis missed the excitement of Amen House and Charles
Williams. In November she wrote plaintively, 'Am I still Celia?' He replied,
'The answer is that you are. Quite clearly, quite certainly, you are all that
I ever said.'[726]

Meanwhile, Anne nursed her secret love for him. On holiday in Paris in
September 1934, she could no longer hold back. She wrote to tell him that
she loved him. Williams replied with a warning:

I always seem to hurt those that love me—*testibus*[727] Michal & Celia—I don't
want to hurt you more than I shall. I shall, of course: in ways foreseen or
unforeseen. But not more than the world would anyhow, & you will forgive
me more easily than the world.[728]

But almost at once—each wrote daily for a week—his tone became rapturous:

> The dynamite explosion of this week, my adorable tenderness, has so shaken
> me that your envelopes move me more than anything [. . .] A page of you is a
> more tempestuous glory of colour and sound than ever a wandering musician
> ran into before. [. . .] And your poem—
>
> No-one's written me a poem before. [. . .] I was moved & thrilled,—I loved
> you for it: there! And I like your wanting to be kissed—there! and if that is
> egotism I can't help it.[729]

And:

> Here am I, almost fumbling your envelopes, like a boy of seventeen. I have had
> so much love, & yet—as not for eight years—I stammer over it, so fresh, so
> strong, so overpowering a marvel. . . When the earth drops from one's feet, &
> at the same moment over one the heavens open in fire, to say what shall one
> *do* seems inadequate. [. . .]
>
> Goodness, child, do you suppose I easily think people are in love with me? [. . .]
> Let me say then that I love you for it. . . ah that sounds so solemn—'for it'; I
> love you.[730]

So the words were said. He wrote poems for Anne, deciding that she would
be 'Ianthe':

> Ianthe lay on the cushions, with her feet up;
> a tree-cat among the green,
> eyes bright as a tree-cat's,
> eyes and person all energy, thrilled
> from steel-bright passion;
> languish of power departed, in power's assent
> to lie in the power of the moment –
> the lion and the lamb lay down –
> swift as a tree-cat's the eyes, lithe the limbs
> stretched in an ease of power.
> The moment remained; I saw
> one more to one and another added
> of those few stanzas,
> rare, reciprocal,
> written in the song of my brain;
> the rare, few stanzas of women
> that astonish, now as then, the brain of my body [. . .] behold,
> Ianthe lies,
> a tree-cat stretched on the green,
> a sudden new stanza,
> a barbarian splendour ablaze in the Roman encampment.[731]

For gradually Williams's Arthurian myth was permeating his daily life. He 'played with the idea' of having 'a Druid figure—a young priestess, for Taliessin to correspond with. But all that is in the future.'[732] Increasingly, he would become Taliessin; and many of those he knew would be drawn into the myth.

As intimacy with Anne increased, some of the old bizarre fantasies began to surface:

> I will call you *darling* without thinking you are my wife—or anyone but your-self. Anyone. I will call you other names too—'Witch, Hyena, Mermaid, Devil'—or (still more fantastically) Idiot, Stupid—no, not even in pretence. No one, my Anne, ever offered you a greater tribute than is this letter. Kiss me then, darling.[733]

And, sending a poem for comment,

> The last section [...] is admirable; if you deny it, I will send you to a blasted heath to gather twigs without buds, and scourge you with them on the bare back for three times three repetitions of the *Dixi custodiam*. Or no, not if you deny but if you affirm, for certainly no-one should be permitted to praise a poem but in immediate threat of torment, so awful is the integrity of divine Apollo; or if in public he permits relaxation of the Heliconian laws, in private the bees of Hymettus sit on your shoulders and rage with ordeal of stings if you rashly speak well.[734]

But whilst Williams might enjoy a love that made no demands on him, Anne was suffering. In November she wrote for advice to Williams's closest friend, D.H.S. Nicholson. He replied:

> You know, of course, Charles' scheme of substitution: the taking on of A's bother by B, with the idea that B can possibly deal with it better because the *immediate* personal tangle is less urgent. And I have no doubt at all that you are doing this, as regards him & the Celia letters. And have told him that you are doing it? So, also, will I: not only with regard to Charles-Celia, but as regards you-Charles as well.[735]

In a further letter he advised her that:

> while pain is there, it isn't so much Love that one is feeling as want—the reversal of all Omnipotence.
>   Lord! yes: [the pain] is huge. [...] But hasn't it been, also for you, quite defi-nitely the greatest good that has ever happened to you? [...] And if that is so, can one return [...] anything but gratitude, & gladness, & your own love-filled & uplifted heart?
>   You can't, I think, anyhow, make a lovelier gift—or a more efficacious one—to Charles.[736]

So Anne bore it as best she could. In mid-1934 Gollancz commissioned Williams to edit *A New Book of English Verse*, an anthology which they hoped would become a standard work: it was to contain nothing that appeared in either *The Oxford Book of English Verse* or Palgrave's *Golden Treasury*, but 'every poem included should be of poetic importance'.[737] Anne was enlisted to help, and the result was a very fine anthology with a typically brilliant and eccentric 'Introduction' by Williams, bubbling with ideas: on the decline of mythology in English poetry, on poetic cant, and—most centrally—on what Williams called 'the Celian moment': the moment in Restoration poetry 'which contains, almost equally, the actual and the potential'—a point of balance between Elizabethan and Romantic poetry. Taking the figure of Celia from Marvell's 'The Match', Williams's 'Introduction' develops the theory of Celia as the ideal figure of woman in poetry, the poetic Muse.[738] Concealed in the most public of places, it was a last wistful message to Phyllis in her distant exile.

Routine work at the Press was as demanding as ever. There were permissions to clear, meetings to vet quotations for 'Q', manuscripts to appraise, introductions to commission. He wrote asking George Bernard Shaw:

> Would you care, and would the morals of your literary life permit you, to contribute to the proposed edition of Butler's *Way of All Flesh* in the *World's Classics*? I carefully avoid asking for a Preface or Introduction, because I seem to remember that those terms in relation to you have a technical meaning for the world, but if it were possible to have either I should be very glad.[739]

The letter was signed by Milford, but the style is unmistakable. Williams's charm did the trick; Shaw duly contributed an 'Essay'. Meanwhile, Williams told Anne, he was encouraging one of the Press's cleaning ladies to memorize *Paradise Lost*: 'I have begun to find that—incredible fact!—she is moved by Milton. So I am making her learn a few lines at a time, beginning at the end: it was the last two lines that got her.'[740]

And there was Geoffrey Grigson—a case-study in how adeptly Williams handled his critics. Grigson had criticized Williams's *New Book* ferociously in the *Morning Post*.[741] Williams invited him to the office ('I rather liked him', he reported, 'though I think he takes his views a little too seriously once he gets into print'). Soon Williams was backing Grigson's proposal for a book on Cornwall, recommending him as a good person to write the 'Introduction' to Bacon's *Essays* for the World's Classics, and inviting him to propose an anthology of folk song.[742] The hostile critic had become a potential ally and OUP author.

One of the biggest challenges was the *Oxford Book of Modern Verse*. By October 1934 Lascelles Abercrombie, the editor, was too ill to complete it; he gave it up, and Williams hunted for a solution. 'Unless a Name is regarded as very important', he proposed, Anne Bradby might edit it; Dylan Thomas could check the selection; Abercrombie could be paid off. The result, he pointed out, would be cheap: 'Pay [Thomas] £15, Lascelles £10, Anne another £25—making £75 in all, and no royalty to anyone.' But Milford, and Sisam, his opposite number at Oxford, wanted a 'Name'. Williams considered Eliot, De la Mare, Aldous Huxley ('I'm rather attracted by the idea!'), Herbert Read, Robert Graves. Or, again, Dylan Thomas, who 'has been to see me two or three times and shown me some more of his stuff—chiefly short stories [...] His own verse is physiologically modern.' Or they could try Yeats: 'He is 69, but when I met him last year he was vivid and entertaining.' Williams thought that Yeats would probably not take it on, but if he did he 'would awe all sides'.

Yeats, as it turned out, was interested. Now there was another anxiety at the Press: would Yeats, in view of his recent obscure poetry, be too highbrow? Yeats, Sisam told Milford, must be made to see that 'a popular book which ordinary people will enjoy is intended: that, even if "The Fiddler of Dooney" is inferior to his latest hard and high thinking, you (at least in your capacity as publisher) expect him to fiddle.' Once Yeats's selections began to come in, anxieties ran the other way. Was Yeats being too conservative? Even eccentric? Williams wrote to ask why, of the Americans, he had omitted H.D., Robert Frost, and Stephen Benet? Yeats refused to explain in detail, but said he had found H.D. 'empty, mere style', adding for good measure that he intended to exclude T.E. Hulme (merely 'the leader of a school') and Wilfred Owen. In April 1936, with the material all in, Williams summed up: 'The whole book varies most amazingly from the most imbecile simple poems of Masefield and Drinkwater to Mr Empson. You cannot, however, say that it has not a great deal of very popular stuff in it.' On publication, reviewers condemned the anthology as eccentric and unrepresentative. Sales were poor. To complete the mess, Yeats neglected to send out copies to some of the poets. Williams had to do it, adding a letter 'to the general effect that it was all W.B.Y's fault but the publishers are doing what the poet should have done.'[743]

★   ★   ★

In autumn 1934 Williams started lecturing on 'Orthodoxy in Literature' at the City Lit, and on 'English Prose from Malory' at Tooting.[744] He was beginning his biography of the libertine Earl of Rochester. On 26 September he shared his ideas with Anne:

> I think Rochester is to be an 'enthusiast' unknown to himself, & that his riots & exaltations are the enthusiasms of a spirit capable of a world in which he wasn't living [...] so at last he has a little spiritual explosion all inside him, & gets converted. We will not be religious but psychological: I mean, we will play with that side. [...] And now I must pretend to work. You, I may add in passing, get prettier every day.[745]

The publisher Duckworth asked him to write a book for a 'Great Lives' series, and sent a list of subjects. Williams chose Queen Elizabeth. And he made a half-hearted effort to interest the Clarendon Press in an update of *Poetry at Present*—'this pathetic attempt of my immaturity', he called it, not very enticingly. He would add 'Auden, Spender, perhaps one or two more of the new', but commented 'I think I should omit the [verse] endpieces for fear of failing with Auden.'[746] The Press was not persuaded.

His main concern now was to write the Arthurian poems. He shared his ideas, however abstruse, with Anne, almost in a stream of consciousness:

> Palomides in a cycle of Arthurian poems was to pass from Dualism—which was Good and Evil, but as much as sensations as morals—[...] to the Unity of Mahomet and Allah...—and so on to Iseult and Christendom and Logres, where one might very well symbolize the unity of life by marriage, so that all the Saracenic femininities become *one*, by the operation of the will. Since I darkly begin to believe that the operation of the will is necessary for this work, & that most of us do not achieve it because our will never operates.[747]

By February 1935 he was discussing possible titles for a collection of Taliessin poems and sending a draft of 'Galahad at Carbonek':

> Galahad stood in the gate of Carbonek;
> the folk of Pelleas ran to greet him;
> Christ was before him, behind the [*illegible*] silk of the sun.
> His eyes were vacant; he sighed *Bless me, Lord Percivale* [...]

He discussed titles for the sequence, suggesting *Taliessin through Logres* ('Do you not think that "through" is better than "-in in"', he asked Anne, 'and that it sounds far more modern & mysterious?').[748] Later in the year he added, 'I love that title; why? O it sounds romantic and vague and is almost classically exact.'[749] It did not strike him that readers might find the title both incomprehensible and unpronounceable, a likely hindrance to sales.

He confessed to profound frustration that his work and ideas were not being taken seriously. 'The Listener', he complained—when the BBC's weekly magazine reviewed *Reason and Beauty*—'says I am vague. O Ianthe-Nan-Anne, what the hell am I? I can't be anything. The answer is that until I've created "the people of C.W." I shan't be understood.'[750]

★   ★   ★

In fact, 'the people of C.W.' were already assembling. Mostly they were members of his lecture audiences. Besides Anne Bradby, there were Thelma Shuttleworth (formerly Mills) and Raymond Hunt; at the Press there was Alice Mary Smyth. In 1933 or 1934 they were joined by Joan Wallis and her fiancé Richard Wallis (unrelated, despite the shared surname). Deciding to take a class in English Literature, the couple arrived at the evening centre in Tooting to be told that the lecturer had recently been in hospital and was still not entirely well. The lecture went ahead, but a lady brought a cup of tea for the tutor, who, Joan recalled, 'practically bent on the ground [...] to say thank you, and with great salaams'—Williams's customary display of ceremonious courtesy. At first sight she 'thought he was a drastically ill man', but 'he was a very good lecturer [and] it was very much an hour's lecture and a discussion. Which, poor man! went on for ever and ever and ever— [...] you know, you get people interested, and they never let you go!'[751] Soon she and Richard were staying after the lectures to discuss not only literature but their ideas, aspirations, and personal lives. That the Wallises were Quakers did not stop them from treating Williams as a spiritual adviser, a role he was happy to take on. From this it was a short step for Joan to begin meeting Williams in the city, where she worked at the Prudential Assurance offices in Holborn. He would meet her train at Holborn Viaduct Station on the way to work, his appearance less than suave, since his hand-tremor prevented him from shaving himself, and he would see her to her office, talking all the way, before going to a barber for a shave and then on to Amen House. Of these meetings, Joan recalled:

> this curious unshaven person used to wait for me at Holborn Station. And then he'd walk back with me, and I'd say, 'I mustn't be late because I mustn't sign below the line or I shall lose my job,' or something. He took no notice

whatever, he was in the middle of Milton! And of course all the unkind people I worked with were treading on my heels and shoving me.[752]

At the office they would ask her about 'that man with a cockney accent'.

But perhaps when Williams spoke of 'the people of C.W.' he meant something more, and was following up a suggestion of Anne's. They had a running joke about her being his 'secretary'. 'My secretaries [...] become, anyhow for awhile, quite the most beautiful women in the Town',[753] he told her; and:

I can't spare you. I must have some-one to be a secretary, & my secretary's duties, sweetness, are of a very complex & tiring kind. For besides writing books for themselves, which is a very important part of their duties to me [...] and becoming Distinguished Careers, they have to be looking up my references, & searching in Museums, & reading my MSS., and commenting on my verse; [...] and also they have never to cease from the thought of sanctity, and the desire of lucidity, & the study of the divinities. And what they get for it in the end, God knows.[754]

As Williams, in 1934 and 1935, came to inhabit his Arthurian and Byzantine visions more and more intensely, the 'secretary' fantasy proliferated, and in the midst of letters to Anne he would wander off into elaborate digressions. Here is just one sample:

Where was I? where were the Secretaries? I could tell the second easier than the first; the secretaries were listening attentively, and waiting an opportunity to say But—All but the Barbarian maid, who, supposing the Prince & the Secretaries to be more or less indefinitely set, had slipped out of the marble door into the Court of the quincunx of Fountains, and was flirting with the sentinel on guard: who was taking part in the military theatricals & had decided that the part of the Young Recruit was the silliest he ever read—but it took him some time to explain, so that through the twilight of the evening the Palace was hushed, except where the Secretaries sat patiently listening to the voice of the Prince, & the maid—less patiently—to the voice of the soldier; & the paraquet that sat on the cornice of the marble door heard a voice within & a voice without, & put its head under its wing & went to sleep.[755]

The fantasies make it clear that when Williams refers pointedly to 'Secretaries' and the like, he is talking about Anne. This is interesting, because in an undated letter, probably of 1934, he writes:

though mystical and sacramental communications exist, and are to be valued, yet the method which the Sacred Secretariat [...] proposed as an implicit Order, would be [...] setting the individual experience above the common morality of the Church.[756]

What this means is not clear; but Williams had lent Anne (the 'Sacred Secretariat') a typescript of *Romantic Theology* in September 1934.[757] He also encouraged her to read Waite's *Secret Doctrine in Israel*.[758] Did she suggest that he should establish some kind of mystical Order—an Order, perhaps, of those who had known the kind of love described in *Romantic Theology*? Now, he rejected the idea. But perhaps the notion stayed with him and took root. Meanwhile, the people who confided in him and discussed his ideas merged with his vision of the Arthurian court, the king's 'household'. In August 1935, for example, he told Anne, jokingly, that after the age of sixty he would never utter an opinion on poetry, and had sworn to this by 'the loves of the strange women that visit Us (but not of Our Household)'.[759] Whatever this means, it implies an inner circle of confidantes; and it uses the royal (or papal?) 'We'.

Certainly he felt, not altogether happily, that life and myth were becoming one. 'Ianthe', he addressed Anne:

> you are creating a myth: I'm becoming a myth to myself. Admirable disciple! it is what I have done for others. I have given them myths which they have kept. I am Phoebus, the maker of myths.[760]

Like other twentieth-century poets—Graves, Yeats, even Eliot—Williams needed a muse. He had found one in Anne Bradby. But she may not have been the only one.

★   ★   ★

Who was Olive Speake? She is working in the OUP's Music Department in the summer of 1935. By the end of 1936 she has left, but Williams continues to write to her until 1942. Then she vanishes. Nothing else is certain. But to Williams, she was 'Stella', the Star; and, for a time, essential to his poetry. In July 1935 he was working on what would become 'The Star of Percivale':

> By the magical western door in the king's hall
> the Lord Percivale harped; he added no voice;
> between string and string, all accumulated distance of sound,
> a star rode by, through the round window, in the sky of Camelot

– and imaginatively he connected her with the star: 'the Stella of the verses has got so mixed up with the Star of Percivale that—but then you will know nothing of the Star of Percivale, will you? which is his coat of arms in my cycle', he told her, adding that he had written a poem about 'Stella and

Rome', which he would show her at Amen House the next day, if she 'had a moment to spare when the clock's needle pricks through 5.30'.[761]

The poem celebrates the inspiration she has given, enabling him to realize his imaginative conception of Rome in poetry:

> Between the early morn and the fuller morn,
> by a window of vision, looking over trees,
> I saw the Empire floating beyond the world;
> here, there, held to it by magnetic attraction,
> yet always soaring away at the point of Rome,
> the point of lovely manual necessity:
> suddenly among the trees reflected in my thought
> Stella's hands lay; the Empire
> was drawn to them; they lay on the trees,
> a machine of trees, an instrument of publication;
> they, typing, were the art of the Emperor.
>
> Reasonless, as reasonless as a chance sweetmeat,
> as an ostentation of pencil-crossed palms,
> as wit that clamoured & was clinched in the flesh,
> (Tolerable mark on a tolerable clarity)
> reasonless the hands came, yet they came.
>
> Nine months, uncertainly pausing,
> I had looked and waited for Rome –
> suddenly I saw it.
>
> Ignorant of the need of the poem,
> alien, negligent, preoccupied,
> in the morning, between two thoughts in the poem,
> the sudden clear arms and hands,
> thrusting, made the link of connexion.
> I cried through the trees & the morning: *Rome*.
>
> I turned & completed the poem.[762]

This poem was for Olive's eyes only. But the 'completed' poem it refers to is one intended for publication, called 'The Vision of the Empire'. The 'nine months' were from October 1934, when he had shown Anne its first draft, to July 1935, when it was finished. He had found his inspiration in 'hands': Olive's hands at the typewriter had linked, imaginatively, with the hands of scribes writing out the decrees of the Emperor; with 'the heart-breaking manual acts of the Pope' as he consecrated the bread of the Mass; and with the hands of the human body, which is also the Empire itself:

> O you shoulders, elbows, wrists,
> bless him, praise him, magnify him for ever;

you fittings of thumbs and fingers,
bless ye the Lord[.]

But why are Olive's hands 'pencil-crossed'? Other letters make this clear.
Williams was playing with her the games of pain and punishment he had
discovered with Phyllis. The 'pencil-crossed' palms have been struck, hard,
with pencils. Other private poems show 'Stella, fixed in a corner, fac[ing]
the wall [...] Her hands behind her the exposed palms of obedience'; or 'her
wrists [...] corded', or 'girt [...] with a handsomeness of hurt'.[763] And this
was not merely for fun, for a fugitive sexual pleasure. It was happening
because Williams had come to believe that it was necessary to enable him to
write poetry.

This is conveyed in another poem written secretly for Olive, where he
shows her objecting to his treatment of her:

'You think too much of control & penance,' she said;
   'I show not my strife to the fashion of a selfish mind.'
And I: 'Have your will; I dispute not at all; from your hand
   let fall the crownet of verse; be the vision resigned.'

Yet for a moment she yielded, she sank to the pose
   of a serious folly, 'twixt doubt and belief and scorn;
yet, ere she broke from the song, she paused; there rose
   through her, beyond her, the house of the Golden Horn.[764]

The Golden Horn is the strait of Byzantium, the centre of Williams's poetic
vision. Williams is seeing it imaginatively 'through her'. But he also tells her,
with a hint of moral blackmail, that she is perfectly free to stop playing these
games of 'control & penance'—so long as she understands that by doing so
she will 'let fall the crownet of verse' and the vision will be gone. But if she
wants to be his muse, she must submit to the rituals. And that these acts *were*
rituals is made clear by yet another of these private verses:

In the controlled ritual, nay, scourged in pretence,
   she emerged out of herself, into shape by shade;
a maid played with a thought on the stair of porphyry,
   in the rare glory, origin of spirit and sense.[765]

The lines are obscure, but some things are clear. The 'stair of porphyry', in
the published poems, is the staircase that leads to the Emperor's throne
room; by means of a 'controlled ritual' of pretended scourging, Olive
becomes a part of Williams's Arthurian–Byzantine vision, a 'maid' in a creative radiance of 'spirit and sense'.

How had Williams come to believe that to write his best poems he must engage in sadistic rituals with a young woman? Ever since reading Patmore's *The Unknown Eros*, he had been fascinated by the possibilities of 'transmuting' sexual energy. His most intense poetic outpourings in the past—*The Silver Stair*, written for Michal during their first love; the *Century of Poems*, written for Phyllis—had come when his attraction to a woman was combined with sexual frustration. There had been discussion with Nicholson and Lee about Eastern and Western 'tantric' techniques. He had come to believe that sexual arousal enhanced his poetry. Phyllis was gone; he could not use her. Anne Bradby, who truly loved him and applied her critical intelligence to his poems, would not co-operate. But he had found a substitute in Olive.

And one *can* speak of his 'using' her, because it is his own expression. In 1942, in his last surviving letter to Olive, he says, 'I look forward still to writing verse a little—better, with luck, than I have done: "the best is yet to be". If you were here, I should certainly be selfish and use you: how? you very well know; why? because it speeds me to my work[.]' And Olive (though her own letters have not survived) seems to have been quite happy to be 'used'. The sheer duration of the relationship—over seven years—suggests as much; moreover, Williams quotes Olive herself. Sending her, for example, two stamps, value 1½d each, and apologizing for the extra penny:

> because the last time we dealt with each other, you said, 'Leave the penny on, because it stings more like that' [...] So here the two pennies are—one for each hand: and I really shall give you six on each as soon as possible.[766]

Sure enough, in his next letter, he mentions that Olive has returned a penny stamp, explaining 'because I only have two hands'.[767]

There were other rituals too. In the joking tone he usually adopts when proposing what are evidently magical practices to his women friends, Williams meditates on the morning and evening stars, Phosphor and Vesper, and modulates into devising an initiatory ritual for Olive / Stella:

> [You are] personified with the movement of the light, of which your arms are the paths: but which is Vesper and which is Phosphor? The left must be Phosphor, because otherwise it would go *against* the path of the sun—which is forbidden by all occult tradition. So the path must be down the left arm for the dawn and up the right for the evening, which are the Morning and Evening Joy, of which I will tell you sometime. But come now—or rather come as soon as possible—& I will make of you in a ritual the Double Staircase of the Path, which I have just invented, and yet it is a mystery and a sacrament, only you must ask, for that is a necessity of Initiation: & it is by binding the

wrists together, first in front, and then behind, so that the figure is, as it were, encompassed: was not that why elastic bands were made? No doubt it should strictly be the binding of the hands to the thighs, & of the ankles together, but that might be (according to modern etiquette) inconvenient, so the other shall serve. And thus you will remember that you are indeed the Path of the Light, & if people annoy you or your mother hurts you it is because you are not yet perfectly the Path, & you will not be so deeply troubled. But since ritual should have a little speech, we will create dialogue in versicles, so:

> Are you the Star?
> —I am the path of the Star.
> What do you desire?
> – To be utterly the Star.
> Is it possible?
> – All things are possible.
> Be glorious in the Star.
> – Amen.

Which is said between the binding and the loosing, at the front & the back.

This is the first ritual I have written, if you except the *Rite of the Passion*, which is like yet unlike—and a pretty little bit of work, & most significant. And it will be very proper of you to mean it; indeed, how could you better spend those two sentences of which we were talking [. . .] and then you could put them in an envelope & seal it & address it to me and put it on my table or keep it ready at any moment, and let me have it[.][768]

The 'two sentences' are mentioned earlier in the letter, where he asks her to 'make an answer of no more than two sentences'. Of course, the full meaning of all this is lost to us in a world of private jokes and discussions.

It was to Olive that Williams hastened first to report a small triumph. He had given some of his recent poems, including 'The Crowning of Arthur', to the Irish poet and novelist James Stephens. A few days later he spotted Stephens on the escalator at the Tube station at Tottenham Court Road. Stephens hailed him exuberantly: 'Well, you're a very lucky man, to have *that* in your pocket! No-one will thank you or praise you, probably no-one alive will want it; but this is it, and you know it!' Stephens added, 'How paltry Eliot's work seems by that!' 'I wouldn't go that far', Williams later recalled modestly, adding that to Stephens he had 'demurred—I hope sincerely—but he [Stephens] only said, "but of course you know it is", & ran away'.[769] Williams told Phyllis too, in a letter. He was pleased to be placed above Eliot, and equally to find Stephens concurring with his own instinct: 'This is it, and you know it!' He was writing real poetry at last.

★   ★   ★

As 1934 drew to its end Williams was as busy as ever: lecturing to the English Association in London and Oxford, dealing with proofs of his *Ring and the Book*, fending off the usual hopeful visitors to the Press (including a Mr Longbridge, who announced himself as 'becoming the foremost lyricist of the world').[770]

Above all, he was struggling with *Rochester.* 'I have decided', he told Anne, 'that the *Life of Lord John Wilmot, Earl of Rochester* shall not be about the Lord J.W., at all. It will be about me. [...] This will destroy all our Mr. Barker's hopes of it selling, but he won't know the inner truth.' He amused himself with analysing the Restoration rake Kabbalistically ('I doubt if my lord had reached Tiphereth, or even Netzach—though perhaps he had dimly mounted to Yesod, though not the Yesod of Dante') but he was finding it increasingly hard to grind out the words. And he was pledged, on finishing *Rochester*, to start work on a life of Queen Elizabeth:

> If it were not for finance, I should like at moments to feel I couldn't write. [...] I slept this afternoon [...] and I have written 7½ pages of this kind, & I will write, if God wills, another 2½, making about two thousand words; & if I can manage 15 to-morrow, that will be five thousand in all: & you have about 20 or 25—that would be ten thousand. [...] Goodness of God, here is a seventh done! What am I grumbling about? And a thousand a day—on average—would take? say 60 days—say 9 weeks. Christmas. Well, if I got the first draft done by Christmas.. but I shan't. [...] Still, by the end of the year? and *Elizabeth* is only to be facts, & only 31,000—so that oughtn't to take more than a month[.][771]

He concluded ruefully, 'if I wrote another page to you [...] I should have written 7,000 words this week-end'.

Soon he was grumbling again:

> How this damn book is ever going to reach 75,000 words I don't know— God may. [...] We have reached 17,000, & all the best bits except the repentance. [...] My present motto is: *Keep Milton out;* if he once gets in, we're lost. If I get all the other stuff in the next 17,000, there'll be nothing for it but to make two words grow where only one grew before.[772]

He battled on over Christmas, and in February was able to report that 'Barker approves of Rochester so far [and] Miss Butts in three pages, bless her, becomes lyrical'[773]—for he was now meeting, and corresponding with, the novelist and reviewer Mary Butts.

But as he struggled to the end of *Rochester*, new challenges appeared. Early in 1935, the Press was contacted by Alexander Dru, the translator of Kierkegaard. The Danish philosopher and theologian was then hardly known in the

English-speaking world; Dru proposed that the Press publish a ten-volume edition of Kierkegaard in English. Williams was intrigued. Never having heard of Kierkegaard, he read an American selection—the only one available—and proposed that the OUP bring out its own volume of selected works. Dru, wanting ten volumes, was displeased, but Williams soothed him: 'We are of course a little hampered here by not having any of Kierkegaard's actual work before us. [...] Kierkegaard is no doubt frightfully important but we would not promise to publish a manuscript by St Thomas or Socrates without seeing it.'[774]

The Press tested the water by publishing *Philosophical Fragments* in 1936. A series of Kierkegaard volumes followed: *Journals* (1938), *Christian Discourses* (1939),*Stages on Life's Way* and *The Present Age* (1940), *The Sickness Unto Death* (1941), *Repetition* (1942), and many others, continuing into the 1960s. Publishing Kiekegaard in English became an important part of Williams's work for the rest of his life.

★ ★ ★

Just as the Kierkegaard venture began, he heard from George Bell, Bishop of Chichester. Bell was passionate about the arts, and had arranged the commissioning of T.S. Eliot's play *Murder in the Cathedral* for the Canterbury Festival of June 1935. Bell was writing a biography of Randall Davidson, the previous Archbishop of Canterbury, and Williams was to oversee its publication. On 18 February 1935 he told Anne Bradby:

> The first four MS. volumes of the Lord Archbishop's life have just come [...] He suggests I shall go & spend a night at the PALACE; I think I shall. I have a vague vision of putting *Romantic Theology* over the Bishop, & thus over the C. of E. But my proposals for myself so rarely come off; God generally manages differently—& no doubt better.[775]

At this point, his confidence in *Romantic Theology* had returned, and he had recently lent it to Anne, to Raymond Hunt, and to L.H. Myers, besides submitting it (unsuccessfully) to Gollancz.[776]

The visit took place soon afterwards. Williams explained Romantic Theology to the Bishop: after all, he reflected, Bell might one day become Archbishop of Canterbury! Bell did not adopt Romantic Theology, but he did something perhaps as important: he recommended Williams as playwright for the next year's Canterbury Festival. He made the suggestion to E. Martin Browne, the producer in charge of religious drama in the diocese. Browne had already been deeply impressed by hearing Williams lecture.[777] He endorsed the recommendation and passed it to Margaret Babington, who ran the Friends of Canterbury Cathedral; and on 6 July, two weeks after *Murder in the Cathedral* finished its run at Canterbury, Williams came home from the office with a letter from Miss Babington. Years later, he reminded Michal of how 'I came home one Saturday [...] & told you I had been asked to do a play for Canterbury & they might not pay much, and you said that of course it must be done.'[778]

Soon afterwards, Michal and Michael saw him off from Victoria Station—'The first morning of my Dramatic Career', he told Michal proudly[779]—to Canterbury, where he was greeted by Martin Browne, who took him to meet the remarkable Miss Babington: 'tall and very, very slim, correct in her behaviour as a vicar's daughter' (which she was), soft-spoken as a young girl; but tireless, equipped with steely determination, and devoted to the Cathedral and its culture. According to Browne, 'she said "Mr Williams, I have one request to make. So far, every festival hero has been carried out dead from the Chapter House: could you choose one who needn't be?" Charles did not hesitate for a moment: "Cranmer: he ran to his death."'[780] As compiler of the *Book of Common Prayer* and presumed author of the Thirty-Nine Articles, Cranmer (Archbishop of Canterbury from 1533 to 1555) was an Anglican theologian of fundamental importance, and a tormented figure, caught in the Tudor controversies over monarchy and religion. His story was full of the tensions and ambiguities which appealed to the dramatist in Williams. And Williams was intrigued by the odd detail that, according to eyewitnesses, Cranmer *ran* to the stake, as if eager for martyrdom.

Whether the subject was really chosen quite so easily is uncertain. Williams told Anne:

We went, & We conversed with Miss Babington, & We surveyed the Chapter House. [...] We also exposed Cranmer. As the afternoon wore on We became aware that Cranmer was tending to increase: for not only Miss B., but We Ourselves became aware that *all* their plays had been medieval, & that the history of the Church was not in effect confined to coat armour and spear points. [...] Also We were attracted by the possibility of King Henry VIII in a Crown and golden mask, thus presenting (i) Henry (ii) the King (iii) the Glory of the World (iv) the Terror of life. [...] We have arranged to extract some money from Canterbury, & We propose to extract more from the imperial loveliness of Caesar.[781]

He was given a free hand, and for the remainder of the summer he toiled away, now having *Cranmer* to write besides the Taliessin poems, the *New Book of English Verse*, the proofs of *Rochester* (due for publication in September) and *Queen Elizabeth*, alongside his usual OUP work.

He worked on *Cranmer*—the title at some point evolving into *Thomas Cranmer of Canterbury*—with Anne, also consulting Fred Page ('Colin'). Anne's help was especially needed, as he wanted to evolve a suitable style of verse for the play and was having trouble dragging himself away from the influence of Lascelles Abercrombie's turgid verse plays. He intended to use 'the Skeleton', an enigmatic spokesperson, to raise disturbing issues in the play, and told Anne:

> Colin thinks there is too much Skeleton. [. . .] I rather agree, but it's difficult to cut nicely. [. . .] As for Cranmer—[. . .] you observed what I myself had acutely & peevishly remarked—viz., the curious Abercrombieness of some of it. If you ask me, Cranmer's own very first line was far too Lascellian: I can't think why. [. . .] I don't quite know what to do: irregular speeches & stanzaic arrangements are awkward. [. . .] I grow more and more inclined to call it a Masque; there would be something not inappropriate in substituting this for the ineffective Third.[782]

Eventually, in the programme but not in the published script, the play was subtitled 'A Masque', and though Williams's notion that it somehow stood in place of the 'ineffective Third' *Masque of Amen House* remained a private fancy, he was determined to retain a stylized element in the play. 'There is something to be said for doing the Reformation as a kind of frieze or dance', he told Anne. 'I a little like the notion of the Death & the Life [...] racing up & down the steps of the stage while the crowned and gold-masked figure of Mary moves rather slowly up the central aisle from the door.'[783]

★   ★   ★

Despite the intensity of this work, and the trysts with Olive Speake, Williams had not forgotten Phyllis. Life with Michal, he told Anne Bradby, had settled down:

> the occasional allusions here seem for the moment to have faded. [. . .] It was only a couple of weeks ago that it occurred to me how nicely (I do mean that) things were going on. And I was almost inclined to think I should have to give up my favourite part as a Tragic—

But, after digressing a little, he continues:

> On Monday night I was a little haunted, & last night. And for the first time
> since the first beginning [...] I was provoked by a temptation to wish nothing
> had ever happened. And that surprised me. In fact, I might almost have been
> capable of repenting, but as it would lead nowhere, I decided not to.
>
> I do wish sometimes I could honestly prefer someone else's happiness to
> mine. You seem to do it, as by nature.[784]

And he continued writing desperately to Phyllis:

> My own dearest Celia,
> It seems more like tuberculosis to me—some thing living has gone out of
> the air, and my lungs don't breathe properly. When it isn't nightmares—there
> was a nightmare of you in Charing Cross Rd. the other day, a thin ghost of you
> that wasn't you, and another on Haverstock Hill; and the second did cross my
> mind with the question 'Wouldn't you rather it had none of it happened?' and
> it was nearer a temptation than ever to say 'Yes', so horrid are the empty
> images of you. [...] I think sometimes we were given three warnings—your
> leg, and my guts, and this; and that this is the last.
> One can, it seems, telephone to Java. It costs five pounds for three minutes,
> & cheap too.[785]

He oscillated between picking over the past and ruminating on her connections with the new poems he was writing:

> I sometimes wish all your other lovers hadn't been so much richer than I—it
> put me at a disadvantage, my sweet comrade. And I sometimes wonder if you
> hadn't been so preoccupied when my household did nearly break up, whether
> I shouldn't have helped it. After all when one has struck...
> Did I tell you that on the day before Christmas I bought a guide to Rome
> secondhand because it had several pages about the Caelian Hill? This led me
> elsewhere & I found that the Hill was named after Coelius Vibenna, an
> Etruscan. Now the Etruscans were great magicians, so I have taken the Coe- as
> Etruscan magic and desire, & the Cae- as Christian & Lateran, & celestial &
> Celian; & in a poem I have written:
>
> > The doctrine triumphs in the change of the diphthong,
> > in the heartrending manual acts of the Pope.
> > the Caelian hands fracture the Host.
>
> But the poem is not written yet.[786]

And again:

> There is no bottom, no fact, about my world. Michal tells me I have lost inter-
> est in everything [...] It is true if I ever stop being busy I am lost in nightmares,
> and even the busyness is sick.

About the poems [...] I will say this. The root of them is you and me in love, & Love. It is personal, & it is (I hope) also universalised, because that is what poetry does. But the fact is the relation of your world & my world, and roughly those are the worlds of sensation & intellect. Together, with other worlds, they become the Empire [...] Circassia is sensation; Logres is Intellect [...] And Taliessin is Logres in speech. [...] Have you never understood, my own, that I was trying to do a new thing in poetry & in the Graal legend? And to do it I needed you, & your utter goodwill, as much as you needed me.

    Celia, I adore you, I love you, I need you. I need you as much as any of the others do. I shall die sooner than you will fade from me.[787]

If Phyllis failed to write, he would become anxious and depressed.[788] He even tried a kind of magical visualization to bring her closer:

I will shut the eyes of my spirit that stare at you as an alien-choosing star, and open its ears to hear the voice that is so huskily-sweet on the telephone saying 'write what you are thinking', & I draw a straight line of wall on each side from me to you, and mark it with the pentagram of safety and the monogram of Celia, to shut out the devils, & proceed.[789]

At the end of August a letter came, and 'not a particularly happy letter'. Phyllis was expecting a baby in January, and she was bored to tears:

what with climate, & pregnancy, & monotony, & gossip, & games (I gather there is an intolerable amount of watching games), the world is pretty disgusting. Everyone says that 'life will be quite different after the baby is born.' Perhaps it will.

Her marriage, little more than a year old, was already in trouble. Williams continued, 'I don't think I mind much about the baby—or the preceding acts. [...] We are in the way of necessity, and only God knows what will emerge in the end. She is in the headless place, & only the Emperor can move.'[790]

    That last, cryptic statement shows Williams entering once more into his own mythology. Brooding on Phyllis's exile in Java, he had developed a grim imaginative counterpoise to the living and fruitful realm of Arthurian Britain and the orderly hierarchy of the Empire. Scrutinizing historical maps in the library, investigating the region where Phyllis had gone, he fixed on P'o-lu, a medieval Chinese name for present-day Barus in north-west Sumatra.[791] He imagined P'o-lu as a vile realm of repulsive dissolution and formlessness: everything that Logres—Arthur's Britain—was not. He filled out the vision with an image from Procopius, the Byzantine historian: 'Some [...] said that the Emperor suddenly rose from his throne and walked about [...] and immediately Justinian's head vanished, while the rest of his body seemed to ebb and flow; whereat the beholder stood aghast and fearful.'[792] In the recently written 'Vision of the Empire' this became:

> Inarticulate always on an inarticulate sea
> beyond P'o-lu the headless Emperor moves,
> the octopuses round him; lost are the Roman hands;
> lost are the substantial instruments of being.

He consoled himself by offering Anne a Christmas present, and suggesting for himself:

a pocket Lady Julian, if such a thing is obtainable still. [...] The Archdeacon [in *War in Heaven*], I remember, read her, and now I am approaching his age, though without his achievement, I might read her again: I did once, mostly.[793]

The *Revelations of Divine Love* of Dame Julian of Norwich would become one of his favourite books.

Meanwhile, at Amen House—despite the disarray of his own private life—Williams's readiness to listen, his penetratingly intelligent advice, and his unshockability led him to be regarded as a fount of wisdom on personal and spiritual matters, a role he found tiresome at times. After an affair with the indefatigable Gerry Hopkins,[794] Alice Mary Smyth had married Peter Miller in April 1935 but by August was involved with an OUP employee, John Anderson. Both parties insisted on consulting Williams. Alice Mary, he told Phyllis:

has been going about looking (Goffin said) 'like death'. She told me she didn't mind the prospect of the days—it was the nights that horrified her. [...] Meanwhile, presenting my world-famous deific act—'C.W. featuring God'—I talk to J.A. I am a little tired of featuring God, but it seems I am bound to it for the run of the piece, the other more agreeable parts being taken. Of course, the contract can be torn up—sometimes, since last year, it has seemed as if I too can throw away my birthright [...] and as if I were choosing between cerebral and actual masturbation & poetry—& not choosing poetry.

Explaining all this to Phyllis, he ended, 'I love you; I am tired of saying I need you; and anyhow we mean quite different things by "love", and they never meet. Goodbye. O I hate, hate, hate everything—the world and myself and you—I hate it for months, and it grows. Blessing, be blessed.'[795] Still

Phyllis managed to add a note of bathos. By the end of the year she had written to Milford, and, Williams told Anne, was proposing to call her baby, if a girl, Penelope:

> but if a boy—Humphrey. It is sublime—& worthy Celia: can one say more? The Imperial mind seemed pleased; and so it very well might. Billy, Gerry, me [...] and the fine flower of our labours and our passions—behold a little Humphrey! [...] Conceive Gerry and me, in years to come, saying, 'How are you, Humphrey?'[796]

Williams makes it sound as if he, Gerry, and Billy had been equally involved in the child's conception. Perhaps, in some metaphysical way, he thought they had.

★   ★   ★

In 1935 two of Willams's best friends became fatally ill. Eugene Mason, the Catholic poet and critic, was dying of cancer at Felixstowe. He was alone in the world, and Williams not only visited him but nursed him tenderly, spending the weekend of 10 and 11 August at his bedside and returning the following weekend to do what he could, including fetching painkillers. 'I am writing from poor little Eugene Mason's [room]', he told Phyllis:

> He has been ill for two years, & after last August had another operation & [...] now he is dying. [...] He is conscious & moaning a little; I shall get some heroin presently—to ease the departure from this world of fools. I have said the Cymbeline Dirge, though he couldn't hear it—and a little of his pet Nightingale Ode on the chance of some rhythm penetrating. But even those things cannot perhaps cure now, any more than—alone—they can save the soul, whatever one means by *that*.[797]

Early in 1936 Daniel Nicholson too died. Williams had known him since 1915: Nicholson was, he said, 'the dearest of my male friends'.[798] Nicholson died in London on 25 January, and for Williams his passing made an epoch, for he had also been friendly with Phyllis, sharing her lively sense of the ridiculous—his death broke another link with her. Returning to his office after the funeral, Williams was touched to find a note of sympathy from Milford on his desk. The result was two poems addressed to Milford, expressing his sense that Milford had somehow presided over his love for Phyllis and made it possible—a notion which now merged with his personal Arthurian–Byzantine myth:

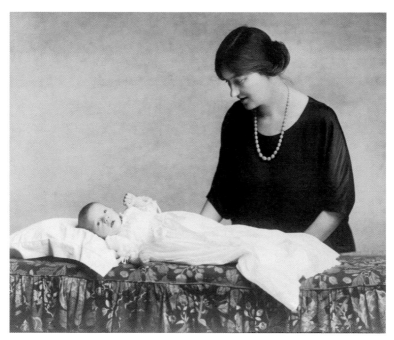

Plate 1. 'Michal' (Florence) Williams, with Michael

Plate 2. Charles aged about 18 months: a studio portrait

Plate 3. North London poverty: in the backyard at 76 Canonbury Road

Plate 4. Charles and Edith with their mother: a studio portrait

Plate 5. Charles and Edith in the garden at 36 Victoria Street, St Albans

Plate 6. Bohemian uncle: Charles Wall in the garden at St Albans

Plate 7. Amateur theatricals: Charles in costume with his father

Plate 8. Florence Conway in medieval costume for the St Albans pageant, 1907

Plate 9. Charles Williams, c. 1910

Plate 10. The quizzical father: Charles Williams in the park with Michael, c. 1922

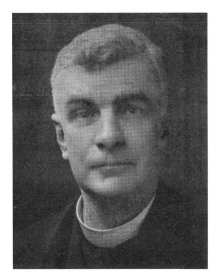

Plate 11. Arthur Hugh Evelyn Lee, Vicar and Magician

Plate 12. A.E. Waite

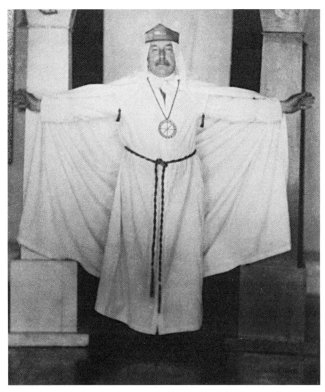

Plate 13. Waite in his robes as Imperator of the Fellowship of the Rosy Cross

Plate 14. Amen House [1924]

Plate 15. The Library at Amen House

Plate 16. Phyllis Jones

Plate 17. Benign despot: Humphrey
Milford, *alias* Caesar

Plate 18. Anne Bradby

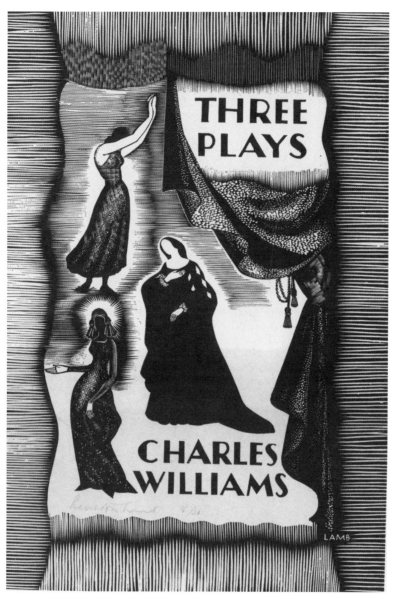

THREE
PLAYS

CHARLES
WILLIAMS

Plate 19. Cover design for *Three Plays*: woodcut by Lynton Lamb

Plate 20. The serious author: publicity portrait, 1930s

Plate 21. *Cranmer:* production photograph, 1936

Plate 22. The Londoner: Williams snapped by
a street photographer, 1930s

Plate 23. Charles Williams reading aloud: drawing by E.G.
Pierce, 1936

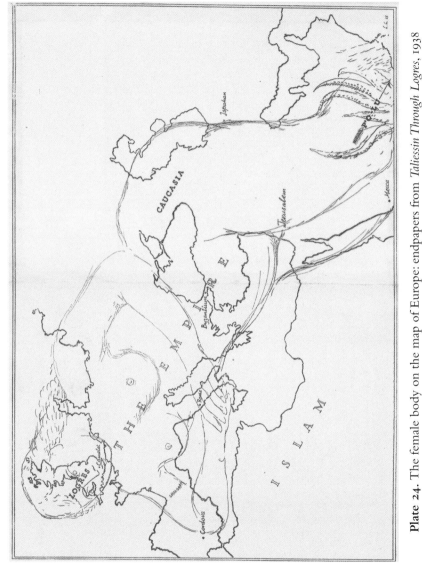

Plate 24. The female body on the map of Europe: endpapers from *Taliessin Through Logres*, 1938

Plate 25. Michal Williams in middle age

Plate 26. Michael Williams as a young man

Plate 27. Charles Williams on the terrace at 9 South Parks Road, Oxford

Plate 28. Nine South Parks Road: wrapper for a portfolio of drawings by Anne Spalding, 1942

Plate 29. In full conversational flight: Charles Williams sketched by an unknown artist

Plate 30. Charles Williams reading: drawing by Anne Spalding, 1942

Plate 31. Gerry Hopkins at 9 South Parks Road, drawing by Anne Spalding, 1942

Plate 32. Ruth Spalding, drawing by Anne Spalding, 1942

Plate 33. Lois Lang-Sims: drawing by Chattie Salaman

Plate 34. At work, with the inevitable cigarette: unknown artist

Plate 35. Writing on the terrace at 9 South Parks Road

Plate 36. The last photograph: Charles Williams outside Southfield House, wartime winter

On returning from a Funeral

About the body the commendatory rite
passed; my mind, with its nine years' habit, cried,
as in all genesis, all crisis, all conclusion,
Celia, and so, returning, found, my Dear Lord,
your single word. I remembered your earlier word,
that spoke of the nine years genesis in verse
and the candle I lit, and thought (wise repetition!)
how inconceivable, yet how conceivable,
it was that things should be other: easy chance
that Celia or you or I should not be there—
but that chance granted, what else? And I saw
under the candled years that winter of joy,
when all that neither of us, your creatures, knew
flourished in the Empire; the crown of our lives' love
was fiercely twisted round the gold of yours [. . .]

—and so on. The second poem was more anguished:

They buried the dead; Celia and I, long since,
buried the living; our hands beat on our coffins;
but there was always air, for God and Caesar
ruled: in any government but yours,
ill might—it is blasphemy—have conquered good.

They buried the dead, and we grow old; my verse
is mightier & darker: still the latest holds
the Emperor's image—the Emperor in Byzantium
and the Vessel that holds us: but if for awhile some minds
delay upon my verse, and the poems within it,
they muse on the Emperor sitting on the throne
over the Golden Horn, and say 'what is he?'
And I: 'It is.. if it is.. it has relation
to Justinian, and [the power of verse deleted] Shakespeare, & the Spirit
and[799]

'But O I forget how I made it end!' Williams jotted on the copy he gave to
Anne Bradby. Probably neither poem was shown to Milford. They were
essentially personal meditations.

There was one more change. Late in 1935 Anne found a place as secretary
to Richard de la Mare, a director of Faber and Faber. She was, she recalled:

thrilled at the prospect, for was not Faber the foremost publisher of modern
poetry, and was not T.S. Eliot a Director? I had already hung about near the

entrance to their office [...] hoping to see Eliot emerge at 5.30, and had been rewarded with a sight of him.[800]

She started just after Christmas, and a year later accepted 'with joy' an invitation to become Eliot's secretary. Surprisingly, Williams showed no jealousy. He was never possessive of Anne as he had been of Phyllis, and perhaps liked having a link with his fellow publisher-poet—possibly even, at times, a spy in the other camp.

But Anne's move to Faber had further consequences. There she met the printer David Bland. He asked her out; but in David's company she met his best friend, Vivian Ridler. Soon Anne and Vivian were in love. Anne felt disloyal to David, and took her trouble to Williams, who responded by chanting the old music hall song: 'Never interdooce yer donah to a pal, 'cos the odds is ten to one he sneaks yer gal!'—'donah' being Cockney slang for 'girlfriend'.[801] He assured her it was all in the normal course of things. He met and liked Vivian, who worked as an Assistant Printer at the OUP. Anne and Vivian married in 1938 and Williams composed a series of collects for their wedding:

> Almighty and most merciful God, who by the glorious Incarnation and Atonement of Christ Jesus hast made men capable of eternal life: Increase among us the knowledge of the exchanges of Thy love, and from the common agony of our lives redeem us to the universal joy of Thy only City [...]
>
> May the Sacred and Incarnate Intelligence excite in us the graces of belief and disbelief, of labour and humility, of clarity and devotion, of faith, hope, and love[.][802]

★ ★ ★

1936 had begun inauspiciously. Michal's back pain was worse than ever,[803] and she underwent X-rays to find the cause.[804] The family was so short of money that, on 7 January, Williams was forced to borrow money from Raymond Hunt.[805] He also took on the usual odd jobs: the Press paid him £20 to retell, in prose, *The Story of the Aeneid* for the Indian market[806]—a distraction from urgent work on the Canterbury play, which had proved extremely difficult to write. In September 1935 he had told Anne, '*Cranmer* remains more or less suspended: I toy with it, but nothing happens',[807] and a few weeks later, as he struggled with 'proofs and proofs and proofs', 'I look at Cranmer over an abyss of English literature, but do nothing.'[808] Still, a text of *Cranmer* was ready for the beginning of rehearsals in March.

The moment it was complete Williams began a series of six articles, 'Letters to Peter', for *G.K.'s Weekly*, the magazine run by the Catholic novelist and journalist G. K. Chesterton. The 'Letters' (addressed to a fictional version of the now fourteen-year-old Michael) were, nominally, book reviews; they were really discursive essays on whatever came into Williams's head. A noticeable political thread runs through them: he quotes with approval Jane Harrison's dictum, 'The upper classes, everywhere and at all times, have worshipped themselves.' And he confesses, 'the yoke of wage-slavery has pressed very lightly on me [...] But I have never forgotten the edge of the abyss and how near it might be; my head swims to look into it and see the skulls and bones at the bottom.'

Several 'Letters' offer aphorisms on theology in Williams's inimitable style. He denounces 'that dreadful thing [...] the Hearty Adventure of Religion', typified by 'a distinguished ecclesiastic who said "You wouldn't ask Jesus for a soft job, would you?"' on which Williams comments, 'I cannot think why *not*.' He proposes a Sodality of St Thomas Didymus, Apostle and Sceptic—'Doubting Thomas'—composed equally of Christians-about-to-become-atheists and atheists-about-to-become-Christians, because 'Scepticism is [...] a necessary part of [...] religion. It was the Blessed Virgin who said: "How shall these things be?"' And he warned: 'Be very careful what you ask of the universe, for, by the glory which is about us! the universe will probably give you what you ask. [...] One of the most terrifying phrases in the New Testament is "Ask, and it shall be given you". And then—what?'[809] In these short pieces he began to develop a style of reflection which would have a powerful impact when he came to write books on theology.

In the penultimate 'Letter', published on 18 June 1936, he lamented the death of Chesterton himself four days earlier. Recalling the thrill of reading *The Napoleon of Notting Hill* 'one summer evening on the pier at Southend', and how he instantly 'turned back and re-read it', he concluded: 'The last of my lords is dead.'[810] But providentially, as it might seem, even as one 'lord' departed, another was making himself known. The previous year Williams had told Anne that his colleague Ray Goffin was writing an introduction to Chaucer's *Troilus & Criseyde*:

He is dealing with the Courts of Love; & neither he nor anyone else can tell me why or how this whole romantic, courtly, & generally adulterous business grew up & flourished in the full daylight of the Church. It's almost as if the Church system & the love system existed side by side.[811]

The relationship between the 'Church system & the love system' was of course the great enigma of Williams's life, the matter of his daily and hourly thought. He did not expect much enlightenment about it from Goffin. But in the spring of 1936 the proofs of a forthcoming book from the Clarendon Press arrived on his desk, with requests for a blurb and publicity material. To his astonished delight the new book dealt, precisely, with the medieval 'love system'. A deeply learned history of the literature of courtly love, it was provisionally called *The Allegorical Love Poem*. Its author was C.S. Lewis.

15

'The Staff Work of
the Omnipotence'

The name C. S. Lewis meant nothing to Williams. But reading the opening chapter of *The Allegorical Love Poem*, he was entranced. The author of this supremely well-written history of courtly love poetry acknowledged the possibility that 'the love religion' might 'find a *modus vivendi* with Christianity and produce a noble fusion of sexual and religious experience'. It must have seemed to him that this unknown author was speaking his own private language.

He drafted publicity material for the book, and considered the title. Lewis's own choice—*The House of Busirane: an essay on the erotic allegory of the Middle Ages*—was impossible. Williams came up with *The Allegory of Love: A Study in Medieval Tradition*. Then, on 12 March, a letter arrived:

[Dear Mr Williams,][812]

I never know about writing to an author. If you are older than I, I don't want to seem impertinent: if you are younger, I don't want to seem patronizing. But I feel I must risk it.

A book sometimes crosses ones path which is so like the sound of ones native language in a strange country that it feels almost uncivil not to wave some kind of flag in answer. I have just read your *Place of the Lion* and it is to me one of the major literary events of my life—comparable to my first discovery of George Macdonald, G.K. Chesterton, or Wm. Morris. There are layers and layers—first the pleasure that any good fantasy gives me: then, what is rarely (tho' not so very rarely) combined with this, the pleasure of a real philosophical and theological stimulus: thirdly, characters: fourthly, what I neither expected nor desired, substantial edification.

I mean the latter with perfect seriousness. I know Damaris very well: in fact I was in course of becoming Damaris (but you have pulled me up). [...] Not only is your diagnosis good: but the very way in which you force one to look at the matter is itself the beginning of a cure. Honestly, I didn't think there was anyone now alive in England who could do it.

Coghill of Exeter put me on to the book: I have put Tolkien (the Professor of Anglo Saxon and a papist) and my brother. So there are three dons and one soldier all buzzing with excited admiration. We have a sort of informal club called the Inklings: the qualifications (as they have informally evolved) are a tendency to write, and Christianity. Can you come down some day next term (preferably *not* Sat. or Sunday), spend the night as my guest in College, eat with us at a chop house, and talk with us until the small hours. Meantime, a thousand thanks.

[C. S. Lewis.][813]

Williams replied at once:

My dear Mr Lewis,

If you had delayed writing another 24 hours our letters would have crossed. It has never before happened to me to be admiring an author of a book while he at the same time was admiring me. My admiration for the staff work of the Omnipotence rises every day.

To be exact, I finished on Saturday looking—too hastily—at proofs of your *Allegorical Love Poem*. I had been asked to write something about it for the travellers and booksellers and people so I read it first. I permit myself to enclose a copy of what I said [...] I wrote this on Monday and yesterday our Sir Humphrey told me in the afternoon that he understood you had been reading my *Lion*.[814] So if ever I was drawn to anyone—imagine!

I admit that I fell for the *Allegorical Love Poem* so heavily because it is an aspect of the subject with which my mind has always been playing; [...] and I regard your book as practically the only one that I have ever come across, since Dante, that shows the slightest understanding of what this very peculiar identity of love and religion means. I know there is Coventry Patmore, but he rather left the identity to be deduced.

After vacillating a good deal I permit myself to believe in your letter and in the interests of the subject so far as to send you a copy of one of my early books of verse [*Poems of Conformity*] , because the poems from pages 42–page 81 may interest you. I blush nowadays for a good deal of the book, and indeed for some part of those poems, but I don't think I blush for the general fundamental idea. You will excuse all this; it arises only because of what I suspect is the very profound importance of the subject of your own book. As to your letter, what can I say? The public for all these novels has been so severely limited (though I admit in some cases passionate) that it gives me very high pleasure to feel that you liked the *Lion*. I have felt so much danger of Damaris hovering around me that she came, so to speak, from the heart. I do think it was extremely good of you to write and extraordinarily kind of the Omnipotence to arrange the coincidence. You must be in London sometimes. Do let me know and come and have lunch or dinner. I am here practically every day for all the day, and if you will send me a post card first I will see that

I am. I should like very much to come to Oxford as you suggest; the only thing is that I am a little uncertain about next term because I may be at Canterbury off and on to see the rehearsals of the Play I have written for the friends of the Cathedral to do in June. [...] Do forgive this too long letter, but after all to write about your *Love Poem* and my *Lion* and both our Romantic Theology in one letter takes some paragraphs.

Very gratefully yours,
Charles Williams.

P.S. I have only one grudge; you make me feel I have been unfair to Spenser in one of my critical books. You even convince me that I have.

P.P.S. And I am 49—so you can decide whether that makes me too old or too young.[815]

Clive Staples Lewis ('Jack' to his family and friends) was twelve years younger than Charles Williams. Born in Belfast but educated mainly in England, he had spent eight months as a student at Oxford before being sent to the Western Front in November 1917. Wounded at the Battle of Arras in April 1918, he was sent back to England and by the time he had recovered, the war was over. He returned to Oxford, taking First Class degrees in 'Greats' (classics, ancient history, and philosophy) and English. Since 1925 he had been Fellow in English at Magdalen College, Oxford. Spiritually, he had moved during his years at Oxford from a rather self-satisfied agnosticism to belief in God and thence to Christianity. Two years before completing *The Allegory of Love*, he had published *The Pilgrim's Regress*, a satirically tinged allegory about religious conversion and the obstacles it faces in the world.

To Lewis, friendship was of massive importance. His religious views had been worked out in discussion with (amongst others) his lifelong friend Arthur Greeves, whom he had known since schooldays; the solicitor and philosopher Owen Barfield, a disciple of Rudolph Steiner's Anthroposophy, who had been Lewis's fellow-undergraduate; and J. R. R. Tolkien, Professor of Anglo-Saxon, a Roman Catholic with whom Lewis had formed a close friendship after taking up his Fellowship at Magdalen. A part had also been played by the Chaucer specialist Nevill Coghill at Exeter College. Sharing books was as essential to Lewis's circle as the debating of ideas, and it was natural that he should have come into contact with Williams through a network of friends and contacts. His letter told Williams that he had been 'put on to' *The Place of the Lion* by 'Coghill of Exeter'. But things were not quite so simple.

Lewis had first heard of Williams when Dr R. W. Chapman had recommended his novels,[816] as 'spiritual shockers'.[817] Chapman was Secretary to
the Clarendon Press: he did in Oxford what Milford did in London, and
had probably heard about Williams's novels from Milford. Lewis 'made a
mental note [. . .] but did nothing about it'. It was only 'a few years later',
visiting Coghill in February 1936 and finding him 'full of a book he had just
read called *The Place of the Lion*', that Lewis borrowed the book and was
deeply excited by it. On 26 February he wrote to Arthur Greeves:

> I have just read what I think is a really great book, 'The Place of the Lion' by
> Charles Williams. [. . .]
>   It is not only a most exciting fantasy, but a deeply religious and (unobtru-
> sively) a profoundly learned book. The reading of it has been a good prepar-
> ation for Lent as far as I am concerned: for it shows me (through the heroine)
> the special sin of abuse of intellect to which all my profession are liable, more
> clearly than I ever saw it before. I have learned more than I ever knew yet
> about humility. In fact it has been a big experience. [. . .] It isn't often now-a-
> days you get a *Christian* fantasy.[818]

Lewis waited until 9 March before telling Chapman:

> Do you remember advising me to read Charles Williams? Well, I have—*The
> Place of the Lion* and *Many Dimensions*. It is 'beyond expectation, beyond desire'.
> To have a rattling good thriller, and on top of that a learned machinery, and
> after that a theology, and real characters, and a real Katharsis—I never thought
> to read it. Amazing man! Is he still in Oxford? is he so senior that an approach
> on my part would look like impudence, or so junior that it would look like
> patronage?
>   Coghill put me on to him, and I have put on Tolkien. All three hum with
> excited approval.[819]

Chapman evidently not only encouraged Lewis to write to Williams,
but passed on the substance of his note to Milford, which explains why
Williams, responding to Lewis, could write 'Sir Humphrey told me in the
afternoon that he understood you had been reading my *Lion*.' Indeed,
one wonders just why Williams in London was, unusually, asked to deal
with Lewis's Clarendon Press book. It is plausible that Chapman, with
Milford's co-operation, was making a second attempt to bring the two
men together. To some extent, it seems, the conjunction of Lewis and
Williams was gently nudged into place by watchful senior figures in the
two branches of the Press.

Reading Williams's letter and *Poems of Conformity*, Lewis perceived that caution was required. On 23 March he wrote:

[Dear Williams,]

This is going to be a complicated matter. To make a clean breast of it, that particular species of romanticism which you found in my book and which is expressed in the poems you send me, is not my kind at all. I see quite clearly why you think it is—the subject of the book, the at any rate respectful treatment of the sentiment, the apparently tell-tale familiarity with Coventry Patmore—it all fits in perfectly and must seem to you almost like a trap [...] I think you will find that I nowhere commit myself to a definite approval of this blend of erotic and religious feeling. I treat it with respect: I display: I don't venture very far.

Praising some of Williams's poems, he firmly rejected others:

Orthodoxy and *Ecclesia Docens* I definitely disliked. (I embrace the opportunity of establishing the precedent of brutal frankness, without which our acquaintance begun like this would easily be a mere butter bath!) [...]

I have read *Many Dimensions* with an enormous enjoyment—not that it's as good as the *Lion*, but then in a sense it hardly means to be. By Jove, it is an experience when this time-travelling business is done by a man who really thinks it out.

He repeated his invitation to Oxford, suggesting the week of 18 May. 'Of course', he added, 'I realise that this letter, for more than one cause, may have quenched all wish for a meeting: but acting on the pleasanter hypothesis—'[820]

And so it happened. Williams told Olive Willis, 'On Monday [18 May] I am going to Oxford to meet a Don who admires me, in fact, two. Don't think that such journeys are habitual; there is a fantastic incident behind this one'[821]—the 'incident' being the apparent coincidence of their reading each other's books. The other 'Don' was probably Tolkien, possibly Coghill. Nothing is known of the meeting but clearly it went well, and Lewis discerned what he most valued in a friend: enough agreement to make profound and affectionate communication possible, and enough disagreement to provide endless fodder for debate. Williams visited Oxford again briefly at the beginning of November, for unknown purposes. It may well have been to see Lewis, and perhaps to attend the 'Inklings'.[822]

★ ★ ★

As rehearsals of *Cranmer* began, in March 1936, Williams heard from a Phyllis Potter, a director who wanted to perform a shortened version of *The Rite of the Passion*. Williams, delighted, immediately granted use of the *Rite*, without payment. A week later he and Phyllis Potter arranged to meet near Amen House for tea.[823]

Little is known about Phyllis Potter, although she was an important figure in the religious drama movement of the 1930s and 1940s. Born in 1886 in South Kensington, daughter of a wealthy shipowner, she trained as a Sunday-school teacher before joining with Leila Rendel in 1911 to found the Caldecott Community, a nursery school for children of women working in a London factory. The Community grew into a charity providing residential care for vulnerable children. But Phyllis Potter became an Anglo-Catholic, and disagreements over religious practice in the community led to her leaving in 1931. 'Brimming with dramatic energy and creative imagination',[824] by 1934 she had become Director of the Chelmsford Diocesan Drama Guild, which performed religious plays in church halls around Essex.

Williams and Potter immediately took to one another, and after a lively discussion Williams came away having promised to write a new play for the Drama Guild. It was the start of a collaboration which would stimulate some of his best dramatic writing. Phyllis Potter wanted a nativity play: an *interesting* nativity play that did not simply rehash the usual elements; and given Williams's interest in the Incarnation, with its profound implications for the potential sacredness of the human body, he was certainly the writer to take it on. So work on *Taliessin Through Logres* stopped again while he began the verse play that would become *Seed of Adam*. Just how unconventional his approach would be was hinted at in a letter to Anne Bradby in late May, where he mentions working on a passage about 'the negress who is one of the seeds in the apple'.[825]

At Canterbury, rehearsals for *Cranmer* were well advanced under the direction of E. Martin Browne. Things were not straightforward. Williams, in Browne's words, 'achieved a kaleidoscopic compression of history'; lest the audience be confused, Browne 'had a boy in one corner turning over the leaves of a calendar of dates and events' to make things clearer. The play would be performed in the Chapter House; both Williams and Browne wanted a stylized, masque-like effect. But when the costumes arrived they found the designer had created heavy, realistic costumes, with Henry VIII's based on the famous Holbein portrait: just what they had *not* wanted. The play was too long and had to be cut, losing a 'magnificent' scene at the end of Part I. Even so, Browne had a moment of horror at the dress rehearsal:

> In fear of Miss Babington's one-and-a-half-hour stop-watch, I asked one of the invited audience to time it for me. Returning from my final run out I asked, 'How long?' 'Two hours and twenty minutes.' I can still remember the chill… 'No, I'm sorry, I'd lost all sense of time: *one* hour and twenty minutes.'

Williams's play was distinctly experimental. It used a stressed, alliterative verse, close to the style of the new *Taliessin* poems, which Browne found 'extremely good to speak and effective to hear'.[826] Eschewing realism for symbolism, the play focuses on Cranmer's inner tensions as he is gradually drawn into the religious and political conflicts of his time, to die, after much vacillation and loss of nerve, a Protestant martyr.

There are only four named characters: Cranmer himself, Henry VIII, Anne Boleyn, and Queen Mary. The others are representative or symbolic figures—lords, commons, a priest (conservative), a preacher (radical), a bishop, and some singers. Williams's great creation, and much the best part in the play, is the Skeleton. The Skeleton is magnificent yet curiously difficult to define. He is ominously knowledgeable about what will happen to Cranmer; he knows just what Cranmer thinks and what illusions he cherishes; his unsparing views and sometimes gloating tone suggest utter cynicism; yet his task is to lead Cranmer to honesty and self-knowledge.

The Skeleton acts as a chorus, commenting on the action; pointing out, for example, that getting what you ask for may not be pleasant:

> Populous with prayers is the plain of Paradise,
> skirring after the men who prayed, whose cries
> beseech heaven to refrain; heaven hears not twice

—or remarking how easy it is to recite prayers, without realizing what they might mean in reality:

> Ah how the sweet words ring their beauty:
> *it is meet, right and our bounden duty.*
> But will you sing it with unchanged faces
> when God shall change the times and the places?

The Skeleton is as challenging to the audience as to Cranmer.

The play opened on 19 June. Williams went with Michael and Michal; Anne Bradby was there, and T.S. Eliot, come to see the successor to his own *Murder in the Cathedral*. The Chapter House was packed. E. Martin

Browne played the Skeleton—in black, with white *appliqué* bones, a skull for the upper half of the face, and a black cloak 'lined throughout with the green of spring, which appear[ed] again as ivy-leaves round the brow'—the one costume the designer had got exactly right. Browne recalled that: 'The Skeleton, as a part, gave me a satisfaction more complete than any other in my acting career.'[827] Given the historical complexities, and Williams's pell-mell mixing of literal and metaphorical in his verse, the play must have been difficult for the audience to follow in detail, but its impact was undeniable. Communicating the stunning energy of the production, Alice Mary Miller in the *Cathedral Chronicle* compared the play to a 'hurricane':

> one remembered horrors and delights [...] the growing oppression of a trap, closing in on Cranmer and on the mind [...] black gowned and masked Executioners with flames licking in their hands; Cranmer running, stumbling into the arms of the Skeleton, the final appalling clarity, and then the cries, 'Speed! Speed!' and the rush of the flames down the aisle and Cranmer, pursued by the Skeleton, flying after them. [...] The play silenced both approval and censure into acknowledgement of greatness.[828]

Williams told Anne Bradby:

> Indeed I never thought it could have that kind of earth- (our earth-) shaking effect. [...] I loved your being there, [...] & I loved seeing you after—& I would not be sorry I was caught in such a whirl of Deans & T.S.E.s & people, for I would not wish anything different. [...] I was moved so much by others' lordliness [...] T.S.E., when I rashly suggested he & M. B. might lunch one day, saying: 'Lunch.. tea.. dinner.. supper.. or breakfast.. at any time.' And Speaight, while he was being praised, saying: 'Yes, but the author gave us everything'[.][829]

He promised to arrange seats for himself and Anne to see the play again the following Saturday; it would, he told her with relish, be 'frightfully packed'. And he sent Browne a sonnet:

> Must you show me the Skeleton then, not only in art
> by one part played and other parts designed,
> but by the bony fingers probing the heart,
> chilling and determining the pretentious mind?
> Must you show me, I say, the way I hate to go,
> yet lately drew in a chart, of such neat lines?
> 'Things spoken seem unfamiliar'—o but no,
> familiar enough this, though my will inclines

little to the bitter warmth of that true cold.
Nor a week ago could I think, Martin, to behold
such neatness in your exact mathematical sight;
not merely cancelling your rightness (that, though much,
were little in truth), but with a rarer touch
forbidding the better rightness to think itself right.[830]

Press response was mostly very favourable, though one clergyman thought the play 'blasphemous' and a local paper called the language 'obstruse' [*sic*].[831] The *Times* opined that Eliot and Williams together had established a 'new school of drama'.

Blasphemous or not, Williams's *Cranmer* was mentioned in a sermon at Westminster Abbey, for on 4 August he cheerfully told Canon Charles Smyth, 'To think that I might have heard myself preached on in Westminster Abbey and did not will always be one of the greater minor sorrows of my life.'[832] And in the autumn, Williams himself was asked to give something approaching a sermon on *Cranmer*, for he sent Raymond Hunt his notes from 'the Sunday address, which sailed over the heads (possibly in both senses) of a peaceful, silent & immovable congregation'. Probably it was at Chichester, for he went on:

Chichester ran me so low that I seem to have all my credit pledged and no money. Could you, without inconvenience, add another ten pounds to what I owe you? I daren't make any promise of when I shall pay you: it may be before, or when, *Descent into H* gets published—if...[833]

He had told Hunt that he was thinking of writing a 'temporary Shakespeare book [...] in order to make a little money out of Oxford',[834] but nothing came of it.

★   ★   ★

Williams was already hard at work on the nativity play, which would be called *Seed of Adam*. He finished a prose draft by the end of July,[835] and on 2 September told Raymond Hunt it was finished, adding gleefully, 'it is the least like a Nativity play that ever I heard. There is a grand moment when the Blessed Virgin dancing with a negress amid the flashes of a scimitar breaks into song with this triumphant line: "parturition is upon me; blessed be He!" '[836]

He sent a draft to Phyllis Potter two days later.[837] But it was far from finished. In mid-October he went to Chichester for discussions, finding some of the diocesan authorities tiresome ('I think between ourselves that outside his own subject Dr Philp is rather a loony, and I detest his laugh. But we got on admirably', he reported),[838] and a week later told Phyllis Potter, 'My novel [*Descent into Hell*] and my Taliessin Poems and your *Nativity* contend wildly in my brain and I do little bits to all when I ought to attend to each in turn.'[839] Phyllis Potter approached Eliot to ask if he would speak after one of the performances. Eliot replied that he would do 'anything' to support production of a play by Williams, and would happily speak from the stage.[840]

Seed of Adam was finished in November 1936, the final chorus arriving just a week before it opened at Chelmsford.[841] Profoundly imaginative and visually spectacular, it abandons realism even more completely than *Cranmer*. It resembles a mummers' play, with the characters announcing themselves forthrightly on entrance. Thus the King of Gold (who also represents the body, the Earth element, and the material world) introduces himself:

> I am Gaspar, Tsar of Caucasia;
> I sprang from our father Adam's loins
> in a bright emission of coins; Eve's need
> of gilded adornment nourished me to dig and dive.
> Pearls I brought up; springs I let forth: who
> will be beautiful now? who profitable then?
> Men thrive and I take my fee.
> Tricked out in riches half the world follow me;
> who fall, crawl or are kicked into dry ditches.

The King of Frankincense, the Sultan of Bagdad, [*sic*] represents Air, intellect, and human culture. But the third King, the King of Myrrh, and his daughter, are astonishing creations—though perhaps they might now be politically impossible to present as written. They are (Williams says, in the parlance of the day) 'a Negro' and 'a Negress', and seem, at first, to represent Death and Hell. The daughter, Mother Myrrh, carries a scimitar and threatens to eat the Chorus (representing humankind) and in particular Mary, whom she chases around the stage with her blade:

> *The movement of the two women quickens and becomes a dance; the scimitar flashing round them in a white fire. The* CHORUS *sway to the movement,* ADAM *only remaining motionless.*
>
> MARY [*suddenly breaking into song*]. Parturition is upon me: blessed be He!
>
> > Sing, brothers; sing, sisters; sing, Father Adam.
> > My soul magnifies the Lord.

Mary catches Mother Myrrh's hand in hers, and a few lines later Mother Myrrh is acting as midwife to the birth. She and her father are revealed as also part of the divine plan: time, death, and the fallen world are part of the process of redemption.

The use of dance, ritual, and wonderfully speakable verse make *Seed of Adam* a minor masterpiece. The premiere on 14 November was hugely enjoyed, not least by the playwright, who told Phyllis Potter, 'I shall never be able to thank you enough for the wild pleasure of Saturday. [...] I never expected the Rural Dean. Nor the Champagne. Nor the Mothers' Union. Nor anything of that wild and intoxicating medley which has blest me with Chelmsford and its surroundings forever.'[842] Eliot was as good as his word, and spoke after one of the performances. 'All went very well', Williams told Anne Bradby, 'though I don't remember what T.S.E. said very clearly, only that we were all extremely pleasant, arguable, & intimate. My wife discussing the Agamemnon chorus with him was a marvellous sight. [...] A fantastic day: & thanks to you for your share in it.'[843]

Seed of Adam became a staple of religious drama for many years, with countless performances around England every winter. After an October 1937 performance in Colchester, Williams gave a lecture on the play. His notes survive,[844] revealing both his creative processes and, incidentally, what an engaging lecturer he was. He admits to having wanted at first to give the play a political dimension. The shepherds would represent the poor; but then that would imply making the kings 'the rich, i.e. the great capitalists, which I was very ill-disposed to do [...] because I did not wish to save the capitalists easily in view of Christ's remarks about the rich—at the Crucifixion perhaps but not just at the Nativity.' So the shepherds were merged into the Chorus. 'Mr. Eliot has made choruses a little difficult. I know all about the Greeks, but they do not prevent one being told one is copying Mr. Eliot.' Then there was the question of how to make things *interesting*:

> Which do you find most *interesting*—I don't say which do you think most important—the Nativity or the latest murder? Well, *if* you found the Nativity most interesting you would be reading theology. And do you? No. I am like you. And as I considered this my attention hung about the third K[ing].

'Meanwhile', he told his audience, 'I had in my usual way, abolished Time and Space. I was prepared to bring in anyone. After all, the Nativity was a local event, besides being universal.' So Augustus Caesar came in, played by Adam; and as for Joseph—well, says Williams, 'the old man leading a devout girl on a donkey was not for this play.' But 'was there not a Mohammedan tradition that [Joseph] was young? I hope there is; I thought there was—good: let us have a young Mohammedan Joseph, and let us (incidentally) make the second King a Sultan.' And he admits that he added a description of a cavalry battle 'as a picturesque extra, though it fitted so well with poetry that I have done it again in my Taliessin poems' (it became 'Mount Badon'). One catches a sense of the sheer exuberance with which he wrote his best work.

★   ★   ★

At the Press there was the usual crop of World's Classics to be nurtured into life, and the continuing cycle of meetings as 'Q' wound its way through the alphabet of quotable authors. On certain Sunday evenings there were the meetings at Lee's vicarage. Williams's brief biography *Queen Elizabeth* would be published by Duckworth in December. And with the faithful Raymond Hunt busy collecting his manuscripts and taking notes at his lectures, he discussed the 'half-fantastic, half-serious' notion that Hunt might write 'a small book' about him: 'I should like to read, before I die, a lucid statement of how I do appear to another male mind, who at least belongs to the same kind of effort.'[845] Wishing Hunt happiness in his impending marriage, he ended with what had become a favourite phrase: 'This also is Thou; neither is this Thou.' God is to be found in everything; yet nothing must be mistaken for God.

He was planning a year-long series of lectures, beginning in the autumn at the City Lit, on 'Poetry and the Pattern of Life'.[846] It would open with 'The Idea of Salvation: Virgil', followed by two lectures on the *Aeneid*. Then would come several on the Bible, including one on 'The Apocalypse and the Song of Solomon: the Consummation' followed by seven on Dante's works. Williams had been reading Dante since at least 1912, but this was the first time he had lectured on him in detail. He discussed his ideas stage by stage with Hunt, who by the end of the year was urging him to write a book on Dante,[847] an idea eventually fulfilled in 1943 by *The Figure of Beatrice*. By then, however, Williams would be well known as a writer on theology. To understand how that happened, we must step back almost three years.

In January 1934, Williams had received a letter from the novelist Mary Butts. It was an agitated compound of enthusiasm and anxiety:

> Three of your books, but chiefly *The Place of the Lion* are of the utmost delight, and what used to be called 'spiritual consolation' to me. [But] I have just been

told, by the usual 'friend of a friend' of yours, that you repudiate those books, rather in the spirit of a Giles Tumulty. [...] There is hardly anything I would rather not believe. If some error has crept into this information, or if it is all bosh—do not trouble to answer this. But if it should be true, I am sure Sir Giles would have an appropriate comment.[848]

Born in 1890, Mary Butts was the great-granddaughter of Blake's patron Thomas Butts, and had grown up in a Dorset country house surrounded by original Blake paintings and engravings. After graduating from the London School of Economics and completing a visionary novel, *Ashe of Rings*, she spent several years among bohemian circles in Paris, where she became friendly with Jean Cocteau and studied with Aleister Crowley. After three months in 1921 at Crowley's 'Abbey of Thelema' in Cefalù, Sicily, she left declaring that 'the place was a "sham" and Crowley a fanatic'—a compliment Crowley returned Tumulty-style, calling her 'a large white red-haired maggot'.[849] Whether or not Crowley was responsible, Mary Butts was also thereafter addicted to opiates: first heroin, later home-grown poppy-head tea. Nonetheless she became a successful novelist. Her short stories were widely praised; *Ashe of Rings* and *Armed with Madness* (a novel about the Grail) won critical though not popular success.

By 1934 she was living in the remote Cornish village of Sennen Cove and had recently become a Christian. Williams's novels had hit her at a vulnerable time. 'I wish it were possible to tell you—I would if I could find decent language, what your books do for one's life and work. But this is true. That it makes the very best of which one is capable very much nearer realisation', she wrote.[850] She told Williams that she had recently 'just finished *Many Dimensions*, and was full up with the joy of it', when someone—it is not clear who—had reported 'with some malice' that Williams had written the books as a kind of hoax, 'with [his] tongue in [his] cheek', and had 'repudiated' them:

> I'll never forget, as he said it, how the room went round and began to dissolve into space corridors—rather like it did when Lord Arglay used the Stone; and I heard myself from somewhere the other side of space, uttering civilities; not allowing him to know the meaning of what he said.[851]

'I felt very strange indeed', she confided. 'For I felt that, if it were true, something of what that would have implied would happen to me. [...] So, I was really frightened.' She added 'Why did you kill Giles Tumulty? I thought when I read it that you'd need him again.'

This alarming letter reached Williams on 9 January after the last post had gone. Feeling a need to reassure at once, he sent a telegram: 'Repudiation all nonsense. Charles Williams.' Next day he wrote more fully:

> I have never repudiated, never could and never should dream of repudiating (by God's mercy) anything real in the novels. What I have probably done, 'at divers times and in divers places', is (i) to make small jokes about them (ii) to refuse to lie about them. It seems to me extraordinary that if anyone says 'Why did you write *The Place of the Lion?*' and I say: 'To pay my child's school fees', then (as I have found happens) there is a sort of feeling that I am being frivolous or mocking or downright diabolical. There is a temporal occasion for everything [...] But why the temporal occasion should be supposed to negative all spiritual existence I cannot see. Why, after all, did the Blessed Virgin go to Bethlehem? To fill up the census papers. [...] I suppose some people would think she ought to have said: 'To be the Mother of God.'[852]

He ended, 'But I wish—O how I wish!—that I hadn't killed Sir Giles.'
Soon Williams heard from the publisher Methuen, with a questionnaire:

> Have you ever had a queer experience that you consider supernatural? The Editors are collecting authentic experiences for a book which Messrs. Methuen will publish if the response justifies it [...] Some of the headings under which these might fall are: prevision, and vision of the past; supernormal powers; magic; consciousness out of the body; awareness of the presence of a spirit; ghost stories etc.[853]

Responses were to be addressed to Mary Butts, who had nominated Williams (other respondents included E.M. Forster, Havelock Ellis, and Lord Dunsany). Williams told her he had nothing to offer:

> I mean one cannot describe the dissemination of light which accompanies (what you will let me call) romantic love, or the successful relation of some difficulty to the power of the Omnipotence as super-natural, can one? It would I feel, be certain to be disappointing to Methuen and to their readers, though you and I might easily repose a greater attention on such things than on any number of ghosts, pterodactyls, werewolves and snowstorms. My wife has a firm conviction that she had a semi-ghostly experience in a flat we used to inhabit; on the other hand, my wife is not, in the terms of Methuen's letter, a distinguished personage! Thus, gloomily contemplating exclusion, I nevertheless take a good deal of pleasure in writing to you about it.[854]

The other editor of the proposed volume, which never saw the light, was the critic Richard Ellis Roberts, a committed Christian and friend of Mary Butts. Roberts was attempting a literary counterattack against secularism, including a series to be called *In Defence of the Supernatural,* for which he was urging Mary Butts to contribute a short book under the title *And Was Crucified.* In late September 1936 he approached Williams, inviting him to write a short book on another phrase from the Nicene Creed: *Came Down from Heaven.* The plan—surely very unbusinesslike—was to commission essays from a group of writers, and to publish them together in one volume (under the title *I Believe*), and also individually as separate small books. The other contributors were writers now largely forgotten: J.D. Beresford, Gerald Bullett, and Kenneth Ingram, all writers of fantasy fiction; and Renée Haynes, a novelist with an interest in the paranormal. It was probably Mary Butts who suggested Williams as a contributor.

Williams accepted the commission eagerly, hoping the deadline would not be too short. 'I am struggling to reorganize a novel at the moment which is called *Descent into Hell* and admirably counters the title of your proposed book', he told Roberts in September.[855] By this time, he had sent Mary Butts copies of almost all his books, and she had written an enthusiastic review of *Cranmer* for *Time and Tide*.[856] Williams told Anne Bradby somewhat wearily:

> Miss Mary Butts [...] faintly hopes [...] to do her proper share in honouring the prophet in his own country. My own view is that prophets are abortions who have gone on living by mistake; the super-foetation of the womb of time. However, not to disadvantage the public, I keep this quiet, only mentioning the truth to an intimate or two.[857]

The next year Mary Butts was begging his help in getting books to review: she had found this work increasingly scarce, and, now ill and alcoholic, was succumbing to racial paranoia with regard to the causes:

> D'you remember how I burst in on you one day six months ago?—with an agitated tale about a Jew-boy's [book] I'd been given to review for the S[unday] T[imes]? How it had been given to me, and then Edith Sitwell had done it? [...] Charles Williams, am I being conceited, or is there some dirty work going on? I mean against us all because of what we believe, and especially perhaps if we attack the Jews?[858]

Williams, who had never 'attacked the Jews', thought the incident more likely to come from 'the pure inefficiency of periodicals'.[859] Mary Butts, however, was not to be mollified:

> If a great paper won't take criticism of the Jews, then, as Belloc pointed out, the Fascists *will* in time have it all their own way. What good is it to pretend

there is no Jewish question? A visit I paid to Berlin some years ago did more
to explain Hitler than a score of books.[860]

She told him that she had had flu, and that the kitchen ceiling had just col-
lapsed on her head; but that after clearing up the mess she had turned to
Many Dimensions, 'the greatest mystical work of our age as I've always been
persuaded', and been comforted by the Hadji's words: 'The way to the Stone
is in the Stone.'

Williams replied on 6 March 1937, ignoring the fantasies about Jews and
expressing sympathy for her 'most appalling morning'. He added:

> For a moment as I read I thought you were going to say that the ceiling fell
> down and killed you and that you were writing from some more advanced
> state of being. I suppose my rational consciousness would object, if I ever
> got such a letter, and indeed though I would never rule it out as a possibility,
> I should not be in a hurry to accept it.[861]

His intuition was more accurate than he knew. Mary Butts had died the
previous day of diabetes, aged forty-six.

Delusions about 'the Jews' were a grim theme of the time. Since 1934 Hitler
had been German head of state, initiating a headlong process of rearmament.
In March 1936 Germany reoccupied the demilitarized zone in the Rhineland,
and sent troops to Spain to support Franco's military revolt against the
socialist government. German Jews, already deprived of their civil rights,
were expelled from most professions. In Britain some attention was distracted from these frightening developments by the abdication crisis.
Edward VIII, having succeeded his father, George V, as King in January
1936, abandoned the throne in December to marry his twice-divorced
lover, Wallis Simpson.

No doubt such public events worried Williams as much as most people,
but there are few clues. A scrap of Amen House letterhead on which he has
jotted an address for 'relief of Sp[anish] distress' suggests a donation for vic-
tims of the Spanish Civil War. 'The King's Crowning, 12th May, 1937', a
poem in the *St Pancras People's Theatre Magazine*, marked the accession of the
new king, George VI, by setting out a view of the monarch's function. He is
to join 'in alliance' with the commons, and so defeat 'tyrants and tricksters';
to bring 'Mercy and Justice', because 'all else is trapped by gold, / all but the
King's grace that was popular of old'. Proposing the King as the commons'
ally against the rich, Williams manages, idealistically, to reconcile his love of

monarchy with his loyalty to the people. In one respect, however, he felt that the new king fell short:

> talking of Ritual, someone ought to tell the King not to smile while he is crowned & robed. One photograph in the Abbey I thought amazingly good: he had become, like Hadrian VII, a piece of ivory or something: & the face under the Crown looked Carven—a lifted image. [...] But he must needs come out on the balcony of the palace in his majesty and smile, & that ruined all. He became a well-meaning youngish man who had dressed up curiously to please someone else's children, & was gratified at their pleasure but not too happy about it all.[862]

By contrast, his *Henry VII* unexpectedly contains, on page 96, a substantial quotation about bureaucracy from Lenin's *Selected Works*. Since the quotation is not especially memorable, the likelihood is that Williams just happened to be reading Lenin at the time and thought the passage would fit. In 'The Calling of Arthur', one of the recent *Tailessin* poems, the decadent King Cradlemas is defeated by an alliance of the people and the new king, Arthur, in whose support 'the south / is up with hammer and sickle, and holds Thames mouth.' Thus, imaginatively, Williams could conceive the ideal state: a synthesis of communism with medieval monarchy.

He was still wrestling with *Descent into Hell* in late November 1936, when he noted:

> Last night I contemplated [...] my own novel, & thought: 'good or not good? fortunate or not so fortunate?' So I touched my forehead to the Omnipotence & said: 'Sir, my lord—your job?' but a wisp of attention said: 'you do mean that?—even if you found it was a bad book & highly unfortunate? you fall in with that?' So I waived the question and put my wish to intend to prefer to be that in the Omnipotence—*extra quem non salus*.[863]

He was troubled, too, by things he had not been able to incorporate into any of his novels. 'But let us remember', he told Anne, 'all the things we wish to put into *White Martyrdom*, and postpone them till that. [...] I will promise to try & avoid reaction if it should come.. after the remaining chapter has been written...but what do you think the publishers will say? never mind.'[864] Probably *White Martyrdom* was another version of the unwritten 'White Column novel'.

Though he was again writing crime reviews, for the *Daily Telegraph*, he ended 1936 still short of money. 'I wish Ellis and Roberts [sic] would hurry with their series, and pay me a lot of money to write *Came Down from Heaven*', he told Raymond Hunt;[865] and he apologized to Phyllis Potter for missing *Seed of Adam* at Romford: 'if I had had a little more silver in the house I think I should [have gone]. But I had run myself so short of actual cash that until I could get a cheque on Monday morning I felt cribbed, cabined and everything else.'[866] But, summing up the year, he was not dissatisfied:

> I have written *Cranmer*, & [*Seed of Adam*], & rewritten *Descent into Hell*, [...] & I have lectured thrice a week for a lot of the year, & done something in Amen House ... and as for what is good, adored be the Omnipotence, and for what is less than good, may the Omnipotence deign to know it as renovated into good: blessed be It.[867]

Looking ahead, though, he saw a heap of uncompleted projects. *Descent into Hell*, still under continuous revision, had been bouncing back from one publisher after another ever since Gollancz rejected it early in 1934. There were the Taliessin poems: 'Would anyone publish *Taliessin*?' he asked Anne Bradby on New Year's Day. 'I wager you no; you can have them to send & try, if you like. I don't believe you would have a single hesitation about their rejection.' There was the *Rite of the Passion*, which Phyllis Potter was asking him to rewrite, 'only she did not think she ought to ask it (she was right) only again she did think my later verse was so much easier to speak for her people; she did not know if they would manage the *Rite* verse'. Worst of all, he was having 'to grind out Henry VII, by sheer process of cribbing it all from [the historians] Gladys Temperley & Herr Busch'.[868] He hoped to have it done by the end of March but failed, and by May was desperate:

> I have concluded the first twelve thousand words of *Henry*: there will be no time to rewrite it now. [...] If I have any luck I hope to reach the twenty-thousand by Sunday night. I have but one purpose—to write seventy thousand words all more or less about Henry. I hope this will be my last biography for Barker, so I'm not worrying about the result.[869]

A Rite of the Passion was performed (rewritten or not) on 22 and 23 March at the Congregational Church in Duke Street, London.[870] It was, of course, hardly a play at all, more a kind of ritual, and some were dissatisfied, as we know from Williams's poem on the occasion:

FOR T.S.E.
on a performance of the *Rite*.

I am not of those who squabble for a penny;
I never had any conceit; I keep on guard

> always against discontent, but I do think it hard
> on my own day, at my own play
> to be—but a woman, see! came up to me
> afterwards; she looked intently at me for a great while,
> and I looked back with a persistent expectant smile:
> presently she said: 'Do you know Mr. Eliot?'
> I said: 'Yes.'
> More minutes passed: we, enlinked, gazed,
> but I grimly now, partly to save my muscles
> too little used thus, partly because I was no more amused.
> She said: 'Do you know *Murder in the Cathedral*?'
> I said: 'Yes.'
> Time slipped into its crack, and slept, and came back.
> She said: '*That* was a good play.'
> I said: 'Yes.'
> She went away then. That was all. As I say,
> I keep reasonable guard against pride, but I do think it hard.[871]

A wistful sense of rivalry with Eliot often surfaced. Discussing possible lectures on modern poetry with Olive Willis the year before, Williams had confessed:

> I break down before a good deal of modern verse—though when I say so the young always say: *O Charles, you don't?* which, however beautiful, is a lie. But I could talk about the Break-up, and T.S. Eliot—& how we should have done it all without him, anyhow, however good he is[.][872]

But Eliot too was doing his part. After several rejections *Descent into Hell* was submitted to Faber. Anne Bradby was 'on tenterhooks to see what Eliot's report would say'. Eliot, probably aware that she and Charles were friends, 'typed it himself [. . .]. To my relief, he recommended publication, though he did not think the story achieved the momentum "that kept one turning the pages of *War in Heaven*".'[873] On 3 March, Williams told Hunt, 'My agent sends me the proposed terms, & I say "anything—so long as they pay me MONEY".' He was about to lunch with Eliot and Frank Morley, directors of the firm, 'to hear what they would like done on it, I hope nothing much'. They promised publication by the end of the summer.[874]

But family problems loomed. In late April, Michael fell seriously ill with flu, which developed into pneumonia. Williams sat up with him at nights, telling Phyllis Potter wryly, 'I find that a dark room where one cannot smoke at 3 o'clock in the morning does not really help me to write verse as much as I had supposed it might.'[875] Michael's condition was alarming.

On 29 April, Williams told Hunt, 'the infant is not yet out of danger [but] on the whole the improvement since Saturday, when the doctor thought he had really gone, has been maintained'.[876] Michael was still ill in mid-May.

Williams struggled to complete *Henry VII* whilst nursing him. Three days later he wrote again ('Saturday, and let the date go hang'):

> Well and what do you think? [...] on Thursday evening as ever was my wife crashed into something like pneumonia or bronchitis or Something—with a temperature of 103 & oddments in proportion. So the doctor came at 9.30 *P.M.*; & the medicines came at 12.30 *P.M.*—no, A.M.: my mind is going! & we have her in bed in room A & Michael still in bed in room B and another nurse and another nurse by day (a different one, not two—not yet anyhow), and chemists in attendance, & the gas fire all night. *And* so on.

It was soon confirmed that Michal had pneumonia. Williams added to his letter:

> We have just decided to have a night nurse as well; I can do a lot; but I can't give injections, and the arthritis complicates matters.
> 5.0.a.m. [...] I have slept & woke, & talked with the night nurse, & 'she is holding her own' and I feel my pulse for agonies & find none. But our emotions ever are 'different from what we have supposed' and it has occurred to me that in these things it is the 'I' that is affected & not its penumbra.. but what consciously affects me is the thought of the gas fire going steadily. [...] But otherwise I have abandoned finance.. it worries me a little as I plunge more deeply every hour [...] And all this is but the beginning: it must go on for weeks, AND weeks.

Medical care had to be paid for. The gas fire, nurses, and medicines were devouring money. Meanwhile, Williams was expecting proofs of *Descent into Hell* ('it is odd, but out of nowhere the sensation struck me that it was pleasant that that at least was *done*'), trying to complete *Henry VII* for June, hoping Milford would accept a proposed book called *The Passion of Lent* 'partly because I want his money, partly because it might be a good book', and remembering that he was supposed to be lecturing at Welwyn the next Sunday: he could send Hunt, or failing him Fred Page, but 'anyhow I must write the paper more or less in full—it'll take *hours*'. And 'the *Sunday Times* has just delivered a book on Chesterton for review'.[877]

By 20 May they had 'three nurses installed—night, day & a kind of housekeeping one. The doctor has dropped in four times to-day. [...] We have oxygen, & champagne, and medicines innumerable.'[878] Phyllis Potter, hearing of their plight, generously sent money. Williams told her:

> My wife this morning, through her half-coma and slight delirium, said that you were one of the few people who did things whilst others were asking

what they could do. [...] I shall not, as they say in novels, 'insult' you by returning it. Though personally I never met anybody yet who was insulted by money
being returned. Anyone can insult me in that way to any extent they like, and
the more of them the better.[879]

Michal and Michael recovered during June, though Michal was not back to
full health even in late July. By then Williams owed Hunt a good deal of
money: at the end of June he apologized, 'My salary this month exactly
covers what I have borrowed from the Press & the rent, or I would send at
once',[880] but in July he was able to send a cheque for £16. 'All my gratitude',
he wrote. 'Money that can be tossed about seems to fulfill its purpose; it
becomes the elemental matter of goodwill.'[881]

Despite his domestic pressures, Williams managed, in June, to help
Bishop Bell of Chichester, who was involved in international Christian
opposition to Nazism, to plan an ecumenical service for St Paul's Cathedral.
He recommended avoiding the Nicene Creed ('an historical bone of
offence' to the Orthodox churches), and urged that one lesson should be
Ezekiel I: 1–23:

> This is the famous passage about the Wheels, but it does seem to me to be one
> of the few passages in the Bible that suggest the mathematical exactness as well
> as the passion of the Divine Glory. The wild fantasy is part of the aliveness of
> it, and all the better for that.[882]

Family illness had interrupted his reading the proofs of Walter Lowrie's
Kierkegaard,[883] but he continued to push forward the series of translations,
though warning that 'Kierkegaard was a very great man but he did rather
run to length', and Williams could not commit the Press to 'an indefinite
series of books which might mean heavy losses'.[884]

In July, he was in touch with W. H. Auden, who proposed to edit an
Oxford Book of Light Verse. The two poets met in Oxford on 28 July; if it
seems odd that Williams should have travelled there to meet the poet, one
might guess that the previous evening (Tuesday) he had dined with Lewis
and attended an 'Inklings', before staying the night at Magdalen. Be that as
it may, the meeting was a success. Auden, Williams reported:

> is an extraordinarily pleasant creature, and we found ourselves in passionate
> agreement against the more conservative poets, such as Binyon, Richard
> Church, and even a doubtful Wilfred Gibson. [...] My own inclination [...] is
> that it would be quite a good idea to collect Auden's name. He is still generally
> regarded as the most important of the young poets at present, and likely to be
> more important if he develops.[885]

The book was approved, and they met again to sign the contract on 20 September (Auden received £100; *Light Verse* appeared in 1938). Williams noted:

> Auden looked in today (accompanied by Isherwood who, I understand, is the Force Behind). He goes to China in January—he and Isherwood, not to hold any post but to do a similar book to the Iceland volume. I gather that Faber are putting up some money though hardly enough.[886]

Pretending to be secretly dominated by Isherwood was probably one of Auden's many private jokes, but the two meetings with Williams left Auden profoundly impressed. He recalled how:

> for the first time in my life I felt myself in the presence of personal sanctity. I had met many good people before who made me feel ashamed of my own shortcomings, but in the presence of this man—we never discussed anything but literary business—I did not feel ashamed. I felt transformed into a person who was incapable of doing or thinking anything base or unloving. (I later discovered that he had had a similar effect on many people.)[887]

Probably through Williams's agency, Auden began to read Kierkegaard—a major factor in his return to Christianity over the next year or so.

★   ★   ★

Faber published *Descent into Hell* in September 1937. It was the most carefully written and original of Williams's novels so far. Set in 'Battle Hill', a suburb of what is clearly St Albans, it centres on the contrast between generosity and selfishness: between characters willing to offer themselves in 'substituted love' for the sake of others, and those whose egoism isolates and destroys them. The doctrine of substituted love enters by way of the poet Peter Stanhope, an idealized version of Williams, whose verse play is being rehearsed by a group of Battle Hill amateurs. One of the cast, a young woman called Pauline Anstruther, is in a state of secret terror because she keeps seeing her own double approaching distantly in the street. Convinced that if the doppelgänger reaches her she will die, she confides in Stanhope, who, to her surprise, offers to 'carry' the fear for her. 'We all know what fear and trouble are', he explains:

> Very well—when you leave here you'll think of yourself that I've taken the particular trouble over instead of you. You'd do as much for me if I needed it,

or for anyone. And I will give myself to it. I'll think of what comes to you, and imagine it, and know it, and be afraid of it. And then, you see, you won't.[888]

Pauline discovers that it works: she is no longer frightened, and when eventually she does meet her double, it turns out to be a radiant figure of her own potential, the person she can now become. And it enables her to perform a still greater act of substitution, for in a visionary moment she encounters her ancestor, John Struther, a Protestant martyr of the time of Queen Mary. Struther, 'in his foul Marian prison', is terrified at the prospect of his approaching death. Across the centuries, Pauline takes on the burden of his fear, enabling Struther to go to his martyrdom rejoicing. Substituted love, then, can transcend time, reaching past as well as present and future; for ultimately all time is simultaneous.

Counterpoised against Stanhope is the middle-aged historian Lawrence Wentworth, whose life is dominated by two passions: ambition and lust. His desire for fame as a historian has reached a pitch where he is ready to falsify evidence if it will bring him pre-eminence over his chief rival, Austin Moffat. Meanwhile he has come to desire Adela Hunt, a young woman who is also a neighbour on Battle Hill. She is being courted by Hugh Prescott and, obsessed by jealousy, Wentworth (like Williams at the worst point of his infatuation with Phyllis Jones) stalks the couple through the night-time streets. Consolation of a kind is offered by Lily Sammile, a disturbingly restless busybody who wanders Battle Hill, recommending to anyone who will listen that they should 'enjoy themselves' and engage in 'pleasant dreams'— in other words, turn away from engagement with others and retreat into self-pleasing fantasy. Mrs Sammile provides Wentworth with a succubus: a delusive replica of Adela which is really an embodiment of his erotic fantasies. For, beneath her suburban disguise, Lily Sammile is the demon Lilith, mistress of Samael, a dark angel from Hebrew myth, sometimes identified with the angel of death.

Both Peter Stanhope and Lawrence Wentworth are, in their extreme contrasts, polarized self-portraits of Williams. The identification with Stanhope is self-evident; but in 1934 he admitted to Anne Bradby, 'There is—I sometimes think—the smallest flicker of Mr. Wentworth about me.'[889] This is an understatement. To create Wentworth, he drew on the worst remembered horrors of his sexual frustration and jealousy over Phyllis, and on the envy and resentment he was tempted to feel over his career and literary reputation, which stood still whilst Milford gained a knighthood and

Eliot attained worldwide celebrity. It was these aspects of himself which Williams was consigning to Hell in the novel.

Reviews were favourable but, Williams thought, curiously bland: 'quite polite and respectful, and hardly a single one of them has suggested any unusualness. I presume that the whole reviewing world is absolutely acquainted with the general idea of substituted love. I am blanketed with courtesy and the general recognition of extremely able writing.'[890] The Lewis brothers wrote to express their enthusiasm, though again neither mentioned substitution, which was for Williams the book's most important theme. Jack thought it:

> the best book you have given us yet. In the first place I find the form of Evil that you are dealing with much more real than the Evil (with a big E) that appears in the other books and which, though I enjoy it, (like pantomime red fire) in a story, I do not believe in. But [. . .] Wentworth [is] a truly tragic study. Of course he can't in the nature of things be as good *fun* as Sir Giles Tumulty, but he's more important. And Mrs Sammile is excellent too.
>
> In the second place I'm glad to have got off the 'amulet' or 'sacred object' theme.
>
> Thirdly—and I hope this doesn't sound patronising—in sheer writing I think you have gone up, as we examiners say, a whole class. Chapter II is in my opinion your high water mark so far. You have completely overcome a certain flamboyance which I always thought your chief danger: this is crisp as grape nuts, hard as a hammer, clear as glass.

He admitted to disquiet about some of the dialogue between Stanhope and Pauline: 'I'm afraid the interchange of formulae like "Under the Mercy" may sound like a game to people who don't know you. The L.C.M.[891] between Dante and P.G. Wodehouse is a difficult thing to hit and I'm not sure if it's a good thing to aim at.'

But overall, 'This is a thundering good book and a real purgation to read. I shall come back to it again and again. [. . .] I want you to be at the next Inklings probably on 20 or 27 October. Can you keep yourself fairly free about the time? [. . .] I have written a thriller about a journey to Mars on which I urgently want your opinion: also you'd be able to take your revenge!'[892] An enthusiastic letter from Warren ('Warnie') Lewis followed:

> I want to tell you how much I have enjoyed *Descent into Hell*: though on second thoughts perhaps 'enjoyed' is hardly the right word: I should rather say how much I appreciated it. Up to this I have always thought that the death of Sir Giles Tumulty was your high water mark, but the Descent seems to me far

in a way better—it will be a long time before I forget [Lily Sammile's] footsteps pattering through Battle Hill at night!!⁸⁹³

The approval of both brothers, coupled with an invitation to Oxford to discuss *Out of the Silent Planet*, made it quite clear: Williams was now a fully fledged member of the Inklings.

★   ★   ★

Henry VII appeared in November 1937: actually his third book that autumn, for besides *Descent Into Hell* he had managed to write *Stories of Great Names*, a collection of short biographies (Alexander the Great, Julius Caesar, Charlemagne, and others) for the Indian school market. Williams—who never paused or rested—was lecturing two evenings a week ('The Approach to Literature' on Wednesdays and 'Poetry and the Pattern of Life' on Fridays) besides working on *He Came Down from Heaven,* as it was now called. But he still needed money, so despite being thoroughly tired of biography he cast about for another subject. Dickens, perhaps? Though his agent, he told Anne Bradby, 'thinks Collins [the publisher] might like a great ecclesiastic as much as Dickens; can you find me a great ecclesiastic? Not Cranmer, [...] I am tired of Cranmer: [...] and not Newman; and no-one very pious? and no missionary, & no...but you know all this.'⁸⁹⁴

Nothing came of it. More fruitfully, his growing reputation, boosted by *Cranmer*, had brought invitations to write for leading literary journals. In July he had published 'The New Milton' in the *London Mercury*,⁸⁹⁵ arguing against the notion of Milton as an 'organ-throated egotist' and stressing the generosity of his life—giving his wife's noisy royalist family refuge in his house—and the elements of gentleness and even comedy in *Paradise Lost*. And in December he began a long relationship with the weekly *Time and Tide* by reviewing Yeats's *A Vision*, whose second edition had just appeared.⁸⁹⁶ Williams was the ideal person to review Yeats's cosmic–spiritual–historical system, poetically assembled from material supposedly dictated to Mrs Yeats by spirits and recorded in 'automatic writing'. His finely written and perceptive review emphasizes the kinship between his own insights and those of Yeats. 'No other writer', he tells us, 'arouses so easily a sense of reverie moving into accurate power', and, 'In a period when our cleverest men may write wisdom but do not habitually write English, [Yeats's] style is itself a refreshment.' Quoting Yeats on the diagrams in Law's Boehme 'where one lifts a flap of paper to discover both the human entrails and the starry heavens', he comments, thinking of his own *Taliessin* poems:

> In another myth something of the same idea related the spiritual heavens and the womb of the mother of Galahad, and the last porphyry is like the porphyry room in Byzantium where the Emperors were born.

'The most thrilling sentence in the book', he says, is Yeats's quotation from Heraclitus—'dying each other's life, living each other's death'.

> If indeed [Williams comments] the world is founded on an interchange so profound that we have not begun to glimpse it, such sentences for a moment illuminate the abyss. If so, it is the principle of some such exchange that must be sought before all national and international evils can be righted. 'A civilization', Mr. Yeats says, 'is a struggle to keep self-control.' Only by discovery of the principle of exchanged life can we keep our self-control by losing it, and without losing it we cannot keep it.

He found in *A Vision* not only points of correspondence with the mythology of his own still-unpublished Taliessin poems, but intimations of the doctrine of substituted love and what he would come to call 'coinherence'. Yeats was delighted with the review: Williams, he wrote, 'is the only reviewer who has seen what he calls "the greatness and terror" of the diagram'.[897]

16

The Order of the
Co-Inherence

I n January 1938 Charles Williams went to Paris—his one journey abroad.
He was invited, 'Supposing that France is still peaceful', to give 'six lectures at the British Institute and one at the Sorbonne [. . .] on the Romantic Poets'.[898] Always desperate to earn, he offered the lectures to the Press as a small book; and Sisam was cautiously encouraging. Williams, Michael, and Michal packed for the journey, and Belgion advised as to where in Paris they might find an approximation to a decent cup of tea ('you will be lost without tea').[899] The supposition that France would be peaceful was a fragile one. 'The papers', Williams noted, 'are full of pictures of the French military with stacked rifles waiting for trouble!'[900] Hitler's armies were now directly adjacent to France; he was threatening Czechoslovakia and preparing to annexe Austria. The atmosphere was deeply unsettling.

Still, the family spent two weeks in Paris; Williams lectured at the Sorbonne on 'The Alteration of Passion' (Romanticism, and how Pope had anticipated Wordsworth) and to the British Institute on 'Byron and Byronism'—a delightful lecture which evoked much laughter.[901] By 5 February he was back in London,[902] telling Phyllis Potter, 'Paris, I am told was a great success; certainly we all had a very pleasant time. Only I don't want to do anything now but write the more difficult kind of poetry.'[903]

★　★　★

A substantial collection of 'the more difficult kind of poetry', in the form of *Taliessin Through Logres*, had been ready for months; but still Williams made no attempt to publish it. Perhaps he was too busy finishing *He Came Down from Heaven*. That book—his first published excursion into theology—came out in May. Part of a series called *I Believe*, it was much more than a personal credo. Williams offered brief and vivid insights into many of the Bible's most important books, including Genesis, Job, Ecclesiastes, Ezekiel, the Gospels, and Revelation, finding fresh and cogent things to say about these texts which had been discussed, exhaustively, for millennia. We may address God, he pointed out, as 'Our Father', but we should remember that 'he does not exist primarily for us'. God exists, first, in and for himself. There was only, ever, goodness to know; but evil came into the world because humans 'wish[ed] to know an antagonism in the good, to find out what the good would be like if a contradiction were introduced into it'. God could safely know this, because he knows all things without necessarily creating them; but for man, 'to be as gods, knowing good and evil' meant knowing it by experience, and that was 'the deprivation of the good, the slow destruction of the good, and of themselves with the good'.

The book contains some very personal ideas. Chapter V expounds 'The Theology of Romantic Love', by means of a discussion of Dante. Chapter VI, 'The Practice of Substituted Love', suggests that St Paul's injunction, 'bear ye one another's burdens', be read almost literally: we can, with agreement on both sides, take over the troubles of others, and we should; though with regard to illness, 'Most men [...] ought not, whatever their goodwill, to contemplate the carrying of the burden of paralysis or consumption or even lesser things.'[904] And he claims that substituted love can act across time as well as space: 'The past and future are subject to interchange, as the present with both, the dead with the living, the living with the dead.'[905] All things are part of a great 'web' of exchange. The book bubbles with stimulating ideas, aphorisms, and insights. Williams had been longing for years to put these thoughts on paper, and this short book could hardly contain them.

Lewis wrote at once, congratulating him 'on producing a really great book':

> And it's so *clear*, which at one time I would never have expected a book of yours to be. Damn you, you go on getting steadily better ever since you first crossed my path: how do you do it? I begin to suspect that we are living in the 'age of Williams' and our friendship with you will be our only passport to fame. I've a good mind to punch your head when we next meet.[906]

They met a few weeks later: Lewis brought brother Warnie and friend Hugo Dyson to Amen House for what was effectively a London meeting of the Inklings. They went to Williams's favourite wine bar for 'an immortal lunch', after which Williams signed with a flourish Lewis's copy of *He Came Down*: 'At Shirreffs, 2.10, 4th July 1938'.[907] 'An almost Platonic discussion [...] followed for about two hours in St Paul's churchyard.'[908]

Lewis's enthusiasm meant the more to Williams because the press seemed blind to the originality of his work. 'The most orthodox ecclesiastical papers are polite to *He Came Down From Heaven* without apparently seeing anything in it',[909] he told Hunt.

★　★　★

Europe was moving towards war. On 12 March 1938 German troops marched into Austria. Clearly Czechoslovakia would be next. It seemed only a matter of time before all Europe would be at war. In Britain, trenches were dug in parks and anti-aircraft guns positioned around industrial cities. Against this backdrop, and even before *He Came Down* reached publication, Williams found himself writing what he came to think of as 'a history of Christendom'.

It may have been precipitated by a report on *Doctrine in the Church of England*, which appeared early in 1938: in April Williams was dictating to Alice Mary notes for a critique of the report.[910] Perhaps he took the idea of a book on Christian doctrine to his agents. Anyhow, in late May he asked Phyllis Potter, 'Did I tell you that I have almost fixed up to write a History of Christendom?'[911] About the same time he was lecturing at Welwyn on 'The Reputed Failure of the Church To-day'.[912] Well-known through *Cranmer* and *He Came Down From Heaven*, he had found himself launched on a new phase of his career, as a public speaker on religion. In mid-August he reported, 'I have written the first 8,000 words of the History of Christendom.'[913] The 'History' soon became, more specifically, *The Descent of the Dove: A History of the Holy Spirit in the Church*; it would be published by Longman's.

Williams was given extra inspiration by the Kierkegaard edition. Early in 1938 the *Journals* were being printed; *Fear and Trembling* and *Repetition* were ready to follow.[914] Williams kept in close touch with Dru and Lowrie, the translators; Lowrie even subsidized publication—a fine arrangement for the Press. Williams read Kierkegaard's *Journals* avidly,[915] and by May was unofficially committing the Press to 'a complete Kierkegaard'.[916] He was also trying to keep the prices down, in order to get the books into more readers' hands.[917] Unfortunately, Lowrie found the Press's New York office unhelpful, and threatened to take his translations to Princeton University Press. Only Williams's sympathy and diplomacy induced him to carry on with Oxford, for the time being. It was a tricky relationship, requiring constant attention.

Another project was a 'volume of maps' for the World's Classics. Someone had suggested a historical atlas, and Williams judged that 'if "Everyman's" can risk five volumes at 2/- each we might stand a chance of cutting them out with one volume at 2/-'.[918] It was soon decided to produce 'a literary atlas with some historical maps': Williams and two others drafted a provisional list; a retired schoolteacher was engaged as editor; and whilst in the real world the map of Europe was thrown into violent disarray, a small group at Amen House debated maps, actual or projected, of Trollope's Barsetshire and Pilgrim's Progress, Hardy's Wessex, 'Victorian London c. 1850, showing modern suburbs as then', Moscow ('?Intourist'), Scott ('Perhaps Grierson will suggest what's wanted?'), 'Quantocks and Lorna Doone', 'Lawrence and Arabs', and much else. But the project faltered and sank during the war.[919]

Meanwhile, though Europe grew ever more dangerous, Phyllis Somervaille, whose marriage to Billy had broken down, could no longer bear life in Java. The Dutch colonists, she said, 'never read a book in their lives', and she longed to be home. Some time in 1938, with her two-year-old daughter Penelope, she boarded a Dutch boat to Genoa, and from there travelled overland across Europe to one of the channel ports and thence to England. It was a courageous journey, and she recalled later that 'one of the best moments of her life was meeting a British customs officer' on arrival.[920] Her timing was fortunate: had she stayed and been cut off by the war, she might have been in Java when the Japanese invaded in 1942. Once back in England she resumed part-time work on the *Oxford Dictionary of Quotations* but saw Williams only rarely.

★   ★   ★

Williams was now writing regularly for *Time and Tide*. A leading weekly magazine, it made his name and opinions well known. Between 1937 and 1945 it published more than 100 of his articles and reviews: on literature, history, theology, and occasionally politics.

He also reviewed literature and biography every three or four weeks for the *Sunday Times*. In June the paper published a letter expressing his anxiety (also felt by George Orwell) that pressure from the dire political situation was encouraging a dishonest use of language:

There is at present a general excited rush to protect liberty. We are all urged to register, in this or that body, to defend liberty. [But] men who agree to agree commonly find that determination becoming of more importance to them than their original agreement. [...] A certain intellectual honesty begins to be lost. [...] The immediate result is around us today; words lose their meaning.

Quite intelligent people talk as if the words democracy, freedom, peace, and (even) art all meant the same thing, and inevitably existed together. It is, apparently, seriously maintained that great art—the art of Dante, of Shakespeare, of Racine, of Bach—can only exist in a democratic state. It is nonsense, and (which is my point) it is guilty nonsense.

Is it quite impossible to establish some sort of precaution against the spreading panic? It sounds, I know, ridiculous to propose a little attention to the English language, to style, as a help towards order and peace. Yet it is something that everyone could assist. [...] It is the best and most certain organisation of liberty, and almost the only living shape—for the English—that the divine thing we call intellectual freedom [...] will at all endure.[921]

In Essex, Phyllis Potter kept him busy with productions of his work. 'I am going to Chingford to-night', he told Anne Bradby in April:

to see the *Rite* & possibly to read a bit, because a voice is said to have failed. It goes on MOVING people: my wife says she is moved—she says it is a privilege to have seen it—& she says some stranger was so MOVED that he or she put a ten-shilling note in the Collection. [...] Mr Lakin of the *Sunday Times* told me (G.H. witnessing) that Mr. Lloyd George says I have one of the twelve best brains in England. Yes. Why? How? My dear girl, I don't know.

At the *Rite* on Sunday immense possibilities—actual but undefined—of poetry flung themselves open before me for a moment.[922]

Phyllis Potter was also pressing Williams to accept a commission. The Diocese of Chelmsford would celebrate its twenty-fifth anniversary in 1939, and she wanted a play for the occasion. It was to be a community event; and, perhaps recalling the St Albans Pageant of 1929, Williams offered to write not a play, but a pageant. It would be called *Judgement at Chelmsford*, and he would write it under the name of 'Peter Stanhope'.

The motives for this curious decision remain mysterious. It was perhaps natural that he should want to identify with his idealized self-portrait from *Descent into Hell*; but 'Charles Williams' was now a well-known name and might be expected to boost the pageant. However, the charade was followed through: planning a visit to rehearsals the following spring, Williams asked Phyllis Potter: 'Do I come as Peter Stanhope or C.W.? Stanhope, I suppose.'[923] And it caused problems—as when he invited a priest from Chelmsford 'to come and see me at the Oxford Press completely forgetting that if he does he will be told there is no Mr Stanhope here'. Hubert Foss was let into the secret and told to deflect Stanhope's visitors (and his mail) to Williams.[924]

★   ★   ★

In the summer of 1938, *Taliessin Through Logres* was accepted for publication by the Oxford University Press. The details are unknown, except that on 12 August Williams announced, 'I have sent the Taliessin proofs to the printer and am promised [second] proofs in a fortnight or so.'[925]

To clarify the poems' microcosmic vision—the way in which Williams envisaged correspondence between the human body and the Empire (with hints of the Sephirotic Tree of the Kabbala behind that in turn)—an end-paper was added showing the map of Europe, with a reclining nude female figure superimposed over it. The drawing showed the head superimposed on Logres (Britain), breasts on France, hands on Rome, buttocks on Caucasia, and genitals at Jerusalem. Sketched by Lynton Lamb, a designer who often worked for the Press, it may well have been drawn on an outline map used in planning the World's Classics 'volume of maps'. The endpaper added to the cost; and with Milford doubtful about likely sales, Williams was paid nothing.[926] But at least the poems would be published.

He was working at his usual headlong pace on *The Descent of the Dove*— 'the Holy Ghost', as he now called it:

> I have sketched the first draft in about 8,000 words of the Holy Ghost, though I cannot say that he comes in much yet. But I have feverishly looked up as many of my earlier lectures as I can find in order to use them all over again and save myself thinking of something fresh. Meanwhile you will be pleased to know that an Irish friend of C.S. Lewis's [Arthur Greeves] thinks that my novels suggest to him 'a really *good* man engaged in work which is somehow mysterious and lovely and devotional even, beyond its obvious meaning.' I have asked my wife if she recognizes the really good man; she replied with tact beyond description but a little ambiguously.[927]

He combined writing *The Dove* with a new series of thirty-five lectures on 'The Christian Idea in Literature', to run at the City Lit from September 1938 to June 1939. The first term would start with 'The History of the Church' and go on via the Church Fathers through the medieval mystics, Luther and Calvin, Loyola and Montaigne, Fox, Pascal, Law, Blake, Kierkegaard, Patmore, Barth, and 'Conclusion (TSE Fam. Reunion)'—of which the students would give a dramatic reading. The second term would deal with the *Dream of the Rood*, *Pearl*, *Piers Plowman*, the *Romance of the Rose*, 'The Matter of Britain, The Grail, Malory, Tennyson, Swinburne and Morris, The Arthurian Myth', and 'Conclusion (reading of *Judgement at Chelmsford*)'.[928] The outline shows clearly how, for Williams, religion, literature, and myth formed a seamless whole, and how he saw Eliot and himself as continuing the tradition.

In early September, when Phyllis Potter received the first sketch of *Judgement at Chelmsford*,[929] Hitler was actively threatening Czechoslovakia. There was a general sense that war was imminent. Civilians were issued with gas masks, and instructions for air raids were announced. Many people had signed up as air-raid wardens, since it was assumed that the outbreak of war would be followed immediately by the bombing of London, perhaps with poison gas. The rear basement at Amen House was converted into an air-raid shelter. Neville Chamberlain's government dithered, hoping that one more concession might satisfy Hitler. Chamberlain met him in mid-September, agreed to let him have the Sudetenland unopposed and returned to report that Hitler 'was a man who could be relied upon when he had given his word'.[930] In London there was general relief. Nonetheless, on 20 September Williams sent Raymond Hunt a set of *Taliessin* proofs, advising: 'You can put them in your safe, and if Hampstead and the Oxford Press are blown up into smithereens, perhaps Welwyn will escape.'[931] Ten days later Chamberlain returned from a final conference with Hitler in Munich, bringing a signed agreement expressing 'the desire of our two peoples never to go to war again'. He was greeted by jubilant crowds.

Williams freely admitted later that he had 'thoroughly approved'—and been 'regarded as a cowardly wretch' by some.[932] He thought one last effort worthwhile to avert the impending catastrophe. But he was far from complacent. In the increasingly unreal atmosphere of a war that seemed inevitable but never actually began, he and Phyllis continued planning *Judgement at Chelmsford* and simultaneously considering what to do if war started. The pageant still needed Diocesan approval. He had talked with someone called Mortlock, he told Phyllis, and:

We have agreed that the real thing to do, supposing Czecho-slovakia allows anything to be done, is for him to make it clear to the Bishop (1) that I am the goods, (2) that it is very proper to use another name, as many distinguished people do it, (3) though I will not be controlled by a committee. [...] If things come to the worst politically, and I still vaguely hope they won't, I have been wondering whether I ought to be doing anything. It is quite useless to try and do any ordinary work in the A.R.P. [Air Raid Precautions] business and so on, because my past experience shows that I should not carry through. But it did occur to me the other night that you know all sorts of distinguished people in the Home Office and things and I wondered whether I might perhaps—or you might for me—suggest to one of them that if there was any literary work that they wanted done, as they did in the last War, I should be very glad to put myself at their disposal in any humble way.[933]

Judgement at Chelmsford developed steadily. The plan was to present the diocese of Chelmsford personified as a young woman, challenged to justify herself and presenting a series of historical scenes, as examples of 'how far and with what energy she has followed God'. In late October Williams told Phyllis Potter:

I have the honour to report that I have drafted the plan of the conversation for the Witch episode. Omnipotence directing me, I picked up in Charing Cross Road for sixpence a little thing by Montague Summers which refers to the Chelmsford Witches in 1646. This gives us an admirable 17th century episode.[934]

The sixpenny book was Montague Summers's *The Discovery of Witches*, a study of Essex witchfinder Matthew Hopkins. In December, Williams was still elaborating the episode, working into it a dance and some verse from the trial of the North Berwick witches; he complained, 'These songs are the most difficult to do, especially in my present period when I have abandoned traditional stanzas.'[935]

Kierkegaard was also going ahead steadily. 'Now that it looks as if we shall live a little longer, and even publish books for a little longer', Williams commented, he asked if Lowrie might write a book about his personal experience of Kierkegaard:

We would give a good deal now to have a MS., say, by a Roman gentleman who had been very strongly affected by St Paul, or to know in so many words how the letters of Abelard first struck a close contemporary. [...] You could supply that sort of book before *he becomes fashionable*.[936]

Williams was as ready as ever to offer unconventional advice. Raymond Hunt, depressed towards the end of the year, wondered if this was the Dark Night of the Soul. Williams advised him to read Coleridge's 'Dejection', adding:

It was not after all the custom of St John of the Cross or the Lady Julian to get up in the morning and say 'I am now about to experience that simple mystical state known as the dark night of the soul.' They merely got up feeling incredibly sterile, incredibly hopeless, incredibly dull, incredibly bad-tempered. So they said 'How odd!' [...] I do think we ought shyly to remember that these ordinary glooms are as much the Way as extraordinary tragedy.[937]

Perhaps Hunt cheered up a little when Williams returned £10 that he owed.[938]

Taliessin Through Logres was published in December 1938. Williams took Alice Mary to celebrate at Shirreff's and they drank a toast, 'standing up, to the book and to Taliessin'.[939] It was not the Arthurian epic Williams had once dreamed of, but something better: a sequence of poems in an absolutely distinctive voice. Its style combined the best features of modernism—flexibility, expressive fragmentation, suggestive juxtaposition of images—with powerful elements of rhyme and rhythm, giving it a strong, distinctive music. Williams had taken episodes from the Arthurian myth and made a lens through which the contemporary world, the history of Europe, and intense personal experience all came into focus. These were poems which could stand with confidence alongside the work of Eliot, Yeats, and Dylan Thomas.

The critic Naomi Royde-Smith gave one of the most perceptive early reactions. Admitting the initial difficulty of the poems, she noted that they demanded to be read aloud; and once assimilated, they:

become at once lucid and alarming. They take on the concrete value of a popular ballad [and] the efficacy of a rune. The mind cannot escape from them. In sleep they return, not with the echoes and remembered imagery of their own themes, but evoking other shapes and other associations. It is as if, steeped in the lore of Taliessin, the poet had acquired a bardic gift and, whether he knew it or was involuntarily possessed by it, had exercised it in the physical inspirations and respirations proper to the full exercise of his manifestly occult prosody.[940]

The *Times Literary Supplement*, though complaining that 'poetic expression comes dangerously near to being submerged in occult argument', admitted that 'the verse is close-knitted and sinewy' and found at least some of the poems 'simple and profound'.[941] And Lewis told Williams, 'My opinion of the poems, except for "The Coming of Galahad", which I think mannered, went up and up. A great work, full of glory.' Reviewing the poems for *Theology*, he conceded that, at times, 'the obscurities are to me impenetrable', but praised the work's 'jagged weight and soaring movement, [...] its prevailing quality of glory—its blaze', as well as 'the fresh, harsh energy of

its unstalled diction and the headlight sharpness of its vision'. He concluded
that Williams 'has written a great poem [...] really "classic" and central'.[942]
Lewis's considered verdict on this book and its sequel, expressed seven years
later, was that 'they seem to me, both for the soaring and gorgeous novelty
of their technique and for their profound wisdom, to be among the two or
three most valuable books of verse produced in the century'.[943]

★   ★   ★

Williams now had special responsibility for religious books at the Press. The
beginning of 1939 saw the publication of *The Passion of Christ*, a small
anthology which gave the narrative from the Gospels, with quotations from
Christian writers—Augustine, William Law, Julian of Norwich, and others,
including, here and there, Williams himself. He was not overenthusiastic
about the outcome. Sending a sample copy to the monk and writer George
Every, he explained:

> the book [...] was decided on by us, three-quarters as Christians and one-quar-
> ter as publishers, in order to make some effort to provide a substitute for all the
> dreadful little books of piety which the hierarchies too often encourage dur-
> ing Lent. We shall not make much money out of it and therefore we have
> permitted ourselves to submit it to any distinguished Christians we know in
> some faint hope that they may be able to put it over the faithful. We feel in
> general here that it could not help but do the faithful some good, unless of
> course it drove them mad. Personally I dare not look at it again.[944]

He was editing a collection of C.S. Lewis's essays, *Rehabilitations*, and later in
the year would see through the OUP's publication of *The Personal Heresy*, a
debate on literary theory between Lewis and E.M.W. Tillyard.

In March, Germany occupied Czechoslovakia. The euphoria generated by
Chamberlain's earlier Munich visit had long evaporated. Now Hitler was
threatening Poland. Britain and France guaranteed Poland's independence.
Final plans were made to evacuate children from London and other cities;
blackout instructions were issued, air-raid shelters were prepared, and civilians practised donning their gas masks. In April young men were made subject
to compulsory military training. As foreboding deepened, those of Williams's
friends who relied on him for help and advice urged him to set up some
formal organization whose members could not just draw comfort from his
ideas but put 'substituted love' into practice at a time when it might be
supremely needed. Writing to Anne Bradby in 1934, Williams had rejected

the idea of 'an implicit Order'. A letter to Phyllis Potter written in 'September', probably of 1937, shows that by then he had altered his ideas radically:

> In relation to the Priesthood, I have changed my mind. I think it must be an Order, probably of unmarried persons, for various reasons pledged, either permanently or for a period, (a) not to make use for their personal advantage of the police, of the law, or any such things, (b) not to blame anyone beyond a formal assent to the fact that crime or sin has been committed. I don't think this necessarily would prevent them being in the army or even assenting to war if necessary; I mean it would not be the usual pacifist position. What we have to aim at is the disuse by Christians of the machinery of the State for their advantage.[945]

Nothing had come of this either. But demands from his students and friends mounted, and now he decided to form a group. On 19 April he told one of them, Ursula Grundy:

> I am [...] proposing to make this small step towards the Order. I have gone as far as making up six short statements as a beginning, and I am disposed at least to promulgate them among the household. It is a curiously mixed business, but I have a slight feeling that it is desirable from every point of view.[946]

On the evening of Friday, 21 April he met Raymond Hunt at King's Cross Station and presented him with a note, and an attached paper. The note read:

> The Order of the Co-Inherence.
> I attach a draft of the Promulgation, dated as from the Feast of the Annunciation in this year; it is proposed that the formal Foundation (in so far as this can be) shall be recognized as from the Feast of Trinity next.
> I invite any comments or recommendations. It is intended that the revised draft shall be submitted if possible to episcopal consideration. It may be found desirable to provide some sort of summary of the principles of the Order, but the present draft is proposed only to those who are already acquainted with it.
> C.W.[947]

The document, on which he had probably been working for some weeks (the Feast of the Annunciation is 25 March) read:

> 1. The Order has no constitution except its members. As it was said: *Others he saved, himself he cannot save.*
> 2. It recommends nevertheless that its members shall make a formal act of union with it and of recognition of their own nature. As it was said: *Am I my brother's keeper?*

3. Its concern is the practice of the apprehension of Co-inherence both as a natural and a supernatural principle. As it was said: *Let us make man in Our image.*

4. It is therefore, *per necessitatem*, Christian. As it was said: *And who ever says there was when this was not, let him be anathema.*

5. It recommends therefore the study, on the contemplative side, of the Co-inherence of the Holy and Blessed Trinity, of the Two Natures in the Single Person, of the Mother and Son, of the communicated Eucharist, and of the whole Catholic Church. As it was said: *figlia del tuo figlio.* And on the active side, of methods of exchange, in the State, in all forms of love, and in all natural things, such as child-birth. As it was said: *Bear ye one another's burdens.*

6. It concludes in the Divine Substitution of Messias all forms of exchange and substitution, and it invokes this Act as the root of all. As it was said: *He must become, as it were, a double man.*

7. The Order will associate itself primarily with four feasts: the Feast of the Annunciation, the Feast of the Blessed Trinity, the Feast of the Transfigur- ation, and the Commemoration of All Souls. As it was said: *Another will be in me and I in him.*

At some point an alternative draft of clause 2 was written. It reads:

> It proposes to those members a recognition of their proper natures, a private act of union with all other Companions and with all men, and an activity consistent. It puts itself entirely at the disposal of Almighty God, and it leaves to Holy Luck communication between its members and any enlargement of the Companionship. As it is said: *Am I my brother's keeper?* and again: *Others have laboured and ye are entered into their labours.*[948]

But this was not used.

'Co-inherence' was a term Williams had developed in his work on *The Descent of the Dove.* It had been used before in theology for the relationship between humanity and God in Christ—each inhering in the other. But for Williams, co-inherence represented the insight that we all inhere in one another: we are profoundly interdependent, we are what we are because of one another; we are inseparable from others, and from God. Co-inherence is what makes 'substitution' in Williams's sense possible: we can take on each other's burdens because at a deep level we *are* one another. Christ ('Messias') can atone for our sins because he is us and we are him. 'Episcopal consid- eration' perhaps meant Bishop Bell. The paper was sent to many close friends—Anne Ridler, Thelma Shuttleworth, Alice Mary Miller, Richard and Joan Wallis—and an increasing circle of friends and sympathetic con- tacts. Preparing to dine with Eliot in November 1939, he told Charles

Hadfield that 'I shall try & find an opportunity to tell him that the Order exists',[949] implying that he thought Eliot might wish to join. Williams continued to propagate his 'Order' until the end of his life—and it would long outlive him.

He was as ready as ever to put its principles into practice. Sometime in 1939 Thelma Shuttleworth, about to travel to Scotland to rejoin her actor husband after four months' separation, was seized with nerves. She telephoned Williams, and as she recalled:

> We had a conversation like that of Peter Stanhope and Pauline in *Descent into Hell*. [...] Charles said—about my jellied state—that I was not to worry, he would see to that. I must simply attend to my affairs, setting all in order and then leaving it to Love. No problem. If I needed to, I must ring again. I was to be not afraid amazedly, enjoy myself, go with God. All will be most well. . . . And it was, instantly![950]

Practising substitution in this manner became a normal part of life for members of Williams's new Order, the 'Companions of the Co-Inherence'.

★　★　★

Throughout the year Williams grappled with the task of writing *Judgement at Chelmsford*. It required him to integrate historical episodes with his own mystical view of Christianity and the demands of the Diocesan authorities, a three-way tussle which sometimes drove him to distraction. 'Damn and blast the Rural Dean!' he fumed to Phyllis Potter, when yet another rewrite was demanded. 'However, I forgive him; he means well.'[951] The opening was to be wholly contemporary, with noise of aeroplanes and bombs, modulating into a song by discontented factory workers. 'I have particularly avoided using at least three obscene words in this', he explained, 'which will no doubt all occur to you and would make the song sound real. No bourgeois song can ever, apart from that, sound convincing to the proletariat. But I think this might serve.'[952] Other episodes included the 'discovery' of the Chelmsford witches by Matthew Hopkins, and the Peasants' Revolt of 1381—a politically charged scene in which John Ball announces: 'This is how we know the Kingdom of God, / That the rich make themselves poorer and not richer.' The episode contains a pointed reference to Thaxted as a place where the Christian spirit has 'cried / that the people must be saved in earth as in Heaven / and the angels dash pride into the pit.' Thaxted was famous as the parish of the 'Red Vicar', Conrad Noel, a founding member of the British Socialist Party, who had hung the Red Flag in his church. Williams was making a firm political point.

He wanted a medieval pageant of the Seven Deadly Sins, set in the convent at Barking; but church authorities proved squeamish:

> If Widdrington objects to the seven deadly sins being presented by girls under the guardianship of nuns I shall think he is introducing modern views. I don't believe that a medieval or Renaissance nunnery would really have avoided the mention of lechery. [...] The alternative would be to produce a lesson in the girls' school at the Convent. But I am not very much moved by that. [...] Unless of course you could have a riot—but there are too many riots in the play already. Or unless you could have one of the girls chastised (like Lady Jane Grey), but your people might not like that. Modern morals are so difficult.[953]

He negotiated objections from the Rural Dean, making the Sins acceptable by changing 'Lechery' to 'Luxury'.

Here and there Williams's private fantasies emerge. The pageant's climax, where the young woman representing Chelmsford is bound to a cross, illustrates how complex were the links between his erotic imaginings and his mystical theology. The image of the crucified woman undoubtedly appealed to his mildly sadistic tendencies; but it also represented the archetypal Christian soul taking on the Cross, mystically participating in the sacrifice of Christ. Moreover, it replicated the Rosicrucian Adeptus Minor initiation of twenty years before, in which Williams had been 'raised on the cross of Tiphereth'. He was quite ready to analyse *Judgement at Chelmsford* Kabbalistically, telling Phyllis Potter:

> I was moved during the weekend to [...] do a kind of brief sketch of the Pageant from (what low creatures call) the spiritual point of view. [...] It can of course be enlarged by a little meditation, but I have laid down the general principles. [...] It becomes clearer to me that the whole thing represents the Sephirotic Tree. Never mind about that if you don't happen to know it; the point is that there is a Pillar of Judgement on one side and a Pillar of Mercy on another and the Union of the two in the middle way is called the Pillar of Benignity. [The Pageant] begins in the present world which is Malkuth and it goes up to Kether which is—It. So there we all are.[954]

Not all his fantasies, however, were sublimated into creative work. He was still in touch with Olive Speake, now working at the Federation of Rural

Music Schools in Gloucester Place, London. In March 1939 she wrote to apologize for missing some appointment (was she still visiting Amen House?) and he replied that it was unimportant, but:

> You shall be [*illegible*] for that failing too, so you can type out on a neat slip of paper: 'Stella is reported for being late and is to have the ruler six times on her hands'—and you shall keep it until I come and then stand up with it for me; [...] Every woman, in order to be a goddess, must be treated like a schoolgirl, but no one ought to treat her like a schoolgirl who does not admire in her a divinity: neither alone is sufficient, so the gaiety of your chastising is the gate of your glory.[955]

★   ★   ★

Whilst work on *Judgement at Chelmsford* went on, there was the likelihood of a new commission, this time from Faber. A brief note survives from Eliot to Williams, dated 29 March 1939, to the effect that the 'outline' looks very satisfactory, though the title is 'possibly a bit high-flown', and something more down-to-earth might be better.[956] There are no further details, but probably this refers to the book about magic, which would become *Witchcraft*, and which Faber would publish in 1941.

A new production of *Seed of Adam* was also imminent: in February Williams had been contacted by Ruth Spalding, a theatrical producer who lived in Oxford and wanted to direct the play.[957] He gave his blessing, and Ruth became as close a friend as Phyllis Potter. He took a deep interest in her production, advising in May, 'Remember that Adam has to say "ankle" instead of "anus"—The Censor insisted that the latter word must not be allowed on the stage—thus completely de-christianizing the body. However, that is not my affair.' Miss Gotch ('is that her name?') has been to Amen House to discuss costumes: 'I have pressed as far as possible for an inhuman angel and I have insisted that Mary must look like the kind of young woman with whom a man might fall desperately in love.'[958] In mid-June he took Michal to Oxford to see the play. They found the production 'admirable [...] beautiful and moving', and stayed overnight at 9 South Parks Road, where Ruth Spalding lived with her sister Anne.

The Williams family was in the midst of changing flats, moving the short distance from Parkhill Road to 12a Antrim Mansions, a tall and oddly ill-proportioned block just off Haverstock Hill, one of Hampstead's main streets. Phyllis Potter was convinced that he was overworking, and wrote urging him to take a holiday:

> I am very concerned about your not having a proper holiday. It is all very well for you to say you are all right, but I know people cannot go on being all right without breaks away from London, and my doctor Ward has already noticed your tremor.[959]

Williams naturally fended this off. 'Thank you', he wrote:

> but if your Dr Ward had known me at 20 she would have seen a positive earth-quake. I have had to put up with it all my life, and a damn nuisance it has been. It is a little worse since the operation but it does not get any worse through a little work.[960]

As his year-long series of lectures on 'The Christian Idea in Literature' drew to a close in June, air-raid shelters were being installed in back gardens, and city skylines decorated with barrage balloons; fish-shaped, silver-coloured, and the size of a house, they were filled with hydrogen and floated on cables designed to cut the wings of low-flying aircraft. The OUP at Amen House finalized its plans for evacuation. In case of war it would join its parent institution at Oxford. Charles Williams thought of Ruth Spalding and wrote to her, asking for help:

> I understand that if by any chance there is a war I shall be moved to Oxford. I suppose you don't happen to know any small and cheap house near you where three people could take rooms at least for two or three weeks until things straightened out? That is the worst of us family men. This (he added hastily) is not to suggest that you should give yourself any trouble; it is only that you might know some house where they did not want evacuated children and yet could put up somebody.[961]

Ruth consulted her sister Anne. The Spalding parents were temporarily in America, so the sisters wrote, asking them whom they would rather house if war began: Charles Williams and colleagues from the Press, or evacuated children. The answer was a telegram of memorable brevity: 'Greatly prefer Charles Williams.'[962]

During the summer—a hot one, when many people nervously snatched what might well be their last peacetime holiday—Williams beguiled his loneliness at the office by writing long letters to Alice Mary, who was at home caring for her new baby, Laura. He was working, he said, on more Taliessin poems; but 'I am as heavy and helpless and bored with Taliessin as ever a woman with a baby; the thing fills me and will NOT emerge, except in imbecilities like sickness itself.'[963] He broke off to look up a passage about the Tetragrammaton in the 1931 Simon and Sperling translation of the *Zohar*, telling Alice Mary:

> I wish I had read it before I wrote *Descent into Hell*, my little succubus would have been made more attractive. For it seems that the female spirits who disport with men in their dreams subsequently give birth. The creatures thus produced are called 'plagues of mankind'; they appear always under the forms of human beings, *but they have no hair on their heads*. I trust—damn, I have forgotten its name—has, by now.

(Alice Mary forgave him for forgetting Laura's sex and name.) Sensing that an era at Amen House was drawing to a close, he reflected uneasily on the past:

> It struck me with a shock how *little* Amen House has done! We did have, after all, a very high chance—and where are we? After all, Gerry & F.P. & H.S.M. are not mere incapable fools, nor I; and why has nothing been produced higher and greater, even in sheer *mind*, than has been? Could we not have made something of criticism or something? I know I hampered it for years, but even so—. Damn it, we are intelligent, aren't we?

Naturally this led to thoughts of 'Phillida':

> It occurred to me one night that one really ought *not* to go about feeling that one debâcle—even a serious debâcle—was quite enough and that one's life had—what shall I say? Done its share! God send no more! Still—you see what I mean? But that may be the effect of the international situation; I think it partly is. Also—O Alice Mary, I blush; yes, I do—it is partly, I fear, painted finger-nails. I didn't know they repulsed me; it seems they do. A peevish reason!

His feelings for Phyllis had largely cooled. They saw one another occasionally around Amen House, but what had once seemed a divine passion was now, often, merely mild irritation on both sides. He was even drawn into negotiations over her approaching divorce from Billy Somervaille:

> our Miss Wilkinson told me that Mrs. Somervaile [*sic*] doesn't like me reading aloud, and Miss W. thinks Mrs Somervaile thinks me too conceited. [...] I have been consulted on a small financial point, raised by Billy, and have considered and discussed it. You will no doubt be told of it. The only thing that worried me was that Phillida began talking of her principles. There is nothing wrong, but something dangerous in it. I permitted myself to remark that Billy no doubt regarded himself as having been led up the garden[.]

There was also a momentary fantasy that the King might join the Companions. Williams had talked, he said, with a Canon of St Paul's, London, after the Oxford performance of *Seed of Adam*. The Canon was full of enthusiasm for the play, and:

> He is, I hear, a Chaplain to His Majesty: I save the Order of the Co-inherence for him when he is back [from his holiday]; he can lay it before the Throne. How right if the Exalted Majesty became, say, the seventeenth member! No? no. Yet wilder things are at hand all the time.

Closing a letter on 23 August, his usual ceremonious style modulated into ominous tones:

> The British Ambassador is flying to Hitler, and Ribbentrop to Moscow; and shall I not send you a note? Who knows which means more? [...]
> I am a little afraid of my mere physical organism breaking; it would be silly of it, but it has never really stood wear well. It is not exactly fear; it is sheer incapacity. Even now, nothing may happen; I half believe it. But if it does, then, somehow or other, in all that happens is the glory and the joy.[964]

That day, the Russian and German foreign ministers signed the Nazi–Soviet Non-Aggression Pact. With Russia's agreement not to oppose Germany, the last bulwark against Nazi aggression was gone. For Britain, war was now almost inevitable. Two days later, with *Judgement at Chelmsford* far on in rehearsal, Amen House quivering on the brink of evacuation, and *The Descent of the Dove* being printed and selected as Christmas choice for the 6,000 members of the Religious Book Club, Williams told Phyllis Potter:

> Goodness only knows whether we shall see the Pageant or not. And where I shall be in the next week. [...] I feel I shall probably be blown to bits in Oxford at precisely the moment that six thousand people, or more, if you include the ordinary sale, are brooding over the Co-inherence. Blessed for ever be the fantastic design of the Omnipotent.[965]

Amen House was in chaos, cluttered with packing cases and poised for evacuation. At 5 p.m. daily everything used in work—books, ledgers, paper-work—had to be repacked. Less work was done each day as staff spent more and more time discussing the impending war. On 29 August, Williams was considering 'dispatching' Michal and Michael to the Spaldings' house in Oxford to settle matters, for the time being at least.[966] The experiment was tried, but it was a disaster. Michal and Michael travelled down a day or so later and turned up at the Spalding residence, but Anne and Ruth were away, having left their ferocious Aunt Becky and gentle brother John in charge of the house. The aunt, assuming them to be uninvited refugees, interrogated them on the doorstep: 'Can you cook? Can you wash? Can you mend?'[967] Michal was deeply offended and the pair returned to London, their relationship with the Spaldings permanently soured.

By Friday, 1 September, business at the Press had become, according to one observer, 'a farce, and we were literally twiddling our thumbs until 11 a.m. [...] when the balloon went up, as it were': Ray Goffin came into the office carrying a special edition of the *Evening Standard*, which he placed before Helen Peacock with the words 'What do you think of that?'— Germany had invaded Poland. 'Shall we pack up?' someone asked. 'Yes', said Miss Peacock, 'I think we'd better.' The call for action was a relief. Throughout the building it was, one witness recalls:

> Coats off, sleeves up, and in some cases (mine certainly) collars off. Into the cases went all the paraphernalia of office life. Hammers rose and fell, ropes were drawn tighter, feet hurried, doors were flung wide open, trolleys trundelled, and the lifts were 'going up' and 'going down' in approved fashion.[968]

Vans from the Press's distribution centre at Neasden arrived to ferry everything to Oxford. They departed 'loaded down to the back axles with all the stuff we could lay hands on'. The move would take several days.

Meanwhile, the British and French governments presented Von Ribbentrop with an ultimatum, which was ignored. On Sunday, 3 September, came Britain's declaration of war on Germany. The next morning Charles Williams, like the rest of the staff from Amen House, travelled to Oxford.

17

'A Kind of Parody of London'

On the train to Oxford, Williams read St John of the Cross. At Oxford he took a taxi to leave his luggage at 9 South Parks Road, the Spaldings' home, then went on to Southfield House, a mansion on the city's eastern outskirts where the Press's London business was setting up wartime offices. Dating from the seventeenth century, Southfield House maintained the Press's high architectural standards. A member of staff wrote:

> One enters by a graceful double pillared doorway into a small annexe which continues into a larger hall with a beautiful, but simply carved, staircase immediately to the left. All the rooms have high ceilings and long windows, and walls tastefully covered with oil and water colour paintings. [...] [The owner] has given permission for us to use the wireless, gramophone, and piano inside the house; and, outside, to have the run of the gardens, putting green, and a delightful badminton court inside the barn. [...] We have put aside the gloom which overshadowed us at Amen House, and look forward to the peace and quiet of the countryside. Wars may come and wars may go, but they will be undetected so far as Southfield House is concerned![969]

Despite this idyllic picture, Southfield House was far from ideal. Its upper floors were crowded and inconvenient. Until 11 December, there were no telephones.[970] 'Everything is [...] in complete disorder', Williams wrote; 'some sort of work is being done; but the corners & tables & boards & general absurdity is [sic] indescribable. [...] Every room has six or seven people in it, and all crowded.'[971]

His first office is best described in the words of Hubert Foss. It was:

> A spacious bathroom. [...] We observe in the darker part a man in his early fifties writing in pencil on a pad, verses about the Arthurian legend. At the table by the window overlooking a handsome and well-kept rose garden sits a slightly younger man dictating letters and handling papers about music. The third occupant of the room is a bright-eyed young girl with red hair who is

typing away as if for dear life. The poet is Charles Williams, the musician the writer of this paper. A few minutes before our entry to view the scene the two men were standing at the window planning in imagination an amateur production in the rose-garden of the Malvolio scenes from *Twelfth Night*. Nearly all the traces of the room's original ablutionary functions have been covered up by shelves of rough wood, and in their place we see files of papers, MSS. and stationery, for wartime has decreed that this is no longer a bathroom but a publisher's office. At any moment tall grey Sir Humphrey Milford may join the company and ask his incisive questions.[972]

The plank-covered bath served as Williams's desk for several months. The other furniture 'came from a Church Hall'.[973]

Williams soon settled in at South Parks Road, and was joined a few days later by Gerry Hopkins. He made contact with C.S. Lewis, who introduced him to Adam Fox, Inkling and Professor of Poetry, and offered his rooms at Magdalen College as a weekend refuge from the crowded Spalding household. Williams began to feel a little more comfortable. 'If ever our Order could hold together spiritually', he wrote to Anne Ridler:

> this is the time. Our coinherence in Hitler & his in us; and in Christ; & in each other; & so on. [...] This is but a shabby note, but I hurl myself into whatever I meant by the Order: now, if ever, let us think of it. I feel that dark point deeper than all their talk of causes and principles; there, there, we are one.

Michal did not want to come to Oxford; he suggested Anne telephone her; and 'Give my love to T.S.E.; I wish he were here and you; you first & then he. Tell him he is the only male love of my life since Nicholson died. And for you, believe much more.' 'Would you believe it?' he added, 'Celia turned up here to-day; [...]—the divorce, Gerry tells me, was made absolute to-day; as soon as M[cDougall] can get leave they will be married.'[974] Phyllis married Archibald McDougall on 22 September at Dover, where he was a Lieutenant Commander in the Royal Naval Volunteer Reserve (RNVR).

Charles Williams's new home was a substantial Victorian detached house with a large garden, in a side road some half-hour's walk from his new workplace. With its highly polished furniture, valuable oil paintings on the walls, and gong in the hall, which summoned residents to dinner each evening, it offered surroundings distinctly more opulent than those he had been used to. It was the home of Henry Norman Spalding and his wife Nellie. Spalding was fascinated by Eastern philosophy, and the family fortune—derived from guano mined from a remote Pacific island by Mrs Spalding's father—enabled the couple to establish academic posts in Oriental Religions at several universities. The Spaldings had gone for a six-month visit to the United States and now found themselves marooned there 'for the duration'. The house had been left in the charge of their son John, a medical student now called up as a 'medical orderly', and their daughters, Ruth and Anne. Anne, age twenty-eight, was an artist and graduate of the Ruskin School of Art; her sister Ruth, twenty-five, was already an actress and 'travelling producer' with the Religious Drama Society. On the outbreak of war, the government had closed all theatres, so Martin Browne at Canterbury had organized the Pilgrim Players, a company ready to perform in barns, church halls, schools, pubs—'Plays any time, anywhere'. Ruth Spalding contacted Browne, and with his encouragement set up the Oxford Pilgrim Players, based at her home. Days after hostilities began, the house could boast a dramatist, a producer, and (though only occasionally in residence) a theatre company.

In the course of the war the house sheltered a great variety of people, though Williams, Hopkins (known as 'Hop'), and the Spaldings were the only long-term residents. At first Dick Milford (Vicar of St Mary's; no relation to Sir Humphrey) stayed there with his children. Later lodgers included Michal (for brief visits), Michael (for much longer), Dorothy Sayers (occasionally), and many actors, refugees, and evacuees, Hungarian, Russian, Austrian, and other. With Ruth often on tour, housekeeping fell to Anne. Though 'very shy of running a house', she quickly settled into her role as landlady and did her best to keep the mercurial lodgers under control. 'The household was run pretty much as a co-operative effort', she recalled, 'in that everyone pitched in and helped with the jobs and the housework and so on', though it cannot have been very onerous, for there were a gardener, a cook, and two maids. Williams encouraged the view that the house was a monarchy with Anne as queen, and himself and Gerry as ministers, advising but not insisting. The queen's job was 'a demanding one, with food rationing, strangers lodging, meals needed at different times and, once fire-watching [...] had begun, members of the household up regularly at odd hours of the night'.[975] The servants found it hard to adapt to the new and varied residents, causing further difficulties. When it all became too trying, 'Well', said Anne, 'we used to have a little sort of committee meeting.'[976] Williams turned out to be quite domesticated:

He was never late for meals [...] He cut the bread for everybody, in spite of his shaky hands, opened windows to air the room after meals, plumped up all the cushions every night before bed. He was a faithful-drier-up, and would break up the most absorbing theological talk to dry the 9 p.m. cups of tea—unless [...] the conversation was of real moment to the visitor, a condition he sensed with accuracy.[977]

When Eliot visited, the two poets compared bed-making techniques, in which they both took pride.

At first Williams spent the evenings working in his bedroom, but owing to coal rationing had no heating. As autumn went on he joined everyone else in the sitting room. He and Hopkins tended to dominate evening conversation, sometimes arguing about religion (Hopkins was an atheist) and drawing everyone else into the debate. A favourite pastime was the board game halma, which Anne taught Williams, after which 'he and I played halma *every* evening, far into the night', Williams lying on the floor, his long legs entangled with the feet of the chairs. Much writing also went on. 'We all sat round the fire', Anne recalls: 'we had just the one fire because there was a war on and so everybody was doing everything at the same time. Hop was going bang bang bang on our very ancient typewriter', while Williams scribbled away, his reporter's pad balanced on one knee as he lay back in an armchair, invariably smoking ('he smoked us out of house and home!'). Once, finding a scrap of broken lithographic stone (unobtainable in wartime) at the art school, Anne brought it home and sketched both men, intent on their work; the prints are now in the National Portrait Gallery. On another occasion, when Williams was out of the house, a visitor insisted that the company experiment with a Ouija board, which (Anne recalled) 'wasn't what we wanted to do at all [...] but we did it because, you know, we had to humour our visitor'. The result was 'slow, uninteresting' until 'Charles came in in the middle and joined in, and the thing just went mad! [...] The thing went absolutely batty! [...] Just shot around the board like *that*!'[978] There is, sadly, no record of any message received.

Sometimes Williams returned to London for weekends: on 29 October 1939, for example, he planned to dine with Eliot and Belgion on Friday evening, then on Saturday take Michal for lunch with Anne and Vivian Ridler and for tea with 'Henry' Lee, before returning to Oxford. More often, he was alone in Lewis's rooms at Magdalen College: bleak enough at first, despite Lewis's thoughtful leaving of milk, tea, and an electric kettle, since all books had been removed, on mistaken orders that the rooms would be requisitioned for government use. Lewis retrieved his books a month later. Eventually Williams reconciled himself to staying mostly at South

Parks Road. On Sundays he attended St Cross Church. On his first weekend in the house, 'Anne asked him if he wanted to be called for early church. He said no, thank you, he would leave it to the Holy Ghost whether he should go or not.'[979] His letters show that the Holy Ghost was unpredictable; he sometimes overslept, and it did not worry him greatly. At church he 'sang vigorously [...] with rhythm but no knowledge of intonation. The Creed and Gloria seemed to arouse his special enthusiasm, and he crossed himself with large swift gestures.'[980] Anne often noticed his smoker's cough as he emerged from church, pausing to light another cigarette. He generally 'look[ed] very surprised at the Eucharist. He always found Christianity surprising although he belonged to it', she remembered, and would mutter '"Well. Well. Well!" in evident astonishment at what had taken place.'[981]

On weekdays he would walk into Oxford with Gerry, carrying his gas mask, turning aside to a barber for his daily shave; he noted grimly that this was 'the one quarter of an hour I get to myself [...] until ten at night'.[982] Then he went on to Southfield House, passing on the way a piece of open ground whose typical Oxford signboard—'Reserved for Jesus and Trinity'— amused him greatly.[983] Michal stayed in London, 'not really liking Oxford', he told Phyllis Potter, 'and feeling very strongly that if she has to pay the rent of a flat [in London] she may as well live in it'. More bluntly, Williams told Raymond Hunt that she had 'firmly refused to come to Oxford if she can possibly avoid it. I sympathize with her; I wish I had the chance of doing the same thing.'[984] Michal's determination was perhaps strengthened by accidentally hearing, when she called at Amen House to collect something of Charles's, that 'Celia' was now working at Southfield House—something he had not mentioned. Phyllis kept her remarriage in September a secret: at the Press she was still 'Mrs Somervaille' and, in October, Williams wrote of her as 'between two marriages'.[985]

He was far from comfortable about her presence in Oxford, finding his feelings painfully ambivalent. After her colonial experiences Phyllis was more sophisticated, as well as older; he sneered to Alice Mary about her 'absolutely foul' nail varnish, her 'smartness', and 'signs of middle-age';[986] but, he told Thelma in October 1939, 'Even now—even after ten years' exile—my heart flutters when some menial's voice says: "Mrs Somervaile". I ought to be of some use while the future husband is on the high seas. I simply *cannot*: I cannot move my physical organism to go down to her.' And he quoted Milton:

The void profound
Of unessential Night receives him next,

> Wide-gaping, and with utter loss of being
> Threatens him, plunged in that abortive gulf

– adding:

> I shouldn't expect you to read [that] for comfort, there is none. But all the darker side of my own work is an image of that—precisely that. The road from the Women's Institute to Clapham Common is still part of that 'abortive gulf'. The tumultuous and insane agony of the nothing.[987]

And he lamented, 'O I wish I were free! I sometimes think Celia can't realize how much pain she causes.'[988]

Naturally, Michal was suspicious. When Williams learned with surprise that one of his plays would be performed at Southfield House in December 1939, he reassured her that 'no-one will be here about whom you might faintly be dubious'[989]—in other words, that Phyllis would not be coming. Still, both he and Phyllis showed signs of sliding back into their old roles: he confessed to Alice Mary in March 1940 that Phyllis had:

> appeared here three—two—weeks ago, and between 6.45 and 7 when I was down at Magdalen drunk on sherry. So I went all We, and said she had better write to Us every week. So yesterday there came a brief letter apologising for not having written the first week, which might mean anything, but saying that it was not forgotten, and she was trying. I do not know what else to do or be. I realize (Althea, do I trust you!) that all sorts of details I dislike in her, phenomenally, will be likely to develop: her voice will get harder and shriller, and so on[990]

Nevertheless, the obsession persisted.

★ ★ ★

Williams settled into work on Kierkegaard, with *The Point of View*, *Christian Discourses*, and *The Present Age* going through the Press. 'We work between gas-masks and sirens', he told Lowry, adding—for a paper shortage loomed—'K may rebuild civilization, but we shall have to be more economical than ever in building K.'[991] *Judgement at Chelmsford* had been cancelled, and he condoled with Phyllis Potter: 'I have been more sorry for you, I think, than for myself. For I have had so much of the pleasure and you have had all the labour.'[992] A consolation was Eliot's admiration for *The Descent of the Dove*, to be published in mid-October: Eliot signed a copy of *The Idea of a Christian Society* 'to Charles Williams with the humble respects of T.S. Eliot, 19 Oct 1939'.[993]

Eliot had commissioned Williams to write a book on the history of magic for Faber, so as soon as final proofs of the *Dove* were sent off, he buckled down to this new project, as yet known simply as *Magic*. He worked at his usual headlong pace: on 6 October he told Anne Ridler that he had:

> done a little [...] towards *Magic*, and cleared off St. Joan and what they thought was wrong with her, and [am] now trying with an inadequate biography to deal with her contemporary Gilles de Rais: all about the strange beauty of youth and witches strangling babies, and Gilles's devotion to St. Joan and to the Holy Innocents between his sadistic murders. I feel a faint sympathy with Gilles; not being a medieval and very rich prince, I haven't his opportunities nor his callousness, but otherwise... Of course I disapprove, but then so did he! However, if the question turns up, let your people know that I am going on. I propose to get hold of the *Malleus* and devote a chapter to that. I do not know which is the more detestable—the covens or the courts.[994]

By mid-autumn he was also working on two new plays, *The House by the Stable* and *The Death of Good Fortune*, for the Oxford Pilgrim Players.[995] He told Phyllis Potter apologetically, 'I cannot bear to live in a house where people are going out to do tiresome plays, and therefore I have written something for them.'[996] And Dick Milford wanted a Passion play for St Mary's.[997]

He wrote *The House by the Stable* between 14 and 26 October, giving the finished text to Ruth Spalding, handwritten on one of his sixpenny note-pads. In November he undertook to edit for the Press, by June 1940, a cal-endar-based devotional anthology, *The New Christian Year*. He asked Michal, Anne Ridler, and others to contribute quotations for it. It would be compiled unpaid, to reimburse money that the Press had lent him during the past year. Finally, untroubled by this colossal workload, he offered the City Lit a lecture course 'once in three weeks on Saturday afternoons'. Fortunately the proposal was turned down.

Williams had long been a workaholic. Radiating kindness and giving unstinting attention to others, he was often deeply unhappy, and inclined to bury his unhappiness in work. Oxford intensified this. He found it 'a dread-ful place to work in—heavy and relaxed',[998] and was continually homesick for London, to which he relentlessly compared it. He told Michal, 'Outside Lewis, I never want to see anyone of Oxford or in Oxford again! [...] I have a nostalgia for walking round the block in London—the City & the Dome; the flat and you.' When Sir Humphrey said that 'if he could choose he would never live in Oxford', Williams and Hopkins heartily agreed.[999] Even the architecture failed to delight him. 'I cannot think that Oxford is very attractive—in rain', he told Alice Mary.[1000] 'It rains', he told Michal, 'heavily and continuously. Oxford, they say, is like this all through the winter. [. . .] Rain in London is bad; rain in Oxford—.'[1001] To Anne Ridler he could only concede that 'Oxford is beautiful so long as one lives in London.'[1002] And when he began to receive invitations to the colleges, he remained unimpressed, comparing the public-school company to that of old days at Amen House: 'Winchester and New Colleges produce—what? A copy (as it were) of the rest of us, without the colour & with as much boredom, I suspect. [. . .] Oxford, however nice, is still a kind of *parody* of London.'[1003]

Despite tensions in his relationship with Michal, he deeply missed her company and care. 'I cannot say how I wish I were being looked after by you', he told her.[1004] Though the Press now paid an extra £1 a week,[1005] he was perpetually short of money, harvesting every penny he could for wife and son, with a new coat or pair of shoes being a major purchase. And he owed money to Humphrey Milford, to Hunt, to others. Every book contract, every review, meant money. It could also mean reputation. He felt undervalued; but each new book or play might be enough to draw serious attention, to put his reputation where he felt it should be—alongside that of Eliot. Somehow, in every predicament of his uncomfortable life, work seemed the best answer.

★ ★ ★

The one great consolation was the friendship of Lewis and the Inklings. Williams had always enjoyed discussion with male groups: the Theological Smokers in St Albans, Fred Page's debating society, 'Henry' Lee's Sunday group (which still met, though Williams could no longer go).[1006] The Inklings offered an oasis of friendship. Lewis's appetite for his company was boundless. Besides lending his college rooms at weekends so that Williams could escape the overcrowding, the play readings, and the madrigal singing at South Parks Road ('more madrigals to-night; fortunately I don't sing, so I sit in a chair and think about witchcraft'),[1007] Lewis established a routine of lunching with him on Tuesdays and Thursdays in a pub, and made him welcome, those same evenings, at meetings of the Inklings.

Never a formal group, but simply a gathering of Lewis's friends held together by mutual liking and shared interests, literary and theological, the Inklings had become—probably some time in the mid-1930s—aware of themselves as 'a sort of informal club'. They met twice a week in Lewis's college rooms, to read from their recent work—though not all were writers—and to discuss literature, ideas, everything under the sun and beyond it. Besides Lewis, the central members of the group when Williams joined it were J. R. R. Tolkien, the Rawlinson and Bosworth Professor of Anglo-Saxon; C. L. Wrenn, another Anglo-Saxon scholar and fellow of Pembroke College; H. V. D. ('Hugo') Dyson, lecturer in English at Reading University; and R. E. Havard, Lewis's medical practitioner. Occasional visitors, some of whom had formerly been central members of the group, included Adam Fox, Professor of Poetry and Dean of Divinity; Nevill Coghill, Fellow in English at Exeter College; and the writer and philosopher Owen Barfield, whose work as a solicitor in London prevented his attending regularly. He and Williams did meet sometimes, however. Barfield was an Anthroposophist—a follower of Rudolph Steiner's teachings—and when they first met, Williams, knowing nothing of Barfield's beliefs, announced 'I have just been talking to someone who told me I was an Anthroposophist.' Sadly, the conversation was diverted, and a potentially fascinating discussion lost.[1008] Lewis's brother Warren, known as 'Warnie', was absent when Williams arrived: a reserve Captain in the Royal Army Service Corps, he had been mobilized on the outbreak of war, and posted to Le Havre in October. He returned to Oxford in August 1940. During November 1939 Gerry Hopkins also attended the meetings, but he soon dropped out.[1009]

John Wain described the ambience of those Thursday evenings at Magdalen as they were a few years later (the rooms a little drabber, the participants a little less lively than in 1939):

> the electric fire pumping heat into the dank air, the faded screen that broke some of the keener drafts, the enamel beer-jug on the table, the well-worn sofa and armchairs, and the men drifting in (those from distant colleges would be later), leaving overcoats and hats in any corner and coming over to warm their hands before finding a chair. There was no fixed etiquette, but the rudimentary honours would be done partly by Lewis and partly by his brother, W.H. Lewis, a man who stays in my mind as the most courteous I have ever met—not with mere politeness, but with a genial, self-forgetful considerateness that was as instinctive to him as breathing. Sometimes [...] the evening would fall flat; but the best of them were as good as anything I shall live to see.[1010]

Williams fitted effortlessly into the group. His friendliness, his razor-sharp intelligence, his quirkily original views, his profound religious faith, and his huge range of literary knowledge were just what was wanted. 'Before he came', Lewis remembered:

> I had passed for our best conduit of quotations: but he easily outstripped me. He delighted to repeat favourite passages, and nearly always both his voice and the context got something new out of them. He excelled at showing you the little grain of truth or felicity in some passage generally quoted for ridicule, while at the same time he fully enjoyed the absurdity: or, contrariwise, at detecting the little falsity or dash of silliness in a passage which you, and he also, admired.[1011]

Delighting in Williams's company, Lewis assumed that others would too. And the evidence is that they did. With the much-loved Warnie absent, and the anxieties of war about them, the group found in Williams's idiosyncratic vitality just the required stimulus, his clanging London–Hertfordshire vowels a strange but apt complement to the ringing dogmatic tones of Lewis and the rapid-fire intensity of Tolkien, who sometimes spoke so fast and so quietly that no one could understand what he was saying.

When Williams joined the group, Lewis was reading aloud weekly from *The Problem of Pain*,[1012] and Tolkien from what the group called 'the new Hobbit'—the manuscript of *The Lord of the Rings*. He had reached the Council of Elrond, at which Frodo volunteers to become the ring-bearer. In November, Williams read *The House by the Stable* to the group. Lewis—far from uncritical of Williams's writing—called it 'unusually intelligible for him'.[1013] But not all Inklings' debate was literary. On 28 September, Lewis told 'Warnie' that during 'a pleasant evening [...] with Williams, Tolkien, and Wrenn' they discussed 'the most distressing text in the Bible ("narrow is the way and few they be that find it")'. In the course of the debate:

> Wrenn *almost* seriously expressed a strong wish to burn Williams, or at least maintained that conversation with Williams enabled him to understand how inquisitors had felt it right to burn people. Tolkien and I agreed afterwards that we knew *just* what he meant: that as some people at school [...] are eminently kickable, so Williams is eminently combustible.[1014]

Far from causing trouble, this kind of thing added zest to the meetings.

Many years later, Tolkien would express deep reservations about Williams, and stress that they 'had nothing to say to each other at deeper (or higher) levels'.[1015] But that was in the 1960s, when Tolkien had become distant from

Lewis and may also have learned, from Alice Mary's account of Williams's life, things that disturbed him. His letters written during Williams's life consistently suggest that, however different their minds, they were close friends. He showed no jealousy over Lewis's new friendship. If there was jealousy, it was on the part of Michal: Williams had to reassure her that although Lewis and his circle were 'good for my mind, [...] I have always said that all enjoyments depend on your centredness'.[1016] As the source of his inspiration she would, he told her naïvely, 'be attended—you—by the masculine minds: great minds, strong males, brothers of our energy—those who know our work—Lewis & Eliot & Raymond & Tolkien'.[1017] Lewis, he said, was the only person in Oxford who really understood the symbolism of his *Taliessin* poems.[1018] And after hearing Lewis lecture on Tasso and Milton, he told Michal how 'very good' it had been: 'it is years since I have heard anyone talk intelligently on poetry. Even T.S.E. is unsound on Milton.'[1019]

But the Inklings were not his only Oxford friends. The young playwright Christopher Fry had just become artistic director at the Oxford Playhouse. Fry had met Williams and Hopkins when the Press published his play *Boy with a Cart*; he also knew the Oxford bookseller Basil Blackwell. Williams, Hopkins, Fry, and Blackwell met weekly for lunch in the Eastgate Hotel, discussing poetry, theatre, and the book trade. Until late 1940, when Fry, a conscientious objector, was conscripted into the Non-Combatant Corps, the meetings were as much of a fixture in Williams's week as the Inklings.

There were also Isabel and Margaret Douglas. Although they became important in Williams's life, little is known about them. Isabel is said to have been a pianist. Her unmarried daughter Margaret was a skilled typist. They met Williams, perhaps through his lectures, in 1937.[1020] They were his devoted followers; they had left London and its likely air raids for Stratford, and, Williams reported, 'want to come and set up a communal establishment with me here. But I really don't think it can happen. I simply cannot at the moment anyhow take on that beautiful burden. I fear this is selfishness but if so it must just go on being selfishness.'[1021] Deflected from South Parks Road, the Douglases opted, like many wealthy people, to sit out the war comfortably in a hotel. After various trials, they settled on the Randolph Hotel, then (as now) Oxford's grandest. They had their own corner table in the dining room, and invited Williams to use it, whether they were there or not, at their expense. He often dined with them, and the table in the Randolph became his chosen place for meeting friends and disciples over lunch, on days when the Douglases were elsewhere. Margaret became his typist, almost his private secretary, knowing his personal life more intimately than anyone else. Through his agency she also came to type material for Tolkien.

★   ★   ★

In late October 1939, *The Descent of the Dove: A Short History of the Holy Spirit in the Church* was published by Longman's and the Religious Book Club. It is Charles Williams's most difficult and demanding book, offering a history of Christianity in terms of its impulses and movements of faith and thought. It was also something of a personal manifesto, emphasizing two fundamental ideas. The first is co-inherence: the perception that we are not isolated units but 'members of one another' and of God. The second is the need for the 'Way of Affirmation' as well as the 'Way of Negation'. Williams discerns co-inherence not only in the general truths that God is present in humanity, and humanity—through Christ—in God, but also in many individual sayings and teachings. He finds a perfect example in the saying of the second-century martyr Felicitas, who explained her courage at the prospect of death in the arena by saying 'then another will be in me who will suffer for me, as I shall suffer for him'.[1022]

As for the Affirmative and Negative Ways, both of which Williams believes to be necessary, he finds the Affirmative Way represented by the fourth-century Athanasian Creed, which stresses the incarnation, affirming that Christ is 'perfect God and perfect Man, [...] not by conversion of the Godhead into flesh but by taking of the manhood into God'. Williams expands this to indicate that all of our sensory experiences can have a spiritual value: 'All images are, in their degree, to be carried on; mind is never to put off matter; all experience is to be gathered in.'[1023] But equally important is the Negative Way. He represents this through the writings of the fifth- or sixth-century mystic Dionysius, for whom the way to God is to put aside all ideas and images whatsoever, because the Divine 'is not knowledge or truth; nor is It kingship or wisdom; nor is It one, nor is It unity [...] nor is It any other thing such as we or any other being can have knowledge of'.[1024] Williams argues that both Ways are necessary, for different people and at different times. Either is incomplete without the other. In this sense Christianity is essentially paradoxical. Each view requires its opposite.

Other aspects of *The Descent of the Dove* are deeply personal. Williams devotes four pages to a discussion of *subintroductae*, women who in the early Christian period vowed virginity but lived in 'spiritual marriage' with male ascetics, sharing their houses and sometimes even their beds, whilst maintaining strict celibacy.[1025] This is a topic many theologians and church historians have preferred to pass over in silence; not so Williams, who clearly saw in it a parallel to his own experiences of 'transmutation of energy' with Phyllis Jones and other women. Conceding that in the fourth century 'The great experiment had to be abandoned because of "scandal"', he remarks that 'it is a pity that the Church [...] should be so nervously alive to scandals.' The loss of the practice was, he wrote:

> the loss, so early, of a tradition whose departure left the Church rather over-aware of sex, when it might have been creating a polarity with which sex is only partly coincident. The use of sex, in this experiment, might have been to pass below itself and release the dark gods of D.H. Lawrence directly into the kingdom of Messias.[1026]

The Descent of the Dove began with a dedication 'To the Companions of the Co-inherence' and ended with a Postscript which proposed the need for 'an Order within the Christian Church' whose purpose, 'in our present distresses, of international and social schism', would be to affirm the 'pattern' of co-inherence and the 'substitutions in love' which co-inherence makes possible. Williams perhaps hoped that readers would ask to join. Whether they did is unknown.

Eliot reviewed the book warmly in the *New Statesman*,[1027] commending Williams's thrillers and later poetry before remarking that 'a heresy from Mr. Williams would be, in its result, [...] a real contribution to the explication of orthodoxy'. He praised the *Dove* as 'not only a valuable book, but a very readable one' for those inside or outside the Church. When it came out on 20 October, Williams at once sent copies to his friends. Enclosing the constitution of the Companions with Olive Willis's copy, he told her the book was 'all about the History of Christendom, but [...] particularly about the Order of the Co-inherence, which I have just established'.[1028] And he told Alice Mary that she and Joan Wallis were 'pillars of the serious Order'.[1029] On the same day, as if to emphasize the importance of co-inherence, *Time and Tide* published an article by Williams arguing that the Church should preach union with, and 'dependence on' the Germans, even as the state should demand separation from, and killing of, Germans. 'The soldiers are fulfilling one duty', he concluded; 'let the priesthood announce the other. This is Christendom at war.'

By now Williams was far advanced with his Christmas double-bill for the Oxford Pilgrim Players, *The House by the Stable* and *The Death of Good Fortune*. Both are short one-act pieces in the manner of medieval 'morality' plays. In *The House by the Stable*, Hell, presented as a crafty trickster, persuades Man to gamble for his soul (a 'jewel' that Man has never really valued), and loads the dice. Man is saved because, though grudgingly, he has allowed a distressed couple, Mary and Joseph, to spend the night in his stable, where their baby has been born. The play is vivid and straightforward.

The Death of Good Fortune, however, is among the most puzzling of all Williams's works. On a fine day, a King brings a god, Good Fortune, to visit the town. Almost everyone is feeling lucky and expecting good things: the youth hopes for a happy day at the fair, the lover for his lady's favour, the old woman for a home of her own, and the King for victory against invaders of his kingdom. The only ones who refuse to worship Good Fortune are a girl who feels 'Despair', and Mary, the mother of Jesus. Mary announces that Good Fortune is half-blinded, and that 'it is time that he should die'. Good Fortune does indeed die. Thereupon the fairground falls silent, the lover returns disappointed, the old woman finds her expected home gone, and the King's magician sees clairvoyantly that the invaders are coming, victorious.

The characters react in different ways. The King advocates a passive stoicism: 'Resign yourselves; be strong.' But the lover resolves on irrational defiance:

> 'I will not be content; it is all untrue,
> this content, this resignation: love must live,
> and if a woman curls up in another's heart
> and spoils love's accidents, love's substance must gather head,
> I do not see how, but somehow: love must live.'

Mary explains that 'When your god Good Fortune dies, the only thing / is to bid your god Good Fortune rise again.' She brings him back to life, and as he recovers he sees his heart being twisted (or *untwisted*, as Mary corrects) in the hands of Jesus. Alive once more, Good Fortune announces that 'All luck is good.' Yet nothing is changed in the material world. The characters are simply presented with a choice: they can regard what befalls them as good, or they can choose to see it as bad. It is up to them. The

Lover, the Girl, and the Magician accept this, and declare despite their suffering that 'All luck is good.' The King and the Old Woman refuse, and depart resentfully. Mary concludes the play by confronting the audience with the same choice:

> And you, great ones, you must always make your choice,
> or always, at least, know that the choice exists—
> all luck is good—or not; even when the ninth
> step is nine times as difficult as that.

It is hard to see how this strange play could have been successful on stage, but it was performed many times during the war, and must somehow have worked. Perhaps its paradoxical message was given meaning by the feelings of a wartime audience who had to endure fear, bereavement, and countless daily difficulties—and choose to make the best of them. For Williams, seeing all luck as good was a strategy for surviving his unhappy love-life, his exile in Oxford, and other privations. But the idea had one very clear source: Boethius's medieval *Consolation of Philosophy* (IV: 7), where Lady Philosophy tells the narrator, 'That all fortune is absolutely good'—a passage Williams had discussed at length in *The Descent of the Dove*.[1030]

On 14 November something very important happened, when for the first time Lewis heard Williams lecture. He told Warnie:

> on Tuesday evening I went to [...] St Hugh's to hear Williams read a paper—or rather not 'read' but 'spout'—i.e. deliver without a single note a perfectly coherent and impassioned meditation, variegated with quotations in his incantatory manner. A most wonderful performance and impressed his audience, specially the young women, very much. And it really *is* remarkable how that ugly, almost simian, face, becomes transfigured.[1031]

Lewis had already thought of trying to involve Williams in university lecturing. Now he became determined 'to smuggle him onto the Oxford lecture list, so that we might have some advantage from the great man's accidental presence in Oxford'.[1032] Normally, Williams's lack of a degree would have ruled him out, but the wartime shortage of lecturers provided both need and opportunity. With Tolkien's help Lewis set to work, and Williams was engaged to lecture for the Oxford English Faculty from January 1940.

★   ★   ★

In October 1939, the editor of *Theology* had asked Williams to submit a poem for the journal's Christmas number. 'I have half a mind to try', he told Anne Ridler: it would be:

all about the Empire & the Pope. But it may not come off. I add however—no, I will complain first. There is no-one (NO-ONE) in Oxford to whom I can talk about Taliessin. This is a serious blow [...] I have been spoilt, I know, but I was a little taken aback when I wanted to say 'and do you think the Pope, who is young, with white hair, brilliant, the image of Merlin (only M. has black hair), might be Merlin + loss?' If you get me. The Pope (let us say) is time losing its beauties (by deprivation or will, not by mere passing change) but affirmatively. O I write it badly; why are you not here to dispute, confirm & correct?[1033]

He missed Anne's constant critique as he wrote. Still, he told Michal later, 'poetry is still more me than I am; and the coming of great lines is less one's work than—something. If I could do as I chose and yet had to be down here, I would do nothing but think of the next *Taliessin* group.'[1034] By the end of the month he was able to send a draft to Anne Ridler and Belgion; possibly also to Eliot. The poem was called 'Divites Dimisit'—words from the Magnificat and Luke's Gospel (1:53): 'the rich he hath sent [empty] away'. The poem satisfied no one. Belgion, Williams told Anne, 'says [...] that the end is not clear, & that he doesn't know if Eliot would approve of the jumping about'.[1035] Anne had doubts, which Williams shared. 'I will admit to you', he confessed:

but not to M.B., that it is composite [*illegible*] of work, as it were—with bits put in, and, as I said, very *ad hoc*, and it cannot, as it is, form part of the series. It might perhaps be a little improvised [*sic*], & used as a Prelude; if not, it will have to be dropped. But it will serve for *Theology*, and it saved me doing a quite different poem.[1036]

Five years later, much revised, it would appear as the concluding poem of his final poetic volume, *The Region of the Summer Stars*. But in this early version, it was, amongst other things, yet another announcement of the Companions of the Co-inherence:

[...] Only Taliessin, in the west with the King, smiled
to think how the household had founded a new Order,
known by no name, least their own,
grounded in the law of the Empire, the acts of the Throne,
                    [...] their salutation
was everywhere the promulgation of the Co-inherence.

Theology's request had inspired him to start work seriously on a new collection of *Taliessin* poems. The rose garden beneath his window at Southfield House had entered his imagination, even prompting him to research roses, looking for symbolic resonance. He told Anne:

> I want to do a longer poem—the one about Lancelot & Helayne & [...] the
> *Encyclopedia Britannica* helpfully assures me that there is a kind of rose which is
> 'derived from a district of the Caucasus'. Most charming! It is, it seems, the
> cabbage-rose. And what marks the cabbage-rose? it is a dark red colour, and
> unlike most roses it has a heart under its petals! Does not that seem to you
> attractive? And do you not think that Blanchefleur might walk in the rose-
> gardens of the king when she talks with the lord Taliessin before she goes
> into the convent at Almesbury—thus doing in the Lord Taliessin completely?
> and then we could sweep on to the tournament at Lonezep, or Caerleon? For
> I have been vaguely looking for roses for some time, and I feel the rose is
> suitable to blood and things; and that is a kind of unifying richness which
> would relate to Caucasia and Blanchefleur. I play with pointing out that cab-
> bages have hearts, and that men feed on them. On the other hand Taliessin and
> Palomides and Lancelot all endure the loss: though I suppose it made least
> difference to the king's poet. I wish I were the king's poet; I am gnawed a little
> at heart still by the complete frustration of it all, but that may partly be from
> trying to think of the poem.
>
> With Merlin going white-haired and Caucasia going rose-lordly, I feel a
> change going over the spirit of my dream. I remember saying to you months
> ago that one would have to re-imagine everything; this, I suppose, is the
> movement.[1037]

It would be another year before the poem, 'Taliessin in the Rose-Garden', was finished.

At the end of 1939 the OUP published *Judgement at Chelmsford* as a pamph-let, giving the author's name as Peter Stanhope. Williams sent copies to the Companions, telling Margaret Douglas:

> I am sending the *Judgement* to the Order this Christmas, not as any personal
> communication but as a mere kind of sign. [...] The making of the Order
> proceeds slowly, individually, troublesomely, exquisitely: it is not a mere estab-
> lishment but a growth. A hundred years are only a beginning.[1038]

He felt he needed to nurture the group, and that it was immensely import-ant. Only half in jest, he wrote to Michal, 'I shall convert the Church of England yet—secretly, & rather like a Dove.'[1039]

★ ★ ★

He spent Christmas in London with Michal and Michael, returning to Oxford on 27 December to prepare his Milton lectures. The task was not altogether welcome. 'It will make me read *Paradise Lost* again', he told Raymond Hunt:

> and you know how passionately I agree with the sinking of your own heart on the great occasion when you found you had nothing but Milton to read on a railway journey. This is no doubt another proof of the Fall, but that cannot agitate us now.[1040]

However, with *Magic* lagging behind schedule despite pressure from Faber, he abandoned the idea, admitting, 'I shall merely repeat all that we have said at the C.L.I. for the last few years. But then, oddly enough, Oxford, so far as I can find, is completely ignorant of such things.'[1041]

First he had to go to Pleshey, where he was to speak at the Chelmsford Diocese Retreat House. Here, retreats were regularly directed by Evelyn Underhill, a lay contemplative whose book *Mysticism* (1911) was and remains a classic study of the subject. Phyllis Potter was a friend of Underhill's, and had urged her to invite Williams. He was asked to speak at a conference there between 20 and 24 January 1940.[1042] What he said is unknown, though in some way he seems to have used material from the unperformed *Judgement at Chelmsford*, which would have had local resonance, and he must have emphasized Romantic Theology, for he told Phyllis Potter:

> I came back here almost overwhelmed by the fact that apparently two clergy-men were going back to their respective parishes with every intention of telling people things in an entirely new way. The women of Wanstead and the lovers of Romford may be indebted to you and Pleshey more than they will ever know.[1043]

More vividly, he told Anne Ridler that a vicar from Romford and a curate from Wanstead had:

> swallowed everything.. in a kind of illumination; adoration, moments of glory, contradictions, exchange, substitution, co-inherence, the City, to say nothing of little details like women & the Crucifixion, & so on; and they have— apparently—gone back to their parishes to hint all these things to any odd parishioner. This, I think, is quite right, and the way it should work.[1044]

And then, on Monday, 29 January, came his first lecture for the Oxford English Faculty. It was scheduled for 11 a.m.; he walked into town through the falling snow with Gerry Hopkins, calling at Magdalen to meet Lewis and Tolkien. The group went together up the High Street, turning into Catte Street and making for the Divinity School, where the lecture would take place. Having heard that by the second term 'everyone is sick of lectures', Williams speculated that, 'Of course there may be no-one there! But I suppose in the grand Oxford Tradition, one lectures anyhow!'[1045]

He need not have worried. Entering the sublimely beautiful fifteenth-century hall with its fan-vaulted roof of golden stone—the University's oldest lecture room—he found 'a reasonably large audience of undergraduates', mostly female. His friends escorted him to the front: an odd figure, tall, angular, and skinny in his slate-blue business suit, between the black gowns of Lewis and Tolkien. They took their seats in the front row, and as Williams stepped onto the platform he must have felt his spirits rise, lifted by the soaring magnificence of the room and the expectation on the faces of his young audience. The enthusiasm that had carried him through so many hours of lecturing in London surged up and he launched into an intense discussion—not, immediately, of Milton, but of poetry as such. 'There are a few passages on poetry in general to which I should like to turn', he told them, 'passages in poetry itself.' He reminded them of Hippolyta's speech in *A Midsummer Night's Dream* ('something of great constancy, / But howsoever strange and admirable') and Wordsworth's pronouncements on poetry in *The Prelude*: among them, his dream of the shell, which was:

> a god, yea, many gods
> Had voices more than all the winds with power
> To exhilarate the spirit, and to soothe
> Through every clime, the heart of human kind.

It is that 'constancy' and that 'power' that we experience, he told his audience, when we encounter great poetry. What else he said, we don't know: the surviving notes give only his starting point for the lecture.[1046] He went on to discuss 'Lycidas', but his main purpose was to change his audience's whole attitude to poetry, as a foundation for reading Milton's major poems.

The lecture was certainly 'something strange and admirable': admirable not least in the old sense of 'arousing wonder'. Accustomed to lectures delivered in the lofty drawl of the educated 'Oxford accent', the students were startled at first by Williams's plebeian voice. A few simply rejected it and waited impatiently for the lecture to end. Most quickly adjusted, and were swept up by the intensity of Williams's delivery. For rather than detached interpretation, or a calm recital of facts and dates, here was a lecturer who regarded poetry as a matter of personal urgency, who was insisting that they must learn *from*, and not merely *about*, the great poets: that they themselves could benefit from, and be disturbed by, the strangeness and the power of poetry. This was something novel and even intoxicating. As the audience left the hall at the end of the hour, bubbling with suppressed amusement, puzzlement, and enthusiasm, and eager for debate, many felt keen to come back for more. Lewis, who must have watched his protégé's performance with some anxiety, was relieved. 'I think he will retain most of his audience', he told Warnie.[1047] Afterwards he, Williams, Tolkien, and Hopkins went to the Mitre to celebrate with sherry.

A week later it was clear that Williams had more than 'retained' his audience. Rumours had got about: the Divinity School was crowded and there was an air of expectancy. This time the lecture was on *Comus*: Milton's masque about temptation, which Williams saw as 'a kind of philosophical ballet', in which a young woman—'and this sense of youth is one of the great things about *Comus*'—is confronted by Comus, 'a black enchanter of the worst kind', who nonetheless 'keeps on talking heavenly poetry'. And, Williams asked his audience, 'what is this ballet about? It might be called "an outrage attempted on a mystery"—if those words have not become completely meaningless to you.' And that 'mystery' is chastity:

> Of course the main theme of *Comus* is chastity, and chastity taken seriously, both morally and poetically. There is a great tradition of this in verse as everywhere else. It is pre-Christian—it is Christian. To understand *Comus* you must give yourself up to that imagination: the imagination of Pallas, & the Vestals, & our Lady St Mary, and Dante's heaven, and Galahad, and Isabella, and the Lady here [in *Comus*]. It is, of course, possible that this terrific tradition is wrong; that chastity means inhibitions and frustrations & so on. All one can say is that the Greeks & Romans, that Shakespeare, Dante, Spenser, & Milton did not think so. They imagined chastity as a positive & transmuting thing. It is, in fact, power: power to what? Milton told us:
>
> > So dear to heaven is saintly chastity
> > That, when a soul is found sincerely so,
> > A thousand liveried angels lackey her,
> > Driving far off each thing of sin and guilt,
> > And in clear dream and solemn vision
> > Tell her of things that no gross ear can hear;
> > Till oft converse with heavenly habitants
> > Begin to cast a beam on the outward shape,

> The unpolluted temple of the mind,
> And turns it by degrees to the soul's essence,
> Till all be made immortal.

'It is', Williams told his audience, 'this transmutation of which Comus [the enchanter] is completely unaware.'[1048]

For Williams, Milton's masque was less about physical virginity than about transmutation, about the changing of sexual energy into spiritual power. It justified what he had undergone with Phyllis, and what he still believed to be a path to poetic inspiration. His discussion of *Comus* was fired with a fervour derived from the long efforts and sufferings of his personal history. Lewis, who probably understood nothing of this, was overwhelmed. 'Simply as criticism it was superb', he told Warnie:

> —because here was a man who really started from the same point of view as Milton and really cared with every fibre of his being about 'the sage and serious doctrine of virginity' which it would never occur to the ordinary modern reader to take seriously. But it was more important still as a sermon. It was a beautiful sight to see a whole room full of modern young men and women sitting in that absolute silence which can *not* be faked, very puzzled, but spellbound [...] he forced them to lap it up and I think many, by the end, liked the taste more than they expected to. It was 'borne in upon me' that that beautiful carved room had probably not witnessed anything so important since some of the great medieval or Renaissance lectures. I have at last, if only for once, seen a university doing what it was founded to do: teaching Wisdom.[1049]

And Williams wrote to Phyllis Potter, 'You will like to know that my lecture on *Comus* turned into a discourse on Chastity, which (our Mr. Lewis said) "was the most important thing that has happened in the Divinity Schools for a hundred years, or is likely to happen for the next hundred." To tell you is sheer conceit—no, it isn't; it is half-amusement and half-shame!'[1050]

18

'Bitter Is the Brew
of Exchange'

Williams was becoming a force at Oxford. But inwardly, though still only fifty-three, he was conscious of flagging energies. 'I am (as they say) "living on my nerves"',[1051] he told Michal. He had, he said, 'a hovering sense that my work is all but done'.[1052] He struggled with an 'increasing physical difficulty of writing':[1053] his thumb would not 'do its job properly'.[1054] Perhaps it was incipient arthritis. His handwriting now became tiny. There were recurrent sore throats, as well as slight but worrying stomach problems.[1055] He also found the blackout a severe trial. While Gerry surged ahead with impunity in the pitch-dark streets, Williams was prone to accidents. Early in 1941 he had a collision with a lamppost in the Cowley Road, cutting his eyebrow, bruising his chest, and breaking a tooth, which required costly dental treatment.[1056] Later that year he told Michal that 'the very hairs of my head are weary'.

By then the war, initially in Britain a perplexing state of anxiety rather than action, had become a pressing reality; 1940 was a terrible year. In spring Germany invaded Denmark, Norway, Holland, Belgium, and Luxembourg. When the assault on France began in May, Chamberlain's indecisive government was replaced by a coalition under Churchill, who authorized the bombing of Berlin. Soon afterwards came the precipitous evacuation of the British Expeditionary Force from Dunkirk. People in Britain began to realize that they might not merely lose the war but face a German invasion. In mid-August began the Battle of Britain, a month of desperate fighting between British and German aircraft over south-east England. This was followed in September by the first major bombing raids on London: 'the Blitz'.

Oxford's sirens gave occasional warnings and a few bombs fell near the outskirts, but the city remained unscathed, although car factories at Cowley were being used for aircraft production. It was rumoured that Hitler spared Oxford, planning to use it as his headquarters after conquering Britain. For whatever reason, the city was a relatively tranquil oasis. In May, the War Office called for volunteers to join the Local Defence (anti-parachute) Volunteer Corps, whose task in case of invasion would be to shoot enemy paratroops as they descended into the fields. Williams considered volunteering, but realized that 'my eyes wouldn't let me discern the parachutes!'[1057] Instead he learned to deal with incendiary bombs and spent night-time hours firewatching at Southfield House.

His main work in 1940 was the book that would become *Witchcraft*. Having written the history of Christianity, he was now, with constant urging from T.S. Eliot, writing the history of magic, giving each chapter to Margaret Douglas to type as he finished it. The book should have been complete by the end of 1939 but was predictably late. In October, dealing with Lucius Apuleius and Simon Magus, he had told Anne Ridler that it was 'all going to be about Power & Images':[1058] magic was a perversion of the Way of Affirmation, whereby images were indulged in and obsessed over. In December he studied *Malleus Maleficarum*, the notorious fifteenth-century handbook for witch trials. 'It is an oddly attractive document', he told Hunt:

> once one has allowed the hypothesis. I think it gets the stresses all wrong, but any talk about it being the work of sexual perverts is entire nonsense. They were hard-thinking men, but a little out of proportion. Much like the Baconians, only of course the results were far more unpleasant, and even damnable.[1059]

Mostly the writing was done at weekends, usually alongside other work: in June he told Michal that over the weekend he had 'done a review and about 4,000 words of Magic, [so] as you will see I have stuck at it'.[1060] He was desperate to finish the book because he owed money, including a large tax bill. He told Anne Ridler in May:

> I have been toying with the idea of writing to Faber's that if they could pay half of the remaining whatever, it would be gratifying—or at least £20, which is what I want at the end of the month. [...] My only point is that they might pay perhaps exactly what I want to settle the rest of the Inland Revenue, & the rest when the rest [of the book] comes. [...] I think I shall write to T.S.E on

these lines next week. It would (as all your authors and our authors say) make 'all the difference'.[1061]

And he asked Phyllis Potter to undertake 'substitution' for him, carrying his anxiety about the book; in February he told her, 'I am very much indebted to you for your leaping into the breach as far as this unfortunate book on Witchcraft is concerned. [...] It was good of you to do what you did. Let me relieve you now of the burden.'[1062] He sent a complete typescript to Faber in late April and on the 28th told Michal that Eliot was reading it and would report after Faber's book committee had met.[1063] The outcome was a payment from Faber but also a request for extensive rewriting.[1064] Six months later he was still labouring over the final chapter, telling Hunt, 'It is a dull book anyhow, and I have no interest in it whatever; it is just worth doing, and that is all one can say.'[1065] The revised typescript went to Faber at the end of October.[1066]

★　★　★

Substitution—undertaking it, requesting it, arranging it—played an increasingly important part in his life. In February 1940 he wrote to Olive Speake, telling her, 'I was asked the other day whether the Companions of the Co-inherence could do anything for a woman in Italy whom I don't know.' The woman, he explained, was at times threatening suicide:

> The more I thought, the more it seemed to me that if the Order was to do anything, then you were the person to do it. It matters nothing that neither you nor I know her; in these things relationship is of no importance, and friends are not always (though they are sometimes) the best people to act.
> I want you to present all your particular distress to Almighty God as a substitution for, and a lightening of, the distress of this unknown woman's [*sic*]. I want you to bear yours as if you were bearing hers—not 'as if'; I want you to believe that, in the Co-inherence of substitutions, it is yours which carries hers and relieves hers. Always under God.
> So, if you really want to help me, you can do that. If you want to be part of the movement of—call it the Order, then you can obey the Headship in me... I am not It, but there is no one else at the moment to direct the charges laid upon all of us within that scope. I am quite clear it will not always be easy; I am quite aware that you may resent it at times. [...] I am asking you because [...] you are the only person I can think of who can make the offering if you will; because, so, your experience is a part of the mystical life of our Lord—of Love, of *Caritas*.[1067]

He added, 'I am not really "asking" you at all. I am telling you. You can, of course, refuse. But if you do you will disobey a perfectly clear command. I do not think you will.'

He also speculated about unconscious substitution: could one person's suffering relieve someone else's, by 'exchange'? He and Michal had worried about Michael's sight; in March 1940, reflecting on his wife's chronic back pain, Williams wrote, 'I have, once or twice, wondered if your back might not have saved his eyes.'[1068] Later in the year he himself practised substitution for some 'worry' of Phyllis McDougall's. She was living away from Oxford but often visiting the Press, working on the *Dictionary of Quotations* (to be published in 1941) and *Poetry and Prose of Robert Browning*, for the World's Classics, ostensibly edited by Milford but actually assembled by Phyllis. Williams in turn helped Phyllis with the work. 'Last week she came down for the day, & we discussed R.B. and her introduction for an hour', he told Alice Mary; adding sardonically, when the *Poetry and Prose* was complete, that he and Milford had 'adequately concluded Browning, and thus, as it were, helped to produce twins by different fathers. No sex disturbances this time—I have not even attempted rape on the stairs. All *most* as was wanted. It is true I am, you will discern, in a foul temper.'[1069] The attachment to Phyllis remained strong and painful. When the devoted Raymond Hunt proposed writing his biography, Williams sent a brief outline of his life, centring on a paradox: his love for Phyllis was of immeasurable value, yet it must never be mentioned. 'If I were asked to choose now, I should, I fear, still say: "Never, never *that*. Let all the work go; let us lose *Taliessin* & the *Dove* and the *E.P.M.* & all—only never *that*." ' But 'for God Almighty's sake never mention it to anyone unless I say they are safe. And especially never to my wife.' And he stipulated, 'no word like Celia or Celian or Phillida or Phillidan should appear in your MS. and any reference to the Masques should be small. I don't like saying so for myself; I would write it over the earth & sky. But there are others.'[1070]

Then there was Sir Humphrey's son Robin. A 37-year-old musician and composer, Robin Milford suffered from depression. After joining the army in 1939 he suffered a breakdown and was invalided out. Soon afterwards his five-year-old son was killed in a road accident. Milford broke down again and attempted suicide. Sir Humphrey asked Williams to help. Williams told Phyllis Potter:

Robin turned a great tendency to gloom on to Christianity, and began to brood over Sin and Hell and so on. [...] Every now and then he has had conversations with me, but they were only conversations. If he had been one of my class people in London, I might have been more use. But occasional talks, with his father, and my employer, sort of in the neighbourhood—all very unsatisfactory. [. . .]

Rather unwisely, I talked to him about the general ideas of exchange and substitution, & so on. And now he wants to know if something can be done for him. [. . .] He has two main worries (i) the burden of his sins (ii) the impulses towards suicide. I don't wish you to be darkened by the complete burden of either—because I am not clear that he is in a position to trust it, and unless he is, we shall merely have you burdened and him still rushing round for more miracles. But I think it would be a very good idea if you could present to our Lord the possibility of them being carried by you or me or Him, if and as necessary. I would not (with the suicide possibility) ask this of anyone who had not what we call faith fairly established. [. . .] On the other hand, as things are, I am loath not to do something with a sense of responsibility.[1071]

Phyllis Potter undertook the task; in an undated letter to her Williams writes, 'I do think the operation on Robin is profoundly useful and profit-able.'[1072] Nothing more is known. Milford continued to teach and compose until his death in 1959.

★ ★ ★

In March a note came from Auden, who was rediscovering his Christian faith. He wanted to tell Williams how much he had been 'moved' by *The Descent of the Dove*.[1073] In July he wrote again, in the tones of an ardent fan:

> As soon as I get back to New York, I will get hold of Taliessin, which will require courage as I don't know how to pronounce it. [. . .] I am trying to learn a little about the Practice of the Presence, but O dear, the spirit and the flesh are as unwilling as they are weak. I wish you were here to help. My day-dream is that you will be sent over to the New York branch.[1074]

Williams was flattered, but the next piece of news aroused mixed feelings. 'It will amuse you', he told Phyllis Potter, 'to know that W.H. Auden has been so moved by the *Dove* that he is writing a long poem which, he says, owes a great deal to it, and that he is calling his book *The Double Man*. I foresee that everyone will attribute the ideas to Mr. Auden. Adored in all ways be the Omnipotence!'[1075] But in due course he reviewed Auden's poem enthusiastically, calling it 'a pattern of the Way', quoting approvingly 'O every day in sleep or labour / Our life and death are with our neigh-bour', and admitting that he was mentioned in the notes.[1076]

He continued to work with his usual intensity. In March he wrote a 'sermon' or prologue for the Pilgrim Players' performance of Gheon's *Way of the Cross*. When Dru's war work prevented him from writing an introduction to Kierkegaard's *The Present Age*, Williams stepped in and wrote it himself. In April he wrote *Terror of Light*, a play about Pentecost, again for Ruth Spalding's company. He read it to the Inklings on 2 May; Lewis thought it 'a mixture of very good stuff and some deplorable errors in taste'.[1077] Williams agreed that 'the scenes about Mary Magdalene and John need a little toning up or down or something', and that the play was 'too like a drawing room comedy'.[1078]

It was performed the same month, at St Mary's Church in Oxford. Michal came for the weekend and saw two performances, but predictably there were difficulties. Charles's devotees Isabel and Margaret Douglas came to the opening; Isabel asked Michal what she thought of the play, and Michal replied, 'I think it is dreadful.' Williams worked on the play over the weekend to improve it, whilst the Douglases gave Michal tea at the Randolph, where they criticized her roundly for 'hurting' Charles by her negative comments. When she saw the play again on Monday she thought it 'really good', but she went home in a huff. 'I am sorry I upset the Douglases', she told Phyllis Potter, 'but I fled from Oxford at the earliest opportunity. I knew it would be a mistake to go. But they have entire possession of Charles again & that should make them happy.'[1079] Williams did his best to placate her, telling her 'I feel more friendly to Oxford now that you have been there: it [was] the first time we have been at all alone in it.'[1080] But she remained distrustful of any female Oxford friends.

The pressure to produce lectures, articles, and reviews mounted steadily. Asked to speak to a Greek Orthodox group and write for the (Catholic) *Tablet*, the *Dublin Review*, and the (Anglican) *Theology*, he was feeling, he said, like 'a little Reunion of Christendom'.[1081] He told Phyllis Potter, 'There are moments when I feel that I am losing my proper job of verse under the pressure of a large number of intrusive Christians. But I have no doubt that it is all right *really*.'[1082] Yet he never liked to turn down paid work. When 'a thing called the *St Martin's Review*', edited by 'a nincompoop', offered him three guineas to write an article on 'The Church Looks Forward', Williams commented wearily 'I probably shall; though what the Church is looking forward to, I don't know. But I daresay I shall discover three guineas' worth of prophecy.'[1083]

In July he was writing both a new Introduction for the World's Classics *Milton*, and a pamphlet on *The Way of Exchange*, commissioned by R.H. Ward for a series called *New Foundations*.[1084] The pamphlet set out his views on exchange and substitution: that we *necessarily* live—whether we like it or not—from and in one another, and God; and that therefore we can, if willing, agree to take over each other's 'troubles, and worries, and distresses, as simply and effectually as an assent is given to the carrying of a parcel'.[1085] Encouraged by Graham Greene at the Ministry of Information he also drafted (but never completed) a pamphlet about *Courage*, to help the war effort.[1086]

★ ★ ★

The war was now directly affecting the Companions. Williams had long treated Alice Mary Miller as one of his closest confidantes, admitting that 'whenever I think of women's minds being as good as men's, I think of you'.[1087] Especially he confided in her his feelings about the war, which stirred painful memories. 'There is to me', he told her, 'an insane sense of reliving one's earlier life; the chief difference is that I now have no friends to be killed.'[1088] And, in the ceremonious style he often adopted when writing to her, he reflected:

> Your Highness will *not* remember 1914 and 1918. I have seen all Europe on the edge of absorption twice and each time saved by—by a miracle? At least by five minutes and five yards. I see no reason why it should happen again, of course. But I do not think I feel worse. [...] I hope for nothing but more retreats and then, in God, the last turn at the last moment. It may not be, but it may.[1089]

He also trusted her with his most intimate thoughts about the Order. On 10 May he wrote casually, 'It was odd, though pleasant, to see you on Saturday. But it was good of you to come—both to an Initiation and to tea',[1090] which suggests that there may have been some rite of acceptance into the Companions. And he alluded, cryptically, to techniques of 'transmutation':

> I have wondered if the technique of loving God in our—genitals, was sound? It grows on me that we ought to try & love; & his immanence (as things are) is hostile to his transcendence—but that is our state; he cannot be. So we must see it together, and as much there as anywhere. The conflict is perhaps the crucifixion of his Humanity.[1091]

He also allowed himself wild speculations. Speaking of Hitler, he wrote:

> If I permitted myself to be melodramatic I should think of Antichrist. I do not;
> history forbids. Once or twice I have all but toyed with the notion that we
> have set a thing going which provokes, as it were, a destructiveness, a wild
> contradiction: that, of course, is silly, but let us indulge ourselves—let us for a
> moment pretend that Hitler is organized chaos frenzied by the movement of
> things into light. No; don't let's: too many errors have begun so.[1092]

Williams firmly believed that the founding of the Companions, re-establishing
the forgotten doctrine of co-inherence, might inaugurate a new era in
Christianity; could Hitler's evil be a dark reaction against this new force?
The notion was hinted at, but instantly dropped.

Alice Mary's husband Peter Miller had been sent to France in the spring
of 1940. In May he was killed during the retreat to Dunkirk.[1093] Alice Mary
and Peter had a one-year-old daughter but their marriage had broken down
and she was overwhelmed with guilt as well as grief. 'My dear, I am so
sorry', Williams wrote:

> you always let me feel that there was a...tradition? a past with Peter; for all
> that has gone by, you did, you know, leave me with a feeling that something
> more than comfort linked you.
>
> He did not find a bad fortune—to die at the height of his imagination... 'If
> it were now to die 'Twere now to be most happy—' Do not (you will let me
> say so) blame yourself just now, directly or indirectly. Pray for him. I am—
> truly—unhappy for you. It is shattering. Loss and again loss.[1094]

And again he thought of co-inherence:

> On Peter, on you, and on me, the house is built: we, I was thinking after read-
> ing your letter, are its props [...] He dies for my life, and I live his actual death;
> in a way, perhaps he lived through—if not my death, at least my pain: and both
> of us mysteriously live and die through you.
>
> The past is our food: what you had you have. No damned nostalgia. The
> phrases of Communion at the Eucharist hold it: 'The body...which was
> given for thee, preserve...unto everlasting life. Take and eat this.' Eat it:
> Peter & me.
>
> [...] I do not presume to be sorry for you—but I cried at Hampstead when
> they said my wife was dying of pneumonia.[1095]

Later, he followed these thoughts further, admitting:

> I darkly suspect that a kind of co-inherence lies [...] even beyond what the
> Order has so far considered—even perhaps to our Companions being willing

to take death as for each other. Anyhow if anything happens to you or me we might consider it so?[1096]

Alice Mary was working in London with refugees, but her brother in the Navy, based in the West Indies, suggested that for her daughter's sake she consider going to Bermuda, where he could find her work at Admiralty House. Williams agreed:

> I find myself envisaging the faint possibility of a temporary German invasion. I do not think it really likely, and yet...like the P.M. I just look at it & away again. And anything would be preferable than to have a growing child in *that* atmosphere.
>
> I do not think you would be less involved in the struggle for the City in Bermuda; and I do rather feel that I should like to know that, if the worst happened here, the City was rallying the reserves. [...] If we were all trampled or shot—or apostatised—you would be there to carry on...everything. Your mind would be the Order and your heart the Church. [...] I shall miss you very acutely, and ECRH.[1097]

'ECRH' was [Ellis] Charles [Raymond] Hadfield, with whom Alice Mary was in love and whom she hoped to marry. A departmental manager at the Press, Hadfield now worked for the London Fire Service. The decision was a hard one but she decided to go. Williams wrote her a reference and saw her off on the boat.[1098]

Some months earlier he had told her:

> It was, for all our sakes, a good day when you came to Amen House—a good day and a secret; fair secrets but very hidden when we first met on the stairs. Most admired, you little thought what was coming to you then, nor I what true help and certain loyalty [...] lay there. Since you and I were left alone in Amen House I have trusted you—personally as well for myself as you—and shall; and you never have failed.[1099]

Later he added, 'Am I not to leave my reputation in your care? Do I not depend on you to prevent me being called a thousand things—sentimentalist, philanderer, and the rest?'[1100] In future years she would feel this as a heavy responsibility.

★ ★ ★

In June 1940, Michael Williams would be eighteen. Charles and Michael had never been close; tensions over Phyllis Jones—though probably never fully discussed at home—had alienated them further, whilst drawing son and mother ever closer. A gauche, sensitive boy, tall and gangly, with thick glasses and all his father's oddity but little of his charm and none of his confidence, Michael had no plans for the future, and no academic aspirations. His preoccupations were the movies, and a romantic attachment to the idea of America. With nineteen-year-olds liable to conscription, it was hard to think clearly about his future.

Charles decided to see if he could find Michael a job connected with films or film criticism. He made enquiries at the *Economist* and arranged for Michael to lunch with the *Sunday Times* film critic Dilys Powell.[1101] Then he tackled Basil Blackwell about work in the book trade.[1102] Michael came to Oxford to meet Blackwell, who agreed 'to take Michael on a kind of "apprenticeship"'.[1103] This would give Michael only a nominal salary, but in three years he would gain excellent book-trade skills and, probably, a job at Blackwell's world-famous bookshop. In theory, at least; but there was the threat of conscription[1104]—and the question of whether Michael, temperamental, difficult, subject to unexplained minor ailments, would stick to the work. But on 29 May 1940, in a ceremony which had changed little since the Middle Ages, Michael and Basil Blackwell signed the indentures; Charles, and Blackwell's business partner, were witnesses. 'I will not say *nothing* could have been better', Williams told Michal, 'but I cannot think of anything. [. . .] "It is the Lord's doing and it is marvellous in our eyes." '[1105] Michael would have a qualification; and if he did not stay with Blackwell in the long term, there might be a job for him with the Press—perhaps even at its New York branch.

So Michael joined the household at South Parks Road. Charles, unused to parental responsibilities, looked after him carefully, made sure he woke each day in time to get to work, washed in cold water himself so that Michael could use the limited supply of hot,[1106] took him to the theatre, and gave support as best he could. Michael began well, but he was not easy-going. Soon he was falling out with fellow-workers at the shop, grumbling about the dusty books, and expressing surprise at the fact (obvious all along) that he was committed to Blackwell's for three years. He also had some nervous difficulties about sleeping: by July he was, Charles told Michal, 'displaying some symptoms of suggesting sleeping in my room: which I think would be a mistake. But I cannot, if he comes to it, very well refuse if you aren't in the bed!'[1107] If that happened, Charles's last scrap of privacy would be gone. They waited, uncomfortably, to see if he would be called up. 'I can't believe he will care for the Army', reflected Williams, 'or the Army—much—for him!'[1108]

★ ★ ★

On 5 February 1941, 'Henry' Lee died of pneumonia. Williams had seen him occasionally in London since the war began, but had not attended his *soirées*. Lee left £30 to Michael Williams, his godson, and to Charles Williams 'any books he cares to have from my library'. Charles wrote an obituary for the *Church Times*:

> He was a man—and he was a priest—of very real energy and very wide interests. His orthodoxy was firm [...] But his intelligence was as wide as his orthodoxy was deep, and though he never compromised he was always willing to discuss the Faith. He was profoundly interested in the mystical schools of all kinds, although he tested their final value by their fruits in the Christian sense. [...]
>
> He had and practised a very high capacity for friendship. The knowledge of him over many years which his friends had—I myself over more than twenty, and others for many more—were, I suppose, completely unclouded by any dispute beyond the intellectual discussions in which he, as well as we, delighted. For the greater part of those twenty years he and I and two others met for an evening once a fortnight or so, when there was nothing to do but talk; and those evenings were always happy.
>
> His concern with Plato, with Paracelsus, with the remote learning of Eleusis or the possible symbolism of alchemy, were not, however, thrust on those who did not want them. He could be as easy at a Sunday School treat as in the Museum Reading Room, and he put himself at the disposal of all[.][1109]

Lee's papers (apart from a single notebook now in the Warburg Institute) seem to have been destroyed. Among them perished, probably, many letters from D.H.S. Nicholson and Charles Williams, and much that bore on the history of the Stella Matutina and on Williams's early esoteric training. We shall never really know what happened on those Sunday evenings.

Proofs of *Witchcraft* had arrived in January 1941.[1110] Williams hastily corrected them and indexed the book, in time for publication in April. *Witchcraft* is a vivid and readable account of magic through the ages, with emphasis on the witch trials of the sixteenth and seventeenth centuries (it supplied most of the material for Christopher Fry's post-war comedy *The Lady's Not For Burning*). It ends with the Salem witch trials of 1692. Williams neither confirms nor denies the reality of magic, but is clear that most of those accused of witchcraft had never attempted anything of the sort. The book also contains some strikingly personal passages. An interest in magic, he suggests, stems from:

> a moment which seems to be of fairly common experience—the moment when it seems that anything might turn into anything else. [...] A room, a street, a field, becomes unsure. The edge of a possibility of utter alienation intrudes. A door, untouched, might close; a picture might walk; a tree might speak; an animal might not be an animal; a man might not be a man. One may be with a friend, and a terror will take one even while his admirable voice is speaking; one will be with a lover and the hand will become a different and terrifying thing, moving in one's own like a malicious intruder.

Secondly, more positively, 'there is the human body, and the movements of the human body'. At times, the body can be 'a phenomenon [...] laden with universal meaning. A hand lighting a cigarette is the explanation of everything; a foot stepping from a train is the rock of all existence.' Both kinds of experience, Williams says, 'overthrow a simple trust that phenomena are what phenomena seem'.[1111] Such perceptions, though probably less common than he believed, were familiar and deeply important to Williams himself. He attributed the roots of magic to experiences which were alive and vivid to his own experience.

Later in the book, discussing the seventeenth-century philosophical magic of Thomas Vaughan, he quotes his favourite passage about chastity from *Comus* and, paraphrasing Vaughan's 'complicated terminology', explains that:

> The movement of the sex energy, the very flow of semen itself, was to be turned, purified, divinitized, in Christ. Through the spirit and the soul, the Divine Grace was to descend upon that Matter. [...] It rooted the Cross in the place of generation, and it proposed to itself the discovery of a method by which, through the Divine Salvation, the glory of the Resurrection should be known in the flesh.[1112]

He sees Vaughan as describing that 'transmutation of energy' which he himself had always found so fascinating.

Witchcraft's opening sentence describes magic as a 'perverted way of the soul'. But how far was Charles Williams himself practising magic? It all depends on what is meant by magic. Whether or not 'substitution' counts as magic is debatable. Williams argued that it was merely obedience, on a spiritual level, to St Paul's injunction 'bear ye one another's burdens, and so fulfil the law of Christ'. But what about the 'energy' which he believed he raised, for poetry or other purposes, through ritual activity with young women? He had not left these activities behind him in London. In March 1940, finishing the first draft of *Witchcraft*, he wrote a friendly letter to Thelma Shuttleworth about her personal difficulties, and about theology:

I am convinced that there must be a Redemption of Sin. It is not enough to leave either personal or public sins behind; your very selfishness, my anger, must be redeemed, and we must know them as redeemed, and Poland, and the Germans, and us. This, all this, must be known in the good.

When the weather is a little steadier, so that we can sit in the open [...] you shall come down here, & we will talk.

Then he added:

You will get a pencil and draw three lines on each hand, and if and when we come through—or before if we anyhow can—you shall be punished—hard—on them. And you will write out that you have done it, and what you will get presently for it. Five times, please—in different phrases each time. War or no war, pain or no pain, separation or no separation, you are pledged to that.[1113]

The following month, after the proposed visit, in a letter containing an intricate argument about pacifism he concluded with:

you got away with it pretty well in Addison's walk & Magdalene, didn't you? I hadn't realized till afterwards how much you had—insolence intertwined with insolence! Celestially, of course, but still... One of these days, and as soon as possible, you shall have five on each hand with a cane for all that. It would, I think, be agreeable if you wrote me a dramatic description—a brief playlet—of Thelma being had into her master's study for cheek and given those stripes: if you do it neatly, I will write you a sonnet on the subject too! There is an offer for you![1114]

None of this disturbed Thelma. Many years later she annotated the letter, as if for posterity: 'He lifted his walking stick at me in M[agdalene] cloisters, & an elderly lady erupted at us and interrupted—I thought it an uproarious joke. The sonnet (which I never had) was owed from as early as this.' She remained a lifelong advocate of his work and ideas, continuing to practise 'substitution' when she deemed it appropriate.

How far these activities with Thelma were related to his creative work is not clear. But Joan Wallis, who had known him well since at least 1934, believed that: 'For those who were willing to pay the personal price, the aim was to enable him to get the poems written, and he needed some kind of physical release to do it.'[1115] For Joan, now a budding writer and art critic, Williams had long been a mentor and spiritual adviser; but the price was that she had occasionally to submit to his personal rituals. This began in London, shortly before the war. In August 1939, at the end of a letter, Williams wrote that he would hold her to 'a seven years' service':

> And I formally and finally, from that time, annexe and possess (subject only to the laws of God and the Empire) all the territory hereinafter defined, holding it for that purpose; namely (a) the head and face (b) the whole back from the neck to the feet—including the soles of those feet (c) the arms from the shoulders to the fingers-tips, back and front; (d) the whole frontal district from the waist to the knees. The rest I leave to your autonomy, exercising meekly an indirect suzerainty.[1116]

Joan would visit him in his office; and sometimes, after their discussion, he would ask her to go to the cupboard. There would be an umbrella or stick— or a sword. She would bring it, and he would make her bend over and would gently spank her with it. There would be no explanation. After the move to Oxford he sometimes telephoned to summon her, insisting that she must put off any social engagements in order to see him, saying, 'You must come. I am stuck and need you to help me over it.' A letter of 11 December 1940 shows how directly he believed these rituals helped his work: he writes:

> Like it or not, approve it or not, it is likely that, if you were to give yourself to me for an afternoon with your princely care to be satisfying, I should work much better.[1117]

As she summed up many years later, 'it had a sexual element, but the restrained sexual element seemed to be a means of releasing the energy he needed to find the means to write'.[1118] And he told her, 'I am undoubtedly your war-work; at least I and my poetry—the junction between me and the lord Taliessin—are your war-work. As we have decided—seriously.'[1119]

Was this a kind of magic? It certainly seems closely related to the kind of 'transmutation' of energies advocated (in Williams's view) by Thomas Vaughan. But how had Williams acquired a sword? Perhaps it came from D.H.S. Nicholson. Ritual swords were certainly used in the Stella Matutina, the branch of the Golden Dawn to which Nicholson had belonged. When he died in 1936, Nicholson's will had given 'Henry' Lee the right to take any books he wished from his library. Perhaps Lee also removed Nicholson's magical equipment, and passed on the sword to Williams.

In a chatty letter of 4 October 1940, Williams addresses Joan by five names: Theodora, Anthea, Tessa, Helena, and Joan. After some gossip about his recent lectures, he continues:

The names—yes. They remind me of the Banishing Pentagram; also of the lower part of the Sephirotic Tree. I do not suppose you ever reminded anyone of *that*—not habitually. But the five would fit wonderfully, thus:[1120]

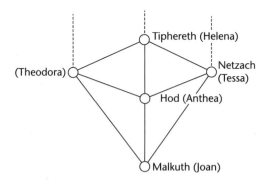

Shall I explain that now? no; take it merely. But the Banishing Pentagram you can yourself make, and we will propose it now: thus—

Do you stand up now, properly poised and firmly; and lift your left hand open and level with the shoulder that the five stars may glow from its palm (this is an addition of our own), and let the right arm be stretched across your body diagonally but a little outwards—as it were a couple of feet from the left thigh; so, and now move it upwards and diagonally to the right, and pause, and bring it straight across left, and then down and diagonally right: thus—

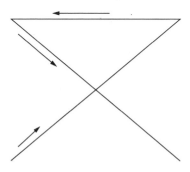

and then upwards and higher actually, thus—

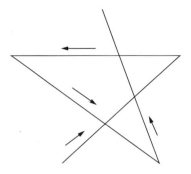

and then close the Pentagram to the original point thus—

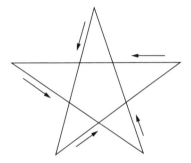

Do you see? and now I will name the points in your terms, which are indeed a part of the Blessing, though the Blessing is more—

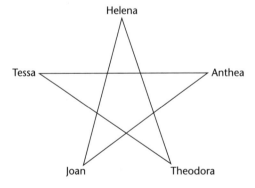

Is not that strange and beautiful and true? For, in its degree, it banishes all evil spirits, and is a part of High Magic, and identifies the worker of it with the Powers of—true worlds. And do you do it every evening, and whenever you fear; for though its proper working is with the magical rod, yet it may well be done with the arm alone; and though it is properly at the full stretch of the arm, yet it may well be done with a finger secretly, if you are in company, and no-one will see, but the Form and the Figure and the Power will be there.[1121]

And so, as he completed his history of magic, Williams taught magic to his disciple.

He trusted Joan implicitly, and in January 1941 she went with him to clear the remaining papers from his desk at Amen House—including confidential materials he wanted no one else to see, among them a photograph of Phyllis, which he destroyed.[1122] But Joan thoroughly disliked the rituals with the sword. In February 1944 she asked firmly to be released from her 'seven years' service'. Williams agreed:

> It is, I gather, something of a burden and not enough of a delight. Alas, once we rushed—did we?—to such things; now? [. . .] Say, till the last Tuesday of this month. When you come, I shall set you free: yes, it's time.[1123]

Joan was never reconciled to what Williams had imposed upon her. Yet her final view was more than sympathetic. His need for the rituals must, she thought, 'have caused him a great deal of pain and bewilderment'. But:

> he remains the most remarkable and good man I've ever met. I've never met anyone who honoured goodness more than Charles. [He] prepared me for recognising strains of goodness in people, and the strains in Charles were pure gold.[1124]

★ ★ ★

Early in October 1939, a second-year undergraduate called Anne Renwick went to the English Club to hear a talk on 'The Image of the City in English Verse'. She had read Lewis's review of *Taliessin Through Logres* and expected Charles Williams, the Arthurian poet, to be 'young & romantic'. Instead, she recognized him as 'the odd-looking man who always sits in the same place at Lewis's lectures & laughs at all the jokes'.[1125] At first she could hardly understand what he was saying. 'All his vowels seemed to be diphthongs', she recalled:

> his 'rs' were not exactly 'ws', but were slurred and softened; and he spoke with extreme rapidity and energy. [. . .] He would be almost shouting one minute, almost whispering the next, and when he quoted passages of poetry, which he did with every other sentence, he marked the metre and rhythm so strongly

that he chanted rather than spoke. But [...] what he was saying was not in the least like anything I had ever heard before. To listen to him was like finding oneself in a place where everything was a different colour and shape and size, lit by a different light.

I came away from the talk quite certain that the only thing I wanted to do was to listen to him again.[1126]

The next time Lewis lectured she arrived early, sat down next to the seat that Williams usually occupied, and waited. When he appeared, she gave him a beaming smile. 'He smiled back, and immediately began to talk, exactly as if he were picking up a conversation which had been briefly interrupted a few minutes previously.'

They soon became close friends, and Williams was so impressed by Anne's intelligence that he began, unofficially, to tutor her: 'a breath-taking and sometimes nerve-racking experience for a very green and ignorant undergraduate', as she remembered.[1127] She would visit him at Southfield House and take her essays, already seen by her official tutor, for him to read. But from the beginning it was more than an academic relationship. In October 1940 Williams writes, 'If *Time & Tide* have sent me a cheque, we will go & have lunch; and if *not*, we will merely drink. And you shall go to sleep over Middle English'—for she had a Chaucer tutorial afterwards. He lent her books, including the inevitable *Hadrian VII*, whose protagonist he perhaps saw as a role model. And the usual games developed. Her essays, he tells her, are excellent; but 'each of them ends exactly where it ought to begin':

What? Yes, I know you only had an hour for each ... Irene, is this a dialogue or a monologue?—and now, when I ask you to speak, you don't! this is sheer impertinence. Bring me the cane. Irene went and fetched (and the details of what then followed you can write to me yourself: *detail*. Let us see if your attention thrives.)

On another occasion he tells her to 'Prostrate on the floor to-night, Irene, adore & say three times: "Almighty God, save us all from the pit, and strengthen in me your honour & my lord's own."'[1128]

When her final examinations came, Lewis, who happened to be marking the papers (which were not anonymous), telephoned Williams and read out a passage from one of Anne's answers. 'Is this yours?' Lewis asked. 'Heaven, no', said Williams. 'Then', said Lewis, 'she writes like an angel and thinks like a sage.' She gained a first class degree and stayed in Oxford for two years after her graduation. They continued to meet, and he persuaded her that she should write a book about Blake, even telling her:

> Sometime during October a review in *Time and Tide* will mention casually, in referring to Blake, that for 'a knowledge of his mystical geography, as for his mystical anatomy, we must wait for the study by Miss Anne Renwick'.[1129]

But the book was never written. Williams sent Anne several verse letters and was deeply attached to her. After she had left Oxford, he sent a poem recalling their relationship:

> *After Telephoning*
> Nay, if it comes to pictures, I too
> could easily call up more than one day;
> say, Magdalen first and you, and I talking;
> or I walking by Rose Lane and finding
> you suddenly [...]
> Then St Mary's, & you suddenly in the aisle;
> or (no, you did not see me then!) you
> running down the Cornmarket; a step or two
> I took backward, but you (too fleet!) were gone;
> or you magnificent at the entrance to this very room
> (or modestly glancing sideways at the joyous doom
> on my table; or swiftly & warmly kissing the rod
> or—but those would need another poem;
> ask me for it, if you please); in Holy Cross
> I, unexpectedly moved, laying you on the altar
> whole and bound and glorious in the Holy Ghost,
> and writing it to you that day [...] & you
> quoting Coleridge, & thus & thus distinguishing
> on the delicate question of whether Taliessin could fall
> on the palace-steps—since he is named, I will say
> that no-one, I think, has touched my heart more
> or made those poems seem more worth while
> than you; so may God grant that to you & me
> they remain—good? Yes, but an intimacy too.
> Camelot would be much duller without you.[1130]

Did Williams actually lay Anne, bound, on the altar of St Cross Church ('Holy Cross')? It seems incredible. Perhaps it was merely a mental operation, a form of prayer. Certainly Anne never resented, and never mentioned, the bizarre aspects of their relationship, though she kept his letters and eventually made them available without restriction. She married, became a

Catholic, moved to London, and worked as a teacher. Her admiration for Williams never faded and she continued for many years to speak, write, and broadcast on him and his work.

Charles Williams now had behind him a long series of sado-masochistic relationships with young women. He believed these were necessary for his creativity: they enabled him to 'transmute' energy for his poetry. And most of the women involved believed he had transformed their lives for the better; they kept a lifelong enthusiasm for him and his work, and had no doubts that it had been worthwhile. But on his side, a compulsive pattern of dependency had developed. It had become an addiction.

★　★　★

Williams's overarching concern during the early war years was the wish to write more *Taliessin* poems. During the summer of 1940 he set Margaret Douglas to typing his older, unpublished Arthurian poems.[1131] He called the resulting typescript, finished in August, *The Advent of Galahad*. He had no intention of publishing it; probably these unsatisfactory poems were typed simply so that he could lay them to rest. He had written one new poem, 'Dives Dimisit', for Christmas 1939, but was dissatisfied with it. It was not until July 1940 that he was able to return to poetry with full concentration. Then, inspired by the rose garden under his window at Southfield House, he completed 'Taliessin in the Rose-Garden', a 200-line poem in which the poet watches Guinevere walking amongst roses:

> Hazel-lithe she stood, in a green gown;
> bare against the green, her arm was tinged
> with faint rose-veins, and golden-flecked
> as the massed fair hair under the gold
> circlet of Logres; on one hand was the ring
> of the consort of Logres; deep-rose-royal
> it drew the rose-alleys to the magical square.

The poet enters a visionary state in which the roses, and the queen's ruby ring, turn to a tide of blood: the blood of the battle which will destroy Arthur's kingdom, the blood that drips from the wounded king of the Grail Castle at Carbonek, the saving blood of Christ, and the menstrual blood of women, which is also shed in the cause of life—for women 'share with the Sacrifice the victimization of blood' and 'women's flesh lives the quest of the Grail'. The body's processes unconsciously symbolize eternal truths:

> Flesh knows what spirit knows,
> but spirit knows it knows [...]—women's travel
> holds in the natural the image of the supernatural[.]

A profound meditation upon blood and its meanings, the poem is complex and magnificent, and implicitly a manifestation of the terrible year of war in which it was written. As difficult as any poem by Yeats or Dylan Thomas, 'Taliessin in the Rose-Garden' demands close and repeated reading, and challenges the reader to reflection. The *Dublin Review* published it in September 1940.

But, as so often, Williams was deeply frustrated by his colleagues' bland inability to make anything of it. He told Alice Mary:

> Gerry thought that if he read it several times he would follow it, though he did not think it particularly obscure; and F.P. said that he could not find anything intelligent to say about it except that he 'seemed to be moving in a region of beautiful ideas'. Phyllis—it is odd how strange that name seems—took some trouble over it, but she confessed that though she understood both the words and the ideas she couldn't all the same 'get it'; [...] I have promised to read it out loud some time, but when she is over here she is so tied up with HSM that it is difficult to find time.[1132]

Phyllis, indeed, spent so much time with Milford that Williams could not avoid jealousy: 'I suspect an affair as near an affair as both their present positions allow', he concluded. He found it painful to see his former protégée giving her attention to Milford, who was publishing his poems without payment. As he wrote in this new poem:

> bitter is the brew of exchange.
> We buy for others; we make beauty for others;
> and the beauty made is not the beauty meant:
> shent is pride while the rose-King bleeds at Carbonek.

By mid-December he was working on another poem, 'The Departure of Blanchfleur', in which Percivale's sister leaves the court at Camelot to become a nun at Amesbury, where she will one day foster Lancelot's son Galahad. This poem centres on the question of freedom and constraint. As Blanchfleur leaves to take the veil—giving up the normal kind of freedom in exchange for commitment to a spiritual discipline—a slave-girl at the court, who has the right to opt for freedom, wonders whether to choose a return to her native Athens, or marriage, or to renew her bondage for a further seven years. Clearly the poem is, on one level, a fantasy vehicle for

Williams's feelings about the women who accepted, or rejected, the 'discipline' he imposed upon them. Predictably therefore, seeing Blanchfleur opt for the convent, the slave-girl chooses freely to renew her own servitude—a decision that Williams no doubt wished certain young women had also made. But the poem goes far deeper than that, into his own religious commitment, and Williams produces a haunting aphorism:

> They only can do it with my lord who can do it without him,
> and I know he will have about him only those.

The words express his sense of the need to persist stoically through times when God seems to have withdrawn all sense of His presence; but they were also a message to his followers, as he came to feel that he might not be with them much longer.

Thereafter, poetry eluded him. In May 1941 he told Thelma Shuttleworth:

> Verse delays its coming; I have written no more Taliessin poems—that, I hope, is not the war. I should simply hate to believe that the war had overcome poetry: which ought to include war and everything: the greater the crisis, the greater the verse, or so at least it ought to be—though that is perhaps for the Very Great. It would, at least, be proper that one's greatest power should be reached at the moment of death. Yeats was very nearly like that.[1133]

There seemed to be no time to concentrate. 'I *want* to spend a year on poetry', he told Michal, 'but don't see how I can. Yet unless I do I shall never get down to the second Taliessin book.'[1134] He had pipe-dreams of persuading Milford to allow him two or three months' paid leave to work on new poems—an unlikely prospect, since sales of the first *Taliessin* book had been poor and the Press had paid him nothing for it. But 'I shall never manage the longer *narrative* poems I want till I can get down to them steadily.' He thought of calling the new book 'either *Jupiter over Carbonek* or *The Household of Taliessin*' and even speculated about a 'third (and perhaps last) Taliessin volume, on the Quest itself'.[1135]

For the moment, all this seemed fantasy. But there were occasional moments of encouragement. Visiting Michal in London in September 1941, he found a copy of *Taliessin Through Logres* 'more or less hidden away in the bedroom',[1136] and discovered she had been reading it at night during air raids. He was deeply touched. And the Inklings continued to be a sustaining resource. In October 1941 he read two poems—probably 'Taliessin in the Rose-Garden' and 'The Departure of Blanchfleur'—to Lewis and Tolkien, he told Anne Renwick, 'with immense effect... They both went on as if—I become foolish!'[1137] When, reflecting deeply on Arthurian mythology, he suddenly understood 'what exactly the gentleman in the burning tomb whom Galahad freed symbolized', he declared to Michal that 'if you think ANY human creature in Oxford—except perhaps C.S.L.—would understand me there, you are *wrong*'.[1138]

★　★　★

In September 1940 the Blitz had begun. For seven months, British cities were bombed heavily night after night—London for more than fifty consecutive nights, with the destruction of a million homes. Familiar landmarks disappeared. 'Did you see that Bourne and Hollingsworth's was bombed?' Williams lamented to Michal. 'To think that we were there a week ago today! O you my heart and London my love! It is shocking not to be there.'[1139] He joined her in early October and told Alice Mary:

> I have been in London for five nights of the bombing, which shook me to jitters—plain panic, unbecoming and obscene, but just so. Not that I wasn't capable of walking, speaking, & making tea: but that below, my heart ran along my nerves like a diabolic tight-rope dancer.[1140]

To Anne Ridler he wrote:

> I feel now a wistful pleasure that I was in London for five nights, and saw from the Hampstead balcony the great fire in the docks on the Saturday afternoon. We spent most of the nights in the flat on the ground floor by the stairs, where on the Tuesday my wife slept peacefully for an hour through the raid. That was the night before the larger guns opened—and was I in the sheer jitters! [...] I detested hearing the things grunting and jerking about the sky. We looked out at one point and saw the flares dropped and hanging in the sky—& so on & so on. You will have heard it all—from people who did something about it, instead of... never mind. I discovered however that I can still be a little fussed about my wife; because I went up on Friday and came down on Monday, and went up again on Tuesday—Cumberledge said that they weren't allowing people to go to London and scared me out of what wits I had left—sat down in the flat, and said to my wife 'Here I stop until you are out of London'. Much against her will—incredible woman! I don't think she *is* afraid—she gave way, went to her sister's in Lutterworth, & came here for this last week-end.[1141]

The experience raised still higher his admiration of Michal's courage. In December much of the old City of London was obliterated. Ralph Binfield, on leave from the army, went to see if Amen House was still there. The devastation was, he found, 'far worse than I had ever imagined', but he bumped into Foss, who reassured him that Amen House, amazingly, was still standing. Everything around it was gone:

> From Amen House to the corner of Warwick Square is a blank. Stanley the newsagent opposite is gone. The whole east side of Ave Maria Lane, the whole of Paternoster Square and Paternoster Row, Ivy Lane, Panyer Alley—nothing stands but tottering walls. The streets themselves, which were piled high with debris have been cleared by the pioneers but only steel-helmeted policemen patrolled about and we were several times ordered out. [. . .] Newgate Street is derelict. The Post Office is gone—all the shops are shattered or burned.

Binfield met a former colleague, who had seen the building on fire the previous day and 'was praying for a fire brigade when up came one and an officer jumped down into the square and a young cheerful voice said "It's all right Bingo, we've come to save the Oxford Press!"'[1142] Quick use of the hose had saved Amen House and prevented the blaze spreading to publishers Hodder and Stoughton next door. A few weeks later the Bunhill Press, where Vivian Ridler now worked, was bombed: Vivian turned up one morning to find the street strewn with magenta-coloured covers of Anne Ridler's poems, which Bunhill was printing for OUP.

Henceforth Michal spent much of her time at Lutterworth, helping in the nursing home where her sister worked. Charles and Michael went up to check on the empty Hampstead flat in late November. They found it unscathed, though a few windows in the block, broken by bombing, were boarded up. They cleaned the flat, and then (Williams told Michal):

> Michael—much to my private surprise—suggested we should say a blessing on it: so when we were ready to go, about 2.15, we went through it and into every room, and then we both knelt down by your bed, and we both said, out loud and together, the Lord's Prayer, and the Hail Mary, and I said might it and we (meaning you) and everyone all be blessed, and he said Amen, and we came away.[1143]

This blessing of the flat may help elucidate a curious incident that took place in 1942, when Miss Cattell, a Press employee, temporarily living on the top floor of the Press's bookshop, on Oxford's High Street, suspected the place to be haunted and found that 'to be alone at nights with only ghosts of the past for company was rather a terrifying thought'. Accordingly, a Press employee remembered:

> after careful pondering on the subject, it seemed that some sort of exorcism was indicated. Consequently the Bishop of Oxford, who is one of the perpetual

Delegates of the Press, was approached by me as to the possibility of the flat being blessed. The Bishop most kindly offered to come himself, and one warm summer Sunday afternoon, despite his many engagements, his Lordship arrived with 'bell, book, and candle' to perform the ceremony, with [...] Mr. Charles Williams as the chief acolyte. It was certainly a comfort to know that the 'Thinges that go bumpe in the nighte' were all laid to rest. To sceptics it may appear superstitious, perhaps, but who of us is not superstitious in one way or another?[1144]

It was probably not a formal exorcism. No doubt Williams joined the Bishop in saying some prayers; perhaps he added a banishing pentagram for good measure.

19

A Pioneer for the Young Poets

The success of his Milton lectures in early 1940 ensured that Williams was asked to lecture again. Milton was followed by Wordsworth, and he gave annual courses on the two poets until 1944, when Wordsworth was replaced by 'Eighteenth-Century Poetry'. From 1943 a series on Shakespeare was added. Williams's rhetorical fireworks became famous, and the lectures were packed. More than fifty years later, former students remembered him vividly: 'Mounting the steps at a bound and launching straight into a flood of quotation'; 'telling students "Never mind what Mr. so-and-so says about it, read the text and think for yourself!"'; 'declaiming like an Old Testament prophet or an enthusiastic evangelical preacher'; 'Leaping from one side of the stage to the other, and acting in turn the part of each character he was talking about'; 'clutch[ing] his copy of Wordsworth, once almost throwing it into the air, but luckily catching it again [. . .] totally absorbed in his fascination with the subject'; 'Pacing up and down the platform [. . .] return[ing] to its centre table three times to bang on it three times with his fist to impress on his audience that "Eternity—forbids thee—to forget"'. In short, 'Electrifying!'[1145] Some of those students went on to become teachers of English and throughout their careers returned to their notes on those lectures for inspiration.

The lectures brought requests to speak to student societies, which he always tried to accept. In 1941–42 alone he addressed the English Society, the International Society, the Celtic Society (twice), the Fine Arts Society, the Makers Society, the Martlets, and the Socratic Club. Outside invitations also proliferated. He lectured on Milton in Bristol; he addressed the Association of Librarians, the Student Christian Movement, the Fellowship of Reconciliation, and St Mary's Convent School, Wantage; he spoke on 'Why I Read' in a London air-raid shelter. He led a debate with Gerry Hopkins on 'Is Cinema an Art?' at the Greenford Ordnance Depot. Then there were religious societies: he addressed Anglo-Catholics at Oxford's Pusey House, Dominicans at Blackfriars, Anglican Sisters at Springfield St Mary; the Fellowship of St Alban and St Sergius, the Church Union, the Chelmsford Diocesan Youth Conference, the Society of St Francis.[1146] Through Phyllis Potter he became a regular speaker to the clergy at conferences at the Pleshey Retreat House, where Evelyn Underhill often led retreats. In October 1942 he even preached a sermon, entitled 'The Weight of Glory', at St Andrew's Church, Cambridge.

Everywhere he made a powerful impression. In November 1940 he spoke on 'Love and Substitution' to theology students in Lincoln. Christopher Evans, a tutor at the theological college:

> was deputed to fetch him by car from Peterborough and drive him back to Lincoln. Travelling was uncertain, the train was late and it was night. Driving through the darkness Christopher remembered as being one of the most extraordinary experiences of his life. Williams smoked all the time and sitting next to him he had a sense that 'lightning might flash out from the ends of his fingers at any moment'.[1147]

Yet often Williams found it a strain. 'I have to take Middleton Murry's place at the Summer School of Sociology here', he told Anne Ridler. 'And what do I speak on? Dearest Anne, "The Recovery of Spiritual Initiative"—yes, faith! pompous fools! I shall fail utterly; what do I know of "The R. of S.I."? However, there it is—for next Wednesday, & I must go through with it.'[1148]

Given a set title, he would usually subvert it. Asked to speak on 'The Church Looks Forward', he pointed out that the Church 'does not, [...] even on earth, look forward. She looks centrally', and proceeded to speak on the spiritual significance of the body and the material world. When the title was 'The Conversion of the Heathen', he addressed the lack of spirituality among self-styled Christians. But he confessed to Alice Mary that he felt he was being forced into a false role. 'I find myself approached to speak at odd sorts of religious conferences or groups—it is all wrong. I was never meant for that kind of thing.'[1149] Yet every invitation meant a chance to communicate his ideas, and perhaps to tell suitable individuals about the Companions of the Co-inherence. Periodically, he would promise to give it up. In June 1941, agreeing to give four addresses at Pleshey, he told Phyllis Potter:

> After this I shall try and extricate myself from the clergy, with whom I appear to be getting mixed up, or I shall find myself continually delivering short

speeches on the Christian Order or something fantastic when my proper job ought to be writing novels, criticism and poetry.[1150]

But the process had a momentum of its own. Besides his work for the Press, his university lectures, his efforts to write more *Taliessin* poems, and his regular reviewing for *Time and Tide* and the *Sunday Times*, he had become, de facto, a spiritual director for a steadily growing circle of people who considered themselves 'Companions' and looked to him for help and advice as they headed for divorce, or contemplated going over to Rome, or considered suicide, or faced death in the forces, the fire services, the air raids. There were constant visits, letters, telephone calls. It is not surprising if he found himself turning to private rituals aimed at 'transmutation of energy'. And he did not follow the example of C.S. Lewis, who in 1940 began to make regular confession to a priest. Giving advice and comfort to many others, Williams carried his whole psychological and spiritual burden alone— perhaps because he knew that full confession would result in firm advice to change course. The writer and actor R.H. Ward, who joined the Oxford Pilgrim Players in 1940 and acted in *The Death of Good Fortune*, met Williams around this time and heartily disliked him: they were naturally antipathetic, and Ward was a difficult and opinionated man. But his suggestion, many years later, that Williams may have 'suffered intolerable conflicts, [that] he may have been unhappy in some secret and insupportable way',[1151] was perhaps the simple truth.

★   ★   ★

Late in 1940 the publisher Ashley Sampson, who had commissioned *The Problem of Pain* from Lewis the previous year, proposed that Williams write a book on *The Forgiveness of Sins*. Williams took it on, though in February 1941 he told Phyllis Potter 'at the moment I don't feel very competent to produce 40,000 words on the subject',[1152] and postponed the task for a few months to write a play for Ruth Spalding's company. The play (working titles varied between *Frontiers of Hell*, *How the Devil*, *The Lady and the Witch*, and *The Devil and the Lady*) was to be a 'thriller', drawing on *Witchcraft*. It had its origin in an idea which had cropped up during his lectures on *Paradise Lost*: that 'Satan was obsessed by the idea of becoming incarnate'.[1153] The play might be classed as 'drawing-room horror': Lady Endicott and her lover, the black magician Smetham, plot to sacrifice their daughter in a Satanic ritual which will bind Lady Endicott's *protégée* Alison to her 'Little

Master', the Devil, with the ultimate aim of enabling Alison to bear his child so that Satan may become incarnate upon earth. Their scheme is foiled, in a somewhat perfunctory ending; but the play contains some truly horrific moments and its portrayal of evil is disturbing. The flavour is suggested by a note from Williams to Ruth (not all of these details survived into the final version):

> The idea is that Phoebe's body is to be re-inlived by a Familiar; her soul is to be at Lady E's disposal in the other world. I will make this clear in Act III if desirable. Yes—her, Phoebe's, birth is a pledge to hell; Lady E. & S. had meant it so. [...] She can't be burnt because her body is needed. They are not sure whether this will happen; if the Familiar doesn't come, they will be left with a dead body on their hands.[1154]

The play was never performed: as Ruth Spalding put it, 'Being war time, nobody asked for a performance of this gloomy work so it has never been produced.'[1155] It is not a very good play and would have made uncomfortable fare for a company used to staging religious drama with a distinctly positive tone. As so often, Williams was ahead of his time. Thirty years later, in the era of *Rosemary's Baby* and *The Omen*, his play's premise would become a prominent theme of cinematic horror.

Finishing the play in early April, Williams went on without a pause to produce an essay on 'The Cross' for a symposium called *What the Cross Means to Me*. It is his most powerful and honest theological essay. It is, he says, 'revolting to our sense of justice' that God should deliberately maintain his creation, as he does, in a state of agony. The only indication of justice is the fact that God chose himself to share the suffering—although 'His life was short. His pains (humanly speaking) comparatively brief.' As for those who crucified him, 'it is often said that He was put to death by evil men'. Williams will have none of this. There was nothing exceptionally evil about those responsible: we have no right to blame them, for such destructiveness is 'common to our experience':

> Caiaphas and Pilate were each of them doing his best in the duty presented to them. The high priest was condemning a blasphemer. The Roman governor was attempting to maintain the peace. At the present time, for example, it is clear that one man must suffer for the people—and many more than one man, whether they consent or not.

In other words, innocent people in Germany are being bombed—for the greater good. 'We can hardly blame those earlier supporters of the same

law. Humanly speaking, they were doing the best they could. [...] Certainly
our sins and faults destroy the good. But our efforts after the good also
destroy it.'[1156]

There is, of course, Easter. But how much does the prospect of resurrection and eternal life really mean to us? Williams was honest about his own
lack of enthusiasm:

> There are those who find it easy to look forward to immortality and those
> who do not. I admit that, for myself, I do not. It is true that the gradual stupe-
> faction of the faculties which normally overcomes a man as he grows older
> seems to make—if not the idea of immortality more attractive—at least the
> idea of annihilation less so. [...] But I cannot say I find the idea of immortality,
> even of a joyous immortality, much more attractive; I admit, of course, that this
> is a failure of intelligence[.]

The Gospel, Williams adds, contains 'really terrifying attacks upon the
Gospel': for example, Jesus's 'incredible comment on Judas: "it were good
for that man if he had not been born." And who [Williams asks] caused
him to be born?' Who but God? Rarely has a theologian raised so many
disturbing questions in so short an essay. It is a distillation of Williams's
feelings at this time: a mixture of profound faith with the sense that life is
almost unbearable; the two experiences existing as paradox, side by side.
Finishing the essay, he told the editor, 'If it were possible for the fee for the
essay to be paid now, as on delivery of the manuscript, it would be a great
convenience.'[1157] A tax bill was due and, as usual, he was alarmingly short
of money.

Finishing 'The Cross', he spent the next ten days writing a pamphlet
titled *Religion and Love in Dante: The Theology of Romantic Love* for a series
called *Dacre Papers*. Based largely on lectures given to his London classes, the
pamphlet is a discussion of key episodes from the *Divine Comedy*, but
Williams emphasizes that the poem is an idealized account of the spiritual
'way' of Romantic Love: 'People are still, it seems, "falling in love"', and 'if
Dante is right' then this may be the beginning, for the lovers, of 'a Way of
Sanctity'.[1158] And so, at last, his theology of romantic love found its way, if
only in brief *précis*, into print.

This torrent of writing would have exhausted most people, but in May
Williams took up his promise to write *The Forgiveness of Sins* and over the
summer produced a 40,000-word book. Beginning with a discussion of
forgiveness in Shakespeare, it goes on to reflect on redemption through

sacrifice: the blood sacrifice of the Hebrew temple, and the sacrifice of Christ. Characteristically, Williams is far from conventional in his approach, discussing, for example, the problem of things which one feels *cannot* be forgiven, and the matter of how unpleasant it is to need forgiveness oneself. A final chapter discusses 'The Present Time'—that is, the war. Can we forgive the Germans? Williams points out that forgiveness can only occur when we find a particular individual responsible for a particular injury to ourselves. Forgiveness on behalf of others means nothing: 'The fact that many of us resent injuries on behalf of others is generally a convenient way of indulging our resentments with an appearance of justice.'[1159] After the war, legal redress and a kind of justice might be possible, he suggests, by bringing the Nazi leaders to a tribunal; but it could not be a legal trial, for there was then no pre-existing law which they had broken (a point on which he may have been mistaken). If they were executed, it would have to be as a sacrifice for the benefit of the future, and it should be called such, rather than a judicial execution. The essay ends by returning to the personal dimension and focusing on the Lord's Prayer: 'Forgive us our trespasses, *as we forgive them that trespass against us*'. It is a matter of co-inherence: if we fail to forgive, we shut ourselves out of 'the act in which, more than any other, the mortal co-inheres with the divine'.[1160] Having finished the book early in August and dedicated it 'To the Inklings', he turned to drama again and spent the rest of the month writing another of his short, masque-like religious plays, for Ruth Spalding.[1161] *Grab and Grace*, a sequel to *The House by the Stable*, is a minor work with a simplistic plot: Man is again tempted by Pride but, with the help of Grace, rejects her. Faith has, however, one striking speech, which sounds like a personal utterance from Williams:

> I can say nothing now to cheer
> a broken heart; only that mine too
> broke; we are not adult till then –
> we are not even young; the second step,
> the perseverance into the province of death,
> is a hard thing; then there is no return.

In late 1941 he contributed a short essay to a book titled *Russia and the West*, edited by C.A. Dawson. Since June of that year, when Germany invaded the USSR, Russia had been, perforce, an important ally: Williams recalled the 'strangeness' of hearing Churchill's speech announcing it on the radio in the lounge of the opulent Randolph Hotel. His contribution, 'Ourselves and the Revolution', gives a rare glimpse of his political sympathies, recalling the anxieties of childhood poverty and his youthful sense that when the Bolshevik Revolution broke out, 'the earth shouted against' the iron sky of oppression, 'and it broke'. He goes on to balance food and freedom in terms of co-inherence:

> The Russians of late have been (one gathers) reasonably fed but not altogether free; we have been reasonably free, but not anything like enough fed. The metaphor of food may be pressed; we must learn to consume and be consumed, to eat and to be eaten. [...] The great social maxim—'from each according to his power; to each according to his need'—is its definition. This is common; let us take it so. If the Revolution and the English can indeed [...] mutually 'eat and be eaten,' Europe might—one does not know, but Europe might—be noble, fed, and free, even yet.[1162]

Whilst writing *The Forgiveness of Sins*, Williams had decided to try a full-length book on Dante; Faber 'agreed warmly', so before the end of November he began work.[1163] He was also writing another long poem ('The Working of Porphyry', eventually published as 'The Calling of Taliessin') for the next *Taliessin* volume. Its tone was authoritative and flawless, making natural and rhythmical use of its Celtic material:

> By some it was said that Taliessin
> was a child of Henwg the saint, bred in Caerleon,
> and thence come, miracle-commissioned; by some
> that he sprang from the bards, the ancient guards of the cauldron
> called of Ceridwen; she goddess or priestess,
> Tydeg Voel's wife, whose life was legend,
> and if he her son then so by magic: none
> knew; no clue showed when he rode down the Wye
> coracle-cradled, and at the weir was seen
> by Elphin the son of Gwyddno and drawn to shore.

How Williams managed to produce this serene and magnificent poetry amidst the turmoil of his life and the pressures of almost incredible overwork remains a mystery.

In November's *New Statesman* he reviewed two volumes of *Carmina Gadelica*, Alexander Carmichael's enormous compendium of Celtic magic spells and invocations, which he thought a work 'of high importance'.[1164] And completing a prodigious year's output, in December he began, encouraged by a BBC producer, an abridgement of Milton's *Samson Agonistes*, and a play, *The Three Temptations*. He sent a sonnet, 'Christmas 1941', to Isabel Douglas. Its tone is elegiac:

> The wings fold; the ways end; this
> is as certain as simple; we shall be mourned for a day
> while others put right the things we have done amiss
> and others remember the words we used to say.[1165]

But by then he was immersed in another crisis.

★   ★   ★

Michael had been working, half-heartedly, at Blackwell's since May 1940, living at South Parks Road. He and Charles lived in uneasy proximity, their most comfortable moments being the evenings when they went together to the theatre. But in July 1941, as Michael's nineteenth birthday approached, he had to register for military service. At first he heard nothing, and enjoyed his Blackwell's job more than before, but in early November the inevitable happened. Williams told Phyllis Potter:

> My son is being swept into the Air Force this week, much to everyone's gloom. Fools say 'it will make a man of him'; wiser people, like me and his mother, sit, agnostically hoping it may not make a beast. Indeed, I am not foolishly pessimistic, but
>> There is a kind of fighting in my heart
>> Which will not let me sleep.
> He is in a very bad temper. He goes (I ask you!) to Penarth, in Glamorganshire, on Saturday. Is it fun?![1166]

Michael was soon transferred to RAF Weston-super-Mare in Somerset. In late November Williams reported, 'Michael is, or seems to be, taking the Air Force more nobly than I had any right to expect.' But soon Michael was depressed and disturbed. His father did his best to help, sending movie magazines and writing long letters drawing on his own experience of prolonged unhappiness:

> I don't in the least underrate what you are going through. [...] In the worst times of one's living, one does really feel 'I can't bear it'. [...] I go back a little to what I said about your courage. [...] What I can tell you with the most certain conviction is that the going through hell does quite certainly result in giving one *power*, if one waits and believes. I am the least of God's creatures, but I have done something in my time, and I only did it through having

suffered. [...] Two or three times in my life I have felt I should really go off my head; did I? no; and (beyond all my beliefs) the result is greater than anything. Adored *always* be the Omnipotence.

And he confided in Michael, as he had never done before, about his own activities:

As to the Order—it really needs a good deal of explanation, and you won't want a full autobiography. [...] You have to grasp [...] that I do lead, in a way, 'a double life'. I have had to be a kind of teacher (not only with women!), and altogether it's been very unexpected and strange; though, mind you, it didn't begin till I had gone through at different times what seemed like the curious mechanics of several different hells. Anyhow about three years ago I established & founded a small Order called the 'Order of the Co-Inherence' which means living in & from each other. I will send you the note I made for it when I can find one. The point of it was that the Companions (as I called them) did believe in it and work in it; they might not know each other, for there is no organization but God, but they practised that belief—exchange & substitution & all that. And when you went I caused certain of them to offer their prayers for you—Margaret & Anne Ridler & one or two more. And I have been rather wondering if I ought to do more. [...] I have been wondering if I should ask Anne Renwick who flung herself into it with devotion. I have to consider who is doing what, & have, when I take steps, to do it carefully. It does mean a *belief* on your part; it means that you must not revolt (not that you do) but allow the situation to be, and then be held—you particularly and individually—by God, the Church, and the Order, and whoever carries your burden or helps to carry it.

Anyhow, there it is, if you wish![1167]

Soon, however, Michael was telephoning his father in great distress: Williams told Anne Ridler of dreadful calls 'with him half-sobbing in Weston-super-Mare and the operator saying that this couldn't go on and all hell gnawing one's nerves'.[1168] Soon Michael had a full-scale nervous breakdown. As Williams summarized in January 1942:

he went through his training, had a collapse of some kind (we are not yet clear as to its nature), was thrown into an R.A.F. hospital, & looks like being discharged as useless to the Services. This may mean anything; myself, I do not expect it to mean much beyond what we knew before—that at a certain point he breaks under tension. No particular discredit to him; [...] I always knew that once he was involved anything might happen![1169]

After a few weeks he was discharged from the RAF and back in Oxford, working at Blackwell's. But he was prone to hysterical outbursts: Anne Spalding remembered him 'lying on the floor in the spare bedroom and hammering with his heels. He was in a very poor way.'[1170] Charles too described himself as 'suffering from a severe re-action' and 'a good deal shaken'.[1171] The question of Michael's future remained unresolved.

The debacle brought other difficulties. When Michael joined the RAF, Michal had given up the London flat and moved in at South Parks Road, though spending much time with her sister at Lutterworth. Charles found this 'a little nerve-racking', he told Anne Ridler: 'I never know which day in the week C[elia] is likely to come in, and I refuse to tell Michal never to come to the office except on Saturday mornings.'[1172] However, since Phyllis came only about once in six weeks, the risk was small. But once Michael left the RAF the psychological pressures must have been formidable. Michal stayed on sporadically with Charles and Michael until September, when, after a furious row with Charles,[1173] Michael returned to London, staying with friends and working at Bumpus's bookshop on Oxford Street. A new flat was found, finally, in February 1943, at 23 Antrim Mansions, Hampstead, a few yards from their previous home. Michal settled there, and Michael joined her, leaving Charles once more alone in Oxford.

★ ★ ★

Many people expected Williams to be a pacifist, but he was not. In April 1940 Thelma Shuttleworth, both pacifist and agnostic, asked him for his views, and he sent her a long letter:

> As far as 'something after death' goes—then yes, I do. At least, I believe in two things. I believe that every soul experiences and understands fully the entire and living Justice of the universe. I believe that Justice to be a living, responsive and intelligent Existence—and one with Almighty Love. [...] It is aware of, and present at, all points of time. Now I myself, as you know, have no passion for everlasting life. I would, I think, die contented to die out. But I do not consider that my personal wishes govern the universe; and—because of all the above—because Justice-in-Love exists, I believe in a Judgement, an Accounting. Or, to put it another way, I believe that we shall see our thoughts, words, & actions in that lucid Justice—that the past lives there, and we shall jolly well know it, where we have sinned and where not, and so on. [...]
>
> So. And as to war? [...] I cannot go so far as to say that the use of physical force against another is always wrong; nor can I say that to take life is always wrong. [...] I think that, in the last resort, a set of people has the right (and I fear the duty) to say something like this: the conditions under which you insist that we and others shall live are, quite simply, intolerable. You are breaking all

possible laws under which men have found it possible to live together. We do not
hate you; but we propose to stop you. It is quite possible for you to stop first. If
you do, very well. But if you do not, if you insist on death and destruction, then
we shall accept your decision. [...] We propose to do our best to remain in a state
of love towards you. But we do not conceive that this means that we must do
whatever you tell us to do at any moment [...] if you try and kill us, we shall
reluctantly accept your decision, and try and kill you until you stop.[1174]

He had no real fears that Germany would win. And he found prophetic
indications in his poems, telling Raymond Hunt in November 1941 that
'once Hitler reaches the Caucasus, the war is as good as won. Have you not
read—actually, in the ordinary papers—"An Imperial Army is preparing to
defend the Caucasus?" And look at p. 60 of Taliessin!'[1175]

The page reads, in part:

> The Emperor in Byzantium nodded to the exarchs;
> it was night still when the army began to move, [...] the wheels
> of the furnished lorries rolling on the roads to the east, [...]
> the City on the march to renew the allegiance of Caucasia.

Occasionally, he played self-mockingly with the idea that his poems could
affect the course of the war. 'I almost feel', he told Anne Ridler the following year, 'I had better write a poem about archangels destroying octopuses—
merely to ensure general Macarthur (MacArthur—dearest Anne!) conquering
in the East.'[1176] Anne Renwick recalled Williams working on 'The Prayers of
the Pope':

> speaking of the difficulty of devising some method of defeat for the octopus
> & saying, of course playfully but seriously in the game, that points in the
> Taliessin poems had coincided with points in the war so often that he must
> hurry up and do it, or the Japanese would have taken India before he had
> thought how to stop them.[1177]

For on 7 December 1941, as Williams was immersed in Michael's problems,
the Japanese had attacked Pearl Harbor, making it certain that the United
States would enter the war. There was now little doubt of an Allied victory;
the questions were how soon it would come, and at what cost.

Soon after Lee's death, Williams found the horoscope his friend had commissioned for him twenty years before. 'It has some odd things', he told
Anne Ridler:

> It prophesies great commercial success—no, sorry, financial: that is its chief
> error. But it also says that at 41 I 'enter the period of Mars which will remain

operative until 56 years of age'. Mars! Venus is weak: I might be 'happier & more successful unmarried' (only I should have done nothing), but I 'may remain celibate throughout my life unless at 57 I come under the influence of Jupiter's greater periods'.[1178]

This was appropriate: he thought of calling the new volume of Taliessin poems *Jupiter over Carbonek*. Jupiter, the planet of Jove, was a godlike planet, and its Great Red Spot like a wound, linking it symbolically to Christ. He would be fifty-six in September and had mixed feelings about the horoscope. 'This alarms me and yet pleases—pleases that Mars will disappear.... Alarms.. what is Jupiter about to do? There is sure to be a catch in it somewhere.'

He decided to get on with the book on Dante, and tried to draft it from scratch; but soon told Raymond Hunt, 'After playing about with Dante for some time I have come to the gloomy conclusion that I had better have all my original notes and, if possible, anything that you recorded of what I actually said.' Using the notes would not get in the way of his developing new ideas: 'If you could only feel, my dear Raymond, how little I want to trouble to say something different.' A few days later he added, 'It is a hideous confession, but the fact is that I do *not* want to read Dante through again! I ought to, of course, but—'[1179] His desire to write the book was fighting against a deep tiredness. But he was cheered by meeting Gervase Mathew, a Dominican friar and occasional Inkling, who said 'he thought there was nothing nearer Dante's real thought than the pamphlet [*Religion and Love in Dante*] and the chapter in *He Came Down*'.[1180] By June the book was well on the way. 'I labour here at the Dante book', he told Anne Ridler: 'we are (of course!) behind-hand, but a few more weeks should do it. [...] But it interferes with the poems.'[1181] On 28 July he sent off the manuscript, at this stage called, cumbersomely, *The Way of the Affirmation of Images*, but it left him dissatisfied. 'It is a sad fact', he told Anne Renwick, 'that it has slid from being what it ought to be down to what I could make it. [...] I suffered when I had finished it from an acute re-action and heaviness.'[1182] He waited anxiously for a verdict from Faber. At first, all he heard was that 'Eliot is supposed to be going through it "in order to make it a trifle more popular".'[1183] It amused him that the hyperintellectual Eliot was trying to popularize his work.

When Eliot's response came, it was not uncritical. Moreover, he objected to the fact that every chapter title contained the word 'Image':

What puzzled me to begin with was that practically everything except God appears to be an image and if it is an image one is tempted to say, 'An image of

what?' It seems to me to belong to a kind of personal language of your own. [...]
Later on [...] you mention co-inherence quite placidly as if it were something
that everybody ought to understand. [...] I am not at all sure what co-inherence
means myself. [...] Need I say more? If so, I will do so.[1184]

Meanwhile, Williams had been reading the book to the Inklings. He told
Anne Ridler:

> Your Mr. Eliot is being a Pest. He says the introductory chapter to *Dante* is
> most obscure & difficult & must be re-written. Now Lewis says it is the clear-
> est thing I have ever written and forbids me to touch it. He even told my wife
> that the whole book was extraordinarily clear, 'which has not always been, Mrs
> Williams, a virtue of your husband's work.' I shall have to [...] rewrite it, of
> course; Faber's having paid the money.[1185]

★   ★   ★

Williams was perhaps unique in being on equally good terms with Eliot
and Lewis. Appreciating both men's kindness and intellectual brilliance,
and sharing their 'high' Anglicanism, he could enjoy Eliot's poetic adventur-
ousness (which Lewis profoundly distrusted) and Lewis's tinge of popularist
vulgarity (which repelled Eliot). He was pleased that both admired his
work—'I must be about the only living person whom both CSL and
TSE urge on to more and more', he told Anne Ridler—and toyed with
schemes of bringing them together, perhaps for a radio broadcast: 'I do
think that three or four of us—Lewis, and perhaps Eliot and so on let
loose on the question of what Love is for twenty minutes each would be
amusing.'[1186] When he eventually succeeded in getting them together, for
tea at Oxford's Mitre Hotel, in the spring of 1945, it was a disaster. Eliot,
overcome by nerves, opened the conversation with 'Mr Lewis, you are a
much *older* man than you appear in photographs', a grand piece of tact-
lessness which he followed with, 'I must tell you, Mr Lewis, that I consider
your *Preface to Paradise Lost* your best book.' Since that book had been
highly critical of Eliot's views, Lewis was baffled. The conversation stalled,
though Williams is said to have enjoyed the occasion as an instance of
grim social comedy.[1187]

    With Eliot as friend, rival poet, and publisher, Williams found the rela-
tionship, though valued, unsettling. Envy was a frequent theme. 'Why
doesn't T.S.E. write to me?' he asked Anne Ridler in 1940. 'I envy him

profoundly—being in London & writing poetry & seeing you & so on.'[1188] When Eliot made a partial move from London to Surrey, it was no better:

> TSE came here to see me the other day—being in Oxford. It seems he is now living about five miles from Guildford—in a house where, he said gravely, there are generally 18 women & no men. He never leaves his room before mid-day because he spends the morning at work—lucky man![1189]

He was delighted by Eliot's many favourable comments on his work, telling Joan Wallis, for example:

> Mr. Eliot in a letter says 'I must repeat that as far as I know you are the only person living who has anything intelligent to say about Milton'; he adds that I am also the only person who has observed the limitations of his own references to J.M. He begins (I can't resist telling you): 'My dear Charles, (unless you are to be addressed as the Blessed Charles, but our Decretarial Etiquette Book contains no guidance for formal approach to the presently Beatified)'—Now, lots of people would keep that (I mean, that letter) dark—out of decency—but I don't know—to tell you seems to bless TSE and me and you at once.[1190]

They met during Williams's brief visits to London, and Eliot wrote amusing letters, often in a teasing tone. When Williams contributed a 'supplement' for the short-lived *Christian News Letter*, Eliot told him that certain people had found it unintelligible, so, 'I, being supposed to be fitted for the task by my experience in writing blurbs about witchcraft and hell, am expected to provide [...] some prefatory matter which will put readers in the right frame of mind to approach your supplement.'[1191]

But Williams knew that while Eliot would publish his criticism, theology, and fiction, he would not take on his poetry. He told Anne Ridler:

> Last week in London I talked to T.S.E. for ten minutes about this and that. He was most warm & intimate (as it were), but the amusing thing was that he said I was not to let anything stand in the way of the Taliessin poems; & when I pointed out I was not paid for them, he said, 'No, of course not'—but I was touched by his almost earnestness.[1192]

'I could wish either Faber's or the Press would pay me for verse', he lamented.[1193] But it never happened.

Even with Lewis, friendship mingled with other feelings. They attended each other's lectures, and met regularly as Inklings, usually at the Eagle and Child for lunch on Tuesdays or Wednesdays, and at Magdalen on Thursday nights. They read their work to each other, and Williams valued Lewis as a receptive hearer and critic. But his feelings about Lewis's enthusiasm for his ideas were mixed. After listening to a reading of *That Hideous Strength* at the Inklings, he told Anne Renwick:

> Lewis is becoming a mere disciple; he is now collecting the doctrine of exchange in the last chapter of the new novel. 'That,' he says, 'is all yours'—I do not deny it, but no-one else will think so; I shall be thought his follower everywhere. 'Rejoice always; again I say, Rejoice!'[1194]

As with Auden, the problem with having a famous disciple was that the disciple might get credit for the ideas; and Williams was tired of his own relative obscurity. He was pleased when Lewis dedicated his excellent short book *A Preface to Paradise Lost* to him, with lavish praise of his Oxford lectures; but Lewis's wording, on close scrutiny, belied the dedication's fulsome tone. Williams, he wrote, 'partly anticipated, partly confirmed, and most of all clarified what I had long been thinking about Milton'. The words seemed designed (even against logic; for how can one 'anticipate' what someone 'had long been thinking'?) to deny Williams's originality. 'You will not think me reluctant to acknowledge the great value of the book', he told Hunt:

> But I have seen so many reviews of it all treating it as the real original exploration & instruction that I was driven to say lightly even to [Lewis] the other day that our people—yours & mine—were reading M[ilton] so while his undergraduates were still in comparative outer darkness. [...] I have a faint feeling that the same thing is going to happen—with him or another—about Dante. It's extraordinary how an adult can still hanker—hanker? no; perhaps not so much as that—for ... for being called chief.[1195]

When Lewis published *The Screwtape Letters*, supposedly letters from an experienced devil advising his nephew on how to tempt a human soul, Williams reviewed it wittily for *Time and Tide*. Writing as 'Snigsnozzle', a fellow devil, he snarled at Lewis for revealing the secrets of infernal temptation and called for an official investigation: 'Letters from devil to devil are not meant for earth. [...] If many of the [human] wretches read them, we must be prepared for a serious increase in virtue.' He concluded, 'You will send someone, some very tactful devils—to see after Lewis?'[1196] Yet Lewis, invited to review Williams's pamphlet on Dante, telephoned to say that they 'had better not review each other's books any more'.[1197] Ostensibly Lewis was afraid of appearing biased; but did he have private doubts about Williams's views on Dante? Williams recommended Anne Ridler instead.

He remained quietly confident that his spiritual understanding was subtler than Lewis's. Telling Anne that he had been 'run after' by two young women looking for religious guidance, he added, 'Both of them began by admiring C.S.L.; both of them (he said blushing) convey somehow a faint impression of advancing in the grades'—that last phrase a distant echo of his Rosicrucian days. He told Anne that he missed her as a critic of his poems: 'No-one of a vivid brain ever talks to me about them. [...] CSL admires them & alludes to them, but—'[1198] Certainly he did not always accept Lewis's judgements. Finishing 'The Founding of the Company' in May 1943, he told Anne Renwick, 'C.S.L. says [it] is *not* very good. But I think he a little has decided what kind of stuff I ought to do, or anyhow I think I shall keep it.'[1199] There was, possibly, just a little class-consciousness in his view of the other Inklings: 'The educated, leisured, capable, cultured classes never produce either you or me', he remarked to Hunt. 'Well—I exaggerate, but near enough, near enough. Keats? "The ill-bred son of a livery stable keeper".'[1200]

And despite giving radio talks himself, for example one on the Authorized Version of the Bible in a series on 'Books that Made History', he had doubts about Lewis's hugely popular broadcasts. 'One has to be too rashly general', he remarked to Hunt:

> I have observed how even C.S.L. has to omit (because of time) points of some seriousness. For example, he made some play with this business of trusting Reason: 'If you trust Reason...' and so on. I reminded him of the pure agnostic answer: 'But I do not trust reason, not so far'. But there was not 'time'. Quite true, but if I had been a listener I should have lost all real interest when I realised that he had just left it out. [...] I do not much want the B.B.C. to use me. [...] I have a terrible fear that I shall be popularised, and then, when Romantic Love is Taken Up, and we are all Romantics on principle [...] what *then*?[1201]

For his part, Lewis found Williams continually fascinating. Often wrong, often guilty of bad taste, but never predictable, never under control. He remembered Williams, in a lecture, speaking of the tradition that Milton had made his daughters read Homer to him without understanding Greek, and 'went on to show us what it would have sounded like, in a misunderstanding and cockney voice', prefacing the performance with 'Of course I can't do the cockney very well'—which Lewis thought 'an example of wonderful self-ignorance'.[1202] But was Williams teasing his audience, engaging in a double-bluff? He was quite capable of it. One senses a distinct frisson reading Lewis's account of how, expounding a relentlessly pessimistic theology, Williams had argued that one should never tell people that they were 'not so unhappy as they thought', pointing out that in the story of Job:

> the weight of the divine displeasure had been reserved for the 'comforters', the self-appointed advocates on God's side, the people who tried to show that all was well—'the sort of people,' he said, immeasurably dropping his lower jaw and fixing me with his eyes—'the sort of people who wrote books on the Problem of Pain'.[1203]

At such moments Lewis felt that Williams was seeing through him, and beyond him.

But the Inklings remained essential to Williams, and it was not only Lewis who rejoiced in his company. It was perhaps in 1942, since it mentions his work on Dante, that Tolkien addressed a long poem to Williams, in the friendliest terms:

> Our dear Charles Williams many guises shows:
> the novelist comes first. I find his prose
> obscure at times. Not easily it flows;
> too often are his lights held up in brackets.
> Yet error, should he spot it, he'll attack its
> sources and head, exposing ramps and rackets,
> the tortuous byways of the wicked heart
> and intellect corrupt. [. . .]
> But heavenly footsteps, too, can Williams trace,
> and after Dante, plunging, soaring, race
> up to the threshold of Eternal Grace.

The poem mocks the obscurity of the Taliessin poems ('The thrones, the war-lords, and the logothetes'), but its affection is unmistakable. Addressing Williams as 'beloved druid-poet', Tolkien declares:

> Your laugh
> in my heart echoes, when with you I quaff
> the pint that goes down quicker than a half,
> because you're near. So heed me not; I swear
> when you with tattered papers take your chair
> and read (for hours maybe), I would be there.[1204]

Occasionally the Inklings hosted other congenial writers. In February 1943 the fantasy writer E.R. Eddison visited, and in October 1944 the South

African poet Roy Campbell, Lewis's former student—though there is no word of what Williams thought of them. Without such gatherings, he might have been consigned to the less than sparkling company of Gerry Hopkins and Fred Page, and the incessant demands of his disciples. The Inklings were, literally, a Godsend.

★   ★   ★

Not all of Williams's younger disciples had spiritual interests. He was naturally an inspiration to budding authors. Twenty-year-old Bruce Montgomery, reading Modern Languages at St John's College, met Williams when he submitted his book *Romanticism and the World Crisis* to the Press—he was the 'young man' who, Williams told Anne Ridler:

> wrote a book all about the shocking results of Romanticism—with which I disagreed in many places, because I should have called what he meant pseudo-Romanticism. But both Gerry & I thought it very good, & had him here to talk to. Your uncle [Milford] won't publish it, nor will Fabers—which I think a pity.

Montgomery went away, read Williams's poetry, and 'now writes to say he has done an exegesis of *Taliessin*. He babbled about writing a book, but [...] I headed him off; besides, learned as he seems to be—at 20?'[1205] Soon Montgomery would be known as a composer, and more widely as the detective novelist 'Edmund Crispin'. He became a friend, lunching with Williams and occasionally attending the Inklings, where he heard Tolkien read from *The Lord of the Rings*. Montgomery delighted in Williams's conversation, and 'was entertained by the habit Williams had of continuing at the next meeting with the half sentence he had broken off with as he caught his bus at the end of their previous encounter ("As I was saying, my dear fellah . . .").'[1206] Montgomery lent him crime novels by John Dickson Carr, and Williams introduced the young writer to his own literary agent. Montgomery repaid the favour by taking Williams as his model for the playwright Robert Warner in his first-published novel, *The Case of the Gilded Fly*. In August 1943 Williams sent him details of the Companions, presumably with an invitation to join; Montgomery's response is unknown.

He did, however, introduce Williams to his friends, Kingsley Amis and Philip Larkin, both reading English at St John's. Larkin was not much impressed by Williams's lectures, but he was writing a novel, *Jill*, whose plot—the moral and mental collapse of a student, centring on obsession with a fantasy girl who becomes disconcertingly real—owes something to Wentworth's story in *Descent into Hell*. When Larkin completed it in May 1944 Montgomery urged him to send the manuscript to Williams, who might read it and recommend it to Eliot at Faber—which Larkin described as 'such a tenuous and dizzying chain of impossibilities that I don't place much faith in it'. He was right, for Williams 'said he couldn't help'[1207]— though Faber eventually published the book anyway. Amis was called up in 1942 after just one year at Oxford, but Larkin was rejected for military service owing to poor eyesight and stayed at Oxford for a full three years. He came to know Williams quite well: in October 1943 he told Amis:

> Bruce [Montgomery] had to go on Thursday but we had lunch in the King's Arms with Charles Williams, who drank and wheezed and talked and beamed and produced proofs of his new poems and handed them round. I admire Charles Williams a good deal as a literary critic, and as a 'Pillar of the Swiss', as Dylan Thomas would spoonerize, but I don't give a fart for his poetry. This I endeavoured to conceal.[1208]

But he continued to admire Williams's fiction: in 1947 he told a friend, 'I am reading a 'new' Charles Williams—*Many Dimensions*—which I will lend you in due course.'[1209] In Larkin's memory, Williams would become a lively comic caricature, 'crazy as a coot', his lectures 'always full of the wildest misquotations. The one

> 'Tis chastity, my brother, chastity,
> That fortress built by nature for herself
> Against infection and the hand of war...

may be apocryphal, but I have personally heard him declaim "Oh, blind, blind, blind, amid the blaze of noon".'[1210]

Larkin may have been immune to the qualities of *Taliessin*, but other young poets were not. John Heath-Stubbs, who stayed on after his first degree to study for a B. Litt (blindness ruling him out for military service), attended Williams's Wordsworth lectures in 1940 and was impressed by their vivid originality, especially when Williams discussed the apocalyptic dream of the Arab with the stone and the shell in Book V of *The Prelude*. 'One of the meanings of this passage', Williams said, 'is this: if bombs were to fall on Oxford at this moment and Wordsworth were among us, he would grab the most important volume of poems he could find and endeavour to save it from the cataclysm. Being Wordsworth, he would probably seize his own poems—and he would probably be right.'[1211] He heard Williams read his *Taliessin* poems to the University Celtic Society, and they met properly when both were invited to give a public reading. Heath-Stubbs gave Williams a copy of his first book, *Wounded Thammuz*, in 1942, and, leaving Oxford the next year, followed it with his second, *Beauty and the Beast*. He visited Williams at the Press: they discussed Victorian poets, and agreed in disliking Herbert Read's psychoanalytic approach to Wordsworth. Heath-Stubbs would remain a notable poet and advocate for Williams's work until his death in 2006.

Heath-Stubbs was the centre of a group of student poets: there were Drummond Allison and Sidney Keyes, who came to read history at Queen's College in 1939 and 1940 respectively, and Ian Davie,[1212] who edited *Oxford Poetry 1942–3* for publication by Blackwell. They would meet for conversation, which was a 'brimming buzz of allusions to saints, kings, martyrs, myths, miracles, bishops, ghosts and quotations'.[1213] Naturally, Williams's work was congenial to them. Keyes, having already based his poem 'Gilles de Retz' on material from *Witchcraft*, met Williams during his last term and was hugely impressed, listing Williams, Eliot, Graves, and Heath-Stubbs as 'the only living writers I accept entirely'. Called up in 1942 and killed in Tunisia seven months later, aged twenty, Keyes completed two important volumes of poems, *The Iron Laurel* and *The Cruel Solstice*; his last poem, 'The Grail', is about Blanchefleur, and took its imagery from *Taliessin Through Logres*. Drummond Allison, like the young Williams, dreamed of writing 'a long Arthurian epic':[1214] his sequence of bleak Arthurian poems (he was called up and killed in 1943) is probably also a response to *Taliessin*. Contact with these poets made Williams feel that he was contributing to the future of English poetry. 'I was told the other day, quite gravely', he wrote to Hunt, 'that I had done the pioneer work for the young poets. Most gratifying, and possibly true.'[1215] And to Michal he quoted Kipling: 'After me cometh a builder; tell him I too have known.'[1216] Through such writers, despite in some cases their tragically brief lives, he became an influence on the British poetic movement known as 'Neo-Romanticism' or 'the New Apocalypse'. 'One young man', he reported to Michal, 'told me that every public-house in Oxford has heard bits of my "geometrical verse" spoken!'[1217]

One tangential connection is worth mentioning. At some point the future actor Christopher Lee, then working as an office junior in London, attended Williams's lectures and visited him at the Press.[1218] Lee knew of

Alice Mary, who was living in Bermuda, for on 1 July 1940 Williams wrote
to her:

> By the way Christopher Lee is in Oxford for a week or two and asked (shyly)
> after that 'most attractive and intelligent lady in the Library'. So I told him all
> and he is very startled and is sending you his good wishes.[1219]

Sixty years later, Lee would play Saruman in the films of *The Lord of the Rings*.

★   ★   ★

Williams's chief concern continued to be the *Taliessin* poems. Increasingly
they drew directly on his life with the Companions; he told Anne Ridler,
'the household (in the Myth) seems to loom over this group [of poems] so
far even more. I am playing with another called *The Founding of the Company*.
But the more serious narrations remain to be done.'[1220] When complete,
'The Founding of the Company' mythologized the Companions of the
Co-Inherence as a kind of knightly order, 'the king's poet's household', an
organization which has:

> no decision, no vote or admission
> but for the single note that any soul
> took of its own election of the Way[.]

The 'household' has three levels: first, those who practise ordinary goodness,
who:

> lived by a frankness of honourable exchange,
> labour in the kingdom, devotion in the Church, the need
> each had of other;

—but 'The Company's second mode' involves those who practise substitution:

> it exchanged the proper self
> and wherever need was drew breath daily
> in another's place, according to the grace of the Spirit
> 'dying each other's life, living each other's death'.
> Terrible and lovely is the general substitution of souls[.]

The third level seems—though Williams's lines are hard to interpret—to be
that of the few who experience mystical vision:

> where the full salvation of all souls
> is seen, and their co-inhering, as when the Trinity

> first made man in Their image, and now restored
> by the one adored substitution; there men
> were known, each alone and none alone,
> bearing and borne, as the Flesh-taking sufficed
> the God-bearer to make her a sharer in Itself.

He had written *Taliessin Through Logres* in close dialogue with Anne Ridler. Now he found her absence a handicap. 'I brood on & off on the new poems', he told her in late 1942:

> but nothing much gets done. You have to remember that you are not here. [...] And no one else can correct, challenge, expand, modify, rebuke. My wife obscurely loves and often reads, but her excellent Highness is either silent or devastating (generally with justice). [...] I shall continue to believe that your most constant Femininity's love did a great deal more for Taliessin than ever you believed[.][1221]

Still, inspiration had at times come from other quarters. When Anne Renwick, who had now left Oxford, wrote to him in April 1943, asking for the Companions to undertake substitution for her sister, who was seriously ill, he told her, 'I will do something about that; what, I do not quite know, and we may, of course, see no result. But the Companions shall be brought secretly to bear.' He continued:

> I have taken those two sets of verse which I wrote for you and you typed for me and out of various bits of each I have made a formal Taliessin poem. It is called *The Queen's Servant*, & isn't bad; and when a gentleman called Tambimuttu asked me for a poem for a thing called *Poetry (London)*, I sent him it, & he says he would love to print it. [...] There is some talk of Tambimuttu doing a pamphlet of Taliessin poems.[1222]

Meary James Thurairajah Tambimuttu had come to London from Ceylon in 1938. A poet and editor of erratic brilliance, he had established *Poetry London* as a leading literary journal. Twenty-seven years old, he knew everyone in bohemian London, and though impecunious and unsystematic, published an astonishing array of important and innovative writers during the war years: the contents pages of his magazine, and its book-publishing offshoot, Editions Poetry London, are a roll-call of the liveliest poets, novelists, and critics of the day. Probably Anne Ridler had told Tambimuttu about Williams: Tambi had recently published her pamphlet *A Dream Observed*. Williams was far from seeing Tambimuttu as the answer to his poetry-publishing problems. On the contrary, he hoped to bring out a full-sized volume from a mainstream publisher; in May 1943, trying to write 'a poem on Taliessin taking Camelot', he told Michal, 'it is absolutely necessary for me to get rid of these odd poems somehow; they clog me, & I must get on to the Dolorous Blow and the Conception of Galahad'. Clearly these were meant for a subsequent and larger book.[1223]

Still, a pamphlet from Editions Poetry London would make a fine interim publication. He planned to include eight poems. Rather than following in narrative chronology those in *Taliessin Through Logres*, they fitted, in narrative sequence, between the poems already published. Besides 'Taliessin in the Rose Garden', 'The Founding of the Company', 'The Queen's Servant', and 'The Prayers of the Pope' (a revised version of 'Dives Dimisit') they included a 'Prelude' setting out the geography of the imagined Arthurian world; 'The Calling of Taliessin' on the bard's early life and travels; and 'The Meditation of Mordred', a masterpiece of cynicism in which Arthur's illegitimate son, doomed to kill him in battle, displays his contempt for all the values of the Arthurian kingdom:

> My father dwelled on the thought of the Grail for his luck,
> but I can manage without such fairy mechanism.
> If it does prove to be, which is no likely thought,
> I will send my own dozen of knights to pull it in.

[...]

> Here, as in the antipodean seas,
> I will have my choice, and be adored for the having;
> when my father King Arthur has fallen in the wood of his elms,
> I will sit here alone in a kingdom of Paradise.

The pamphlet would be called *The Region of the Summer Stars*—a phrase from the medieval Welsh *Song of Taliesin*. Lewis later wrote, 'I doubt if C.W. attached more than an "emotive" significance to it',[1224] but he could not have been more wrong. As 'The Calling of Taliessin' (lines 250–7) makes clear, Williams associated the phrase with the sphere of Venus as described by Dante in the *Paradiso*; with the 'third heaven' mentioned by St Paul;[1225] and with the 'feeling intellect' of the Snowdon episode in Book 14 of Wordsworth's *Prelude*.[1226] It was the realm of loving and creative vision from which, as a poet, he aspired to view the world.

Characteristically, Tambimuttu took his time over the book: by late August 1943 Williams had heard nothing. He told Joan Wallis:

> I wait—with slight impatience—for the proofs of the eight poems which are to make up *The Region of the Summer Stars*: there are some good things in it.

But I need...I do not know what I need; yes, I do. C.S.L. *et hoc genus omne* are admirable, but (in a way) useless. You have done, in your time, more towards the creation of great verse than all the Great. [...] Oxford is friendly, but sterile; I have known you encourage fruit; smoke your next cigarette to that.[1227]

But it would be well over a year before the new book saw the light of day. And those hints to Joan Wallis ('I do not know what I need; yes, I do') made it clear that Williams believed as strongly as ever that to produce his best work, he required female assistance and 'transmutation of energy'.

★ ★ ★

The writer and mystic Evelyn Underhill had died in London on 15 June 1941, just after Williams arrived to address a conference of clergy at Pleshey, the retreat house where she had taught. They had met more than once, though we know only that they discussed *Descent into Hell* and substitution: Underhill told Williams that he was mistaken in thinking it impossible for one human being to take on the sins of another. 'Oh', she said, 'but the saints do—they say they do. St. Catherine said: "I will bear your sins".'[1228] Soon there were suggestions that he should edit Underhill's letters—though he resisted any idea of writing a biography.[1229] The publisher Longman wanted a selected volume of letters, so he undertook it, though not without grumbling: 'To such hack jobs do we all come', he sighed to Joan Wallis.[1230] It proved difficult. Underhill naturally had disciples, many with strong views of their own. 'The Underhill letters are proving to be a minefield', he told Phyllis Potter, adding—with an allusion to *The Old Curiosity Shop*:

> Everyone is explaining to me (a) Codlin is the friend and not Short, (b) the truth about E's attitude to the Roman Church, (c) that there are numbers of intimate letters which they do not want published but which would help me to understand, (d) that there are people in the back-ground whose advice would be useful to me, (e) that I shall, of course, do it wonderfully and (f) that if I don't they will be able to put it right.[1231]

His long introduction to the letters, finished in mid-February 1943 and published in November, was carefully uncontroversial, but made the interesting suggestion that Underhill's classic book *Mysticism* had been written out of an 'impossibility': the point when Underhill, profoundly drawn to the Roman Catholic Church but repelled by the Pope's encyclical against

'Modernism', had remained an Anglican whilst feeling that she could not accept Anglicanism. 'One is apparently left to live alone', Williams wrote:

> with an Impossibility. It is imperative, and in the end possible, to believe that the Impossibility does its own impossible work; to believe so, in whatever form the crisis takes, is of the substance of faith; especially if we add to it Kierkegaard's phrase that, in any resolution of the crisis, so far as the human spirit is concerned, 'before God man is always in the wrong.' [Though] we should add to it the opposite and complementary truth that, also before God, man is always in the right[.][1232]

So Underhill's development was linked to his own critical theory, and his painfully achieved view of his own life.

★   ★   ★

Slowly, signs of public recognition were coming his way. In April 1942 he and Michal were invited to Canterbury to attend the enthronement of William Temple as Archbishop. And early in 1943 he heard that Oxford University proposed to give him an honorary MA. He was pleased, and broke the news romantically to Michal on Magdalen Bridge before telling anyone else. But he had niggling doubts. At first he assumed he owed the honour mainly to Lewis and Tolkien, but then he heard rumours that it was more a matter of courtesy to the Press: honorary degrees had been given to 'certain old servants of the Clarendon Press',[1233] and now they were doing the same with the London branch. This changed his feelings. 'In my worst moments', he told Michal, 'I do not wish to owe the Press a pin's head, & I most certainly do not wish to be patronised by Chapman and Milford.'[1234] When Milford offered to pay any fees that might be due, Williams's hackles rose again; he suspected the money might be withheld from any payment he received for a future book. But then he heard that the Vice-Chancellor himself had been keen on his receiving the degree, which cheered him up. And the Douglases offered to pay for hiring his academic gown.

He greatly enjoyed the ceremony, held on 27 February. Michal came from London, and the Latin citation praised him not only as critic and publisher but as 'a distinguished poet' who 'has recently received great acclaim', and as a lecturer: 'With what sharpness of mind he expounded, with what fervour of spirit he recited!'[1235] His ritual training came in useful: Lewis later reported hearing that Williams appeared to be 'the only Graduate who understood what a Ceremony was, & what it was about'.[1236] The *Times* carried a report, mentioning 'the well-known lecturer and critic, Mr. Charles Williams'.[1237] Charles and Michal had lunch afterwards with the Vice-Chancellor and other dignitaries.

20

'It Is Not Yet Too Late'

Despite his dislike of radio, the broadcast of *The Three Temptations* in November 1942 showed that Williams had a dramatic grasp of the medium. Remarkably, the play manages to compress the baptism of Jesus by John the Baptist, the temptation in the wilderness, and the crucifixion, all quite coherently into thirty minutes. It is notable for presenting Judas as Everyman: wanting only a comfortable life, he simply does what, the play suggests, most people would be capable of doing. There is no separate spokesperson for the dramatist. Instead, commentary is provided by Herod's unsparing view of his own actions, together with the comments of Caiaphas the high priest and Pilate the Roman governor. As Herod puts it:

> My dear Caiaphas,
> We all depend on Everyman. Why shouldn't Everyman
> have his place in damnation as well as we?
> If you think it damnation. I do,
> and prefer it. You do—and pretend it's faith.
> Pilate does, and he pretends it's duty.
> Judas Iscariot is of the same flesh as we,
> and prefers the quiet temporary comfort of damnation
> to the crucifixion of glory: don't you, Judas?

Remarkably powerful, the play shows how dark Williams's theology had become. He now had little faith in either established institutions or the impulses of most human beings: something which may reflect engagement both with Kierkegaard and the 'crisis theology' of Karl Barth, whom he had quoted extensively in *The New Christian Year*.

He continued, however, to believe in the value of prayer and the sacraments. In 1944, for example, writing to Michael, he emphasized the importance of:

prayers.. not meaning petitions, but a small effort towards life in grace. [. . .]

Besides life-in-grace is the only really bearable life. Life without grace is a wearing and irritating and intensely egotistic proceeding. It's an odd fact that, though concentration on a thing is necessary in order to get it, yet concentration on oneself is certain to ruin oneself. It's like always staring in a mirror; one sees everything out of proportion. Grace, among other things, means attention to things as they are. Myself, I think that the Eucharist is of high value there, because that does, over a period, work: it provides one point of heaven to which to attach oneself freely and firmly[.][1238]

On another occasion he told Michael:

There are two kinds of prayer chiefly: with words, and without, both important, but that with words meant (generally) to lead up to the other. An important thing is regularity. And another important thing (which you will know) is that one's immediate wishes or re-actions are *un*important & irrelevant. I mean that, for example, whether one *wishes* at any moment to pray is quite immaterial. It is asserted (and I agree) by everyone who does it that there is more not-wanting than wanting. No one can begin to do the right thing without being interfered with: ourselves? the Devil? God knows, but there it is.[1239]

★ ★ ★

After much revision *The Figure of Beatrice* was published in June 1943. Offering a detailed reading of Dante, it was best suited to be read alongside Dante's text: something readers could use for comment and interpretation as they made their way through Dante's works. Less startling than some of Williams's earlier criticism, it is full of insight. Lewis called it:

a book every student of Dante must reckon with—the sort of book which may offend narrow experts as much by its merits as by its faults. If [Williams] knows less than they about Florentine politics and the history of the language, he knew a good deal more about poetry and love—possibly about Heaven and Hell.[1240]

The reviews were equally good. Christopher Hollis in the *Tablet* said it should be 'read and re-read until it becomes part of the furniture of the mind'.[1241] The *Times Literary Supplement* ran a full-page review praising Williams's 'delicate sensitiveness to [...] Dante's mighty argument', and crediting him with 'a work that continually evokes rays of fresh light from facets of Dante's jewel'.[1242] Reviewing the book for *Time and Tide* Anne Ridler, clear-headed as always, kept her feet on the ground, praising his treatment of the *Inferno* and *Purgatorio* but calling his discussion of the *Paradiso* 'somewhat repetitive' and 'a little disappointing', and the writing 'mannered'.[1243] Privately, Williams admitted that she was right:

> I said [...] when the book was finished, that the last third was merely chat. [...] The crown of a holy life would be to comment properly on the *P[aradiso]*; so it's not unnatural that a non-holy life shouldn't be able to. But we needn't tell everyone that.[1244]

The book's achievement was widely recognized, even in Oxford, where it led to his being invited to join the highly respected Dante Society. The outspoken Maurice Bowra of Wadham declared it 'scandalous' and 'a condemnation of our whole system' that he had not been offered a Fellowship.[1245] It remains unknown whether Bowra, not yet head of his college, tried to get Williams a fellowship.

Even before *The Figure of Beatrice* appeared, Williams was talking to Eliot about possible sequels: in April he proposed one on Wordsworth, to be called *The Figure of Power*,[1246] and in June one on King Arthur,[1247] to be called *The Figure of Arthur*. Had they been completed, the books would have formed a trilogy dealing with the central themes of his life: the spiritual way of romantic love, the power of poetry, and the Arthurian myth. Eliot showed enough interest to keep the ideas alive, but made it clear that Faber really wanted another novel. So Williams submitted a proposal for *The Figure of Power*, based on his university lectures, to Milford instead. He negotiated through his agent, Nancy Pearn: not something he normally did with the OUP. It was a mistake, as he told Anne Ridler:

> I said it would save [Milford] discussing money with me—which he hates doing, if my Miss Pearn wrote to his Miss Peacock. So he agreed, and so she did, asking for the terms Fabers give me—nothing very shattering. And after awhile I get a letter from Miss Pearn, quoting Miss Peacock: 'Sir H. M. would have liked to publish Mr. C.W.'s lectures, but he could not consider these terms. As you say these are the terms Mr. W. gets, no doubt you will be able to dispose of the book elsewhere.'
>
> This, after so many years, seems to me a little unkind. It has not, of course, been mentioned between us; our conversation being largely concerned with what I am to do about Robin. But I am Embittered, and more clear than ever that.. O never mind![1248]

It was a cruel snub, and crassly phrased (referring to 'lectures' rather than a book, as if Williams had submitted a bundle of notes). Still organizing 'substitution' for Robin Milford's depression, he might have expected at least

more tact. It strengthened his perception that at the Press he was unappreciated and treated with scant respect.

His main concern, however, was with the batch of *Taliessin* poems he had
submitted to Tambimuttu. It was not only that he wanted to see the poems
in print. He also wanted, simply, to get them 'out of the way'—a phrase he
used repeatedly[1249]—so that he could move on to other poems. There would
be, he wrote to Michal, a 'third *Taliessin* volume', and he would dedicate it
to her.[1250] He wanted, he confessed to Joan Wallis, to 'get on to the longer
ones'[1251]—poems which would be 'graver than our last'[1252] and, he thought,
better. The unpublished poems 'clog me; and I must get on to the Dolorous
Blow and the Conception of Galahad'.[1253] He felt a painful sense of urgency.
'There is not all *that* time to do what must be done',[1254] he told Michal; and
again, 'It is not yet too late for me to beat all the rest of my generation at
their own game.'[1255]

Sometimes his conception of future poems took a playful tone. In
December 1943 he suggested to Anne Renwick:

> One of these days I will write you another Taliessin poem…I may even write
> it about whatever equivalent of a bath-room they had in Camelot or Almesbury,
> or indeed Carbonek…that is not a bad idea, Irene. We might write one about
> the princess Helayne bathing.. yes; we might. And the Dolorous Blow, by a
> process of substitution.. m'm, yes; you see? I am rather taken with the idea!
> but the bathing should be before the Blow or after the Healing. Well—keep
> me to it.[1256]

Meanwhile, Tambimuttu was infuriatingly slow. He published one poem,
'The Queen's Servant', in *Poetry London* in July,[1257] alongside work by Keith
Douglas, Alun Lewis, Louis Macneice, Stephen Spender, and others. But
proofs of the book did not arrive until early October.[1258] And though
Williams, speedy as ever, returned them corrected a week later, chaos duly
followed. Nothing was heard for nearly nine months. Then Tambi got in
touch to say he had lost the proofs. 'At least, he says "the printer"', Williams
reported; 'but I know that printer.'[1259] Enclosing a new set of proofs for correction, Tambi said he 'could not give any date' for publication.[1260] Williams's
comment—'tiresome creature!'—was a masterpiece of self-control.

The more so, as he found writing increasingly hard. 'I cannot quite
describe the extreme effort which the act of writing now seems to demand',
he had told Thelma in April 1943.[1261] This was especially true of poetry: to
Michal he confessed, 'I could write a book in less time than it takes to revise
a dozen lines of verse'; though 'more capable of writing' than he had been

for the past two years, he 'positively loathe[d] the writing'.[1262] Some of this was sheer mental exhaustion. Through 1943 he continued the relentless round of lectures, talks, and readings, combining Press and university work with speaking at conferences at Pleshey, and addressing students at Reading, pupils at Radley, Catholics at Pusey House, naval cadets at Balliol, poetry enthusiasts at St Mary's Church, the Fellowship Of Reconciliation ('whatever that is')[1263] at Ferry Hinksey, and many more.

His physical health was also suffering. He had to wear elastic stockings for varicose veins,[1264] and there were occasional ominous twinges of stomach pain: he put them down to 'wind' but the pain was bad enough, one morning, to make him wonder if he would be able to lecture; however, it passed off.[1265] The constant speaking, after travelling on cold, dark, delayed wartime trains, 'takes it out of me more', he told Michal; 'and there's nowhere to relax afterwards. I could cry with pity for myself; [...] And my back is a little aching, and my legs are very much aching, and I want to be taken care of!'[1266] He tried not to burden her with complaints, but it was hard.

★　★　★

In the background lurked the matter of the novel. In the summer of 1943 it was nearly six years since *Descent into Hell* had appeared. Williams had been hankering for years to write another, but for the first time had trouble finding his theme. As long ago as June 1940 he had asked Michal to 'think of a subject for a new novel. [...] Let it be supernatural this time, because I am more certain there.'[1267] Slowly something crystallized. In July 1940 he told Thelma Shuttleworth that:

> the difficulty is that the theme must be beyond *Descent [into Hell]*—it should be, I think, an account of heaven, & I doubt if I can do heaven. An account of the timeless in terms of time is bound to seem silly.[1268]

By September it had drawn in some ideas which would be used in his play *Frontiers of Hell*. He told Anne Ridler:

> It has occurred to me that a novel might arise: the cause was—(a) the bombing of London (b) air (c) Raphael, the archangel of Air (d) archangels (e) archangels— spirit—close to and ruling matter but not in it (f) the 'lost archangel' wanting to get in (g) but according to his own nature which is disturbance (h) disturbance and hate (i) man disturbed (j) bombs. But I don't know. If I saw my way, and could write or had ever been able to write, it might be a good book. But everyone would say it was not a novel.[1269]

To Joan Wallis he added that he had:

> a half-mind to make the human figure a man, of approaching middle-age, and [. . .] a painter. But I cannot see how to get him among the archangels, even if we should begin or end with the bombing—and with his unknown death?[1270]

At the end of 1940 he had written to Eliot with a sketch of his ideas, to see if Faber might be interested. Eliot was cautious, stressing the need for the novel to fit a familiar *genre*. The ideas, he said, were of 'great interest', but:

> what *qua* publisher and blurb-writer I am concerned with, is the slickness of the detective-story-thriller machinery which remains to be built up. That you can accomplish this feat I know; but don't forget its importance in selling the book. And after all, one of your most important functions in life (which I have endeavoured to emulate in *The Family Reunion*) is to instill sound doctrine into people (tinged sometimes with heresy, of course, but the very best heresy) without their knowing it.[1271]

Williams sent a synopsis in January,[1272] but the book went no further for the time being.

In June 1943, however, having sent his poems to Tambimuttu, he turned back to the novel, rereading *Descent into Hell* and *Witchcraft* to attune his imagination. He had discussed it again with Eliot, who was 'more than receptive', indeed 'eager' for it.[1273] Soon imaginative conceptions were stirring, and Williams would 'lie at night [. . .] with a kind of ghostly skeleton of a novel, and wake scared and unrefreshed'.[1274] By the end of the month he was writing, and had introduced a painting and 'light', though still without much notion of a plot;[1275] in early July he told Anne Renwick, 'I cannot, so far, get things to happen—I cannot *think* of anything. I stumble about in the first chapter.' He seems to have hoped that she might inspire the novel as Phyllis had inspired *Many Dimensions*. 'I need you to flatter me', he told her:

> —flatter? No; say, feed with a dance of words. These things are always easier if one has an alert and charming Intelligence at disposal [. . .] I am not quite certain that I will not write the novel to you, as it were, though the world will never know; but then you must dance for me as and how it can be. . .[1276]

Things moved slowly. A week later, he was 'agreeably engaged with a haunted house—only not really haunted, but all rather horrid—'[1277] but mostly he felt frustrated and gloomy. 'I am being forced into a novel', he complained to Joan Wallis: 'I push the sentences before me like bricks in a wheelbarrow; 'tis a glum prospect, but it's the only thing I can get paid for at the moment. The best thing so far is the title to the first chapter; which is called "The Noises that were not there".'[1278]

At that stage the draft certainly looked like a promising thriller. It began with the finding of the naked body of a dead girl in a deserted London house said locally to be haunted. It is just after the end of the war, and Challis, the policeman making the discovery, reports that he heard a bomb exploding but entered the house to find no damage and only a heap of sand which appeared to move and then somehow assembled itself into the corpse. Clarissa Drayton, a 33-year-old psychic investigator, is unofficially called in (her uncle is Assistant Commissioner at Scotland Yard). She is not surprised to hear that, at the post mortem, the body has dissolved with a gust of wind into a small pool of fluid 'held together by a dusty scum'. Clarissa predicts that analysis will reveal only dust and water. 'The air's gone', she comments, 'and there was very little fire.' She deduces that the material is the residue of a fiendish experiment: 'the devil trying to make a body'. It had failed, and the demon's explosion of rage was what Challis heard as a bomb. When Clarissa and Challis spend a night in the 'haunted' house, Challis (whose wife has been killed in the Blitz) falls in love with Clarissa; but soon it becomes clear that during the night he has been invaded by a demonic entity.

Meanwhile we are introduced to Clarissa's brother Jonathan, an artist. He has just completed a painting of a London scene after an air raid: it is a landscape of rubble and wreckage but also of radiant light. Jonathan, we are told, had wanted to call the picture 'Marriage', but his wife 'pointed out that a wild stretch of rubble and a few shadows under the name of *Marriage* might give quite a lot of people the wrong idea'. Jonathan's response is that in fifty years' time, people will understand.' "In fifty years", Marjorie answered, "I may not mind being represented by a devastating stretch of rubbish. But meanwhile—".'[1279] One suspects that Marjorie is a portrait of Michal, and that the picture, with its profound ambiguity, represents a view of Williams's own marriage. Perhaps Clarissa is intended as a portrait of Anne Renwick, whose 'alert and charming Intelligence' he hoped would inspire his work.[1280]

But the novel, entitled at this stage *Clarissa*, went little further. The plot was promising, but he wanted to introduce larger themes; and here lay the difficulty. He hatched a somewhat bizarre idea, which would be difficult to integrate with what he had already written:

> I have been toying with the idea of putting some-one rather like Anti-Christ into the new novel and making him a Jew, on the general opinion that not until the Jews have produced this figure as well as the Divine figure can their destiny be achieved. In which case there will have to be a long and purple passage explaining all that. The advantage of this is that it will take up several pages and save my bothering about the people in the novel.[1281]

Perhaps unwisely, he showed the draft to Michal. Her comments—not just on this, but on his previous novels too—left him shaken. 'I was very much struck', he told her tactfully on 3 September:

> by your remarks yesterday on my novels. You have still a little . . . devastation (let us say) in your language, but I realize that there is something profoundly true—an insight of the most accurate—in your comments on the wives, &c. (Mind you, they weren't *meant* like that, and I doubt if they strike men quite in the same way.) It's a weakness in the books, but that (I admit) only means that I can't do women—and never could. You were terribly right. [. . .] Three quarters of my mind is delighted that we are so at one about my discarded chapters; the other quarter is sad about the wasted work. Two months almost thrown away! But perhaps something better may come.[1282]

He started again. By mid-October he had written 'almost a quarter' of a new version, but still feared Michal's displeasure. 'I am worried about the "consolation" you required & I promised', he told her; 'perhaps it will appear. At present it seems rather sinister. However, there are ¾ of it to go, but I am so anxious to please you with it that I fuss a little.'[1283] Michal would have been even less pleased had she known that the previous month her husband had enlisted Anne Renwick as a power-supply for both the novel and some possible new poems. Apparently this could work over the telephone: Anne was now employed in London, and Williams wrote:

> I should like a little, at least until next June, to have you and your Image in mind occasionally as a background for the novel on which I labour, and the future poems on which I do not. If you are well and it can conveniently be done at any time, I would ring you up either at the Ministry or at home—give me the numbers and a suitable hour.[1284]

★ ★ ★

The novel, however, had by then become less urgent, because of an unexpected commission. He had been approached in August by Mrs Sarah Flecker, mother of the poet James Elroy Flecker, who had died of tuberculosis in 1915, aged thirty-one. Mrs Flecker wanted to commission a biography: not of her well-known son, but of her far less famous husband, Dr William Herman Flecker, Anglican clergyman and headmaster of Dean Close School, Cheltenham, who had died in 1941. Perhaps Mrs Flecker knew Milford: Williams told Anne Ridler that he was going to write the book 'For cash; all Caesar's fault, bless him!'[1285] Whether this meant the commission had come through Milford, or just that he was forced to take it because Milford didn't pay him enough, is unclear. Anyway, he buckled down without much enthusiasm: 'After the lovers of Florence, the old boys of England!' he sighed to Joan Wallis.[1286] He was uncomfortable with Mrs Flecker's demands for a fervent Evangelical style,[1287] but by the end of September had, he told Michal, 'the Flecker money in (we hope!) full view'.[1288] Canterbury Press commissioned the book, and by October he was settling to the work, cheerfully telling Michal that his life of Flecker *père* would be:

> a discourse on the theme of Responsibility—its necessity, the late Victorian version of it, the perversion of it, the serious and lofty passion of it, & it in Dr. Flecker. Now there is the first synopsis for you! do approve.[1289]

Of course, no sooner had he committed himself to Flecker than another commission appeared. The Bishop of Chichester was approached by Margaret Sinclair, who was looking for someone to write a play for the drama group of the United Council for Missionary Education. The Bishop passed her on to Williams in early October. She wanted something topical, relating to current events in the Far East:

> From all accounts [she wrote], the Japanese do seem to go to enormous trouble, in the South Sea Islands, [...] to hunt down the missionaries, who have moved out into the bush, with their Christian groups and have lived there for months.[1290]

They met in London in mid-October,[1291] and he told her he could write the play between March and September of the following year, 1944. Having by now learnt to drive a hardish bargain, he explained, 'My family as well as I depend on my writing for part of their necessities', so he would want £100 in advance, half in April and half on completion of the play. It would be in verse, he told her, but 'My own recent style does not make the stuff difficult to say. We are so colloquial nowadays.'[1292] To his delight, the Committee accepted his terms, so he told Michal he would hand over detailed negotiations to his agent, '& indulge myself with the prospect of the money. And of you & me going—yes, really!—after the war to see a New Play of mine'[1293]— for there were rumours that the war might be over within a year.

★   ★   ★

In September 1943 Williams received, unexpectedly, a letter from a young lady called Lois Lang-Sims. Twenty-seven years old and living in Canterbury, Lois had read a good many of his books, and been deeply impressed by hearing *The Three Temptations* on the radio. Earlier that summer she had bought *The Figure of Beatrice* and 'read it carefully more than once'.[1294] Since she was in the throes of an unhappy love affair, the book's discussion of romantic love as a spiritual path was of intense interest to her. But she wrote now with a question which went to the root of Williams's view of love: *Who*, in reality, is the object of the ideal lover's love? 'According to Charles', she explained:

> as I understood it, the human Beatrice of the here and now, [...] with all her faults, was not *in herself* the object of her lover's adoration, which was fixed upon Beatrice 'in her glory', the ideal Beatrice of the heavenly state. But, as I pointed out, one could not be absolutely certain that Beatrice was, ever had been, or ever would be, in that state.[1295]

If Wentworth, for example, in *Descent into Hell*, was damned, then 'what became of his "glory"?' If he had ever been loveable, then since his glory was never fulfilled, anyone loving him must have loved something which never existed. 'I did not want to be in love with an hypothesis', Lois confessed. With innocent deviousness, she posited a hypothetical 'Jane' who might be in love with a man, and might want to know who or what it was that, ultimately, she loved. Could Williams enlighten her?

Unwittingly, Lois had asked exactly the right question. It was a question that had the potential to crack open Williams's armour: the mythology that he placed around people and around his own life; the new names that he gave his friends and lovers, fitting a stylized version of each into his imaginative world; his unconscious reluctance to allow others to be fully what they inconveniently were. Lois's letter promised a salutary shock.

To his credit, he took it seriously and sent a careful reply, admitting that he didn't know what would happen to Jane's 'glory' if she ever reached hell, but suggesting that in the meantime what one would love would be 'Jane as God devised her', though, 'When Jane snaps her sister's head off, or indulges in malicious gossip, or whatever, it is clear that Jane is not being as God devised her. I do not find myself able to deny either fact.'[1296] He added that if we sometimes find Jane maddening, 'The maddeningness of Jane is generally due to our fallen nature as much as to hers. Or more.'[1297] Somehow this perfectly orthodox and sensible answer failed to satisfy Lois, and she wrote again. This time she revealed something about her own spiritual practice, and Williams perceived things that chimed with his own ideas about substitution and co-inherence. On 20 September (his fifty-seventh birthday) he replied, briefly taking up again the argument about love, but moving on to what perhaps interested him more:

> Some years ago there was begun a Company.. scattered and unknown to each other.. called of the Co-inherence, and when I can find a copy of the Promulgation I will, if you choose, send it. It involves you in nothing more than you are already involved in; that is its great charm.[1298]

He suggested she meet him for lunch in Oxford or, possibly, in London one weekend.

'Of course', Lois recalls, 'I accepted his invitation.'[1299] They arranged to meet for lunch in Oxford on 14 October, Williams stipulating, a little oddly, that they should meet beforehand at South Parks Road so that they could 'see each other first'. He may have meant exactly that: his poor sight might have difficulty spotting a stranger looking for him in a large room. Lois duly turned up just as the hall clock was striking ten. She had heard Williams described by her cousin, many years before, as a kind of clown who gave performances at Downe House. More recently, reading his books, she had envisaged him as a white-bearded sage. When the door was flung open she saw 'a grey-haired, fragile-looking man, with a deeply-creased, abnormally-sensitive face'. He wore a pinstripe suit, and as he stood above her 'in an attitude at once deferential and authoritarian', she found herself 'held by his gaze, which had a quality of intent stillness wholly at variance with the rapid flow of words and the constant jerky movement of his limbs and the muscles of his face'. So stunned by his presence that she could hardly take in what he was saying, she followed him into the house, and he flung himself 'sideways into a chair, his legs over the arm' in a strangely contorted posture.[1300]

Lois had the impression that she 'was, for some reason, greatly approved', and that she need do nothing but sit still and pay attention—not so much to what he said, which in any case she could scarcely follow, as to the mere fact that she was being addressed. When at last she was 'courteously dismissed' to wander into town whilst Williams set out for the office, she was surprised to find that she felt, in some strange way, 'committed' to Williams, though she had no idea what that might mean. 'Love and veneration', she recalled, 'had been aroused in me without my knowing how or why'; she also felt, uncomfortably, that she had been 'enspelled'. But more than anything, she felt 'a sharp-stinging ache of compassion for a being who had violently impressed me as being, humanly speaking, *alone*'.[1301]

At one o'clock they lunched at his usual table in the Randolph. They talked of Dante, but also of the spiritual 'task' which Williams seemed to assume Lois had, by virtue of being in love, already undertaken. He took it for granted that she was a member of the Company, and that ('in deadly earnest and yet as a kind of game') she would obey him. After lunch, as they sat in the lounge, he took her wrist, his hand 'quiver[ing] as if from a succession of electric shocks', and counted out on her fingers the command: 'Love—obey—pray—play—and be intelligent.' (She did not know it, but Williams was drawing on the traditional planetary attributions, beginning from the thumb, to Venus, Jupiter, Saturn, Apollo, and Mercury.) It was a mnemonic or spell that would echo in her mind. He also turned her hand over and made the motion of invisibly writing something on her palm. (One recalls his asking Thelma Shuttleworth, in 1930, 'have you ever [...] arranged for a pencilled message or name on your hands?')[1302] Perhaps he was already assigning her a new name. Soon he flung wide the hotel's doors and, as they reached the street, bent 'with a combination of ritual solemnity, old-fashioned courtesy, and whimsical playfulness' to kiss her hand, before disappearing into the crowd.[1303]

Lois was a young, beautiful, sensitive, and intelligent woman. Her account of her meeting with Williams shows how intoxicating, and how dangerous, his presence could be; and how easily his blend of natural charisma, spiritual power, and magical training could win disciples. Lois went away with her mind in a whirl: 'one felt a bit crazy after sessions with Charles', she reflected later.

Their correspondence, of course, continued, with Williams setting Lois 'tasks' and expecting what he unequivocally called 'obedience': for, he told her, 'you are at work, within the Church, for the Company, and for (kissing your hand on it) Us'.[1304] She was instructed to visualize the man she loved as he was, and as he might become at his perfect best, and to hold 'the twin images [...] before God' in her mind; she was to practise goodwill towards his mother, and towards her own; she was to practise substitution (how, he did not explain) and not to be surprised if as a result she found herself in 'some unexpected jam' (which would be the effect of a trouble from which she was relieving some other person). More ominously, Williams told her, 'You are engaged to report—as a mythical slave or schoolgirl should— yes?—on [these] four jobs'; and if she was 'lazy or inattentive or negligent or a truant', she was to tell him quite frankly, and 'I warn you I will have you, as frankly, pay for it.' He added that if she were willing to commit her- self for a year to 'making this movement? daring this discipline? practising this ritual? playing this game?'—then she was to write back, listing the five commands he had given for her fingers, and also finding five words to sum up the new tasks (the fifth being to report on the other four). She was, he told her, 'in the Myth', 'Blanchefleur (who was Percivale's sister and foster-warden of Galahad) and a girl slave'.[1305]

The correspondence shows how deeply erotic fantasy and spiritual direction were blended in Williams's mind. Much of the advice he gave was good, even traditional, and certainly well-intentioned. Yet it was framed within a fantasy of sexually charged control, and by asking Lois to reply in ritualized form Williams was ensuring that she felt psychologically com- mitted by her own act to the relationship as he defined it. Moreover, there can be little doubt that he expected to use the relationship as a source of energy for his creative work. From any point of view this was wrong. Yet Williams was far from being a cynical man. The fact that he could not clearly see the damage he was likely to cause indicates the depth of confu- sion which he had now reached. Fortunately, Lois turned out to be a match for him.

Over the following weeks, Williams set her specific tasks: for example, to copy out Shakespeare's Sonnet 116 six times, adding 'I shall have my ears soundly boxed for disobedience' (for she had committed some now- forgotten 'offence').[1306] But he also shared with her frankly his own memories of the agonies of unrequited love: 'have I not almost shrieked in the streets? and walked because I could not sit? and sat because I could not walk? and as for knocking one's head or biting the carpet—?'[1307] And he told her she was 'a serious neophyte and initiate, and an example to Us'.[1308] Early in December she visited him again in Oxford. She had already wondered whether anything would come of the punishments he had promised for various small lapses in her 'obedience', and had read in *Taliessin* of the slave girl who is beaten with a hazel rod for some fault:

> But I was not really expecting this poetic image to be carried over into actual life, until Charles picked up the heavy ruler from his desk and demanded that I should stand before him and hold out the palm of my hand. I did so at once. He struck the palm of my hand with the ruler, courteously and ceremoniously, but hard so that it hurt.
>
> 'What have you to say now?' he asked.
>
> I stood quite still and looked him straight in the eyes. 'Thank you,' I said. I was half angry and totally astonished; but I had no intention of revealing my astonishment.[1309]

Whilst Lois stood there in a state of shock, Williams put down the ruler and strode about the room, talking volubly and with intense agitation. At that moment Sir Humphrey Milford walked in. Williams, 'caught in the full spate of his daemonic inspiration',[1310] presented Lois to him in his usual courtly manner. Milford appeared quite unsurprised.

Lois returned home with a copy of *Paradise Lost* and instructions to write an essay on it, which she did. Soon other demands followed—most notably, the demand that she should undertake substitution for 'one of our people', as Williams put it, who was returning by sea from Bermuda with her child, and was extremely anxious about the voyage. This was Alice Mary, whom Lois had never met and of whom she knew nothing. Lois found it extraordinary that Williams should expect her to 'present [her]self shyly to Almighty God in exchange for' some total stranger, and be prepared to undergo this other person's fear—'including', she reflected, 'perhaps the terror of an actual disaster', in a sea beset by German U-boats. How could Williams ask this of her? Reluctantly she did her best, praying for Alice Mary, with 'a half-hearted codicil to the effect that here I was'.[1311] She experienced nothing out of the ordinary,[1312] but Alice Mary arrived safely. And Lois retaliated by asking Charles to take on her nervousness about teaching a Sunday-school class. Rather startled, he agreed to do it, and experienced 'something of a depression' during the day, which he accepted as the burden he had assumed.

So Lois kept something of the initiative. Moreover, her essay on Milton was so good that Williams read it aloud in the White Horse pub to Tolkien, Warnie, and Jack Lewis, who 'approved highly'.[1313] By this time, Williams had taken to calling her 'Lalage' (three syllables, with a soft 'g'), after a girl in Horace's Ode I.22. Lois was now convinced that she was in love with him, yet remained 'slightly resentful and very much perplexed'.[1314] The relation-ship was pervaded by a sense of unreality: she sensed that she had been conscripted into Williams's myth, 'a bubble which must not be pricked at any point'.[1315] And the price exacted was growing heavier. When she next visited him in Oxford, having again been threatened with punishment, 'after I had kissed his hand, kneeling on one knee, and he had kissed mine, he told me to bend over a chair and lift up my skirt. When I did so, he took the ruler and struck me hard on the behind. I stood up, feeling bruised in more senses than one.'[1316] Williams again strode about the room, talking at an immense rate, and then 'paused in front of me and, putting his arms about me, held me close to him in a strange stillness, a silence that could not have been more unlike his usual excitement'. At no time did he show any sign of sex-ual arousal. Lois was utterly perplexed. She returned home 'in a state of dangerous exhaustion, and almost immediately became seriously ill'.[1317] In retrospect she had no doubt that this was a result of Williams's actions.

Years later, when Lois had contact with Tibetan religious culture, she recognized that Williams had involved her in something resembling tantric practice—a practice he had imposed without her knowledge or consent. But in the immediate aftermath, she continued to write to him—even sug-gesting that he should have punished her more. By the spring of 1944 she was 'too weak to get across the room without [her] mother's help [and] could hardly lift a knife and fork'.[1318] Even then she went on writing to Williams, who sent letters teaching her the banishing pentagram ('for the banishing of Evil Spirits or Elementals and the stabilizing of the good'), and the Hebrew Tetragrammaton.

The question with which Lois had started returned ever more insistently. Did 'Lalage' have anything to do with the real Lois? How far did Williams's feelings for people really relate to *them*, and how far had he constructed fantasies which obliterated his awareness of their actuality? In May 1944, feeling rather stronger, she arranged to meet him again in Oxford, deter-mined to demand an answer, and to tell him that she could not continue their relationship on its current terms. Over lunch, she suggested to him that the Dantean way of love, as he interpreted it, was 'impersonal, inhuman, unconcerned with the actuality of its supposed object'.[1319] To her astonish-ment, Williams at once agreed. He offered no defence. Yet he seemed 'very much perturbed', and towards the end of the meal he asked Lois what she would suggest might be put in the place of such a love. 'Why', said Lois, 'a human relationship.' Williams's reply was as devastating as it was enigmatic.

'But child, what if his humanity were not human? How then could he have a human relationship?' They walked to Southfield House. In his office, Lois told Williams that she could not continue her 'obedience'. Almost to her shock, he accepted this. 'Springing to his feet and pacing the room, he declared that, of course, naturally, I must be loosed at once.' He gave her, 'seemingly at random', a copy of *Christian Symbolism*, kissed her hand, and bowed her out, murmuring 'Go with God'. Lois found herself alone on the street. She wept as she walked back to the station.

Months later she saw him by chance on the London Tube, reading a manuscript. She touched his arm and greeted him. Williams 'gave a violent start and blushed literally to the roots of his hair'. Yet again, Lois had challenged him, catching him outside his dramatic role. He grasped her hand warmly, said something she could not take in, and left the train at the next station. She met him once more, in Oxford early in 1945. She had been considering (but for the present decided against) becoming a Roman Catholic; also, the man she loved had announced his engagement to someone she knew, though not very well. She wanted to discuss both matters with Williams. They lunched in the Randolph (significantly, perhaps, at a different table from the one they had previously used), and she hoped for 'some trace [. . .] of his former tenderness and warmth'. But now nothing was the same— except for the flourish with which he kissed her hand on parting. They never met again.

★   ★   ★

'What if his humanity were not human?' Superficially, Williams's question referred to Dante; but patently, it was a personal confession. At that moment, then, Williams did not consider himself ('his humanity') to be human. What could he have meant? Lois connected it with lines from 'The Calling of Taliessin':

> 'It is a doubt if my body is flesh or fish,'
> he sang in his grief; 'hapless the woman who loves me,
> hapless I[.]'

We should be cautious about reading this as simply a personal statement, since the crucial first line is taken directly from the *Mabinogion*. Still, a possible interpretation is that Williams thought himself incapable of love— sexual love in particular, and perhaps all love. In 1943 he had told Thelma

Shuttleworth, "'At eventide," wrote St John of the Cross, "they will examine thee in love." I shall not perhaps pass very well; in fact, I shan't.'[1320] But perhaps he meant something else. Did he mean that he had suffered so much and so long that he was no longer human? Or did he mean that by long practice of 'transmutation of energy' he had become something *more* than human? We shall never know; but the words, and their sequel—'How then could he have a human relationship?'—sound desolate, the words of someone who felt himself utterly alone.[1321]

However, he was as busy as ever organizing substitution and prayer for Companions and others. Thelma Shuttleworth needed his support, especially in the summer of 1943, having been arrested for some offence connected with her pacifism. The details are not clear, but Williams was 'profoundly shocked and distressed', and, in line with the principle of co-inherence, told her:

> I feel, as it were, half-responsible, and as if you were paying the price of my freedom. So, of course, you are; that is, in some strange way, true; as much as the people who are dying for my safety. But that doesn't cut any ice in the ordinary sense. [...] I will have prayers said and thoughts sent for you.[1322]

He was haunted, he said, by the thought of Thelma in prison—and of Belgion, a prisoner of war in Germany ('so much can different ways lead to the same fate').[1323]

Anne Renwick's sister had been in hospital, and several Companions were at work 'carrying' her illness. And, by the divine irony which Williams so often recognized, he was called upon to arrange help for—of all people—Commander McDougall, Phyllis's husband, who had been suffering from severe depression—'having fits of melancholy, & wouldn't go to London alone, & wouldn't drive a car, & so on & so on'. Williams had the brilliant, if convoluted, idea that Robin Milford, whose depression the Companions were already trying to alleviate, might be asked to 'offer' his own melancholy on behalf of McDougall. Thus, one depressed person might help himself by helping another. 'I don't quite see [how] at the moment..if the [Commander] & Robin knew each other, it would be perhaps easier', he reflected. 'I am convinced still that along that way lies a great operation.'[1324] But by September he had found a solution and, he told Anne Ridler, had:

> proposed—well, rather more, I have demanded—that [Robin] shall put his glooms and griefs at my disposal, if and when he has them. [...]But what do I do with them? Fantasy beyond fantasy, substitution beyond substitution, death beyond death! I cause them to be offered for Celia's Commander!

This required the involvement of Margaret Douglas, apparently as a kind of link. Perhaps she knew both men. Anyhow:

I have caused one of the Companions—Margaret Douglas, a good woman, 49, fat, mindless, and seriously good; a faintly comic spinster, middle-agedly in love with me; *and* a pillar of spiritual purpose, of intended high generosities, probably a saint—odd!—I have caused her to be the knot of the Milford-MacDougall, the Robin-Archibald union.[1325]

So the complex web of substitution continued to ramify.

★   ★   ★

In November 1943, Williams received a letter from Eleanor Plumer, Principal of St Anne's College, asking if he would take Shakespeare tutorials for the college. Learning that he would be paid between twelve and sixteen guineas a term, he readily agreed, and for the rest of the war taught between two and four tutorials every week during term. His classes were much sought-after: when it became known that he would be teaching, under-graduates began 'hammering away' at their college tutors to be put into his classes.[1326] Owing to his OUP commitments, he taught in the evenings; and, St Anne's being then in South Parks Road, pupils came to No. 9 for their tutorials. The sessions began in January 1944.

Arriving at 8 p.m. students would be greeted by Williams, who seemed to be alone in the house: mysteriously, he contrived that other residents were never seen, though the Spalding sisters sometimes hung out of an upstairs window to get a glimpse of the visitors. He would take his pupils along the hall into a sitting room with armchairs, rugs, and many books. He would smoke incessantly as they read their essays, then stride about the room discussing the week's topic, pausing every so often to light a new cig-arette with shaking hands, throwing failed matches into the hearth when his tremor extinguished them. In winter a gas fire would be burning. In sum-mer, students might be invited out onto the veranda, and even offered a glass of sherry. At first they were nervous, but they soon found Williams a delightful and illuminating tutor. 'He had a very exceptionally courteous kind of address towards the person he was with', recalled one former pupil:

and [...] if you made a point in your essay [...] 'Oh, just stop there a minute,' he said, 'and let's think about that'—this statement whatever it was you'd made—and he'd turn it round and put it inside out and bring in 3 or 4 other instances from somewhere and then perhaps one or other of us would make a

little tiny offering that added to it, you know, and then he would calmly sort
of hand it back to you, and say 'Thank you very much, that was very interesting,' as though you'd provided it all, you know!'[1327]

'He didn't seem to mind', recalled another, 'that we were callow trembling
youthful immature people...not industrious enough for a start, and not
clever enough, to get as much as we should have got.'[1328] The emphasis of his
teaching was always on the text—'Go back to the text always and test it out,
don't rely on quoting from someone'—and on the student's own response:

> The whole message of the way he taught was, that what was important was
> your response to the piece of literature that you were reading. Nothing else
> mattered, [...] not having read the accepted critics wouldn't matter, it wasn't
> the point. The point was, what is *your* response to it? And that has stayed with
> one all one's life and been a guiding principle.[1329]

His enthusiasm seemed completely genuine. 'He was *really* interested, I think,
in poetry', recalled another pupil. 'He was really interested in "How does
the poet do this?"' And there was the stimulus of Williams's extraordinary
presence:

> I would sit there, entranced by his amazing personality. He was fire and
> air, immensely exciting; poetry seemed to take on a whole new meaning.
> I remember him saying—peering intensely at us—'My dear young ladies' (as
> he often called us) 'you must get poetry into your blood and your bones! And
> *especially* into your blood and your bones!' Though our subject was ostensibly
> I think Shakespeare and Jacobean dramatists, he would range over a wide
> variety of writers pouring forth lines from memory in his effortless intense
> magical way. He seemed seldom still. Everything he said seemed new and
> enriching to me.
>
> Individual words could be a treasure trove. He once set us an essay to write
> on the word 'strange' as used in Congreve's 'Let us be very strange and well-
> bred', *Midsummer Night's Dream*'s 'And grows to something of great constancy,
> But howsoever strange and admirable,' and a third which I think may have
> been Donne's 'By our first strange and fatal interview'—but I'm not certain
> about that.
>
> One emerged from the hour with him elated: seemingly on a different
> plane from that of everyday life, having been in touch with some visionary,
> more real world.[1330]

Not the least exciting aspect of these visits was his habit of flinging open the
house door with some remarkable utterance. One undergraduate recalled
being greeted with 'Why do you think the Elizabethans were so obsessed

with illegitimate children?' On another occasion it was, 'I want to say to my wife, "O star of eve . . . "'—or words to that effect.[1331] And there were references to Michal in pre-tutorial conversation:

> he would mention that he'd just *heard* from his wife, or he was *writing* to his wife, or he was *going* there this weekend, and he would always refer to her in a rather elaborate way, as though she were [. . .] a lady to whom all honour was due, you know. [. . .] It was a little bit *forced* . . . [. . .]—over the top, somehow, one sometimes felt. On the other hand *we* used to look at one other afterwards, and say, 'Why the hell aren't they living together?'[1332]

He was unstinting of his time, and pupils were only too eager to stay as long as they could:

> The first [. . .] two or three times [. . .] when we surreptitiously glanced at our watches and saw it was past nine o'clock we made kind of polite gestures, tentative movements, as though we understood we—but 'No, no, my dear young ladies, you don't need to go now!'—And then [. . .] he kept us there sometimes till 11 o'clock; and it was marvellous of course.[1333]

Afterwards, they would leave the house 'sort of elated, [. . .] living in a different world [. . .] afire with enthusiasm for what we were studying, which—however good the other lecturers were, and they were very good—we didn't get that.'[1334] For many of his pupils the question 'What would Williams have said about this?' became 'a touchstone for one's thinking about literature.'[1335] As Joy Stephenson summed up:

> He was, I suppose, the most remarkable person I ever met in my life, the most unusual person. [. . .] He didn't in the least make you feel how inadequate you were in comparison with him, he somehow kind of lifted you up there into this other plane with him, which was just so lovely.[1336]

During these tutorials there was never a hint of anything religious, magical, or sexual. Williams stuck strictly to tutorial business, and did it incomparably well. The inspiration and enlightenment he brought remained lifelong: in one former pupil's words, 'unforgettable, unforgotten'.[1337]

21

'Into the Province of Death'

On 1 December 1943 Charles Wall died at Leyton. In recent years Williams had rarely seen his uncle, who had been editing a fervently Anglo-Catholic monthly, *Credo*—later called *The Fiery Cross*. He left little money; his books went to Charles, who kept 'two or three' on Arthurian subjects and sold the rest.[1338]

He was again preoccupied with Michael. Now twenty-one, Michael had been living in Hampstead with his mother since early 1943 and working in Bumpus's bookshop. The emotional storms seemed to have settled: Michal was 'working wonders' with him and Charles sensed 'a kind of peace emanating' from their London flat.[1339] With his mother there to get him up, fed, and out of the house each morning, Michael seemed better for 'the relief and the care and the regularity'.[1340] But Michael was discontented. He didn't want to spend the rest of his life working in bookshops, but neither had he any idea of what he would rather do. He vaguely considered taking evening classes. 'I thought the Spanish a very good idea', Charles assured him in June 1943; 'South America will grow more & more important.'[1341] Three months later, Charles was writing to a friend at County Hall to see what was available: 'He has general ideas of a rather vague kind on the history of drama, Spanish, salesmanship, and I have added to these the possibility of whatever courses are given, if any, on cinemas [sic].' Charles added that unless he wrote on his son's behalf, Michael 'will mean to up to the next moment after the last'.[1342] Even university was vaguely considered—perhaps a degree in English at the University of London—though how this would be financed is not clear.[1343]

Meanwhile, Charles coached Michael in literary journalism and introduced him to Theodora Bosanquet, literary editor of *Time and Tide*. In June

1943, he suggested Michael write 'a short notice of *Case 27* [a play], and send it to Theodora':

> I think you ought to keep up your contact there, & here with an all but first night is a good opportunity. Keep it shortish and leave it (if you can) at the office on Monday. [...] She was quite sincere when she said she wanted to see more of your work.[1344]

By the end of the year Michael was regularly reviewing theatre and biography for *Time and Tide*. He chose the pen name 'Michael Blain', and in August 1944 the magazine published reviews by father and son on the same page.[1345] 'There are both your men together, and both quite good. Absurd, but gratifying', Charles rejoiced to Michal.[1346]

But emotional problems recurred. Michael had periods of depression, and outbursts of anger which became violent. In October 1943, Charles told Michal, 'I'm so nerve-ridden over Michael and his goings-on [...] that I can't get on with writing.'[1347] In June 1944, after an evening at Oxford, Michael 'made trouble' in a way that caused physical destruction at the flat. 'I don't know what damage happened to the place', Charles wrote to Michal, 'but after the workmen'—for they had been having building work—'this must have been a nice thing to happen!'[1348] He wrote in carefully soothing terms to Michael:

> I'm sorry—very sorry—about your sensations and emotions. Seeing one kind of life and being imprisoned in another is a very difficult thing; [...] I have felt much the same, though that won't help you. But one is in a state of helpless and irritable revolt, and apt to say and do all sorts of silly and useless—not to say cruel—things. [...]
>
> You need not tell me that I myself don't manage it terribly well. I know that. Our nerves, our longings, our tempers, our secret powers, are all at odds. But even if I have crashed very often, if I have failed to...well, never mind; but I was going to say that I have tried not to tyrannise. By which I mean not to 'take it out' of others. [...]
>
> I hope all this will not merely annoy you. I know just as well as you the maddening horror of gloom that takes one. I know also that, *if* one can hold through it, what are called 'the child' or Grace or Love—something quite certain and fixed and absolute—looks through it; and one is, perhaps only for a moment, different.[1349]

Trying to keep Michael on an even keel by letter was a persistent concern. Charles tried to boost his son's self-confidence, and his confidence in his father's love. 'I have for you an admiration much in excess of what many fathers feel', he told Michael on his twenty-first birthday in June 1943. 'You have real personal talents—wit, intelligence, charm, and (if you will let me say so) a certain free goodness. [. . .] I admire you and I love you, and it is a solid fact that, in your best form, I could wish for no better companion.'[1350] And in May 1944:

> One of your own great capacities is a kind and intelligent mind. You are as clear-headed in things of the spirit as you are in business. And I could dream of no better gift! [. . .] I salute in you the undoubted marks of the Way. It is a long Way, but (unless everything is lunatic, which I do not believe) the End is quite certain.[1351]

These protestations could not compensate for a childhood in which Michael had been largely neglected by his father. Moreover, Michael was tormented by anxieties about his sexuality. Cryptic passages in letters from Charles suggest that Michael was confiding in him about encounters that troubled him; though the details remain unclear. 'I am sorry about the other incident', writes Charles on 10 December 1943:

> and very glad you told me. I think, from all you said, you behaved admirably, and had the re-action which (if I may put it like that) a gentleman should. [. . .] If you find yourself disposed to avoid the unfortunate creature (I mean 'unfortunate') then, as much as you can, I should. If not, then don't; treat it as a remark for which you have absolutely no use, and (as it were) drop it delicately and firmly overboard, with perhaps the faintest obviousness. It is, after all, a legal offence, and wretched poor men are had up by the police. But discreetly avoid being à deux with him. Firmness—even decisiveness—and courtesy.[1352]

Again, in March 1944, when Michael has been invited out for the evening, his father writes:

> I should certainly go. [. . .] At the very worst, there can be nothing but a slight disagreeableness. Even in these days, very few girls are seduced unless they fundamentally wish, and no man. [. . .] There are a number of men who are not fully homosexuals who yet like to play, as it were, at a distance with the emotion. King James I, I fancy, is an example. [. . .] This has nothing to do with your problem, except that any apparent advance may not mean The Worst. It may mean no more than itself. But of course it has, I know, to be avoided or checked.
>
> I do feel that *not* to go would be, as it were, a retreat, and I do not wish you to retreat. One way or another, you are on a moving tide, and you can deal with it as a gentleman should.[1353]

There are other letters, equally cryptic. The truth, whether or not Michael recognized it as yet, was that he was gay; and at a time when homosexual behaviour, however private, was a criminal offence. Both Anne Ridler and Joan Wallis had heard from Charles that a proposition from an American serviceman had precipitated Michael's problems in the Royal Air Force.[1354] Charles's attitude to homosexuality, ultimately, is not known, though John Heath-Stubbs recalled him saying that 'one must be very kind' to such people.[1355] Perhaps he was thinking of Michael.

★   ★   ★

Returning to his novel in the autumn of 1943, Williams made steady progress. Certain things had became clear. Nine years earlier he had fancifully told Anne Ridler, 'I will write my seventh novel about the mind in space—about the intellectual space in which we follow our paths; but the intellectual space is the abyss of God.'[1356] Now the prediction was fulfilled: he realized that his new novel should be set in the afterlife. His central character would be dead when the narrative opened. So when he resumed writing, he introduced his heroine, Lester, and her mean-spirited companion, Evelyn: two young women who have just been killed by a plane crashing on the Thames embankment in London. For Betty—a young woman whose unmarried mother keeps her as a servant and plots with her lover, Betty's father, to use her for evil purposes—Williams drew on his unperformed play, *The Devil and the Lady*. Betty's wicked father would also be the false Messiah that Williams had wanted to portray. Named Simon the Clerk, he would be a black magician and guru with ambitions for world domination, and would send his hapless daughter out on psychic quests to gain information about the future. In the course of these shadowy travels in the spirit realm, Betty would meet Lester and Evelyn, and Lester would save her.

Adding to these ingredients Betty's *fiancé*, a painter making art from the aftermath of the London Blitz, who is the best friend of Lester's newly bereaved widower, he had a rich brew that could combine horror and suspense with commentary on the fanaticisms of the contemporary world, allowing him to venture imaginatively into the twilight realm of the newly dead and explore the redemptive power of love.

He read the draft to Lewis and Tolkien as he wrote, making 'very great changes'—according to Tolkien—in response to their comments.[1357] Working with such strange materials, he felt his way with extreme difficulty. 'I've got to a point where the dead young woman has just met Antichrist', he told Michal wryly on 9 December, 'and what they say to each other I simply cannot begin to think.'[1358] He was troubled by persistent doubts about the book's style. 'A style suitable to us in our last period takes some finding', he lamented a few days later. 'I have [...] a dark feeling that there is something I ought to be saying, a kind of unity of all—but don't know what it is.'[1359] And he continued to enlist Anne Renwick's help, on (so to speak) the astral plane:

> I owe you a box on the ears; for I lay awake last night brooding over the novel, till I had to box your ears in order to dismiss it and sleep. (Do you—if we come to remembering—remember your rather proud remark [...] when I said I should send for you at such moments? 'You had better,' you said naughtily.)[1360]

Writing the novel was not made easier by the simultaneous chore of writing the life of William Flecker. 'I am relatively bored with the novel and absolutely bored with Mr. Flecker', he told Anne Ridler.[1361] As spring came he worked on the novel and the biography alternately, usually linking them in his letters: 'I worked steadily ALL yesterday: Flecker in the morning: on novel in the afternoon & evening'; or 'almost finished copying another chapter of the novel. To-night I shall go back to Mrs. F. [sic].'[1362] By the end of January he believed he had the novel more than half complete; but the more he wrote, the less confident he felt. 'It lacks—something', he sighed in March. 'I sometimes wonder if I have finished all.'[1363] To Hunt he wrote, 'About the novel, the less said the better; personally I think it lousy, though it has no doubt possibilities of virtue. So long as I get it past Fabers, it's all (he said untruthfully) I care.'[1364] By mid-April he had fixed on the title *All Hallows' Eve*. He told Phyllis Potter, 'The Novel nears its weary end. Its principle is all right, but its details are unexciting. Here and there I am shocked to say it becomes almost Beautiful. In fact, I hope it is better than I fear. But that I alone, of all people, shall never know.'[1365] He spent the first weekend of May in 'a maniacal effort to get it finished',[1366] and a few days later sent it off to Faber. 'I am', he told Michal, 'bitterly disappointed in it.'[1367] To Anne Ridler, he wrote:

> it has some quite good hints for a novel in it, and a younger man would have made a Great [*illegible*] for it. It's about two dead girls, an unconvincing magician, infant baptism, and the resurrection of the past. But I'm a little scared in

case F&F go dubious. If they do take it (according to contract), in the late autumn I shall approach them about the [*illegible*] Arthur book.[1368]

Then it was back to Flecker. It took until the end of June,[1369] and Williams never grew excited about it. A straightforward portrait of a hardworking headmaster, written under his widow's scrutiny, it could hardly be very exciting, though Williams was frank about the conflict between Dr Flecker and his poet son, who had had a youthful atheist phase. Really little more than a commemorative pamphlet, *Flecker of Dean Close* appeared in 1946.

★ ★ ★

Whilst Tambimuttu dawdled over publication of *The Region of the Summer Stars*, Williams was cheered by a sense that his reputation and influence were growing. In March the *Sunday Times*, reviewing 'contemporary young poets', remarked testily that 'after being expected to admire *The Waste Land*, we [are] now expected to admire Taliessin's Logres'.[1370] To be mentioned in the same breath as Eliot soothed a long-standing sense of rivalry. He was acquiring 'a positive library' of books sent by young poet-admirers.[1371] Robin Milford said he was learning the *Taliessin* poems by heart and greatly enjoying them:

> Each poem is a fresh experience whilst completely belonging to all the others. [...] I have not forgotten that you [...] asked me [...] to write a work for the Order. I have had the form of the work now in my head for some time and if I have the health I intend to start working on it at the beginning of next year.[1372]

In April he was invited, with Eliot and Dorothy Sayers, 'to get together and [...] prepare a year's cycle of services for the Church in Country parts'.[1373] The project never reached completion, but it may have been during a preliminary meeting in London that an episode related by John Heath-Stubbs and Anne Ridler took place:

> Williams moved that the phrase 'from the desire of damnation, Good Lord deliver us', be inserted in the litany. The bishop who was presiding over the meeting pooh-poohed the idea, saying that he could not understand what the phrase could mean.

According to Heath-Stubbs, Williams and Eliot stood up and 'testified that they had both frequently been tempted to desire damnation'. In Anne

Ridler's version, Williams and Eliot merely exchanged significant glances, agreeing that they knew only too well what it meant.[1374]

The Company, meanwhile, was 'steadily enlarging itself'; and a 'study group' had been formed at Lady Margaret Hall to read Williams's theological works: 'They have been reading the *Dove*, & c.', he told Anne Ridler, 'and they feel something must be done (the dears!) about this blinding truth; it must be shown in their lives. [. . .] What blinding truth? They have heard it all in sermons. However, I shall go & see them.'[1375] The women's colleges appreciated his teaching so much that they sent him a 'personal gift' of £50 'as a tangible expression of their gratitude'.[1376] Perhaps this was instigated by Helen Gardner, Fellow in English at St Hilda's, who also told Williams that 'one or two of the Birmingham people had raised the possibility of offering [him] a Chair there'.[1377] Williams was flattered, but when the post was advertised he decided against applying: if he left the Press he would forfeit his pension and find himself a few years later with no retirement income. Nor did he want to live in Birmingham.[1378]

Certainly, retirement from the Press was in his thoughts. He would be fifty-eight in September 1944, which would give him, if his health lasted, another seven years. He thought:

> how admirable it would be if I could get a Readership here when I retire. I know it may be only a dream; on the other hand, CSL & Tolkien are [. . .] likely to take [. . .] trouble over a project which would enable them to see a good deal more of me [. . .] And I think, in the future, they *may* take steps. [. .] And Oxford might . . . it just might . . . want me.[1379]

'Let me know your reaction', he urged Michal: 'You shall not live anywhere you do not wish.' He remained ambivalent, however, about Oxford. 'The English upper classes sitting cosily round the divine poets agonizing over their task always has and always will rile me', he told Michal. 'This flatulence is all round one here; and it maddens me. I except Magdalen. And I don't know how it's to be cured; but I know very well that I will never encourage it.'[1380] In Oxford he felt driven more than ever by 'my students, my disciples, my readers' to adopt a self-protective armour:

> A carapace—which is what a turtle has—shuts slowly round me, once I get to this town. It's a quite nice carapace, a shell almost lustrous, but a shell it is. I can feel myself getting out of the train without it, all naked and open to assault, and as I go through Oxford my armour grows round me.[1381]

In general, signs of stress were mounting. It was harder to face tutorials ('When I shrink alarmed, I say to myself "Come, come, £20! And probably more easily earned than most!"');[1382] nor were lectures easy. In February he was awake late at night 'trying to think of something to say about *Antony [and Cleopatra]*—& I may say I failed, so it was *not* a good lecture'.[1383] He wanted to write more poetry, but there never seemed to be time. Taliessin, he told Hunt, 'has been stuck on a horse at Verulam for the last nine months, and there remains'.[1384] When Robin Milford asked him if he ever felt as if he couldn't relax, Williams snapped back, 'Ever feel! I never can.'[1385] On some days, for no apparent reason, he felt sick after breakfast,[1386] though the feeling always passed. In May, he gave his last lecture of the academic year. He thought his performance 'a little woolly here and there', and told Michal: 'I felt curiously as if it were my last lecture in Oxford. If there ever are any more, you must come to the first, & start me off properly. But I don't think there will be, somehow. I daresay that's nonsense, but it's how I feel.'[1387] On 6 July he discussed with Helen Peacock the question of what pension would come to Michal in case of his death.[1388] The following day he drafted, on an OUP letterhead, a codicil to his will, appointing Michael, and failing him Hunt, as his literary executor, adding:

> I do not [*inserted above line*: in general] wish that anything written before [*inserted above line*: about] 1939 shall be published until the expiration of copyright (after which the question will probably not arise), except for such occasional short poems or prose pieces as my literary executor may decide, with the consent of my wife if living. [*deleted:* Any vagueness in this paragraph is to be interpret][1389]

The codicil was never added to the will. Its sheer vagueness would have rendered it worthless. He probably meant it to apply to unpublished materials only: a starting-date of 1939 would have ruled out nearly all his best published work, including *Taliessin Through Logres* and *Descent into Hell*. Perhaps he meant to ensure that the poems to Phyllis, retyped during the war by Margaret Douglas, could not be published.

He knew already that Hunt hoped to write his biography and had made a chronology of his writings and lectures. On 10 March 1944, the twentieth anniversary of the day 'Phyllida' arrived at Amen House, he drew up a brief chronology of his relationship with her, for Hunt's private use. He noted such things as the dates of the *Masques*, the *Century of Poems*, her riding accident, her marriages and sojourn in Java, and, finally, 'the vicarious

operation for McD[ougall]' in 1943.[1390] The question of biography sometimes worried him. An undated fragment in Michal's hand survives:

> Do you remember [...] I think it was in 1943 & Charles was spending a week
> end at home. We were discussing the poetry of a younger poet & I at least was
> not enthralled by the poets work. Charles somewhat abruptly broke into my
> dispraise & said 'I say, You wont ever write my biography will you?' Somewhat
> surprised.[1391]

⋆　⋆　⋆

At the end of May he spoke on 'The Index of the Body' to medical students
from St Bartholomew's Hospital, temporarily evacuated to Oxford. (The talk
was so successful that he was invited back in June, and in November spoke on
'Wordsworth and the Body' at the London School of Medicine for Women.)[1392]
Then he began work on *The House of the Octopus*, his play for the Missionary
Council.[1393] He was in a bad mood and feeling unwell. 'If one allows one's
temper to get twisted', he wrote to Michal, 'it's hardly surprising that one's
body should follow suit and one should have cramp and wakefulness.' He had
'pushed through' his tutorials, and was 'feverishly' reading manuscripts for the
Sylvan Press. He had been feeling 'embittered', and 'hate[d] people's faces'. His
newly completed novel was 'an abortion of intelligence'. He resolved to make
his new play 'as bitter as I know how. I'll show them what I think of men.'[1394]

It was hard going: in August he was struggling with the play, and asked
Michal to 'invoke the Blessed Trinity, to whom I profess I have (like the
Black Prince) a devotion, to encourage it. And quickly.'[1395] By the end of the
month he was still pushing 'slowly—O slowly—on with the Second Act'.[1396]
At least, he reflected, the play would pay for some false teeth he needed.
'This play will always mean Teeth to me.'[1397] Somehow *The House of the
Octopus* was finished: he had proofs in February 1945,[1398] and it was performed in London. But—despite articulating some fascinating ideas—it
remains one of his weakest plays: the speeches often verbose, the verse slack,
the characters flat. Margaret Sinclair had asked for something reflecting the
suppression of Christianity by the Japanese in the Pacific; Williams chose to
express this through the evil empire of his own mythology, P'o-L'u, with its
associated octopus imagery. In the visionary world of *Taliessin* this had been
more or less acceptable; but in the play's more realistic setting, threats of
giving Christians to the 'cephalopods' verge on the ludicrous (and incidentally reveal Williams's ignorance of biology).

This is a pity, for the play contains some deeply original views, expressed particularly through Ayalu, a young islander who, early in the play, renounces her Christianity through fear of the invaders, just before she is killed. Anthony, the missionary, denounces her as an apostate, but the islanders refuse to condemn her:

> She died, even if she lied; she is still a witness.
> Might not, sir, her first baptismal vow
> have swallowed her fault instead of her fault her vow?
> If God is outside time, is it so certain
> that we know which moments of time count with him,
> and how?

They explain that:

> We in these isles
> live in our people—no man's life his own—
> from birth and initiation. [. . .] No sin,
> no death through sin, no death in sin, parts us.
> It is sin, you say, our Lord redeems
> in his Church; how if he now redeem this?

Ayalu's ghost appears later; and—in substitution—she takes on Anthony's fear when he faces martyrdom. As for Anthony, the missionary, it is revealed that he wanted the people to be more dependent on him than on God. Williams was not letting the Missionary Council off easily. But he sensed the play's shortcomings: in early September he told Dorothy Sayers it was 'not very good, and I shall have to copy it all out again and make it sound a little more exciting'. Associating the ghostly Ayalu with *All Hallows' Eve*, he added, 'It is a little touched by my more recent habit of talking about the Dead and the characters tending to be dead before they appear at all. My next novel will be even more like that than the one for the proofs of which I am waiting.'[1399]

★   ★   ★

Even as he worked on *The House of the Octopus*, Williams felt he must take on other tasks to support himself and his family. In August he hoped to review detective novels for *Time and Tide*, and had a commission from Faber to make a selection of poems by the elderly 'Georgian' poet Wilfrid Wilson Gibson. Eliot claimed to be 'a wee bit vexed' that Williams had accepted this, because it would delay his writing *The Figure of Arthur* (which Faber had now commissioned); but Williams recalled Gibson telling him it had been Eliot's idea. 'One cannot suspect the Great of lying', he remarked, 'but one of them must have got mixed. I suspect W.G. and neither mentions the fee—I bet it'll be £5, but it won't really be a long job.'[1400] He postponed the task until December, finishing it within the month.[1401] It would appear in 1945 as *Solway Ford and Other Poems*. He also agreed, at the end of August, to give a radio talk for the BBC's Indian service on 'Julius Caesar— Shakespeare & Politics'. He was unenthusiastic, 'But it means a Fee.'[1402]

Meanwhile, in June, he had received a letter from Robert Graves. Forced from his home in Mallorca by the Spanish Civil War, the English poet and novelist was now living in Devon. Graves and Williams had been sporadically in touch since February 1943, when Williams had reviewed Graves's novel *Wife to Mr Milton*, in a witty pastiche of seventeenth-century prose, pretending to be a friend of Milton's defending the poet against Graves's very hostile portrait. Graves had written to him, and Williams replied:

> My dear Robert Graves,
>   I only hope I made clear [...] how much I admired your book. On the other hand I hope you do not think that I am entirely trammelled by the old academic views of Milton. The truth, I think, lies somewhere between your novel and my own (rather too extreme) opposition. I am permitting myself the pleasure of sending you a copy of the World's Classics Milton with my Introduction, which you may think untrue. You will however see that I think the poetry there discussed must have sprung from something real in Milton, and that that reality has still to be sought for. But I don't at all deny that there were times when he must have been quite intolerable.[1403]

Now, Graves told Williams he had been writing about Taliesin (as he spelled it), and was about to submit a manuscript. Williams felt a little apprehensive: he liked Graves's poetry, and thought him 'a sound man, if perverse. But I could faintly wish he had not happened on the same Celtic poet!!'[1404]

The manuscript arrived. It was a draft of what would become *The White Goddess*, written the previous year in a fever of inspiration and setting forth Graves's view of the poet as priest of the Triple Muse-Goddess. The book contained a discussion of the 'Hanes Taliesin' from the *Mabinogion*, a cryptic poem which Graves believed concealed an ancient bardic alphabet. None of this trespassed on Williams's own *Taliessin*. He found the book delightful, and strongly recommended it to Milford—but in vain. Milford returned the typescript to Graves's agent, conceding that Williams 'liked it very much and was much in favour of my publishing it', but pleading the wartime paper shortage and the Press's commitment to 'specialist works' such as 'the [Oxford] History of English Literature, and so on'. He added, a little patronisingly, 'I am far from denying that Mr Graves's book is worthy to stand by these. But the Press is already committed to these works of scholarship and not to his study of the poetic mind.'[1405] Those last words seem significant: did Milford recall Williams's *Poetic Mind* books and foresee similar commercial failure? Williams himself wrote sadly to Graves:

My Dear Robert Graves,

I had better say at once that I have failed. I am very sorry indeed, not that it will make any difference to you, because you will get the book published easily enough, but because I should very much have liked the Press to publish it. [...]

I read the book with very great interest indeed. It seemed to me a thrilling description of the way the poetic mind works, and very valuable on that account. The mere etching of Taliessin reading *The Book of Enoch* in an Ethiopian translation was astonishing and moving. It's so exactly the kind of thing my own Taliessin might have done that I felt as if you knew more of my own invention when he was travelling through Caucasia than I did myself.

So with all the collations; I mention this because it was so intimate to me. But I know no other prose book that so suggests the annexations, as it were, of poetic genius. Lowe's *Road to Xanadu* had a touch of it, but had not the same power of individual approach. I do very profoundly regret that we can't do it. I have said all this here, and pressed it as far as I can. But, as Sir Humphrey has written to Mr. Watt, we are more hampered than any other publisher with learned works of the past and present to which we are committed.

I very greatly admired your attitude towards scholarship. But, wise though that was, it was the whole scope of your pursuit [...] that so fascinated me. As soon as my own new Taliessin poems (which are indeed from that riddle), "The Region of the Summer Stars" appear, I shall do myself the honour of sending you a copy merely as a humble salute.

It is, of course, impossible for me to write like this and not to feel something of a fool when I know the MS. is going back to Watt. But there I must rely on your generosity. The Press is not free to do all that it would, nor I even within the Press.

Most regretfully and sincerely yours,
CW.

In due course *The White Goddess* was taken by Eliot for Faber. It has been in print, and regarded as something of a classic, ever since.

★   ★   ★

Williams had been in occasional contact with Dorothy L. Sayers since 1934, when he had praised *The Nine Tailors* as 'a marvellous book [of] high imagination'.[1406] She had written *The Zeal of Thy House* as the Canterbury play to follow his *Cranmer*, and they had read over parts of it together.[1407] Sometime in late 1943 or early 1944, happening to be in Oxford, she came to see him at South Parks Road. According to Anne Spalding, 'Somebody told Dorothy Sayers that our house was warmer than the house of her friends round the corner so she pushed herself upon us'.[1408] 'When she arrived, she was very much the successful author, lecturing C.W. on how he ought to get his books into mass circulation by doing this and that with publishers and agents. Twenty-four hours later she was his disciple, sitting at his feet.'[1409] She went away and read *The Figure of Beatrice*, 'not because it was about Dante, but because it was by Charles Williams'.[1410] Soon she was writing him long letters about theology. Amongst other things they discussed the ordination of women: it was, Williams thought:

> due to something very much more than masculine arrogance that women are kept from the priesthood. They are, physically, too like the Victim in the shedding of blood.
>
> But that is a secret mania of my own. [...] Anyhow, in my new novel, practically all the useful activity is in the women. [...] It is true that one of them is dead all through the book, but her activity is very much her own all the same.[1411]

Sayers, who admitted that she had 'nobody to talk to here',[1412] adopted a somewhat flirtatious tone, signing herself 'your faithful & affectionate pupil, Topsy'; Williams reciprocated: 'Always yours adoringly'. Her frequent letters were voluminous: one ran to thirty-six pages, and another began 'Dear Charles, Me again! You must dread the sight of my handwriting'.[1413] Williams hinted that he could not answer at similar length: 'Something in me', he told her tactfully, 'yearns to sit down and answer [you] at much fuller length, and something else says to me "Charles, you know you won't"', to which she replied—in a twelve-page letter—'Of course I don't expect you to write me reams and reams.'[1414] She visited him in Oxford several times, and turned out to be hard work. 'I got in from Magdalen last night about 12 and found her sitting up', he told Michal in February 1944. 'We conversed until 2.15. I like the old dear, but she's rather heavy going. I should find 2.15 late for one's dearest friends—but what can one do?'[1415] He also grumbled about being press-ganged into 'Dorothy Sayers's committees for explaining or defending or promulgating or elucidating or doing something or other to the Faith. I do not love the Faith so much as all that; though I trust...yes I do trust.'[1416]

Still he was pleased by her interest in his theology, and felt she might spread the word about co-inherence. Then, in mid-August, she announced, 'I have embarked upon an arduous enterprise for which you are entirely responsible.'[1417] The 'enterprise' was the reading of the entire *Divine Comedy*, to which she had been inspired by *The Figure of Beatrice*. Finding a parallel text, she devoured the poem in twenty-one days, pouring out her thoughts to Williams in long letters as she went. Essentially she was writing a commentary for herself. Williams did not respond in detail to her views, but (apparently without irony) suggested that he edit her letters for publication: '[People] might have their whole consciousness of Dante altered by reading you, and turned into a much happier and more truthful apprehension.[...] we need to encourage [...] less catholic culture and more poetic intelligence.'[1418]

In December, Sayers announced dramatically that she had 'fallen into the clutches of a monster',[1419] meaning that she had begun translating the poem. She sent the first five cantos, and Williams encouraged her: 'Consider that you have done five already out of the 100 [...] I wait with thrilling expectation for the next batch.'[1420] The following spring, Sayers persuaded E.V. Rieu, editor of the new Penguin Classics Series, to commission the work. It became the twentieth century's most popular English Dante translation.

★ ★ ★

In June, as Williams worked on *The House of the Octopus*, the D-Day landings had taken place. In August, Paris was liberated. The war was nearing its end: on 7 September he donned his 'tin hat' for one last night of fire watching, and a week later Oxford's street lights came on for the first time since 1939.[1421] Milford, having left his Oxford house and staying briefly at South Parks Road, talked of retiring when the London branch left Oxford. Williams expected to go back, at least for a few years. After that the future was uncertain. He reflected that he would soon have been at the Press for thirty-seven years.[1422] Hearing of a plan to 're-arrange all the offices', he had, he told Alice Mary, 'a horrid fear that I shan't get mine; & on the whole, I'd as soon that as any. But so long as they don't ask me to share—'.[1423]

Foss asked him to write an introduction for John Webster's *The Duchess of Malfi*, which the Sylvan Press would publish with illustrations by an exciting young artist, Michael Ayrton. Williams was pleased: 'I should like to do that really well', he told Michal: 'after poetry, criticism is my real work'.[1424] It was mostly done in November,[1425] and proved problematic: Foss wanted him to write on the play's poetry, but George Rylands, asked to discuss staging, wrote on the poetry as well, compelling Williams to rework his piece in order to avoid duplication.[1426]

Tambimuttu had finally promised *The Region of the Summer Stars* for September, but by the end of the month it was still not out. Williams set off for a conference at Pleshey on 'Worship and the Arts'. 'I am to talk on the Pagan Contribution to Art', he told Anne Renwick; 'and I shall begin by saying that "the Pagan Contribution to Art was, quite simply, art." Which there is no getting over—chronologically.' He was working, he added, on new poems, and had, 'for the first time for a year, written a score of lines for Taliessin. It is when he has killed Cradlemas, and he is then seized with a sense of guilt; though it was right, he feels it is sin.'[1427]

At last, on 11 October, *The Region of the Summer Stars* was published. Containing a Preface and eight poems, the book ran to just over sixty pages. Magnificent, complex, and musical, it contained definitive statements of many of Williams's themes. Besides 'The Calling of Taliessin', 'Taliessin in the Rose-Garden', 'The Founding of the Company', and 'The Meditation of Mordred', it included 'Prelude', placing the Arthurian world in the context of early Christian history; 'The Departure of Dindrane', in which the Princess Dindrane's decision to enter a convent becomes an image of voluntary service to a spiritual commitment and hence, paradoxically, of freedom; and 'The Queen's Servant', the poem written for Anne Renwick on her departure from Oxford, in which Taliessin sends a girl as a secretary to the Queen. The volume's final poem, 'The Prayers of the Pope', is one of Williams's greatest and most surprising achievements. Essentially a cosmic prayer for the last phases of the Second World War, it also intimates the end of Williams's active leadership of the Companions.

'Early on the feast of Christmas the young Pope / knelt in Lateran; [...] he prayed / alone and aloud in the candled shroud of the dark.' Around him the closing stages of a European war are vividly evoked in Dark Age terms:

> The consuls and lords fought for the fords and towns,
> but over the Rhine, over the Vistula and Danube
> pressed the grand tribes; the land shook
> as band after band stamped into darkness cities
> whose burning had lamped their path; their wrath grew
> with vengeance and victory; they looked to no returning.

Meanwhile, Taliessin ('Shining Brow' in Welsh) makes his final farewell to his Company:

> Taliessin gathered his people before the battle.
> 'Peers of the household,' the king's poet said,
> 'dead now, save Lancelot, are the great lords
> and the Table may end to-morrow; if it live,
> it shall have new names in a new report.
> Short is Our time, though that time prove eternal.
> Therefore'—he lifted his hands to the level of his brow,
> the hands that had written and harped the king's music;
> there the ageing began ere the hair was grey,
> or the tongue tired of song, or the brain fey;
> O but the Bright Forehead was once young!
> 'Therefore we now dissolve the former bonds—'
> the voice sounded, the hands descended—'We dissolve
> the outer bonds; [. . .] We restore
> again to God the once-permitted lieutenancy'[.]

'The Prayers of the Pope'—reworking Williams's earlier version, 'Dives Dimisit' ('the rich He hath sent empty away')—reinterprets the idea of riches: here they become the 'riches' of 'sorrow', of 'heart's heaviness', 'the double wealth of repentance', 'the riches of loss'. The poem's refrain, and its concluding line, is 'Send not, send not the rich empty away.' It is a moving and magnificent final statement.

Williams gave, or sent, a copy of the book at once to Michal, enclosing another poem for her:

> Long ago—is it?—we first spoke
> (wearing lightly then the yoke of union),
> of such poems as these. And I, in that communion,
> knew little, nor you, from what depth of soil,
> grew the shape of futurity. O if the toil
> of these—yes, these—is more yours than mine,
> yet to-day let us think of the joy,
> blessing each other. This is a shape. I know
> they are not important, say, as the mouth closed
> on a curse, or the heart on worse things. Yet you,
> you all the time not only believed but goaded.
> Loaded was I with gloom? but you lit it;
> Burnt was I with envy? You checked it;
> I have learnt something of—glory? Let the world
> say as it choose; but you . . . I will come to you,

> shy yet myself, saying 'These are the new
> poems; darling, do you like them? and if, be kind;
> kiss me, lunch with me, and ever bind
> more closely hearts and hands to each other assigned.

The book brought, at last, some public recognition of Williams's poetic achievement. The reviews were mixed: as he summed up:

> The *Stars* has had very few reviews. The *T.L.S.*—was the *T.L.S.*; *T&T* was (inevitably!) good; the *Birmingham Post* didn't like it; Mr. Richard Church in *John o' London's* said he wouldn't say anything because he didn't understand it; and the *Tribune* says it marks 'a new high-water level of tedium in last year's verse'. But then the *Tribune* alludes to the Grail-quest as 'This simple subject'—which gives me soft and continued joy.[1428]

But Auden wrote:

> You're the only one since Dante who has found out how to make poetry of theology and history. [...] I can say this all the more wholeheartedly because I start with a terrific handicap, namely a roast-beef-and-Yorkshire-pudding Philistine distaste for the whole Matter of Britain. [...] I would never have dreamed that a poet could excite me with such material as a base, and here you come and do it.[1429]

By 23 November, 800 copies had been sold. Before Christmas the whole edition was gone: Nicholson and Watson, publishing the book under the 'Editions Poetry London' imprint, planned to reprint in the New Year. They were, Williams told Michal:

> clamouring for more; they'd 'like to follow it up with a further selection from your Taliessin poems.' [...] They also want to know if they can take over the original *T. in* [sic] *Logres*, if the O.U.P. are not re-publishing.
>   This selling of & passion for my verse is something altogether new, and I want to cry a little—if you were here I should. I don't say it's much...but we have waited so long since the *Silver Stair* for something of the kind: [it] is all a little shaking. I would ring you up, but in 3 minutes I could hardly explain, tho' I know you'd understand.[1430]

★ ★ ★

Williams's emotional reaction reveals not only his tiredness, but the way in which, during these Oxford years, he had come to re-evaluate his marriage. Loneliness in Oxford had shown him how much he valued his wife's support and kindness: the snacks and cups of tea she brought him when he was working late at night, the dose of common sense she could bring to his wilder states of mind (she had, he said, saved him from 'persecution manias, false fancies, & all the rest').[1431] Sometimes, waking suddenly, he would believe he was at home with Michal beside him, and would speak to her: 'It might have been a scene from one of my novels',[1432] he reflected after one such episode. The psychic connection between them, he believed, was very strong. When a troublesome pain in his shoulder went away, he wrote 'I wish I could think that your new pain hadn't come back'[1433]—assuming that they continually practised substitution for one another. In their relationship he found a 'mutual exchange of unseen life', a 'steady unnoticeable nourishment and repose'.[1434]

It worried him that she was still in London, threatened by the new V2 missiles. Impressed by her sangfroid, he could not share it. He told Joan Wallis, 'It seems I grow no more courageous with age, for I find I leave tube stations with a faint regret, and when my wife says she thinks we had better get away from the windows, I do not like it.'[1435] Without Michal's care he often did not eat properly: he bought sandwiches, or went without food from breakfast until he could have a piece of cake at 4 p.m. He also came to realize afresh what she had contributed, at great cost, to his ability to write poetry. 'O language, language!' he lamented: 'language has ruined me and hurt you. I would give up all my poetry to make you happy.'[1436] But he also believed, now, that she wanted him to write:

> The odd thing is that you would, I do most passionately believe, sacrifice with goodwill & gaiety more for my best verse than I! On the other hand, I have to go through the writing of it, which is more exertion than fun—so perhaps we sway level in the union.[1437]

A surviving letter from Michal to him shows a deep tenderness. Woken at 5.30 a.m. by 'five wretched bombs' which fortunately fell far away, she writes to him whilst she drinks a cup of tea, 'wishing how I'm wishing you were here', then 'pausing while I fill my cup & cut you more bread & butter'—as if he were really there. He has called her the night before: 'You have a charming phone voice', she tells him; adding (no doubt at the suggestion of an episode in the still-unpublished *All Hallows' Eve*), 'I wish after death one could phone to the other one. Imagine...' But the next page is lost.[1438] And he was deeply touched by advance gifts she gave him in August 1944 for his fifty-eighth birthday ('the tie has a kind of subdued richness which I always adore. [...] The cake is wonderful too')[1439] and, he told

Dorothy Sayers, he looked forward to 'taking my wife to Lyons' Coventry Street Corner House [...] for a Bottle of Claret, [...] and going to sleep in a Deanna Durbin film afterwards'.[1440] On these brief visits he was, he said, 'renewing, as far as I can, the last period of marriage'.[1441] When Phyllis Potter suggested meeting in London he refused, explaining that he must spend all possible time with Michal—'This is not negligence nor lack of affection, but only the curious necessity which lies at the root of all my verse.'[1442] It was his wife's company that was now essential for creativity. He speculated about getting the Oxford Chair of Poetry—a five-year role that would have suited him perfectly and, though unpaid, might bring a Fellowship in its wake—after which they could retire to Oxford. It was a mark of how much he had changed that London no longer cast a spell. 'I have no place-attachment now', he told Michal. 'This Oxford period has broken all that.'[1443]

Besides Michal, it was the Inklings who sustained him. During summer 1944, Tolkien had read aloud the perilous journey of Frodo, Sam, and Gollum into Mordor from *The Lord of the Rings*, and Lewis had read from *Who Goes Home?* (afterwards *The Great Divorce*), a theological fantasy set in an afterlife not unlike that of *All Hallows' Eve*.[1444] In September, at Lewis's suggestion, Williams brought Raymond Hunt to the Inklings.[1445] And one October morning, when Williams and Tolkien strolled into the Eagle and Child for their Tuesday morning gathering, they noticed a strange, tall, gaunt man in a 'wide-awake' hat, who unexpectedly joined the conversation—'like Trotter at the Prancing Pony', Tolkien observed. It was Lewis's former student, the poet Roy Campbell, who was at once invited for Thursday evening.[1446]

Tolkien and Williams were as close as ever. If Lewis did not turn up on a Tuesday morning they drank and talked together, and in September the pair walked home discussing, sceptically, 'what common factors existed in the notions associated with *freedom*, as used at present'.[1447] Both were deeply weary of wartime propaganda. Tolkien noted that it was sometimes hard to recall his discussions with Lewis and Williams 'because we all agree so'.[1448] Unlike some Inklings, Williams took a keen interest in the development of *The Lord of the Rings*, perhaps because in the *Taliessin* poems he had created his own fantasy world. He was the first person to read a large part of the work in continuous typescript, when Tolkien lent him, in November or December 1944, the first four books—ending with Sam and Frodo's crossing of the river at Amon Lhaw and their departure into the grey hills, heading for Mordor. They discussed the book in some depth: 'C. Williams who is reading it all', Tolkien reported:

> says the great thing is that its *centre* is not in strife and war and heroism (though they are all understood and depicted) but in freedom, peace, ordinary life and good living. Yet he agrees that these very things require the existence of a great world outside the Shire—lest they should grow stale by custom and turn into humdrum.[1449]

On 6 November, Tolkien recorded, 'I saw C.S.L. and C.W. from about 10.40 to 12.50 [...] It was a bright morning, and the mulberry tree in the grove just outside C.S.L.'s window shone like fallow gold against cobalt blue sky.'[1450] Ten days later Tolkien joined Williams, Lewis, and others for dinner in Magdalen with Owen Barfield—a joyfully contentious evening during which they debated chance, ghosts, hymns, and many other things.[1451] They all knew that this happy companionship could not last much longer. With the war's end, Williams must return to London. It was perhaps now, at the end of 1944, that Lewis, Tolkien, and others began in secret to plan a *Festschrift*, a book of essays in his honour which they could present to him as some consolation for his departure into what now loomed as a kind of exile.

As the year ended, Williams was feeling less than exuberant. He told Thelma Shuttleworth:

> Everything, these days, has to be done.. I was going to say *deliberately*, but that's hardly enough. I could say, daring to borrow from Wordsworth, that all action lies on me
>   With a weight
>   Heavy as frost and deep almost as life.
> [...] Just as verse now has to be thought and planned and considered and re-considered; just as prose needs writing two or three times when once was formerly enough; just as one can no more lecture on what one knows, but has to re-read what one *did* know.. [...] Like the Red Queen one has to run so very fast even to remain in the same place.
>   I cannot make it too clear that I am not *grumbling* at this. I only say, it happens—and so, no doubt, it should. At 60 one ought not to be 'a boy at heart', and I'm very glad I'm not. And I go into it now because the growth of it increases. The war? I don't believe it. Life was always like that; all mankind kills and is weary of killing; we are slayers from our mothers' wombs. No; I do not think it is the war.[1452]

★ ★ ★

After Christmas in London, he was back at Southfield House for New Year 1945. The weather was freezing, the pavements icy. In his spare time he worked on *The Figure of Arthur*, telling Michal on 2 January that he was 'madly reading in [Darwell Stone's] History of the Doctrine of the Eucharist in order to push something into my book about the grail in history'.[1453] With Milton lectures approaching and Arthurian matters in mind, he thought he should look at Spenser, so:

> driven by [a] sense of duty, I embarked on *The Faerie Queene*, and have cleared up the first two books. [...] But I do not seem to be filled with new ideas about Milton. I keep on tending to lose myself in fairies and fantasies, & have less & less inclination to do a thing other.[1454]

'Will you tell me', he asked Michal, 'why every book seems more difficult than the one before?'[1455]

He was thinking of further poems for his Arthurian sequence. He wrote to Joan Wallis, requesting her psychic assistance and offering to send a symbolic ten shillings in exchange: the fact that he had 'freed' her didn't mean, he pointed out, that he couldn't enlist her temporarily for particular purposes. And he needed her advice as an art historian: 'I may want the Lord Bors to have a drawing of his wife Elaine, done by someone (I think) in the train of the Imperial Nuncio.'[1456] What material would they have used? Ivory? Vellum? He knew individual portraits were an anachronism, but didn't see why Bors shouldn't have one in the poem.

Faber had promised publication of *All Hallows' Eve* 'early in the New Year'. It appeared on 19 January. Williams continued to have serious doubts about it and was anxious about the reviews—'to tell you the truth', he confessed to Michal, 'I'm a little afraid of them...generally nowadays I don't mind. But this is all wrong somehow, & I don't wish to be told so.' The next day he added, 'the novel really gnaws me. I feel as if everybody would sneer at it. This is silly because you liked a lot of it, and T.S.E. liked it, but there it is!'[1457] But reviews were mostly good. The *TLS* was predictably sniffy ('the whole confection will no doubt have its appeal for those whose imagination best resembles the author's') but the popular press—which could generate sales—was thoroughly positive, with excellent notices in the *Daily Herald*, *Daily Mail*, and *Birmingham Post*.[1458] In the *New Statesman* the poet Henry Reed called Williams 'one of the most important writers of our time'. Despite having 'most of the faults a novel can contain—including vagueness, dead characterisation' (an unfortunate choice of words in the context) 'and over-stated climaxes', *All Hallows' Eve*, he thought, 'yet emerges as ten times more interesting than most novels'. Williams was 'so much more richly versed in human nature than most authors that their observations seem adolescent compared to his'. It was, Reed, wrote, 'a peculiarly wonderful book'.[1459]

All Hallows' Eve was topical: set at the end of the war, still actually some months away, its representation of the experience of the newly dead, in a timeless, shadowy version of drab wartime London, was remarkably convincing. At a time when almost everyone had lost close family or friends to violent death, such a vision was less odd than it might seem now (the novel has much in common with the famous Powell and Pressburger film *A Matter of Life and Death*, released the following year). There were also political resonances. The evil guru, Simon the Clerk, creates magical replicas of himself with large followings in Russia and China; at the end of the novel, all three are being invited to an international peace conference—though the living hero and dead heroine save the world from their malign domination just in time.

Nonetheless, the novel is certainly flawed. Its plot is convoluted, and its climax veers into the gothic, becoming grotesque rather than poignantly uncanny. A scene where the dead Lester's consciousness voluntarily enters a dwarfish replica of a human body magically created by Simon the Clerk, and manipulates it to make a telephone call in her own voice, is especially hard to accept. The conventions of the horror story, and the aspirations of a metaphysical fiction about love and redemption, refuse to blend.

More successfully, the novel resolves the theme of the guru or charismatic magician which Williams had broached in his first-written novel, *Shadows of Ecstasy*. Simon the Clerk is very similar to Considine, the dangerous adept of that novel. Like Considine, Simon is centuries old; like him he tries to charm and seduce an artist (in Considine's case a poet, in Simon's a painter) into following him. But whereas Williams had remained ambivalent about Considine, refusing to condemn him and leaving open the possibility that he might be right, in the case of Simon there is no doubt. Having refused compassion and love in the name of power, Simon destroys himself—imploding into a spiritual hell of fire and blood representing his determination to separate himself from others, his refusal of co-inherence. If Williams had ever been tempted by the figure of the guru—in himself or others—he now decisively rejected it.

Still, he recognized that the novel's elements were not adequately integrated. 'The two parts don't quite fit', he told Phyllis Potter; 'I am convinced [there] is an unsatisfactory link up.'[1460] He resolved to 'do better next time': he was already thinking of another novel, to be set even more completely in the realm of the dead.[1461] It would, he told Anne Ridler, deal amongst other things with 'parting':

> the essentials of the one Way are the accidents of the other. [...] Speaking mystically, there must be, sooner or later, some sort of seclusion of the soul to the Omnipotence. [...] The Rejection aims at this; the Affirmation endures it, when it comes. [...] I have it vaguely in mind to go on to something like this in another novel. But unless my poor style improves and my devotion, I shan't dare. (Or so I hope.)[1462]

★ ★ ★

On 23 January he trudged through the snow to the Taylorian to give his first Milton lecture. A packed hall awaited the well-known performance; he felt a little like a music-hall artiste: 'Mr Williams in his now famous advocacy of Chastity [...] and his Instruction in Miltonic Virtues, "as given before crowned heads".'[1463] Tutorials were beginning, and the list of topics, ranging from Malory to Keats, 'almost frightens me', he confessed to Michal.[1464] And there was the usual daunting programme of talks: 'Personification in English Verse' at Birmingham University; 'Blake' at Mansfield College; 'Poetry in War-Time' at Balliol. He addressed the Women's Royal Naval Service (WRNS) on 'The Appreciation of Poetry', and students from Westfield College on 'Shakespeare and the Supernatural'[1465]—all this in January and February. During the same period the Vicar of Headington asked him to join the parish's 'Moral Welfare Council' ('the last body I ever thought to find myself on!', Williams reflected),[1466] the BBC commissioned him to script a five-minute broadcast on 'Evidence' for transmission in March,[1467] and the theatre at Stratford booked him for a week of talks on Shakespeare for servicemen in July.[1468] In March he gave a series of Passiontide addresses ('generally on Substitution') to theology students at Lincoln,[1469] and took part in a poetry reading at St Anne's House, Soho.[1470] In April he spoke to seventy service personnel about *Twelfth Night*, and to a reading group at Robin Milford's house about *All Hallows' Eve*. 'What do they want to know?' he asked Michal, rhetorically. 'God knows. But I will play my part.'[1471] He also accepted an invitation to preach at St Mary's, Oxford's University Church, on Whit Sunday, 20 May.

Alongside this relentless programme there were requests for books. The Religious Drama Society wanted him to collect his religious plays into a volume; and the British Council offered £50 for a book on religious drama.[1472] There even seems to have been a suggestion that he might write a life of Jesus: he told Michal he had discussed the idea with Gervase Mathew, who joked that it 'was quite simple: all I had to do was to have the 4th Gospel typed out & send it in as mine. He added that nothing was a more exact C.W. style than "In the beginning was the Word," & St. John was clearly my disciple as well as Our Lord's.'[1473]

He told his agent that after the war he would like to return to reviewing crime fiction.[1474] Meanwhile, he urgently needed to finish *The Figure of Arthur*. In February, Eliot had asked when it would be ready, and, Williams reflected wryly, 'There being only 3000 words done out of 90,000, it doesn't seem as if the answer was *Soon*.'[1475] He worked doggedly in the evenings, and by Easter had two chapters ready for the Inklings. Lewis sketches the scene:

> Picture to yourself an upstairs sitting-room with windows looking out into the 'grove' of Magdalen College on a sunshiny Monday morning in vacation at about ten o'clock. The Professor [Tolkien] and I, both on the chesterfield, lit our pipes and stretched our legs. Williams in the arm-chair opposite to us threw his cigarette into the grate, took up a pile of the extremely small, loose sheets on which he habitually wrote—they came, I think, from a twopenny pad for memoranda—and began[.][1476]

What he began to read was, first, a brisk and vivid survey of everything known from the earliest chronicles about the supposed Arthur; and, in the second chapter, a long historical discussion of the Eucharist, as prelude to an account of the Grail. But there was still much more to write.

★ ★ ★

Away from the Inklings, Williams found himself ever more out of sympathy with those around him. He liked and trusted the devoted Margaret Douglas, but found her domineering mother Isabel, with her conventional thinking and snobbish 'cultured' attitudes, increasingly hard to tolerate. 'Culture avenges itself at last', he growled to Michal; 'you must serve it with more than your class-emotions if it is to serve you. There are a million women like her—dangers to the great arts. [. . .] They have done more harm than they can ever know!!'[1477] Isabel was, he thought:

> a dreadful example of the English upper classes being kind to Culture. I startled her the other day by saying that it was arguable that every great artist had done more harm than good. So it is, but her kind of circle does not think in those terms. So with other things. 'But, Charles, by Liberty you don't mean License?' 'But, my dear, Isabel, I do—exactly.' And so on . . . yet she means well.[1478]

He felt equally uncomfortable at the Press. An editorial meeting one morning in late April brought his feelings to a head, when it emerged—he told Michal ironically—that 'a problem had arisen':

> Whom should we ask to write a book on Shakespeare for the Home University Library? Would you think there could be—*here*—more than one answer? There could; there could, in fact, be any answer but that. We discussed A, B, & C, anyone except . . . Except . . . Of course they may think of me yet, but I think it unlikely. Or—let's be fair—they may want a different kind of book from mine. But it's a little strange to be superfluous where one has been Someone; in all the literary world there is no place where I am as negligible—in the most charming way—as here. This is a rebuke to egotism. I allow that Sir H. was not in on it, but I doubt if Sir H—[1479]

—the rest of the letter is missing, but the meaning is clear: even Caesar would not have put in a word for him. He told Alice Mary a few days later:

> If in a couple of years [Oxford] found or made a Readership or whatever, I very likely would take it: for certainly at the Press after this year I shall be lagging superfluously on the stage. G[erry Hopkins] & JC & I get on very well, but we have no use for each other.[1480]

He had been promised his old office again in London, but it now had little attraction. 'I shall linger there', he sighed to Michal, 'a superfluous but kindly treated . . . O well, don't let's be bad-tempered and resentful. We shall see how everything works out.'[1481] Colin Hardie of Magdalen had asked him 'what [he] would feel about a tutorship',[1482] but he did not really expect anything from that direction. The only ray of light was that a representative from the Press's New York branch had been positive about finding a job there for Michael, whose fascination with America was undiminished.[1483]

At South Parks Road, as at the Press, a sense of war's approaching end unsettled everything. The Spalding parents were expected, and their possessions were brought out of store. 'Putting Mr. Spalding's evening shoes back in what used to be M[ichael]'s room', Williams confessed, 'I was seized with almost a terror of everything that had happened there [...] and I looked at the room, but I refrained from cursing, and thought it wiser to try & praise God.'[1484] At Southfield House, expecting to leave by September, he set himself to tidy his bathroom office, 'throwing away papers and sending books back to stock'.[1485] He did not relish a return to the 'revolting' London flat, which was damp and uncomfortable.[1486] 'Oxford now begins to look really beautiful to me', he told Michal.[1487] The transience of his surroundings encouraged a sense of his own insubstantiality. He reflected:

> I was always pretty much of a slightly non-personal figure, and all my 'interests' rather in figures than in people. Perhaps the people in my novels grow more real as my consciousness of actual people decreases. [...] Somehow, except at home...and perhaps at Magdalen or with Eliot...I am always aware of a gulf. My voice—or my style—goes across it, but my heart doesn't. [...] I do think it's very important that I should finish my job, find my last style, make my last shapes in verse or prose or public comments. But that is all.[1488]

As war's grip on Europe relaxed, old acquaintances turned up: Monty Belgion, gaunt from years as a prisoner-of-war in Germany, but gossipy and grandiose as ever;[1489] and (much more welcome) Christopher Fry, released from his pacifist's war work. Williams and Fry shared a happy afternoon in a pub, where they agreed that life had, after all, been well worth living. 'I saw him to his bus', Fry recalled:

> and as we parted he said to me—[...] it was shouted from the tailboard of the moving bus, over the heads of pedestrians and bicyclists outside the Midland Station, Oxford—'When we're dead we shall have the sensation of having enjoyed life altogether, whatever has happened to us.' The distance between us widened, and he leaned out into the space so that his voice should reach me: 'Even if we've been murdered, what a pleasure to have been capable of it!'[1490]

★   ★   ★

Trinity term began in late April. Before tutorials started, he reviewed Owen Barfield's *Romanticism Comes of Age* for the *New English Weekly*, in what was really a brief essay on Wordsworth.[1491] It was perhaps on 1 May that Michal, now writing daily and with an end to the long separation in sight, wrote one of her tenderest letters:

> Darling,
>   A day nearer to your home coming. You shall be cossetted & spoilt you shall quote & quote your Milton & I'll try not to swear or throw things

about—only come. because Im no Jacob it was Jacob wasnt it who thought seven years as nothing for the love he bore? I have found the years I have been without you just hideous. I want our eventide to be lovely as was our morning time. And the afternoon of our life? Why that has been lovely too but sometimes cloudy. & that we would wish, to save smugness.

Good night & till tomorrow

Michal.[1492]

Alice Mary planned to visit him, and he wrote explaining that he would certainly not be in Oxford much longer. He offered some books, and lamented that with 'tutorials every day and two more on Fridays', he was getting little writing done, either of poems or the *Arthur* book. 'It's a good thing, most noble lady, that whatever was done was done when it was done', he concluded. 'Now we rather carry on with—No. I talk nonsense. Even now "the feeling intellect" pervades Oxford—a little to my alarm. Intercede for Oxford!'[1493]

On Saturday morning, 5 May, he joined Michal in London, and although on Sunday morning he felt unwell, by noon he was better and they lunched with his Aunt Alice at Leyton. He took the midnight train back to Oxford. It was full, so he had to stand all the way, and did not get to bed until 2.30 a.m.[1494] On Monday the midday papers came into the Press with news that the German U-boats had ceased resistance and the air force was surrendering. 'They've failed', Williams wrote to Michal; 'they've been broken. And you—especially—have helped to do it. Victory depended on you.'[1495] He bumped into Gervase Mathew in the street, and after chatting about literary matters Williams asked him to say a Mass 'for anyone I have ever loved in any way'. Mathew, surprised, promised to do it. The government had declared the following day, Tuesday 8 May, a national holiday—'Victory in Europe Day'. Most of the staff at Southfield House were going to London to celebrate, but Williams said to Helen Peacock, 'Well, you and I, Dorinda, will be there as usual at our desks.'[1496] In the event, with no one else at work, it was pointless to stay, so after 'exchanging a word with Miss Peacock', Williams 'drifted to Magdalen' and had a drink with the Lewis brothers and Colin Hardie, after which he had lunch with the Douglases at the Randolph. Then he returned to South Parks Road, and wrote to Michal:

It's very quiet & silent now. It's also pouring with rain. I'm sitting on the balcony alone in the house. [...] And it's done. I've a dim sense of relief—it *might* have been your mercy; the awful days when I thought the enemy might for ever be between me & you didn't come to the worst. The mourning & the burying are done. [...] There couldn't have been a better Peace Sunday than last. I wish we were together, but that was very good. And now it is nice to be done.[1497]

A group of students telephoned, uncertain whether their tutorial would take place that evening. 'My *dear* young ladies!' said Williams, 'Of course you must do *exactly* what you want to do.' The students (Brenda Tee recalled) 'had talked it over and thought, well, poor chap! He must be glad of a night off, surely, you know! So we said "All right, thank you very much, we have got something to celebrate; so it really would be quite nice this time not to come".'[1498]

With peaceful hours before him, Williams settled to work on *The Figure of Arthur*. Much later, Anne Spalding came home. Together they wandered around Oxford, enjoying the festivities in the streets, the bonfires along the middle of the High Street. Then they walked home and celebrated Peace by switching on the porch light for the first time in six years. From the dark street a voice, probably that of a passing student, intoned, 'Put out the light, and then put out the light!' Williams was ecstatic: it was his favourite line from *Othello*.[1499]

He went to work as usual on 9 May and met the Douglases for lunch at the Randolph. But he seemed unwell, and though he ate a little it became obvious that he was in pain. He told Margaret that he had a severe pain in his stomach. Very concerned, she insisted on walking back to South Parks Road with him and sending him to bed. Anne Spalding telephoned for a doctor but the first was unavailable; only the fifth doctor she called was able to come. By 6 p.m. Williams was feeling so bad that he telephoned Michal, who at once came to Oxford. She did not think at first that he was seriously ill,[1500] and Williams himself made light of it. The doctor, apparently not fully informed of the medical history, diagnosed 'acute constipation and inflammation of the colon', and prescribed medicines. Over the next few days the pain grew much less; but according to Margaret 'he could not keep anything down, nor would any medicine relieve his constipation'.[1501] On Friday, Michal, who had rushed up from London without making any arrangements for the helpless Michael, returned home to attend to domestic matters. On Sunday, since medicines were having no effect, the doctor began to talk about sending Williams to hospital, though the patient himself resisted the idea.[1502] On Monday, 14 May, about noon, he was taken to Oxford's public hospital, the Radcliffe Infirmary. An operation was performed in the evening and, at around 9 p.m., Michal, again staying at South Parks Road, left a message at the Randolph: 'operation performed, condition satisfactory'. She had been told to telephone the hospital at 9 a.m. The doctors were cautiously optimistic: it was the old problem again—intussusception caused by adhesions in the gut. Williams had come well through a similar operation in 1933. However, a member of the medical staff recalled, 'At his operation many adhesions were cut but there was a limit to the amount of searching that could be done and no certainty that all were divided. He was moreover dehydrated from vomiting.'[1503]

In the morning, as Michal was about to make her call, the telephone rang: it was the hospital, asking her to come urgently. Williams had survived the night and even regained consciousness. But, Margaret Douglas reported, 'I understand that there was a sudden collapse, and that he became unconscious just about as she arrived, and died soon after.' Charles Williams died at about 9.30 in the morning on 15 May 1945.[1504]

Epilogue

A t Southfield House, the switchboard took the brief and shocking message from the hospital and transferred the call to Helen Peacock.[1505] Miss Peacock took the news to Milford. She also told Gerry Hopkins and Fred Page. Stunned though they were, they realized that there might be things in Williams's office which would cause Michal pain, so hasty preventive action was taken. Williams had put most of his papers into two large cardboard boxes, ready for return to London, asking Helen Peacock to deal with these 'if anything happened'. The friends collected the other personal papers in his office and added them to the boxes, apparently expecting Miss Peacock to sort them and destroy anything likely to cause trouble. A tearful Margaret Douglas also arrived and 'swept away' a 'packet of Phillida's letters' which, she later recalled, Milford had 'overlooked'[1506]—implying that even Sir Humphrey was involved in the operation. Gerry would later go through one of the boxes, removing some poems and lecture notes; otherwise it seems that the contents were destroyed. All of Phyllis's letters, however—and Williams had kept every one—were returned to her.

Already news of Charles Williams's death was spreading through Oxford. A group of his tutorial students, hearing that he was in hospital, had gone there quite early in the morning, hoping for news. The hospital receptionist had sent them up to his ward, where they were met by the ward sister, who told them that he had died shortly before. They returned home in tears and, from the St Anne's student hostel, telephoned to tell other friends.[1507] John Wain, an English student who thirty-eight years later would become Professor of Poetry at Oxford, recalled:

> I was walking from Longwall Street, where I lodged, towards St. John's, and had just reached the Clarendon Building when a girl I knew by sight came pedalling fast and agitatedly on her bicycle round the corner from New

College Lane. 'John,' she called out, 'Charles Williams is dead.' She had never spoken to me before, and normally would have avoided using my Christian name. But this was a general disaster, like an air-raid, and a touch of comradeliness was right. I asked her for details, but she knew nothing except that he was dead. In any case, she could not talk; she was only just not crying.

I walked on towards St. John's. The war with Germany was over. Charles Williams was dead. And suddenly Oxford was a different place.[1508]

Lewis had set out that morning intending to call on Williams at the hospital on his way to the Eagle and Child, where he would meet Tolkien and others for a drink. He recalled:

I heard of [Williams's] death at the Infirmary itself, having walked up there with a book I wanted to lend him, expecting this news that day as little (almost) as I expected to die that day myself. [...] I thought he would have given me messages to take on to the other [Inklings]. When I joined them with my actual message—it was only a few minutes' walk from the Infirmary but, I remember, the very streets looked different—I had some difficulty in making them believe or even understand what had happened. The world seemed to us at that moment primarily a *strange* one.[1509]

Warnie received the news whilst typing in his brother's rooms at Magdalen:

At 12.50 [...] the telephone rang, and a woman's voice asked if I would take a message for J[ack]—'Mr. Charles Williams died in the Acland this morning'.[1510] One often reads of people being 'stunned' by bad news, and reflects idly on the absurdity of the expression; but there is more than a little truth in it. I felt just as if I had slipped and come down on my head on the pavement. J had told me when I came into College that Charles was ill, and it would mean a serious operation: and then went off to see him: I haven't seen him since. I felt dazed and restless, and went out to get a drink: choosing unfortunately the King's Arms, where during the winter Charles and I more than once drank a pint after leaving Tollers at the Mitre, with much glee at 'clearing one's throat of varnish with good honest beer': as Charles used to say.

There will be no more pints with Charles: no more 'Bird and Baby': the blackout has fallen, and the Inklings can never be the same again. I knew him better than any of the others, by virtue of his being the most constant attendant. I hear his voice as I write, and can see his thin form in his blue suit, opening his cigarette box with trembling hands. These rooms will always hold his ghost for me. There is something horrible, something *unfair* about death, which no religious conviction can overcome. 'Well, goodbye, see you on Tuesday Charles' one says—and you have in fact though you don't know it, said goodbye for ever. He passes up the lamplit street, and passes out of your life for ever. [...] And so vanishes one of the best and nicest men it has ever been my good fortune to meet. May God receive him into His everlasting happiness.[1511]

Back at the Randolph, the faithful Margaret Douglas had telephoned Alice Mary, and Phyllis McDougall. Then she set to work, serving her hero as she had so often done, by typing: for he had given her a list of people who should be told in case of his death—not an unusual step to take in wartime. Now Margaret wrote to one after another of the Companions and close friends. She also telephoned Joan Wallis, for whom Charles Williams had left one last mission.

Michal, meanwhile, went about the bleak task of registering her husband's death. The causes were given as '(a) Acute Intestinal Obstruction (b) Adhesions (c) Previous operation for obstruction and Tuberculous glands in mesentery'. The seeds of his death had been sown in childhood, swallowed with the cheap unpasteurized milk drunk by the poor.

At the Press, Milford telephoned Faber and Faber, but failing to reach either Eliot or Geoffrey Faber, he sent a brief note:

My dear Faber,
I tried to speak first to Eliot on the telephone this afternoon, but your secretary told me he was in Paris, and afterwards to you, but you were out, to tell you the very sad and entirely sudden news of Charles Williams' death this morning after an operation. As in a paper of instructions which Williams left he asked specially that Eliot should be told I am writing this letter to you as it is the nearest I can do to carrying out his wishes.
Yours sincerely,
HS Milford.[1512]

Some time in the afternoon Joan Wallis arrived, having taken a train from London. Already known at Southfield House, she was allowed into Charles's office, where she removed from the cupboard his magical regalia—the sword she had so much disliked, his Rosicrucian robes, and perhaps other items. She took them to 9 South Parks Road where, with the co-operation of Anne Spalding, she buried them in the garden.[1513] House and garden are now gone, replaced since 1970 by new university buildings.

★   ★   ★

The funeral was arranged for Friday, 18 May, to take place in the beautiful twelfth-century St Cross Church, where Charles Williams had so often worshipped. We can picture the scene, as the priest enters, walking ahead of the coffin, which is covered with roses,[1514] and proclaiming 'I am the resurrection and the life, saith the Lord: he that believeth in me, though he were dead, yet shall he live: and whosoever liveth and believeth in me shall never die.' The church is crowded with friends, colleagues (Press and University), and undergraduates who have valued Williams's teaching. Milford, Fred Page, and Gerry Hopkins are of course there. Charles Williams's mother is too frail to attend: she has stayed in St Albans, cared for by her sister-in-law, Alice Wall. But here is Edith, Charles's sister. She will continue to live near St Albans Abbey, running a secretarial school until the 1960s. A regular churchgoer, she will be known in her later years as a quietly contemplative—almost a saintly—woman. With her is Alice Mary Miller, who in October will marry Charles Hadfield. A keen Companion, she will remain devoted to Williams's memory and teaching, and will publish two books about him. Some will think her too vehement in her advocacy—not understanding how heavily Williams's question ('Am I not to leave my reputation in your care?') continues to weigh upon her.[1515] Among the many students stands an older man, Robin Milford, who has cycled here with lines by Williams—

> 'The entire point of the thrice co-inherent Trinity
> When every crown & every choir is vanished
> And all the sight & hearing is nothing else'

– echoing in his head.[1516] Milford will continue to compose music, and to fight against depression, until 1956, when he will take his own life. And here are Isabel and Margaret Douglas. Margaret—who has loved Williams devotedly—is utterly bereft. Soon they will leave Oxford for their flat in Maida Vale, where Margaret will continue to study Williams's works and meet his friends. With them is Anne Ridler, who has come up from London.[1517] She will become a well-known poet, critic, and librettist, and a prominent advocate for Williams's literary work. She will return to Oxford with her husband Vivian, who will become Printer to the University of Oxford and a world-renowned typographer. Anne will die in 2001.

Tolkien is there: a devout Roman Catholic, nothing prevents him from attending an Anglican funeral. Beside him is Fr Gervase Mathew, who will say a Mass for Williams the next day, at which Tolkien himself will serve. It will be nine years before *The Fellowship of the Ring* will appear, setting Tolkien on the path to unforeseen international fame. But his friendship with Lewis will gradually cool; and looking back, in the 1960s, he will blame 'the sudden apparition of Charles Williams' as well as Lewis's marriage in 1956. Naturally, Jack and Warnie are present. Jack may be shaken, but his faith is not. Soon he will write to Michal:

> My friendship is not ended. His death has had the very unexpected effect of making death itself look different: I believe in the next life ten times more strongly than I did then. At moments it seems almost tangible [...] he seems, in some indefinable way, to be all around us now.[1518]

A student will recall seeing Lewis, after the service—to her astonishment—'leap neatly over a grave, like a 20 yr. old, to say hello, [...] clearly celebrating a triumphant entry into Heaven of such a dear friend'.[1519] The writer Reneée Haynes, there to represent *Time and Tide*, felt the same: 'I don't know, I think he *must* have been at that funeral—I came away that afternoon really reassured that that immense, felicitous and dedicated vitality isn't gone, not even out of reach.' And she remembers his kindness: how he calmed her 'panic' before she became a Roman Catholic; how he 'help[ed] to carry a baby in a pushcart up the steps of a Tube station—an entirely unknown baby'.[1520]

In a front pew, with Edith, are Michal and Michael. Michal is elegant and stoical as always; still in a state of shock, she is nonetheless determined to carry out the plans she made with Charles in his last months. 'I am going to live at Oxford', she will tell Anne Ridler:

> Charles & I had decided to spend his retirement there & we had made such wonderful plans. I dont want Michael to be tied to me. I have seen so many sons trapped that way & he should be independent. [...] I thought it would be nice to settle at Oxford & all of you who loved Charles could come & visit me.[1521]

But none of this will happen. She and Michael will continue to live together in the Hampstead flat on her widow's pension, the small royalties from Charles's books, and Michael's irregular earnings from bookshops. The prospect of a publishing job in New York will fade away, Michael will write no more literary journalism, and he will never settle into any determined career. Nor will he form any other long-term personal relationship. At times he will share a bedroom with his mother; at times, too, he will seek psychiatric help.

Michal will wait for the literary world to rediscover her husband's work, but will have no truck with biographers—whose output, she believes, is 'the genteel woman's News of the World' and would inevitably draw attention

to 'Charles moral & spiritual lapse'.[1522] This attitude, and the cautious dila-
toriness of Raymond Hunt, with whom Michal will have frequent disagreements, will hinder the propagation of Williams's work. A project to publish
his wartime letters to Michal will be tinkered with for almost half a century.
They will appear only in 2002, one year after Michael's death and thirty-two years after Michal's.

Raymond Hunt, for some reason, is not at the funeral. Nor is Phyllis
McDougall. Hubert Foss will hear of his friend's death only that day. He will
write to Michal:

> I cannot express [to] you the terrible grief I feel at this disastrous news of
> Charles's death. I am numbed with the shock and the sadness of it. No pen
> lesser than that of Milton Shelley or Arnold could attempt to speak of the love
> and admiration in which I had held Charles for nearly twenty-five years. [...]
> Only a day or two ago I was dreaming in the early morning of the delight that
> now the war is over, that I should find in the return of Charles to London and
> the renewal, as I was hoping, of that long association of poet & master of words
> with printer & musician which has been all my working life a source of so
> much inspiration to me.[1523]

Foss will live a short and brilliant life; he will die in 1953, aged fifty-four.

Charles Williams will be buried in Holywell cemetery, the small rural
burial-ground beside the church. His gravestone will be cut with a decora-
tive wreath designed by Vivian Ridler, and the words:

CHARLES WALTER STANSBY WILLIAMS
Poet
20 Sep. 1886
15 May 1945
UNDER THE MERCY

In due course the remains of Michal and Michael will also lie there. Perhaps
the finest literary tribute to Charles will be a sonnet by Anne Ridler, 'Charles
Williams: In Anamnesis'

> This is a likeness but it does not speak.
> The words are echoes, the image looks from the wall
> Of many minds, kindling in each the spark
> Of passionate joy, yet silent in them all.
> Pupils grow older, but a long-dead master
> Stands where they parted, ageless on his hill.
> The child grows to be father of his father,
> Yet keeps relation, kneels in homage still.

What is the speech of the dead? Words on a page
Where Taliessin launched his lines of glory
Capture for him a poet's immortality
As every reader wakes them. So the image
Speaks through a living mind, as he in life
Would use from each the little that each could give.[1524]

And so often the dead return in dreams. In 1948 C.S. Lewis wrote to Michal:

It began as a nightmare. I was being followed through a house of many passages by lions and came out down a backstair onto a moonlit lawn. A figure
approached—touched my hand—'Hallo Jack!'—and it was Charles. And
I knew that everything (lions included) was ALL RIGHT. I live on him almost
every day. Sometimes I have felt he was just beside me and almost heard him
say, with his inimitable gaiety, 'You know, the only reason I don't *appear* is that
it would be . . . well, bad manners.'[1525]

Michal too would catch one last glimpse of him in a dream. In 1958 she told
a friend:

I dreamt of Charles the other night. He was standing on a niche in a cathedral
I could not identify. His garments were beyond whiteness & he looked very
very grave & he looked & looked at me.[1526]

Endnotes

1. Hadfield (1959) p. 14; Hadfield, who interviewed Charles Williams's sister about her early memories, is an essential source for much information about Charles Williams's childhood, which cannot now be attested from other sources.
2. *Witchcraft*, p. 77.
3. 'Disillusion in Literature', *Sunday Times*, 1 May 1939.
4. Hadfield (1983) p. 3.
5. 1891 census.
6. Edith Williams, 'Memories of Early Days at Home', CWSA.
7. 1861 census.
8. Edith Williams, 'Memories of Early Days at Home', CWSA.
9. 1861, 1871, 1891 censuses.
10. Amended birth certificate of R.W.S Williams, Wade, WFPA 48.
11. Wade, WFPA 48.
12. Hadfield (1959) p. 13.
13. Hadfield (1983) p. 5.
14. Hadfield (1983) p. 5.
15. Wade, WFPA 35.
16. Ridler (1958) p. xii.
17. Invoices in Wall's papers at the Society of Antiquaries of London.
18. Charles Wall, *Shrines of British Saints*, pp. ix, x.
19. King, p. 114.
20. Hadfield (1983) p. 6.
21. Edith Williams, 'Memories of Early Days at Home', CWSA.
22. Hadfield (1983) p. 6.
23. Ridler (1958) p. xii.
24. Edith Williams, 'Memories of Early Days at Home', CWSA.
25. Ridler (1958) p. xii.
26. Edith Williams, 'Memories of Early Days at Home', CWSA.
27. Edith Williams, 'Memories of Early Days at Home', CWSA.
28. Edith Williams, 'Memories of Early Days at Home', CWSA.
29. Alice Goodman, *The Story of the Abbey School*.
30. Hadfield (1959) p. 14.
31. Edith Williams, 'Memories of Early Days at Home', CWSA.

32. *Divorce*, p. 8.
33. MS poem in Christmas card sent to Hubert Foss, 1924; courtesy of Diana Sparkes.
34. Hadfield (1959) pp. 21–2.
35. Elsie Toms, *The Story of St Albans*, p. 178.
36. Toms, *The Story of St Albans*, p. 176.
37. Toms, *The Story of St Albans*, p. 177.
38. St Albans School entry register.
39. Frank I. Kilvington, *A Short History of St Albans School*, p. 70.
40. Kilvington, *A Short History of St Albans School*, p. 71.
41. Hadfield (1959) p. 20.
42. Hadfield (1959) p. 19.
43. Ridler (1958) p. xii.
44. Hadfield (1959) p. 19.
45. Hadfield (1983) p. 8.
46. Hadfield (1959) p. 17.
47. *Divorce*, p. 8.
48. Wade, WFPA 62.
49. Hadfield (1959) p. 20.
50. Wade, CWMS 113.
51. Hadfield (1959) p. 21.
52. Hadfield (1959) p. 20.
53. Hadfield (1959) p. 22.
54. Hadfield (1959) p. 20.
55. *The Albanian*, July 1902.
56. *The Albanian*, July 1903.
57. Hadfield (1983) p. 11 gives the wrong date.
58. George Robinson to Anne Ridler, undated, Bodleian, ARP.
59. UCL *Calendar*, 1902.
60. Entrance forms, UCL Records Office.
61. Hadfield (1959) p. 11.
62. CW to Alice Wall, 2 June 1902, Wade, CWP 83.
63. UCL *Calendar*.
64. Ridler (1958) p. xiv.
65. Wade, CWP 172.
66. Wade, CWP 172.
67. Wade, CWP 172.
68. Wade, CWP 172.
69. George Robinson to Anne Ridler, undated, Bodleian ARP.
70. Hadfield (1959) p. 23.
71. *The Albanian*, July 1903; Hadfield (1959) p. 22.
72. George Robinson to Anne Ridler, undated, Bodleian ARP.
73. UCL *Calendar*.

74. UCL entrance forms.

75. Ridler (1958) pp. xiv–xv.

76. George Robinson to Anne Ridler, undated, Bodleian, ARP.

77. Ridler (1958) p. xiv.

78. Hadfield (1983) pp. 11–12, quoting Edith Williams.

79. Hadfield (1983) p. 12.

80. Hadfield (1983) p. 12 credits Alice Wall; George Robinson to Anne Ridler, undated, Bodleian, ARP, credits Charles Wall.

81. Hadfield (1983) p. 12.

82. 'Letters to Peter', *GK's Weekly*, 18 June 1936.

83. Hadfield (1959) p. 26.

84. Frederick Page to Anne Ridler, undated, Bodleian, ARP.

85. George Robinson to Anne Ridler, undated, Bodleian, ARP.

86. Hadfield (1959) p. 26.

87. CW to Anne Renwick, 20 May 1941, Bodleian, MS. Eng. Lett. d. 452.

88. Wade, CWP 87b.

89. *St Albans Pageant, July 1907* [official brochure], Gibbs and Bamforth, St Albans.

90. Toms, *The Story of St Albans*, pp. 179–80.

91. Wade, Charles Williams Photo Collection.

92. Wade, CWMS 101.

93. Michal Williams, 'As I Remember', Wade, WFPA 41.

94. *Poems of Conformity*, p. 43.

95. *Kelly's Post Office Directory* 1883, 1884, 1885.

96. Wade, WFPA 73.

97. Wade, WFPA 73.

98. Wade, WFPA 41.

99. Wade, WFPA 41.

100. Hadfield (1959) p. 31.

101. Hadfield (1983) p. 13.

102. Hadfield (1959) p. 35.

103. Peter Sutcliffe, *The Oxford University Press*, p. 164.

104. Coventry Patmore, 'To the Body', lines 11–12.

105. Derek Patmore, *The Life and Times of Coventry Patmore*, p. 196.

106. Coventry Patmore, 'The Contract', lines 59–67, 75–6.

107. Coventry Patmore, 'Deliciae Sapientiae de Amore', lines 57–8, 61–6, 69–71.

108. Coventry Patmore, 'The Child's Purchase', lines 96–7.

109. Edmund Gosse, *Coventry Patmore*, pp. 169–70.

110. Claude Colleer Abbott, ed., *Further Letters of Gerard Manley Hopkins*, p. xxxvi.

111. Claude Colleer Abbott, ed., *Further Letters of Gerard Manley Hopkins*, p. 365.

112. Gosse, *Coventry Patmore*, pp. 167–70.

113. Wade, WFPA 41.

114. *The Silver Stair*, XVI.

115. *The Silver Stair*, XX.

116. *The Silver Stair*, XXXIX.
117. Wade, WFPA 39.
118. Wade, WFPA 41.
119. 2 Samuel 6: 14–16.
120. 2 Samuel 6: 23.
121. Frederick Page to Alice Meynell, 3 May 1911, Greatham.
122. CW to Alice Wall, 4 June 1911, Wade, CWP 83.
123. CW to Alice Wall, 4 June 1911, Wade, CWP 83.
124. CW to Alice Meynell, Bodleian, MS. Eng.c. 2724, f.85.
125. CW to Wilfrid Meynell, 7 July 1911, Greatham.
126. CW to Alice Meynell, 6 Nov 1911, Greatham.
127. Alice Meynell to CW, 16 Feb [1912], Wade, CWP 369.
128. CW to Alice Meynell, 17 Feb 1912, Greatham.
129. CW to Alice Meynell, 25 Mar 1912, Greatham.
130. Wilfrid Meynell to CW, 24 July 1912, Wade, CWP 371.
131. CW to Wilfrid Meynell, 27 July 1912, Greatham.
132. Wilfrid Meynell to CW, 14 Oct 1912, Wade, CWP 371.
133. CW to Wilfrid Meynell, 12 Nov 1912, Greatham.
134. Greatham.
135. Viola Meynell, *Alice Meynell: A Memoir*, p. 258.
136. Walter Raleigh to H.S. Milford, 22 Nov 1912, Greatham.
137. Wade, CWMS 39.
138. Wade, CWMS 39.
139. Wade, CWMS 39.
140. Alice Meynell to CW, 28 May [1915], Wade, CWP 369.
141. Ridler (1958) pp. 179–80.
142. Frederick Page to Anne Ridler, undated, Bodleian, ARP.
143. Bodleian, MS Eng. e. 2012.
144. Bodleian, MS Eng. e. 2012, p. 65.
145. *Letters of Evelyn Underhill*, ed. Charles Williams, p. 15.
146. Roger Simpson, 'Arthurian Pageants in Twentieth-Century Britain', *Arthuriana*, XVIII (2008), pp. 63-87.
147. 5 July 1913, Fred Page to Alice Meynell, Greatham.
148. Alice Meynell to CW, 10 July 1914, Wade, CWP 369.
149. Alice Meynell to CW, 10 July 1914, Wade, CWP 369.
150. CW to Dorothy L. Sayers, 7 Sept 1944, Wade, Dorothy L. Sayers Papers, 116.
151. Andrew Frisardi, 'Selections from the *Vita Nuova*', *Temenos Academy Review*, 10 (2010), p. 29.
152. FP to CW 29 July 1914, Wade, CWP 392.
153. Hadfield (1983) p. 23; E. M. Forster, 'E.K. Bennett', *The Caian*, V, p. 124.
154. Wade, CWMS 244.
155. Wade, WFPA 35.
156. Sutcliffe, *Oxford University Press*, p. 172.

157. *Poems of Conformity*, p. 25.
158. Hadfield (1983) pp. 24–5.
159. 27 Oct 1917, CW to Wilfrid Meynell, Greatham.
160. 8 Dec 1917, CW to Wilfrid Meynell, Greatham.
161. CW to Wilfrid Meynell, 14 July 1916, Greatham.
162. 20 May 1917, CW to Olive Willis, Bodleian, E. Martin Browne Literary Papers, Box 4.
163. Hadfield (1983) p. 23.
164. Alice Meynell to CW, 5 Dec [1914], Greatham.
165. Alice Meynell to CW, 11 Sept [1915], Wade, CWP 369.
166. CW to Alice Meynell, 14 July 1916, Greatham.
167. CW to Alice Meynell, 9 Nov 1916, Greatham.
168. Alice Meynell to CW, 14 Nov [1916], Wade CWP 369.
169. 17 Nov 1916, CW to Alice Meynell, Greatham.
170. Hadfield (1983) p. 25.
171. Sutcliffe, *Oxford University Press*, p. 165.
172. Hadfield (1983) p. 25.
173. CW to Wilfrid Meynell, 21 Feb 1917, Greatham.
174. OUP Archive, *Amen Corner Letters Copied*, Vol. 46, p. 729.
175. Wade, WFPA, [Lindop G. 34].
176. 14 July 1916, CW to Alice, Meynell, Greatham.
177. 14 July 1916, CW to Alice, Meynell, Greatham.
178. 21 Feb 1917, CW to Wilfrid, Meynell, Greatham.
179. 28 Feb 1917, CW to Wilfrid, Meynell, Greatham.
180. Wilfrid Meynell to CW, 26 Feb 1917, Wade, CWP 372.
181. CW to Wilfrid Meynell, 28 Feb 1917, Greatham.
182. Hadfield (1983) p. 25.
183. CW to Wilfrid Meynell, 13 Apr 1917, Greatham.
184. CW to Olive Willis, 20 May 1917, Bodleian, E. Martin Browne Literary Papers, Box 4.
185. CW to Alice Meynell, 3 July 1917, Greatham.
186. OUP Archive, OP 3457/22911.
187. Ellic Howe, *The Magicians of the Golden Dawn*, p. 57.
188. R.A. Gilbert, *Golden Dawn Companion*, pp. 171, 173.
189. OUP Archive, OP 3457/22911.
190. A.E. Waite, *Hidden Church of the Holy Graal*, p. 679.
191. Gilbert, *A.E. Waite*, p. 148.
192. Gilbert, *A.E. Waite*, p. 123.
193. Gilbert *A.E. Waite*, p. 148.
194. Waite, *Hidden Church of the Holy Graal*, p. 636.
195. Gilbert, *A.E. Waite*, p. 13.
196. MS Diary of A.E. Waite, private collection.
197. A.E. Waite to CW, 14 July 1917, Wade CWP.

198. FRC Form of Profession, private collection.

199. A.E. Waite, *Real History of the Rosicrucians*, p. 426.

200. Waite, *Hidden Church of the Holy Graal*, p. 679.

201. Waite, *Hidden Church of the Holy Graal*, p. 637.

202. A.E. Waite to CW, 6 Sept 1917, Wade, CWP 457.

203. This reconstruction is based on Anonymous [A.E. Waite,] *The First Order of the Rosy Cross. World of Action Part I. The Ceremony of Reception into the Grade of Neophyte, o = o*. Privately Printed, 1916.

204. Gilbert, *Golden Dawn Companion*, p. 171.

205. Obituary of A.H.E. Lee by CW, *Church Times*, 14 Mar 1941.

206. Charles Williams and R.R. Graves, *In Memoriam: Arthur Hugh Evelyn Lee, Priest*, [memorial service programme, sheet, 1941] Wade Center Article File, 2pp., CW-MISC.

207. R.A. Gilbert to Grevel Lindop, 6 May 2011, updating his *Golden Dawn Companion*.

208. A.H.E. Lee's will.

209. King, pp. 30, 111, 112.

210. Warburg Institute Library, Yorke Collection, NS 32.

211. Francis King, ed., *Astral Projection, Ritual Magic and Alchemy, passim*.

212. Anne Ridler Interview 2.

213. Ridler (1958), p. xxiv.

214. 'Ourselves and the Revolution', p. 10.

215. CW to Olive Willis, 2 July 1918, Wade, CWP 156; CW to Olive Willis, 18 Oct 1918, Bodleian, E. Martin Browne Literary Papers, Box 4.

216. Anne Ridler, *Olive Willis and Downe House*, p. 66.

217. Anne Ridler, *Memoirs*, p. 60.

218. CW to Olive Willis, 11 Aug 1918, Bodleian, E. Martin Browne Literary Papers, Box 4.

219. Wade, WFPA 39, pp. iii–iv.

220. CW to Olive Willis, 11 Aug 1918, Bodleian, E. Martin Browne Literary Papers, Box 4.

221. CW to Olive Willis, 11 Aug 1918, Bodleian, E. Martin Browne Literary Papers Box 4.

222. Michal Williams to Glen Cavaliero, 22 July 1955 and 25 July 1955.

223. Michal Williams to Anne Ridler, 25 June 1957, Bodleian, ARP.

224. Michal Williams to Anne Ridler, 25 June 1957, Bodleian, ARP.

225. Michal to Anne Ridler, undated, Bodleian ARP.

226. Hadfield (1959) p. 53.

227. Michal Williams, *Christian Symbolism*, p. 6.

228. Lois Lang–Sims, *Letters to Lalage*, p. 80.

229. Michal Williams to Glen Cavaliero, 18 July 1955.

230. 30 July 1918, CW to Alice Meynell, Greatham.

231. Hadfield (1929) p. 58.

232. Hadfield (1959) p. 58.

233. Alice Meynell to CW, Mar 8 [?1919], Wade, CWP 369.

234. Alice Meynell to CW, 19 Nov [?1919], Wade, CWP 369.

235. OUP Archive, OP 1364/10108.

236. CW to Aylmer Maude, 14 May 1921, OUP Archive, OP 1365.

237. OUP Archive, OP 1365.

238. J.S. Philllimore, 'The Poet Williams', *New Witness*, 10 Jan 1918.

239. Theodore Maynard, 'The Satanist', *New Witness*, 7 Feb 1918.

240. Theodore Maynard, 'The Poetry of Charles Williams', *North American Review*, 1919, Vol. CCX (No. 766), p. 26.

241. Theodore Maynard, 'The Poetry of Charles Williams', *North American Review*, 1919, Vol. CCX (No. 766), p. 26.

242. CW to Alice Meynell, 30 July 1918, Greatham.

243. CW to Olive Willis, 24 July 1918, Bodleian, E. Martin Browne Literary Papers, Box 4.

244. John Pellow's Diary, Bodleian, MS Facs. c. 134.

245. 'Grade of Neophyte', Anonymous [A.E. Waite,] *FRC: Points of Contemplation Preliminary to All Grades*, privately printed, [London] 1923.

246. Anonymous [A.E. Waite], *The Third Order of the Rosy Cross: World of Formation Part II. The Pontifical Ceremony of Admission to the Grade of Adeptus Minor, 5=6*, Privately Printed, [London], 1917. p. 55.

247. Waite, *Record of the Holy House*, MS, private collection.

248. R.A. Gilbert, *A.E. Waite*, p. 149.

249. Ridler (1958), pp. xxiv–xxv.

250. *The English Poetic Mind*, pp. 116–17.

251. Michal Williams to Anne Ridler, undated, Bodleian, ARP.

252. CW to Phyllis Jones, Bodleian, MS Res. c. 320 mixed undated II, 60a-d.

253. Atwood, *A Suggestive Enquiry into the Hermetic Mystery*, 1850, rpt. 1918, *passim*.

254. Henry Proctor, *Evolution and Regeneration,* p. 62.

255. Henry Proctor, *The Secret of Life*, pp. 116–17.

256. Proctor, *The Secret of Life*, p. 77.

257. D.H.S. Nicholson, *The Mysticism of St Francis of Assisi*, p. 193.

258. Nicholson, *The Mysticism of St Francis of Assisi*, pp. 193–6.

259. CW to Olive Willis, 18 Oct 1918, Bodleian, E. Martin Browne Literary Papers Box 4.

260. Wade, CWMS 139.

261. Alice Meynell to CW, 8 Mar?1919, Wade, CWMS 139.

262. Greatham.

263. CWSN, 7, Autumn 1977, p. 2.

264. CWSN, 7, Autumn 1977, p. 2.

265. John Pellow's Diary, Bodleian, MS Facs. c. 134.

266. John Pellow to CW, 19 Apr 1921, Wade.

267. CW to JP, undated (?Oct 1921), Wade, CWP 54.

268. CW to JP, 8 Oct 1921, Wade, CWP 54.

269. CW to John Pellow, undated, Wade, CWP 54.
270. John Pellow's Diary, 22 Nov 1923, Bodleian, MS Facs. 134.
271. John Pellow's Diary, 28 Apr 1923, Bodleian, MS Facs. c. 134.
272. CW to John Pellow, 26 Apr 23 1923, Wade, CWMS 54.
273. CW to John Pellow, 6 Oct. 1921, Wade, CWMS 54.
274. CWSN, 7, Autumn 1977, p. 1.
275. CW to John Pellow, 18 Jan 1922, Wade, CWP 54.
276. Sutcliffe, *The Oxford University Press*, p. 210.
277. CW to John Pellow, 6 July 1922, Wade, CWP 54.
278. CW to John Pellow, undated [1922], Wade, CWP 54.
279. CW to Olive Willis, undated [1922], Bodleian, E. Martin Browne Literary Papers, Box 4.
280. CWSN 7, Autumn 1977, p. 2.
281. CW to John Pellow, 12 Sept 1923, Wade, CWP 54.
282. John Pellow's Diary, 21 Nov 1923, Bodleian MS Facs. c. 134.
283. John Pellow's Diary, 3 July 1925, Bodleian MS Facs. c. 134.
284. CW to John Pellow, 4 July 1925, Wade, CWP 54.
285. John Pellow's Diary, 15 Sept 1923, Bodleian, MS Facs. c. 134.
286. John Pellow's Diary, 3 May 1924, Bodleian MS Facs. c. 134.
287. CW to John Pellow, undated [1922], Wade, CWP 54.
288. CW to John Pellow, 21 Sept [1922], Wade, CWP 54.
289. CW to John Pellow, 19 Dec 1923, Wade, CWP 54.
290. CW to John Pellow, undated [?1923], Wade, CWP 54; John Pellow's Diary, 6 July 1923, Bodleian, MS Facs. c. 134.
291. John Pellow's Diary, 6 July 1923, Bodleian, MS Facs. c. 134.
292. CW to Olive Willis, 12 Aug 1923, Bodleian, E. Martin Browne Literary Papers, Box 4.
293. CW to Olive Willias, undated, Bodleian E. Martin Browne Literary Papers Box 4.
294. Thelma Shuttleworth, 'Love and Friendship', CWSN 27, Autumn 1982, p. 3.
295. Eric Maskell, *Saraband*, quoted in CWSN, 70, Summer 1993, p. 12.
296. CWSN 27, Autumn 1982, p. 3.
297. CWSN 6, Summer 1977, p. 8; CWSN 27, Autumn 1982, p. 5.
298. Michal Williams to Glen Cavaliero, 18 July 1955.
299. Anonymous [A.E. Waite], *FRC Grade of Adeptus Exemptus*, privately printed, 1917.
300. Anonymous [Waite, A.E.], *FRC: Grade of Adeptus Exemptus* [London], privately printed, 1917.
301. Michal Williams to Anne Ridler, undated, Bodleian, ARP.
302. Ridler (1958), p. xxv.
303. CW to Anne Bradby, 13 Apr 1934, Bodleian, ARP.
304. CW to Anne Ridler, 25 Mar 1942, Bodleian, ARP.
305. CW to John Pellow, Dec [?1924], Wade, CWP 54.
306. Commonplace Book, Bodleian, MS Eng. E. 2012, pp. 22, 170.

307. CW to Olive Willis, 24 Oct 1918, Bodleian E. Martin Browne Literary Papers, Box 4.

308. John Pellow's Diary, May 3 1924, Bodleian, MS Facs. c. 134.

309. John Pellow's Diary, 21 Nov 1923, Bodleian, MS Facs. c. 134.

310. CW to John Pellow, 5 Oct 1923, Wade, CWP 54; John Pellow's Diary, 21 Aug 1924, Bodleian, MS Facs. c. 134.

311. John Pellow's Diary, 3 Apr 1924, Bodleian, MS Facs. c. 134.

312. John Pellow's Diary, 19 Nov 1923, Bodleian, MS Facs. c. 134.

313. John Pellow's Diary, 8 May 1923, Bodleian, MS Facs. c. 134.

314. John Pellow's Diary: 28 Apr 1923, Bodleian, MS Facs. c. 134.

315. Waite, *The Way of Divine Union*, pp. 287–8.

316. John Pellow's Diary, 15 Sept 1923, Bodleian, MS Facs. c. 134.

317. CW to John Pellow, 5 Sept 1924, Wade, CWP 54.

318. John Pellow's Diary, quoted in Dodds, 'The Chapel of the Thorn: An Unknown Poetic Drama by Charles Williams', *Inklings-Jahrbuch* 5 (1987), 133.

319. John Pellow's Diary, 24 Aug 1924, Bodleian, MS Facs. c. 134.

320. Charles Hadfield, CWSN 19, Autumn 1980, p. 3.

321. Charles Hadfield, CWSN 19, Autumn 1980, p. 3.

322. Wade, CWMS 417.

323. Charles Hadfield, CWSN 19, Autumn 1980, p. 3.

324. Leslie Taylor, CWSN 21, Spring 1981, p. 5.

325. Charles Hadfield, CWSN 19, Autumn 1980, p. 3.

326. Charles Hadfield, CWSN 19, Autumn 1980, p. 3.

327. Kenneth Day, CWSN 21, Spring 1981, pp. 4–5.

328. Ralph Binfield, CWSN 9, Spring 1978, p. 3.

329. Ralph Binfield, CWSN 9, Spring 1978, p. 3.

330. Ralph Binfield, CWSN 9, Spring 1978, p. 3.

331. J. W. [*sic*], *The Record* [OUP] 9, Dec 1964.

332. Charles Hadfield, CWSN 19, Autumn 1980, p. 3.

333. Johanne Schuller Interview.

334. Ralph Binfield, CWSN 9, Spring 1978, p. 3.

335. Hadfield (1983) p. 56.

336. Ralph Binfield, unpublished essay, 'Working With Charles Williams', courtesy of Joy Cooper.

337. OUP Archive, OP 1365/10110.

338. OUP Archive, OP 1365/10110.

339. OUP Archive, OP 1365/10110.

340. CW to Olive Willis, undated [late 1922], Bodleian, E. Martin Browne Literary Papers, Box 4.

341. CW to Olive Willis, 14 May 1923, Bodleian, E. Martin Browne Literary Papers, Box 4.

342. CW to John Pellow, 5 Oct 1923, Wade, CWP 54.

343. CW to John Pellow, 14 Apr 1924, Wade, CWP 54.

344. John Pellow's Diary, Bodleian MS Facs. c. 134.
345. CW to John Pellow, 5 Sept 1924, Wade, CWP 54.
346. CW to John Pellow, 6 Sept 24, Wade, CWP 54.
347. CW to John Pellow, 16 Sept 1924, Wade, CWP 54.
348. CW to John Pellow, 3 Oct 1924, Wade, CWP 54.
349. *Outlines of Romantic Theology*, p. 7.
350. *Outlines of Romantic Theology*, p. 10.
351. *Outlines of Romantic Theology*, p. 14.
352. *Outlines of Romantic Theology*, p. 25.
353. *Outlines of Romantic Theology*, p. 48.
354. *Outlines of Romantic Theology*, p. 44.
355. Waite, *The Secret Doctrine in Israel*, p. 239.
356. *Outlines of Romantic Theology*, p. 55 n.
357. *Outlines of Romantic Theology*, p. 24.
358. Nicholson, *The Marriage-Craft*, p. 7.
359. Nicholson, *The Marriage-Craft*, p. 8.
360. Nicholson's will and codicil.
361. Nicholson, *The Marriage-Craft*, p. 34.
362. Nicholson, *The Marriage-Craft*, p. 207.
363. Nicholson, *The Marriage-Craft*, p. 210.
364. Nicholson, *The Marriage-Craft*, p. 215.
365. Nicholson, *The Marriage-Craft*, p. 225.
366. OUP Archive, *Amen Corner Letters Copied*, Vol 58.
367. Wilfrid Meynell to CW, 8 Jan 1925, Wade, CWP 371.
368. A.E. Housman to CW, 12 Jan 1925, Wade, CWP 282.
369. CW to John Pellow, 16 June 1925, Wade, CWP 54.
370. CW to Olive Willis, 12 Aug 1923, Bodleian, E. Martin Browne Literary Papers, Box 4.
371. John Pellow's Diary, 22 June 1925, Bodleian MS Facs. c. 134.
372. John Pellow's Diary, 22 June 1925, Bodleian MS Facs. c. 134.
373. John Pellow's Diary, 26 July 1925, Bodleian MS Facs. c. 134.
374. John Pellow's Diary, 28 July 1925, Bodleian MS Facs. c. 134.
375. CW to John Pellow, 2 Nov 1925, Wade, CWP 54.
376. *Detective Fiction Reviews*, p. 104.
377. CW to Olive Willis, 23 Dec 1925, Bodleian E. Martin Browne Literary Papers, Box 4.
378. CW to John Pellow, 17 July 1925, Wade, CWP 54.
379. CW to John Pellow, Monday [Aug] 1925, Wade, CWP 54.
380. Gilbert, *A.E. Waite*, p. 149.
381. *Shadows of Ecstasy*, Chapter 3.
382. *Shadows of Ecstasy*, Chapter 7.
383. *Shadows of Ecstasy*, Chapter 5.
384. Irene Smith, CWSNL 21, Spring 1981, p. 6.

385. Hadfield (1983) p. 78.

386. Ralph Binfield, 'Charles Williams as I Knew Him', CWSNL, 2, Summer 1976, p. 9; 'Working with Charles Williams', courtesy of Joy Cooper.

387. CW to OW, 23 Dec 1925, Bodleian E. Martin Browne Literary Papers, Box 4.

388. John Pellow's Diary, Jan 2 1926. Bodleian MS Facs. c. 134.

389. John Pellow's Diary, 4 Jan 1926, Bodleian MS Facs. c. 134.

390. John Pellow's Diary, 5 Jan 1926, Bodleian MS Facs. c. 134.

391. Phyllis McDougall Interview.

392. CW to Phyllis Jones, undated, Bodleian MS Res. c. 320, mixed undated XII 350c.

393. CW to John Pellow, May 1926, Wade, CWP.

394. Duncan Hinnells, *An Extraordinary Performance*, p. 26.

395. Charles Hadfield, CWSNL 19, Autumn 1980, p. 4.

396. GRO, Probate records.

397. Hadfield (1983) p. 56.

398. Phyllis Jones to CW, Bodleian MS Res. c. 320, Mixed undated II, c. 1929–30, F47a.

399. Phyllis McDougall Interview.

400. Phyllis McDougall Interview.

401. Hadfield (1983) p. 56.

402. Phyllis McDougall Interview.

403. CW to Phyllis Jones, Bodleian, MS Res. c. 320/VIII, letter 211.

404. CW to Edith Williams, undated Wade, CWP [Lindop R.10].

405. CW to Phyllis Jones, 1 Aug 1926, Bodleian MS Res. c. 320/VIII, letter 222.

406. Phyllis Jones to CW, undated, Bodleian MS Res. c. 321.

407. Hadfield (1983) p.60.

408. *Times* Index, 6 Dec 1926.

409. Phyllis McDougall Interview.

410. *The Chaste Wanton*, scene III, in *Three Plays*.

411. Hadfield (1983) p. 72.

412. CW to Raymond Hunt, 1 Mar 1940, Wade, CWP 30.

413. Phyllis Jones to CW, Bodleian MS Res. c. 320, Mixed undated II, c. 1929–30, f. 47a.

414. Bodleian MS Res. c. 137.

415. Nicholson, *The Marriage-Craft*, p. 225.

416. Wade, CWMS 392.

417. CW to Raymond Hunt, 1 Mar 1940, Wade, CWP 30.

418. CWSN 27, Autumn 1982, p.3.

419. Phyllis McDougall Interview; I follow CW's dates in Wade CWMS 417 rather than Hadfield's.

420. Phyllis McDougall Interview.

421. CW to Hubert Foss, 26 Jan 1927; courtesy Diana Sparkes.

422. Ralph Binfield, 'Charles Williams as I knew Him', CWSN 2, Summer 1976, p. 9.

423. CWSN 21, Spring 1981, p. 7.
424. CW to Phyllis Jones, undated [1927], Bodleian, MS Res. c. 320, mixed undated VII, 197a.
425. CW to Raymond Hunt, 1 Mar 1940, Wade, CWP 30.
426. D.H.S. Nicholson to Anne Bradby, 28 Nov 1934, Bodleian, ARP.
427. CW to John Pellow, 2 Dec [1926], Wade, CWP 54.
428. CW to Olive Willis, Dec [1926], Bodleian E. Martin Browne Literary Papers, Box 4.
429. Phyllis Jones to CW, Bodleian, MS Res. c. 320, Mixed undated II, f60.
430. Phyllis Jones to CW, undated, Bodleian, MS Res. c. 321.
431. CW to H.S. Milford, 28 Feb 1930, Wade MS 182.
432. CW to Phyllis Jones, Bodleian MS Res. c. 320.1/VIII, 211.
433. CW to Phyllis Jones, Bodleian MS Res. c. 320, mixed undated VIII, 212e.
434. Hadfield (1983) p. 60.
435. Phyllis McDougall Interview.
436. Phyllis Jones to CW, Bodleian, MS Res. c. 320, mixed undated II, 55b.
437. CW to Phyllis Jones, undated, Bodleian MS Res. c. 321.
438. CW to Phyllis Jones, Bodleian MS Res. c. 320/I, letter 18.
439. Phyllis Jones to CW, Bodleian MS Res. c. 320, mixed undated II, f47.
440. Phyllis Jones to CW, Bodleian MS Res. c. 321.
441. Phyllis Jones to CW, Bodleian MS Res. c. 321.
442. Phyllis Jones to CW, undated, Bodleian MS Res. c. 321.
443. CW to Phyllis Jones, undated, Bodleian MS Res. c. 320, VII 204b.
444. Phyllis Jones to CW, Bodleian MS Res. c. 320, mixed undated II 60, a–d.
445. Phyllis Jones to CW, undated, Bodleian MS Res. c. 321, XIII.
446. *The Masques of Amen House*, p. 127.
447. *The Masques of Amen House*, p. 123.
448. Phyllis Jones to CW, undated, Bodleian MS Res. c. 320/XIII, unnumbered.
449. Phyllis Jones to CW, undated, Bodleian MS Res. c. 321.
450. Bodleian MS Res. c. 137.
451. R.A. Gilbert to Grevel Lindop, 7 July 2009.
452. Michal Williams to Anne Ridler, undated, Bodleian, ARP.
453. Hadfield (1983) pp. 72–3.
454. Wade, CWMS 182.
455. Phyllis McDougall Interview.
456. *Descent into Hell*, Chapter 3.
457. Phyllis Jones to CW, undated, Bodleian, MS Res. c. 320/I, letter 51.
458. CW to Phyllis Jones, undated, Bodleian, MS Res. c. 320/VIII, letter 210.
459. Phyllis Jones to CW, undated, Bodleian, MS Res. c. 320/XIII, unnumbered.
460. CW to Phyllis Jones, undated, Bodleian, MS Res. c. 320/VIII, letter 200.
461. Phyllis Jones to CW, Bodleian, MS Res. c. 320/XIII, unnumbered.
462. Phyllis Jones to CW, undated, Bodleian MS Res. c. 320/I, letter 23.
463. Phyllis Jones to CW, undated, Bodleian MS Res. c. 320/II, letter 41.

464. Phyllis Jones to CW, undated, Bodleian MS Res. c. 320/XIII, unnumbered.
465. Michal Williams to CW, undated, Bodleian MS Res. c. 320/XIII, unnumbered.
466. CW to Raymond Hunt, 1 Mar 1940, Wade, CWP 30.
467. CW to Jean Smith, 13 June 1927, courtesy of Prof Martin Smith.
468. CW to A.E. Housman, 18 Sept 1929, OUP Archive.
469. *A Book of Victorian Narrative Verse*, p. x.
470. *Oxford Book of Regency Verse*, pp. v, vi–vii, viii.
471. Phyllis Jones to CW, undated, Bodleian MS Res. c. 320/XIII, unnumbered.
472. Phyllis Jones to CW, undated, Bodleian MS Res. c. 320/II, letter 53a.
473. *The Dominant* I, Dec 1927, p. 11.
474. Bodleian MS Res. c. 137.
475. Bodleian, Charles Williams/Hadfield papers, Box 3: envelope 35, K45.1.
476. *Detective Fiction Reviews*, pp. 58–9.
477. CW to Phyllis Jones, Aug 1935, Bodleian MS Res. c. 320/XIII, letter 358.
478. Hubert Foss to Dora Foss, 30 Jan 1929; courtesy of Diana Sparkes.
479. CW to Phyllis Jones, Jan 1929, Bodleian MS Res. c. 320/I, letter 34.
480. CW to Thelma Mills, ?1929, Bodleian MS Eng. Lett. e. 136, f24.
481. CWSNL, 27, Autumn 1982, p. 4.
482. CW to Thelma Mills, ?1929, Bodleian MS Eng. Lett. e. 136, f24.
483. CW to Thelma Mills, '26 June', Bodleian MS Eng. Lett. e. 136, f95.
484. Thelma Shuttleworth to Gillian Lunn, 11 Feb 1984, courtesy of Gillian Lunn.
485. D.H.S. Nicholson to Anne Ridler, 28 Nov 1934, Bodleian, ARP.
486. Thelma Shuttleworth to Gillian Lunn, 11 Feb 1984.
487. Thelma Shuttleworth to Gillian Lunn, 11 Feb 1984.
488. CW to Phyllis Jones, undated, Bodleian MS Res. c. 320/VI, 151b.
489. Dodds, *The Arthurian Poems of Charles Williams*, p. 205.
490. Hadfield (1983) p. 82.
491. CW to Thelma Shuttleworth, [1930], Bodleian MS Eng. Lett. e. 136. f83.
492. CW to Phyllis Jones, Bodleian MS Eng. Res. c. 320/III letter 87d.
493. CW to Phyllis Jones, Bodleian MS Eng. Res. c. 320/III letter 146a.
494. CW to Phyllis Jones, [25 Oct 1930], Bodleian MS Eng. Res. c. 320/II letter 63a.
495. CW to H.S. Milford, 28 Feb 1930, Wade CWMS 182.
496. CW to Raymond Hunt, 1 Mar 1940, Wade CWP.
497. *Poetry at Present*, p. viii.
498. *Poetry at Present*, p. 165.
499. Stanford, *Selected Letters of Robert Bridges*, II, pp. 900–1.
500. CW to Thelma Mills, Bodleian MS Eng. Lett. e. 136. f63.
501. *Poems of Gerard Manley Hopkins*, p. x.
502. *Poems of Gerard Manley Hopkins*, p. xii.
503. *Poems of Gerard Manley Hopkins*, p. xi.

504. *Poems of Gerard Manley Hopkins,* p. xiv.

505. *Poems of Gerard Manley Hopkins,* p. xiii.

506. *Poems of Gerard Manley Hopkins,* p. xvi.

507. Bodleian, Charles Williams/Hadfield papers, Box 2, K19.

508. H.S. Milford to Secretary, 11 Mar 1930, OUP Archive, Milford Letters, Vol 135 p. 436.

509. CWSN 4, Winter 1976, pp. 10–11.

510. Hadfield (1959), p. 83; CWSN 4, Winter 1976, pp. 10–11.

511. Victor Gollancz to CW, 19 Mar 1930, Wade, CWP 257.

512. *War in Heaven,* Chapter 3.

513. CW to Phyllis Jones, Bodleian MS Res. c. 320/VII, letter 180.

514. Hadfield (1983) p. 92.

515. Hadfield (1983) p. 92.

516. CW to Olive Willis, 12 July 1930, Bodleian, E. Martin Browne Literary Papers, Box 4.

517. Anne Ridler Interview 2.

518. Anne Ridler, *Memoirs,* pp. 60–1; Anne Ridler Interview 2; there are minor inconsistencies between the two sources.

519. Anne Ridler Interview 2.

520. CW to Phyllis Jones, undated, Bodleian MS Res. c. 320/I letter 12.

521. 'Epilogue in Somerset: A Song of the Myths', *Three Plays,* p. 199.

522. Mary Guillemard Interview.

523. CW to Phyllis Jones, Bodleian MS Res. c. 320/I letter 13.

524. Ridler (1958), p. xxvii.

525. Anne Ridler Interview 2.

526. CW to Anne Bradby, 12 Aug 1930, Bodleian, ARP.

527. CW to Anne Bradby, 21 Aug 1930, Bodleian, ARP.

528. CW to Phyllis Jones, undated, Bodleian MS Res. c. 320/I letter 10.

529. *The Masques of Amen House,* p. 27.

530. CW to Thelma Mills, 6 Feb 1930, Bodleian MS Eng. Lett. e. 136, f53.

531. CWSN 27, Autumn 1982, p. 4.

532. Hadfield (1983) p. 84.

533. Phyllis Jones to CW, undated, Bodleian MS Res. c. 320/II, letter 49.

534. Hadfield (1983) p. 83.

535. *Outlines of Romantic Theology,* pp. 19–20.

536. Phyllis Jones to CW, undated, Bodleian MS Res. c. 321/XIII, unnumbered.

537. Hadfield (1983) p. 86.

538. CW to Phyllis Jones, undated, MS Res. c. 320/IV, letter 106.

539. CW to Phyllis Jones, undated [postmark 24 Nov 1930], MS Res. c. 320/X, letter 273.

540. Michal Williams to Glen Cavaliero, 22 Oct 1956.

541. Michal Williams to Anne Ridler, undated, Bodleian, ARP.

542. Wade Center Oral Histories.

543. CW to Phyllis Jones, undated, Bodleian MS Res. c. 320/II, letter 73.

544. CW to Phyllis Jones, undated, Bodleian MS Res. c. 320/II, letter 89.

545. Hadfield (1983) p. 86.

546. Phyllis Jones to CW, undated, Bodleian MS Res. c. 321/XIII, unnumbered.

547. Phyllis Jones to CW, undated, Bodleian MS Res. c. 321, unnumbered.

548. Waite, *The Secret Doctrine in Israel*, p. 63.

549. A.H.E. Lee, 'Time and Mr. Dunne'; *The Speculative Mason*, Vol. XXXI, Nos. 2: Apr 1939, pp. 43–50, and 3: July 1939, pp. 93–6.

550. *Many Dimensions*, Chapter 6.

551. *Many Dimensions*, Chapter 2.

552. *Many Dimensions*, Chapter 3.

553. CW to Phyllis Jones, 10 Sept 1930, Bodleian MS Res. c. 320/II, 89.

554. *Many Dimensions*, Chapter 16.

555. CW to Phyllis Jones, 10–12 Sept 1930, Bodleian MS Res. c. 320/II, 89.

556. CW to Phyllis Jones, 14 Sept 1930, Bodleian MS Res. c. 320/II, 76.

557. CW to Phyllis Jones, undated, Bodleian MS Res. c. 320/VII, 180.

558. CW to Phyllis Jones, undated, Bodleian MS Res. c. 320/II, letter 39.

559. Hadfield (1983) p. 86.

560. Phyllis Jones to CW, undated, Bodleian MS Res. c. 321/XIII, unnumbered.

561. CW to Phyllis Jones, undated, Bodleian MS Res, c. 320/V, 138.

562. Phyllis McDougall Interview.

563. CW to Phyllis Jones, undated, Bodleian MS Res. c. 320/V, letter 138.

564. Phyllis Jones to CW, undated, MS Res. c. 320/XIII, unnumbered.

565. CW to Phyllis Jones, undated, MS Res. c. 320/IV, letter 105.

566. CW to Phyllis Jones, undated, Bodleian MS Res. c. 320/V, letter 140.

567. Phyllis Jones to CW, undated, Bodleian MS Res. c. 320/XIII, unnumbered.

568. CW to Phyllis Jones, undated, Bodleian MS Res. c. 320/VIII, 204.

569. Anne Ridler, *Memoirs*, p. 55.

570. Anne Ridler, *Memoirs,* pp. 55–6.

571. Anne Ridler, *Memoirs*, p. 72.

572. CW to Anne Bradby, 22 Dec 1930, Bodleian, ARP.

573. Phyllis Jones to CW, undated, Bodleian MS Res. c. 320/I, 6.

574. Phyllis Jones to CW, undated, Bodleian MS Res. c. 320/I, 38.

575. Phyllis Jones to CW, undated, Bodleian MS Res. c. 320/XIII, unnumbered.

576. Phyllis Jones to CW, undated, Bodleian MS Res. c. 320/II, 45.

577. CW to Olive Willis, 12 Jan 1931, Bodleian E. Martin Browne literary papers, Box 4.

578. Phyllis Jones to CW, 27 Apr 1931, Bodleian, MS Res. c. 320/XIII, unnumbered.

579. Phyllis Jones to CW, undated, Bodleian MS Res. c. 320/I, 30.

580. Phyllis Jones to CW, Bodleian MS Res. c. 320/XIII, unnumbered.

581. Bodleian, Charles Williams/Hadfield papers, Box 3, B67.

582. CW to Thelma Mills, 2 Sept 1932, Bodleian MS Eng. Lett. e. 136.

583. CW to Thelma Mills, 15 July 1932, Bodleian MS Eng. Lett. e. 136.

584. CW to Thelma Mills, undated, Bodleian MS Eng. Lett. e. 136, f1.

585. CW to Thelma Mills, undated, Bodleian MS Eng. Lett. e. 136, f12.

586. CW to Thelma Mills, Apr 1931, Bodleian MS Eng. Lett. e. 136, f91.

587. Thelma Shuttleworth, note added to CW to Thelma Mills, 30 Apr 1940, Bodleian MS Eng. Lett. e. 136, f91.

588. Wade Oral Histories: Thelma Shuttleworth.

589. CW to Thelma Mills, undated, Bodleian MS Eng. Lett. E. 136, f5.

590. Anne Ridler, *Memoirs*, p. 77.

591. CW to Anne Bradby, 24 Nov 1931, Bodleian, ARP.

592. CW to Olive Willis, 12 Jan 1931, photocopy, Bodleian, ARP.

593. CW to Phyllis Jones, undated, Bodleian MS Res. c. 320/VII, 173.

594. Michal to Glen Cavaliero, 30 July 1955.

595. Michal to Glen Cavaliero, 22 Oct 1956.

596. CW to Frederick Page, 26 Sept 1931, Bodleian MS Res. c. 136.3.

597. Note by Alice Mary Hadfield on CW to Phyllis Jones, 'letter 137', CWSA.

598. J.W. Dunne, *An Experiment with Time*, Chapter XII.

599. MS courtesy of Diana Sparkes.

600. *The Place of the Lion*, Chapter 10.

601. CW to Phyllis Jones, undated, Bodleian MS Res. c. 320/III, 88.

602. CW to Olive Willis, 22 June 1931, Bodleian E. Martin Browne Literary Papers, Box 4.

603. CW to Lewis Chase, 23 July 1931, Wade, CWP 7.

604. CW to Olive Willis, 5 May 1931, Bodleian E. Martin Browne Literary Papers, Box 4.

605. CW to Kenneth Sisam, 22 Sept 1931; transcript in CWSA.

606. CW to Anne Bradby, 10 Nov 1931, Bodleian ARP.

607. *The English Poetic Mind*, p. 27.

608. *The English Poetic Mind*, p. 191.

609. *The English Poetic Mind*, pp. vi–vii.

610. *The English Poetic Mind*, p. 9.

611. *TLS* 1932, p. 443; the anonymous reviewer was Basil De Selincourt.

612. Geoffrey Hill, *Collected Critical Writings*, pp. 562–3.

613. Gilbert, *A.E. Waite*, p. 138.

614. CW to Phyllis Jones, undated, Bodleian MS Res. c. 321/III, 93.

615. *The Greater Trumps*, Chapter 14.

616. CW to Phyllis Jones, undated, Bodleian MS Res. c. 320/XIII, 363.

617. *The Greater Trumps*, Chapter 14.

618. Hadfield (1983) p. 99.

619. *Letters to Lalage*, pp. 21–2.

620. CW to Olive Willis, 13 July 1932, Bodleian E. Martin Brown Literary Papers, Box 4.

621. CW to Anne Bradby, 26 Aug 1931, Bodleian ARP.

622. *News Chronicle*, 16 Mar 1932.

623. E. Martin Browne with Henzie Browne, *Two in One*, p. 72.
624. CW to Anne Bradby, 12 Sept 1932, Bodleian ARP.
625. CWSA.
626. Hadfield (1983) p. 109.
627. CW to Olive Willis, 22 Dec 1932, Bodleian E. Martin Browne Literary Papers, Box 4.
628. Hadfield (1959), p. 114.
629. Hadfield (1959), p. 115.
630. Hadfield (1959), pp. 115–16.
631. Hadfield (1959), p. 117.
632. German white wine.
633. Hadfield (1983) pp. 108–9.
634. CW to Phyllis Jones, undated, Bodleian MS Res. c. 320/V, 140.
635. CW to Phyllis Jones, undated, Bodleian MS Res. c. 320/XI, 296.
636. CW to Phyllis Jones, undated, Bodleian MS Res. c. 320/X, 292.
637. Hopkins, *Nor Fish Nor Flesh*, p. 18.
638. Hopkins, *Nor Fish Nor Flesh*, p. 19.
639. Hopkins, *Nor Fish Nor Flesh,* p. 83.
640. Hadfield (1983) p. 117.
641. CW to Phyllis Jones, undated, Bodleian MS Res. c. 320/V, 171.
642. Hadfield (1983) p. 117.
643. Kenneth Sisam to CW, 23 June 1933, Wade, CWP 428.
644. T.S. Eliot, 'Introduction' to *All Hallows' Eve*.
645. CW to Phyllis Jones, undated, Bodleian MS Res. c. 320/II, 68.
646. Bodleian, Charles Williams/Hadfield papers, Box 3/29, ff D.65–7.
647. Anne Ridler, *Memoirs*, p. 85.
648. CW to Anne Bradby, 13 Apr 1933, Bodleian ARP.
649. CW to Anne Bradby, 13 July 1933, Bodleian ARP.
650. An asymptote is a line that approaches closer and closer to a curve but never meets it. Its significance for Williams is not clear.
651. CW to Anne Bradby, 17 Aug 1933, Bodleian ARP.
652. CW to Raymond Hunt, 21 Aug 1933, Wade, CWP 16.
653. Private information.
654. CW to Phyllis Jones, 4 Sep 1933, Bodleian MS Res. c. 320/V.
655. CW to Anne Bradby, 4 Sept 1934, Bodleian ARP.
656. Anne Ridler Interview 1.
657. CW to Phyllis Jones, undated, Bodleian MS Res. c. 320/V, 171.
658. King, p. 65.
659. CW to Anne Bradby, 17 Sept 1933, Bodleian ARP.
660. CW to Raymond Hunt, 28 Sept 1933, Wade, CWP 16.
661. CW to Phyllis Jones, undated, Bodleian MS Res. c. 320/V, 171.
662. CW to R.W. Chapman, 28 Sept 1933, Bodleian MS Eng. Lett. c. 766, ff 84–5.

663. CW to Anne Bradby, 2 Oct 1933, Bodleian ARP.

664. CW to John Pellow, 11 Nov [?1933], Wade, CWP 54.

665. Montgomery Belgion to CW, 18 Oct 1933, Wade, CWP 167.

666. Hadfield (1983) p. 79.

667. T.S. Eliot, *For Lancelot Andrewes: Essays on Style and Order.*

668. T.S. Eliot, 'Introduction' to *All Hallows' Eve.*

669. CW to Phyllis Jones, 28 Nov 1934, Bodleian MS Res. c. 321/XIII, 356–6.

670. Lyndall Gordon, *Eliot's New Life*, p. 100.

671. T.S. Eliot to CW, 7 Oct 1934, Bodleian MS Res. c. 136.3 (photocopy).

672. Helen Gardner, *The Composition of* Four Quartets, p. 85.

673. Ralph Binfield, 'Charles Williams at the O.U.P.', MS in possession of Joy Cooper; Ralph Binfield, 'Amen House and "Caesar"', CWSN 9, Spring 1978, p. 4.

674. Ridler (1958), p. xx.

675. Paul Ferris, ed., *Dylan Thomas: The Collected Letters*, p. 90.

676. CW to Raymond Hunt, 16 Mar 1936, Wade, CWP 23.

677. Paul Ferris, ed., *Dylan Thomas: The Collected Letters* pp. 320, 327.

678. Paul Ferris, ed., *Dylan Thomas: The Collected Letters*, p. 391.

679. *Reason and Beauty in the Poetic Mind*, p. 5.

680. CW to Anne Bradby, 5 July 1934, Bodleian ARP.

681. Untraced; the review is not in *Scrutiny.*

682. Edith Sitwell to CW, 4 Feb 1934, Bodleian MS Res. c. 136.3.

683. 'Autocriticism', *Week-End Review*, 18 Nov 1933.

684. Ridler, *Memoirs*, p. 95.

685. Anne Ridler Interview 2.

686. Ridler, *Memoirs* p. 97.

687. Ridler, *Memoirs*, p. 97; CW to Anne Bradby, 23 May 1934, Bodleian ARP.

688. Ridler, *Memoirs* p. 96.

689. Anne Ridler Interview 2.

690. CW to Anne Bradby, 28 Feb 1934, Bodleian ARP.

691. CW to Anne Bradby, 16 Nov 1933, Bodleian ARP.

692. CW to Anne Bradby, 9 Jan 1934, Bodleian ARP.

693. CW to Anne Bradby, 15 Jan 1934 Bodleian ARP.

694. CW to Anne Bradby, July 1934, Bodleian ARP.

695. CW to Anne Bradby, July 6 1934, Bodleian ARP.

696. CW to Anne Bradby, 13 Aug 1934, Bodleian ARP.

697. CW to Anne Bradby, 13 Aug 1934, Bodleian ARP.

698. CW to Anne Bradby, 13 Aug 1934, Bodleian ARP.

699. CW to Anne Bradby, [Spring 1934], Bodleian ARP.

700. CW to Anne Bradby, 23 May 1934, Bodleian ARP.

701. CW to Anne Bradby, 13 Apr 1934, Bodleian ARP.

702. Anne Ridler Interview 2.

703. CW to Anne Bradby, 15 May 1934, Bodleian ARP.

704. CW to Anne Bradby, 31 July 1934, Bodleian ARP.
705. Anne Ridler Interview 2.
706. CW to Anne Bradby, 24 Aug 1934, Bodleian ARP.
707. CW to Anne Bradby, 1 Sept 1934, Bodleian ARP.
708. CW to Anne Bradby, 29 Aug 1934, Bodleian ARP.
709. CW to Anne Bradby, 29 Aug 1934, Bodleian ARP.
710. CW to Anne Bradby, 30 Aug 1934, Bodleian ARP.
711. CW to Anne Bradby, [?1 Sept 1934], Bodleian ARP.
712. CW to Anne Bradby, 4 Sept 1934, Bodleian ARP.
713. Hadfield (1983) p. 117.
714. CW to Anne Bradby, 4 Sept 1934, Bodleian ARP.
715. CW to Anne Bradby, 4 Sept 1934, Bodleian ARP.
716. CW to Anne Bradby, 6 Sept 1934, Bodleian ARP.
717. CW to Anne Bradby, 9 July 1934, Bodleian ARP.
718. CW to Anne Bradby, 24 Aug 1934, Bodleian ARP.
719. Anne Ridler Interview 2.
720. CW to Anne Bradby, undated (in sequence as at late 1934), Bodleian ARP.
721. Anne Bradby to CW, undated, Bodleian ARP.
722. CW to Anne Bradby, 6 Aug 1935, Bodleian ARP.
723. CW to Anne Bradby [?1935], Bodleian ARP.
724. CW to Anne Bradby, undated, Bodleian ARP.
725. CW to Anne Bradby, 15 Sept 1934, Bodleian ARP.
726. CW to Phyllis Somervaille, 23 Nov 1934, Bodleian MS Res. c. 321/XIII, 356.
727. 'as witness'.
728. CW to Anne Bradby, 11 Sept 1934, Bodleian ARP.
729. CW to Anne Bradby, 13 Sept 1934, Bodleian ARP.
730. CW to Anne Bradby, 14 Sept 1934, Bodleian ARP.
731. CW to Anne Bradby, undated, Bodleian ARP.
732. CW to Anne Bradby, 15 Sept 1934, Bodleian ARP.
733. CW to Anne Bradby, 12 Sept 1934, Bodleian ARP.
734. CW to Anne Bradby, 30 Sept 1934, Bodleian ARP.
735. D.H.S. Nicholson to Anne Bradby, 28 Nov 1934, Bodleian ARP.
736. D.H.S. Nicholson to Anne Bradby, 30 Nov 1934, Bodleian ARP.
737. Hadfield (1983) p. 122.
738. *A New Book of English Verse*, p. 14.
739. CW to G.B. Shaw, 15 Apr 1935, OUP Archive, OP1366/01034.
740. CW to Anne Bradby, 12 Aug 1935, Bodleian ARP.
741. 'The *New Book of English Verse*: Criticism and Counter-Criticism', *Morning Post*, 11 Nov 1935.
742. Memo, CW to H.S. Milford, 16 Dec 1935, OUP Archive, OP1364/010091.
743. OUP Archive PB/ED/004932, Box OP 702.
744. Raymond Hunt Chronology, Bodleian Bodleian MS Res. c. 136/3.
745. CW to AB, 26 Sept. 1934, AR papers.

746. CW to Kenneth Sisam, 20 June 1935, CWSA.

747. CW to Anne Bradby, ['Sept or Oct 1934'], Bodleian ARP.

748. CW to Anne Bradby, 15 Feb 1935, Bodleian ARP.

749. Ridler (1958), p. lxiii.

750. CW to Anne Bradby, 11 Oct 1934, Bodleian ARP.

751. Joan Wallis Interview 2.

752. Joan Wallis Interview 1.

753. CW to Anne Bradby, 6 Sept 1934, Bodleian ARP.

754. CW to Anne Bradby, 15 Sept 1934, Bodleian ARP.

755. CW to Anne Bradby, ['1934'], Bodleian ARP.

756. CW to Anne Bradby, ['1934'], Bodleian ARP.

757. CW to Anne Bradby, [postmarked 12 Sept 1934], Bodleian ARP.

758. Ridler (1958), p. xxv.

759. CW to Anne Bradby, 28 Aug 1935, Bodleian ARP.

760. CW to Anne Bradby, undated [?1934], Bodleian ARP.

761. CW to Olive Speake, 3 July 1935, Wade, CWP 78.

762. Wade, CWMS 28.

763. Wade, CWMS 28.

764. Wade, CWMS 28.

765. Wade, CWMS 28.

766. CW to Olive Speake, 24 Apr 1940, Wade, CWP 78.

767. CW to Olive Speake, 18 May 1940, Wade, CWP 78.

768. CW to Olive Speake, 10 July 1935, Wade, CWP 78.

769. Wade CWMS 28; CW to Phyllis Somervaille, Bodleian MS Res. c. 321/XIII, 363, 364, 365.

770. CW to Anne Bradby, 5 Dec 1934, Bodleian ARP.

771. CW to Anne Bradby, 'St John Lateran' [9 Nov] 1934, Bodleian ARP.

772. CW to Anne Bradby [late 1934], Bodleian ARP.

773. CW to Anne Bradby [postmarked 15 Feb 1935], Bodleian ARP.

774. Hadfield (1983) p. 124.

775. CW to Anne Bradby, 18 Feb 1935, Bodleian ARP.

776. CW to Raymond Hunt, 5 Nov 1934 and 21 Mar 1935, Wade, CWP 17, 18; CW to Anne Bradby, 12 Sept 1934, Bodleian ARP.

777. Browne, *Two in One*, p. 101.

778. King, p. 84.

779. King, p. 84.

780. Browne, *Two in One*, p. 103.

781. CW to Anne Bradby, 28 Aug 1935, Bodleian ARP.

782. CW to Anne Bradby, ['Summer 1935'], Bodleian ARP.

783. CW to Anne Bradby, [?Oct 1935], Bodleian ARP.

784. CW to Anne Bradby, 15 Feb 1935, Bodleian ARP.

785. CW to Phyllis Somervaille, 4 Mar 1935, Bodleian MS Res. c. 320/V, 124.

786. CW to Phyllis Somervaille, 26 Mar 1935, Bodleian MS Res. c. 321/XIII, 356.

787. CW to Phyllis Somervaille, undated [?early Apr 1935], Bodleian MS Res. c. 321/XIII, 357.
788. CW to Anne Bradby, 9 July 1935, Bodleian ARP.
789. CW to Phyllis Somervaille, 29 Aug 1935, Bodleian MS Res. c. 321./XIII, 361.
790. CW to Anne Bradby, 30 Aug 1935, Bodleian ARP.
791. Jane Drakard, *A Malay Frontier*, pp. 3–4.
792. Procopius of Caesarea, *The Secret History*, XII.
793. CW to Anne Bradby, 15 Dec 1935, Bodleian ARP.
794. Anne Ridler Interview 2.
795. CW to Phyllis Somervaille, 29 Aug 1935, Bodleian MS Res. c. 321/XIII, 361.
796. CW to Anne Bradby, 24 Dec 1935, Bodleian ARP.
797. CW to Phyllis Somervaille, Aug 1935, Bodleian MS Res. c. 321/XIII, 358.
798. Hadfield (1983) p. 183.
799. Bodleian ARP.
800. Anne Ridler, *Memoirs*, pp. 102–3.
801. Anne Ridler Interview 2.
802. *Image of the City*, p. 195.
803. CW to Raymond Hunt, 2 Jan 1936, Wade CWP 19.
804. Unfortunately nothing is known about the causes of Michal's back problems, or of what the X-rays revealed.
805. CW to Raymond Hunt, 7 Jan 1936, Wade CWP 19.
806. CW to Anne Bradby, 4 Feb 1936, Bodleian ARP.
807. CW to Anne Bradby, 11 Sept 1935, Bodleian ARP.
808. CW to Anne Bradby, [Sept/Oct 1935], Bodleian ARP.
809. *GK's Weekly*, 5 Mar, 1936.
810. *GK's Weekly*, 18 June 1936.
811. CW to Anne Bradby, undated ['1934'], Bodleian ARP.
812. The letter survives only as a typed copy, which lacks both salutation and valediction.
813. C.S. Lewis, *Collected Letters* II, pp. 183–4.
814. Milford had received a knighthood in the 1936 New Year's Honours.
815. CW to C.S. Lewis, 12 Mar 1936, Bodleian MS Eng. c. 6825, ff48–9.
816. Not R.W. Chambers, as erroneously stated in the Green and Hooper biography of Lewis (p. 133).
817. C.S. Lewis, *Essays Presented to Charles Williams*, p. viii.
818. C.S. Lewis, *Collected Letters* II, pp. 180–1.
819. C.S. Lewis to R.W. Chapman, 9 Mar [1936], Bodleian MS Res. c. 136/3.
820. Lewis, *Letters*, II, pp. 185–7.
821. CW to Olive Willis, 11 May 1936, Bodleian E. Martin Browne literary papers, Box 4.
822. CW to Phyllis Potter, 6 Nov 1936, Bodleian MS Res. c. 58.
823. CW to Phyllis Potter, 5 and 12 Mar 1936, Bodleian MS Res. c. 58.

824. Michael Little and Siobhan Kelly, *A Life Without Problems?*, p. 19.
825. CW to Anne Bradby, 27 May 1936, Bodleian ARP.
826. Browne, *Two in One*, p. 106.
827. Browne, *Two in One,* pp. 104, 107.
828. Typescript in CWSA.
829. CW to Anne Bradby, 22 June 1936, Bodleian ARP.
830. Browne, *Two in One*, p. 107.
831. Pickering, *Drama in the Cathedral*, pp. 197–8.
832. CW to Rev Canon Charles Smyth, 4 Aug 1936, Wade, CWP 433.
833. 14 Oct 36 CW to Raymond Hunt, Wade, CWP 20.
834. 2 Sept 36 CW to Raymond Hunt, Wade, CWP 20.
835. CW to Phyllis Potter, 31 July 1936, Bodleian MS Res. c. 58.
836. CW to Raymond Hunt, 2 Sept 1936, Wade, CWP 20.
837. CW to Phyllis Potter, 4 Sept 1936, Bodleian MS Res. c. 58.
838. CW to Phyllis Potter, 21 Oct 1936, Bodleian MS Res. c. 58.
839. CW to Phyllis Potter, 29 Oct 1936, Bodleian MS Res. c. 58.
840. T.S. Eliot to Phyllis Potter, 27 Oct 1936, Wade CWP 243.
841. CW to Phyllis Potter, 10 Nov 1936, Bodleian MS Res. c. 58.
842. CW to Phyllis Potter, 16 Nov 1936, Bodleian MS Res. c. 58.
843. CW to Anne Bradby, undated, Bodleian ARP.
844. *Collected Plays*, pp. 174–5.
845. CW to Raymond Hunt, 19 Nov 1936, Wade, CWP 21.
846. 'Poetry folder', Wade, CWP.
847. CW to Raymond Hunt, 23 Dec 1936, Wade, CWP 21.
848. Mary Butts to CW, 6 Jan 1934, Wade, CWP 181.
849. Nathalie Blondel, *Mary Butts: Scenes from the Life*, p. 106.
850. Mary Butts to CW, 13 Jan 1934, Wade, CWP 181.
851. Mary Butts to CW, 11 Feb 1935, Wade, CWP 181.
852. CW to Mary Butts, 10 Jan 1934, Beinecke Library.
853. Blondel, *Mary Butts*, p. 369.
854. CW to Mary Butts, 15 Jan 1935, Beinecke Library.
855. CW to Ellis Roberts, 29 Sept 1936, Wade, CWP 36.
856. *Time and Tide*, 4 Aug 1936.
857. CW to Phyllis Jones, 29 Aug 1935, Bodleian MS Res. c. 321. XIII.
858. Mary Butts to CW, 2 Jan 1937, Wade CWP 181.
859. CW to Mary Butts, 15 Jan 1937, Beinecke Library.
860. Mary Butts to CW, undated [1937], Wade CWP 181.
861. CW to Mary Butts, 6 Mar 1937, Beinecke Library.
862. CW to Anne Bradby, 13 May 1937, Bodleian ARP.
863. CW to Anne Bradby, 27 Nov 1936, Bodleian ARP.
864. CW to Anne Bradby, 3 Dec 1936, Bodleian ARP.
865. CW to RH, 23. Dec 36, Wade, CWP 21.
866. CW to Phyllis Potter, Bodleian MS Res. c. 58.

867. CW to Raymond Hunt, 'Vigil of the Feast of the Fructiferous Incarnation' [24 Dec] 1936, Wade, CWP 21.
868. CW to Anne Bradby, 1 Jan 1937, Bodleian ARP.
869. CW to Anne Bradby, 13 May 1937, Bodleian ARP.
870. Programme in Bodleian ARP.
871. Bodleian, Charles Williams/Hadfield Box 4, f90.
872. CW to Olive Willis, 11 May 1936, Bodleian E. Martin Browne literary papers, Box 4.
873. Anne Ridler, *Memoirs*, p. 114.
874. CW to Raymond Hunt, 3 Mar 1937, Wade, CWP 23.
875. CW to Phyllis Potter, 27 Apr 1937, Bodleian MS Res. c. 58.
876. CW to Raymond Hunt, 29 Apr 1937, Wade, CWP 23.
877. CW to Anne Bradby, 16 May 1937, Bodleian ARP.
878. CW to Raymond Hunt, 20 May 1937, Wade, CWP 24.
879. CW to Phyllis Potter, 21 May 1937, Bodleian MS Res. c. 58.
880. CW to Raymond Hunt, 29 June 1937, Wade, CWP 24.
881. CW to Raymond Hunt, 7 July 1937, Wade, CWP 25.
882. CW to the Bishop of Chichester, 2 June 1937, Wade, CWP 4.
883. CW to Walter Lowrie, 4 June 1937, Walter Lowrie Papers, Princeton University Library.
884. CW to Walter Lowrie, 21 Dec 1937, Walter Lowrie Papers, Princeton University Library.
885. OUP Archive, PB/ED/004927, OP 701.
886. OUP Archive, PB/ED/004927, OP 701.
887. James A. Pike, ed., *Modern Canterbury Pilgrims*, p. 41.
888. *Descent into Hell*, Chapter 6.
889. CW to Anne Bradby, 30 Aug 1934, Bodleian ARP.
890. CW to Phyllis Potter, 11 Oct 1937, Bodleian MS Res. c.58.
891. 'Lowest Common Multiple'.
892. C.S. Lewis, *Collected Letters* II, pp. 218–19.
893. W.H. Lewis to CW, 19 Oct 1937, CWP 355.
894. CW to Anne Bradby, 31 Aug 1937, Bodleian ARP.
895. *London Mercury,* July 1937, 36: 213, pp. 255–61.
896. *Time and Tide,* 4 Dec 1937, pp. 1674–6.
897. Roy Foster, *W.B. Yeats: A Life: II: The Arch-Poet,* p. 607.
898. CW to Kenneth Sisam, 17 Jan 1938, Wade, CWP 71.
899. Montgomery Belgion to CW, 20 Jan 1938, Wade, CWP 167.
900. CW to Phyllis Potter, 15 Jan 1938, Bodleian MS Res. c. 58.
901. CW to Phyllis Potter, 15 Jan 1938, Bodleian MS Res. c. 58.
902. Raymond Hunt's Chronology, Bodleian MS Res. c. 136.3.
903. CW to Phyllis Potter, 8 Feb 1938, Bodleian MS Res. c. 58.
904. *He Came Down From Heaven*, p. 127.
905. *He Came Down From Heaven*, p. 130.

906. C.S. Lewis, *Collected Letters* II, pp. 227–8.

907. Hadfield (1983) pp. 164–5.

908. *Essays Presented to Charles Williams*, p. viii.

909. CW to Raymond Hunt, 11 July 1938, Wade, CWP 26.

910. Bodleian Charles Williams/Hadfield, Box 4 Env. 36, K46.1 and K46.2. The notes are handwritten, on OUP letterhead, with a typed copy. Both copies state that they were 'dictated to Alice Mary Smyth in Apr 1932' but this cannot be correct. Alice Mary did not set foot in the OUP until 1933; and the notes mention a recent 'report on doctrine of the church of England': there was no such report in 1932. Evidently both sets of notes are later copies and Alice Mary, or someone else, misread her handwritten '8' as a '2'.

911. CW to Phyllis Potter, 20 May 1938, Bodleian MS Res. c. 58.

912. Raymond Hunt's Chronology, Bodleian MS Res. c. 136.3.

913. CW to Phyllis Potter, 19 Aug 1938, Bodleian MS Res. c. 58.

914. CW to Walter Lowrie, 21 Jan 1938, Princeton University Library.

915. Information from Geoffrey Hill.

916. CW to Walter Lowrie, 6 May 1938, Princeton University Library.

917. CW to Walter Lowrie, 20 May 1938, Princeton University Library.

918. OUP Archive: internal memo, 27 June 1938.

919. OUP Archive, World's Classics Suggestions, Loge 000 266 LG35.

920. Information from Roddy McDougall.

921. 'Defeating Its Own End', Letter to Editor, *Sunday Times*, 12 June 1938.

922. CW to Anne Bradby, Apr 1938, AR papers.

923. CW to Phyllis Potter, 11 May 1939, Bodleian MS Res. c. 58.

924. CW to Phyllis Potter, 16 May 1939; Phyllis Potter to CW, 13 June 1939, Bodleian MS Res. c. 58.

925. CW to Raymond Hunt, 12 Aug 1938, Wade CWP 26.

926. OUP Archive: LOCA 003784 CA 54.

927. CW to Raymond Hunt, 12 Aug 1938, Wade CWP 26.

928. Bodleian MS Eng. c. 2791/1.

929. CW to Phyllis Potter, 7 Sept 38, Bodleian MS Res. c. 58.

930. Graham Macklin, *Chamberlain*, p. 69.

931. CW to Raymond Hunt, 20 Sept 1938, Wade, CWP 26.

932. CW to Thelma Shuttleworth, 30 Apr 1940, Bodleian MS Eng. Lett. e. 136.

933. CW to Phyllis Potter, 27 Sept 38, Bodleian MS Res. c. 58.

934. CW to Phyllis Potter, 28 Oct 1938, Bodleian MS Res. c. 58.

935. CW to Phyllis Potter, 12 and 13 Dec 1938, Bodleian MS Res. c. 58.

936. CW to Walter Lowrie, 4 Nov 1938, Princeton University Library.

937. CW to Raymond Hunt, 3 Oct 1938, Wade, CWP 26.

938. CW to Raymond Hunt, 28 Dec 1938, Wade, CWP 26.

939. Hadfield (1983) p. 194.

940. Cutting, dated 17 Dec 1938, source unidentified; Bodleian MS Res. c. 137.

941. *TLS*, 17 Dec 1938, p. 804.
942. *Theology*, 38 (Apr 1939), pp. 268–75.
943. *Essays Presented to Charles Williams*, p. vii.
944. CW to George Every, 3 Feb 1939, CWSA.
945. CW to Phyllis Potter, 'September', Bodleian MS Res. c. 58.
946. Hadfield (1983) p. 173.
947. Wade, CWMS 77.
948. Bodleian MS Res. c. 136.3.
949. CW to Charles Hadfield, 1 Nov 1939 [misdated '1943'], Bodleian Charles Williams/Hadfield papers, Box 2, K.15.2.
950. CWSN, 27, Autumn 1982, p.6.
951. CW to Phyllis Potter, 13 Feb 1939, Bodleian MS Res. c. 58.
952. CW to Phyllis Potter, 20 Feb 1939, Bodleian MS Res. c. 58.
953. CW to Phyllis Potter, 27 Jan 1939, Bodleian MS Res. c. 58.
954. CW to Phyllis Potter, 8 Aug 1939, Bodleian MS Res. c. 58.
955. CW to Olive Speake, 24 Mar 1939, Wade, CWP 78.
956. T.S. Eliot to CW, 29 Mar 1939, Wade CWP 244.
957. CW to Phyllis Potter, 23 Feb 1939, Wade CWP 59.
958. CW to Ruth Spalding, 24 May 1939, Wade CWP 76.
959. Phyllis Potter to CW, 13 June 1939, Bodleian MS Res c. 58.
960. CW to Phyllis Potter, 14 June 1939, Bodleian MS Res. c. 58.
961. CW to Ruth Spalding, 8 Aug 1939, Wade CWMS 76.
962. Ruth Spalding Interview.
963. CW to Alice Mary Miller, undated [1939], Bodleian Charles Williams/Hadfield papers, Box 2, K27.3.
964. Bodleian, Charles Williams/Hadfield Box 2, K.27.5.
965. CW to Phyllis Potter, 25 Aug 1939, Bodleian MS Res. c. 58.
966. CW to Phyllis Potter, 29 Aug 1939, Bodleian MS Res. c. 58.
967. Anne Spalding Interview.
968. 'T.H.H.', 'Amen House Transfers to Oxford', *The Lantern*, Vol. XII, No. 3, Oct 1939, pp. 68–71.
969. 'T.H.H.', 'Amen House Transfers to Oxford'.
970. King, pp. 36–7.
971. King, pp. 15, 16.
972. Hubert Foss's Commonplace Book, courtesy of Diana Sparkes.
973. CW to Michal Williams, 22 Sept 1939, Wade, CWP 97.
974. CW to Anne Ridler, Sept 1939 [dated by Anne Ridler 'Outbreak of War' but written from Southfield House], Bodleian ARP.
975. Hadfield (1983) p. 178.
976. Anne Spalding Interview.
977. Hadfield (1983) p. 178.
978. Anne Spalding Interview.
979. Hadfield (1983) p. 178.

980. Hadfield (1983) p. 178.

981. Anne Spalding Interview, CWSNL 7, Autumn 1977, p. 4.

982. King, p. 24.

983. Anne Spalding Interview.

984. CW to Raymond Hunt, 13 Sept 1939, Wade, CWP 27.

985. CW to Thelma Shuttleworth, Oct 1939, Bodleian MS Eng. Lett. e. 136.

986. Hadfield (1983) p. 164.

987. CW to Thelma Shuttleworth, Oct 1939, Bodleian MS Eng. Lett. e. 136.

988. CW to Alice Mary Miller, 23 Oct 1939, Bodleian, Charles Williams/Hadfield papers, Box 2, K.27.7.

989. King, p. 37.

990. CW to Alice Mary Miller, 14 Mar 1940, Bodleian, Charles Williams/Hadfield, Box 2, K27.9.

991. CW to Walter Lowrie, 7 Sept 1939, Princeton University Library.

992. CW to Phyllis Potter, 8 Sept 1939, Bodleian MS Res. c. 58.

993. Information from Maggs Bros Ltd.

994. CW to Anne Ridler, 6 Oct 1939, Bodleian ARP.

995. Hadfield (1983) p. 195.

996. CW to Phyllis Potter, 15 Nov 1939, Bodleian MS Res. c. 58.

997. King, p. 23.

998. CW to Michal Williams, 24 Sept 1939, Wade, CWP 97.

999. King, p. 24.

1000. CW to Alice Mary Miller, 20 Oct 1939, Bodleian, Charles Williams/Hadfield, Box 2, K.27.6.

1001. King, p. 33.

1002. CW to Anne Ridler, 30 Oct 1939, Bodleian ARP.

1003. CW to Alice Mary Miller, 6 Apr 1940, Bodleian, Charles Williams/Hadfield, Box 2, K.27.10.

1004. King, p. 21.

1005. King, p. 17.

1006. King, p. 25.

1007. King, p. 24.

1008. Carpenter, p. 155n.

1009. C.S. Lewis, *Collected Letters* II, p. 294.

1010. John Wain, *Sprightly Running*, p. 184.

1011. *Essays Presented to Charles Williams*, p. xi.

1012. Carpenter, p. 173.

1013. C.S. Lewis, *Collected Letters* II, p. 289.

1014. C.S. Lewis, *Collected Letters* II, p. 283.

1015. J.R.R. Tolkien, *Letters*, p. 362.

1016. King, pp. 89–90.

1017. King, pp. 50–1.

1018. King, pp. 124.

1019. King, pp. 27.

1020. Margaret Douglas to Anne Ridler, Whit Sunday 1945, Bodleian ARP.

1021. CW to Phyllis Potter, 13 Sept 1939, Bodleian MS Res. c. 58.

1022. *Descent of the Dove*, p. 28.

1023. *Descent of the Dove,* p. 59.

1024. *Descent of the Dove,* p. 61.

1025. Elizabeth A. Clark, 'John Chrysostom and the *Subintroductae*', *Church History*, Vol. 46, No. 2. (June 1977), pp. 171–85.

1026. *Descent of the Dove*, p. 13.

1027. *New Statesman*, 9 Dec 1939.

1028. CW to Olive Willis, 26 Sept 1939, Bodleian E. Martin Browne literary papers, Box 4.

1029. CW to Alice Mary Miller, 20 Oct 1939, Bodleian, Charles Williams/Hadfield, Box 2, K.27.6.

1030. *Descent of the Dove*, p. 183.

1031. C.S. Lewis, *Collected Letters* II, p. 293.

1032. C.S. Lewis, *Collected Letters* II, p. 335.

1033. CW to Anne Ridler, 6 Oct 1939, Bodleian ARP.

1034. Carpenter, p. 172.

1035. CW to Anne Ridler, 27 Oct 1939, Bodleian ARP.

1036. CW to Anne Ridler, 30 Oct 1939, Bodleian ARP.

1037. CW to Anne Ridler, 30 Oct 1939, Bodleian ARP.

1038. CW to Margaret Douglas, 19 Dec 1939, Wade, CWP 11.

1039. King, p. 36.

1040. CW to Raymond Hunt, 21 Nov 1939, Wade, CWP 28.

1041. CW to Raymond Hunt, 5 Jan 1940, Wade, CWP 29.

1042. CW to Phyllis Potter, 21 Nov 1939, Bodleian MS Res. c. 58.

1043. CW to Phyllis Potter, 26 Jan 1940, Bodleian MS Res. c. 58.

1044. CW to Anne Ridler, 9 Feb 1940, Bodleian ARP.

1045. King, p. 42.

1046. Wade, CWMS 356.

1047. C.S. Lewis, *Collected Letters* II, p. 339.

1048. Wade, CWMS 356; fragment on Comus, Bodleian MS Res. c. pp. 136–7.

1049. C.S. Lewis, *Collected Letters* II, pp. 345–6.

1050. CW to Phyllis Potter, 18 Feb 1940, Bodleian MS Res. c. 58.

1051. King, p. 52.

1052. CW to Raymond Hunt, 9 Feb 1940, Wade, CWP 29.

1053. CW to Alice Mary Miller, 6 Apr 1940, Bodleian, Charles Williams/Hadfield papers, Box 2, K.27.10.

1054. CW to Anne Ridler, 28 Mar 1940, Bodleian ARP.

1055. e.g. King, p. 118.

1056. King, pp.108, 110; CW to Alice Mary Miller, 3 Mar 1941, Bodleian, Charles Williams/Hadfield papers, Box 2, K27.26.

1057. King, p. 44.

1058. CW to Anne Ridler, 27 Oct 1939, Bodleian ARP.

1059. CW to Raymond Hunt, 21 Dec 1939, Wade, CWP 28.

1060. King, p. 72.

1061. CW to Anne Ridler, 15 Feb 1940, Bodleian ARP.

1062. CW to Phyllis Potter, 13 Feb 1940, Bodleian MS Res. c. 58.

1063. King, pp. 57–8.

1064. King, p. 70.

1065. CW to Raymond Hunt, 17 Oct 1940, Wade, CWP 32.

1066. King, p. 101.

1067. CW to Olive Speake, 22 Feb 1940, Wade, CWP 78.

1068. King, p. 51.

1069. CW to Alice Mary Miller, 1 July 1940, Bodleian, Charles Williams/Hadfield, K27/19.

1070. CW to Raymond Hunt, 1 Mar 1940, Wade, CWP 30.

1071. CW to Phyllis Potter, 10 Oct 1941, Bodleian MS Res. c. 58.

1072. CW to Phyllis Potter, undated, Bodleian MS Res c. 58.

1073. CW to Alice Mary Miller, 14 Mar 1940, Bodleian, Charles Williams/Hadfield papers, Box 2, K27.9.

1074. W.H. Auden to CW, 14 July 1940, Wade, CWP 163.

1075. CW to Phyllis Potter, 19 July 1940, Bodleian MS Res. c. 58.

1076. *Dublin Review*, 1940, pp. 99–101.

1077. C.S. Lewis, *Collected Letters* II, p. 410.

1078. CW to Ruth Spalding, 3 May 1940; courtesy of Jeannie Moyo.

1079. Michal Williams to Phyllis Potter, 16 May 1940, Bodleian MS Res. c. 58.

1080. King, p. 60.

1081. King, p. 58.

1082. CW to Phyllis Potter, 15 May 1940, Bodleian MS Res. c. 58.

1083. King, p. 53.

1084. Raymond Hunt's Chronology, Bodleian MS Res. c. 136/3.

1085. Ridler (1958) p. 154.

1086. King, pp. 70, 71.

1087. CW to Alice Mary Miller, 14 Mar and 6 Apr 1940, Bodleian, Charles Williams/Hadfield, Box 2, K.27.10.

1088. CW to Alice Mary Miller, 10 May 1940, Bodleian, Charles Williams/Hadfield papers, Box 2, K.27.10.

1089. CW to Alice Mary Miller, 16 May 1940, Bodleian, Charles Williams/Hadfield papers, Box 2, K.27.10.

1090. CW to Alice Mary Miller, 10 May 1940, Bodleian, Charles Williams/Hadfield papers, Box 2, K.27.10.

1091. CW to Alice Mary Miller, 10 May 1940, Bodleian, Charles Williams/Hadfield papers, Box 2, K.27.10.

1092. CW to Alice Mary Miller, 16 May 1940, Bodleian, Charles Williams/ Hadfield papers, Box 2, K.27.13.

1093. Hadfield (1983) p. 192.

1094. CW to Alice Mary Miller, 17 June 1940, Bodleian, Charles Williams/ Hadfield papers, Box 2, K27.16.

1095. CW to Alice Mary Miller, 25 June 1940, Bodleian, Charles Williams/ Hadfield papers, Box 2, K27.17.

1096. CW to Alice Mary Miller, 17 July 1940, Bodleian, Charles Williams/Hadfield papers, Box 2, K27.17.

1097. CW to Alice Mary Miller, 5 June 1940, Bodleian, Charles Williams/Hadfield papers, Box 2, K27.17.

1098. CW to Alice Mary Miller, 1 July 1940, Bodleian, Charles Williams/Hadfield papers, Box 2, K27.17.

1099. CW to Alice Mary Miller, 3 Mar 1941, Bodleian, Charles Williams/Hadfield papers, Box 2, K27.17.

1100. CW to Alice Mary Miller, 22 May 1940, Bodleian, Charles Williams/ Hadfield papers, Box 2, K.27.15.

1101. King, p. 45; CW to Michael Williams, 14 Feb 1940, Wade, CWP 103.

1102. King, p. 46.

1103. King, p. 48.

1104. King, p. 60.

1105. King, p. 66.

1106. King, p. 79.

1107. King, p. 74.

1108. CW to Raymond Hunt, 31 Mar 1940, Wade, CWP 31.

1109. *Church Times*, 14 Mar 1941.

1110. King, p. 106.

1111. *Witchcraft*, pp. 77–8.

1112. *Witchcraft*, pp. 231–2.

1113. CW to Thelma Shuttleworth, 1 Mar 1940, Bodleian MS Eng. Lett. e. 136.

1114. CW to Thelma Shuttleworth, 30 Apr 1940, Bodleian MS Eng. Lett. e. 136.

1115. Joan Wallis Interview 1.

1116. CW to Joan Wallis, 30 Aug 1939, Wade, CWP 84.

1117. CW to Joan Wallis, 11 Dec 1940, Wade, CWP 85.

1118. Joan Wallis Interview 1.

1119. CW to Joan Wallis, 28 Oct 1939, Wade, CWP 84.

1120. The oddest feature of this diagram is its simple inaccuracy. The sphere labelled 'Hod' should be Yesod; the unlabelled sphere by the name 'Theodora' is properly Hod.

1121. CW to Joan Wallis, 4 Oct 1940, Wade, CWP 84.

1122. CW to Joan Wallis, 10 Jan 1941, Wade, CWP 85; Joan Wallis Interview 1.

1123. CW to Joan Wallis, 4 Feb 1944, Wade, CWP 86.

1124. Joan Wallis Interview 1.

1125. Lewis *Collected Letters*, II, p. 1714.

1126. 'Charles Williams as I knew him', CWSN 3, Autumn 1976.

1127. CWSN 3, Autumn 1976.

1128. CW to Anne Renwick, undated, Bodleian MS Eng. Lett. d. 452.

1129. CW to Anne Renwick, 30 Sept 1941, Bodleian MS Eng. Lett. d. 452.

1130. Bodleian MS Eng. Lett. d. 452, f127.

1131. Raymond Hunt's Chronology, Bodleian MS Res. c. 136/3.

1132. CW to Alice Mary Miller, 29 Oct 1940, Bodleian, Charles Williams/Hadfield, Box 2, K27.24.

1133. CW to Thelma Shuttleworth, 12 May 1941, Bodleian MS Eng. Lett. d. 452. f142.

1134. King, p. 124.

1135. CW to Anne Renwick, 29 Nov 1941, Bodleian MS Eng. Lett. d. 452.

1136. CW to AMH, 20 Sept 1941, Bodleian, Charles Williams/Hadfield papers, Box 2, K27.28.

1137. CW to Anne Renwick, 22 Oct 1941, Bodleian MS. Eng. Lett. d. 452.

1138. King, p. 124.

1139. Carpenter, p. 178.

1140. CW to Alice Mary Miller, 7 Oct 1940, Bodleian, Charles Williams/Hadfield papers, Box 2, K27.23.

1141. CW to Anne Ridler, 26 Sept 1940, Bodleian ARP.

1142. Ralph Binfield, letter courtesy of Joy Cooper.

1143. King, p. 99.

1144. 'ELC', 'The Oxford Depot', *The Clarendonian*, Vol. IV, No. 1 (new series), Mar, 1950, pp. 13–17.

1145. Information from Brenda Boughton; Anne Grimwade; Margaret Routley; Noël Welch; Anne Wallace-Hadrill.

1146. Raymond Hunt's Chronology, Bodleian MS Res. c. 136/3.

1147. Information from Brian Horne.

1148. CW to Anne Ridler, 26 Sept 1940, Bodleian ARP.

1149. CW to Alice Mary Miller, 29 Oct 1940, Bodleian, Charles Williams/Hadfield papers, Box 2, K27.24.

1150. CW to Phyllis Potter, 6 June 1941, Bodleian MS Res. c. 58.

1151. R.H. Ward, *Names and Natures*, 179.

1152. CW to Phyllis Potter, 6 Feb 1941, Bodleian MS Res. c. 58.

1153. Information from Joan Light.

1154. CW to Ruth Spalding, 3 Apr 1941, Wade CWP, 75.

1155. Ruth Spalding to Stephen Barber, 10 Oct 1995, courtesy of Jeanie Moyo.

1156. Ridler (1958) p. 133.

1157. CW to A. Douglas Millard, 22 Apr 1941; courtesy of Malcolm Guite.

1158. *Religion and Love in Dante*, p. 111.

1159. *The Forgiveness of Sins,* p. 191.

1160. *The Forgiveness of Sins,* p.199.
1161. Hadfield (1983) p. 202.
1162. 'Ourselves and the Revolution', p. 10.
1163. Raymond Hunt's Chronology, Bodleian MS Res. c. 136/3.
1164. 'Gaelic Incantations', *New Statesman*, XXII, 29 Nov 1941, p. 461.
1165. Bodleian, Charles Williams/Hadfield papers, Box 4, Ring binder 30, B113.
1166. CW to Phyllis Potter, 6 Nov 1941, Bodleian MS Eng. Lett. d. 452, f144.
1167. CW to Michael Williams, 8 Dec 1941, Wade, CWP [Lindop E.64].
1168. CW to Anne Ridler, 27 Oct 1942, Bodleian ARP.
1169. CW to Thelma Shuttleworth, Bodleian MS Eng. Lett. d. 452., f144.
1170. Anne Spalding Interview.
1171. King, p. 136.
1172. CW to Anne Ridler, 23 Dec 1941, Bodleian ARP.
1173. King, p. 248.
1174. CW to Thelma Shuttleworth, 30 Apr 1940, Bodleian MS Eng. Lett. e. 136.
1175. CW to Raymond Hunt, 29 Nov 1941, Wade, CWP 33.
1176. CW to Anne Ridler, 25 Mar 1942, Bodleian ARP.
1177. C.S. Lewis, *Collected Letters* II, p. 218n.
1178. CW to Anne Ridler, 25 Mar 1942, Bodleian ARP.
1179. CW to Raymond Hunt, 5 and 12 Feb 1942, Wade, CWP 34.
1180. CW to Raymond Hunt, 1 June 1942, Wade, CWP 36.
1181. CW to Anne Ridler, 22 June 1942, Bodleian ARP.
1182. CW to Anne Renwick, 30 July 1942, Bodleian MS Eng. Lett. d. 452.
1183. CW to Bruce Montgomery, 1 Sept 1942, Bodleian MS Eng. c. 3858, ff56–66.
1184. T.S. Eliot to CW, 5 Sept 1942, Wade, CWP 244.
1185. CW to Anne Ridler, 30 Sept 1942, Bodleian ARP.
1186. CW to Phyllis Potter, 6 Feb 1941, Bodleian MS Res. c. 58.
1187. Green and Hooper, *C.S. Lewis: A Biography*, pp. 223–4.
1188. CW to Anne Ridler, 28 Mar 1940, Bodleian ARP.
1189. CW to Joan Wallis, 11 Nov 1940, Wade, CWP 85.
1190. CW to Joan Wallis, 19 Dec 1940, Wade, CWP 85.
1191. T.S. Eliot to CW, 20 May 1941, typed transcript, Bodleian MS Res. c. 136.3.
1192. CW to Anne Ridler, 25 Mar 1942, Bodleian ARP.
1193. CW to Anne Ridler, 13 July 1943, Bodleian ARP.
1194. CW to Anne Renwick, 13 May 1942, Bodleian MS Eng. Lett. d. 452.
1195. CW to Raymond Hunt, 21 Dec 1942, Wade, CWP 38.
1196. 'Letters in Hell', *Time and Tide*, Mar, 1942, p. 22.
1197. King, p. 143.
1198. CW to Anne Ridler, 30 Sept 1942, Bodleian ARP.
1199. CW to Anne Renwick, 4 May 1943, Bodleian MS Eng. Lett. d. 452.
1200. CW to Raymond Hunt, 29 Apr 1942, Wade, CWP 35.
1201. CW to Raymond Hunt, 31 July 42, Wade, CWP 36.
1202. Lewis *Letters* II, 360.

1203. *Essays Presented to Charles Williams*, p. xiii.

1204. Carpenter, pp. 123, 126.

1205. CW to Anne Ridler, 30 Sept 1942, Bodleian ARP.

1206. David Whittle, *Bruce Montgomery/Edmund Crispin: A Life in Music and Books*, pp. 26–7.

1207. Andrew Motion, *Philip Larkin*, pp. 124–5.

1208. *Selected Letters of Philip Larkin: 1940–1985*, ed. Anthony Thwaite, p. 79.

1209. *Selected Letters of Philip Larkin*, p. 141.

1210. *Selected Letters of Philip Larkin*, p. 641.

1211. John Heath-Stubbs, *Hindsights: An Autobiography*, p. 97.

1212. King, p. 160.

1213. Ross Davies, *Drummond Allison: Come, Let us Pity Death*, p. 43.

1214. Davies, *Drummond Allison: Come, Let us Pity Death*, p. 44.

1215. CW to Raymond Hunt, 15 May 1943, Wade, CWP 39.

1216. King, p. 160.

1217. King, p. 160.

1218. Hadfield (1959), p. 157.

1219. CW to Alice Mary Miller, 1 July 1940, Bodleian, Charles Williams/Hadfield papers, Box 2, K27.19.

1220. CW to Anne Ridler, 23 Dec 1941, Bodleian ARP.

1221. CW to Anne Ridler, 30 Sept 1942, Bodleian ARP.

1222. CW to Anne Renwick, 12 Apr 1943, Bodleian MS Eng. Lett. d. 452.

1223. King, p. 159.

1224. C.S. Lewis, *Collected Letters* II, p. 902.

1225. 2 Corinthians, 12:2.

1226. Stephen Barber, 'Metaphysical and Romantic in the Taliessin Poems', *Seven: An Anglo-American Literary Review*, XX, 2003, pp. 76–8.

1227. CW to Joan Wallis, 20 Aug 1943, Wade, CWP 86.

1228. *The Letters of Evelyn Underhill*, p. 21.

1229. CW to Phyllis Potter, 23 July 1942, Bodleian MS Res. c. 58.

1230. CW to Joan Wallis, 23 Dec 1942, Wade CWP 85.

1231. CW to Phyllis Potter, 24 Aug 1942, Bodleian MS Res. c. 58.

1232. *The Letters of Evelyn Underhill*, p. 15.

1233. CW to Raymond Hunt, 20 Feb 1943, Wade, CWP 39.

1234. King, p. 148.

1235. Translation by Stephen Barber.

1236. King, p. 151.

1237. *The Times*, Mar 1 1943.

1238. CW to Michael Williams, 18 Nov 1944, Wade, CWP [Lindop E 64].

1239. CW to Michael Williams, 14 Sept 1943, Wade, CWP [Lindop E. 64].

1240. C.S. Lewis, *Collected Letters*, Vol III, p. 1031.

1241. Carpenter, p. 188.

1242. *TLS*, 24 July 1943, p. 358.

1243. *Time and Tide*, 31 July 1943, pp. 633–4.

1244. CW to Anne Ridler, 13 July 1943, Bodleian ARP.

1245. Carpenter, p. 188.

1246. King, p. 153.

1247. King, p. 161.

1248. 13 July 1943, CW to Anne Ridler, Bodleian ARP.

1249. King p. 155; CW to Joan Wallis, 27 May 1943, Wade, CWP 86; CW to Anne Ridler, 21 Sept 1943, Bodleian ARP.

1250. King, p. 153.

1251. CW to Joan Wallis, 27 May 43, Wade, CWP 86.

1252. CW to Margaret Douglas, 29 July 1943, Wade, CWP 14.

1253. King, p. 159.

1254. King, p. 155.

1255. King p. 159 [King misreads 'beat' as 'best'].

1256. CW to Anne Renwick, 20 Dec 1943, Bodleian MS Eng. Lett. d. 452.

1257. *Poetry London*, IX, 1944.

1258. King, p. 171.

1259. CW to Joan Wallis, 5 July 1944, Wade, CWP 86.

1260. CW to Anne Renwick, 5 July 1944, Bodleian MS Eng. Lett. d. 452.

1261. Carpenter, p. 197.

1262. King, p. 154.

1263. King, p. 160.

1264. King, p. 161.

1265. King, p. 179.

1266. King, p. 180.

1267. King, p. 73.

1268. CW to Thelma Shuttleworth, 30 July 1940, Bodleian MS Eng. Lett. e. 136.

1269. CW to AR, 26 Sept 1940, Bodleian ARP.

1270. CW to Joan Wallis, 30 Sept 1940, Wade CWP 86.

1271. T.S. Eliot to CW, 14 Dec 1940, typed transcript, Bodleian MS Res. c. 137.

1272. Raymond Hunt's Chronology, Bodleian MS Res. c. 136.3.

1273. King, p. 162.

1274. King, p. 163.

1275. King, p. 163.

1276. CW to Anne Renwick, 6 July 1943, Bodleian MS Eng. Lett. d. 452.

1277. CW to Anne Ridler, 13 July 1943, Bodleian ARP.

1278. CW to Joan Wallis, 23 July, 1943, Wade, CWP 86.

1279. *The Noises That Weren't There:* Fragment, Wade CWMS 134.

1280. CW to Anne Renwick, 6 July 1943, Bodleian MS Eng. Lett. d. 452.

1281. CW to Dorothy L. Sayers, 13 Aug 1943, Wade, Dorothy L. Sayers Papers, 115 b.

1282. King, p. 168.

1283. King, p. 174.

1284. CW to Anne Renwick, 24 Sept 1943, Bodleian MS Eng. Lett. d. 452.

1285. CW to Anne Ridler, 21 Sept 1943, Bodleian ARP.

1286. CW to Joan Wallis, 20 Aug 1943, Wade, CWP 86.

1287. King, p. 168.

1288. CW to Michal, 22 Sept 1943, Wade, CWP [Lindop E.64].

1289. King, p. 170.

1290. Margaret Sinclair to the Bishop of Chichester, 29 Sept 1943, Wade, CWP 425.

1291. CW to Margaret Sinclair, 14 Oct 1943, Wade, CWP 70.

1292. CW to Margaret Sinclair, 28 Oct 1943, Wade, CWP 70.

1293. King, p. 180.

1294. *Letters to Lalage*, p. 23.

1295. *Letters to Lalage*, p. 23.

1296. *Letters to Lalage*, p. 25.

1297. *Letters to Lalage*, p. 26.

1298. *Letters to Lalage*, p. 27.

1299. *Letters to Lalage*, p. 29.

1300. *Letters to Lalage*, p. 31.

1301. *Letters to Lalage*, pp. 32–3.

1302. CW to Thelma Shuttleworth, '1930', Bodleian MS Eng. Lett. e. 136, f83.

1303. *Letters to Lalage*, p. 95.

1304. *Letters to Lalage*, pp. 35–6.

1305. *Letters to Lalage*, pp. 36–7.

1306. *Letters to Lalage*, p. 39.

1307. *Letters to Lalage*, p. 41.

1308. *Letters to Lalage*, p.42.

1309. *Letters to Lalage*, p. 47.

1310. *Letters to Lalage*, p. 48.

1311. *Letters to Lalage*, p. 54.

1312. Lois Lang-Sims Interview.

1313. *Letters to Lalage*, p. 63.

1314. *Letters to Lalage*, p. 67.

1315. *Letters to Lalage*, p. 68.

1316. *Letters to Lalage*, p. 68.

1317. *Letters to Lalage*, p. 70.

1318. *Letters to Lalage*, p. 72.

1319. *Letters to Lalage*, p. 79.

1320. CW to Thelma Shuttleworth, 10 Aug 1943, Bodleian MS Eng. Lett. e. 136, f148.

1321. On such a baffling matter, it may be worth mentioning one perhaps relevant parallel. In 'No. 2 The Pines', his well-known essay on Swinburne, written in 1914, Max Beerbohm writes of the poet, 'He was not a thinker: his mind rose ever away from reason to rhapsody; neither was he human. He was a king

crowned but not throned.' The context offers no further elucidation of
Beerbohm's meaning. Possibly the phrase stuck in Williams's memory.

1322. CW to Thelma Shuttleworth, 10 Aug 1943, Bodleian MS Eng. Lett.
d. 452, f148.

1323. CW to Thelma Shuttleworth, 24 Sept 1943, Bodleian MS Eng. Lett.
d. 452. f152.

1324. CW to Anne Ridler, 13 July 1943, Bodleian ARP.

1325. CW to Anne Ridler, 21 Sept 1943, Bodleian ARP.

1326. Brenda Boughton Interview.

1327. Brenda Boughton Interview.

1328. Helen King Interview.

1329. Brenda Boughton Interview.

1330. Joy Stephenson Interview.

1331. Joy Stephenson Interview.

1332. Brenda Boughton Interview.

1333. Brenda Boughton Interview.

1334. Joy Stephenson Interview.

1335. Helen King Interview.

1336. Joy Stephenson Interview.

1337. Joy Stephenson Interview.

1338. King, p. 193.

1339. King, p. 152.

1340. CW to Phyllis Potter, 'Easter Sunday', Apr 1943, Bodleian MS Res. c. 58.

1341. CW to Michael Williams, 16 June 1943, Wade, CWP [Lindop E 64].

1342. CW to Mildred Topliss, 3 Sept 1943, Wade, CWP 81.

1343. CW to Michael Williams, 5 May 1944, Wade, CWP [Lindop E 64].

1344. CW to Michael Williams, 4 June 1943, Wade, CWP [Lindop, D 22 (b)].

1345. King, p. 298 n. 1.

1346. King, p. 220.

1347. King, p. 172.

1348. King, p. 209.

1349. CW to Michael Williams, 30 June 1944, Wade, CWP [Lindop E.64].

1350. CW to Michael Williams, 16 June 1943, Wade, CWP [Lindop E. 64].

1351. CW to Michael Williams, May 1944, Wade, CWP [Lindop E.64].

1352. CW to Michael Williams, 10 Dec 1943, Wade, CWP [Lindop E.64].

1353. CW to Michael Williams, 12 Mar 1944, Wade, CWP [Lindop E. 64].

1354. Anne Ridler Interview 2.

1355. John Heath-Stubbs Interview.

1356. CW to Anne Ridler, undated [1934], Bodleian ARP.

1357. Carpenter, p. 194.

1358. King, p. 182.

1359. Carpenter, p.194.

1360. CW to Anne Renwick, 2 Jan 1944, Bodleian MS Eng. Lett. d. 452.

1361. CW to Anne Ridler, 6 Jan 1944, Bodleian ARP.
1362. King, pp. 192–3.
1363. CW to Alice Mary Miller, 30 Mar 1944, Bodleian, Charles Williams/Hadfield papers, Box 2, K27.35.
1364. CW to Raymond Hunt, 6 Apr 1944, Wade, CWP 41.
1365. CW to Phyllis Potter, 18 Apr 1944, Bodleian MS Res. c. 58.
1366. King, p. 199.
1367. King, p. 200.
1368. CW to Anne Ridler, 25 May 1944, Bodleian ARP.
1369. Raymond Hunt's Chronology, Bodleian MS Res. c. 136/3.
1370. King, p. 192.
1371. King, p. 203.
1372. Robin Milford to CW, 18 Mar 1944, Wade, CWP 378.
1373. King, p. 198.
1374. Heath-Stubbs, *Hindsights*, pp. 172–3; information from Anne Ridler.
1375. CW to Anne Ridler, 6 Jan 1944, Bodleian ARP.
1376. King, p. 195.
1377. King, p. 197.
1378. King, p. 208.
1379. King, p. 189.
1380. King, p. 187.
1381. CW to Michal, 10 Jan 1944, Wade, CWP 136.
1382. King, p. 187.
1383. King, p. 190.
1384. CW to Raymond Hunt, 6 Apr 1944, Wade, CWP 41.
1385. King, p. 192.
1386. King, p. 209.
1387. King, p. 202.
1388. King, p. 211.
1389. Draft codicil to CW's will, Wade, CWP [Lindop A. 3].
1390. Wade, CWMS 417.
1391. Michal Williams, fragment, Wade, CWP [Lindop E.57].
1392. Raymond Hunt's Chronology, Bodleian MS Res. c. 136.3.
1393. Raymond Hunt's Chronology, Bodleian MS Res. c. 136.3.
1394. King, pp. 203–4.
1395. King, p. 215.
1396. King, p. 220.
1397. King, p. 221.
1398. King, p. 248.
1399. CW to Dorothy L Sayers, 7 Sept 1944, Wade, Dorothy L. Sayers papers, 115a.
1400. King, p. 213.
1401. King, p. 238.

1402. CW to Michal Williams, Aug 1944, Wade CWP [Lindop E.64].

1403. CW to Robert Graves, 5 Mar 1943, St John's College Robert Graves Trust.

1404. King, p. 209.

1405. Transcribed in W.S. Watt to Robert Graves, 27 July 1944, St John's College Robert Graves Trust.

1406. *The Letters of Dorothy L. Sayers,* I: *1899–1936: The Making of a Detective Novelist,* ed. Barbara Reynolds, p. 340.

1407. *The Letters of Dorothy L. Sayers,* II: *1937–1943: From Novelist to Playwright,* p. 14.

1408. Anne Spalding Interview.

1409. Carpenter, p. 189.

1410. Carpenter, p. 189.

1411. CW to Dorothy L. Sayers, 26 Apr 1944, Wade, Dorothy L. Sayers Papers, 115a.

1412. *The Letters of Dorothy L. Sayers,* III, *1944–50: A Noble Daring,* p. 45.

1413. Dorothy L. Sayers to CW, undated, Wade, Dorothy L. Sayers Papers, 116.

1414. *The Letters of Dorothy L. Sayers,* III, *1944–50: A Noble Daring,* p. 53.

1415. Carpenter, p. 189.

1416. CW to Joan Wallis, 5 July 1944, Wade, CWP 86.

1417. *The Letters of Dorothy L. Sayers,* Volume III: *1943–1950: A Noble Daring,* p. 45.

1418. *The Letters of Dorothy L. Sayers,* Volume III: *1943–1950: A Noble Daring,* p. 75.

1419. *The Letters of Dorothy L. Sayers,* Volume III: *1943–1950: A Noble Daring,* p. 115.

1420. *The Letters of Dorothy L. Sayers,* Volume III: *1943–1950: A Noble Daring,* p. 119.

1421. King, p. 222.

1422. King, p. 220.

1423. CW to Alice Mary Miller, 18 Sept 1944, Bodleian, Charles Williams/Hadfield papers, Box 2, K27.39.

1424. King, p. 223.

1425. Raymond Hunt's Chronology, Bodleian MS Res. c. 136.3.

1426. King, p. 239.

1427. CW to Anne Renwick, 30 Sept 1944, Bodleian MS Eng. Lett. d. 452.

1428. CW to Alice Mary Hadfield, 5 Jan 1945, Bodleian, Charles Williams/Hadfield, Box 2, K27.42.

1429. W.H. Auden to CW, 11 Jan 1945, Bodleian MS Res. c. 136.3.

1430. King, p. 233.

1431. King, p. 228.

1432. King, p. 191.

1433. King, p. 201.

1434. CW to Thelma Shuttleworth, 20 Dec 1944, Bodleian MS Eng. Lett. d. 452, f157.

1435. CW to Joan Wallis, 5 July 1944, Wade, CWP 86.

1436. King, p. 211.

1437. CW to Michal Williams, 25 Sept 1944, Wade, CWP 145.

1438. Michal Williams to CW, 'Wednesday', undated [but before 27 Mar 1945, when the last V2 fell], Wade, CWP [Lindop H. 20].

1439. CW to Michal Williams, 28 Aug 1944, Wade, CWP [Lindop E. 64].

1440. CW to Dorothy L. Sayers, 7 Sept 1944, Wade, Dorothy L. Sayers papers, 116.

1441. CW to Dorothy L. Sayers, 20 Jan 44, Wade, Dorothy L. Sayers papers, 115a.

1442. CW to Phyllis Potter, 19 Dec 1944, Bodleian MS Res. c. 58.

1443. Carpenter, p. 197.

1444. Carpenter, p. 195.

1445. King, p. 221.

1446. Carpenter p. 191.

1447. Humphrey Carpenter, ed., *Letters of J.R.R. Tolkien*, p. 93.

1448. *Letters of J.R.R. Tolkien*, p. 102.

1449. Carpenter, p. 123.

1450. *Letters of J.R.R. Tolkien*, p. 102.

1451. *Letters of J.R.R. Tolkien*, p. 103.

1452. CW to Thelma Shuttleworth, 20 Dec 1944, Bodleian MS Eng. Lett. d. 452, f157.

1453. King, p. 239.

1454. CW to Alice Mary Miller, 5 Jan 1945, Bodleian, Charles Williams/Hadfield papers, Box 2, K27.42.

1455. King, p. 239.

1456. CW to Joan Wallis, 11 Jan 1945, Wade, CWP 87.

1457. King, p. 242.

1458. King, p. 243.

1459. *New Statesman*, 10 Mar 1945, p. 160.

1460. CW to Phyllis Potter, 1 Feb 1945 and 14 Feb 1945, Bodleian MS Res. c. 58.

1461. CW to Dorothy L. Sayers, 7 Sept 1944, Wade, Dorothy L. Sayers papers, 116.

1462. CW to Anne Ridler, 6 Mar 1945, Bodleian ARP.

1463. King, p. 243.

1464. King, p. 242.

1465. Raymond Hunt's Chronology, Bodleian MS Res. c. 136.3.

1466. King, p. 241.

1467. Raymond Hunt's Chronology, Bodleian MS Res. c. 136.3.

1468. King, pp. 251, 253.

1469. CW to Joan Wallis, 26 Mar 1945, Wade, CWP 87.

1470. Raymond Hunt's Chronology, Bodleian MS Res. c. 136.3.

1471. King, p. 256.

1472. King, p. 248.

1473. King, p. 258.

1474. King, p. 255.

1475. King, p. 248.

1476. *Arthurian Torso*, p. 2.

1477. King, pp. 246–7.

1478. CW to Phyllis Potter, 15 Jan 1945, Bodleian MS Res. c. 58.

1479. King, p. 256.

1480. CW to Alice Mary Miller, 4 May 1945, Bodleian, Charles Williams/Hadfield, Box 2, K27.44.

1481. King, p. 257.

1482. King, p. 249.

1483. King, p. 217, 242.

1484. King, p. 249.

1485. King, p. 255.

1486. CW to Phyllis Potter, 15 Jan 1945, Bodleian MS Res. c. 58.

1487. King, p. 254.

1488. King, p. 249.

1489. King, p. 240.

1490. Christopher Fry, 'Charles Williams', *Adelphi*, XXVII, 27 Nov 1950.

1491. *New English Weekly*, 10 May 1945, pp. 33–4.

1492. Michal Williams to CW, 'Tuesday', Wade, CWP [Lindop O.1].

1493. CW to Alice Mary Miller, 4 May 1945, Bodleian, Charles Williams/Hadfield, Box 2, K27.44.

1494. Margaret Douglas to Edith Williams, 21 May, 1945, Wade, CWP [Lindop N. 20]; King p. 257.

1495. King, p. 257.

1496. Hadfield (1983) p. 235.

1497. King, p. 258.

1498. Brenda Boughton Interview.

1499. Anne Spalding Interview.

1500. Anne Spalding, Wade Oral Histories.

1501. Margaret Douglas to Anne Ridler, 15 May 1945, Bodleian ARP.

1502. Anne Spalding, Wade Oral Histories.

1503. Private information.

1504. Margaret Douglas to Edith Williams, 21 May 1945, Wade, CWP [Lindop N. 20].

1505. Ena Sheen to Grevel Lindop, 24 May and 4 June 2006.

1506. Margaret Douglas to Anne Ridler, 30 May 1945, Bodleian ARP.

1507. Helen King Interview.

1508. John Wain, *Sprightly Running*, p. 152.

1509. *Essays Presented to Charles Williams*, pp. xiii–xiv.

1510. A slip on Warnie's part: Williams died in the Radcliffe Infirmary, not the Acland Nursing Home.

1511. W.H. Lewis, *Brothers and Friends*, p. 182.

1512. OUP Archive, Milford Letter Books, Vol. 170, p. 714, H.S. Milford to G.C. Faber, 15 May 1945.

1513. Gavin Ashenden, *Alchemy and Integration* p. 238, n. 32; Anne Spalding, reported by Eileen Mable.

1514. Renée Haynes to Theodora Bosanquet, 18 May 1945, Houghton Library.

1515. CW to Alice Mary Miller, 22 May 1940, Bodleian, Charles Williams/Hadfield papers, Box 2, K.27.14.

1516. Robin Milford to Anne Ridler, 23 May 1945, Bodleian ARP.

1517. Raymond Hunt to Anne Ridler, 24 May 1945, Bodleian ARP.

1518. C.S. Lewis, *Collected Letters* II, p. 653.

1519. Helen Wheeler to Grevel Lindop, undated [2006].

1520. Renée Haynes to Theodora Bosanquet, 18 May 1945, Houghton Library.

1521. Michal Williams to Anne Ridler, 20 May 1945, Bodleian ARP.

1522. Michal Williams to Glen Cavaliero, 18 June 1956 and 30 Nov 1957.

1523. Hubert Foss to Michal Williams, 18 May 1945, Wade, CWP 250.

1524. Anne Ridler, *Collected Poems*, p. 213.

1525. C.S. Lewis to Michal Williams, 15 June 1948, Wade CWP [Lindop D.18].

1526. Michal Williams to Glen Cavaliero, 11 May 1958.

Manuscript Sources

Manuscript sources for Charles Williams's life are mainly in two repositories: the Bodleian Library, Oxford, and the Marion E. Wade Center, Wheaton College, Illinois.

The principal holdings in the Department of Special Collections at the Bodleian (not all of which have been fully catalogued) are as follows:

CW's Commonplace Book: **MS. Eng. e. 2012**

Notes and typescripts relating to CW's works: **MS. Eng. c. 2719**

Papers relating to CW's plays and correspondence with Olive Willis: **E. Martin Browne literary papers, uncatalogued**

Correspondence between CW and Phyllis Jones (later Somervaille, later McDougall): **MS. Res. c. 320**

Letters from CW to Anne Renwick: **MS. Eng. lett. d. 452**

Letters from CW to Thelma Shuttleworth: **MS. Eng. lett. e. 136**

Raymond Hunt's Chronology of CW's life: **MS. Res. c. 136/3**

Papers donated by Alice Mary Hadfield: **Charles Williams/Hadfield papers, uncatalogued**

Photocopies of John Pellow's *Diary*: **MS. Facs. c. 134**

Papers donated by Phyllis Potter: **MS. Res. c. 58**

Papers donated by Anne Ridler: **MS. Res. c. 136–7**

Additional papers bequeathed by Anne Ridler: **Anne Ridler papers, uncatalogued**

The Marion E. Wade Center at Wheaton College, Illinois, holds the following very extensive collections:

Charles Williams Papers (letters to, from, and about CW)

Charles Williams Manuscripts (manuscripts of CW's writings)

Raymond Hunt Papers (materials relating to CW's life and work, including notes on many of his lectures)

Williams Family Papers (materials relating to the Williams and Wall families going back to the mid-nineteenth century)

Wade Oral Histories (transcripts of interviews with many people who knew CW)

The archive of the Charles Williams Society, held at the Centre for Medieval and Renaissance Studies, St Michael's Hall, Shoe Lane, Oxford OX1 2DP, contains many documents relating to CW's life and reputation, including Alice Mary Hadfield's working notes from her two books on Williams. An online catalogue is available at http://www.charleswilliamssociety.org.uk/the-catalog/catalog-papers-list/

The archives of the Oxford University Press, Great Clarendon Street, Oxford OX2 6DP contain a wealth of material on the workings of the Press during CW's time there. The **Amen Corner Letters**, the **Milford Letter Books**, and the files on individual titles published by the Press are especially valuable.

Other important collections are CW's letters to Mary Butts, held in the Beinecke Rare Book and Manuscript Library, Yale, as **Mary Butts Papers, Box 2, folder 46**; and his letters to Theodora Bosanquet held in the Houghton Library, Harvard College, Cambridge, Massachusetts as **bMS Eng 1213.6**. The only known manuscript of Arthur Hugh Evelyn Lee is his notebook, held in the Warburg Institute, London, as **Yorke Collection, NS 32**. Charles Wall's papers are held by the Society of Antiquaries of London, Burlington House, London W1J 0BE. The diaries of A.E. Waite, and his *Record of the Holy House*, are in a private collection.

References

Abbott, Claude Colleer, ed., *Further Letters of Gerard Manley Hopkins, Including his Correspondence with Coventry Patmore*, second edition (London: Oxford University Press, 1956).

Anonymous, [Waite, A.E.], *The First Order of the Rosy Cross. World of Action Part I. The Ceremony of Reception into the Grade of Neophyte, o = o* ([London]: privately printed, 1916).

Anonymous, [Waite, A.E.], *FRC: Grade of Adeptus Exemptus* ([London]: privately printed, 1917).

Anonymous, [Waite, A.E.], *The Third Order of the Rosy Cross: World of Formation Part II. The Pontifical Ceremony of Admission to the Grade of Adeptus Minor, 5=6* ([London]: privately printed, 1917).

Anonymous, [Waite, A.E.], *FRC: Points of Contemplation Preliminary to All Grades* ([London]: privately printed, 1923).

Anonymous, [De Selincourt, Basil], *The English Poetic Mind, Times Literary Supplement*, 1932, p. 443.

Anonymous, report on award of Oxford M.A. degrees, *The Times*, 1 March 1943.

Anonymous, review of *The Figure of Beatrice, Times Literary Supplement*, 24 July 1943, p. 358.

Ashenden, Gavin, *Charles Williams: Alchemy and Integration* (Ohio: Kent State University Press, 2008).

Atwood, Margaret, *A Suggestive Enquiry into the Hermetic Mystery* (London: Trelawny Saunders, 1850).

Auden, W. H., untitled essay in Pike, James A., ed., *Modern Canterbury Pilgrims* (London: Mowbray, 1956).

Barber, Stephen, 'Metaphysical and Romantic in the Taliessin Poems', *Seven: An Anglo-American Literary Review*, XX, 2003, pp. 76–8.

Binfield, Ralph, 'Amen House and "Caesar"', *Charles Williams Society Newsletter*, 9 (Spring 1978), p.4.

Blondel, Nathalie, *Mary Butts: Scenes from the Life* (Kingston, N.Y.: McPherson, 1998).

Browne, E. Martin and Browne, Henzie, *Pilgrim Story: The Pilgrim Players, 1939–1943* (London: Frederick Muller, 1945).

Browne, E. Martin and Browne, Henzie, *Two in One* (Cambridge: Cambridge University Press, 1981).

Butts, Mary, review of *Thomas Cranmer of Canterbury, Time and Tide*, 4 August 1936.

Carpenter, Humphrey, *The Inklings: C.S. Lewis, J.R.R. Tolkien, Charles Williams and Their Friends* (London: Allen and Unwin, 1978).

Carpenter, Humphrey, ed., *Letters of J.R.R. Tolkien: A Selection* (London: Allen and Unwin, 1981).

Champneys, Basil, *Memoirs and Correspondence of Coventry Patmore*, 2 vols (London: George Bell, 1900).

Clark, Elizabeth A., 'John Chrysostom and the *Subintroductae*', *Church History*, 46/2 (June 1977), pp. 171–85.

Davies, Ross, *Drummond Allison: Come, Let us Pity Death* (London: Cecil Woolf, 2008).

Dodds, David Llewellyn, 'The Chapel of the Thorn: An Unknown Poetic Drama by Charles Williams', *Inklings-Jahrbuch,* 5 (1987), pp. 133–54.

Dodds, David Llewellyn, *Arthurian Poets: Charles Williams* (Cambridge: D.S. Brewer, 1991).

Drakard, Jane, *A Malay Frontier: Unity and Duality in a Sumatran Kingdom* (Ithaca: Cornell South East Asia Program, 1990, rpr 2004).

Dunne, J.W., *An Experiment with Time*, 2nd edn (London: Faber and Faber, 1929).

'ELC', 'The Oxford Depot', *The Clarendonian*, IV/1 (new series) (March 1950), pp. 13–17.

Eliot, T.S., *For Lancelot Andrewes: Essays on Style and Order* (London: Faber and Gwyer, 1928).

Eliot, T.S., review of *The Descent of the Dove* by Charles Williams, *New Statesman*, 9 Dec 1939.

Eliot, T.S., 'Introduction' to *All Hallows' Eve* by Charles Williams (New York: Pellegrini and Cudahy, 1948).

Ferris, Paul, ed., *Dylan Thomas: The Collected Letters* (New York: Macmillan, 1985).

Forster, E.M., 'E.K. Bennett', *The Caian*, V, p. 124.

Foster, Roy, *W.B. Yeats: A Life: II: The Arch-Poet* (Oxford: Oxford University Press, 2003).

Frisardi, Andrew, 'Selections from the *Vita Nuova*', *Temenos Academy Review* 10 (2010), p. 29.

Fry, Christopher, 'Charles Williams', *Adelphi*, XXVII, 27 Nov 1950.

Gilbert, R.A., *The Golden Dawn Companion : A guide to the history, structure, and workings of the Hermetic Order of the Golden Dawn* (Wellingborough: Aquarian, 1986).

Gilbert, R.A., *A. E. Waite, Magician of Many Parts* (Wellingborough: Crucible, 1987).

Gordon, Lyndall, *Eliot's New Life* (Oxford: Oxford University Press, 1988).

Gosse, Edmund, *Coventry Patmore* (London: Hodder and Stoughton, 1905).

Green, Roger Lancelyn and Hooper, Walter, *C.S. Lewis: A Biography* (London: Collins, 1974).

Grigson, Geoffrey, 'The New Book of English Verse: Criticism and Counter-Criticism', *Morning Post*, 11 Nov 1935.

Heath-Stubbs, John, *Hindsights: An Autobiography* (London: Hodder and Stoughton, 1993).

Hill, Geoffrey, *Collected Critical Writings*, ed. Kenneth Haynes (Oxford: Oxford University Press, 2008).

Hinnells, Duncan, *An Extraordinary Performance: Hubert Foss, Music Publishing, and the Oxford University Press* (Oxford: Oxford University Press, 1998).

Hooper, Walter, ed., *The Collected Letters of C.S. Lewis*, Volume II: *Books, Broadcasts and the War, 1931–1949* (New York: Harper San Francisco, 2004).

Hopkins, Gerard, *Nor Fish Nor Flesh* (London: Victor Gollancz, 1933).

Howe, Ellic, *The Magicians of the Golden Dawn: A documentary history of a magical order, 1887–1923* (London: Routledge and Kegan Paul, 1972).

J.W., 'Memories of Amen House', *The Record* [OUP], 9 Dec 1964.

King, Francis, ed., *Astral Projection, Ritual Magic and Alchemy; being hitherto unpublished Golden Dawn material*, revised edition (Wellingborough: Aquarian, 1987).

King, Roma, ed., *From Serge to Michal: Letters from Charles Williams to his Wife, Florence, 1939–1945*, (Ohio: Kent State University Press, 2002).

Lee, A.H.E., ed. and trans., *Magnetism and Magic* by Baron du Potet de Sennevoy (London: George Allen and Unwin, 1927).

Lee, A.H.E., 'Time and Mr. Dunne', *The Speculative Mason*, XXXI/2 (April 1939), pp. 43–50, and 3 (July 1939), pp. 93–6.

Lewis, C.S., *The Allegory of Love: A Study in Medieval Tradition* (Oxford: Clarendon Press, 1936).

Lewis, C.S., review of *Taliessin Through Logres, Theology*, 38 (April 1939), pp. 268–75.

Lewis, C.S., *A Preface to Paradise Lost* (London: Oxford University Press, 1942).

Kilby, Clyde S. and Marjorie Lamp Mead, eds, *Brothers & Friends: The Diaries of Major Warren Hamilton Lewis* (San Francisco and London: Harper & Row, 1982).

Little, Michael and Kelly, Siobhan, *A Life Without Problems? The achievements of a therapeutic community* (Aldershot: Arena, 1995).

Macklin, Graham, *Chamberlain* (London: Haus, 2006).

Maskell, Eric, *Saraband* (Leominster: Gracewing, 1992).

Maynard, Theodore, 'The Satanist', *New Witness*, 7 Feb 1918.

Maynard, Theodore, 'The Poetry of Charles Williams', *North American Review*, CCX/766 (1919), p. 26.

Meynell, Viola, *Alice Meynell: A Memoir* (London: Cape, 1929).

Milford, H.S., ed., *The Oxford Book of Regency Verse 1798–1837* (Oxford: Oxford University Press, 1928).

Motion, Andrew, *Philip Larkin: A Writer's Life* (London: Faber and Faber, 1993).

Nicholson, D.H.S., *The Mysticism of St Francis of Assisi* (London: Cape, 1923).

Nicholson, D.H.S. and A.H.E., Lee, *The Oxford Book of English Mystical Verse* (Oxford: Oxford University Press, 1917).

Patmore, Coventry, *The Poems of Coventry Patmore*, ed. Frederick Page (Oxford: Oxford University Press, 1949).

Patmore, Derek, *The Life and Times of Coventry Patmore* (London: Constable, 1949).

Phillimore, J.S., 'The Poet Williams', *New Witness*, 10 Jan 1918.

Pickering, Kenneth, *Drama in the Cathedral : A twentieth century encounter of church and stage* (Colwall: J. Garnet Miller, 2001).

Procopius, *The Secret History*, tr. Richard Atwater (New York: Covici Friede, 1927).

Proctor, Henry, *The Secret of Life* (London: L.N. Fowler, 1911).

Proctor, Henry, *Evolution and Regeneration* (London: L.N. Fowler, 1912).

Reed, Henry, review of *All Hallows' Eve* by Charles Williams, *New Statesman*, 10 Mar 1945, p. 160.

Reynolds, Barbara, ed., *The Letters of Dorothy L. Sayers, Volume I: 1899–1936: The Making of a Detective Novelist* (London: Hodder and Stoughton, 1993).

Reynolds, Barbara, ed., *The Letters of Dorothy L. Sayers, Volume II: 1937–1943: From Novelist to Playwright*, (Cambridge: The Dorothy L. Sayers Society, 1997).

Ridler, Anne, *Olive Willis and Downe House: An Adventure in Education* (London: John Murray, 1967).

Ridler, Anne, review of *The Figure of Beatrice* by Charles Williams, *Time and Tide*, 31 July 1943, pp. 633–4.

Ridler, Anne, *Collected Poems* (Manchester: Carcanet Press, 1994).

Ridler, Anne, *Memoirs* (Oxford: Perpetua Press, 2004).

Stanford, Donald E., ed., *The Selected Letters of Robert Bridges* (London and Toronto: Associated University Presses, 1984).

Sutcliffe, Peter, *The Oxford University Press: An Informal History* (Oxford: Clarendon Press, 1978).

T.H.H., 'Amen House Transfers to Oxford', *The Lantern*, XII/3 (October 1939), pp. 68–71.

Thwaite, Anthony, ed., *Selected Letters of Philip Larkin: 1940–1985* (London: Faber, 1992).

Wain, John, *Sprightly Running: Part of an Autobiography* (London: Macmillan, 1963).

Waite, A.E., *The Real History of the Rosicrucians* (London: George Redway, 1887).

Waite, A.E., *The Hidden Church of the Holy Graal: its legends and symbolism. Considered in their affinity with certain mysteries of initiation and other traces of a secret tradition in Christian times* (London: Rebman, 1909).

Waite, A.E., *The Secret Doctrine in Israel: A Study of the Zohar and its Connections* (London: Rider, 1913).

Waite, A.E., *The Way of Divine Union. Being a doctrine of experience in the life of sanctity, considered on the faith of its testimonies and interpreted after a new manner* (London: Rider, 1915).

Ward, Richard Heron, *Names and Natures: Memories of Ten Men* (London: Victor Gollancz, 1968).

Whittle, David, *Bruce Montgomery/Edmund Crispin: A Life in Music and Books* (Aldershot: Ashgate, 2007).

Williams, Charles, *The Silver Stair* (London: Herbert and Daniel, 1912).

Williams, Charles, *Divorce* (London: Oxford University Press, 1920).

Williams, Charles, *Poems of Conformity* (London: Oxford University Press, 1920).

Williams, Charles and V.H. Collins (ed.) *Poems of Home and Overseas* (Oxford: Clarendon Press, 1921).

Williams, Charles, *Windows of Night* (London: Oxford University Press, 1924).

Williams, Charles, 'The One-Eared Man,' *Dominant* I (Dec 1927), p. 11.

Williams, Charles, (ed.), *A Book of Victorian Narrative Verse* (Oxford: Clarendon Press, 1927).

Williams, Charles, 'The History of Critical Music', *Dominant*, I (Apr 1928), supplement, i–iv.

Williams, Charles, *A Myth of Shakespeare* (London: Oxford University Press, 1929).

Williams, Charles, *Heroes and Kings* (London: Sylvan Press, 1930).

Williams, Charles, (intro.) *Poems of Gerard Manley Hopkins,* edited with notes by Robert Bridges. Second edition with an appendix of additional poems, and a critical introduction by Charles Williams (London: Oxford University Press, 1930).

Williams, Charles, *Poetry at Present* (Oxford: Clarendon Press, 1930).

Williams, Charles, *War in Heaven* (London: Victor Gollancz, 1930).

Williams, Charles, *Many Dimensions* (London: Victor Gollancz, 1931).

Williams, Charles, *The Place of the Lion* (London: Mundanus: Victor Gollancz, 1931).

Williams, Charles, *Three Plays* (London: Oxford University Press, 1931).

Williams, Charles, *The English Poetic Mind* (Oxford: Clarendon Press, 1932).

Williams, Charles, *The Greater Trumps* (London: Victor Gollancz, 1932).

Williams, Charles, 'Autocriticism', *Week-End Review*, 18 Nov, 1933, p. 525.

Williams, Charles, *A Short Life of Shakespeare with Sources* (abridged from E.K. Chambers; London: Oxford University Press, 1933).

Williams, Charles, *Bacon* (London: Arthur Barker, 1933).

Williams, Charles, *Reason and Beauty in the Poetic Mind* (Oxford: Clarendon Press, 1933).

Williams, Charles, *Shadows of Ecstasy* (London: Victor Gollancz, 1933).

Williams, Charles, *James I* (London: Arthur Barker, 1934).

Williams, Charles, *The Ring and the Book by Robert Browning: The story retold* (London: Oxford University Press, 1934).

Williams, Charles, *Rochester* (London: Arthur Barker, 1935).

Williams, Charles, (ed.) *The New Book of English Verse* (London: Gollancz, 1935).

Williams, Charles, 'Letters to Peter' I – VI, *GK's Weekly*, Mar 5, Apr 2, Apr 30, May 28, June 18, and July 23, 1936.

Williams, Charles, *Queen Elizabeth* (London: Duckworth, 1936).

Williams, Charles, *The Story of the Aeneid* (London: Oxford University Press, 1936).

Williams, Charles, 'The New Milton', *St Martin's Review*, 36 (July 1937), pp 255–61.

Williams, Charles, 'Staring at Miracle' [Review of W.B. Yeats, *A Vision*], *Time and Tide*, 4 Dec 1937, pp. 1674–6.

Williams, Charles, *Descent into Hell* (London: Faber and Faber, 1937).

Williams, Charles, *Henry VII* (London: Arthur Barker, 1937).

Williams, Charles, *Stories of Great Names* (London: Oxford University Press, 1937).

Williams, Charles, *He Came Down From Heaven* (I Believe Series, No. 5: London: Heinemann, 1938).

Williams, Charles, *Taliessin Through Logres* (London: Oxford University Press, 1938).

Williams, Charles, *The Descent of the Dove: A Short History of the Holt Spirit in the Church* (London: Longmans, Green, 1939).

Williams, Charles, (ed.) *The Passion of Christ: Being the Gospel and Narrative of the Passion with Short Passages Taken from the Saints and Doctors of the Church* (London: Oxford University Press, 1939).

Williams, Charles, *New Year Letter* [Review of the book by W.H. Auden], *Dublin Review*, 1940, pp. 99–101.

Williams, Charles, 'Arthur Hugh Evelyn Lee' [obituary], *Church Times*, 14 March 1941.

Williams, Charles, 'Gaelic Incantations' [review of Alexander Carmichael, *Carmina Gadelica*, vols. III and IV], *New Statesman*, XXII, 29 Nov 1941, p. 461.

Williams, Charles, *Religion and Love in Dante: The Theology of Romantic Love* (Dacre Papers No. 6, Westminster: Dacre Press, 1941).

Williams, Charles, (ed.) *The New Christian Year* (London: Oxford University Press, 1941).

Williams, Charles, *Witchcraft* (London: Faber and Faber, 1941).

Williams, Charles, 'Letters in Hell' [review of C.S. Lewis, *The Screwtape Letters*], *Time and Tide*, Mar, 1942, p. 22.

Williams, Charles, 'Ourselves and the Revolution', in '*Russia and the West*', ed. C.A. Dawson (London: Changing World Series No. 1, 1942).

Williams, Charles, *The Forgiveness of Sins* (London: G. Bles, 1942).

Williams, Charles, *The Figure of Beatrice* (London: Faber and Faber, 1943).

Williams, Charles, (ed.), *The Letters of Evelyn Underhill* (London: Longmans, 1943).

Williams, Charles, 'The Queen's Servant', in *Poetry London* IX (July 1944).

Williams, Charles, *The Region of the Summer Stars* (London: Nicholson and Watson Editions Poetry London, 1944).

Williams, Charles, *All Hallows' Eve* (London: Faber and Faber, 1945).

Williams, Charles, *Romanticism Comes of Age* [review of the book by Owen Barfield], *New English Weekly*, 10 May 1945, pp. 33–4.

Williams, Charles, (ed.) *Solway Ford and Other Poems by Wilfred Gibson* (London: Faber and Faber, 1945).

Williams, Charles, *Flecker of Dean Close* (London: Canterbury Press, 1946).

Williams, Charles and C.S. Lewis, *Arthurian Torso: Containing the Posthumous Fragment of The Figure of Arthur by Charles Williams and a Commentary on the Arthurian Poems of Charles Williams by C.S. Lewis* (London: Oxford University Press, 1948).

Williams, Charles, *The Image of the City*, ed. Anne Ridler (London: Oxford University Press, 1958).

Williams, Charles, *Collected Plays* (London: Oxford University Press, 1963).

Williams, Charles, *Outlines of Romantic Theology*, ed. Alice Mary Hadfield (Grand Rapids: William B. Eerdmans, 1990).

Williams, Charles, *The Masques of Amen House, together with Amen House Poems and Selections from the Music for the Masques by Hubert J. Foss*, ed. David Bratman (Altadena: Mythopeoic Press, 2000).

Williams, Charles, *The Detective Fiction Reviews of Charles Williams, 1930–1935*, ed. Jared Lobdell (Jefferson, N.C.: McFarland: 2003).

Index